LEAVING CERTIFICATE MATHS
HIGHER LEVEL

GW00417550

Power of
Maths

PAPER
2

Tony Kelly and
Kieran Mills

PUBLISHED BY:
Educate.ie
Walsh Educational Books Ltd
Castleisland, Co. Kerry, Ireland
www.educate.ie

EDITORS:
Ciara McNee and Antoinette Walker

DESIGN:
Kieran O'Donoghue

COVER DESIGN:
Kieran O'Donoghue

LAYOUT:
Compuscript

PRINTED AND BOUND BY:
Walsh Colour Print, Castleisland,
Co. Kerry, Ireland

Copyright © Tony Kelly and Kieran Mills 2016

Without limiting the rights under copyright, this book is sold subject to the condition that it shall not, by way of trade or otherwise, be lent, resold, hired out, reproduced, stored in or introduced into a retrieval system, or transmitted, in any form or by any means (electronic, mechanical, photocopying, recording or otherwise), or otherwise circulated, without the publisher's prior consent, in any form other than that in which it is published and without a similar condition, including this condition, being imposed on the subsequent publisher.

PHOTOGRAPHS AND ILLUSTRATIONS:
Alamy.com; Bigstock.com; iStockphoto.com; Shutterstock.com; Vectorstock.com; Wikicommons (public domain)

The authors and publisher have made every effort to trace all copyright holders. If any have been overlooked, we would be happy to make the necessary arrangements at the first opportunity.

ACKNOWLEDGEMENTS
The authors would like to thank Pat Saville for her invaluable assistance in writing this book. We would also like to thank Ian Wilkinson for providing additional mathematical expertise.

ISBN: 978-1-910052-97-6

Contents

Introduction

Power of Maths is the first new Leaving Certificate Higher Level series since the full implementation and examination of the new Maths syllabus. The new syllabus encourages teachers and students to engage deeply with mathematical content. *Power of Maths* promotes this engagement by developing students' mathematical knowledge and problem-solving skills.

The *Power of Maths Higher Level* package includes two textbooks (with free ebooks), two Activity Books, step-by-step instructional videos and fully worked-out solutions. *Power of Maths* introduces content in a staged and graded manner and ensures that the principles of Maths are firmly established before students are guided through more complex material. Students who use the *Power of Maths* series will be fully prepared for the demands of the most recent Leaving Certificate exam papers.

Content covered in *Power of Maths Paper 1* and *Power of Maths Paper 2*

Power of Maths Paper 1 Higher Level has been divided into 10 major sections: Number, Algebraic Expressions, Algebraic Equations, Sequences and Series, Financial Maths, Complex Numbers, Functions, Differentiation, Integration, and Mathematical Induction. This reflects the content that can be examined in the Higher Level Leaving Certificate Paper 1 examination.

Geometry, Mensuration, Trigonometry, Co-ordinate Geometry, Probability, and Statistics are covered in *Power of Maths Paper 2 Higher Level*. This reflects the content that can be examined in the Higher Level Leaving Certificate Paper 2 examination.

The first three sections of *Power of Maths Paper 1* and *Power of Maths Paper 2* provide the foundations for the rest of the course. We recommend completing Sections 1, 2 and 3 of *Power of Maths Paper 1* first, followed by Sections 1, 2 and 3 of *Power of Maths Paper 2*. Sections can then be completed sequentially, alternating between *Power of Maths Paper 1* and *Power of Maths Paper 2*, as you please.

Key features of *Power of Maths Paper 2*

Learning outcomes

- Each chapter begins with a set of learning outcomes to guide students through the content.

Tips and key terms

- Tip and key term boxes appear throughout to aid understanding.

Examples

- *Power of Maths* is packed with examples. **Worked Examples** explain the reasoning behind a given approach to solving a problem. These examples underpin the philosophy behind the new approach to learning Maths.

- **Numbered Examples** apply the principles learnt to all types of situations. They utilise the more traditional approach to teaching Maths.

- **Short Examples** appear throughout the text and are indicated by a green arrow. These examples give students short and snappy explanations, helping them to undertake the exercises that follow.

Exercises

- Exercises appear at **regular intervals** in the text so that students can carry out questions with a minimum amount of teaching.
- **Questions in the exercises are graded**. Earlier questions provide plenty of practice and rigour to allow students to become totally familiar with the techniques required for carrying out a particular mathematical procedure. Gradually students are asked to use these techniques and **apply them to real-life situations**.

Activity boxes

- Activity boxes in the margin direct students to optional extra activities in the Activity Book.

Digital icons

- Digital icons link to step-by-step instructional videos and other digital resources on **www.educateplus.ie**.

Revision questions

- Revision questions at the end of each section provide plenty of practice of the type of questions examined in the Leaving Certificate examination.

Revision summaries

- Revision summaries at the end of each section reinforce and embed learning.

Activity Book

Power of Maths Paper 2 Higher Level comes with an Activity Book. The optional activities are signposted in the margin of this textbook and are designed to allow students to discover mathematical concepts on their own and to acquire a deeper understanding of the material. This enhances the enjoyment of the subject, allowing students to learn complex material as effortlessly as possible.

Digital resources

Digital icons in the Trigonometry section of this textbook link to step-by-step instructional videos. Students can access the videos by clicking on the icon in the ebook or by visiting **www.educateplus.ie**.

These step-by-step instructional videos are designed to make the learning of difficult concepts as easy as possible. They also provide further exercises to complement the material in the textbook and Activity Book.

Students and teachers also receive a **free ebook** with the textbook. It can be downloaded using the redeem code on the inside front cover of this textbook.

Additional resources for teachers

Fully worked-out solutions for all of the exercises are available for teachers on **www.educateplus.ie**.

Finally, enjoy the experience of learning a beautiful subject.

Tony Kelly and Kieran Mills

SECTION 1

Geometry

Where would engineers and architects be without geometry? Engineers and architects must design and assemble shapes to construct buildings and bridges and to work out the stresses and strains between the component parts.

Golden Gate
Bridge

CHAPTER 1

Review of Euclidean Geometry

Learning Outcomes

- To understand what is meant by theorems, definitions and axioms.
- To understand the types of angle formed by intersecting lines and lines intersecting parallel lines.
- To know the properties of triangles and to understand the conditions necessary for triangles to be congruent.
- To know the properties of parallelograms.

In his book *The Elements*, the Greek mathematician **Euclid** developed the geometry of **flat** space. This has become known as Euclidean geometry. The geometry of **curved** space is the geometry of the universe and resulted from the work of Bernhard **Riemann**.

Euclid 🎧

1.1 Definitions and axioms

In Euclidean geometry, all of the results (theorems) are derived by a sequence of steps (proofs) based on definitions (meanings) and axioms (self-evident truths).

Definitions

KEY TERM

A **definition** is a statement of the meaning of a term.

An example of a definition is the meaning of parallel lines.

Two lines l_1 and l_2 are parallel if they are identical or have no common point.

TIP

The same number of arrows on lines indicates that they are parallel to each other. The symbol for 'is parallel to' is ||.

or

Written mathematically: $l_1 \| l_2 \Rightarrow l_1 = l_2$ *or* $l_1 \cap l_2 = \{\ \ \}$

In words: l_1 is parallel to l_2 implies l_1 is equal to l_2 or l_1 and l_2 have no points in common.

Axioms

> **KEY TERM**
>
> An **axiom** is a statement which is assumed to be true (is universally accepted).

Euclid set out five axioms. Two of these are stated below.

1. There is exactly one line through any two given points.

    This is accepted as a self-evident truth or an axiom.

2. Given any line l and a point A, there is exactly one line through A that is parallel to l.

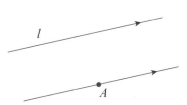

1.2 Angles and lines

> **ACTIVITY 1**
>
> **ACTION**
> Identifying angles
>
> **OBJECTIVE**
> *To name the different types of angles and to understand the meaning of alternate, corresponding and vertically opposite angles*

Vertically opposite angles

> **LINE THEOREM 1**
>
> If l_1 and l_2 are two intersecting lines, the angles opposite each other (vertically opposite angles) are equal.
> It states that $x = z$ and $y = w$.

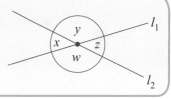

This theorem can be proved from the definitions and axioms of Euclid.

> **KEY TERM**
>
> A **transversal** is a line that crosses two or more other lines.

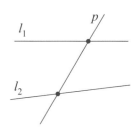

The line p is a transversal of the lines l_1 and l_2.

For two parallel lines l_1 and l_2 and a transversal p, the angles x and y are alternate angles and the angles w and z are alternate angles. They are called alternate angles because they are on opposite sides of the transversal.

> **LINE THEOREM 2**
>
> If l_1 and l_2 are parallel lines ($l_1 \| l_2$) and p is any transversal, then alternate angles are equal: $x = y$ and $w = z$.

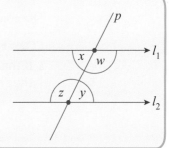

KEY TERM

The **converse** of a stated theorem is formed by taking the conclusion of the stated theorem as the starting point and making the starting point the conclusion.

The **converse** of **line theorem** 2 is also true.

CONVERSE OF LINE THEOREM 2

If a transversal makes equal alternate angles on two lines, then the lines are parallel: $x = y \Rightarrow l_1 \parallel l_2$.

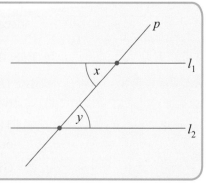

Since line theorem 2 and its converse are both true, we can write $x = y \Leftrightarrow l_1 = l_2$.

The 'equivalent to' sign $\Leftrightarrow$ means that if the statement on one side of the $\Leftrightarrow$ sign is true, the statement on the other side is automatically true and vice versa.

These two statements are equivalent as they are just different ways of saying the same thing.

Corresponding angles

KEY TERM

For two parallel lines l_1 and l_2 and a transversal p, the angles x and a are **corresponding angles** and the angles b and y are also **corresponding angles**.

LINE THEOREM 3

If l_1 and l_2 are parallel lines and p is any transversal, then $x = a$ and $b = y$.
[Corresponding angles are equal.]

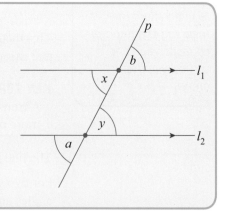

x and a are called corresponding angles as they are in matching positions on the same side of the transversal on each of the parallel lines.

The converse of line theorem 3 is also true.

CONVERSE OF LINE THEOREM 3

If the corresponding angles of a transversal on two lines are equal, then the lines are parallel.

▸ l_1 cannot be parallel to l_2 as $|\angle BEG| = 122° \neq |\angle ABD| = 108°$.

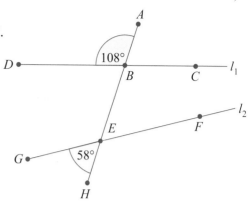

1.3 Triangles

Congruent triangles

In order to prove many geometrical results, you need to understand the idea of congruence. Two triangles are congruent if they are identical in all respects. This means that in both triangles the lengths of the sides and the measures of the angles opposite these sides are the same.

Triangle 1 is congruent to triangle 2 if, when you cut out triangle 1, it will fit on top of triangle 2 perfectly.

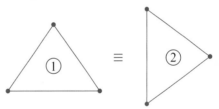

$\equiv$ is the symbol for 'congruent to'.

For two triangles to be congruent, they must satisfy one of the following sets of conditions:

Congruent condition 1 (SSS)

---

1. Side, side, side (**SSS**)

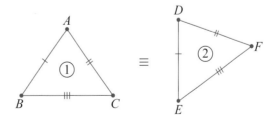

$|AB| = |DE|$ [Side (**S**)]

$|AC| = |DF|$ [Side (**S**)]

$|BC| = |EF|$ [Side (**S**)]

$\Rightarrow \triangle ABC \equiv \triangle DEF$

This means that all angles opposite these sides are also equal in size.

CONGRUENT CONDITION 2 (SAS)	2. Side, angle and side (SAS), where the angle is included between the two sides

$|AB| = |DE|$ [Side (**S**)]

$|\angle ABC| = |\angle DEF|$ [Angle (**A**)]

$|BC| = |EF|$ [Side (**S**)]

$\Rightarrow \Delta ABC \equiv \Delta DEF$

It follows that $|AC| = |DF|$ and the other angles opposite the equal sides are also equal in size.

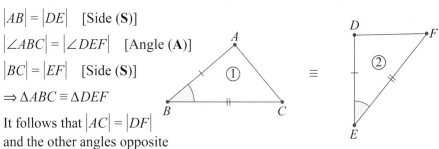

CONGRUENT CONDITION 3 (ASA)	3. Angle, side and angle (ASA), where the angles are connected to the given side

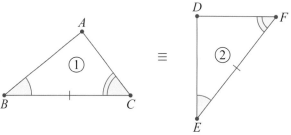

$|\angle ABC| = |\angle DEF|$ [Angle (**A**)]

$|BC| = |EF|$ [Side (**S**)]

$|\angle ACB| = |\angle DFE|$ [Angle (**A**)]

$\Rightarrow \Delta ABC \equiv \Delta DEF$

It follows that $|AC| = |DF|$ and $|AB| = |DE|$.

CONGRUENT CONDITION 4 (RHS)	4. Right angle, hypotenuse and side (RHS)

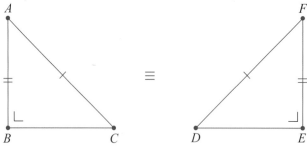

$|\angle ABC| = |\angle DEF| = 90°$ [Right angle (**R**)]

$|AC| = |DF|$ [Hypotenuse (**H**)]

$|AB| = |FE|$ [Side (**S**)]

$\Rightarrow \Delta ABC \equiv \Delta DEF$

It follows that $|BC| = |DE|$ and the angles opposite the equal sides are also equal in size.

The four basic triangle theorems

The sum of the angles in a triangle

TRIANGLE THEOREM 1

The interior angles in any triangle add to 180°.
$x + y + z = 180°$.

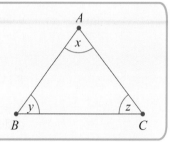

TIP

The sum of the two smaller angles
in a right-angled triangle is always 90°:
$x + y = 90°$

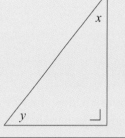

TRIANGLE THEOREM 2

Each exterior angle of a triangle
is equal to the sum of the two interior
opposite angles.

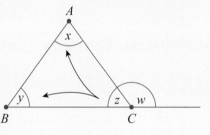

Proof

In the triangle ABC, w is the exterior
angle to the interior angle z adjacent
to it.

$x + y + z = 180°$ [3 angles of a triangle add up to 180°]

$z + w = 180°$ [Straight angle]

$\therefore x + y + z = z + w$

$\Rightarrow w = x + y$

Angles opposite sides of equal length

TRIANGLE THEOREM 3

In an isosceles triangle, the size of the angles
opposite sides of equal length are equal:
$|AB| = |AC| \Rightarrow z = y$.

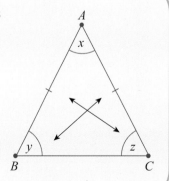

The converse of triangle theorem 3 is also true.

> **CONVERSE OF TRIANGLE THEOREM 3**
>
> If two angles in a triangle are equal, then the lengths of the sides opposite them are equal: $z = y \Rightarrow |AB| = |AC|$.
> So $|AB| = |AC| \Leftrightarrow z = y$.

Proof by contradiction

You will meet a method of proof known as **proof by contradiction** in many different areas of mathematics.

Proof by contradiction is a method of proof in which we assume the conclusion is false.

Let us illustrate the idea here by proving the converse of triangle theorem 3 by contradiction.

EXAMPLE 1

Prove, by contradiction, the statement that if two angles in a triangle are equal in size, the sides opposite them are also equal in length.

Solution

Let us assume that the statement is not true.

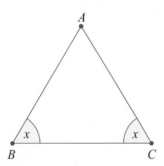

So given $\triangle ABC$ in which $|\angle ABC| = |\angle ACB|$, assume that $AB \neq AC$.

Suppose $|AB| > |AC|$.

Draw CD so that $|DB| = |AC|$.

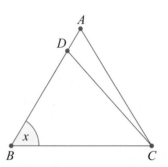

Redraw $\triangle ABC$ and $\triangle DBC$.

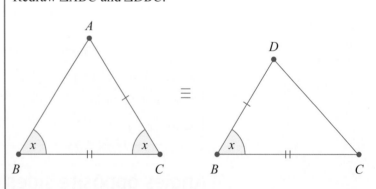

$\triangle ABC \equiv \triangle DBC$ [**SAS**]

Therefore, the smaller triangle $\triangle DBC$ is identical to $\triangle ABC$.

This is not true, so the assumption that $|AB| \neq |AC|$ must be wrong.

So $|AB|$ must be equal to $|AC|$.

Our assumption has been contradicted.

The **converse** of triangle theorem 3 has been proved by the **method of contradiction**.

This method involves assuming the statement made is not true given a set of conditions and deducing that something obviously impossible happens as a result. This leads to the conclusion that the original statement must be true.

This method is also known as '*reductio ad adsurdum*', meaning 'reduction to absurdity'. It arises in many areas of mathematics.

The theorem of Pythagoras

TRIANGLE THEOREM 4

In a right-angled triangle, the square of the length of the hypotenuse is equal to the sum of the squares of the lengths of the other two sides: $r^2 = x^2 + y^2$.

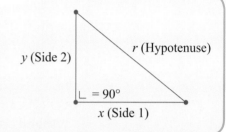

The converse of the theorem of Pythagoras is also true.

CONVERSE OF THE THEOREM OF PYTHAGORAS

If the square of the length of the longest side of a triangle is equal to the sum of the squares of the lengths of the other two sides, then the angle opposite the longest side is 90°.

1.4 Parallelograms

A parallelogram is a quadrilateral with parallel opposite sides. There are two basic parallelogram theorems.

ACTION
Exploring the properties of parallelograms

OBJECTIVE
To draw a parallelogram and discover its properties

Opposite sides and opposite angles in a parallelogram

PARALLELOGRAM THEOREM 1

In a parallelogram, opposite sides are equal in length and opposite angles are equal in size.

Opposite sides are equal in length:
$|AB| = |DC|, |AD| = |BC|$

Opposite angles are equal in size:
$|\angle ADC| = |\angle ABC| = x, |\angle BAD| = |\angle BCD| = y$

There are two **corollaries** of this theorem.

KEY TERM

A **corollary** is a logical deduction from a theorem.

COROLLARY 1

A diagonal of a parallelogram divides it into two congruent triangles.

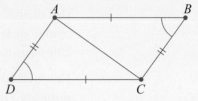

Proof

$[AC]$ is diagonal of the parallelogram $DCBA$.

Consider $\triangle ABC$ and $\triangle ADC$.

$|AB| = |DC|$ [Opposite sides are equal; Side (**S**)]

$|\angle ABC| = |\angle ADC|$ [Opposite angles are equal; Angle (**A**)]

$|BC| = |AD|$ [Opposite sides are equal; Side (**S**)]

$\triangle ABC \equiv \triangle ADC$

COROLLARY 2

The adjacent angles in a parallelogram add to 180°.

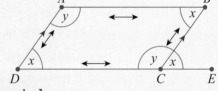

Proof

In the parallelogram $DCBA$:

$|\angle ABC| = |\angle BCE| = x$ [Alternate angles]

But, $|\angle BCE| + |\angle BCD| = 180°$ [Straight angle]

$\therefore |\angle ABC| + |\angle BCE| = x + y = 180°$

The diagonals of a parallelogram

KEY TERM

To **bisect** a line means to divide it into two equal lengths.

PARALLELOGRAM THEOREM 2

The diagonals of a parallelogram bisect each other.

If $[AC]$ and $[BD]$ are the diagonals of the parallelogram $DCBA$, then E is the midpoint of $[AC]$ and $[BD]$. Therefore, $|AE| = |EC|$ and $|DE| = |EB|$

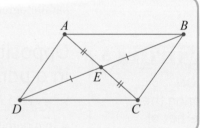

The converse of parallelogram theorem 2 is also true:

CONVERSE

If two intersecting line segments $[AC]$ and $[DB]$ bisect each other, then $DCBA$ is a parallelogram.

$|AE| = |EC|$ and $|DE| = |EB| \Rightarrow DCBA$ is a parallelogram.

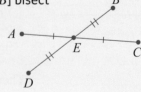

EXERCISE 1

Diagrams are not drawn to scale.

1. Find the missing angles: x, y and z.

   (a)

   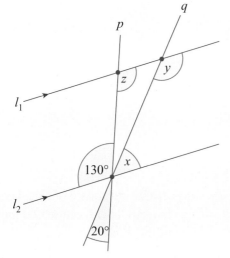

   (b)

   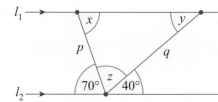

   (c)

   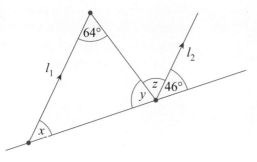

2. **(a)** Is $l_1 \parallel l_2$? How do you know this is the case?

   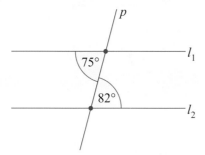

(b) Is $l_1 \parallel l_2$? How do you know this is the case?

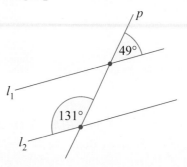

(c) What is the converse of $F \Rightarrow G$?

(d) State $F \Rightarrow G$ in words.

(e) $F \Rightarrow G$ and $G \Rightarrow F$ can be written as
_____.

(f) If a statement and its converse are true, the statements are _____.

3. **(a)** Find x and y.

   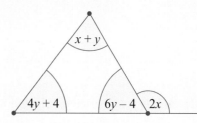

   (b) If $AB \parallel DC$, $DA \parallel CB$ and E is the midpoint of $[DC]$, prove that $\triangle ADE \equiv \triangle EFC$.

   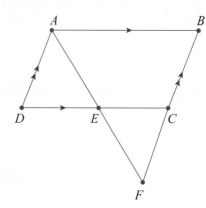

4. **(a)** If $|AD| = |BD| = |DC|$ and if D is on $[BC]$, prove that $x + y = 90°$.

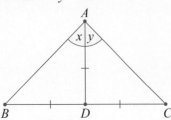

(b) If $|AB| = |AD|$ and $|BD| = |CD|$ and if D is on $[AC]$, prove that $|\angle ABD| = 2x$.

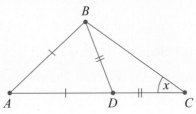

(c) If $|BA| = |BC|$, prove that $y = 90° + \dfrac{x}{2}$.

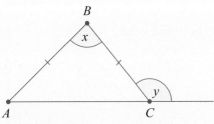

(d) $\triangle FBD$ is an isosceles triangle with $|FB| = |FD|$. Prove that $x = y$.

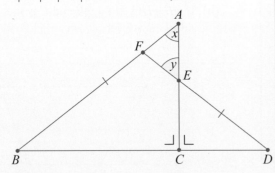

(e) $ADCB$ and $GFED$ are two squares. Show that $\triangle CGD$ and $\triangle AED$ are congruent.

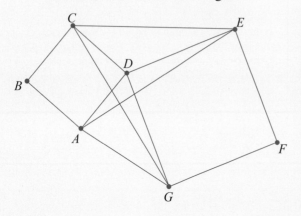

5. Find x and y as required.

(a)

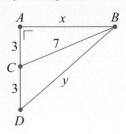

(b)

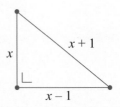

6. **(a)** $ABCD$ is a square of side 4 cm inscribed in a circle with centre O. Find the radius of the circle.

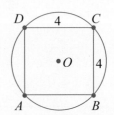

(b) A window consists of a plain glass triangle ABC on top of a square $EDCA$ with a circular stained glass section with centre O inscribed in the square. Find the area of the plain glass, correct to one decimal place.

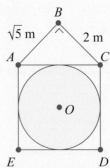

(c) A tightrope walker gets on the rope at A and walks to B. Find the height h of the top of the rope B above the ground, correct to two decimal places.

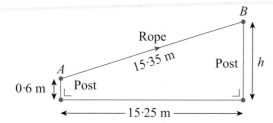

(d) Express the maximum distance d to the Earth that an astronaut can see from a space shuttle in terms of h and R, where h is the height of the shuttle above the Earth and R is the radius of the Earth. Estimate d, to the nearest kilometre, if the shuttle is in orbit 320 km above the Earth and the radius of the earth is 6400 km.

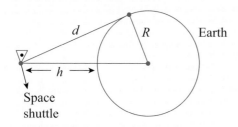

(e) A man travels from an island jetty at A to a house B on the shore along the path ACB.

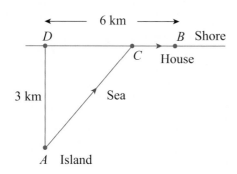

The nearest point D on the shore is 3 km from the jetty A on the island and the house is 6 km along the shore from D. If he lands at C, 2 km from the house, find $|AC|$.

If he can row at 5 km/h and walk at 8 km/h, find the total time for the journey ACB.

(f) An aeroplane P starts taxiing along a runway at a point O which is 92 m from the base of the control tower A.

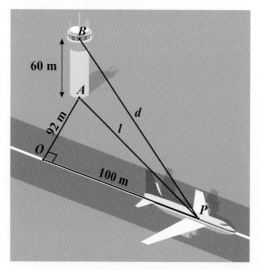

(i) Find distance l the plane is from the base of the control tower when the plane P has moved 100 m down the runway, correct to two decimal places.

(ii) Find d, the distance from the top of the tower B to the plane when it has moved 100 m down the runway, correct to one decimal place. The tower is 60 m high.

7. (a) $ABCD$ is a quadrilateral with $|\angle APD| = 90°$. Show that $|AB|^2 + |CD|^2 = |AD|^2 + |BC|^2$.

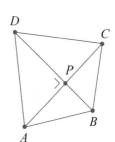

(b) In $\triangle ABC$, $|AB|^2 = |AP|^2 + |PC|^2$ and $BP \perp AC$. Find $|\angle BCP|$.

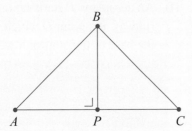

(c) In $\triangle ABC$, prove that $|PB|^2 = |PC|^2 = |OB|^2 - |OC|^2$.

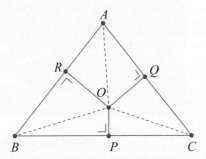

(d) A playing field is in the shape of the quadrilateral $ABCD$ in the plan below. Show that $|\angle ADC|$ is a right angle.

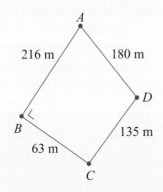

(e) The ferry *Jonathan Swift J* travels due north from Dublin Port P at 80 km/h. The ferry *Ulysses U* sails due east from Dublin Port at 40 km/h. If both leave Dublin Port at the same time, find the distance between them after 2·5 hours, correct to one decimal place.

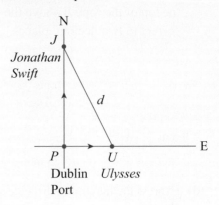

8. (a) Find x and y if $DCBA$ is a parallelogram.

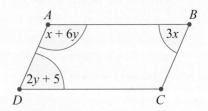

Find $|\angle DCB|$.

(b) $DCBA$ is a parallelogram. $[AE]$ bisects $\angle DAB$. $[FC]$ bisects $\angle BCD$.

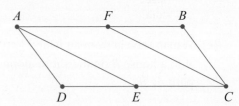

Prove that:

(i) $|AD| = |DE|$

(ii) $|AF| = |EC|$

(c) $DCBA$ is a parallelogram with $[AE]$ perpendicular to $[BD]$ and $[CF]$ perpendicular to $[BD]$. Prove that $\triangle DEA \equiv \triangle CFB$.

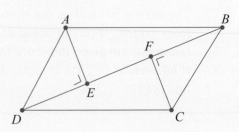

Triangles and Parallelograms

CHAPTER 2

Learning Outcomes

- To understand the relationship between the sizes of angles and the lengths of sides opposite these angles.

- To know whether or not it is possible to draw triangles given their sides.

- To know the properties of the angles and the line segments formed when a transversal cuts parallel lines.

- To understand triangles through a knowledge of the ratio theorem and the properties of similar triangles.

- To prove the required triangle and parallelogram theorems.

- To be able to find the areas of triangles and parallelograms.

2.1 The biggest and smallest angles in a triangle

WORKED EXAMPLE Looking at how angles and sides are related

1. Stepladder

A stepladder with two equal legs, each of length 2 m, is standing on level ground, as shown in **Figure 1**. The legs slip outwards. The distance $|BC|$ between the contact points of the legs on the ground increases, as shown in **Figure 2**.

- In **Figure 1**, $|BC| = 2$ m.
- In **Figure 2**, as the ladder slips, $|BC|$ increases and so does $|\angle BAC|$. The other two angles decrease.
- In **Figure 2**, the biggest angle is opposite the longest side and vice versa (conversely).

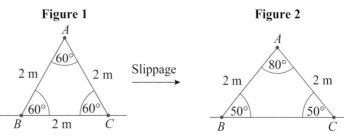

ACTIVITY 6

ACTION
The biggest and smallest angles in a triangle

OBJECTIVE
To explore the relationship between sizes of angles and the lengths of sides opposite these angles

2. Lifting a weight using a pulley

A man B is lifting a weight C off the ground by pulling on the rope $[AB]$.

Figure 3   **Figure 4**   **Figure 5**

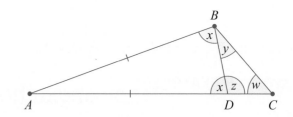

- In **Figure 3**, the biggest angle is $90°$ and the longest side $[AB]$ is opposite it. The smallest angle is $30°$ and the shortest side $[BC]$ is opposite it.
- In **Figure 4**, the biggest angle is $120°$ and the longest side $[AB]$ is opposite it.
- In **Figure 5**, the biggest angle is $135°$ and the longest side $[AB]$ is opposite it. The smallest angle is $15°$ and the shortest side $[AC]$ is opposite it.

EXAMPLE 1

In $\triangle ABC$, $|AC| > |AB|$. $[BD]$ is drawn so that $|AB| = |AD|$.

Show that $|\angle ABC| > |\angle ACB|$.

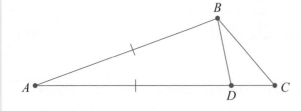

Solution

$|AB| = |AD| \Rightarrow |\angle ABD| = |\angle ADB| = x$ [Isosceles]

$x = y + w$ [Exterior angle]

$|\angle ABC| = x + y = 2y + w > w$

$\Rightarrow |\angle ABC| > |\angle ACB|$

SUMMARY: RELATING ANGLES IN A TRIANGLE TO THEIR SIDES AND VICE VERSA

In any triangle, the biggest angle is always the angle opposite the longest side.

Conversely, the longest side is always the side opposite the biggest angle.

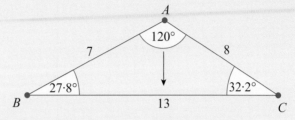

$\angle BAC$ is the biggest angle $\Leftrightarrow$ [BC] is the longest side.

$\angle ABC$ is the smallest angle $\Leftrightarrow$ [AC] is the shortest side.

EXERCISE 2

Diagrams are not drawn to scale.

1. A skateboarder goes from $A \rightarrow B \rightarrow C$ on a ramp as shown.

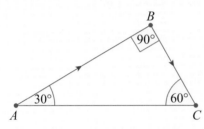

Which is the longer of her two journeys, [AB] or [BC]? Why?

2. A dirt-bike rider goes around the circuit ABC. Which is the biggest angle he turns through: x, y or z?

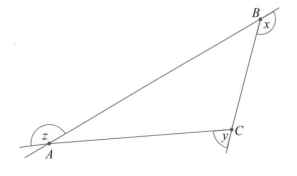

3. (a) In $\triangle ABC$, D is on [BC] such that $|BA| = |BD|$.

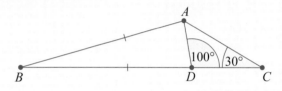

Find:

(i) $\left|\angle ADB\right|$ **(iv)** $\left|\angle DAC\right|$

(ii) $\left|\angle BAD\right|$ **(v)** $\left|\angle BAC\right|$

(iii) $\left|\angle ABD\right|$

Which is the longest side in $\triangle ABC$? Why?

Which is the shortest side in $\triangle ABC$? Why?

(b) A field is shown in the diagram.

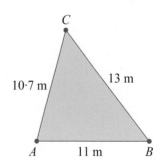

(i) What is the length of the perimeter?

(ii) Name the biggest angle.

(iii) Name the smallest angle.

4. *A* is the centre of circle *s* and $|\angle DBC| = 15°$.

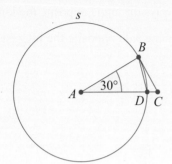

Find:

(a) $|\angle ABD|$

(b) $|\angle ADB|$

(c) $|\angle BDC|$

(d) $|\angle BCD|$

Which is longest side in $\triangle ABC$? Why?

2.2 Constructing triangles

Given the lengths of three line segments, can you always construct a triangle with these as sides?

ACTIVITY 7

ACTION
Can a triangle be drawn?

OBJECTIVE
To use matchsticks to see whether it is possible to construct various triangles

WORKED EXAMPLE Can a triangle be drawn?

1. Given lengths of 5 cm, 4 cm and 7 cm, is it always possible to construct a triangle with these lengths as sides?

Try it with 7 cm as base [*AB*].

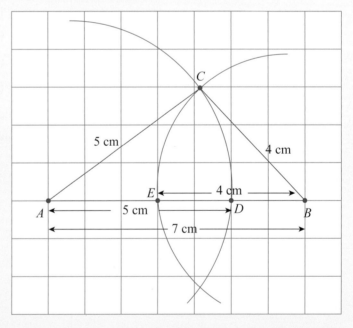

Draw an arc of a circle of radius 5 cm with centre *A* and an arc of a circle of radius 4 cm with centre *B*. These overlap at *C*. So $\triangle ABC$ can be constructed as shown. Clearly the radius of circle with centre $A = |AD|$ = 5 cm and the radius of circle centre $B = |BE| = 4$ cm.

These overlap because $5 + 4 > 7$.

$|AD| = 5$, $|BE| = 4$, $|AB| = 7$

$|AD| + |BE| > |AB|$

2. What would happen if the lengths were 5 cm, 2 cm and 7 cm? Let's try it with 7 cm as base [AB].

Clearly the arcs do not overlap and so a triangle cannot be formed because 5 + 2 = 7. Try it yourself with base $|AB|$ = 5 cm or 2 cm.

$|AD| = 5, |BD| = 2, |AB| = 7$

$|AD| + |BD| = |AB|$

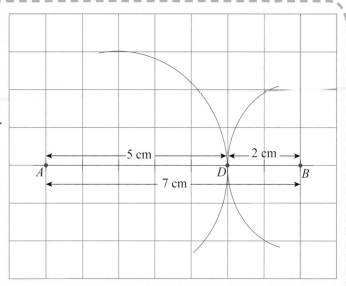

3. Finally, what about the lengths 4 cm, 2 cm and 7 cm? It is not possible to form a triangle with these sides because 4 + 2 < 7. Try it with base $|AB|$ = 7 cm.

$|AD| = 4, |BE| = 2, |AB| = 7$

$|AD| + |BE| < |AB|$

Maybe the wrong side was used as a base. So try it yourself with base of $|AB|$ = 4 cm.

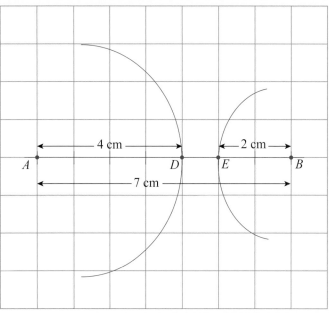

We were able to construct a triangle using the lengths in **1** because 5 + 4 > 7. In order to construct a triangle from three line segments of given lengths, the sum of the lengths of two sides must be bigger than the length of the third. This must be true of any two sides because any of the sides could have been used as the base.

TIP

You can construct a triangle from three line segments of given lengths only if the sum of any two lengths is greater than the third length.

EXAMPLE 2

If $|AB|$ = 9 cm, $|AC|$ = 3 cm and $|BC|$ = 5 cm, is it possible to construct $\triangle ABC$?

Solution

$|AB|$ = 9 cm, $|AC|$ = 3 cm, $|BC|$ = 5 cm

$|AB| + |BC| = 14$ cm > 3 cm = $|AC|$ ✓

$|AB| + |AC| = 12$ cm > 5 cm = $|BC|$ ✓

$|BC| + |AC| = 8$ cm < 9 cm = $|AB|$ ✗

No. The triangle cannot be constructed.

EXAMPLE 3

For $\triangle ABC$ shown, write down three inequalities satisfied by x. Hence, show that $3 < x < 21$. If x is a natural number, find all possible values of x.

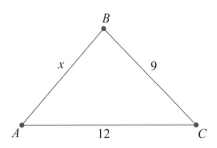

Solution

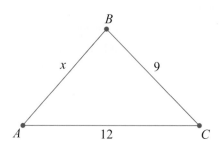

1: $12 + 9 > x \Rightarrow 21 > x$

2: $x + 9 > 12 \Rightarrow x > 3$

3: $x + 12 > 9 \Rightarrow x > -3$

$3 < x < 21$

$x \in \{4, 5, 6, 7, 8, 9, 10, 11, 12, 13, 14, 15, 16, 17, 18, 19, 20\}$

EXAMPLE 4

A mountain bike course is set out in the form of an equilateral triangle as shown.

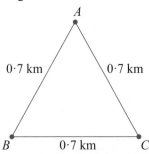

It is proposed to extend this course by lengthening one side only by 1 km but keeping the triangular shape. **(a)** Is this possible? **(b)** What is maximum distance one side can be increased while still keeping the shape, correct to the nearest metre?

Solution

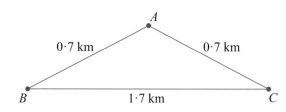

(a) $|AB| + |AC| = 1 \cdot 4 \text{ km} < 1 \cdot 7 \text{ km} = |BC|$

It is not possible.

(b) If $[BC]$ is increased: $|BC| < 0 \cdot 7 \text{ km} + 0 \cdot 7 \text{ km}$

$|BC| < 1 \cdot 4 \text{ km}$

Maximum distance one side can be increased: $< 0 \cdot 7 \text{ km}$

Maximum distance $= 699 \text{ m}$

EXERCISE 3

Diagrams are not drawn to scale.

1. Is it possible to construct $\triangle ABC$ given the following lengths? If not, state why.

    (a) $|AB| = 2 \text{ cm}$, $|BC| = 3 \text{ cm}$, $|AC| = 4 \text{ cm}$

    (b) $|AB| = 5 \text{ cm}$, $|BC| = 4 \text{ cm}$, $|AC| = 3 \cdot 2 \text{ cm}$

    (c) $|AB| = 3 \text{ cm}$, $|BC| = 8 \text{ cm}$, $|AC| = 5 \text{ cm}$

    (d) $|AB| = 11 \text{ cm}$, $|BC| = 18 \text{ cm}$, $|AC| = 6 \text{ cm}$

    (e) $|AB| = a - 1$, $|BC| = a$, $|AC| = (a + 1)$, $(a > 2)$

2. For $\triangle ABC$, find $|AC|$.

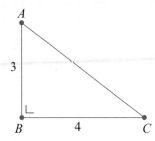

Verify the following:
(a) $|AB| + |AC| > |BC|$
(b) $|AB| + |BC| > |AC|$
(c) $|AC| + |BC| > |AB|$

3. Try to construct $\triangle ABC$ with $|AB| = 4$ cm as the base, $|AC| = 8$ cm and $|BC| = 2$ cm.
   Why can it not be done?

4. Two sides of a triangle are 12 cm and 8 cm. The other side is x.

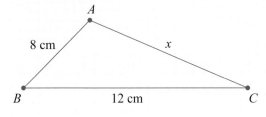

Complete the following:
(a) $x + 8 > \square \Rightarrow x > \square$
(b) $x + 12 > \square \Rightarrow x > \square$
(c) $8 + 12 > x \Rightarrow x < \square$
   $\therefore \square < x < \square$

Write out all the possible whole number values of x.

5. The mast of a crane $[AC]$ is 30 m high. What is the minimum whole number value in metres that the length $|AB|$ can have?

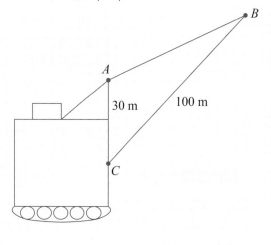

2.3 Transversal lines

A transversal of a set of parallel lines is a line that intersects each of the parallel lines.

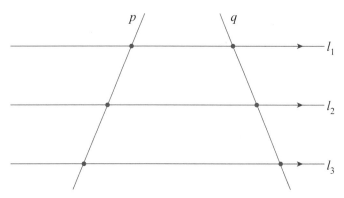

The lines p and q are both transversal lines of the parallel lines l_1, l_2 and l_3.

WORKED EXAMPLE

Properties of transversal lines

A mathematical snooker player is snookered on a red ball as shown.

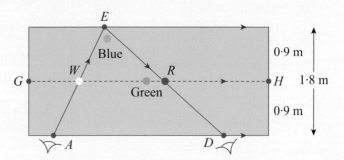

He reckons his path from white (W) to red (R) is $W \rightarrow E \rightarrow R$. The line GH joining white to red is down the middle of the 1·8 m wide table. The snooker player estimates the distance $|AE|$ to be about 2 m and $|ED|$ to be about 3·2 m. What is the length of the path $W \rightarrow E \rightarrow R$?

It is obvious that $|WE| = \frac{1}{2}|AE| \simeq 1$ m and $|ER| = \frac{1}{2}|ED| \simeq 1 \cdot 6$ m.

Therefore, the length of the path $\simeq 2 \cdot 6$ m.

EXAMPLE 5

l_1, l_2 and l_3 are parallel lines with two transversals p and q. The three parallel lines cut off equal segments of length 3 on p. If $|BA| = 4$, find $|AE|$.

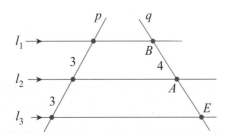

Solution

Translate $p \rightarrow p'$ so that p' passes through A, the point where q crosses l_2.

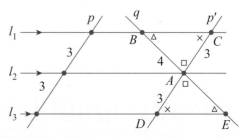

$\triangle ABC$ and $\triangle ADE$ are congruent.
$|AE| = |AB| = 4$

The result in Example 5 can be generalised into the transversal theorem.

TRANSVERSAL THEOREM

If three parallel lines cut off equal segments on the same transversal line, they will cut off equal segments on any other transversal.

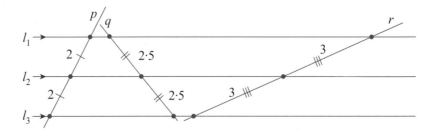

EXAMPLE 6

Find x if the transversals p and q are perpendicular to the three parallel lines l_1, l_2 and l_3.

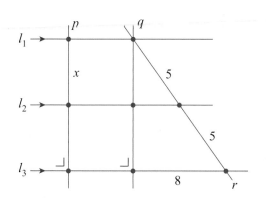

Solution

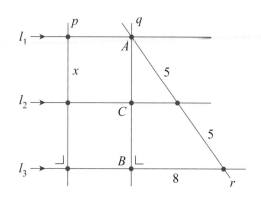

$|AB| = \sqrt{10^2 - 8^2} = \sqrt{36} = 6$ [Pythagoras]

$|AC| = |CB| = 3$ [Transversal theorem]

$\therefore x = |AC| = 3$ [Since $p \parallel q$ and $l_1 \parallel l_2$]

SYLLABUS NOTE

↟ You need to know the proof for the **transversal theorem** for the Leaving Certificate exam.

PROOF OF THE TRANSVERSAL THEOREM

↟ If three parallel lines cut off equal segments on some transversal line, then they will cut off equal intercepts on any other transversal line.

Given: $l_1 \parallel l_2 \parallel l_3$ and $|DE| = |EF|$.

Prove: $|AB| = |BC|$

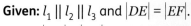

Construction: Draw a line $D'F'$ through B parallel to DF.

Proof:

$DEBD'$ is a parallelogram $\Rightarrow |DE| = |D'B|$

$EFF'B$ is a parallelogram $\Rightarrow |EF| = |BF'|$

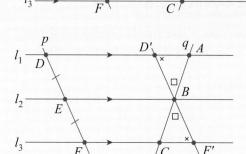

$\therefore |D'B| = |BF'|$ [Because $|DE| = |EF|$]

Now $|\angle AD'B| = |\angle BF'C|$ [Alternate angles **(A)**]

$|D'B| = |BF'|$ [Equal segments **(S)**]

$|\angle ABD'| = |CBF'|$ [Vertically opposite angles **(A)**]

$\therefore \triangle AD'B \equiv \triangle BCF'$

$\therefore |AB| = |BC|$

The transversal theorem inevitably means that, if three parallel lines cut off equal segments on a transversal, they must be equally spaced.

EXAMPLE 7

Show that the parallel lines l_1, l_2 and l_3, are equally spaced by drawing a transversal perpendicular to them.

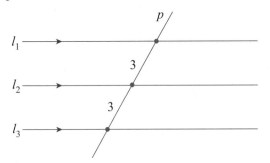

Solution

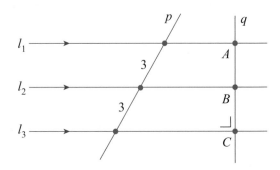

Draw transversal q perpendicular to l_1, l_2 and l_3. If it intersects them at A, B and C respectively, $|AB| = |BC|$ by the transversal theorem and so l_1, l_2 and l_3 are equally spaced.

The transversal theorem can be extended to any number of parallel lines because these lines can be grouped in sets of threes.

EXAMPLE 8

Show that, if five parallel lines cut off equal line segments on the same transversal, they will cut off equal segments on any other transversal.

Solution

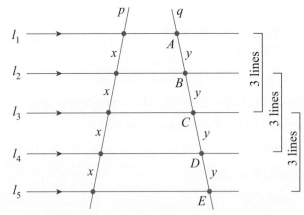

Applying the transversal theorem to lines l_1, l_2 and l_3 means $|AB| = |BC| = y$.

Applying the transversal theorem to lines l_2, l_3 and l_4 means $|BC| = |CD| = y$.

Applying the transversal theorem to lines l_3, l_4 and l_5 means $|CD| = |DE| = y$.

Transversal lines and ratios

Eleven equally spaced lines cut off equal segments of lengths 2 and 3 on transversal p and q.

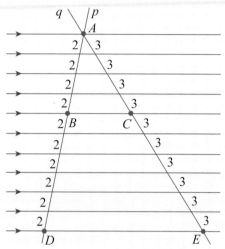

$$\frac{|AB|}{|BD|} = \frac{8}{12} = \frac{2}{3}$$

$$\frac{|AC|}{|CE|} = \frac{12}{18} = \frac{2}{3}$$

$$\Rightarrow \frac{|AB|}{|BD|} = \frac{|AC|}{|CE|}$$

Using the idea in the worked example, we can deduce the transversal theorem for non-equally spaced parallel lines.

EXAMPLE 9

Given three parallel lines l_1, l_2 and l_3 and two transversals p and q such that $|AB| = 2$ and $|BC| = 5$, show that $\dfrac{|AB|}{|BC|} = \dfrac{|DE|}{|EF|}$.

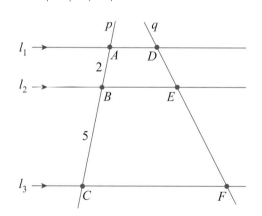

Solution

Draw equally spaced parallel lines between A and C so that $[AC]$ is divided into seven equal segments. The transversal theorem states that $[DF]$ will also be divided into seven equal segments each of length x, say.

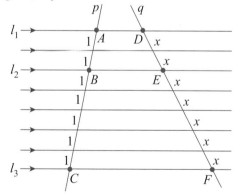

$$\therefore \frac{|AB|}{|BC|} = \frac{2}{5} \text{ and } \frac{|DE|}{|EF|} = \frac{2x}{5x} = \frac{2}{5}$$

$$\Rightarrow \frac{|AB|}{|BC|} = \frac{|DE|}{|EF|}$$

▶ Find y.

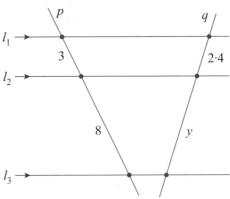

$$\frac{3}{8} = \frac{2 \cdot 4}{y} \Rightarrow y = \frac{8 \times 2 \cdot 4}{3} = 6 \cdot 4$$

EXERCISE 4

Diagrams are not drawn to scale.

1. l_1, l_2 and l_3 are three equally spaced parallel lines. Find $|BC|$ and $|EF|$.

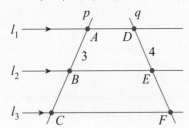

2. **(a)** l_1, l_2 and l_3 are parallel lines. Find $|BC|$.

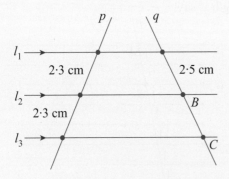

   (b) l_1, l_2 and l_3 are parallel lines. What can you say about these parallel lines?

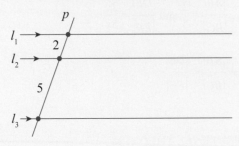

3. Two bridges, AB and CD, cross a river between two parallel banks, AC and BD. Another walkway, EF, joins the bridges. It is parallel to the banks and halfway between the two bridges. A woman walks from C to B along the path $CFEB$.

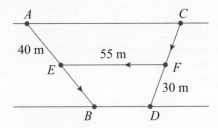

   How far does she walk in crossing the river?

4. l_1, l_2 and l_3 are three equally spaced parallel lines.

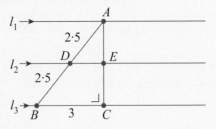

   Find:

   (a) $|AC|$ **(d)** area $\triangle ADE$

   (b) $|AE|$ **(e)** area $\triangle ABC$

   (c) $|DE|$ **(f)** area $\triangle ABC$: area $\triangle ADE$

5. Four houses have their frontage onto a lake. They back onto a road as shown. What is the length of the frontage of each of the four houses if $|AB| = 112 \cdot 92$ m?

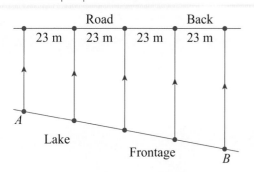

6. l_1, l_2, l_3 and l_4 are four parallel lines.

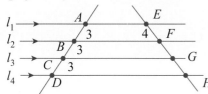

Find:

(a) $|FG|$

(b) $|GH|$

(c) $\dfrac{|AB|}{|BD|}$

(d) $\dfrac{|EF|}{|FH|}$

7. l_1, l_2 and l_3 are parallel lines and p and q are two transversals. Show that $|DE| = 2$ by drawing a line through E parallel to p.

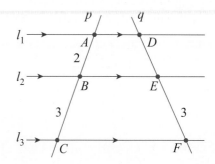

8. Find x if l_1, l_2 and l_3 are parallel lines and p and q are two transversals.

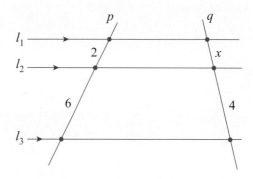

2.4 The ratio theorem

WORKED EXAMPLE

Explaining the ratio theorem

In $\triangle ABC$, $|AB| = 5$ and $|AC| = 10$. A line DE is drawn **parallel** to the **base** so that $|AD| = 3$ and $|DB| = 2$.

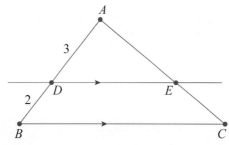

What are $|AE|$ and $|EC|$?

Divide [AB] into five equal segments by drawing equally spaced parallel lines starting at A and ending at B.

According to the transversal theorem [AC] is also divided into 5 equal segments by these lines.

This means the length of each segment is $\frac{10}{5} = 2$.

Therefore, $|AE| = 6$ and $|EC| = 4$.

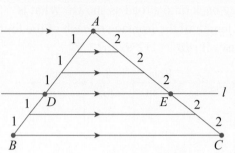

$$\therefore \frac{|AD|}{|DB|} = \frac{3}{2} \text{ and } \frac{|AE|}{|EC|} = \frac{6}{4} \Rightarrow \frac{|AD|}{|DB|} = \frac{|AE|}{|EC|}$$

Also, $\frac{|AD|}{|AB|} = \frac{3}{5}$ and $\frac{|AE|}{|AC|} = \frac{6}{10} \Rightarrow \frac{|AD|}{|AB|} = \frac{|AE|}{|AC|}$

And, of course, $\frac{|DB|}{|AB|} = \frac{2}{5}$ and $\frac{|EC|}{|AC|} = \frac{4}{10} \Rightarrow \frac{|DB|}{|AB|} = \frac{|EC|}{|AC|}$

The idea in this example is the basis of the ratio theorem.

THE RATIO THEOREM

If a line *l* drawn parallel to side [BC] of ΔABC divides [AB] in the ratio *s*:*t*, it also divides [AC] in the ratio *s*:*t* and vice versa.

$$\therefore \frac{|AD|}{|DB|} = \frac{|AE|}{|EC|} = \frac{s}{t}$$

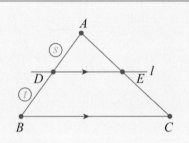

WARNING

Do not mix up the ratio in which a side is divided with the actual lengths of these divisions.

So when you are given a ratio which you wish to mark on the diagram, it is a good idea to put a circle around each number as shown on the triangle above.

TIP

You should use the ratio theorem as follows:

$$\frac{\text{Top}}{\text{Bottom}} = \frac{\text{Top}}{\text{Bottom}}$$

$$\frac{\text{Top}}{\text{Whole}} = \frac{\text{Top}}{\text{Whole}}$$

$$\frac{\text{Bottom}}{\text{Whole}} = \frac{\text{Bottom}}{\text{Whole}}$$

▸ In ΔABC, DE is parallel to AB.

$$\frac{|CD|}{|DA|} = \frac{5}{4} = \frac{|CE|}{|EB|}$$

$$\frac{|CD|}{|CA|} = \frac{5}{9} = \frac{|CE|}{|CB|}$$

$$\frac{|AD|}{|AC|} = \frac{4}{9} = \frac{|BE|}{|BC|}$$

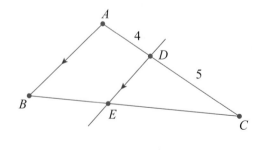

SYLLABUS NOTE

You need to know the proof for the ratio theorem for the Leaving Certificate exam.

PROOF OF THE RATIO THEOREM

In $\triangle ABC$, if a line DE is parallel to BC and cuts $[AB]$ in the ratio $s:t$, then it also cuts $[AC]$ in the same ratio.

Given: $\triangle ABC$ with a line DE parallel to $[BC]$ dividing $[AB]$ in the ratio $s:t$.

Construction: Divide $[AB]$ into $(s + t)$ segments of equal length x by drawing equally spaced parallel lines starting at A and ending at B as shown.

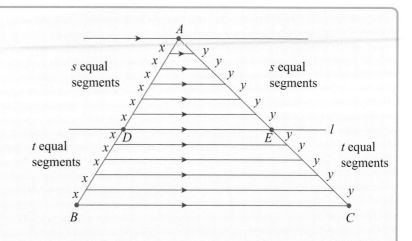

Proof: By the transversal theorem, the segments on $[AC]$ have equal length y.

$$\therefore \frac{|AD|}{|DB|} = \frac{sx}{tx} = \frac{s}{t} \Rightarrow \frac{|AE|}{|EC|} = \frac{sy}{ty} = \frac{s}{t}$$

Therefore, DE divides $[AC]$ in the same ratio.

In words: A line drawn parallel to any side of a triangle divides the other two sides in the same ratio.

The converse of the ratio theorem is also true. Can you state it?

EXAMPLE 10

In $\triangle ABC$, $|AB| = 6$ cm and $|AE| = 2 \cdot 8$ cm. If $|BD|:|DA| = 3:2$ and $[DE] \parallel [BC]$.

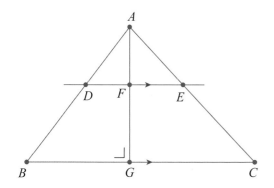

Find:

(a) $|BD|$

(b) $|DA|$

(c) $|EC|$

(d) $|AC|$

(e) $\dfrac{|AF|}{|FG|}$

Solution

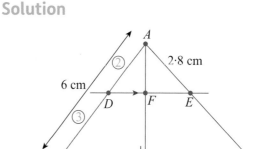

(a) $|BD| = \dfrac{3}{5}|BA| = \dfrac{3}{5} \times 6 = 3 \cdot 6$ cm

(b) $|DA| = \dfrac{2}{5}|BA| = \dfrac{2}{5} \times 6 = 2 \cdot 4$ cm

(c) $\dfrac{|EC|}{|AE|} = \dfrac{3}{2} \Rightarrow |EC| = \dfrac{3}{2} \times 2 \cdot 8 = 3 \times 1 \cdot 4 = 4 \cdot 2$ cm

(d) $|AC| = |AE| + |EC| = 2 \cdot 8 + 4 \cdot 2 = 7$ cm

(e) $\dfrac{|AF|}{|FG|} = \dfrac{2}{3}$

EXAMPLE **11**

A wooden beam $[DE]$ in the roof space of a house is parallel to the floor $[BC]$.

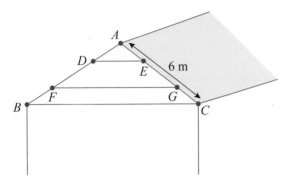

(a) If $|AB| = 7 \cdot 5$ m, $|AC| = 6$ m and $|AD| : |DB| = 1 : 2$, find:

    (i) $|AD|$ **(iii)** $|AE|$

    (ii) $|DB|$ **(iv)** $|EC|$

(b) Another beam $[FG]$ is inserted parallel to $[BC]$ such that $|DF| : |FB| = 3 : 2$, find:

    (i) $|DF|$

    (ii) $|FB|$

    (iii) $|EG|$

    (iv) $|GC|$

Solution

(a)

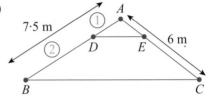

    (i) $|AD| = \frac{1}{3} \times 7 \cdot 5 = 2 \cdot 5$ m

    (ii) $|DB| = \frac{2}{3} \times 7 \cdot 5 = 5$ m

    (iii) $|AE| = \frac{1}{3} \times 6 = 2$ m   [Ratio theorem]

    (iv) $|EC| = \frac{2}{3} \times 6 = 4$ m   [Ratio theorem]

(b)

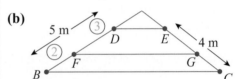

    (i) $|DF| = \frac{3}{5} \times 5 = 3$ m

    (ii) $|FB| = \frac{2}{5} \times 5 = 2$ m

    (iii) $|EG| = \frac{3}{5} \times 4 = 2 \cdot 4$ m

    (iv) $|GC| = \frac{2}{5} \times 4 = 1 \cdot 6$ m

         [Corollary to transversal theorem]

EXAMPLE **12**

In $\triangle ABC$, $[EF] \parallel [BC]$. In $\triangle ACD$, $[FG] \parallel [CD]$. Show that $\frac{x}{y} = \frac{z}{w}$ using the ratio theorem on $\triangle ABC$ and $\triangle ACD$.

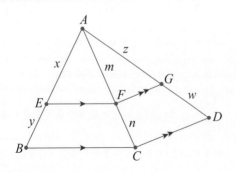

Solution

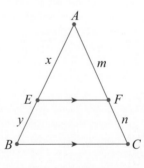

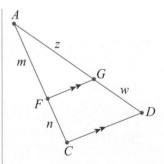

$\frac{x}{y} = \frac{m}{n}$ [Ratio theorem] $\frac{m}{n} = \frac{z}{w}$ [Ratio theorem]

$$\therefore \frac{x}{y} = \frac{z}{w}$$

EXERCISE 5

Diagrams are not drawn to scale.

1. Find *x* in each of the following:

   (a)
   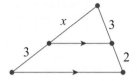

   (b)
   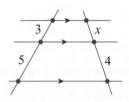

   (c)
   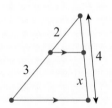

   (d)
   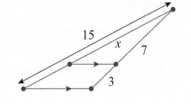

   (e)
   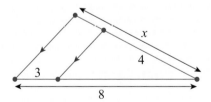

   (f)
   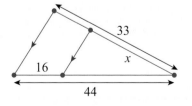

2. **(a)** Find x, $\left|\angle ABC\right|$ and $\dfrac{\text{Area }\triangle ABC}{\text{Area }\triangle ADE}$.

   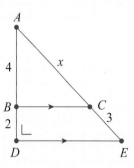

   (b) Find *x* and *y*.

   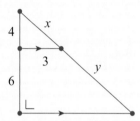

   (c) Find *x*.

   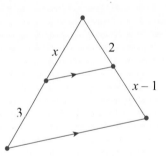

   (d) Find *x* and *y*.

   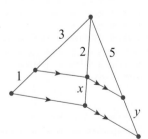

3. In $\triangle ABC$: $\dfrac{|AD|}{|DB|} = \dfrac{4}{5}$.

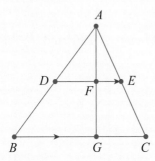

   (i) If $|AB| = 18$ cm, find $|DB|$.

   (ii) If $|AE| = 6$ cm, find $|EC|$.

   (iii) Find $\dfrac{|AF|}{|FG|}$.

4. In $\triangle ACE$: $[BD] \parallel [CE]$. In $\triangle AEG$: $[DF] \parallel [EG]$.

   Show that $\dfrac{|AB|}{|BC|} = \dfrac{|AF|}{|FG|}$.

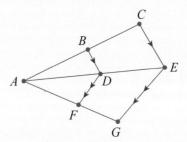

5. In $\triangle ABC$: $[EF] \parallel [BC]$ and $[DF] \parallel [EC]$.

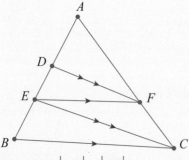

   (a) Show that $\dfrac{|AD|}{|DE|} = \dfrac{|AE|}{|EB|}$.

   (b) If $|AD| = 4$ cm and $|DE| = 2$ cm, find $|EB|$.

6. In $\triangle ADE$: $[BC] \parallel [DE]$ and $[BF] \parallel [DC]$.

   Show that $\dfrac{|AC|}{|CE|} = \dfrac{|AF|}{|FC|}$.

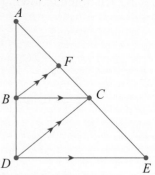

7. In $\triangle ABC$: $[DE] \parallel [BC]$ and $|\angle AED| = |\angle DEB|$.

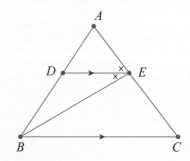

   Show that:

   (a) $|EC| = |EB|$

   (b) $|AD| : |DB| = |AE| : |EB|$

2.5 Similar (equiangular) triangles

If the measures of three angles in one triangle are equal respectively to the measures of the three angles in another triangle, the two triangles are said to be similar (equiangular).

WORKED EXAMPLE

Properties of similar triangles

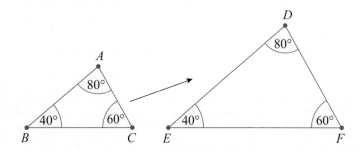

$\triangle ABC$ and $\triangle DEF$ are similar.

If $\triangle ABC$ is moved so that $A \rightarrow D$ and $[AB]$ lies along $[DE]$, then $[AC]$ will lie along $[DF]$ as DF makes an angle of $80°$ with $[DE]$.

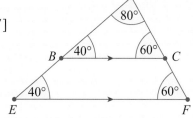

Since $|\angle ABC| = |\angle DEF| = 40°$ and $|\angle ACB| = |\angle DFE| = 60°$ are corresponding angles, it follows that $[BC] \parallel [EF]$.

$|AB|$ is a fraction of $|DE|$, $|AC|$ is a fraction of $|DF|$ and $|BC|$ is a fraction of $|EF|$.

$\triangle DEF$ is just an enlargement (*see* Section 4.2) of $\triangle ABC$.

TIP

You need only two angles to be equal in two triangles for them to be similar as the third angle in each must inevitably be equal.
Do you know why?

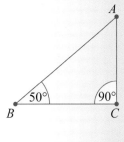
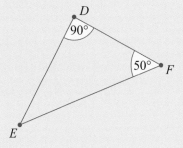

These two triangles are similar because
$|\angle ACB| = 90° = |\angle EDF|$, $|\angle ABC| = 50° = |\angle DFE|$
and hence $|\angle BAC| = 40° = |\angle DEF|$.

WORKED EXAMPLE The ratio of the sides of similar triangles

In the previous worked example $\triangle ABC$ is moved so that $A \to D$.

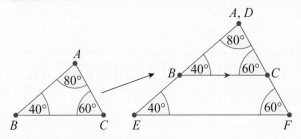

Since $[BC] \parallel [EF]$ we can say by the ratio theorem that $\dfrac{|AB|}{|DE|} = \dfrac{|AC|}{|DF|}$.

Similarly, if $\triangle ABC$ is moved so that $B \to E$ such that $[BA]$ lies along $[ED]$ then $[BC]$ will lie along $[EF]$.

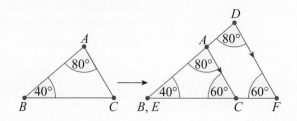

Since $[AC] \parallel [DF]$ we can say by the ratio theorem that $\dfrac{|AB|}{|DE|} = \dfrac{|BC|}{|EF|}$.

$\therefore \dfrac{|AB|}{|DE|} = \dfrac{|BC|}{|EF|} = \dfrac{|AC|}{|DF|}$

This result leads to the similar triangle theorem.

THE SIMILAR TRIANGLE THEOREM

If two triangles ABC and DEF are similar (equiangular), then the lengths of their sides are proportional in order.

In words, the theorem simply says:

The ratio of the lengths of sides opposite angle x

= the ratio of the lengths of sides opposite angle y

= the ratio of the lengths of sides opposite angle z.

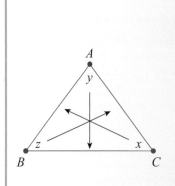
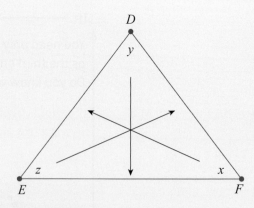

$$\frac{|AB|}{|DE|} = \frac{|BC|}{|EF|} = \frac{|AC|}{|DF|}$$

EXAMPLE 13

Triangles ABC and DEF are similar with $|\angle ABC| = |\angle DEF|$ and $|\angle BAC| = |\angle EDF|$.

Find x and y.

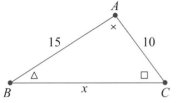 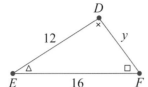

Solution

$$\frac{x}{16} = \frac{15}{12} \Rightarrow x = \frac{15 \times 16}{12} = 20$$

$$\frac{10}{y} = \frac{15}{12} \Rightarrow y = \frac{12 \times 10}{15} = 8$$

EXAMPLE 14

In $\triangle ABD$, $|\angle BAD| = |\angle ECD|$. Find $x = |AE|$ by drawing $\triangle ABD$ and $\triangle ECD$ separately.

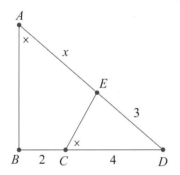

Solution

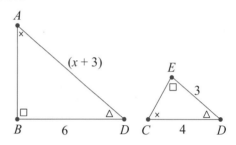

$|\angle BAD| = |\angle ECD|$ [Given]

$|\angle ADB| = |\angle EDC|$ [Common angle]

$\therefore \triangle ABD$ and $\triangle ECD$ are similar.

$$\frac{x+3}{4} = \frac{6}{3}$$

$$x + 3 = 8$$

$$\therefore x = 5$$

EXAMPLE 15

By holding a €1 coin at arm's length, it is possible to cover completely the face of a person standing a certain distance away. (The diagram is not drawn to scale.)

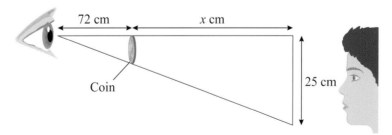

The diameter of a €1 coin is 2·325 cm and the distance from the top of a person's head to her chin is 25 cm. If the coin is held 72 cm from the observer's eye, find the distance from the top of the coin to the top of the person's head.

Solution

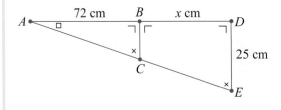

$\triangle ABC$ and $\triangle ADE$ are similar.

$$\therefore \frac{x + 72}{72} = \frac{25}{2\cdot325}$$

$2\cdot325(x + 72) = 72(25)$

$2\cdot325x + 167\cdot4 = 1800$

$2\cdot325x = 1632\cdot6$

$x = \dfrac{1632\cdot6}{2\cdot325} \approx 702 \text{ cm} = 7\cdot02 \text{ m}$

PROOF OF THE SIMILAR TRIANGLE THEOREM

If two triangles ABC and DEF are similar, then their sides are proportional in order.

Given: Two similar triangles $\triangle ABC$ and $\triangle DEF$ with $|\angle ABC| = |\angle DEF|$, $|\angle BAC| = |\angle EDF|$ and $|\angle ACB| = |\angle DFE|$.

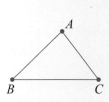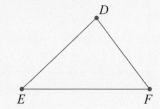

To prove: $\dfrac{|AB|}{|DE|} = \dfrac{|BC|}{|EF|} = \dfrac{|AC|}{|DF|}$

Construction: Draw $\triangle DGH$ in $\triangle DEF$ with $|DG| = |AB|, |\angle GDH| = |\angle BAC|$ and $|DH| = |AC|$.

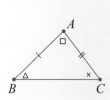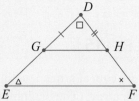

Proof:

$\triangle DGH \equiv \triangle ABC$ [2 sides and included angle (**SAS**)]

$\Rightarrow |\angle DGH| = |\angle ABC| = |\angle DEF|$

$\therefore GH \parallel EF$

$\Rightarrow \dfrac{|DG|}{|DE|} = \dfrac{|DH|}{|DF|}$ [Ratio theorem]

$\therefore \dfrac{|AB|}{|DE|} = \dfrac{|AC|}{|DF|}$

Similarly, by translating $\triangle ABC$ so that $B \to E$ and $[BA]$ lies along $[ED]$ and $[BC]$ along $[EF]$ then

$\dfrac{|BC|}{|EF|} = \dfrac{|AB|}{|DE|}$.

$\therefore \dfrac{|AB|}{|DE|} = \dfrac{|BC|}{|EF|} = \dfrac{|AC|}{|DF|}$

EXERCISE 6

Diagrams are not drawn to scale.

1. Find *x* and *y* for the similar triangles below.

    (a)

    (b)

     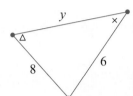

    (c)

    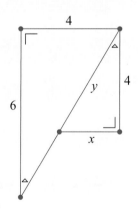

    (d)

    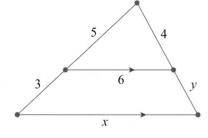

2. Find *x* and *y*.

    (a)

    (image of triangle with sides 5, 4, 3, 6, x, y)

    (b)

    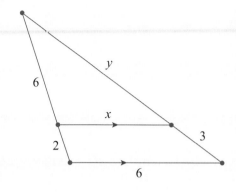

    (c)

    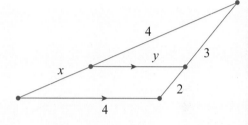

3. Write down the equal angles in △*ABC* and △*DCE* on the figures below and find the missing value(s).

    (a)

    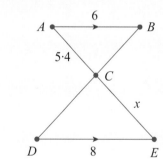

    (b)

    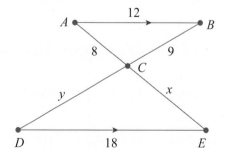

4. (a) Find x and y if $\left|\angle DAB\right| = \left|\angle DBC\right|$ and $\left|\angle BDA\right| = \left|\angle BDC\right|$.

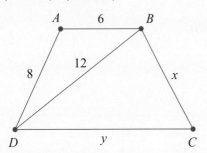

(b) Find $x = \left|AE\right|$ if $\angle EAB = \left|\angle ECD\right|$ and C is on $[BD]$.

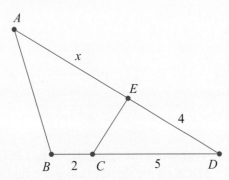

(c) Find x if $\left|\angle ABC\right| = \left|\angle AED\right|$ and D is on $[AB]$.

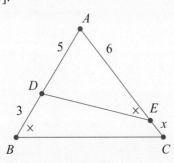

5. Show that $\triangle ABD$ and $\triangle BDC$ are similar if $\left|\angle ABC\right| = 90°$ and $[BD]$ is perpendicular to $[AC]$. Find $\left|DC\right|$ if $\left|AD\right| = 4$ and $\left|BD\right| = 6$.

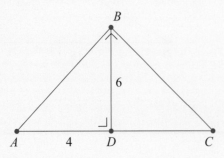

6. Show that $\triangle ABD$ and $\triangle ACD$ are similar if $\left|\angle ABC\right| = \left|\angle CAD\right|$ and C is on $[BD]$. Find x and y.

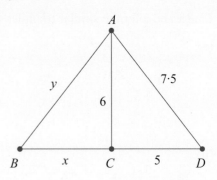

7. In $\triangle ABC$, $\left|\angle CAB\right| = \left|\angle ADB\right| = 90°$. Find $\left|BC\right|$ and $\left|AD\right|$ if $\left|BD\right| = 4$ and $\left|AB\right| = 6$.

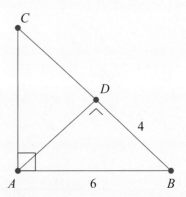

8. The width of a lake between two points A and B has to be measured.

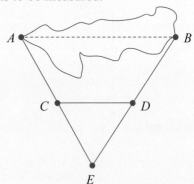

The distances from a point E to A and B are measured using a trundle wheel.

The midpoints C of $[AE]$ and D of $[BE]$ are found and marked with posts C and D.
The distance $\left|CD\right|$ is measured as 148 m.
What is $\left|AB\right|$?

9. Find the value of *h*, the height at which a tennis ball must be hit so that it just passes over the net and lands 5 m from the base of the net.

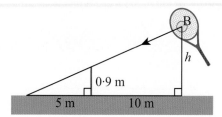

10. To estimate the height of a tree, a man walks 30 m from its base. He places a pole of height 3·0 m vertically in the ground at a point 3·2 m from him so that he can just see the top of the tree. The man's eye is 1·6 m above the ground. Find the height *h* of the tree, correct to one decimal place.

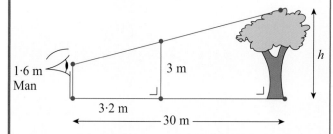

11. A camera takes a photograph of the ground. How high above the ground must the front of the camera be to photograph 60 m of the ground?

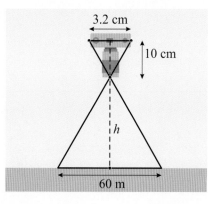

12. An object is placed a distance *d* in front of your eyeball. If *h* is the height of the object and *l* is the length of its image on the retina, find a formula relating *h*, *d* and *l*, where all distances are in metres. If *d* = 5 m and *l* = 1 mm, find *h*.

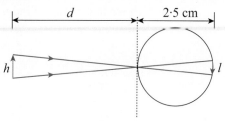

13. Thales calculated the height of the Great Pyramid at Giza. He placed a rod of height 1·2 m at the tip of the pyramid's shadow so that $|\angle ACB| = |\angle ECD|$. Find *h*, correct to the nearest metre.

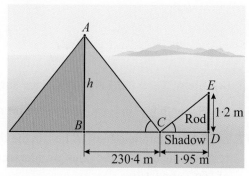

14. A family wish to convert their attic. This involves moving a beam from [*BC*] to [*EF*]. The beam must be parallel to the floor [*GH*]. Find $|EF|$.

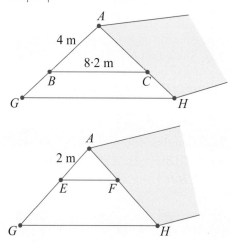

15. A wooden seesaw is hinged at *C* to the top of a vertical post 1·2 m high. The length of the seesaw $|AB| = 6·4$ m.

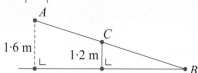

(a) When *B* is on the ground, *A* is 1·6 m above the ground. Find $|AC|$.

(b) When *A* reaches the ground, *B* rises to height *h* above the ground. Find *h*.

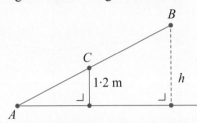

16. *ABCD* is a parallelogram. *E* divides [*AD*] in the ratio 3:2. *F* divides [*BC*] in the ratio 1:1.

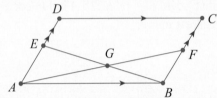

(a) Show that $\triangle EGA$ and $\triangle FGB$ are similar.

(b) Show that *G* divides [*EB*] in the ratio 6:5.

17. *DCBA* is a parallelogram. *E* lies on the line [*CB*] produced. *F* is the point of intersection of [*DE*] and [*AB*].

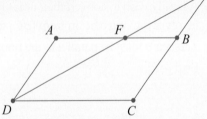

(a) Show that $\triangle AFD$ and $\triangle EFB$ are similar.

(b) If $|AF| = 2\,|FB|$, find $\dfrac{|BC|}{|EC|}$.

18. In $\triangle ACB$, $|\angle CAB| = 90°$ and [*AD*] is perpendicular to [*CB*]. Show that:

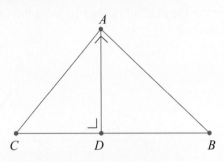

(a) $\triangle ACB$ and $\triangle ADB$ are similar,

(b) $|AB|^2 = |BD| \times |BC|$.

19. In $\triangle ABC$, *M* is the midpoint of [*BC*]. *P* is the midpoint of [*AM*]. *MS* is parallel to [*BQ*] where *S* and *Q* are on [*AC*].

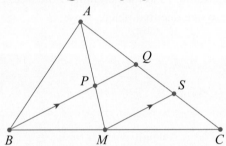

(a) Using $\triangle AMS$ show that $|AQ| = |QS|$.

(b) Using $\triangle BQC$ show that $|QS| = |SC|$.

(c) Show that $\triangle MSC$ is similar to $\triangle BQC$. Hence, show that $|MS| = \tfrac{1}{2}|BQ|$.

20. The triangles *ABC* and *A'B'C'* are similar with $|\angle ABC| = |\angle A'B'C'|$, $|\angle BCA| = |\angle B'C'A'|$ and $|\angle BAC| = |\angle B'A'C'|$.

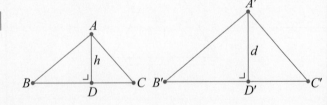

(a) If $\dfrac{|A'B'|}{|AB|} = k$, find $\dfrac{|B'C'|}{|BC|}$ and $\dfrac{|A'C'|}{|AC|}$.

(b) Show that:

   (i) $\triangle ABD$ is similar to $\triangle A'B'D'$ and find $\dfrac{|B'D'|}{|BD|}$ and $\dfrac{d}{h}$,

   (ii) $\triangle ADC$ is similar to $\triangle A'D'C'$ and find $\dfrac{|D'C'|}{|DC|}$ and $\dfrac{d}{h}$.

(c) Show that $\dfrac{\text{Area } \triangle A'B'C'}{\text{Area } \triangle ABC} = k^2$.

21. In the quadrilateral *AEDB*, *DE* is perpendicular to [*AE*] and *F* is on [*DE*]. $|\angle DBC| = |\angle BAC| = |\angle DFB| = 90°$ where *C* is on [*AE*].

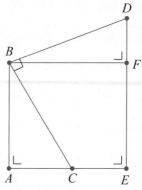

(a) Show that $|\angle FBD| = |\angle ABC|$.

(b) Show that $\triangle BDF$ and $\triangle BCA$ are similar.

(c) If $|BD| = |BC|$, show that $|BF| = |BA|$ and say why *AEFB* is a square.

2.6 Area of triangles and parallelograms

Area of a triangle

The area of a triangle is given by: $\boxed{\text{Area} = \frac{1}{2} \times (\text{Base}) \times (\text{Perpendicular height})}$

WORKED EXAMPLE

Does it matter which side is used as the base?

For $\triangle ABC$, [*AB*] is the base, [*AC*] is the perpendicular height.

$\therefore$ Area $= \frac{1}{2}|AB| \times |AC| = \frac{1}{2} \times 3 \times 4 = 6$

Similarly, if [*AC*] is the base, [*AB*] is the perpendicular height.

$\therefore$ Area $= \frac{1}{2} \times |AC| \times |AB| = \frac{1}{2} \times 4 \times 3 = 6$

What if [*BC*] is used as the base?

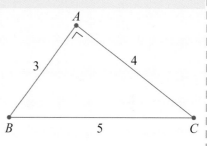

Draw [*AD*] perpendicular to [*BC*].
The perpendicular height $h = |AD|$.
Area $= \frac{1}{2} \times 5 \times h$

Triangles *ABD* and *ABC* are similar. Separate out the similar triangles.

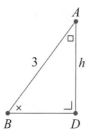
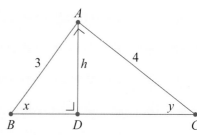

$\therefore \frac{h}{4} = \frac{3}{5} \Rightarrow h = \frac{12}{5}$

Area $= \frac{1}{2} \times 5 \times \frac{12}{5} = 6$

This example is the basis of the area theorem.

THE AREA THEOREM

The area of a triangle is always the same no matter what side you take as the base.

EXAMPLE 16

Find the area of $\triangle ABC$ if $|AB| = 6$ cm, $|BC| = 7.5$ cm, $|AC| = 8$ cm and $|AE| = 5.7$ cm. Hence, find $|CD|$ and $|BF|$, correct to one decimal place where $[CD]$ is perpendicular to $[AB]$ and $[BF]$ is perpendicular to $[AC]$.

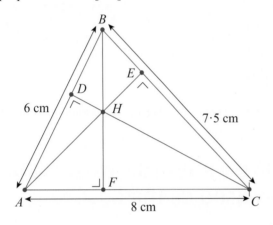

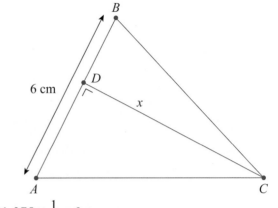

$$21.375 = \frac{1}{2} \times 6 \times x$$

$$x = \frac{21.375}{3} = 7.125 = |CD|$$

$$\therefore x = |CD| \approx 7.1 \text{ cm}$$

Solution

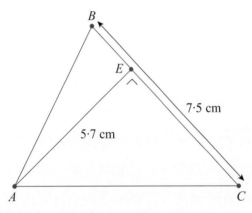

Area $\triangle ABC = \frac{1}{2} \times 7.5 \times 5.7 = 21.375$ cm^2

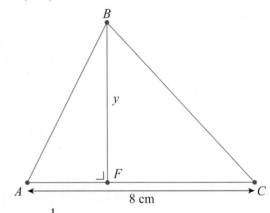

$$21.375 = \frac{1}{2} \times 8y$$

$$\therefore y = \frac{21.375}{4} = 5.344 = |BC|$$

$$\therefore y = |BF| \approx 5.3 \text{ cm}$$

EXAMPLE 17

A field ABC for ploughing is marked out. A second field ADC must be marked out with the same area such that $[BD] \parallel [AC]$. Draw in the perpendicular height for each triangle. Using $[AC]$ as the base:

(a) find the area of $\triangle ABC$,

(b) find the area of $\triangle ADC$,

(c) find the area of $\triangle AEC$ if $|BE| : |EC| = \frac{3}{2}$ if $\triangle AEC$ is left unploughed.

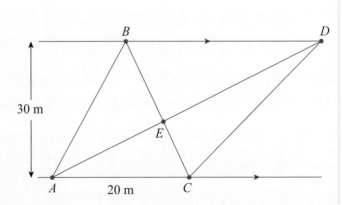

Solution

(a) Area $\triangle ABC = \frac{1}{2} \times 20 \times 30 = 300 \text{ m}^2$

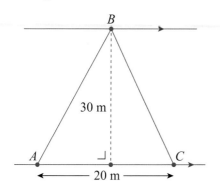

(b) Area $\triangle ADC = \frac{1}{2} \times 20 \times 30 = 300 \text{ m}^2$

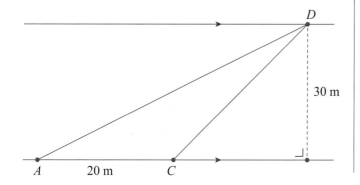

(c) Let h = height of $\triangle AEC$.

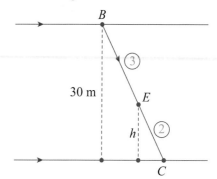

$$\frac{|BC|}{|EC|} = \frac{30}{h} = \frac{5}{2}$$

$$h = \frac{2}{5} \times 30 = 12 \text{ m}$$

$$\therefore \text{ Area of } \triangle AEC = \frac{1}{2} \times 20 \times 12$$
$$= 120 \text{ m}^2$$

EXAMPLE 18

'If two triangles are congruent, they are identical and so they have the same area.'

(a) What is the converse of this statement?

(b) Show the converse is false by an example or drawing.

Solution

(a) The converse statement: 'Two triangles with the same area are congruent.'

(b)

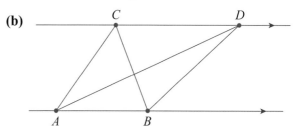

$\triangle ACB$ and $\triangle ADB$ have the same area. They are clearly not congruent.

This is an example of a false converse.

Area of a parallelogram

ACTIVITY 12

ACTION
Finding the area of parallelograms

OBJECTIVE
To find the areas of given parallelograms

We have already shown that a diagonal of a parallelogram divides it into two congruent triangles.

So the area of a parallelogram is divided into two triangles of equal area by a diagonal.

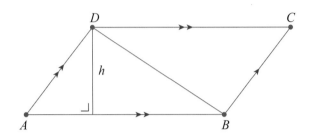

∴ Area of the parallelogram $ABCD$ = 2 × (Area of the $\triangle ABD$)

$$= 2 \times \frac{1}{2} \times |AB| \times h = |AB| \times h = \text{Base} \times \text{perpendicular height}$$

Area of a parallelogram = Base × perpendicular height

EXAMPLE 19

$DCBA$ is a parallelogram.

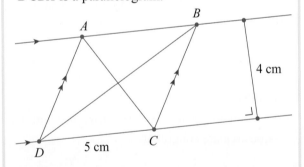

Find the area of:

(a) $\triangle ADC$

(b) $\triangle BDC$

(c) parallelogram $DCBA$

Solution

(a) Area of $\triangle ADC = \frac{1}{2} \times 5 \times 4 = 10$ cm^2

(b) Area of $\triangle BDC = \frac{1}{2} \times 5 \times 4 = 10$ cm^2

(c) Area of parallelogram = $5 \times 4 = 20$ cm^2

EXAMPLE 20

The area of the parallelogram $DCBA$ is 40.

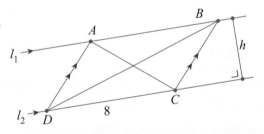

Find the perpendicular distance between the parallel lines l_1 and l_2.

Solution

Area = Base × height

$\Rightarrow 40 = 8 \times h$

$h = 5$

EXAMPLE 21

ABCD is a parallelogram. Find *h*.

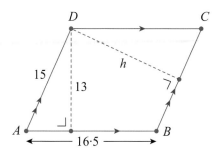

Solution

Area $= 16 \cdot 5 \times 13 = 15 \times h$

$\therefore h = 14 \cdot 3$

EXAMPLE 22

DCBA is a parallelogram with area 15 cm^2.
If $|BE| = 3$ cm, find $|AC|$.

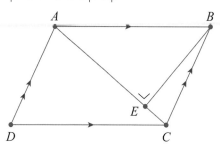

Solution

Area $= 15$ cm$^2 = 2 \times$ Area $\triangle ABC$

$= 2 \times \dfrac{1}{2} \times |AC| \times 15$

$|AC| = 5$ cm

EXAMPLE 23

BDEA is a parallelogram with $|AE| = 2|AB|$.
C is the midpoint of $[BD]$.

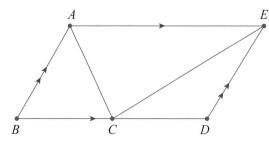

(a) Show that $|\angle ACE| = 90°$.

(b) If $|AB| = |AC| = 4$, find the area of $\triangle ACE$ and, hence, the area of parallelogram *BDEA*.

Solution

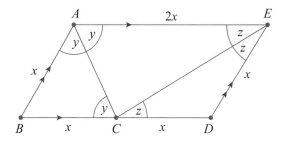

(a) Adjacent angles in a parallelogram add to 180°
$\Rightarrow 2y + 2z = 180°$

$\therefore y + z = 90°$

$\therefore |\angle ACE| = 180° - 90° = 90°$

(b)

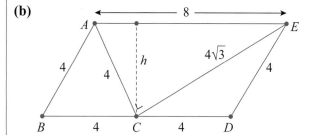

$|CE| = \sqrt{64 - 16} = \sqrt{48} = 4\sqrt{3}$

Area $\triangle ACE = \dfrac{1}{2} \times 4\sqrt{3} \times 4 = 8\sqrt{3}$

$8\sqrt{3} = \dfrac{1}{2} \times 8h$

$h = 2\sqrt{3}$

Area parallelogram $= 8 \times 2\sqrt{3} = 16\sqrt{3}$

or

Area parallelogram $= 2$(area of $\triangle ACE$)

EXERCISE 7

Diagrams are not drawn to scale.

1. Find the area of the triangles shown.

    (a)

    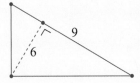

    (b)

    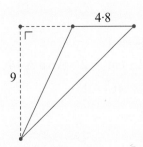

2. **(a)** Find the areas of $\triangle ABC$ and $\triangle DEF$.

    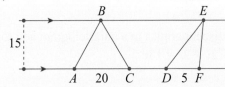

    (b) Find the areas of $\triangle ABC$ and $\triangle ACD$.

    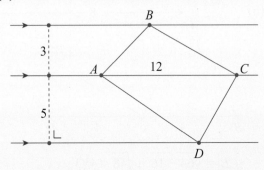

    (c) Find the areas of triangles $\triangle ABC$, $\triangle BCD$ and $\triangle CDE$ if $[AE]$ is parallel to $[BD]$, $[AB]$ is parallel to $[CD]$ and $[BC]$ is parallel to $[DE]$.

    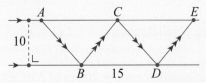

3. **(a)** Find $x = |BC|$ if the area $\triangle ABC = 30$.

    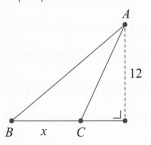

    (b) Find x if $|BC| = 15$, $|AB| = 12$, $|EC| = 14$ and $|AD| = x$.

    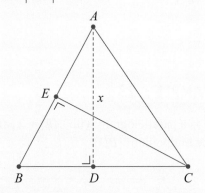

    (c) Find h if the area of the quadrilateral $BDCA$ is 54, $|CD| = 6$ and $|BD| = 8$.

    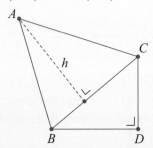

4. **(a)** A surveyor measures the distances $|AB|$, $|AD|$ and $|BD|$ in order to find the area of a plot of land $ADCB$ on which to build a house.

    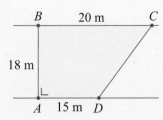

    If $[BC]$ is parallel to $[AD]$ and $[BA]$ is perpendicular to $[AD]$ find the area of $ADCB$.

(b) A trapezium is a quadrilateral with two parallel sides.

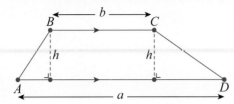

Show that the area of the trapezium is $\frac{1}{2}h(a+b)$.

(This can be remembered as half the sum of the lengths of the parallel sides by the perpendicular distance between the parallel sides.)

(c) A velocity-time curve is a trapezium as shown.

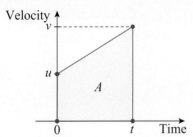

Show that the shaded area A is given by:

$$A = \frac{(u+v)t}{2}.$$

(d) In $\triangle ABC$ is shown, $|AC| = a$, $|BE| = b$, $|BC| = x$ and $|AD| = y$.

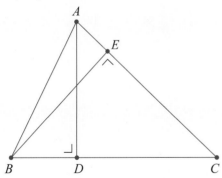

(i) Show that $\triangle BCE$ and $\triangle ACD$ are similar.

(ii) Hence, show that $\dfrac{y}{b} = \dfrac{a}{x}$.

(iii) Show that the area of $\triangle ABC$ with base $[AC]$ equals the area of $\triangle ABC$ with base $[BC]$.

5. Find the area of each parallelogram $ADCB$ below.

(a)

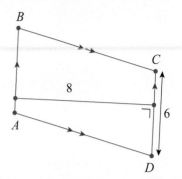

(b)

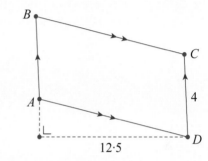

6. Find the perpendicular height h of parallelogram $ADCB$ shown.

Area = 320 and $|BA| = 16$

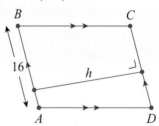

7. **(a)** Find x if $ADCB$ is a parallelogram with $|AB| = 12 \cdot 5$ and $|AD| = 25$.

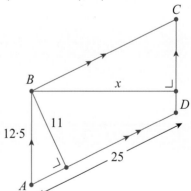

(b) If the perimeter of the parallelogram *ADCB* is 58 and the area is 414, find *x* and *h*.

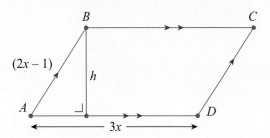

8. *ADCB* is a parallelogram.

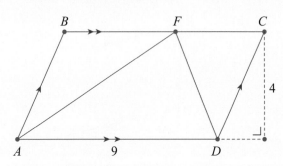

  (a) Find the area of $\triangle AFD$.

  (b) If *F* divides [*BC*] such that [*BF*]:[*FC*] = 2:1, find the area of $\triangle FDC$.

9. *ADCB* is a parallelogram. Find *x* if $|AB| = 15$ and $|AD| = 20$.

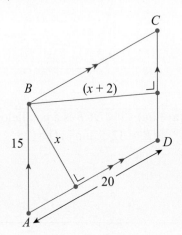

10. *ADCB* is a parallelogram with $|CD| = 5$, $|ED| = 3$ and $|BC| = \sqrt{65}$. Find:

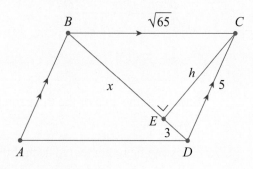

  (a) $h = |CE|$

  (b) $x = |BE|$

  (c) the area of the parallelogram

11. *ADCB* is a rhombus of side 4 with $|\angle BAD| = 60°$. Find its area.

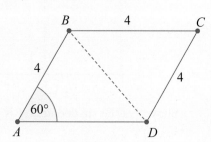

  Hint: Write in all angles in $\triangle ADB$ and find its area.

Circles

Learning Outcomes

- To understand a number of properties of circles.

- To understand the properties of tangents and chords to circles.

3.1 Circles

ACTIVITY 13

ACTION
Angle standing on
an arc of a circle 1

OBJECTIVE
*To find the relationship
between the angle
on a circle and the
angle at the centre of
the circle standing on
the same arc*

Angle standing on an arc

In the circle s_1 with centre O, the shorter of the two arcs joining A to B is known as the **minor** arc ($|\angle OAB| < 180°$) and the longer one is known as the **major** arc ($|\angle OAB| > 180°$).

In the circle s_2 with centre O and radius r, $\angle AOC$ is the angle at the centre standing on the minor arc AC and $\angle ABC$ is the angle at point B on the circle standing on the minor arc AC.

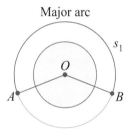
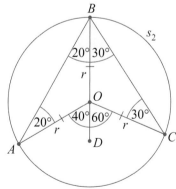

In $\triangle AOB$, $|AO| = |OB| = r$ and $|\angle OAB| = 20°$.

$|\angle AOD| = 20° + 20° = 40°$ [Exterior angle]

In $\triangle COB$, $|OC| = |OB| = r$ and $|\angle OCB| = 30°$.

$|\angle DOC| = 30° + 30° = 60°$ [Exterior angle]

$\therefore |\angle AOC| = 40° + 60° = 100° = 2|\angle ABC|$

This result is a consequence of a more general circle theorem.

THE ARC THEOREM

The size of the angle at the centre of a circle standing on an arc is twice the size of the angle at any point of the circle standing on the same arc.

There are four corollaries of the arc theorem.

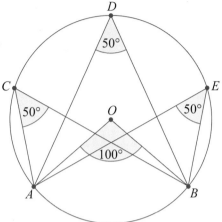

Angles standing on the same arc

Lots of angles can stand on the same arc
of a circle.

All the angles standing on the minor arc *AB*
are half the size of the angle at the centre
standing on the same minor arc *AB*, and
so they are all equal in size.

COROLLARY 1

Angles standing on the same arc are
equal in size.

Angle in a semicircle

An angle in a semicircle is a special case of
what we have discovered above.

The angle $\angle ACB$ standing on the arc *AB*,
where [*AB*] is a diameter of the circle,
is 90° because $|\angle AOB|$ is 180°.

COROLLARY 2

The angle at a point on a circle standing
on an arc *AB* is always 90° if [*AB*] is a
diameter of the circle.

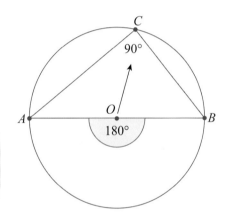

The converse of this corollary is also true.

COROLLARY 3

If the angle standing on a chord [*AB*] at some point of a circle is a
right angle, then [*AB*] is a diameter of this circle.

Cyclic quadrilaterals

A cyclic quadrilateral is a quadrilateral with **all**
four vertices on a circle.

ADCB is a cyclic quadrilateral in a circle with
centre *O*.

$$|\angle ABC| = 80° \Rightarrow x = 160°$$

$$\therefore y = 200° \Rightarrow |\angle ADC| = 100°$$

$$\therefore |\angle ABC| + |\angle ADC| = 180°$$

COROLLARY 4

The opposite angles in a cyclic quadrilateral add to 180°.

The converse of this corollary is also true. Can you state it?

EXAMPLE 1

ADCB is a cyclic quadrilateral of a circle with centre *O* as shown.

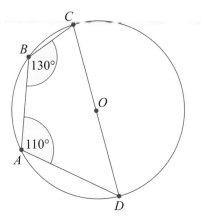

If $|\angle BAD| = 110°$ and $|\angle ABC| = 130°$, find:

(a) $|\angle ADC|$

(b) $|\angle BCD|$

(c) $|\angle CAB|$

Solution

(a) $|\angle ADC| = 180° - 130° = 50°$ [Corollary 4]

(b) $|\angle BCD| = 180° - 110° = 70°$ [Corollary 4]

(c) $|\angle CAB| = 110° - |\angle CAD|$
$= 110° - 90°$ [Corollary 2]
$= 20°$

EXAMPLE 2

BCDA is a cyclic quadrilateral with $|AD| = |AB|$. Find *x* if $|\angle DCE| = x°$.

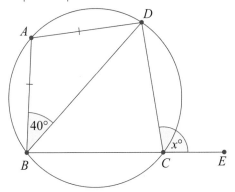

Solution

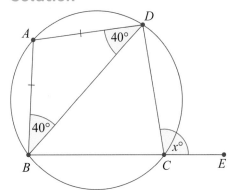

$|\angle ADB| = |\angle ABD| = 40°$ [Isosceles triangle]

$|\angle BAD| = 180° - 80° = 100°$

$\therefore |\angle DCB| = 180° - 100° = 80°$

$x = 100°$

EXAMPLE 3

$[AB]$ and $[CD]$ are two chords of a circle *s* with $|AB| = |CD|$.

(a) Show that $\triangle ABE \equiv \triangle CED$.

(b) Show that $|AD| = |BC|$.

Solution

(a) $|\angle BAD| = |\angle BCD|$ [Standing on the same arc *DB* (Angle **A**)]

      $|AB| = |CD|$ [Given (Side **S**)]

      $|\angle ABC| = |\angle ADC|$ [Standing on the same arc *AC* (Angle **A**)]

      $\therefore \triangle ABE \equiv \triangle CED$ [**ASA**]

(b) $\triangle ABE \equiv \triangle CED$

      $\Rightarrow |AE| = |CE|$

      and $|ED| = |EB|$

      $\therefore |AE| + |ED| = |CE| + |EB|$

      $\therefore |AD| = |BC|$

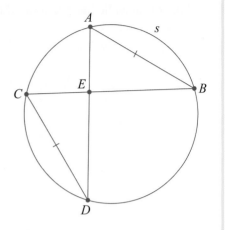

EXERCISE 8

Diagrams are not drawn to scale.

1. Find *x* and *y* as required. All circles have centre *O* when given.

(a)

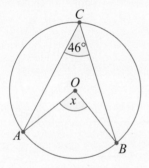

(b)

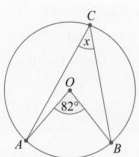

(c)

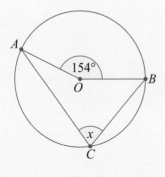

(d)

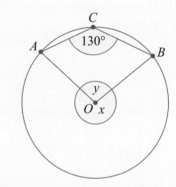

(e)

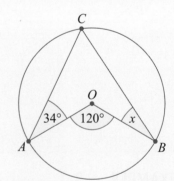

(f)

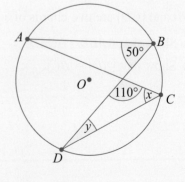

(g)

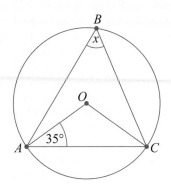

(h)

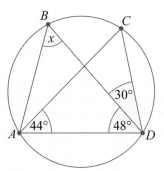

(i)

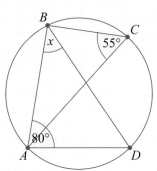

(j)

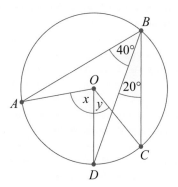

2. Find *x*, *y*, *z* and *w* as required. All circles have centre *O*.

(a)

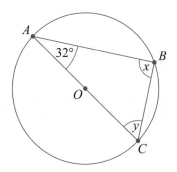

(b)

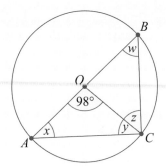

(c)

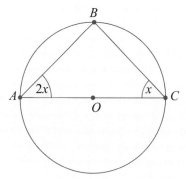

(d)

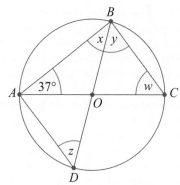

(e)

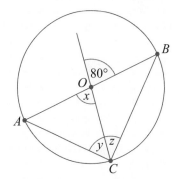

(f)

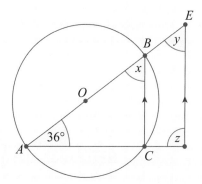

(g) In the circle shown, $|AB| = 15$, $[BC]$ is a diameter and $|BC| = 17$.

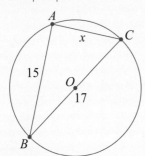

(h) In the circle shown, $|AC| = 2·4$, $[BC]$ is a diameter and $|BO| = 1·3$.

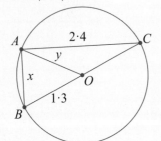

(i)

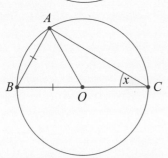

(j) $[AC]$ is a diameter of circle shown.

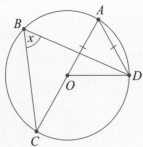

3. Find *x, y,* and *z* as required. *O* is the centre of a circle when given.

(a)

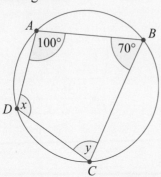

(b)

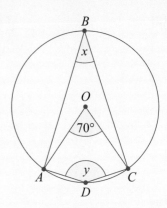

(c)

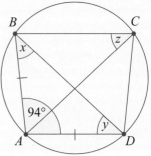

(d)

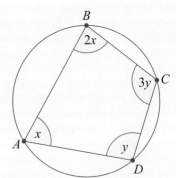

(e)

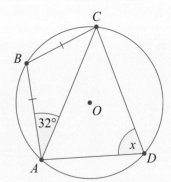

(f)

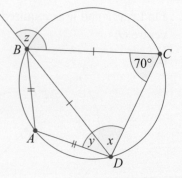

(g)

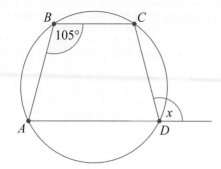

(h)

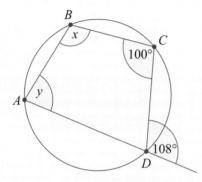

(i)

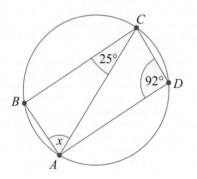

(j)

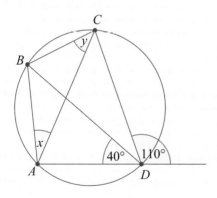

4. (a) *ADCB* is a cyclic quadrilateral. *E* is on the line *AD*.

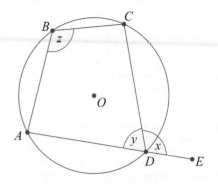

    (i) Express *x* in terms of *y*.

    (ii) Express *z* in terms of *y*.

    What can you deduce about $|\angle CDE|$ from **(i)** and **(ii)**?

(b) [*AB*] is the diameter of a circle with centre *O*.

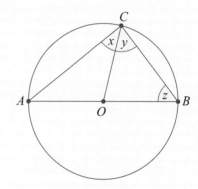

    (i) Express *x* in terms of *y*.

    (ii) Express *z* in terms of *y*.

    Hence, show that $x + z = 90°$.

(c) *ABCD* is a cyclic quadrilateral.

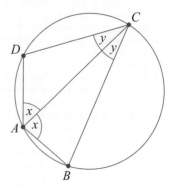

If $|\angle DAC| = |\angle CAB| = x$ and $|\angle ACD| = |\angle ACB| = y$, show that $|\angle ABC| = 90°$.

What does this tell you about [*AC*]?

(d) $BCDA$ is a cyclic quadrilateral with $|BE| = |EC|$. Prove that $BC \parallel AD$.

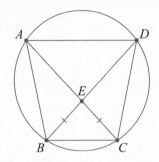

(e) $[AB]$ is a diameter of a circle with centre O with $|BQ| = |BA|$.

(i) Show that $|\angle BPQ| = 90°$.

(ii) Show that $|AP| = |PQ|$ by proving that triangles APB and PQB are congruent.

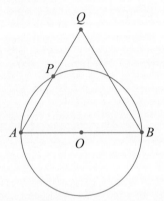

(f) $[AB]$ and $[PQ]$ are diameters of a circle with centre O.

(i) Show that $|\angle APQ| = |\angle PQB|$.

(ii) Say why $AP \parallel QB$.

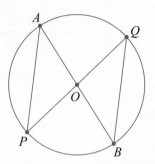

(g) $ABCD$ is a cyclic quadrilateral of circle s. $ABCF$ is a parallelogram. Show that $DEFG$ is a cyclic quadrilateral.

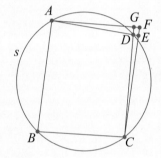

3.2 Tangents

KEY TERM

A **tangent** to a curve is a line (of infinite length, as are all lines) which intersects the curve at one point only.

A tangent to a circle

The circle s shown has centre O. To understand the idea of a tangent to the circle at the point P on the circle, start by drawing a series of successive lines through P that make angles from $0°$ to $180°$ with the diameter $[PP_1]$.

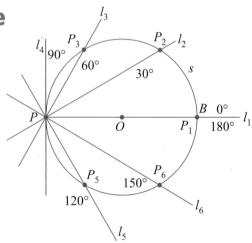

The table on the next page shows the number of points at which each line intersects the circle, as a function of the angle the line makes with the diameter.

Angle	Points	Number of points	Tangent
0°	PP_1	2	No
30°	PP_2	2	No
60°	PP_3	2	No
90°	P	1	Yes
120°	PP_5	2	No
150°	PP_6	2	No
180°	PP_1	2	No

Clearly, the only line which is the tangent at P is the line l_4 through P which makes an angle of 90° with the diameter $[PP_1]$. This is a very important result. The tangent at a point on the circle is perpendicular to the diameter (or radius) that goes to this point of intersection of the tangent and the circle. The point of intersection of the tangent and the circle is known as the point of contact of the tangent.

THE TANGENT THEOREM

Each tangent to a circle is perpendicular to the diameter (or radius) that goes to the point of contact.

PQ is a tangent at P to circle s

$\Rightarrow |\angle OPQ| = 90°$ where O is the centre of the circle.

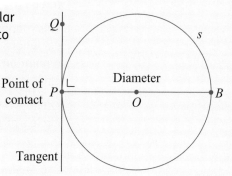

EXAMPLE 4

t is a tangent to the circle with centre O at P. Find x and y.

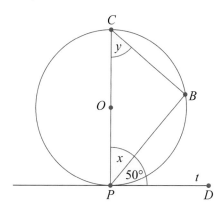

Solution

$|\angle CBP| = 40°$ [Angle standing on diameter]

$x = 90° - 50° = 40°$ [Tangent at P]

$y = 180° - 90° - 40° = 50°$

EXAMPLE 5

If t is a tangent to the circle with centre O at P, find x.

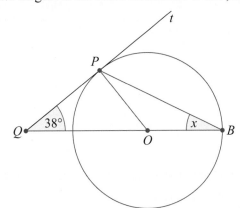

Solution

$|\angle QPO| = 90°$ [t is a tangent at P.]

$|\angle POQ| = 90° - 38° = 52°$

$\therefore |\angle POB| = 180° - 52° = 128°$

$\triangle OPB$ is an isosceles triangle

$\Rightarrow |\angle OPB| = \dfrac{180° - 128°}{2} = \dfrac{52°}{2} = 26°$

The converse of the tangent theorem is also true.

CONVERSE OF THE TANGENT THEOREM

If a point P lies on a circle s with centre O and line PQ is perpendicular to the radius $[OP]$, then PQ is a tangent to the circle at P.

This means that if a line t is drawn perpendicular to OP where O is the centre of a circle s and P is a point on the circle then t is a tangent to the circle s at P.

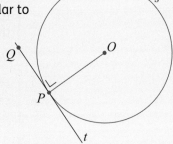

$|\angle OPQ| = 90° \Rightarrow PQ$ is a tangent to circle s at P.

Proof by contradiction

Proof by contradiction is used in many areas of mathematics.
The proof of the tangent theorem is a good example.

PROOF BY CONTRADICTION

Prove, by contradiction, that each tangent to a circle at a point on a circle is perpendicular to the diameter that goes to the point of contact.

Proof: Suppose the point of contact of a diameter of the circle with centre O is P and the tangent t at P **is not** perpendicular to OP. (This is the opposite of the statement of the theorem).

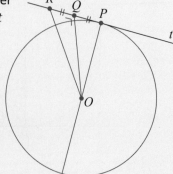

Draw the perpendicular from O to t to meet it at Q. Mark the point R on t such that $|PQ| = |QR|$ and join O to R.

$\triangle ORQ \equiv \triangle OQP$ **[SAS]**

$\Rightarrow |OR| = |OP|$

Therefore, the point R is on the circle.

This means that the line t cannot be a tangent as it goes through two points on the circle.

Therefore, t must be perpendicular to OP for it to be a tangent.

EXAMPLE 6

AB is a diameter of a circle *s* with centre *O* and $|\angle ABC| = 50°$. A line *AD* is drawn at $40°$ to *AC*. Is *AD* a tangent to *s* at *A*?

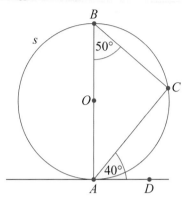

Solution

$|\angle ACB| = 90°$ [Angle standing on a diameter]

$\Rightarrow |\angle BAC| = 180° - 90° - 50° = 40°$

$\therefore |\angle BAD| = 40° + 40° = 80°$

AD is not a tangent to *s* at *A* since $|\angle BAD| \neq 90°$.

EXAMPLE 7

A circle *s* with centre *O* has radius *r*. A line *t* is drawn perpendicular to *OA* where *A* is a point on the circle. Show that no other point *B* which is on *t* can be on the circle *s*. What conclusion can you make about *t*?

Solution

Mark any point *B* on *t* so that $|AB| = x$.

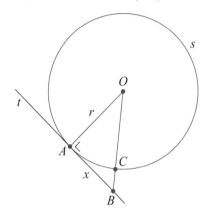

$|OB|^2 = r^2 + x^2 > r^2$

$\therefore |OB| > r$

Therefore, *B* is not on the circle.

Therefore, *t* is a tangent.

Touching circles

Two circles can touch at one point either externally or internally.

Externally

Circles s_1 and s_2 intersect externally at only one point *P*.

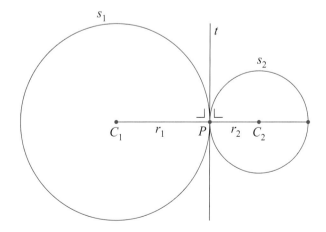

The common tangent *t* at *P* is perpendicular to $C_1 P$ and $C_2 P$, where C_1 is the centre of s_1 and C_2 is the centre of s_2. Therefore, *P*, C_1 and C_2 are collinear.

Internally

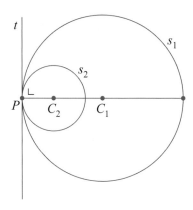

Circles s_1 and s_2 intersect internally at only one point P.

The common tangent t at P is perpendicular to C_1P and C_2P, where C_1 is the centre of s_1 and C_2 is the centre of s_2. Therefore, P, C_1 and C_2 are collinear.

> **TIP**
>
> ⬆ If two circles touch externally or internally, their centres and their point of contact are collinear.

▸ Circles s_1 and s_2 touch at P. If the radius of s_1 is 7 and $|C_1C_2| = 10$, find the radius of s_2, where C_1 is the centre of s_1 and C_2 the centre of s_2.

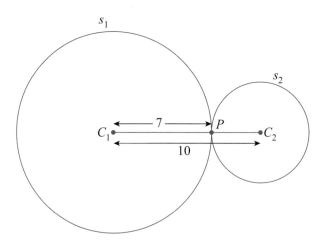

Radius of $s_2 = 10 - 7 = 3$

▸ Circles s_1 and s_2 touch internally. C_1 is the centre of s_1 and C_2 is the centre of s_2. If the length of the diameter of s_2 is 6 and the length of the diameter of s_1 is 18, find $|C_1C_2|$.

$|C_1C_2| = 3 + 3 = 6$

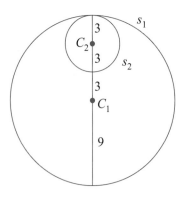

EXERCISE 9

Diagrams are not drawn to scale.

1. Find x and y as required. O is the centre of each circle and t is a tangent to each circle.

(a)

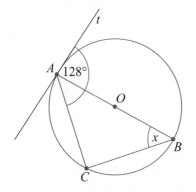

(b)

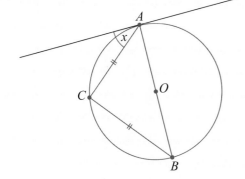

(c)

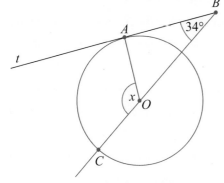

(d)

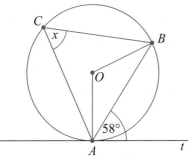

(e)

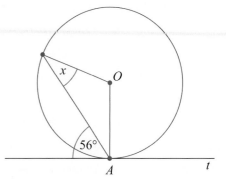

(f)

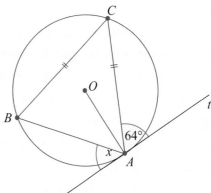

(g)

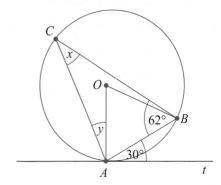

(h) l is a tangent at B.

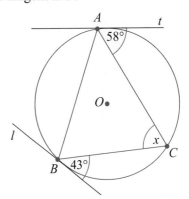

2. *t* is a tangent to the circle *s* at *A*. *O* is the centre of the circle. *B* is a point on *t* such that $|OB| = 10$ and $|AB| = 6$. Find the radius of the circle.

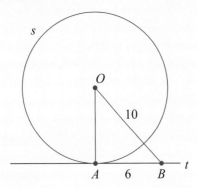

3. (a) $[AB]$ is the diameter of the circle with centre *O* shown. *t* is the tangent at *A*.

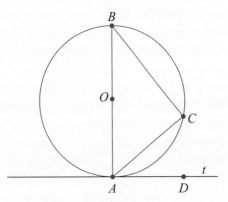

Show that $|\angle DAC| = |\angle ABC|$.

(b) $[AB]$ is a diameter of the circle with centre *O* shown. *t* is a tangent at *A*.

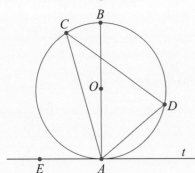

Prove that:

(i) $|\angle EAC| = |\angle ABC|$

(ii) $|\angle EAC| = |\angle ADC|$

4. Circles s_1 and s_2 are touching in each case. C_1 is the centre of s_1 and C_2 is the centre of s_2. r_1 is the radius of s_1 and r_2 is the radius of s_2.

If the distance from C_1 to C_2 is 9 cm and the radius of s_1 is double that of s_2, find the radius of each circle.

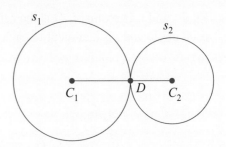

5. The picture shows the circular face s_3 of a new toy with two circular eyes s_1 and s_2. s_3 touches s_1 and s_2. If the radius of s_1 is 5 cm and the radius of s_3 is 9 cm, find the radius of s_2 and hence, find $|C_1C_2|$.

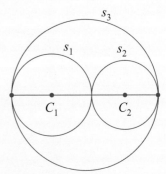

6. Three pipes are stacked as shown.

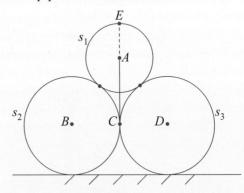

The pipes have circular cross-sections s_1, s_2 and s_3 which touch externally.

s_1 has centre *A* and radius 2 m. s_2 has centre *B* and radius 3 m. s_3 has centre *C* and radius 3 m.

AC is the common tangent of s_2 and s_1.

(i) Find $|AC|$.

(ii) Find the height above the ground of the top *E* of s_1.

3.3 Chords

If a perpendicular line is drawn from the centre O of a circle to any chord $[AB]$ of the circle, two right-angled triangles are formed.

If D is the point at which the perpendicular cuts the chord, the triangles formed are $\triangle AOD$ and $\triangle BOD$.

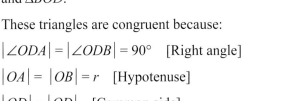

These triangles are congruent because:

$|\angle ODA| = |\angle ODB| = 90°$ [Right angle]

$|OA| = |OB| = r$ [Hypotenuse]

$|OD| = |OD|$ [Common side]

$\therefore |AD| = |DB|$ [The perpendicular line OD divides $[AB]$ into two equal parts.]

 ACTIVITY 15

ACTION
Exploring chords

OBJECTIVE
To examine the properties of chords in circles

THE CHORD THEOREM

A perpendicular drawn from the centre of a circle to any chord of the circle bisects the chord.

EXAMPLE 8

O is the centre of a circle s of radius $\sqrt{13}$. Find the perpendicular distance from O to a chord of length 6.

Solution

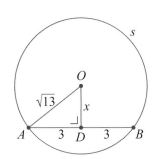

$x = \sqrt{13 - 9} = \sqrt{4} = 2$

$|AB| = 6$

$\therefore |AD| = |DB| = 3$ [OD bisects chord $[AB]$]

$(\sqrt{13})^2 = x^2 + 3^2$ [Pythagoras]

$13 = x^2 + 9$

$x^2 = 4$

$\therefore x = \sqrt{4} = 2$

EXAMPLE 9

O is the centre of a circle. $[AB]$ is a chord with $|AB| = 11$ cm. If the area of $\triangle OAB$ is $72 \cdot 6$ cm^2, find the radius of the circle.

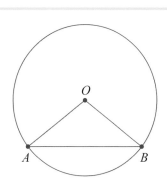

Solution

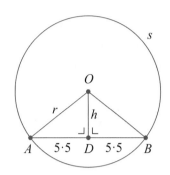

$|AB| = 11$

$\therefore |AD| = |DB| = 5 \cdot 5$ [OD bisects chord $[AB]$]

Area of $\triangle OAB = \dfrac{1}{2} \times 11 \times h = 72 \cdot 6$

$5 \cdot 5h = 72 \cdot 6$ cm

$h = \dfrac{72 \cdot 6}{5 \cdot 5} = 13 \cdot 2$ cm

$r^2 = 5 \cdot 5^2 + 13 \cdot 2^2$ [Pythagoras]

$\therefore r = \sqrt{5 \cdot 5^2 + 13 \cdot 2^2} = 14 \cdot 3$ cm

The converse of the chord theorem is also true.

CONVERSE OF THE CHORD THEOREM

If D is the midpoint of a chord $[AB]$ and a line l through D is drawn perpendicular to $[AB]$, then every point on l will be equidistant from A and B.

Therefore, the centre O of the circle must be on this line l.

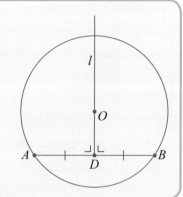

EXERCISE 10

Diagrams are not drawn to scale.

1. O is the centre of the circle s. $[AB]$ is a chord with $|AB| = 30$. If the perpendicular distance from O to $[AB]$ is 8, find the radius of the circle.

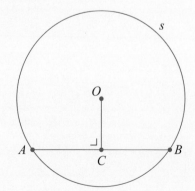

2. O is the centre of the circle s. $[AB]$ is a chord of length 8. $[CD]$ is a chord of length 6 parallel to $[AB]$. If the radius of the circle is 5, find the perpendicular distance between the chords.

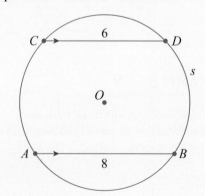

3. O is the centre of the circle s. $[AB]$ is a chord with $|AB| = 48$ cm. The area of ΔOAB is 168 cm^2. Find:

   (a) the perpendicular distance from O to $[AB]$,

   (b) the radius of the circle.

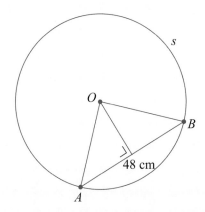

4. A circle s with centre O has a radius of 17 cm. A chord AB of length 30 cm is parallel to the tangent t. Find the perpendicular distance h from AB to t.

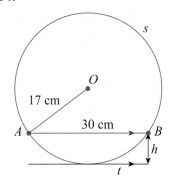

5. AB is a line of length 8 cm and C is the midpoint of $[AB]$. l is the perpendicular bisector of $[AB]$. A point O is chosen on this line such that $|OC| = 2$ cm.

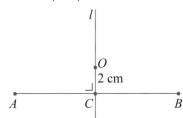

Find:

   (a) $|AC|$ **(c)** $|AO|$

   (b) $|CB|$ **(d)** $|OB|$

If a circle is drawn of radius $|AO|$ with centre O, will B be on the circle? Why?

6. Two circles s_1 and s_2 intersect at A and B as shown. D is the midpoint of $[AB]$ and l is a line drawn perpendicular to AB. If C_1 is the centre of s_1 and C_2 is the centre of s_2, are C_1 and C_2 collinear? Why?

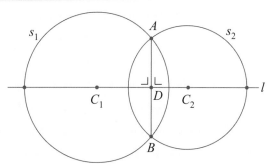

7. s_1 and s_2 are intersecting circles and $[AB]$ is their common chord. C_1 is the centre of s_1 with radius r_1. C_2 is the centre of s_2 with radius r_2. If $r_1 = \sqrt{10}$, $r_2 = \sqrt{5}$ and $|AD| = 1$, show that $|C_1D| : |DC_2| = 3:2$.

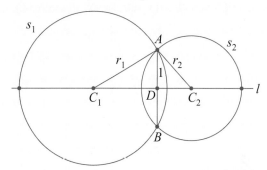

8. $[AB]$ is a diameter of a circle s with centre O. $[CD]$ is a chord perpendicular to $[AB]$ with $|AB| = 26$ and $|CD| = 10$. $[AB]$ intersects $[CD]$ at P.

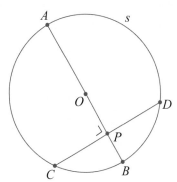

Find:

   (a) $|OC|$ **(c)** $|OP|$

   (b) $|CP|$ **(d)** $|AP|$

If $|AD| = k\sqrt{26}$, find k.

9. *O* is the centre of the circle *s*. [*AB*] is a chord of *s* and [*OP*] ⊥ [*AB*]. |*AB*| = 16 and |*OP*| = 6.

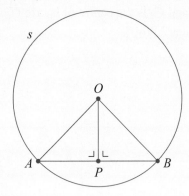

Find:

(a) |*PA*|,

(b) the area of Δ*ABO*,

(c) the length of the diameter of the circle.

10. [*PQ*] is a chord of circle *s* with centre *O*. [*AB*] is a diameter of *s* perpendicular to [*PQ*]. Prove that Δ*POD* ≡ Δ*QOD*. Hence, prove that |*PD*| = |*DQ*|.

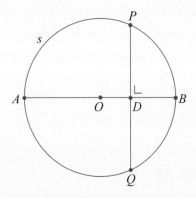

11. Δ*ACD* is an equilateral triangle in circle *s*. *AB* bisects ∠*CAD*.

(a) Show that *AB* is a diameter of circle *s*.

(b) Find |∠*EBC*| if *E* is on the tangent *t* to *s* at *B*.

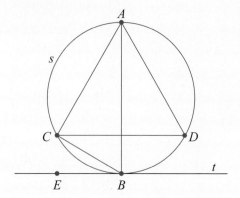

Constructions and Dilations

CHAPTER 4

Learning Outcomes

- To be able to carry out a number of constructions.
- To enlarge and reduce various shapes through a given centre.

4.1 Constructions

ACTION
Constructions

OBJECTIVE
To draw the seven constructions

Using a straight edge, compass, ruler, protractor and set square as appropriate, you must be able to construct the following:

1. The circumcentre and circumcircle of a triangle
2. The incentre and incircle a triangle
3. An angle of 60°
4. A tangent to a circle
5. A parallelogram
6. The centroid of a triangle
7. The orthocentre of a triangle

Construction 1: Finding the circumcentre and circumcircle of a given triangle, using only a straight edge and compass

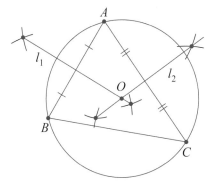

KEY TERMS

The **circumcircle** of a triangle is the circle that passes through its three vertices.

A **circumcentre** of a triangle is the centre of its circumcircle.

Given $\triangle ABC$:

1. Bisect side $[AB]$ perpendicularly by drawing the line l_1.
2. Bisect side $[AC]$ perpendicularly by drawing the line l_2.

3. Mark O, the point of intersection of the lines l_1 and l_2.
   This is the circumcentre of $\triangle ABC$.

4. Draw a circle with centre O with $|OA|$ or $|OB|$ or $|OC|$ as radius.
   This is the circumcircle.

NOTES

1. The perpendicular bisector of a side is known as a mediator. l_1 and l_2 are mediators.

2. The radius r of the circumcircle is given by $r = |OA| = |OB| = |OC|$.

Construction 2: Finding the incentre and incircle of a given triangle, using only a straight edge and compass

KEY TERMS

The **incircle** of a triangle is the circle which touches each of the three sides at one point only.

The **incentre** of a triangle is the centre of its incircle.

Given $\triangle ABC$:

1. Bisect angle $\angle ABC$ by drawing the line l_1.

2. Bisect angle $\angle ACB$ by drawing the line l_2.

3. Mark O, the point of intersection of lines l_1 and l_2.
   This is the incentre.

4. Draw a circle with centre O with $[BC]$ as a tangent.
   This is the incircle.

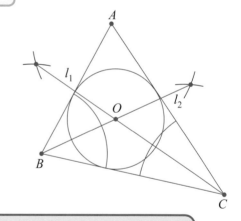

NOTES

1. The radius r of the incircle of $\triangle ABC$ is the perpendicular distance from the centre O to any side.

2. Remember that the bisectors OA, OB and OC divide each vertex angle into two equal parts.

3. The lines l_1 and l_2 are known as the bisectors of the angles.

4. Each side of the triangle is a tangent to the incircle.

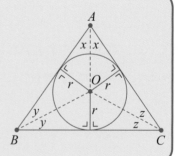

Construction 3: Constructing an angle of 60°, without using a protractor or a set square

1. Draw a line segment $[AB]$ of a given length.

2. Using A as a centre, draw an arc of length $|AB|$.

3. Using B as a centre, draw an arc of length $|AB|$.

4. Mark the point C of intersection of these arcs.

5. Join C to A and C to B.

   $|\angle CAB| = 60°$

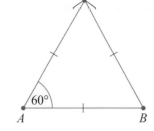

NOTES

1. The $\triangle ABC$ is an equilateral triangle.

2. $|\angle ACB| = |\angle CAB| = |\angle ABC| = 60°$

3. $|AC| = |AB| = |BC|$

Construction 4: Drawing a tangent to a given circle at a given point on it

Given a circle with centre O and a point P:

1. Join O to P and extend it to Q.

2. Using a set square, draw a line t perpendicular to OQ at P. This line t is the tangent to the circle at P.

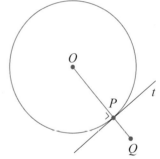

Construction 5: Drawing a parallelogram, given the length of the sides and the measure of the angles

Construct a parallelogram $ABCD$ with $|AB| = 7$ cm, $|AD| = 4$ cm and $|\angle BAD| = 48°$.

1. Using your ruler, draw a line segment $[AB]$ of length 7 cm.

2. Using your protractor, draw a line AE at an angle of 48° with centre A measured anticlockwise from $[AB]$.

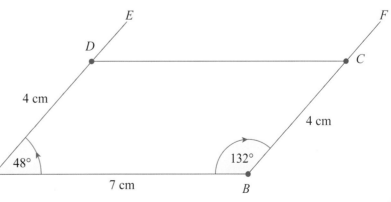

3. Measure out a distance of 4 cm along the line *AE* with your ruler and mark the endpoint *D* of this distance.

4. Using your protractor, draw a line *BF* at an angle of 132° (180° – 48°) with centre *B* measured clockwise from [*AB*].

5. Measure out a distance of 4 cm along the line *AF* with your ruler and mark the endpoint *C*.

6. Join *D* to *C* with your ruler.

NOTE

The adjacent angles in a parallelogram add to 180°.

Construction 6: Finding the centroid of a triangle

KEY TERM

The **centroid** of a triangle is also known as its centre of gravity.

Given $\triangle ABC$:

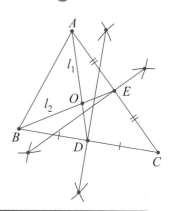

1. Bisect [*BC*] and mark its midpoint *D*. Join *A* to *D*. This is the line l_1.

2. Bisect [*AC*] and mark its midpoint *E*. Join *B* to *E*. This is the line l_2.

3. Mark *O*, the point of intersection of the lines l_1 and l_2. This is the centroid of $\triangle ABC$.

NOTES

1. A median is a line that extends from the vertex of a triangle to the midpoint of the opposite side. l_1 and l_2 are medians. Each triangle has three medians. The third median of $\triangle ABC$ is [*CF*] where *F* is the midpoint of [*AB*].

2. $|BD| = |DC|$, $|AE| = |EC|$ and $|BF| = |FA|$.

3. The centroid *O* divides each median in the ratio 2:1. $|AO|:|OD| = |BO|:|OE| = |CO|:|OF| = 2:1$

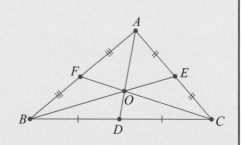

Construction 7: Finding the orthocentre of a triangle

Given $\triangle ABC$:

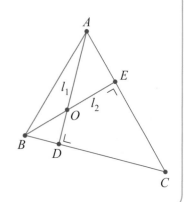

1. Draw the line l_1 from *A* perpendicular to [*BC*] using a set square.

2. Draw the line l_2 from *B* perpendicular to [*AC*] using a set square.

3. Mark *O*, the point of intersection of lines l_1 and l_2. This is the orthocentre of $\triangle ABC$.

NOTES

1. $\triangle ADC$ and $\triangle BCE$ are similar. Can you show that they are similar and hence show that $|BC| \times |AD| = |AC| \times |BE|$?

2. An altitude is a line segment through a vertex that is perpendicular to the side joining the other vertices. l_1 and l_2 are altitudes.

EXERCISE 11

Diagrams are not drawn to scale.

1. Construct an angle of $60°$ using a ruler and compass only.

2. In $\triangle ABC$, $AD \perp BC$, $BE \perp AC$ and $FC \perp AB$.

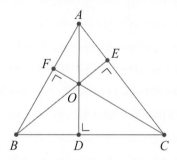

   (a) What are $[AD]$, $[BE]$ and $[FC]$ called?

   (b) What is their point of intersection called?

   (c) Show that $\triangle ADC$ and $\triangle BEC$ are similar.

   Hence, show that $|BC| \times |AD| = |BE| \times |AC|$.

3. Construct a parallelogram $ABCD$ with $|AB| = 9$ cm, $|BC| = 6$ cm and $|\angle ABC| = 105°$. What is $|\angle BAD|$?

4. (a) Construct $\triangle ABC$ with $|AB| = 6$ cm, $|AC| = 7$ cm and $|BC| = 8$ cm.

   (b) Find, by drawing, the circumcentre of $\triangle ABC$.

   (c) Draw the circumcircle of $\triangle ABC$.

   (d) Measure the radius of the circumcircle of $\triangle ABC$, correct to the nearest centimetre.

5. O is the circumcentre of $\triangle ABC$ with $|\angle OAB| = 30°$ and $|\angle OCB| = 35°$.

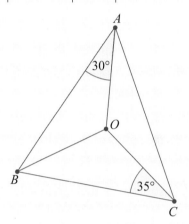

   Find:

   (a) $|\angle OBA|$ (e) $|\angle AOC|$

   (b) $|\angle AOB|$ (f) $|\angle OAC|$

   (c) $|\angle OBC|$ (g) $|\angle OCA|$

   (d) $|\angle BOC|$

6. $\triangle ABC$ is an isosceles triangle with $|AB| = |BC|$. O is the circumcentre of $\triangle ABC$. D is the midpoint of $[BC]$, $[AD]$ is perpendicular to $[BC]$. $|BO| = 13$ and $|OD| = 5$.

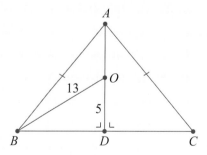

   Find:

   (a) $|BD|$ (b) $|BC|$ (c) $|AD|$

   Hence, find $|AB|$ in surd form.

7. *OC* is the bisector of ∠*AOB*. Perpendiculars are drawn from *C* to *OA* and *C* to *OB*.

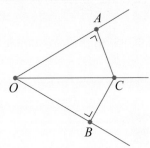

(a) Prove that △*AOC* ≡ △*BOC*.

(b) Deduce that $|AC| = |BC|$.

8. (a) Construct △*ABC* with $|AB| = 7·5$ cm, $|AC| = 6$ cm and $|BC| = 4·5$ cm.

(b) Find, by drawing, the incentre of △*ABC*.

(c) Draw the incircle of △*ABC* and measure the radius of the incircle, correct to one decimal place.

9. Construct a parallelogram *ABCD* with $|AB| = 8$ cm, $|∠ABC| = 120°$ and $|BC| = 6$ cm. Draw the bisectors of ∠*ABC* and ∠*BAD*. If these intersect at *O*, measure $|∠AOB|$.

10. *O* is the incentre of △*ABC* with $|∠BAC| = 100°$. Show that $|∠BOC| = 140°$.

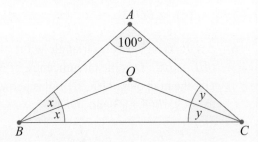

11. The circle with centre *O* is the incircle of the right-angled triangle △*ABC*.

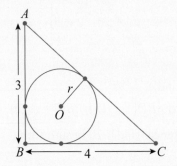

(a) Find $|AC|$.

(b) Find the area of △*ABC*.

(c) Find the radius *r* of the incircle by using the fact that Area △*ABC* = Area △*AOB* + Area △*BOC* + Area △*AOC*.

12. The circle with centre *O* is the incircle of the right-angled triangle △*ABC*. Find the radius *r* of the incircle.

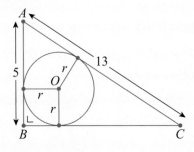

13. The circle with centre *O* is the incircle of △*ABC* and *r* is the radius of its incircle. Show that the area of △*ABC* = $\frac{1}{2}rp$, where *p* is the perimeter of △*ABC*.

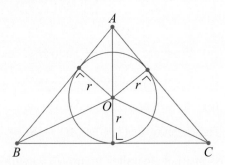

14. (a) Draw a circle *s* with centre *O* and radius 6 cm.

(b) Mark a point *P* on *s* and use your set square to draw a tangent to *s* at *P*.

(c) Draw △*OPQ* where *Q* is on the circle and $|OP| = |PQ|$. What is $|∠POQ|$?

(d) Find the area of △*OPQ* and the area of the sector between the chord [*PQ*] and the circle.

15. (a) Construct △*ABC* with $|AB| = 8$ cm, $|AC| = 7$ cm and $|BC| = 7$ cm.

(b) Find, by drawing, the centroid *G* of △*ABC*.

(c) Measure $|CG|$ and $|GD|$ where *D* is the midpoint of [*AB*]. Show that $|CG|:|GD| = 2:1$.

4.2 Dilations (enlargements and reductions)

ACTIVITY 17

ACTION
Dilations

OBJECTIVE
To carry out the enlargement of a figure

WORKED EXAMPLE Enlarging an object

If you place a point source of light O behind a photograph $ABCD$ and project the image onto a screen so that $|OA'| = 2|OA|$, you get an **enlarged** image of the photograph.

The size of the angles between the sides in the **image** are the same as the size of the angles between the sides in the original, but the length of each side in the image is twice the length of the corresponding side in the original.

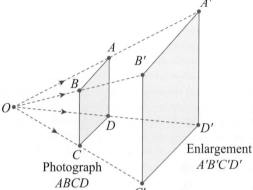

So $|\angle A'B'C'| = |\angle ABC|$ for example but $|C'D'| = 2|CD|$.

O is called the centre of the enlargement as all rays emerge from O.

$A'B'C'D'$ is **similar** to $ABCD$ as all the angles in $A'B'C'D'$ have the same size as all angles in $ABCD$. For example, $|\angle B'C'D'| = |\angle BCD|$.

So, $\dfrac{|OA'|}{|OA|} = \dfrac{|OB'|}{|OB|} = \dfrac{|OC'|}{|OC|} = \dfrac{|OD'|}{|OD|} = 2 = k$

$\Rightarrow \dfrac{|A'B'|}{|AB|} = \dfrac{|B'C'|}{|BC|} = \dfrac{|C'D'|}{|CD|} = \dfrac{|D'A'|}{|DA|} = 2 = k$

k is called the **scale factor** of the enlargement. It is the factor by which each side of the original figure is increased (or decreased) in length.

$$\text{Scale factor} \quad \dfrac{|\text{Image length}|}{|\text{Object length}|}$$

$A'B'C'D'$ is an enlarged version of $ABCD$ in which the lengths of each side are double the length of each side of the original $ABCD$. Each vertex of $A'B'C'D'$ is twice as far from O as each vertex of the original.

The area of the image $A'B'C'D' = |C'D'| \times |B'C'|$

$$= k|CD| \times k|BC| = k^2|CD| \times |BC|$$

$$= k^2 \times \text{Area of object } ABCD$$

$$k^2 = \dfrac{|\text{Image area}|}{|\text{Object area}|}$$

The image produced by **enlarging** or **reducing** a figure is called a **dilation**.
A dilation image is similar to the original figure. Also, the corresponding sides on
the two figures are parallel.

KEY TERM

A **dilation** is the transformation of a figure T, in which each point of the
image T is k times the distance of each point of the original figure (object)
from a fixed point O.

If $k > 1$, the dilation is called an **enlargement**.

If $0 < k < 1$ the dilation is called a **reduction**.

WORKED EXAMPLE Reducing an object

If $\triangle A'B'C'$ is the image of $\triangle ABC$ under a reduction with centre O and
scale factor $0{\cdot}6$,

$$\frac{|OA'|}{|OA|} = \frac{|OB'|}{|OB|} = \frac{|OC'|}{|OC|} = k = 0{\cdot}6$$

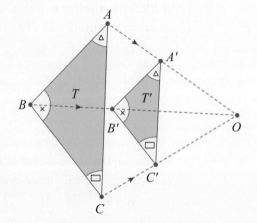

This means that:

1. $[AB] \parallel [A'B']$, $[AC] \parallel [A'C']$, $[BC] \parallel [B'C']$

   Therefore, $\triangle ABC$ and $\triangle A'B'C'$ are similar.

   and so $\dfrac{|A'B'|}{|AB|} = \dfrac{|B'C'|}{|BC|} = \dfrac{|A'C'|}{|AC|} = k = 0{\cdot}6$

2. $\dfrac{\text{Area } \triangle A'B'C'}{\text{Area } \triangle ABC} = k^2 = 0{\cdot}6^2$

4

Construction of an enlargement with centre O and scale factor k

Find the image of $\triangle ABC$ under the enlargement with centre O and scale factor 3.

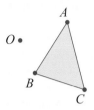

1. Join O to A and continue this line to A' such that $|OA'| = 3|OA|$. Mark A'.

2. Join O to B and continue this line to B' such that $|OB'| = 3|OB|$. Mark B'.

3. Join O to C and continue this line to C' such that $|OC'| = 3|OC|$.

4. Join A' to B' to C' to give the image $\triangle A'B'C'$ of $\triangle ABC$ under this enlargement.

Construction

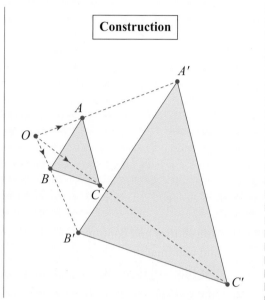

Construction of a reduction with centre O and scale factor k

Find the image of rectangle $ABCD$ under the reduction with centre O and scale factor $\frac{1}{2}$.

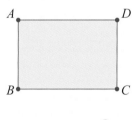

1. Join A to O and continue to A' such that $|OA'| = \frac{1}{2}|OA|$.

2. Join B to O and continue to B' such that $|OB'| = \frac{1}{2}|OB|$.

3. Join C to O and continue to C' such that $|OC'| = \frac{1}{2}|OC|$.

4. Join D to O and continue to D' such that $|OD'| = \frac{1}{2}|OD|$.

5. Join A' to B' to C' to D' to A' to give the image of rectangle $ABCD$ under this reduction.

Construction

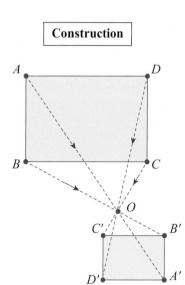

WORKED EXAMPLE   Construction of the centre of a dilation

If $\triangle A'B'C'$ is the image of $\triangle ABC$ under an enlargement with centre O and scale factor k, find O by drawing and calculate k.

| Construction |

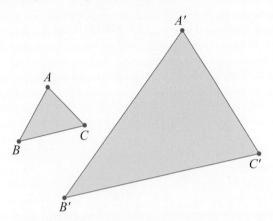

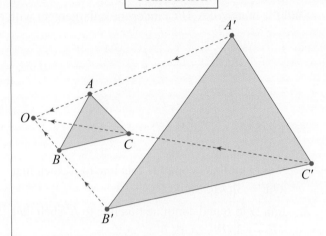

All corresponding angles are equal.

$\left|\angle A'B'C'\right| = \left|\angle ABC\right|$

$\left|\angle A'C'B'\right| = \left|\angle ACB\right|$

$\left|\angle B'A'C'\right| = \left|\angle BAC\right|$

Also, $A'B' \parallel AB$, $A'C' \parallel AC$, $B'C' \parallel BC$

$\dfrac{\text{Image area}}{\text{Object area}} = k^2 = $ scale factor squared

1. Join A' to A and continue this line. Join B' to B and continue this line. Join C' to C and continue this line. All three lines intersect at O.

2. Mark O. This is the centre of the enlargement.

3. To find the scale factor measure the lengths $\left|OA'\right|$ and $\left|OA\right|$.

$\left|OA'\right| = 5{\cdot}6$ cm

$\left|OA\right| = 1{\cdot}6$ cm

$\therefore k = \dfrac{\left|OA'\right|}{\left|OA\right|} = \dfrac{5{\cdot}6}{1{\cdot}6} = 3{\cdot}5$

EXAMPLE   1

$\triangle OCD$ is the image of $\triangle OAB$ under the enlargement with centre O.

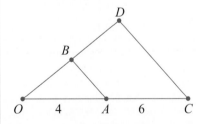

Find:

(a) the scale factor of the enlargement,

(b) the area of $\triangle OCD$ given the area of $\triangle OAB$ is 6 square units.

Solution

(a) $k = \dfrac{\left|OC\right|}{\left|OA\right|} = \dfrac{10}{4} = \dfrac{5}{2} = 2{\cdot}5$

(b) $\dfrac{\text{Area } \triangle OCD}{\text{Area } \triangle OAB} = k^2 = \dfrac{25}{4} = \dfrac{\text{Area } \triangle OCD}{6}$

$\therefore$ Area $\triangle OCD = \dfrac{25}{4} \times 6 = 37{\cdot}5$ square units

EXAMPLE 2

A surgeon produces an X-ray image of a patella
(knee cap) which has been enlarged by a scale factor
of 2. If the image is a circle of radius 4 cm, find:

(a) the radius of the object (the patella),

(b) the area of the patella in terms of π.

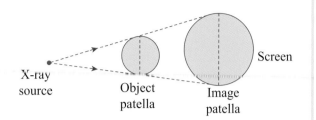

Solution

(a) $\dfrac{\text{Radius of image}}{\text{Radius of object}} = 2 \Rightarrow \dfrac{4}{2} = \text{Radius of object} = 2$ cm

(b) Area of object $= \pi(2)^2 = 4\pi$ cm^2

EXAMPLE 3

$\Delta A'C'B'$ is the image of ΔACB under the enlargement
with centre O and scale factor 2·5
with $|AC| = 4$ and $|A'B'| = 12$.

(a) Find $|A'C'|$.

(b) Find $|AB|$.

(c) If the area of ΔABC is 4·6 square units, find the
area of $\Delta A'B'C'$.

Solution

(a) $\dfrac{|A'C'|}{|AC|} = k \Rightarrow \dfrac{|A'C'|}{4} = 2\!\cdot\!5 \Rightarrow |A'C'| = 10$

(b) $\dfrac{|A'B'|}{|AB|} = k \Rightarrow \dfrac{12}{|AB|} = 2\!\cdot\!5 \Rightarrow |AB| = \dfrac{12}{2\!\cdot\!5} = 4\!\cdot\!8$

(c) $\dfrac{\text{Area } \Delta A'B'C'}{\text{Area } \Delta ABC} = k^2 \Rightarrow$ Area $A'B'C' = (2\!\cdot\!5)^2 \times 4\!\cdot\!6 = 28\!\cdot\!75$ square units

EXAMPLE 4

$\Delta A'B'C$ is the image of the
right-angled triangle ΔABC with
$|AB| = 5$, $|AC| = 7$ and $|\angle BAC| = 90°$
under an enlargement with
centre O and scale factor 2.

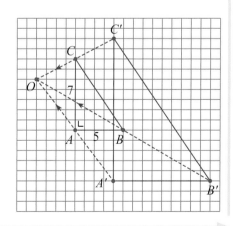

Find:

(a) $|CB|$ (c) $|A'C'|$ (e) the area of $\triangle ABC$

(b) $|A'B'|$ (d) $|B'C'|$ (f) the area of $\triangle A'B'C'$

Show that the area $\triangle A'B'C'$: Area $\triangle ABC = k^2 : 1$.

Solution

(a) $|CB| = \sqrt{5^2 + 7^2} = \sqrt{25 + 49} = \sqrt{74}$ [Pythagoras]

(b) $|A'B'| = k \times |AB| = 2 \times 5 = 10$

(c) $|A'C'| = k \times |AC| = 2 \times 7 = 14$

(d) $|B'C'| = \sqrt{100 + 196} = \sqrt{296} = 2\sqrt{74}$ or $|B'C'| = k \times |BC| = 2 \times \sqrt{74}$

(e) Area of $\triangle ABC = \frac{1}{2} \times 5 \times 7 = 17\cdot5$

(f) Area of $\triangle A'B'C' = \frac{1}{2} \times 10 \times 14 = 70$

$$\frac{\text{Area } \triangle A'B'C'}{\text{Area } \triangle ABC} = \frac{70}{17\cdot5} = 4 = k^2$$

EXERCISE 12

Each square in the diagrams below represents a 5 mm × 5 mm square. Copy these diagrams onto 5 mm × 5 mm grid paper.

1. Draw the image $A'D'C'B'$ of the rectangle $ADCB$ under the enlargement with centre O and scale factor $k = 2$.

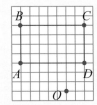

   Show that:

   (a) $\dfrac{|A'B'|}{|AB|} = \dfrac{|B'C'|}{|BC|} = \dfrac{|C'D'|}{|CD|} = \dfrac{|D'A'|}{|DA|} = k$

   (b) $\dfrac{\text{Area } A'B'C'D'}{\text{Area } ABCD} = k^2$

2. Draw the image $A'C'B'$ of the triangle ACB under the reduction with centre O and scale factor $k = \frac{1}{2}$.

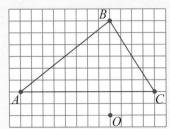

Show that:

(a) $\dfrac{|A'C'|}{|AC|} = k$ (b) $\dfrac{\text{Area } \triangle A'B'C'}{\text{Area } \triangle ABC} = k^2$

3. Draw the image $OD'C'B'$ of the quadrilateral $ODCB$ under the enlargement with centre O and scale factor $k = 3$.

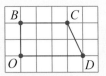

   Show that:

   (a) $\dfrac{|OB'|}{|OB|} = \dfrac{|B'C'|}{|BC|} = \dfrac{|OD'|}{|OD|} = k$

   (b) $\dfrac{\text{Area } \triangle OD'C'B'}{\text{Area } \triangle ODCB} = k^2$

4. Construct the image [CD] of [AB] under the enlargement with centre O and scale factor 2 and the image [EF] of [CD] under the reduction with centre G and scale factor $\frac{1}{2}$.

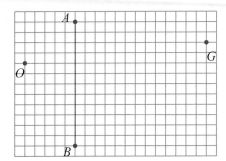

Find in cm:

(a) $|CD|$

(b) $|EF|$

Is $|EF| = |BA|$? Why?

5. (a) Construct the parallelogram ABCD with $|AB| = 9$ cm, $|BC| = 6$ cm and $|\angle DAB| = 60°$ using your compass and ruler.

(b) Draw the diagonals of the parallelogram and mark their point of intersection.

(c) Find the image A'B'C'D' of ABCD under a reduction with centre O and scale factor 0·5.

6. $\triangle A'B'C'$ is the image of $\triangle ABC$ under an enlargement with centre O.

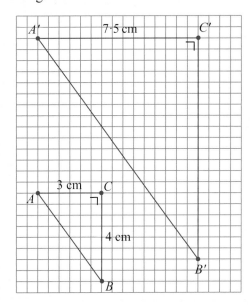

(a) Copy this diagram onto graph paper and find, by drawing, the centre O of the enlargement.

(b) (i) Find the scale factor k of the enlargement.

  (ii) Find $|AB|$ and $|A'B'|$.

(c) Find $|\angle A'C'B'|$ and the areas of $\triangle ABC$ and $\triangle A'B'C'$.

7. (a) Construct a square OBCD with $|OB| = 5$ cm on 5 mm × 5 mm square paper.

(b) On your diagram in part **(a)**, construct the image OB'C'D' of the square OBCD under the enlargement with centre O and scale factor 2.

(c) Find the area of the square OB'C'D' and the area of the region between the two squares.

8. The quadrilateral A'B'C'D' is the enlargement of ABCD with centre O and scale factor k.

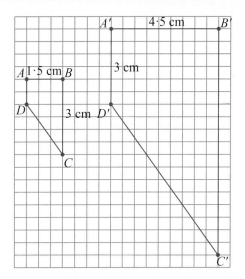

(a) Copy this diagram onto graph paper and find, by drawing, the centre O of the enlargement.

(b) Find the scale factor of the enlargement.

(c) Find $|AD|$ and $|B'C'|$.

(d) Show that the area of A'B'C'D' is k^2 times the area of ABCD.

9. A small rectangle *OABC* on a computer screen is enlarged in area by a certain percentage as shown to become the rectangle *ODEF*.

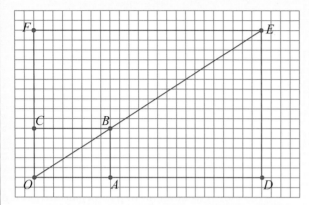

(a) What is the centre of the enlargement?

(b) What is the scale factor of the enlargement?

(c) Find $|DE|$ in cm.

(d) What is the percentage increase in the area of the rectangle *OABC*?

10. $\triangle A'B'C'$ is the image of $\triangle ABC$ under an enlargement with centre *O* and scale factor *k*. $B \in [A'C']$.

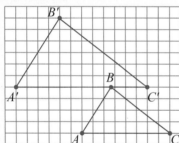

(a) Find *k*.

(b) Find the centre of the enlargement.

(c) Calculate $|BC'|$ in grid units.

11. The triangle *A'B'C'* is the image of the triangle *ABC* under an enlargement.

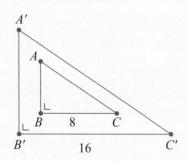

(a) Find the scale factor of the enlargement.

(b) Copy the diagram onto graph paper and show how to find the centre of the enlargement.

(c) Find the area of triangle *ABC* given that the area of *A'B'C* is 84 square units.

(d) Find $|AB|$.

12. (a) Draw a square *OABC* with side 4 cm and label the vertices.

(b) Draw the image of the square under the enlargement with centre *O* and scale factor 2·5.

(c) Calculate the ratio of the area of the image square to the area of the original square.

(d) Another square *OPQR* is the image of the square *OABC* under a different enlargement with centre *O*. The area of *OPQR* is 324 cm². Calculate the scale factor of this enlargement.

13. The pupil of Joe's eye is 4·4 mm in diameter. His optician uses drops to dilate his pupils by a factor of 2·5. Find the diameter of each pupil after dilation.

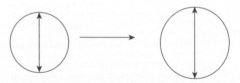

14. Moira enlarged a picture on a photocopier. The original photo was 4 cm × 6 cm. The copy was *x* cm × 8 cm. What is the scale factor of the enlargement? Find *x*.

15. Joe enlarged a photo on a photocopier. The original photo was 4 cm × *x* cm. The copy was *x* cm × 16 cm. Find the scale factor and *x*.

16. The square frame *DCBA* is an enlargement of the square picture *HGFE* with centre *O*.

(a) Find the scale factor *k* if $|AB| = 70$ cm and $|FG| = 42$ cm.

(b) Find $|OB|$ and $|OF|$ in surd form.

(c) Show that $\dfrac{|OB|}{|OF|} = k$.

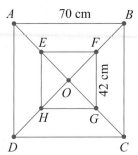

17. $\triangle DFE$ is an enlargement of $\triangle ACB$ under the enlargement with centre O and scale factor k. $|OA| = x$ and $|CD| = 2$.

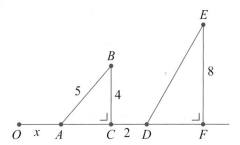

Find:

(a) the scale factor of the enlargement

(b) $|AC|$

(c) $|DE|$

(d) $|DF|$

(e) $x = |OA|$

18. A jewellery designer wishes to design a brooch consisting of two circular rings s_1 and s_2. The bigger circle s_1 one is an enlargement of the smaller circle s_2 with scale factor 3 with centre O.

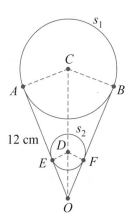

The rings are joined by two silver bars $[OA]$ and $[OB]$ which are tangents to each circle. C is the centre of the larger ring and D is the centre of the smaller ring.

The radius of the smaller circle is 3 cm and $|OA| = 12$ cm.

(a) (i) What is $|\angle CAO|$? Why?

    (ii) What is $|\angle DEO|$? Why?

(b) (i) Explain why $\triangle OED$ and $\triangle OAC$ are similar.

    (ii) Find $|DE|$ and $|OE|$.

    (iii) What is $|OD|$?

(c) (i) What is the radius of the bigger circle s_1?

    (ii) What is $|OC|$?

    (iii) What is $|DC|$?

(d) (i) Find the angle $|\angle DOE|$, correct to two decimal places.

    (ii) Find $|AB|$.

(e) The silver used to make such brooches is supplied in cylinders of pure silver of length 10 cm and cross-sectional area $1\cdot44$ cm^2.

    (i) Find the volume of silver in each cylinder in cm^3.

    (ii) If 1 cm^3 of this pure silver weighs $0\cdot3376$ troy ounces:

    find the number of troy ounces in the piece, correct to two decimal places, and find the cost of each cylinder, correct to the nearest euro, if 1 troy ounce of pure silver costs €50.

REVISION QUESTIONS

1. **(a)** In $\triangle ABC$ shown, if DE is parallel to BC, find x and y.

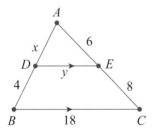

(b) To measure the width of a river between two parallel banks l_1 and l_2, a student lines up two posts A and B with a tree E on the opposite bank l_2. She then walks parallel to the bank l_1 and places a post C on the bank. Finally she walks from post B parallel to the bank l_1 to D and places a post there so that it lines up with C and E. From her measurements, find the width of the river, correct to one decimal place.

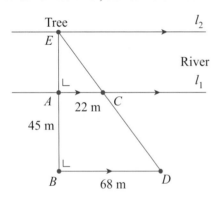

2. k is the perpendicular bisector of $[BC]$. $|\angle ABC| = 30°$ and AC is perpendicular to BC.

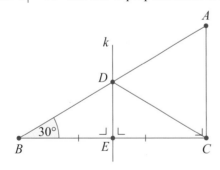

(a) Find $|\angle DCB|$.

(b) Show that $\triangle ADC$ is equilateral.

(c) Show that $\dfrac{\text{Area } \triangle DBE}{\text{Area } \triangle ABC} = \dfrac{1}{4}$.

3. **(a)** A, B, C, D and E are points on a circle s and $|\angle BDE| = 110°$.

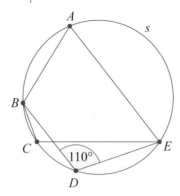

Find:

(i) $|\angle BAE|$ **(ii)** $|\angle BCE|$

(b) AD and BD are tangents to the circle with centre O. $[OD]$ intersects the chord $[AB]$ at C.

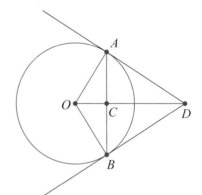

(i) Show that $\triangle ADO$ and $\triangle BDO$ are congruent.

(ii) Prove that $[OD]$ bisects the chord $[AB]$.

4. **(a)** In $\triangle DCA$ shown, $BE \parallel DC$, find:

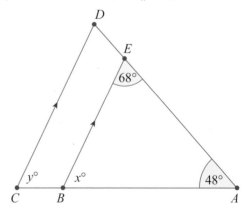

(i) x **(ii)** y

(b) The diagram shows a kite with $|AB| = |AC|$ and $|BD| = |DC|$.

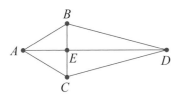

(i) Show that $|\angle BAD| = |\angle CAD|$ by showing that $\triangle ABD \equiv \triangle ACD$.

(ii) Show E is the midpoint of $[BC]$.

5. **(a)** $ADCB$ is a trapezium with $BC \parallel AD$ and $|\angle ADC| = 90°$. Find $|AB|$.

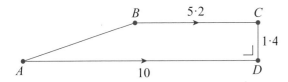

(b) The circular top of a bucket has diameter 34 cm. The circular bottom has diameter 20 cm. The sloping sides are 25 cm in length. Find the depth h of the bucket.

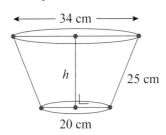

6. ABC is a triangle. AD is the bisector of the angle $\angle BAC$ and $|CE| = |CD|$.

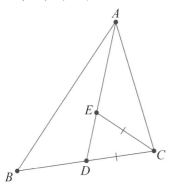

(a) If $|\angle CED| = x$, express the following in terms of x:

(i) $|\angle CDA|$ **(ii)** $|\angle CEA|$ **(iii)** $|\angle ADB|$

(b) If $|\angle CAD| = y$, express $|\angle BAD|$ in terms of y.

(c) Show that $|AD| \times |AC| = |AE| \times |AB|$.

7. **(a)** In $\triangle ACB$ and $\triangle DEF$, $|\angle ABC| = |\angle DFE|$ and $|\angle BCA| = |\angle FED|$.

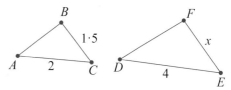

Is $|\angle BAC| = |\angle FDE|$? Why?

What can you say about the two triangles? Find x.

(b) The smallest angle in a triangle is three-quarters the size of the second biggest angle and the second biggest angle is half of the size of the biggest angle. Find the measure of all angles.

8. In $\triangle ABC$, $|\angle ABC| = 80°$ and $|\angle ACB| = 60°$. The bisectors of these angles meet at K. If AK produced meets BC at M, find $|\angle BAK|$ and show that $\triangle BAM$ is isosceles.

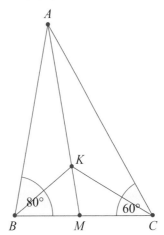

9. In $\triangle ABC$, $|BP| = 3$, $|AP| = 6$, $|AC| = 12$ and $|BC| = 10$. $PQ \parallel AC$ and $QR \parallel BA$.

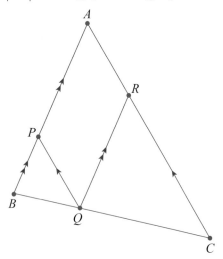

(a) Show that $\triangle PBQ$ and $\triangle ABC$ are similar.

(b) Find $|BQ|$.

(c) Show that $\triangle QRC$ and $\triangle ABC$ are similar.

(d) Find $|RC|$ and $|AR|$.

(e) Show that the area of parallelogram $APQR$ equals the area of $\triangle QRC$.

10. In right-angled triangles $\triangle ABC$ and $\triangle DEB$, $AC \perp BD$ and $DE \perp BE$. $|AC| = |BE| = x$.

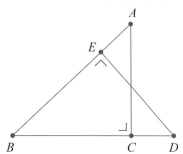

(a) Show that $\triangle ABC$ and $\triangle BED$ are similar.

(b) Show that $|DE| \times |BC| = x^2$.

11. $ABCD$ is a parallelogram with $[AE] \perp [BC]$ and $[CF] \perp [AD]$. Prove that $\triangle ABG \equiv \triangle DHC$.

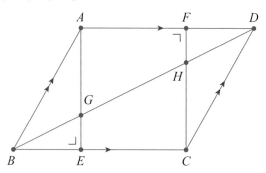

12. (a) $ABDC$ is a rhombus. The diagonals intersect at E.

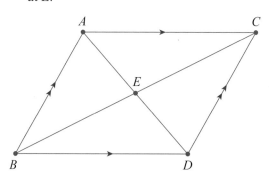

(i) Show that $|\angle AEC| = 90°$.

(ii) Find $|\angle BED|$ and $|\angle DEC|$.

(b) $ABDC$ is a rhombus of side x. $|BC| = 24$ cm. $|AB|$ is 2 cm longer than $|AE|$. Find x.

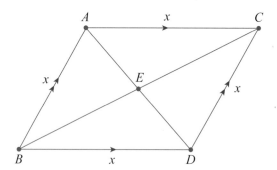

13. In $\triangle ABC$, DG is parallel to AB.

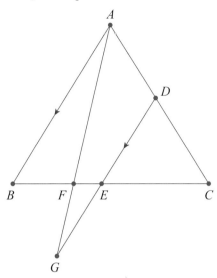

(a) Show that $\dfrac{|AB|}{|EG|} = \dfrac{|BF|}{|FE|}$.

(b) Show that $\triangle DEC$ and $\triangle ABC$ are similar and deduce that $\dfrac{|AB|}{|DE|} = \dfrac{|BC|}{|EC|}$.

(c) If E is the midpoint of $[DG]$ deduce that $\dfrac{|BF|}{|FE|} = \dfrac{|BC|}{|EC|}$.

14. $[BC]$ is the diameter of a circle with centre O. D is a point on the circle and AC is a tangent to the circle at C.

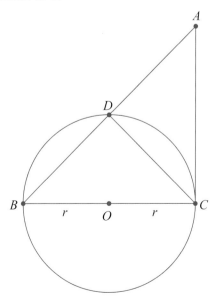

(a) Show that $\triangle BDC$ and $\triangle ABC$ are similar.

(b) If $|BD| = |AD|$, show that $|BD| = \sqrt{2}r$, where r is the radius of the circle.

Find:

(i) $|DC|$ in terms of r

(ii) $|\angle DBC|$

15. ABC is a right-angled triangle with $|\angle ABC| = 90°$. E is on AC such that $BE \perp AC$. D is a point on AB such that $DE \perp AB$. $|AE| = 8$ cm and $|EC| = 7$ cm.

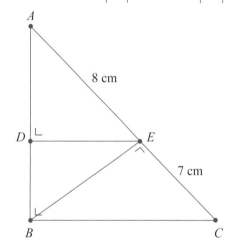

(a) Show that $\triangle BEA$ and $\triangle BEC$ are similar.

(b) Find $|BE|$.

(c) Find $|AD|$.

16. (a) Construct a right-angled triangle CDE with $|CD| = 6$ cm, $|DE| = 8$ cm and $|CE| = 10$ cm.

(b) Construct the incircle of this triangle.

(c) Prove that $A = \dfrac{rp}{2}$ for any $\triangle CED$, where A is the area, p is the perimeter and r is the radius of the incircle.

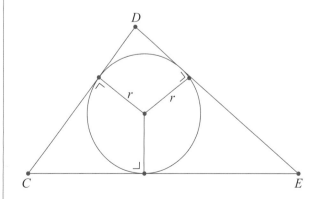

(d) A mobile phone mast F is placed at the same distance from three roads $[CD]$, $[DE]$ and $[CE]$ joining three towns C, D and E.

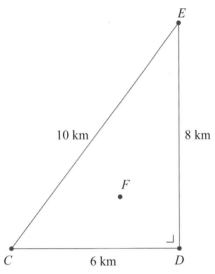

(i) Find how far F is from each road.

(ii) Find how far F is from each town.

(e) Where should the mast be built in order to be equidistant from each town?

(f) If a mobile phone signal travels at 3×10^8 m s^{-1}, how long does it take the signal to go from F to E if F is equidistant from each road, correct to two significant figures?

17. (a) Three towns A, B and C are connected by three roads $[AB]$, $[AC]$ and $[BC]$. What is the length of the shortest route from A to C?

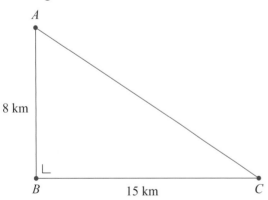

(b) A water company wants to use one pump placed at a position C on the water main DE to pump water to estates F and G using the minimum length of pipe.

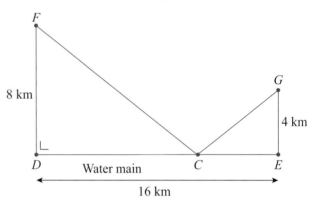

Figure 6

Redraw the diagram in Figure 6 to show how to calculate where C must be placed on $[DE]$ to minimise the total length $|FC| + |CG|$.

(c) If $|DC| = x$, find x to minimise the total length of the pipe system.

(d) Show that $|\angle FCD| = |\angle GCE|$.

(e) Find the minimum length of pipe required.

18. A washer is in the shape of a flat disc of metal between two circles s_1 and s_2 with the same centre O.

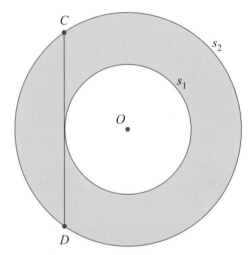

(a) r is the radius of s_1 and R is the radius of s_2. Copy the diagram above, putting r and R on it.

(b) C and D are two points on s_2 such that $|CD| = 16$ mm and $[CD]$ is a tangent to s_1.

    (i) Evaluate $R^2 - r^2$.

    (ii) Find the area of the washer in terms of π.

(c) If the washer is 0·1 mm thick, find the volume of the metal in cm^3.

(d) If 1 cm^3 of the metal has a mass of 5·5 g, find the washer's mass in grams, correct to two decimal places.

(e) If the metal costs €200 per tonne, find the cost of the metal to make 500 000 washers correct to the nearest euro.

(f) A larger type of washer of the same shape is made at the same factory with circles s_3 and s_4 each with centre O. $[AB]$ is a tangent to s_3 with $|AB| = 24$ mm.

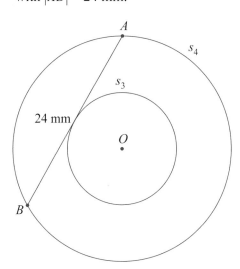

Find the washer's area in terms of π in mm^2.

19. (a) By redrawing the diagram below, explain why $\triangle ABC$ and $\triangle A'B'C'$ are similar.

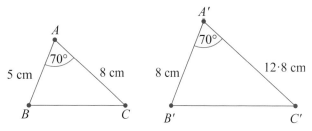

(b) By redrawing the diagrams below, explain why $\triangle AOB$ and $\triangle A'OB'$ are similar.

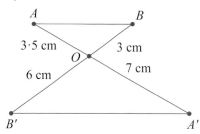

What is $\dfrac{|A'B'|}{|AB|}$?

(c) If $\dfrac{|AB|}{|A'B'|} = \dfrac{|AC|}{|A'C'|}$ and $|\angle BAC| = |\angle B'A'C'|$, prove that $\triangle ABC$ is similar to $\triangle A'B'C'$ by redrawing the diagrams below.

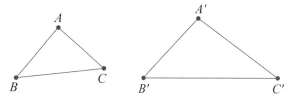

SUMMARY

Geometry

1. Angles and lines:

(a) Vertically opposite angles: $x = y$

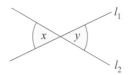

(b) Alternate and corresponding angles

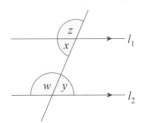

$l_1 \parallel l_2 \Leftrightarrow x = y$ (alternate angles)

$l_1 \parallel l_2 \Leftrightarrow z = w$ (corresponding angles)

2. Triangles:

(a) Congruence: **SSS, SAS, ASA, RHS**

(b)

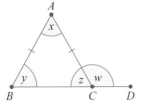

  (i) $x + y + z = 180°$

  (ii) $w = x + y$

(c)

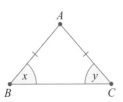

$|AB| = |AC| \Leftrightarrow x = y$

(d) Pythagoras

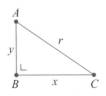

$|\angle ABC| = 90° \Leftrightarrow r^2 = x^2 + y^2$

(e)

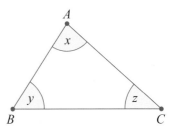

  (i) If $[BC]$ is the longest side $\Leftrightarrow x$ is the biggest angle.

  (ii) Sum of the lengths of any two sides is greater than the length of the other side.

3. Parallelograms: $ABCD$ is a parallelogram.

(a)

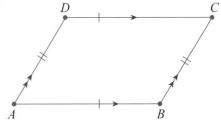

  (i) Opposite sides have equal lengths.

  (ii) Opposite angles are equal in size. Adjacent angles add to $180°$.

(b)

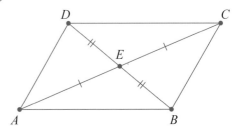

The diagonals bisect each other: $|AE| = |EC|$, and $|DE| = |EB|$

4. Transversals and similar triangles:

(a) Transversals

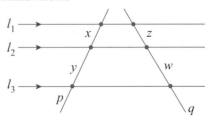

$l_1 \parallel l_2 \parallel l_3 \Leftrightarrow \dfrac{x}{y} = \dfrac{z}{w}$

(b) Ratio theorem

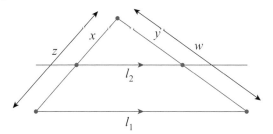

$$l_1 \parallel l_2 \Leftrightarrow \frac{x}{z} = \frac{y}{w}$$

(c) Similar triangles

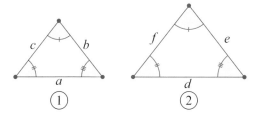

If all the angles in triangle ② are equal in size to all the angles in triangle ①:

$$\frac{a}{d} = \frac{b}{e} = \frac{c}{f}$$

5. Area of a triangle and a parallelogram:

(a) Triangle

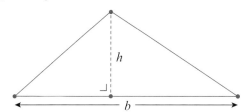

Area $= \frac{1}{2}$ (Base b) × Perpendicular height h

It does not matter which side is used as the base.

(b) Parallelogram

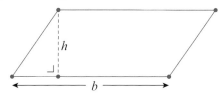

Area = Base b × Perpendicular height h

It does not matter which side is used as the base.

6. Circles:

(a) (i)

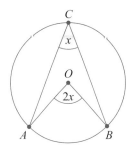

Circle centre O: $\left|\angle AOB\right| = 2\left|\angle ACB\right|$

(ii) Angles standing on the same arc

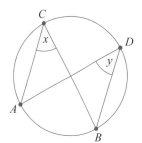

$$\left|\angle ACB\right| = \left|\angle ADB\right|$$

(iii) Angle standing on the diameter

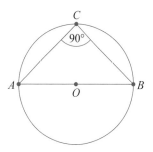

Circle centre O:

$[AB]$ is a diameter $\Leftrightarrow \left|\angle ACB\right| = 90°$

(iv) Cyclic quadrilateral

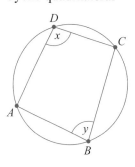

$ABCD$ is a cyclic quadrilateral

$\Leftrightarrow \left|\angle ADC\right| + \left|\angle ABC\right| = 180°$

(b) Tangents and chords

(i) Tangents

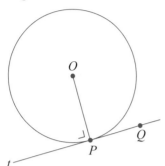

t is a tangent to circle with centre O at $P \Leftrightarrow |\angle OPQ| = 90°$

(ii) Chords

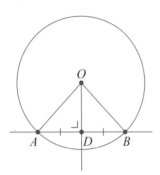

If $[AB]$ is a chord to circle with centre O, then $OD \perp AB \Leftrightarrow |AD| = |DB|$.

(iii) Touching circles

Externally

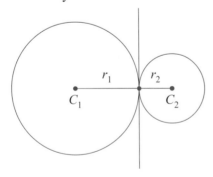

$|C_1 C_2| = r_1 + r_2$

Internally

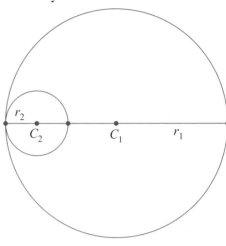

$|C_1 C_2| = r_1 - r_2$

7. Constructions:

1. Circumcentre and circumcircle
2. Incentre and incircle
3. Angle of 60°
4. Tangent to a circle
5. Parallelogram
6. Centroid
7. Orthocentre

8. Dilations:

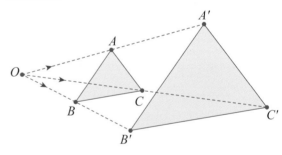

Under a dilation with centre O and scale factor k:

(i) $\dfrac{|OA'|}{|OA|} = \dfrac{|OB'|}{|OB|} = \dfrac{|OC'|}{|OC|} = \dfrac{|A'B'|}{|AB|} = \dfrac{|A'C'|}{|AC|} = \dfrac{|B'C'|}{|BC|} = k$

(ii) Area $\triangle A'B'C' = k^2 \times$ Area $\triangle ABC$

SECTION 2

Mensuration

Mensuration is the study of the perimeter, area and volume of plane and solid figures. It is used extensively in computer imaging in creating animations, designing video games and producing CT and MRI scans.

Two-dimensional Figures

CHAPTER 5

Learning Outcomes

- To know how to find the perimeter and area of polygons.
- To know how to find the perimeter and area of circles.
- To use the trapezoidal rule to estimate areas.

Plane figures are two-dimensional (2D) shapes which can be drawn on a flat surface. They have no thickness or depth. Many mathematical problems are two-dimensional or can be simplified into two dimensions. For example, the flight of a golf ball is essentially two-dimensional as it moves in a two-dimensional vertical plane.

5.1 Perimeter and area of quadrilaterals and triangles

KEY TERM

The **perimeter** l of a 2D plane figure is the length of the boundary of the figure.

The **area** of a 2D plane figure is the amount of space inside the boundary of the plane figure.

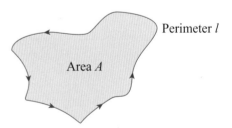

KEY TERM

A **polygon** (*poly* = many, *gon* = angles) is a closed plane shape with a boundary consisting of three or more straight lines.

The polygon *BCDEFG* has six sides and six interior angles.

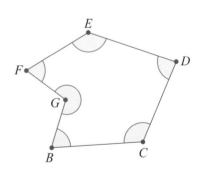

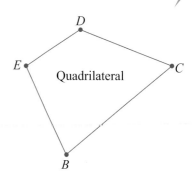

1. Rectangle

Properties

- In a rectangle, the opposite sides are equal in length and are parallel.
- Angles are 90° at each vertex.
- Diagonals are equal in length.
- Diagonals bisect each other.

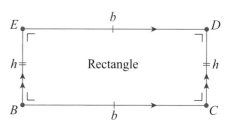

Formulae

Perimeter $l = 2b + 2h \Rightarrow \frac{1}{2}l = b + h$

Area $A = b \times h$

2. Square

Properties

- In a square, all sides are equal in length and opposite sides are parallel.
- Angles are 90° at each vertex.
- Diagonals are equal in length.
- Diagonals bisect each other at 90°.

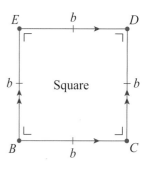

Formulae

Perimeter $l = 4b \Rightarrow \frac{1}{4}l = b$

Area $A = b^2$

3. Parallelogram

Properties

- In a parallelogram, opposite sides are equal in length and are parallel.
- Opposite angles are equal.
- Adjacent angles add up to 180°.
- Diagonals bisect each other.

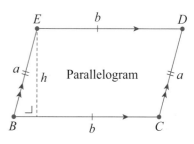

Formulae

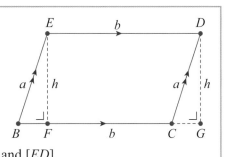

Perimeter $l = 2b + 2a \Rightarrow \frac{1}{2}l = b + a$

Area: The area A of the parallelogram $BCDE$ is the same as the area of the rectangle $FGDE$.

$\therefore A = b \times h = $ base $\times$ height, where h is the perpendicular height and is the distance between the parallel sides $[BC]$ and $[ED]$.

4. Rhombus
Properties

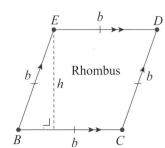

- In a rhombus, all sides are equal in length and opposite sides are parallel.
- Opposite angles are equal.
- Adjacent angles add up to 180°.
- Diagonals bisect each other at 90°.

Formulae

Perimeter $l = 4b$

Area $A = b \times h = $ Base $\times$ perpendicular height

5. Triangle
Properties

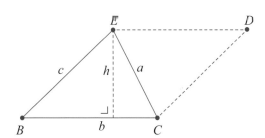

- In a triangle, the interior angles add up to 180°.

Formulae

The perimeter $l = |BC| + |CE| + |EB| = b + a + c$

Area $A = $ Half of the area of the parallelogram $BCDE = \frac{1}{2}b \times h$

$A = \frac{1}{2} \times $ base $\times$ perpendicular height

6. Trapezium

Properties

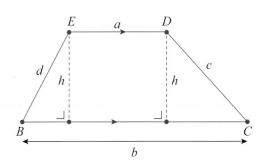

- In a trapezium, one pair of opposite sides is parallel: $[ED] \parallel [BC]$.

Formulae

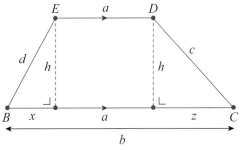

Perimeter $l = |BC| + |CD| + |DE| + |EB| = b + c + a + d$

Area: The area A can be found by finding the sum of two triangles and one rectangle.

$$A = \tfrac{1}{2}xh + ah + \tfrac{1}{2}zh = \tfrac{1}{2}h(x + 2a + z) = \tfrac{1}{2}h((x + a + z) + a) = \left(\frac{b+a}{2}\right)h = \tfrac{1}{2}h(b + a)$$

In words: The area of a trapezium is half of the perpendicular distance between the two parallel sides multiplied by the sum of the lengths of the parallel sides.

7. Other polygons

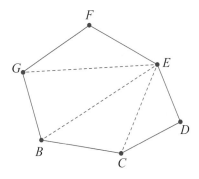

ACTIVITY 1

ACTION
Classifying polygons

OBJECTIVE
To name a number of polygons

Formulae

The perimeter l = Sum of the length of the sides

The area A = Sum of the areas of the triangles into which the polygon can be divided

EXAMPLE 1

Of the two figures shown, which has the **(a)** greater area, **(b)** greater perimeter?

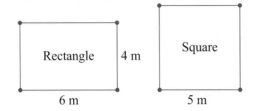

Rectangle   4 m

6 m

Square

5 m

Solution

(a) Area of rectangle = 6 × 4 = 24 m^2

Area of square = 5 × 5 = 25 m^2

The square has the greater area.

(b) Perimeter of rectangle = 2 × 6 + 2 × 4 = 20 m

Perimeter of square = 4 × 5 = 20 m

Their perimeters are the same.

EXAMPLE 2

The cross-section of the wing of a Boeing 747 is in the form of a trapezium $BCDE$ with $[BC] \parallel [ED]$.

Find the area of the trapezium, correct to the nearest m^2.

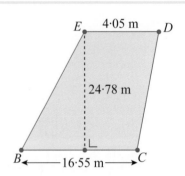

E   4·05 m   D

24·78 m

B ◄——16·55 m——► C

Solution

$A = \frac{1}{2} \times 24 \cdot 78(4 \cdot 05 + 16 \cdot 55) = 255$ m^2

EXAMPLE 3

Find the area of:

(a) $\triangle BCD$

(b) the quadrilateral $BCED$

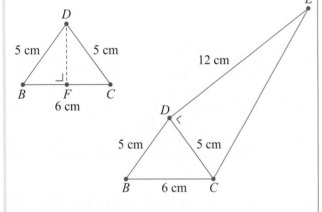

D

5 cm   5 cm

B   F   C

6 cm

E

12 cm

D

5 cm   5 cm

B   6 cm   C

Solution

(a) The triangle is isosceles.

$\left|BF\right| = \left|FC\right| = 3$ cm

$\left|DF\right| = h = 4$ cm   [Using Pythagoras]

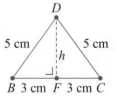

D

5 cm   5 cm

h

B 3 cm   F 3 cm C

Area $\triangle BCD = \frac{1}{2} \times 6 \times 4 = 12$ cm^2

(b) $\triangle DCE$ is a right-angled triangle.

Area of $BCED$ = Area $\triangle BCD$ + Area $\triangle DCE$

$= 12 + \frac{1}{2} \times 5 \times 12$

$= 12 + 30$

$= 42$ cm^2

EXAMPLE 4

(a) Find the area of the rhombus $BCDE$, if $|BD| = 12$ cm and $|EC| = 10$ cm.

(b) In the kite $EBCD$, $|ED| = |EB|$ and $|DC| = |BC|$. Show that $|\angle DFE| = 90°$. Find the area of the kite, if $|EC| = 12$ cm and $|DB| = 6$ cm.

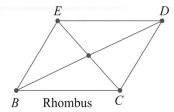

Rhombus

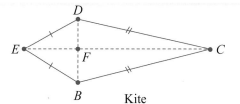

Kite

Solution

(a) Rhombus: The diagonals bisect each other and they intersect at right angles.

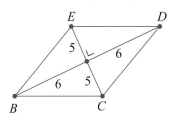

Area of $BCDE = 2($Area $\triangle BDE)$

$A = 2 \times \frac{1}{2} \times 12 \times 5 = 12 \times 5 = 60$ cm^2

Can you make a generalisation about the area of a rhombus?

(b) Kite: $\triangle EDC \equiv \triangle EBC$ [3 sides]

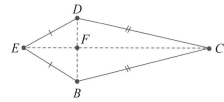

$\Rightarrow |\angle DEF| = |\angle BEF|$

$\therefore \triangle DEF \equiv \triangle BEF$ [**SAS**]

$\therefore |\angle EFD| = |\angle EFB| = 90°$

Area $= 2 \times \frac{1}{2} \times 12 \times 3 = 36$ cm^2

Can you make a generalisation about the area of a kite?

EXERCISE 1

Diagrams in these questions are not necessarily drawn to scale.

1. Find the perimeter l and area A of the shapes shown. Give surd answers correct to one decimal place.

(a)

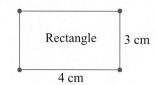

Rectangle   3 cm

4 cm

(b)

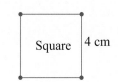

Square   4 cm

(c)

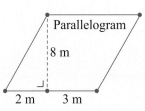

Parallelogram

8 m

2 m   3 m

(d)

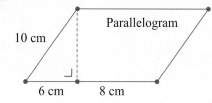

Parallelogram

10 cm

6 cm   8 cm

(e)

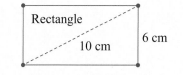

Rectangle

10 cm   6 cm

(f)

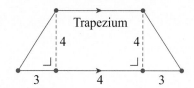

Trapezium

4   4

3   4   3

(g)

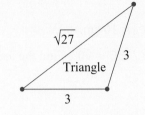

(h)

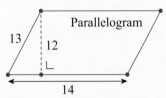

(i)

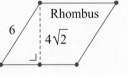

(j)

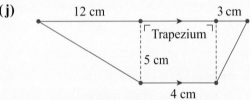

2. Find the area of the shaded regions of the shapes shown.

(a)

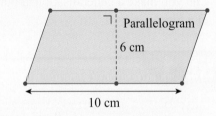

(b)

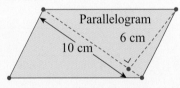

(c)

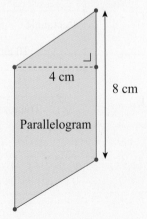

(d)

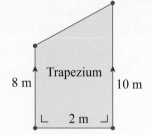

(e)

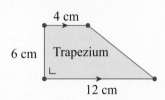

(f) $BCDE$ is a rectangle with $|BF| = |FE|$ and $|CG| = |GD|$.

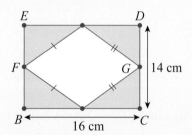

(g) BCE is a triangle with $|BG| = |GC|$, $|BF| = |FE|$ and $|CD| = |DE|$.

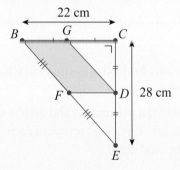

(h) In the rhombus $BCDE$, $|EC| = 14$ cm and $|DB| = 12$ cm.

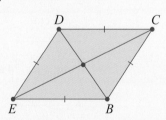

(i) In the rectangle $BCDE$, $|BG| = |GE| = |CF| = |FD| = 4$ cm

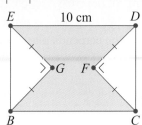

(j) In the quadrilateral $BCDE$, $|DG| = 9$ cm, $|BF| = 18$ cm and $|EC| = 38$ cm.

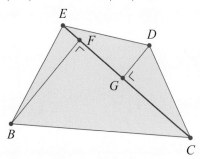

3. Find x in the following:

(a) The perimeter of the rectangle is 30 cm.

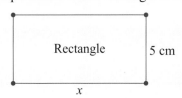

(b) The area of the rectangle is 30 cm^2.

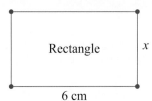

(c) The perimeter of the square is 48 cm.

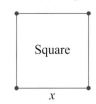

(d) The area of the square is 25 m^2.

(e) The area of the parallelogram is 50 cm^2.

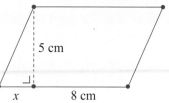

(f) The area of the trapezium is 50 cm^2.

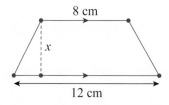

(g) The area of the parallelogram is 100 cm^2.

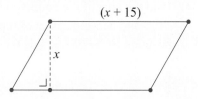

(h) The area of the parallelogram is 24 cm^2.

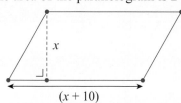

(i) The area of the rhombus is 240 cm^2.

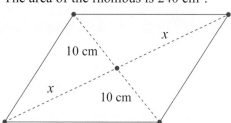

(j) The area of the triangle is 500 cm^2.

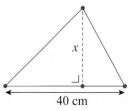

4. **(a)** A wire 4 m long is bent into the shape of a rectangle. The length of the shorter side is 66 cm. Calculate the area enclosed by the rectangle in metres squared.

(b) The perimeter of a rectangular field is 280 m long. If one side measures 60 m, calculate the length of the diagonal of the field.

(c) An isosceles triangle has two sides of length 25 cm and a base of length 14 cm. Calculate the perpendicular height of the triangle and its area.

(d) Find the ratio of the area of the Δ *FDE* to the area of the square *BCDF*.

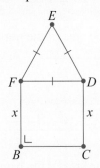

(e) Find the area of the equilateral triangle *BCD* and hence the area of the regular hexagon *BCEFGH* of side 6 cm.

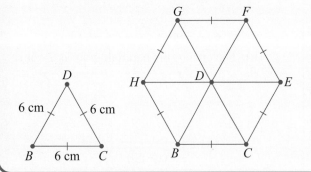

(f) A metal air conditioning system has a cross-section in the shape shown below. Find the area of the cross-section. if [*FC*] ∥ [*AB*], [*CD*] ∥ [*FE*], [*FC*] is perpendicular to [*FE*] and the perpendicular distance from *E* to [*AB*] is 11 m.

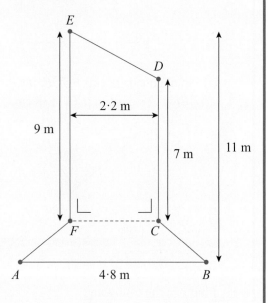

5.2 Perimeter and area of circles

A circle is the set of all points in a plane that are the same distance (the radius) from a given point called the centre of the circle.

Identifying the parts of a circle

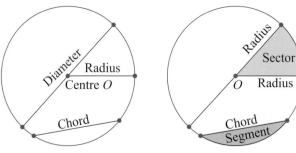

- **Full circle:** A rotation around a full circle from a point *P* back to *P* traces out an angle of 360°.

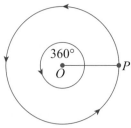

TIP

Depending on the context, diameter and radius can refer to the line segments described by these terms or to their lengths.

- **Radius:** The length of a diameter = $2r$, where r is the length of a radius.

$$r = |OP| = |OQ|$$
$$2r = |PQ|$$

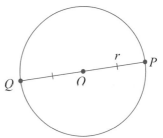

- **Circumference:** The circumference of a circle with radius r is the total length l of the full circle and is given by:

$$l = 2\pi r$$

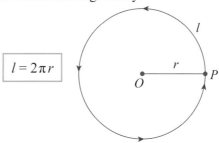

- **The area of a circle:** The area A inside a circle of radius r is given by:

$$A = \pi r^2$$

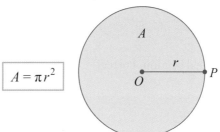

EXAMPLE 5

A circle has a diameter of 12 cm.

Find:

(a) the circumference of the circle, correct to one decimal place,

(b) the area of the circle, correct to the nearest whole number.

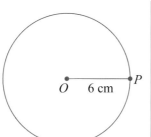

Solution

$d = 2r = 12 \Rightarrow r = 6$ cm

(a) $l = 2\pi r = 2 \times \pi \times 6 = 12\pi$ cm $= 37 \cdot 7$ cm

(b) $A = \pi(r)^2 = \pi(6)^2 = 36\pi$ cm$^2 = 113$ cm^2

ACTIVITY 2

ACTION
Exploring sectors

OBJECTIVE
To write down the fraction of a given sector of the full circle

Sector of a circle

A **sector of a circle** is a slice (pie piece) of a full circle.

The angle $\theta = \angle|POQ|$ at the centre of the circle determines the length of the arc PQ and the area of the sector enclosed by the radii $[OP]$ and $[OQ]$.

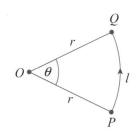

Formulae

The **length** l of the arc PQ of a sector of a circle:

$l = 2\pi r\left(\dfrac{\theta}{360}\right)$, for θ in degrees.

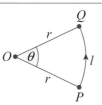

The **area** A of a sector of a circle:

$A = \pi r^2\left(\dfrac{\theta}{360}\right)$, for θ in degrees.

EXAMPLE 6

Find the length of the major arc PQ and the perimeter of the sector of a circle with centre O and radius 10 cm shown, correct to two decimal places.
Find the area of the shaded section, correct to one decimal place.

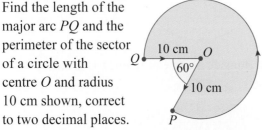

Solution

$\theta = 300°$

Arc length PQ: $l = \dfrac{300}{360} \times 2 \times \pi \times (10) = \dfrac{50\pi}{3}$ cm $= 52\!\cdot\!36$ cm

Perimeter $= l + 2r = 52\!\cdot\!36 + 20 = 72\!\cdot\!36$ cm

Area $A = \dfrac{300}{360} \times \pi \times (10)^2 = \dfrac{250\pi}{3}$ cm$^2 = 261\!\cdot\!8$ cm^2

EXAMPLE 7

$EFGH$ is a rectangle. s_1 and s_2 are two semicircles of radii 3 cm with centres I and J on $[HG]$ and $[EF]$, respectively.
Find the area of the shaded region, correct to two decimal places.

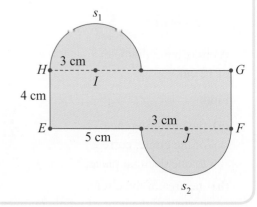

Solution

$A = $ Area of $EFGH + 2($Area of $s_1)$

$A = 4 \times 11 + 2 \times \frac{1}{2}\pi(3)^2 = (44 + 9\pi)$ cm$^2 = 72\!\cdot\!27$ cm^2

EXAMPLE 8

A logo for a New Government Agency (NGA) is shown below coloured in green.

It is obtained by removing the four quarter circles coloured red, with their centres at the vertices of the square $DEFG$, each of radius 40 cm from the square.

(a) Find the length of the side of the square $DEFG$.

(b) Find the area of the logo, correct to two decimal places.

Solution

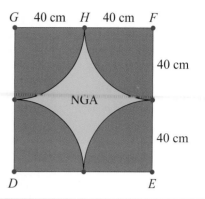

$|GH| = |HF| = 40$ cm

(a) 80 cm

(b) Area of logo = Area of square − area of 4 quarter circles

$$= 80 \times 80 - 4 \times \frac{1}{4} \times \pi (40)^2$$

$$= 1373 \cdot 45 \text{ cm}^2$$

EXERCISE 2

Diagrams are not drawn to scale.

1. Find the circumference l and area A of a circle with:

   (a) a radius of 10 cm in terms of π,

   (b) a diameter of 10 cm in terms of π,

   (c) a radius of $\sqrt{3}$ m in terms of π,

   (d) a diameter of x in terms of π and x.

2. Find the perimeter and area of each of the following sectors of a circle with centre O, correct to two decimal places.

   (a) A semicircular flower-bed of diameter 64 cm.

   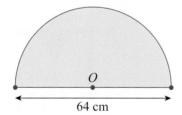

   (b)

   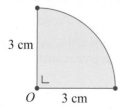

   (c)

   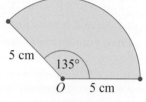

   (d)

   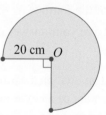

3. **(a)** A sector of a circle has a radius of 6 cm and an angle of 120°. Find the area of the sector in terms of π.

   (b) If the circumference of a circle is 10π cm, find its radius and its area in terms of π.

   (c) If the area of a circle is 9π cm², find its radius and circumference in terms of π.

   (d) A sector of a circle of radius 6 cm has an area of 12π cm². Find, in terms of π:

   (i) the angle in the sector,

   (ii) the length of the arc of the sector,

   (iii) the circumference of the circle.

   (e) A sector of a circle has an arc length of 15 cm and a radius of 10 cm. Find the measure of the angle in the sector, correct to the nearest degree.

4. (a) The base of the trunk of the General Sherman tree in Sequoia National Park, California is a circle of circumference 31 m. If the tree is cut down to the base, what would be the area of its cross-section at the base? Give your answer correct to one decimal place.

(b) A circular merry-go-round has a diameter of 24·6 m. How far does a child travel on an outside horse after 10 full revolutions? Give your answer correct to two decimal places.

(c) Find the circumference of the equator of the Earth if its radius is $6·4 \times 10^6$ m. Give your answer correct to the nearest kilometre.

(d) The boat on a carnival ride travels along an arc of a circle with centre O. The boat is attached to O by a rod 5·8 m long. The rod swings from OA to OB. If the length of the arc AB is 6·8 m, find the angle through which the boat swings, to the nearest degree. If the time to go from A to B is 5 seconds, find its average speed.

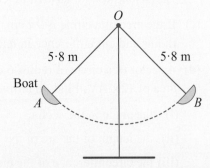

(e) The Millennium Dome at Greenwich in England is a large fabric dome. It covers a circular plot of land of diameter 97·5 m. Find the circumference and area of land it covers, correct to the nearest whole number.

5. (a) Find the perimeter and area of the cross-section of the arch shown, consisting of a semicircle with diameter $[DC]$ on a rectangle $ABCD$, correct to the nearest whole number.

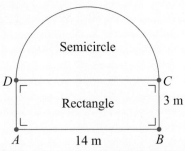

(b) Find the area of the shaded region to the nearest cm^2 if the circle with centre O is inscribed in the square $ABCD$. Give your answer correct to the nearest whole number.

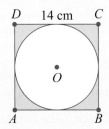

(c) Find the area of the shaded region where s_1 and s_2 are two identical touching circles each of radius 4 cm and t_1 and t_2 are two tangents parallel to $[BD]$. B is the centre of s_1 and D the centre of s_2. Give your answer correct to two decimal places.

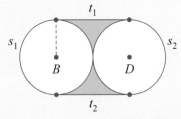

(d) Find the area of the shaded section if s_1 and s_2 are two concentric circles with centre O, of diameters 14 cm and 42 cm respectively. Give your answer in terms of π.

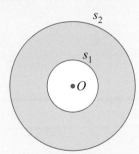

6. (a) The Chicxulub crater in Mexico is believed to be the site of the asteroid impact that killed off the dinosaurs.

It consists of an inner ring of radius 40 km and an outer ring of radius 90 km with the same centre O.

Find:

(i) the perimeter of each ring,

(ii) the area between the rings.

Give answers correct to the nearest whole number.

(b) The pattern for a skirt consists of the sector of a circle with centre O, with $|OR| = |OP| = 0.64$ m and $|OQ| = |OS| = 0.28$ m.

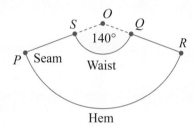

Find:

(i) the length of the waist, correct to three decimal places,

(ii) the length of the hem, correct to three decimal places,

(iii) the area of the material needed for the skirt, correct to one decimal place.

(c) Lucy bought a pack of 50 writeable compact discs (CDs). Each CD can store 700 MB of data.

(i) Calculate the cost of one CD if she paid €22·50 for the pack.

(ii) What is the minimum number of CDs she needs to store 3560 MB of data?

(iii) A CD has a centre hole with centre O and radius $r = 7.5$ mm. The radius $R = |OE|$ of the CD is 58 mm. The writeable area is 85% of the area of the CD. Find the writeable area, correct to the nearest cm^2.

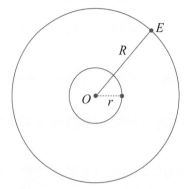

(d) A rectangular yard contains a swimming pool surrounded by a tiled area as shown. The shape of the pool consists of a rectangle of length 12 m and breadth 6 m with two semicircular ends.

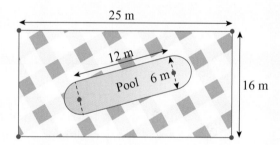

(i) Find the area of the pool, correct to one decimal place.

(ii) Find the area to be tiled, correct to one decimal place.

(iii) If the tiles are 30 cm × 30 cm, find the minimum number of tiles required.

(iv) If 1 m^2 of tiles costs €15 and labour costs are €5 per m^2, find the total cost of the tiling excluding VAT using the minimum number of tiles.

(e) Flower-beds are set out inside a rectangular garden as shown.

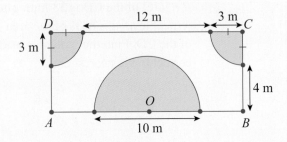

There are three flower-beds, one semicircle with centre O and two quarter circles with centres C and D respectively.

(i) Find the total area of all flower-beds, correct to one decimal place.

(ii) Find the area of the lawn, correct to one decimal place.

5.3 Estimating areas (trapezoidal rule)

The trapezoidal rule is a method for approximating the area of a plane shape with an irregular boundary (curve). This is done by splitting the area into a set of trapeziums with the same base h as shown by drawing equally spaced lines from the boundary perpendicular to a base line.

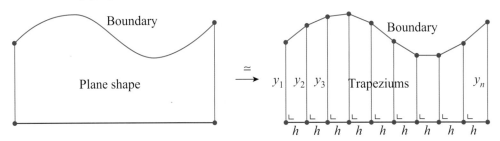

TIP

The area of a trapezium is half the sum of the lengths of the parallel sides multiplied by the perpendicular distance between the parallel sides.

WORKED EXAMPLE

Deriving the trapezoidal rule

Find the area of the polygon $BCDEFGHIJ$.

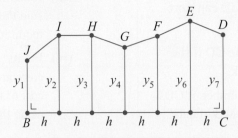

The area enclosed by these six trapeziums is given by:

$$A = \tfrac{1}{2}h(y_1 + y_2) + \tfrac{1}{2}h(y_2 + y_3) + \tfrac{1}{2}h(y_3 + y_4) + \tfrac{1}{2}h(y_4 + y_5) + \tfrac{1}{2}h(y_5 + y_6) + \tfrac{1}{2}h(y_6 + y_7)$$

$$= \tfrac{1}{2}h\{y_1 + y_2 + y_2 + y_3 + y_3 + y_4 + y_4 + y_5 + y_5 + y_6 + y_6 + y_7\}$$

$$= \tfrac{1}{2}h\{(y_1 + y_7) + 2(y_2 + y_3 + y_4 + y_5 + y_6)\}$$

In general, the area A under a curve can be approximated by the trapezoidal rule:

$$A \approx \tfrac{1}{2}h\{y_1 + y_n + 2(y_2 + y_3 + y_4 + \ldots + y_{n-1})\}$$

$$= \left(\frac{\text{Base step } h}{2}\right)\{(\text{First height } y_1 + \text{last height } y_n) + \text{twice (the sum of the other heights)}\}$$

$$A = \tfrac{1}{2}h[y_1 + y_n + 2(y_2 + y_3 + y_4 + \ldots y_{n-1})] \quad \text{[Trapezoidal rule]}$$

ACTIVITY 3

ACTION
Trapezoidal rule

OBJECTIVE
To use the trapezoidal rule to estimate a given area

EXAMPLE 9

The diagram shows the garden of a house. At equal intervals of 3 m along one side of the house, perpendicular lines are drawn to meet the boundary.

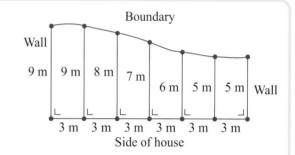

Use the trapezoidal rule to estimate the area of the garden.

Solution

Base step $= h = 3$ m

First height $= 9$ m

Last height $= 5$ m

Area $A = \tfrac{3}{2}\{(9 + 5) + 2(9 + 8 + 7 + 6 + 5)\} = \tfrac{3}{2}\{14 + 70\} = 3(7 + 35) = 126 \text{ m}^2$

EXAMPLE 10

Use the trapezoidal rule to estimate the area A enclosed by the curve c using base step 3.

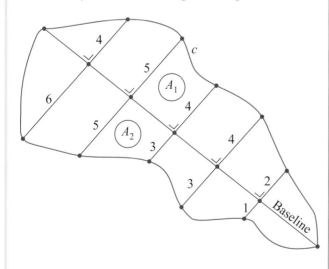

Solution

The area enclosed by c is split into an area A_1 on one side of the baseline and an area A_2 on the other side the baseline. Apply the trapezoidal rule to each area and then add the results or apply the trapezoidal rule to the whole area to find the area in one go.

$h = 3$

Method 1: Separately

Above baseline:

$A_1 = \tfrac{3}{2}[0 + 0 + 2(4 + 5 + 4 + 4 + 2)] = 57$

Below baseline:

$A_2 = \tfrac{3}{2}[0 + 0 + 2(6 + 5 + 3 + 3 + 1)] = 54$

$A = A_1 + A_2 = 57 + 54 = 111$

Method 2: In one go

$A_1 = \tfrac{3}{2}[0 + 0 + 2(10 + 10 + 7 + 7 + 3)] = 111$

EXAMPLE 11

Graph the function $y = f(x) = x^2 + 4$ in the domain $-4 \leq x \leq 4$, $x \in \mathbb{R}$. Use the trapezoidal rule to estimate the area between the curve, the x-axis and the lines $x = -4$ and $x = 4$ by dividing the interval between $x = -4$ to $x = 4$ into eight equal base steps.

Solution

$y = x^2 + 4$

x	−4	−3	−2	−1	0	1	2	3	4
y	20	13	8	5	4	5	8	13	20

Base step = 1

$A = \frac{1}{2}\{(20 + 20) + 2(13 + 8 + 5 + 4 + 5 + 8 + 13)\}$

$\quad = \frac{1}{2}\{40 + 112\} = 20 + 56 = 76$

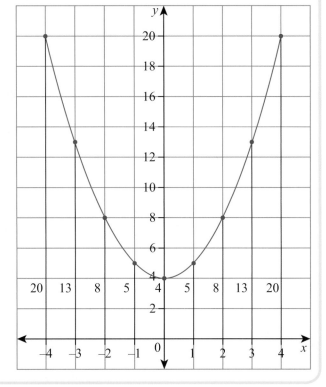

EXERCISE 3

Diagrams are not drawn to scale.

1. Find the area of the plane shapes below. All measurements are in centimetres (cm) unless otherwise stated. The diagrams are not drawn to scale.

   (a) Base step = 3

   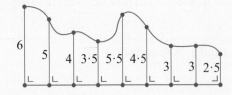

   (b) Base step = 2

   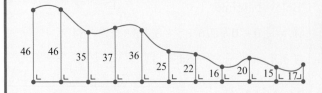

   (c) Base step = 6

   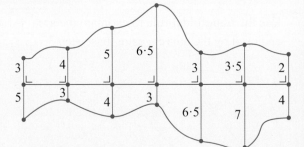

   (d) Base step = 5

   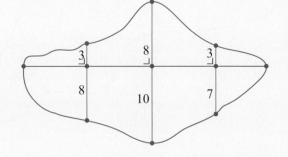

(e) Base step = 1

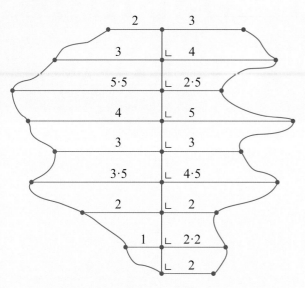

(f) Base step = 4

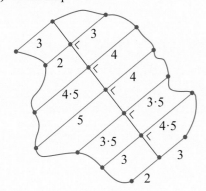

2. (a) Graph the function $f(x) = 2x^2 + 3$, in the domain $0 \leq x \leq 6$, $x \in \mathbb{R}$. Use the trapezoidal rule to calculate the area between the curve, the x-axis and the lines $x = 0$ and $x = 6$ by dividing the interval from 0 to 6 in six equal base steps.

(b) Graph the function $f(x) = x^2 - 2x - 8$, in the domain $-2 \leq x \leq 4$, $x \in \mathbb{R}$. Use the trapezoidal rule to calculate the area between the curve, the x-axis and the lines $x = -2$ and $x = 4$ by dividing the interval from -2 to 4 in six equal base steps.

(c) Graph the function $f(x) = x^3 + 4x^2 - 10x - 8$, in the domain $-5 \leq x \leq -1$, $x \in \mathbb{R}$. Use the trapezoidal rule to calculate the area between the curve, the x-axis and the lines $x = -5$ and $x = -1$ by dividing the interval from $x = -5$ to $x = -1$ in four equal base steps.

Three-dimensional Figures and Nets

Learning Outcomes

- To know how to find the surface area and volume of various solids.

- To understand how to transform 2D nets into their 3D shapes and vice versa.

6.1 Surface area and volume of solids

KEY TERM

A **solid** is any object that takes up space. A solid has a volume.

Types of solids

Solids can be divided into:

1. **Polyhedra:** Solids made up of all flat surfaces (faces),

2. Solids with at least one curved surface.

1. Polyhedra

A polyhedron (plural: polyhedra) is a solid made up of all flat surfaces called **faces**. Cubes and pyramids are examples of polyhedra.

The corner points of a polyhedron are known as **vertices** (singular: vertex).

The intersection of two faces is called a **side**.

- The **cube** has six faces, 12 sides and eight vertices.
  It has a uniform cross-section.

- The **pyramid** has five faces, eight sides and five vertices.

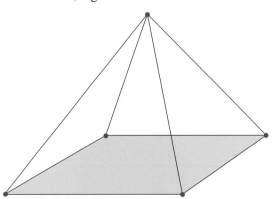

Polyhedra can be divided into prisms and pyramids.

(a) Prisms

A prism is a solid made up of all flat surfaces called faces with a uniform cross-section of the same shape and area as the base of the solid all the way from the bottom to the top of the solid. The shape of the base gives the prism its name.

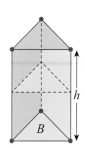

- **Triangular prism:** A triangular prism has a triangular base and cross-section.

- **Rectangular prism:** A cuboid or rectangular prism has a rectangular base and cross-section.

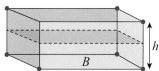

The **surface area** of a prism is equal to the sum of the areas of all faces.

The **volume** V of a prism = Area B of the base × height h of the prism $\Rightarrow V = Bh$

ACTIVITY 4

ACTION
Properties of polyhedra

OBJECTIVE
To write down the number of faces, edges and vertices for various polyhedra

EXAMPLE 1

For the triangular prism shown, find:

(a) the total surface area

(b) the volume

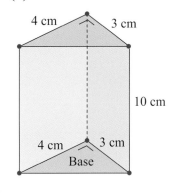

Solution

(a) The base is a right-angle triangle.

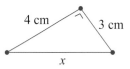

$x = 5$ cm   [Pythagoras]

The prism consists of three rectangles and two right-angled triangles as faces.

$$A = 5 \times 10 + 4 \times 10 + 3 \times 10 + 2 \times \tfrac{1}{2}(4) \times 3$$

$$= 50 + 40 + 30 + 12 = 132 \text{ cm}^2$$

(b) $V = Bh = \left(\tfrac{1}{2} \times 4 \times 3\right) \times 10 = 60 \text{ cm}^3$

(b) Pyramids

A pyramid is a solid with all flat faces and with a cross-section of the same shape as the base. The area tapers from the bottom (base) to the top (apex) of this solid. This means the cross-sectional area decreases from the base to the apex.

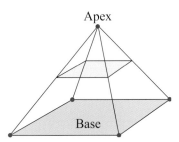

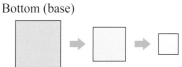

Square-based pyramid

Cross-sectional area decreases from bottom to top

2. Solids with at least one curved surface

(a) Cylinders

A solid cylinder has two flat circular surfaces at the base and top and one curved surface.

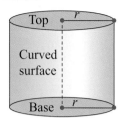

(b) Cones

A solid cone has a circular flat base and a circular cross-section which decreases in area from the base to the apex and one curved surface.

If the line from the apex to the centre of the circular base makes an angle of 90° with any base radius, the cone is known as a **right-circular cone**.

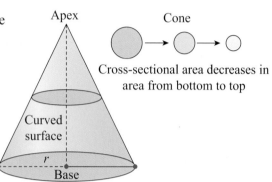

Cross-sectional area decreases in area from bottom to top

(c) Spheres and hemispheres

(i) Sphere: A sphere is a solid that has one curved surface. It is a ball.

(ii) Hemisphere: A hemisphere is half a sphere. It has one flat circular surface and one curved surface.

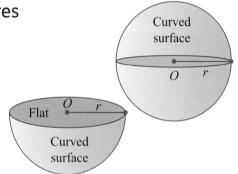

Formulae for solids

1. Triangular prism **Structure:** 5 faces = 3 rectangles and 2 triangles **Uniform cross-sectional area** B **Surface area** A: $A = (ah + bh + ch) + 2B$ **Volume** V: $V = Bh$	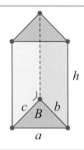

2. Rectangular prism (Cuboid) **Structure:** 6 faces = 6 rectangles **Uniform cross-sectional area** B: $B = a \times b$ **Surface area** A: $A = 2ab + 2bh + 2ah = 2(ab + bh + ah)$ **Volume** V: $V = B \times h = abh$	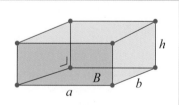

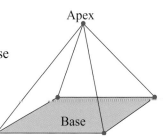

3. **Pyramid**

Structure: Base and 4 faces

Surface area A: A = Area of base + Area of triangular faces attached to the base

4. **Cylinder**

Structure: 2 flat circular faces and 1 curved face which, when opened out, is a rectangle

Uniform cross-sectional area $B = \pi r^2$

r = Radius of the circular base

h = Height of cylinder

Curved surface area $= 2\pi rh$

Total surface area A: $A = 2\pi rh + 2\pi r^2$

Volume V: $V = Bh \Rightarrow V = (\pi r^2)h = \pi r^2 h$

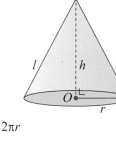

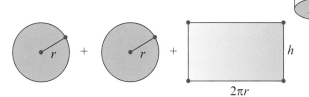

5. **Right-circular cone**

Structure: 1 flat circular face and 1 curved face which, when opened out, is a sector of a circle with centre D, radius l and arc length $2\pi r$.

Non-uniform circular cross-section

r = Radius of circular base

h = Vertical height = distance from the vertex D to the centre O of the circular base

l = Slant height, where $l = \sqrt{h^2 + r^2}$

Curved surface area $= \pi rl$

Surface area A: $A = \pi r^2 + \pi rl$

Volume V: $V = \frac{1}{3}\pi r^2 h$

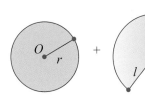

Flat surface area   Curved surface area

6. **Sphere**

Structure: 1 curved surface

r = Radius of the sphere

Total surface area A: $A = 4\pi r^2$

Volume V: $V = \frac{4}{3}\pi r^3$

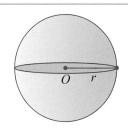

7. **Hemisphere**

Structure: 1 flat surface and 1 curved surface

r = Radius of the hemisphere

Surface area A: $A = \pi r^2 + 2\pi r^2 = 3\pi r^2$ [Flat surface area + curved surface area]

Volume V: $V = \frac{2}{3}\pi r^3$

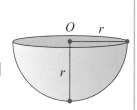

ACTIVITY 5

ACTION
Exploring pyramids and prisms

OBJECTIVE
To be able to distinguish between pyramids and prisms

EXAMPLE 2

Find the surface area of a pyramid *DEFG* with an equilateral triangular base of side 6 cm if the apex is 8 cm vertically above *D*. Give your answer correct to one decimal place.

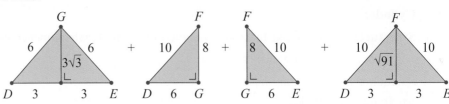

Solution

Faces:

Area $A = \frac{1}{2} \times 6 \times 3\sqrt{3} + 2 \times \frac{1}{2} \times 6 \times 8 + \frac{1}{2} \times 6 \times \sqrt{91}$

$= 9\sqrt{3} + 48 + 3\sqrt{91} = 92 \cdot 2 \text{ cm}^2$

EXAMPLE 3

A cylindrical tube has height 80 cm and base diameter 20 cm. Find, in terms of π:

(a) its curved surface area,

(b) its total external surface area if it has:

    (i) a top only,   **(ii)** a top and a bottom,

(c) its volume.

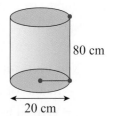
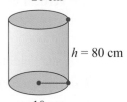

Solution

(a) Curved surface area $= 2\pi rh = 2 \times \pi \times 10 \times 80 = 1600\pi \text{ cm}^2$

(b) (i) Area $= 1600\pi + \pi(10)^2 = 1700\pi \text{ cm}^2$ **(ii)** $A = 1600\pi + 2\pi(10)^2 = 1800\pi \text{ cm}^2$

(c) $V = \pi(r)^2 h = \pi(10)^2 \times 80 = 8000\pi \text{ cm}^3$

EXAMPLE 4

A grain silo consists of a cylinder on an inverted cone as shown. The height of the cylinder is 18 m and the radius of its base is 4 m. The slant height of the cone is 5 m.

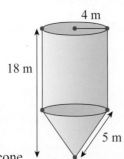

(a) Find the height of the cone.

(b) Find the volume of the cone in terms of π.

(c) Find the volume of the silo in terms of π.

(d) When the volume of the grain is $200\pi \text{ m}^3$, find the height of the surface of the grain above the vertex of the cone.

Solution

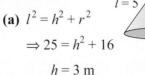

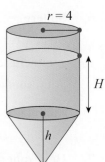

(a) $l^2 = h^2 + r^2$

$\Rightarrow 25 = h^2 + 16$

$h = 3 \text{ m}$

(b) Volume of cone $V_1 = \frac{1}{3}\pi r^2 h$

$= \frac{1}{3}\pi \times 16 \times 3 = 16\pi \text{ m}^3$

(c) Volume of silo $V_2 = 16\pi + \pi(4)^2 \times 18 = 304\pi \text{ m}^3$

(d) Volume of grain $= 200\pi = 16\pi + \pi(16)H$

$16\pi H = 184\pi$

$H = 11 \cdot 5 \text{ m}$

Therefore, the height of grain $= 11 \cdot 5 + 3 = 14 \cdot 5 \text{ m}$

EXAMPLE 5

A salt cellar is in the shape of a hemisphere on a cylinder as shown.

2 cm

If the radius of the hemisphere is 2 cm, find:

(a) the volume V of the hemisphere in terms of π,

(b) the curved surface area A of the hemisphere in terms of π.

(c) If the volume of the hemisphere is half the volume of the cylinder, find the volume of the salt cellar.

Solution

Hemisphere:

$r = 2$ cm

(a) $V = \frac{2}{3}\pi(r)^3 = \frac{2}{3}\pi(2)^3 = \frac{16\pi}{3}$ cm^3

(b) Area $A = 2\pi(r)^2 = 2\pi(2)^2 = 8\pi$ cm^2

(c) Volume of cylinder $= \pi(r)^2 h = \pi(2)^2 h = 4\pi h$

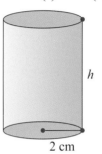

h

2 cm

Volume of hemisphere $= \frac{1}{2} \times$ Volume of cylinder

$\frac{16\pi}{3} = \frac{1}{2} \times 4\pi h \Rightarrow h = \frac{8}{3}$ cm

Volume of cylinder $= 4\pi \times \frac{8}{3} = \frac{32\pi}{3}$ cm^3

Volume of salt cellar $= \frac{16\pi}{3} + \frac{32\pi}{3} = \frac{48\pi}{3} = 16\pi$ cm^3

More challenging problems

1. Recasting

Imagine a solid object is melted down and recast as a new solid object. The volumes of the two objects will be equal once all the material in the melted solid is used in recasting.

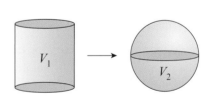

$V_1 = V_2$ (assuming all of V_1 is used)

EXAMPLE 6

The diameter of a solid metal sphere is 24 cm.

(a) Find the volume of the sphere in terms of π.

(b) The sphere is melted down. All of the metal is used to make a solid shape consisting of a cone on top of a cylinder as shown. The height of the cone is 6 cm and that of the cylinder is 8 cm. Find the radius r of the cylinder and cone, correct to one decimal place.

Solution

(a) Sphere

$$V = \frac{4}{3}\pi(r)^3 = \frac{4}{3}\pi(12)^3 = 2304\pi \text{ cm}^3$$

(b) Volume of combined solids $= \pi(r)^2 8 + \frac{1}{3}\pi(r)^2 6$

$$= 8\pi r^2 + 2\pi r^2$$
$$= 10\pi r^2$$

$$10\pi r^2 = 2304\pi$$
$$r^2 = 230.4$$
$$r = 15.2 \text{ cm}$$

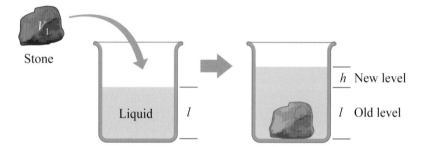

2. Immersion

A liquid takes on the shape of the container into which it is poured.

If a solid object is immersed in a container of liquid with uniform cross-section, it displaces its own volume of liquid and increases the height of the liquid.

> Volume of immersed object = Volume of liquid contained between the old level and the new level

EXAMPLE 7

Find the volume of a sphere of radius 2 cm.

A prism with a right-angled triangular cross-section contains water. Find the increase in the height of the water when an iron sphere of radius 2 cm is completely immersed in the water. Give your answer correct to two decimal places.

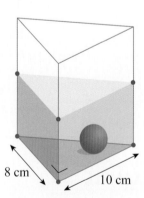

Solution

Volume of the sphere $= \frac{4}{3}\pi(2)^3 = \dfrac{32\pi}{3} \text{ cm}^3$

Volume of liquid between old and new level:

$$V = Bh = \frac{1}{2}(8 \times 10) \times h = 40h$$

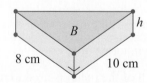

$$40h = \frac{32\pi}{3}$$
$$h = 0.84 \text{ cm}$$

EXAMPLE 8

A wedge of cheese is cut from a cylindrical piece of cheese of base radius 8 cm and thickness 3 cm. It is melted in a cylindrical saucepan of radius 6 cm. To what height does the melted cheese rise in the pan?

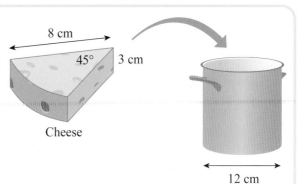

Cheese

12 cm

Saucepan

Solution

Volume of cheese $= \dfrac{45^{\circ}}{360^{\circ}} \times \pi (r)^2 h$

$\dfrac{1}{8} \times \pi (r)^2 h = \dfrac{1}{8} \times \pi (8)^2 \times 3 = 24\pi$ cm^3

The melted cheese forms a cylinder in the pan of radius 6 cm. $\pi (6)^2 h = 24\pi \Rightarrow h = \dfrac{24}{36} = \dfrac{2}{3}$ cm

3. Moving liquids or gases

KEY TERM

The **rate of flow** of a liquid or gas in a pipe is the volume of liquid which passes through the pipe per second.

If a volume V of a liquid or gas takes t seconds to flow through a pipe of uniform cross-sectional area B and length l:

The rate of flow of the liquid or gas in a pipe

$= \dfrac{\text{Volume of pipe } V}{\text{Time } t}$

$= \dfrac{\text{Cross-sectional area of pipe } B \times \text{Length of pipe } l}{\text{Time } t}$

$= \dfrac{B \times l}{t}$

$= B \times v$, where $v = \dfrac{l}{t}$ is the speed of the liquid or gas

$= $ Cross-sectional area $\times$ speed

l

Flow of liquid

B   *B*

TIP
The units of rate of flow are cm^3/s or m^3/s.

Rate of flow in a pipe = Cross-sectional area of the pipe × speed of liquid or gas in the pipe

EXAMPLE 9

TAPS is the Trans-Alaska Pipeline System. Oil flows through this pipe system, which has a circular cross-section, at a speed of 1·7 m/s. If the internal diameter of the pipe is 1·22 m, calculate the rate of flow of oil in the pipe, correct to three decimal places.

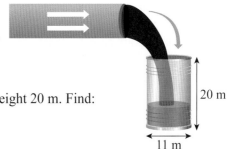

20 m

11 m

The oil is collected in cylindrical tanks of base diameter 11 m and height 20 m. Find:

(a) the volume of such a tank, correct to two decimal places.

(b) the time it takes to fill the tank, correct to the nearest minute.

Solution

Rate of flow of oil $= B \times v = \pi (r)^2 \times v$

$\qquad = \pi \times (0·61)^2 \times 1·7 = 1·987$ m^3/s

(a) Volume of storage tank: $V = \pi (r)^2 h = \pi (5·5)^2 \times 20 = 1900·66$ m^3

(b) Time $= \dfrac{1900·66 \text{ s}}{1·987} \simeq 16$ minutes

EXERCISE 4

Diagrams are not necessarily drawn to scale.

A. Polyhedra

1. The volume of a rectangular block is 1344 cm³. If its length is 14 cm and its breadth is 8 cm, find:

   (a) its height,

   (b) its surface area.

2. The volume of a cube is 27 cm². Find its surface area.

3. The surface area of a cube is 54 cm². Find its volume.

4. How many litres of water can be stored in a rectangular tank measuring 1·2 m by 0·7 m by 0·4 m. (1 litre = 1000 cm³)

5. A plastic door-wedge has a uniform cross-section as shown with $[FG] \parallel [DE]$ and $|FG| = 2$ cm.

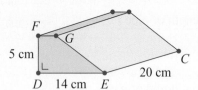

   Find:

   (a) the area of its cross-section,

   (b) the volume of plastic required to manufacture it,

   (c) its total surface area.

6. The diagram shows a tent with a uniform isosceles triangular cross-section of height 2 m.

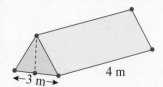

   Calculate:

   (a) the area of its cross-section,

   (b) the volume of air inside the tent,

(c) the surface area of the tent, including the base.

7. The diagram shows the design of a greenhouse with a uniform cross-section $CDEFGH$ with $|GD| = 10$ m.

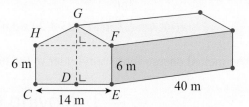

   Calculate:

   (a) the area of its cross-section,

   (b) the volume of air inside the greenhouse.

8. The diagram shows the design of a swimming pool with a uniform cross-section $CDEFG$.

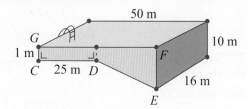

   (a) What is the area of its cross-section?

   (b) Find its capacity in m³.

9. The triangular prism shown has an equilateral triangle as its cross-section and a length of 6 cm.

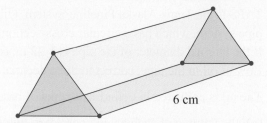

   If its volume is $12\sqrt{3}$ cm³, find:

   (a) the length of each side of the base,

   (b) the total surface area of the prism in surd form.

10. The triangular prism has an isosceles triangle
CDE as its cross-section with
$|CD| = |CE| = 3$ cm and $|DE| = 2$ cm. If its
total surface area is $28\sqrt{2}$ cm^2, find its length l.

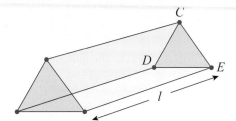

11. Find the area of the isosceles triangle $\triangle CDE$.
Hence, find the surface area of the pyramid
shown where $CDFG$ is a square of side 8 m
and each triangular face is identical to $\triangle CDE$.

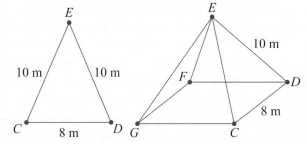

12. Find the surface area of the pyramid consisting
of four triangular faces identical to $\triangle CDG$
with $|CD| = 12$ m, $|GD| = |GC| = 10$ m and
square base $FCDE$.

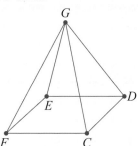

B. Curved surfaces

1. Find the total surface area and volume in
terms of π for the following solids:

   (a) a cylinder of base radius 5 cm and height
8 cm,

   (b) a cone of base radius 6 cm and height 8 cm,

   (c) a sphere of radius 6 cm,

   (d) a hemisphere of radius 9 cm.

2. A sphere has a diameter of 6 cm. Express its
volume in terms of π.

3. A right-circular cone has a height of 12 cm
and a base radius of 6 cm. Find:

   (a) its volume in terms of π,

   (b) its slant height in surd form,

   (c) its curved surface area correct to the
nearest cm^2,

   (d) its total surface area, correct to the
nearest cm^2.

4. A cylinder has a volume of 720π cm^3.
If its radius is 6 cm, calculate:

   (a) its height,

   (b) its total surface area in terms of π.

5. A cylinder has volume of 360π cm^3.
If its height is 10 cm, find:

   (a) its radius,

   (b) its total surface area in terms of π.

6. The curved surface area of a cylinder is 660 cm^2.
If the diameter of the base is 10 cm, find:

   (a) its height correct to the nearest cm,

   (b) its volume, correct to the nearest cm^3.

7. A right-circular cone has a base radius of 6 cm
and a volume of 168π cm^3. Find its height.

8. A right-circular cone has a curved surface area of
34π cm^2. If its base radius is 4 cm, find its height.

9. A right-circular cone has a volume of 16π cm^3.
If its height is 12 cm, find the radius of its base.

10. A hemisphere has a volume of 1152π cm^3.
Find its surface area in terms of π.

11. A polytunnel
of length 12 m
has a
semicircular
cross-section
with centre O
and radius 4 m.

Find, in terms of π:

   (a) the cross-sectional area

   (b) the volume

   (c) the curved surface area

12. (a) A fuel storage tank consists of a cylinder with a hemisphere at each end.

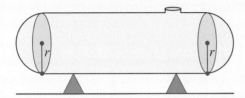

The internal volume of the tank is 90π m³. The ratio of the volume of the cylindrical section to the sum of the volumes of the hemispheres is $3:2$. Find the internal radius of the tank.

(b) A buoy at sea is in the shape of a hemisphere with a cone on top as shown. The height of the cone is $1\cdot2$ m and the radius of its base is $0\cdot9$ m.

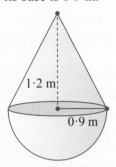

(i) Find the slant height of the buoy.

(ii) Find the total surface area of the buoy in terms of π.

(iii) Find the volume of the buoy in terms of π.

(iv) When it floats, $0\cdot75$ m of the buoy's height is above the water. What volume of the buoy is above the water, correct to two decimal places?

13. A hollow sieve is in the shape of a cylindrical upper part and a conical lower part as shown.

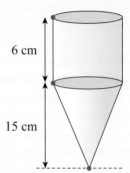

If the total volume is 176π cm³, find the diameter of the cylinder.

14. A test-tube consists of a hemisphere with a cylinder as shown. The radius of the hemisphere is 3 cm. Find the total volume in terms of h and π.

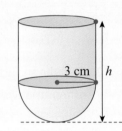

If the volume is 36π cm³, find h.

15. (a) If the volume of the cylinder A is equal to the volume of cylinder B, find h.

(b) A solid lead cylinder of base radius 2 cm and height 15 cm is melted down and recast as a solid cone of base radius 3 cm. Find the height of the cone.

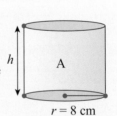
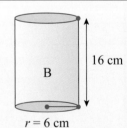

(c) The diameter of a solid hemisphere is 12 cm. Find its volume in terms of π. The metal is melted down and a solid right-circular cone and solid cylinder are formed.

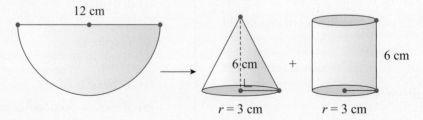

The heights of the cone and cylinder are both 6 cm and their base radii are both 3 cm. Find the percentage of metal that is not used.

16. (a) A solid metal sphere has a radius of 3 cm. Express the volume of the sphere in terms of π. A cylindrical container is partly filled with water. The sphere is completely submerged in this container.

If the level of water in the container rises by 1 cm, calculate the radius of the base of the cylinder.

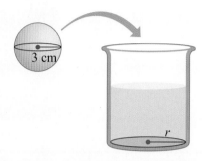

(b) A cylinder has a diameter of 10 cm and contains water. A metal cone of base diameter 8 cm and height 15 cm is lowered into the cylinder so that it is completely immersed in water. Find the rise in the level of the water in the cylinder.

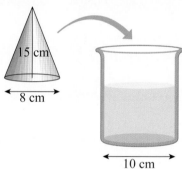

(c) A solid metal sphere of radius 9 cm is completely immersed in a cylinder containing water. The sphere is removed and the level of water drops by 3 cm. Calculate the diameter of the base of the cylinder to nearest cm.

(d) A solid metal hemisphere of radius 4 cm and a cone of height 10 cm and base radius 5 cm are completely immersed in a can containing water. The can has an equilateral triangular cross-section of side length 20 cm. When the hemisphere and the cone are removed, calculate the drop in height of the water level, correct to two decimal places.

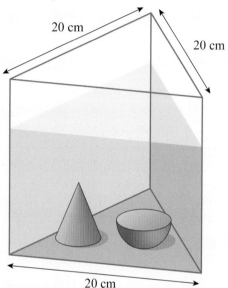

17. (a) Water flows through a cylindrical pipe of internal radius 2 cm at a speed of 10 cm/s. Calculate, in terms of π, the rate of flow of water from the pipe. The water flows into a cylindrical container of base diameter 16 cm and height 100 cm. How long will it take to fill the container?

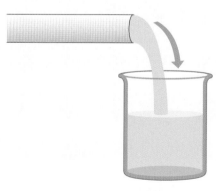

(b) A cone of base diameter 8 cm and height 12 cm is inverted and filled with water. The water then drips from the vertex of the cone at a rate of 1·256 cm³/s.

Calculate the time in seconds until the cone is empty, correct to the nearest second.

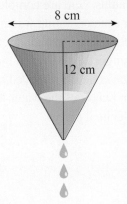

8 cm

12 cm

(c) A drainpipe has a semicircular cross-section of radius 7 cm. On a certain day, it is full of rain water, which flows along it at 8 cm/s.

Find how long it takes to fill a cylindrical water tank of height 80 cm and base diameter 48 cm. Give your answer correct to the nearest minute.

Drainpipe

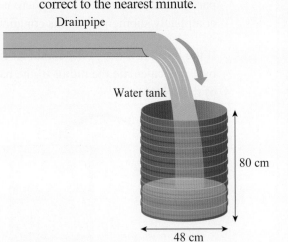

Water tank

80 cm

48 cm

6.2 Nets

ACTIVITY 6

ACTION
Exploring nets

OBJECTIVE
To experiment with a number of figures by building 3D shapes from their 2D nets

A **net** of a solid is a flattened out diagram showing each of its faces on a 2D diagram as a plane shape with the same external surface area as the solid.

If the cube in Figure 1 shown is opened out and laid flat it looks like the diagram in Figure 2.

The surface area is the sum of the areas of the six squares.

If the sides of the cube are of length 5 cm, the surface area = $6 \times 5^2 = 150$ cm^2.

Figure 1

Cube
(6 faces)

Net

Figure 2

The net shows all 6 faces

EXAMPLE 10

The net of a triangular prism is shown. Find its surface area.

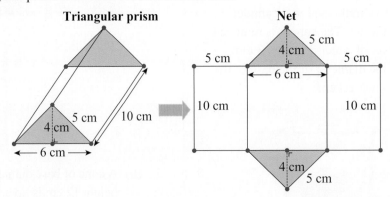

Triangular prism

5 cm
10 cm
5 cm
4 cm
6 cm

Net

5 cm
4 cm
5 cm
5 cm
6 cm
10 cm
10 cm
4 cm
5 cm

Solution

The surface area of the prism = $(5 \times 10) + (6 \times 10) + (5 \times 10) + 2 \times \frac{1}{2}(6 \times 4)$

$\underbrace{\qquad\qquad\qquad\qquad\qquad\qquad}_{\text{3 Rectangles}}$ $\underbrace{\qquad\qquad}_{\text{2 Triangles}}$

$= 160 + 24 = 184$ cm^2

EXAMPLE 11

The net of a pyramid with rectangular base 8 cm by 6 cm and four isosceles triangular faces with equal sides of length 12 cm is shown. Find:
(a) its surface area, **(b)** the height of the pyramid, giving each answer correct to one decimal place.

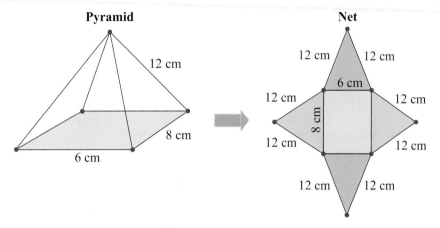

Pyramid   **Net**

Solution

(a) Area = Area of blue rectangle + area of 2 red triangles
+ area of 2 green triangles

$$= 8 \times 6 + 2 \times \frac{1}{2} \times 6 \times \sqrt{135} + 2 \times \frac{1}{2} \times 8 \times \sqrt{128}$$

$$= 48 + 18\sqrt{15} + 64\sqrt{2}$$

$$= 208 \cdot 2 \text{ cm}^2$$

(b) Length of the diagonal of rectangle $= \sqrt{8^2 + 6^2} = 10$ cm

Height of pyramid $h = \sqrt{12^2 - 5^2} = \sqrt{119} = 10 \cdot 9$ cm

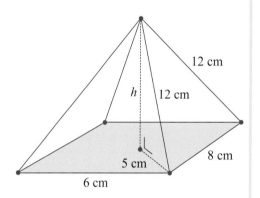

EXAMPLE 12

The net of a cylinder is shown.

(a) Find its curved surface area in terms of π.

(b) Find its total surface area in terms of π.

Solution

(a) Curved surface area $= 8\pi \times 7 = 56\pi$ cm^2

(b) Total surface area $= \pi(4)^2 \times 2 + 56\pi$
$= 88\pi$ cm^2

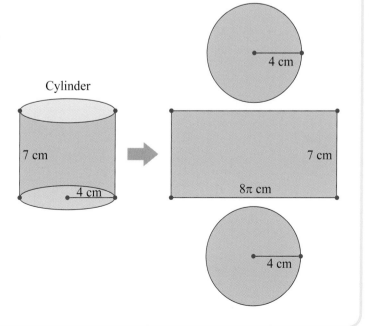

EXAMPLE 13

The net of a cone is shown.

(a) Find its curved surface area in terms of π.

(b) Find its total surface area in terms of π.

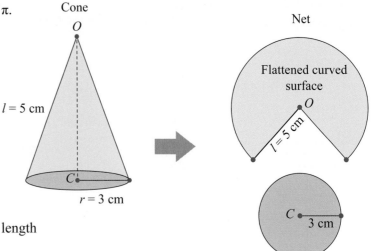

Cone

Net

Solution

When flattened out, the curved surface area is the sector of a circle with centre O and radius 5 cm, with an arc length equal to the circumference of the base of the cone.

Arc length of curved surface when flattened
= Circumference of base of cone
= $2\pi \times 3 = 6\pi$ cm

Now, a full circle of radius 5 cm has an arc length of 10π cm and an area of 25π cm^2.

Therefore, a sector of radius 5 cm and arc length 6π cm has an area of $\dfrac{6\pi}{10\pi} \times 25\pi = 15\pi$ cm^2.

(a) Curved surface area = 15π cm^2 = $\pi \times r \times l$

(b) Total surface = $\pi \times (3)^2 + 15\pi = 24\pi$ cm^2

EXERCISE 5

Diagrams are not drawn to scale.

1. Draw the net of each solid below and hence, find the total surface area of each solid. Write answers involving circles in terms of π.

   (a) Rectangular solid

   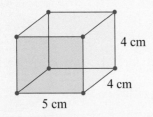

   4 cm
   4 cm
   5 cm

   (b) Triangular prism

   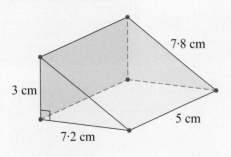

   7·8 cm
   3 cm
   5 cm
   7·2 cm

   (c) Right-circular cone

   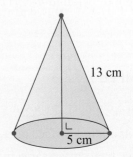

   13 cm
   5 cm

   (d) Cylinder

   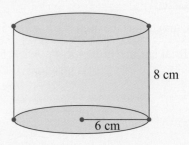

   8 cm
   6 cm

(e) Pyramid consisting of four equilateral
triangles of side 10 cm

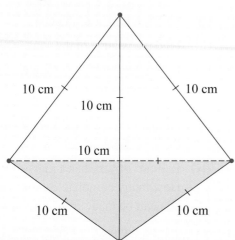

2. For each of the following nets:
   (i) find the total surface area of the solid
   by calculating the area of each of its
   surfaces,

   (ii) draw the shape of the solid with its
   dimensions.

   (a) Rectangle and two circles

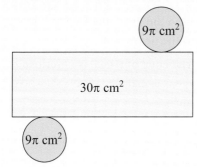

   (b) Square and four isosceles triangles

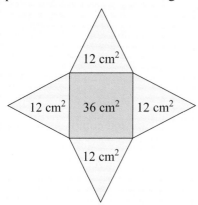

(c) Six squares

		50 cm²		
50 cm²	50 cm²	50 cm²	50 cm²	
		50 cm²		

(d) Sector of a circle and a circle

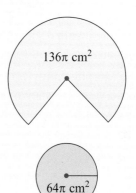

3. Draw the net of a solid with uniform cross-
   section in the form of trapezium $CDEF$ with
   $|CD| = 10$ cm, $|FC| = |ED| = 33$ cm,
   $|FE| = 49.6$ cm, $[FE] \parallel |CD|$ and $|DG| = 70$ cm
   $[DC]$. Find its total surface area, correct to
   two decimal places.

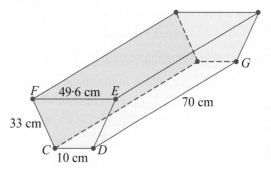

REVISION QUESTIONS

Diagrams are not drawn to scale.

1. **(a)** The floor of a room is in the shape of a trapezium with [DC] ‖ [EF]. What area of carpet is required to cover it?

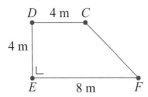

Find the length of the skirting board, giving your answer in surd form.

(b) The Murphy family wants to build a conservatory as shown on a rectangular plot 5 m by 3 m.

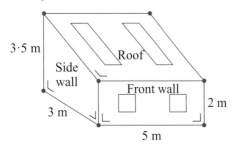

The front wall has a height of 2 m and the back wall has a height of 3·5 m. Find:

(i) the area of a side wall and the area of the front wall,

(ii) the area of the roof, giving your answer in surd form,

(iii) the volume of the conservatory.

(c) A wax candle is in the shape of a cylinder of base diameter 10 mm with a right-circular conical top of slant height 13 mm.

(i) Find the height of the cone.

(ii) Find the volume of the cone in terms of π.

(iii) If the volume of the cylinder is five times the volume of the cone, find the height of the cylinder in cm. Find the volume of the candle in cm^3, correct to three decimal places.

(iv) If 1 cm^3 of wax has a mass of 0·8 g, How many complete candles like this one can be made from 1 kg of wax?

2. **(a)** A running track is made up of two 100 m straights and two semicircular ends, each of diameter 62 m. Find the length of the track, correct to the nearest metre.

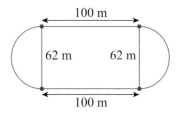

Find the area enclosed by the track, correct to the nearest m^2.

(b) The edge of a lake is described by the equation $y = x^2 + 2$, $0 \le x \le 4$, $x \in R$, where x and y are in metres.

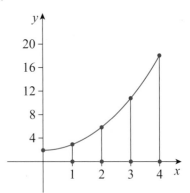

(i) Copy and complete the table below to find the y co-ordinates of the five points on the curve.

x	0	1	2	3	4
y					

(ii) Use the trapezoidal rule to estimate the area of the lake.

(c) Find the volume of a solid sphere of radius 2 cm. A cylindrical vessel has internal base diameter 16 cm and contains water. The surface of the water is 6 cm from the top of the vessel.

How many solid spheres must be totally submerged in order to bring the level of the water to 2 cm from the top of the vessel?

3. (a) The diagram shows the wiper on a car's back window.

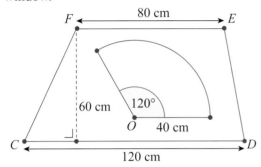

The window is in the form of a trapezium *CDEF* with [*CD*] ∥ [*FE*]. The wiper blade is 40 cm long and traces out the sector of a circle with centre *O* as shown.

Find the area of the window not cleaned by the wiper, correct to one decimal place.

(b) A closed container consists of a cylinder of base radius 12 cm and length 24 cm with a top made up of a hemisphere of radius 12 cm.

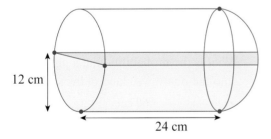

The container rests on a horizontal surface and is exactly half full of water.

(i) Calculate the surface area of the container in contact with the water in terms of π.

(ii) Show that the volume of the water is 2304π cm^3.

(iii) The container is now turned upright so that it stands vertically on a table. Find the depth *h* of the water.

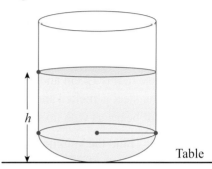

(iv) Finally, the container is inverted again. Find the depth *h* of the water.

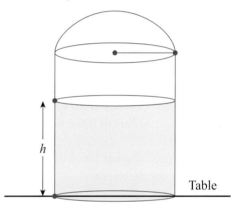

4. (a) Show that in every square the ratio of the length of a side to the length of a diagonal is $1:\sqrt{2}$.

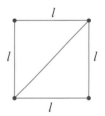

(b) The diagram shows a horseshoe magnet. The shaded cross-section consists of two semicircles of inner and outer radii of 2 cm and 4 cm respectively and two rectangles as shown.

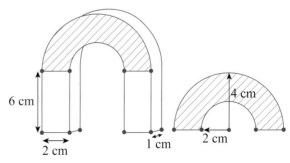

(i) Calculate the cross-sectional area of the magnet, correct to one decimal place.

(ii) Find the volume of metal in the magnet, correct to one decimal place.

(c) To make spherical ball bearings, a steel works uses solid cylindrical steel rods of base radius 12 cm and length 16 m. The steel is melted and recast as spherical ball bearings with no waste.

(i) Find the volume of steel in one rod in terms of π in cm^3.

(ii) Find the volume of a ball bearing in terms of π if its radius is 2 cm.

(iii) How many ball bearings can be made from each rod?

(iv) Another type of ball bearing is produced by this company. If 6400 can be made from a single steel rod, find the radius of these ball bearings.

5. (a) A rectangular piece of metal *CDEF* measures 8 cm by 16 cm.

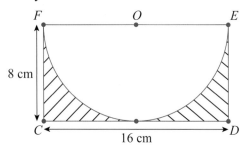

A semicircular section with centre *O* on [*FE*] and radius 8 cm is removed. Find the area of the remaining piece of metal, correct to two decimal places.

(b) The diagram *CDEF* shows a field with one boundary *ED* that is uneven.

At equal intervals of 5 m along *BC*, perpendicular measurements are taken of 7 m, 8 m, 10 m, 12 m, 14 m 15 m and *x* m.

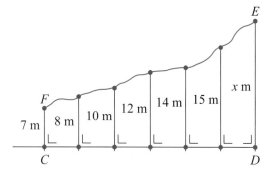

Using the trapezoidal rule, the area of the field is estimated to be 357·5 m^2. Find *x*.

(c) A swimming pool as shown has a length of 25 m and a width of 8 m. The depth is 1·2 m at the shallow end and 2·5 m at the deep end.

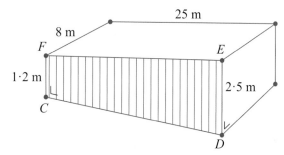

(i) Find the area of the cross-section *CDEF* (a trapezium), in which [*CF*] ∥ [*DE*].

(ii) Find the volume of the pool.

(iii) If the pool is filled to a depth of 0·5 m from the top, find the volume of water in the pool in kilolitres.

6. (a) A rectangular board *CEGH* contains a shaded region *CDFG* in the shape of a quadrilateral. What is the probability that a pin dropped onto the board will land in the shaded area?

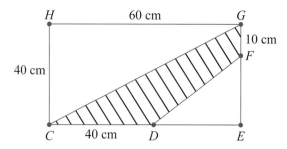

(b) The diagram shows a section of a wall that is to be painted. At equal intervals of 0·6 m along the bottom of the wall perpendicular measurements are made to the uneven edge as shown on the diagram.

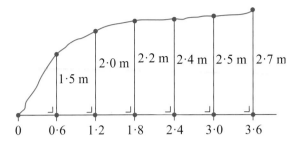

(i) Use the trapezoidal rule to estimate the area of the section of the wall.

(ii) How many litres of paint are needed to paint this section if 1 litre of paint covers $2 \cdot 5$ m^2?

(c) A 3D ornament consists of a hollow hemisphere of clear plastic of diameter 24 cm with a right-circular cone of base diameter 24 cm which fits exactly into the hemisphere. The space between the solids is filled with a liquid. Find the volume of the liquid in terms of π.

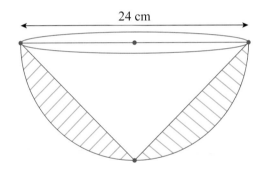

7. (a) In the diagram shown, the three circles s_1, s_2 and s_3 touch each other. If the ratio of the diameter of the largest circle to the smallest circle is 3:1, what fraction of the largest circle is shaded?

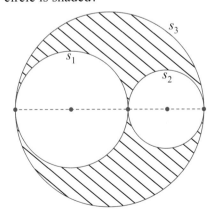

(b) The diagram shows a piece of land which borders the side of a straight section of road [CD] of length 66 m. At equal intervals along

[CD] perpendicular measurements are made to the boundary as shown.

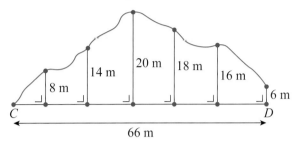

(i) Use the trapezoidal rule to estimate the area of the land.

(ii) The land has a value of €80 000 per hectare. Find the value of the land if 1 hectare = 10 000 m^2.

(c) A driveway consists of an area enclosed by two concentric circles with centre O, with inner radius $2 \cdot 5$ m and width 2 m.

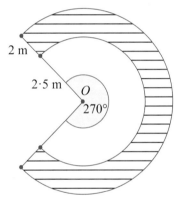

Find the area of the driveway in terms of π. If it is tarred to a depth of 20 cm, find the cost correct to the nearest euro, if the price of tar is €60 per cubic metre.

8. (a) The diagram shows a small square s_2 inside a big square s_1.

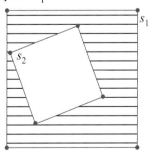

If the area of the shaded region is equal to the area of the small square, find the ratio of the area of the big square to the area of the small square.

(b) The diagram shows the speed-time curve of a body for a journey which takes 10 seconds. The curve is a trapezium with $[OE] \parallel [DC]$.

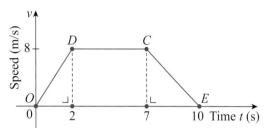

Find:

(i) the initial speed,

(ii) the final speed,

(iii) the distance travelled if the distance is the area of the trapezium,

(iv) the average speed.

(c) A pyramid has a square base *CDEF* of side $6\sqrt{2}$ m. The vertex *G* is 8 m vertically above the point *O* of intersection of the diagonals of the square.

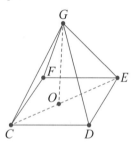

Find $|GC|$ and the area of the four triangular faces, correct to two decimal places.

9. (a) A carton of orange juice with a slogan is a cuboid as shown.

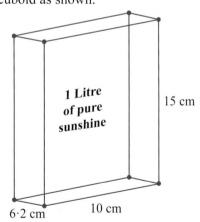

(i) A wary shopper measures the sides of the container with a tape measure. Why is the slogan misleading?

(ii) When the shopper gets home, she pours the juice into a cylindrical jug of base diameter 10 cm. If it occupies half the volume of the jug, find the height of the jug, correct to one decimal place.

(b) Three tennis balls, each of radius 3·5 cm, just fit into a cylindrical container.

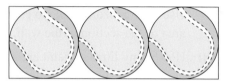

Find:

(i) the volume of the three balls in terms of π,

(ii) the volume of the container in terms of π,

(iii) the percentage volume of the container not filled by the tennis balls.

10. (a) Joe and Peter buy a two-person tent to travel around Europe. Find the volume of the tent when erected, correct to two decimal places. The tent has an isosceles triangular cross-section *CEF* with perpendicular height 1·04 m.

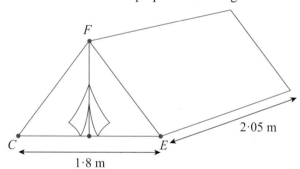

(b) A hollow water can is shown, consisting of a cylinder attached to a cone.

When full, it holds 8 litres of water.

The height of the cylinder is four times the height of the cone.

Find the total height of the container, correct to one decimal place.

(c) Tom and Fiona have a bicycle each.

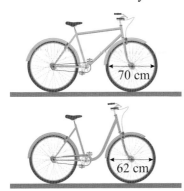

The diameters of the wheels on Tom's bike are 70 cm and the diameters of the wheels on Fiona's bike are 62 cm. Calculate the difference in the number of revolutions of the wheels of each bike over 1 km. Give your answer correct to two significant figures.

11. (a) Find the area of the regular hexagon of side 10 cm.

(b) (i) Using similar triangles, or otherwise, find $h = |EF|$ for the right-circular cone shown if $|ED| = 2$ cm.

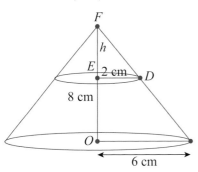

(ii) A frustum is obtained by slicing the top of the cone by a plane parallel to its base. Find the volume of the frustum.

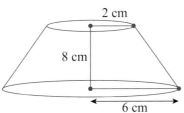

(c) Draw the net for the pyramid with a square base of side 6 cm and all other sides of length 5 cm. Find its total surface area.

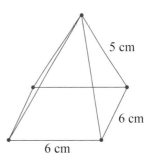

12. (a) Water flows through a pipe with a uniform cross-sectional area of 20 cm^2 at a speed of 2 m/s. Find the volume of water passing through the pipe per second.

(b) How long does it take to fill a rectangular tank 2 m × 1 m × 1 m?

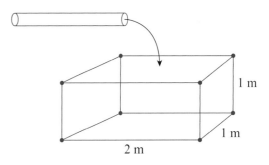

(c) A river runs between parallel banks 18 m wide. The depth h metres of the river measured at the point d metres from one bank is given by $h = \frac{1}{9}d\sqrt{18 - d}$.

(i) Write down an inequality satisfied by d.

(ii) Copy and complete the table giving all answers correct to one decimal place.

d (m)	0	3	6	9	12	15	18
h (m)							

(iii) Plot a graph of h against d on graph paper.

(iv) Use the trapezoidal rule to estimate the cross-sectional area of the river at this point.

(v) If the river flows at 3 m/s, estimate the volume of water passing through this area per second.

SUMMARY

Mensuration

1. 2D shapes:

    (a) Rectangle

    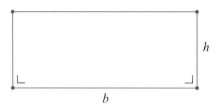

    Perimeter = $2b + 2h$

    Area = $b \times h$

    (b) Square

    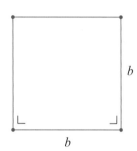

    Perimeter = $4b$

    Area = b^2

    (c) Parallelogram

    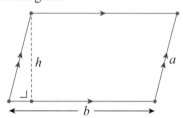

    Perimeter = $2b + 2a$

    Area = $b \times h$

    (d) Rhombus

    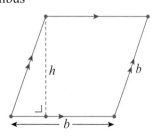

    Perimeter = $4b$

    Area = $b \times h$

(e) Triangle

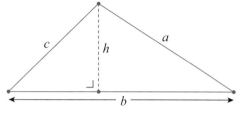

Perimeter = $a + b + c$

Area = $\frac{1}{2} \times b \times h$

(f) Trapezium

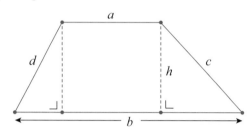

Perimeter = $b + c + a + d$

Area = $\frac{1}{2} h (b + a)$

(g) Circles

   (i) Full circle

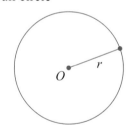

Perimeter = $2\pi r$

Area = πr^2

   (ii) Sector of a circle

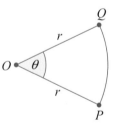

Arc length $PQ = 2\pi r \times \left(\dfrac{\theta}{360}\right)$ [Angle in degrees]

Area = $\pi r^2 \times \left(\dfrac{\theta}{360}\right)$ [Angle in degrees]

2. Trapezoidal rule:

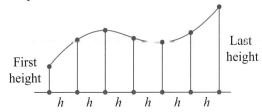

$$\text{Area} \simeq \frac{\text{Base step } h}{2} \{(\text{First height} + \text{last height}) + \text{twice the sum of the other heights}\}$$

3. 3D shapes:

(a) Triangular prism

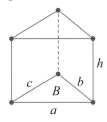

Surface area = Sum of areas of all faces
$$= (ah + bh + ch) + 2B$$

Volume = Cross-sectional area B × height h

(b) Cuboid

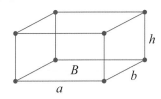

Surface area = $2(ab + bh + ah)$

Volume = $Bh = abh$

(c) Cylinder

Curved surface area = $2\pi rh$

Total surface area = $2\pi rh + 2\pi r^2$

Volume = $\pi r^2 h$

(d) Right-circular cone

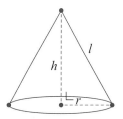

Curved surface area = πrl

Total surface area = $\pi r^2 + \pi rl$

Volume = $\frac{1}{3}\pi r^2 h$

(e) Sphere/Hemisphere

(i) Sphere

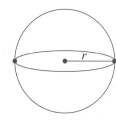

Surface area = $4\pi r^2$

Volume = $\frac{4}{3}\pi r^3$

(ii) Hemisphere

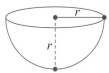

Curved surface area = $2\pi r^2$

Total surface area = $3\pi r^2$

Volume = $\frac{2}{3}\pi r^3$

4. Rate of flow of a liquid or gas:

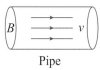

Pipe

Rate of flow = $\dfrac{\text{Volume}}{\text{Time}} = B \times v$, where B is the cross sectional area and v is the speed

SECTION 3

Trigonometry

There are numerous real-life applications of trigonometry. These applications include acoustics, architecture, astronomy, cartography, engineering, medical imaging, oceanography and seismology.

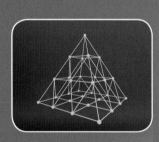

Trigonometry 1

CHAPTER 7

Learning Outcomes

- To define the three trigonometric ratios – cosine (cos), sine (sin) and tangent (tan) – and to understand how these functions change as you go around the circle.
- To work with angles in degrees and radians allowing you to carry out sector calculations.
- To solve right-angled triangles using your knowledge of trigonometry.

KEY TERM

Trigonometry is the study of the relationship between lengths and angles in geometric figures (shapes).

7.1 Trigonometry basics

1. Defining the trigonometric ratios

All **angles** are measured from the positive *x*-axis around a circle. If you stop at any point *P* on a circle with centre *O*, the line *OP* makes an angle with the +*x*-axis. This angle *A* is associated with the point *P* and leads to the definition of the three basic trigonometric ratios (functions).

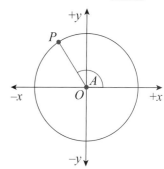

The three basic trigonometric ratios (functions)

ACTION
Examining the three basic trigonometric ratios

OBJECTIVE
To understand how to use the definitions for cos, sin and tan

Consider the point P on a circle of centre O and radius r so that OP makes an angle A to the +x-axis. The co-ordinates of this point are (x, y). The definitions of cosine (cos), sine (sin) and tangent (tan) are as follows:

$$\cos A = \frac{x}{r} = \frac{x \text{ co-ordinate}}{\text{Radius}}$$

$$\sin A = \frac{y}{r} = \frac{y \text{ co-ordinate}}{\text{Radius}}$$

$$\tan A = \frac{y}{x} = \frac{y \text{ co-ordinate}}{x \text{ co-ordinate}} = \frac{\frac{y}{r}}{\frac{x}{r}} = \frac{\sin A}{\cos A}$$

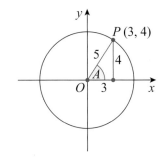

$P(x, y) = (r \cos A, r \sin A)$

TIP

cos A is associated with the x co-ordinate of a point on a circle and sin A is associated with the y co-ordinate of a point on a circle.

▶ For the angle A shown, write down the values of cos A, sin A and tan A.

$$\cos A = \frac{x}{r} = \frac{3}{5}, \sin A = \frac{y}{r} = \frac{4}{5}, \tan A = \frac{y}{x} = \frac{4}{3}$$

$P(3, 4)$

Direction of angles: All angles are measured from the +x-axis.

Anticlockwise angles are **positive**: +A.

Clockwise angles are **negative**: −A.

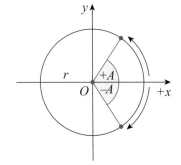

2. Quadrants

Every circle is divided into four equal sectors by the x-axis and the y-axis. Each such sector is called a **quadrant.**

The **first quadrant** extends from 0° to 90°.

The **second quadrant** extends from 90° to 180°.

The **third quadrant** extends from 180° to 270°.

The **fourth quadrant** extends from 270° to 360°.

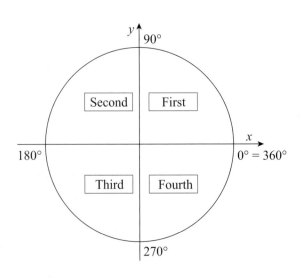

The angles in each quadrant have special names:

1. An angle $0° < A < 90°$ in the first quadrant is called an **acute** angle.

2. An angle $90° < A < 180°$ in the second quadrant is called an **obtuse** angle.

3. An angle $180° < A < 360°$ in the third or fourth quadrant is called a **reflex** angle.

EXAMPLE 1

For the angle A in the third quadrant, find:

(a) the radius of the circle, **(b)** $\cos A$, **(c)** $\sin A$, **(d)** $\tan A$, **(e)** $\dfrac{\cos A}{3}$, **(f)** $\dfrac{1}{2 \sin A}$.

Solution

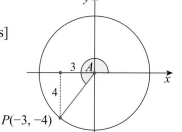

(a) $r = \sqrt{3^2 + 4^2} = 5$ [Pythagoras]

(b) $\cos A = \dfrac{x}{r} = \dfrac{-3}{5} = -\dfrac{3}{5}$

(c) $\sin A = \dfrac{y}{r} = \dfrac{-4}{5} = -\dfrac{4}{5}$

$P(-3, -4)$

(d) $\tan A = \dfrac{y}{x} = \dfrac{-4}{-3} = \dfrac{4}{3}$

(e) $\dfrac{\cos A}{3} = \dfrac{1}{3} \cos A = \dfrac{1}{3} \times -\dfrac{3}{5} = -\dfrac{1}{5}$

(f) $\dfrac{1}{2 \sin A} = \dfrac{1}{2 \times -\dfrac{4}{5}} = \dfrac{1}{-\dfrac{8}{5}} = -\dfrac{5}{8}$

ACTIVITY 2

ACTION
Trigonometric ratios and the size of the circle

OBJECTIVE
To understand that the trigonometric ratios for given angles are independent of the radius of the circle. Hence, a unit circle is usually chosen to obtain the values of cosines, sine and tangent

TIP
↑ The values of $\cos A$, $\sin A$ and $\tan A$ do not depend on the radius of the circle.

This means the unit circle ($r = 1$) can be used to find $\cos A$, $\sin A$ and $\tan A$ for any angle between $0°$ and $360°$.

$r = 1$: $\cos A = \dfrac{x}{r} = \dfrac{x}{1} = x$ and $\sin A = \dfrac{y}{r} = \dfrac{y}{1} = y$.

TIP
↑ $\cos A$ is equal to the x co-ordinate and $\sin A$ is equal to the y co-ordinate for the unit circle.

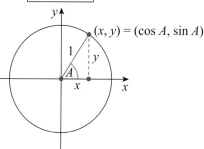

$(x, y) = (\cos A, \sin A)$

ACTIVITY 3

ACTION
Working with unit circles

OBJECTIVE
To understand that in a unit circle $\cos A$ represents the x co-ordinate and $\sin A$ represents the y co-ordinate

WORKED EXAMPLE — Finding trigonometric ratios by measurement

Find $\cos 50°$, $\sin 50°$ and $\tan 50°$.

Try this on square paper by drawing a unit circle where 1 unit = 10 cm.

Draw a circle with centre O with a radius of 1 unit. Measure out the angle $50°$ anticlockwise from the $+x$-axis. Measure $|OQ|$ and $|QP|$.

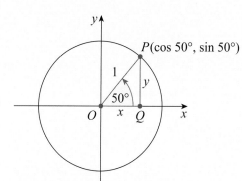

$P(\cos 50°, \sin 50°)$

$\cos 50° = +x = +|OQ| = 0{\cdot}64$

$\sin 50° = +y = +|QP| = 0{\cdot}77$

$\tan 50° = \dfrac{\sin 50°}{\cos 50°} = 1{\cdot}2$

You can use your calculator to find more accurate values for $\cos A$, $\sin A$, $\tan A$ for $0° \leq A \leq 360°$.

EXAMPLE 2

For the angle A in the second quadrant in the unit circle, find x where $x = |OQ|$ and hence find $\cos A$, $\sin A$ and $\tan A$.

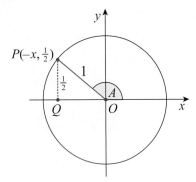

Solution

$$x^2 + \frac{1}{4} = 1^2$$

$$x^2 = \frac{3}{4} \Rightarrow x = \pm\frac{\sqrt{3}}{2}$$

$$\therefore P\left(-\frac{\sqrt{3}}{2}, \frac{1}{2}\right) \text{ as } P \text{ is in the second quadrant.}$$

From the trigonometric definitions:

$$\cos A = -\frac{\sqrt{3}}{2} \quad [x \text{ co-ordinate of a unit circle}]$$

$$\sin A = \frac{1}{2} \quad [y \text{ co-ordinate of a unit circle}]$$

$$\tan A = \frac{\sin A}{\cos A} = \frac{\frac{1}{2}}{-\frac{\sqrt{3}}{2}} = -\frac{1}{\sqrt{3}}$$

Be careful how you manipulate the trigonometric functions.

▸ $3 \sin A = 3 \times \sin A$

▸ $\sin^3 A = (\sin A)^3$

▸ $\dfrac{\cos A}{5} = \dfrac{1}{5} \times \cos A$

▸ $-\left(\dfrac{2\cos^2 A}{5}\right) = -\dfrac{2}{5} \times (\cos A)^2$

EXAMPLE 3

For the angle A in the first quadrant, find $\sin A$, $\cos A$, $\tan A$, $\cos^3 A$ and $\dfrac{25 \tan^2 A}{24}$.

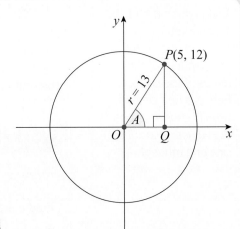

Solution

$$r^2 = 5^2 + 12^2 = 169 \Rightarrow r = \sqrt{169} = 13$$

From the trigonometric definitions:

$$\cos A = \frac{x}{r} = \frac{5}{13}, \ \sin A = \frac{y}{r} = \frac{12}{13}, \ \tan A = \frac{y}{x} = \frac{12}{5}$$

You can simplify this circle approach by extracting the right-angled triangle (RAT) OQP from the circle.

$$\cos A = \frac{x}{r} = \frac{\text{ADJ}}{\text{HYP}} = \frac{5}{13}, \ \sin A = \frac{y}{r} = \frac{\text{OPP}}{\text{HYP}} = \frac{12}{13}, \ \tan A = \frac{y}{x} = \frac{\text{OPP}}{\text{ADJ}} = \frac{12}{5}$$

$$\cos^3 A = (\cos A)^3 = \left(\frac{5}{13}\right)^3 = \frac{125}{2197}$$

$$\frac{25 \tan^2 A}{24} = \frac{25}{24} \times (\tan A)^2 = \frac{25}{24} \times \left(\frac{12}{5}\right)^2 = \frac{25}{24} \times \frac{144}{25} = 6$$

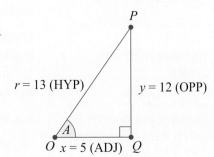

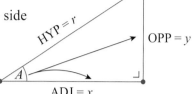

For an acute angle A:

$$\cos A = \frac{x}{r} = \frac{\text{ADJ}}{\text{HYP}}, \quad \sin A = \frac{y}{r} = \frac{\text{OPP}}{\text{HYP}}, \quad \tan A = \frac{y}{x} = \frac{\text{OPP}}{\text{ADJ}}$$

where **ADJ** = the length of the side **adj**acent to the angle,

OPP = the length of the side **opp**osite the angle,

HYP = the **hyp**otenuse, the length of the side opposite the right angle in a RAT.

EXAMPLE 4

An acute angle A is shown in a right-angled triangle. Find **(a)** r, **(b)** $\cos A$, **(c)** $\sin A$, **(d)** $\tan A$, **(e)** A, correct to two decimal places.

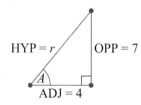

Solution

(a) $r^2 = 4^2 + 7^2 = 16 + 49 = 65 \Rightarrow r = \sqrt{65}$

(b) $\cos A = \dfrac{\text{ADJ}}{\text{HYP}} = \dfrac{4}{\sqrt{65}}$

(c) $\sin A = \dfrac{\text{OPP}}{\text{HYP}} = \dfrac{7}{\sqrt{65}}$

(d) $\tan A = \dfrac{\text{OPP}}{\text{ADJ}} = \dfrac{7}{4}$

(e) The acute angle A can be found using the inverse trigonometric buttons on your calculator.

$$\tan A = \frac{7}{4} \Rightarrow A = \tan^{-1}\left(\frac{7}{4}\right) = 60\cdot25°$$

Try finding A using $\cos^{-1}$ and $\sin^{-1}$.

3. Related angles ⚡

The three trigonometric ratios of angles in the second, third and fourth quadrants can be related to the trigonometric ratios of an angle in the first quadrant known as its **reference angle**.

ASTC

ACTIVITY 4

ACTION
Working with ASTC

OBJECTIVE
To decide in which quadrants a trigonometric ratio exists

Consider four angles θ, E, F and G, one in each quadrant as shown, and their corresponding co-ordinates in the unit circle.

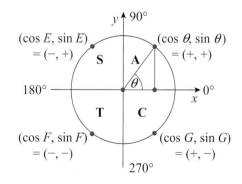

Remember that cos (Angle) is the x co-ordinate, sin (Angle) is the y co-ordinate and tan (Angle) $= \dfrac{y}{x}$.

First: $\theta = 0° \rightarrow 90°$	Second: $E = 90° \rightarrow 180°$	Third: $F = 180° \rightarrow 270°$	Fourth: $G = 270° \rightarrow 360°$
$\cos \theta = +$	$\cos E = -$	$\cos F = -$	$\cos G = +$
$\sin \theta = +$	$\sin E = +$	$\sin F = -$	$\sin G = -$
$\tan \theta = +$	$\tan E = -$	$\tan F = +$	$\tan G = -$
All three trigonometric ratios are +	Only sin is +	Only tan is +	Only cos is +

This leads to the conclusion:

A = **All** three trigonometric ratios are **positive** in the first quadrant.

S = Only **Sine** is **positive** in the second quadrant.

T = Only **Tangent** is **positive** in the third quadrant.

C = Only **Cosine** is **positive** in the fourth quadrant.

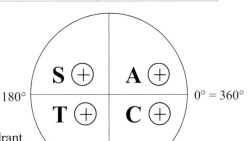

ACTIVITY 5

ACTION
Exploring reference angles

OBJECTIVE
To understand the connection between angles in different quadrants and an angle in the first quadrant

WORKED EXAMPLE
Related angles

For $\tan D = \dfrac{y}{x} = -\dfrac{1}{2}$: The minus sign (ASTC) locates the quadrant in which the angle lies. The minus sign tells you that the angle D is in the second quadrant $P(x = -2, y = 1)$ or in the fourth quadrant $Q(x = 2, y = -1)$ because tan is negative in these quadrants.

The reference angle θ in the first quadrant, which has the same numerical value for $\tan \theta$ as $\tan D$, is shown in the right-angled triangle $\triangle ORS$.

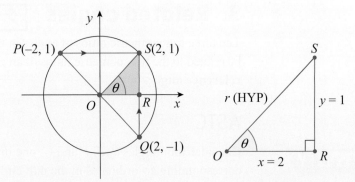

$\tan \theta = \left| \dfrac{y}{x} \right| = \dfrac{1}{2}$ enables you to draw the reference angle θ in the first quadrant in the right-angled triangle ORS. r can be found using the theorem of Pythagoras.

$r^2 = 2^2 + 1^2 = 5 \Rightarrow r = \sqrt{5}$

ACTIVITY 6

ACTION
Using ASTC and right-angled triangles

OBJECTIVE
Using ASTC and a right-angled triangle, you can get all trigonometric functions from one trigonometric function

TIP
You can calculate all trigonometric ratios using the sign found from ASTC and the ratio found from a right-angled triangle (RAT) drawn so that the trigonometric ratio of the reference angle θ is the same as that of the modulus of the trigonometric ratio of the given angle A.

Steps for finding all trigonometric ratios from a given trigonometric ratio

1. Write down the given trigonometric function and quadrant where the angle is located.

2. Draw ASTC and shade in the relevant quadrant.

3. Draw a right-angled triangle with a reference acute angle θ and use the theorem of Pythagoras to work out the missing side.

TIP

Always apply ASTC first to get the sign of the required trigonometric ratio before you read off the value of the ratio from the right-angled triangle.

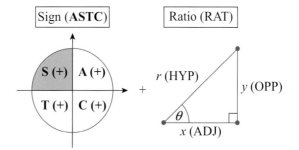

4. Use ASTC to find the signs first and then the right-angled triangle to find the size of the trigonometric functions required.

EXAMPLE 5

If $\cos A = -\frac{1}{3}$, and A is obtuse, find:

(a) $\sin A$,
(b) $\tan A$,
(c) $\dfrac{2}{\cos A}$,
(d) $\cos^2 A + \sin^2 A$.

Solution

1. $\cos A = -\frac{1}{3}$ [A is in the second quadrant.]

2. The negative sign tells you A is in the second or fourth quadrants. Shade in the second quadrant as you are told that A is obtuse.

3. Draw the right-angled triangle with the reference acute angle θ which has the same numerical value for $\cos \theta$ and $\cos A$. Use the theorem of Pythagoras to work out the missing side.

$$\cos \theta = \frac{1}{3} = \frac{x}{r} = \frac{\text{ADJ}}{\text{HYP}}$$

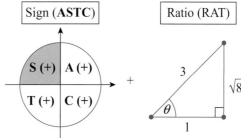

4. Find the trigonometric functions required.

(a) $\sin A = \sin \text{(angle in 2nd quadrant)} = \oplus \dfrac{\sqrt{8}}{3} = \dfrac{2\sqrt{2}}{3}$ [**ASTC** first, ratio second]

(b) $\tan A = \tan \text{(angle in 2nd quadrant)} = \ominus \sqrt{8} = -2\sqrt{2}$

(c) $\dfrac{2}{\cos A} = \dfrac{2}{-\frac{1}{3}} = -6$

(d) $\cos^2 A + \sin^2 A = (\cos A)^2 + (\sin A)^2 = \left(\dfrac{-1}{3}\right)^2 + \left(\dfrac{2\sqrt{2}}{3}\right)^2 = \dfrac{1}{9} + \dfrac{8}{9} = 1$

4. Special angles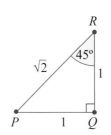

The three trigonometric ratios of the angles $0°$, $30°$, $45°$, $60°$, $90°$, $180°$, $270°$ and $360°$ appear regularly in problems.

45°

A $45°$ angle in a right-angled triangle means the second angle is also $45°$. Therefore, the right-angled triangle is an isosceles triangle.

In triangle PQR:

$$\cos 45° = \frac{\text{ADJ}}{\text{HYP}} = \frac{1}{\sqrt{2}} = \frac{\sqrt{2}}{2}$$

$$\sin 45° = \frac{\text{OPP}}{\text{HYP}} = \frac{1}{\sqrt{2}} = \frac{\sqrt{2}}{2}$$

$$\tan 45° = \frac{\text{OPP}}{\text{ADJ}} = \frac{1}{1} = 1$$

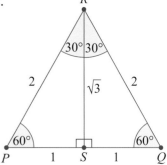

60° and 30°

Using an equilateral triangle, write down in surd form:
$\cos 30°$, $\sin 30°$, $\tan 30°$, $\cos 60°$, $\sin 60°$ and $\tan 60°$.
In the triangle PSR:

$$\cos 30° = \frac{\sqrt{3}}{2}, \quad \sin 30° = \frac{1}{2}, \quad \tan 30° = \frac{1}{\sqrt{3}} = \frac{\sqrt{3}}{3}$$

$$\cos 60° = \frac{1}{2}, \quad \sin 60° = \frac{\sqrt{3}}{2}, \quad \tan 60° = \frac{\sqrt{3}}{1} = \sqrt{3}$$

Borderline angles

The cosine, sine and tangent of angles on the **borderlines** of the quadrants can be calculated easily from the unit circle.

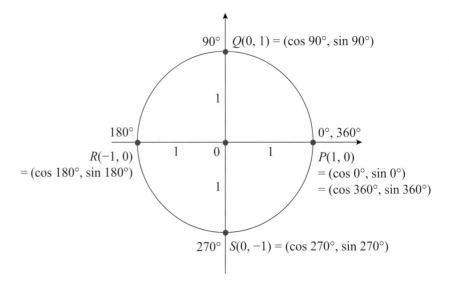

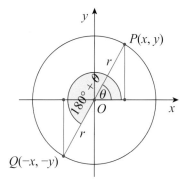

Putting all of these results in a single table, we get:

A	0°	30°	45°	60°	90°	180°	270°
cos A	1	$\dfrac{\sqrt{3}}{2}$	$\dfrac{1}{\sqrt{2}}$	$\dfrac{1}{2}$	0	−1	0
sin A	0	$\dfrac{1}{2}$	$\dfrac{1}{\sqrt{2}}$	$\dfrac{\sqrt{3}}{2}$	1	0	−1
tan A	0	$\dfrac{1}{\sqrt{3}}$	1	$\sqrt{3}$	∞	0	∞

This table is on page 13 of the *Formulae and Tables* book.

> **NOTE**
> The cos, sin and tan of 360° are the same as the cos, sin and tan of 0° respectively as 0° and 360° have identical co-ordinates on the unit circle.

5. Well-behaved and badly behaved angles

Well-behaved angles

Consider the acute reference angle θ and its related angle $(180° + \theta)$ in the third quadrant. If the co-ordinates of a point P in the first quadrant are (x, y), then the co-ordinates of the point rotated through 180° into the third quadrant will be $Q(-x, -y)$.

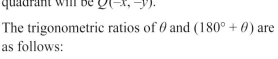

The trigonometric ratios of θ and $(180° + \theta)$ are as follows:

Reference angle θ	Angle $(180° + \theta)$
$\cos \theta = \dfrac{x}{r}$	$\cos (180° + \theta) = -\dfrac{x}{r} = -\cos \theta$
$\sin \theta = \dfrac{y}{r}$	$\sin (180° + \theta) = -\dfrac{y}{r} = -\sin \theta$
$\tan \theta = \dfrac{y}{x}$	$\tan (180° + \theta) = \dfrac{-y}{-x} = \dfrac{y}{x} = \tan \theta$

$(180° + \theta)$ seems 'well behaved' in the sense that its trigonometric ratios have the same numerical value as the trigonometric ratios of the reference angle θ.

Cosine stays as cosine, sine as sine and tangent as tangent.

You can show in the same way that $(180° - \theta)$, $(360° - \theta)$ and $(360° + \theta)$ are also well behaved.

Of course, the signs of the trigonometric ratios of these well-behaved angles $(180° \pm \theta)$ and $(360° \pm \theta)$ can be found using ASTC.

Badly behaved angles

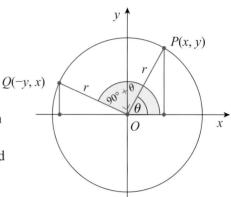

Consider the acute reference angle θ and its related angle $(90° + \theta)$ in the second quadrant. If the co-ordinates of a point P in the first quadrant are (x, y), then the co-ordinates of the point Q obtained when OP is rotated anticlockwise through $90°$ about the origin O are $(-y, x)$ in the second quadrant.

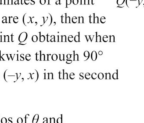

The trigonometric ratios of θ and $(90° + \theta)$ are as follows:

Reference angle θ	Angle $(90° + \theta)$
$\cos \theta = \dfrac{x}{r}$	$\cos (90° + \theta) = -\dfrac{y}{r} = -\sin \theta$
$\sin \theta = \dfrac{y}{r}$	$\sin (90° + \theta) = \dfrac{x}{r} = +\cos \theta$
$\tan \theta = \dfrac{y}{x}$	$\tan (90° + \theta) = -\dfrac{x}{y} = -\dfrac{1}{\tan \theta}$

TIP

When you rotate (x, y) anticlockwise through 90° it becomes $(-y, x)$.

$(90° + \theta)$ seems 'badly behaved' in the sense that its trigonometric ratios have different numerical values to the trigonometric ratios of the reference angle θ.

Cosine changes to sine, sine changes to cosine and tangent changes to one over tangent.

In the same way, you can show that $(90° - \theta)$, $(270° - \theta)$ and $(270° + \theta)$ are also badly behaved.

Of course, the signs of the trigonometric ratios of these badly behaved angles $(90° \pm \theta)$ and $(270° \pm \theta)$ can be found using **ASTC**.

Steps for dealing with the trigonometric ratios of well-behaved and badly behaved angles

1. Use **ASTC** first to determine the sign of the ratio.

2. If the angle is well behaved, i.e. it is of the form $(180° \pm \theta, 360° \pm \theta)$, then the trigonometric ratios are unchanged.

3. If the angle is badly behaved, i.e. it is of the form $(90° \pm \theta, 270° \pm \theta)$, cos changes to sin, sin changes to cos and tan changes to $\dfrac{1}{\tan}$.

Well-behaved angles $(180° \pm \theta, 360° \pm \theta)$	Badly behaved angles $(90° \pm \theta, 270° \pm \theta)$
$\sin \to \sin$	$\sin \to \cos$
$\cos \to \cos$	$\cos \to \sin$
$\tan \to \tan$	$\tan \to \dfrac{1}{\tan}$

▸ Find $\sin(90° + \theta)$, where θ is acute.

$\sin(90° + \theta) = \sin(\text{angle in the second quadrant}) = \oplus$ [Using ASTC]

$(90° + \theta)$ is badly behaved $\Rightarrow \sin \rightarrow \cos$

$\therefore \sin(90° + \theta) = \oplus \cos\theta$

▸ Find $\cos(180° + \theta)$, where θ is acute.

$\cos(180° + \theta) = \cos(\text{angle in the third quadrant}) = \ominus$ [Using ASTC]

$(180° + \theta)$ is well behaved $\Rightarrow \cos \rightarrow \cos$

$\cos(180° + \theta) = \ominus \cos\theta$

▸ Find $\tan(270° - \theta)$, where θ is acute.

$\tan(270° - \theta) = \tan(\text{angle in the third quadrant}) = \oplus$ [Using ASTC]

$(270° - \theta)$ is badly behaved $\Rightarrow \tan \rightarrow \dfrac{1}{\tan}$

$\tan(270° - \theta) = \dfrac{1}{\tan\theta}$ $\left[\cot\theta \text{ is shorthand for } \dfrac{1}{\tan\theta} \right]$

EXAMPLE 6

If $\sin\theta = \dfrac{3}{5}$, and θ is acute, find:

(a) $\cos(90° + \theta)$, **(b)** $\tan(180° + \theta)$, **(c)** $\sin^2(270° - \theta)$, **(d)** $\cos^3(270° + \theta)$.

Solution

Sign (**ASTC**)	Ratio (**RAT**)

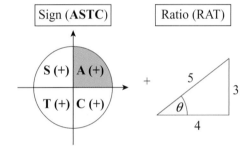

$\sin\theta = \dfrac{3}{5}$, θ acute

(a) $\cos(\underbrace{90° + \theta}_{\text{2nd}}) = -\sin\theta = -\dfrac{3}{5}$ [Badly behaved]

(b) $\tan(\underbrace{180° + \theta}_{\text{3rd}}) = +\tan\theta = \dfrac{3}{4}$ [Well behaved]

(c) $\sin^2(270° - \theta) = [\sin(\underbrace{270° - \theta}_{3^{rd}})]^2 = [-\cos\theta]^2 = \left[-\dfrac{4}{5}\right]^2 = \dfrac{16}{25}$

(d) $\cos^3(270° + \theta) = [\cos(270° + \theta)]^3 = [+\sin\theta]^3 = \left[\dfrac{+3}{5}\right]^3 = \dfrac{27}{125}$

The trigonometric ratios in the second, third and fourth quadrants

Every angle can be related to an angle in the first quadrant using the well-behaved angles: $180° \pm \theta$, $360° \pm \theta$.

TIP

You can always use the 0° – 180° axis (well behaved) to look up trigonometric ratios. By using this line, the trigonometric functions remain unchanged. You need only to worry about the sign which can be found using **ASTC**.

▸ **Second quadrant:** What reference angle θ in the first quadrant relates to 135°?
$135° = 180° - 45°$: $\theta = 45°$

▸ **Third quadrant:** What reference angle θ in the first quadrant relates to 240°?
$240° = 180° + 60°$: $\theta = 60°$

▸ **Fourth quadrant:** What reference angle θ in the first quadrant relates to 300°?
$300° = 360° - 60°$: $\theta = 60°$

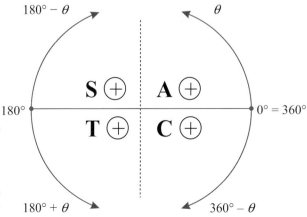

EXAMPLE 7

Find **(a)** sin 240°, **(b)** cos 135°, **(c)** tan 315°, **(d)** sin 120°, **(e)** sin³ 240°.

Solution

(a) $\sin 240° = \sin(180° + 60°) = -\sin 60° = -\dfrac{\sqrt{3}}{2}$

$\underbrace{\qquad\qquad}_{3rd}$

(b) $\cos 135° = \cos(180° - 45°) = -\cos 45° = -\dfrac{1}{\sqrt{2}}$

$\underbrace{\qquad\qquad}_{2nd}$

(c) $\tan 315° = \tan(360° - 45°) = -\tan 45° = -1$

(d) $\sin 120° = \sin(180° - 60°) = +\sin 60° = +\dfrac{\sqrt{3}}{2}$

(e) $\sin^3 240° = [\sin 240°]^3 = \left[-\dfrac{\sqrt{3}}{2}\right]^3 = \dfrac{-3\sqrt{3}}{8}$

You can carry out these calculations on your calculator.

6. Negative angles

Consider the acute reference angle θ and its related negative angle $-\theta$ in the fourth quadrant.
If the co-ordinates of a point P in the first quadrant are (x, y), then the co-ordinates of the point reflected in the x-axis is the point $Q(x, -y)$ in the fourth quadrant.

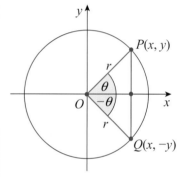

Reference angle θ	Angle $-\theta = (360° - \theta)$
$\cos \theta = \dfrac{x}{r}$	$\cos(-\theta) = \dfrac{x}{r} = \cos \theta$
$\sin \theta = \dfrac{y}{r}$	$\sin(-\theta) = -\dfrac{y}{r} = -\sin \theta$
$\tan \theta = \dfrac{y}{x}$	$\tan(-\theta) = -\dfrac{y}{x} = -\tan \theta$

EXAMPLE 8

If A is an obtuse angle, show that $\cos(-A) = \cos A$.

Solution

A obtuse $\Rightarrow A = 180° - \theta$, where θ is acute.

$\cos(-A) = \cos(360° - A) = \cos(360° - 180° + \theta) = \cos(180° + \theta) = -\cos \theta$

Now $\cos A = \cos(180° - \theta) = -\cos \theta$

$\therefore \cos(-A) = \cos A$

TIP

↑ The result in Example 8 can be generalised for any angle A.

For all negative angles A	
$\cos(-A) = \cos A$	Trick: ⊖ rubs out
$\sin(-A) = -\sin A$	Trick: ⊖ filters out to front
$\tan(-A) = -\tan A$	Trick: ⊖ filters out to front

▸ $\sin(-60°) = -\sin 60° = -\dfrac{\sqrt{3}}{2}$

▸ $\sin(-120°) = -\sin 120° = -\sin 60° = \dfrac{\sqrt{3}}{2}$

▸ $\cos(-240°) = \cos 240° = -\cos 60° = -\dfrac{1}{2}$

▸ $\tan^3(-120°) = [\tan(-120°)]^3 = [-\tan 120°]^3 = [+\tan 60°]^3 = (+\sqrt{3})^3 = 3\sqrt{3}$

You can carry out these calculations on your calculator.

EXAMPLE 9

If $\cos\theta = \dfrac{4}{5}$, and θ is acute, find:

(a) $\cos(180° - \theta)$,   **(b)** $\sin(-\theta)$,   **(c)** $\tan(\theta - 90°)$.

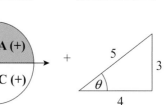

Solution

$\cos\theta = \dfrac{4}{5}$, θ acute

(a) $\cos(180° - \theta) = -\cos\theta = -\dfrac{3}{5}$ [Well behaved]

(b) $\sin(-\theta) = -\sin\theta = -\dfrac{3}{5}$ [Filter out sign]

(c) $\tan(\theta - 90°) = \tan[-(90° - \theta)] = -\tan(90° - \theta) = -\dfrac{1}{\tan\theta} = -\dfrac{1}{\frac{3}{4}} = -\dfrac{4}{3}$

7. The trigonometric ratios of angles greater than 360°

There are 360° in a complete circle. When you add 360° to an angle, you go all the way around and back to the same point on the circle with the same co-ordinates as the original angle.

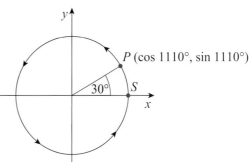

> **TIP**
>
> The trigonometric ratios of an angle A, $360° + A$, $720° + A$, $1080° + A$,... are exactly the same.

▸ Find $\sin 1110°$.

$\dfrac{1110°}{360°} = 3$ remainder $30°$

Starting at S, $1110°$ brings you 3 times (3 by 360°) around the circle back to S and then moves you on to P.

$\therefore \sin 1110° = \sin 30° = \dfrac{1}{2}$

▸ Find $\cos 585°$.

> **TIP**
>
> To find the trigonometric ratios of an angle A greater than 360°, divide A by 360° first and then find the trigonometric ratio of the remainder.

$\dfrac{585°}{360°} = 1$ remainder $225°$

$\cos 585° = \cos 225° = -\cos 45° = -\dfrac{\sqrt{2}}{2}$

8. The fundamental trigonometric identity

An identity is a mathematical result which is true for **all values** of the variable (angle).

The fundamental trigonometric identity states that:

$$\cos^2 A + \sin^2 A = 1 \text{ for every angle } A$$

PROOF

By the distance formula:

$$|OP| = \sqrt{(r\cos A - 0)^2 + (r\sin A - 0)^2} = r$$
$$(r\cos A)^2 + (r\sin A)^2 = r^2$$
$$r^2\cos^2 A + r^2\sin^2 A = r^2$$
$$r^2(\cos^2 A + \sin^2 A) = r^2$$
$$\cos^2 A + \sin^2 A = 1$$

[Diagram: circle centred at $O\,(0,0)$ with radius r, point $P(r\cos A, r\sin A)$, angle A.]

ACTIVITY 8

ACTION
The fundamental trigonometric identity
($\cos^2 A + \sin^2 A = 1$)

OBJECTIVE
To use your calculator to convince yourself of the truth of the fundamental trigonometric identity

Some points to note:

1. This result is true **for any value of** A.

2. This very important trigonometric result is given on page 13 of the *Formulae and Tables*.

3. It will be used many times in this book. It is basically the trigonometric version of the theorem of Pythagoras.

4. It is **true only for the sum of the squares** of cos A and sin A.

    ▸ $\cos^2 5A + \sin^2 5A = 1$
    ▸ $\cos^2(2A - 3B) + \sin^2(2A - 3B) = 1$
    ▸ $\cos^2(180° + 5\theta) + \sin^2(180° + 5\theta) = 1$
    ▸ $\cos^2 73.62° + \sin^2 73.62° = 1$

EXERCISE 1

1. Find the following for the diagram shown:

    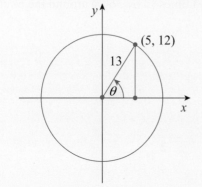

    (a) $\cos\theta$

    (b) $\sin\theta$

    (c) $\tan\theta$

    (d) $3\cos\theta$

    (e) $\dfrac{\sin\theta}{6}$

    (f) $\tan^3\theta$

    (g) $3\sin^2\theta$

    (h) $\dfrac{1}{\cos\theta}$

    (i) $\dfrac{2}{\sin\theta}$

    (j) $-\dfrac{1}{3\tan\theta}$

2. Find the following for the diagram shown:

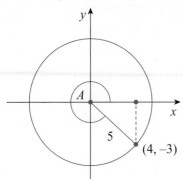

(4, −3)

5

(a) $\sin A$

(b) $\cos A$

(c) $\tan A$

(d) $\sin^2 A$

(e) $-2\cos A$

(f) $\tan^3 A$

(g) $\dfrac{3\sin A}{2}$

(h) $\dfrac{4\sin^3 A}{5}$

(i) $\dfrac{3\cos A - 4\sin A}{-4\sin A + 3\cos A}$

(j) $\cos^2 A + \sin^2 A$

3. Find the point P for the diagram shown. Hence, find the following:

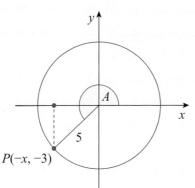

$P(-x, -3)$

5

(a) $\cos A$

(b) $\sin A$

(c) $\tan A$

(d) $4\cos A$

(e) $\dfrac{\sin A}{2}$

(f) $\tan^2 A$

(g) $-\dfrac{3}{4}\sin A$

(h) $\dfrac{\sin A}{\cos A}$

(i) $\dfrac{1}{\cos A}$

(j) $\dfrac{3\sin A - 4\cos A}{4\sin A + 3\cos A}$

4. Find $\cos\theta$, $\sin\theta$, $\tan\theta$ for each right-angled triangle below:

(a)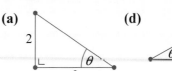

(d)

(b)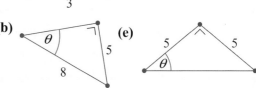

(e)

(c)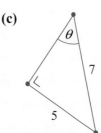

5. Find A in each case, correct to one decimal place.

(a)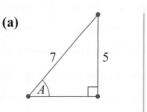

(d)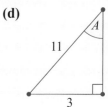

(b)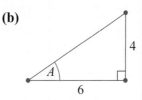

(e)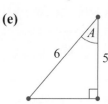

(c)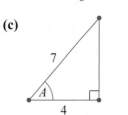

6. (a) If $\cos A = \frac{3}{5}$, and A is acute, find $\sin A$, $\tan A$, $\dfrac{1}{\sin A}$, $\dfrac{1}{\cos A}$ and $\dfrac{1}{\tan A}$.

(b) If $\sin A = \frac{3}{5}$, and A is obtuse, find $\cos A$, $\tan A$, $3\cos A$ and $\tan^3 A$.

(c) If $\dfrac{1}{\cos A} = -2$, and A is obtuse, find $\sin A$, $\tan A$ and $\cos^2 A + \sin^2 A$.

(d) If $\tan A = -3$, and A is in the fourth quadrant, find $\sin A$, $\cos A$ and $\dfrac{1 - \sin^2 A}{1 + \sin^2 A}$.

(e) If $\sin A = \dfrac{5}{13}$, and A is acute, find $\cos A$, $\tan A$, $\dfrac{\sin A}{\cos A}$ and $\sqrt{1 - \cos^2 A}$.

(f) If $\tan A = \dfrac{1}{4}$, and A is in the third quadrant, find $\sin A$, $\cos A$, $\dfrac{1}{\tan A}$ and $\dfrac{\cos A}{\sin A}$.

(g) If $4 \tan A = 9$, and A is acute, find
$$\frac{3 \sin A + 2 \cos A}{2 \sin A - 3 \cos A}.$$

(h) If $\cos A = -\dfrac{5}{13}$, and A is obtuse, find $\sin A$, $\tan A$ and $\dfrac{2}{\tan^3 A}$.

(i) If $3 \tan A = -7$, and A is obtuse, find $\cos A$, $\sin A$ and $\dfrac{3 \sin A + \cos A}{2 \sin A - \cos A}$.

(j) If $13 \cos A + 12 = 0$, and A is obtuse, evaluate $\dfrac{1 - \tan A}{1 + \tan A}$.

7. Use the table of famous angles and the unit circle to answer the following questions:

A	30°	45°	60°
$\cos A$	$\dfrac{\sqrt{3}}{2}$	$\dfrac{1}{\sqrt{2}}$	$\dfrac{1}{2}$
$\sin A$	$\dfrac{1}{2}$	$\dfrac{1}{\sqrt{2}}$	$\dfrac{\sqrt{3}}{2}$
$\tan A$	$\dfrac{1}{\sqrt{3}}$	1	$\sqrt{3}$

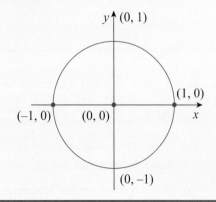

Without using your calculator, find:

(a) $\cos 30°$ **(f)** $\cos 90°$

(b) $\sin 45°$ **(g)** $\sin 180°$

(c) $\tan^2 60°$ **(h)** $\tan 270°$

(d) $4 \cos 60°$ **(i)** $\tan^3 30°$

(e) $\cos^2 60° + \sin^2 60°$ **(j)** $\cos^4 45°$

8. (a) What is the maximum value of **(i)** $\cos A$, **(ii)** $\sin A$, **(iii)** $\tan A$?

(b) What is the minimum value of **(i)** $\cos A$, **(ii)** $\sin A$, **(iii)** $\tan A$?

9. (a) If $\cos A = 0$, what values between 0° and 360° can A have?

(b) If $\sin A = 0$, what values between 0° and 360° can A have?

10. If θ is acute, simplify the following:

(a) $\cos(90° - \theta)$ **(f)** $\tan(270° - \theta)$

(b) $\sin(90° + \theta)$ **(g)** $\cos(180° + \theta)$

(c) $\sin(180° + \theta)$ **(h)** $\tan(90° + \theta)$

(d) $\cos(270° + \theta)$ **(i)** $\sin(360° + \theta)$

(e) $\tan(360° - \theta)$ **(j)** $\cos(180° - \theta)$

11. (a) Evaluate the following without using your calculator:

(i) $\cos 240°$ **(vi)** $\sin^3 300°$

(ii) $\tan 315°$ **(vii)** $\sin 330°$

(iii) $\cos 300°$ **(viii)** $\cos^3 150°$

(iv) $\tan^2 120°$ **(ix)** $\tan^2 210°$

(v) $\tan 225°$ **(x)** $\sin^2 240°$

(b) (i) $\sin(-30°)$ **(vi)** $\tan(-120°)$

(ii) $\tan(-60°)$ **(vii)** $\sin 420°$

(iii) $\cos(-45°)$ **(viii)** $\cos^3(-210°)$

(iv) $\cos(-150°)$ **(ix)** $\tan(-600°)$

(v) $\sin(-330°)$ **(x)** $\sin^3 990°$

Use your calculator to check your answers.

12. If $\tan \theta = \frac{3}{4}$, and θ is acute, evaluate the following:

(a) $\sin \theta$	**(d)** $\cos(180° - \theta)$	**(g)** $\cos^3(180° + \theta)$	**(j)** $\cos(-\theta)$
(b) $\cos \theta$	**(e)** $\tan(360° - \theta)$	**(h)** $\tan(\theta - 180°)$	**(k)** $\tan^3(90° + \theta)$
(c) $\sin(180° + \theta)$	**(f)** $\tan(270° + \theta)$	**(i)** $\sin(-180° - \theta)$	**(l)** $\sin(\theta - 270°)$

7.2 Angles (degrees and radians)

Measurement of angles

Angles are measured using the arc length of a sector of a circle.

KEY TERM

> An angle **subtended** by an arc at the centre of a circle is the angle between the two lines joining the centre of the circle to the end points of the arc.

The measurement of the size of an angle is always based on the same principle: the bigger the arc, the bigger the angle it subtends at the centre of a circle.

The size of an angle is directly proportional to ($\propto$) the length of arc it subtends at the centre of the circle: $\theta \propto l$

> As l increases, θ increases in proportion.

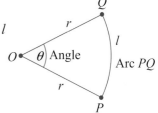

Angles can be measured in degrees or radians.

Degrees

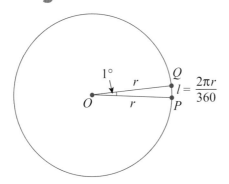

KEY TERM

> $1° =$ The angle subtended at the centre of a circle by an arc length of $\frac{1}{360}$ of the circumference of the circle.

▸ $46{\cdot}7° =$ Angle subtended at the centre of a circle by an arc length $= \dfrac{46{\cdot}7}{360}$ of the circumference of the circle.

Subdivision of degrees

Degrees can be divided into **minutes** and **seconds**.

$1 \text{ minute} = 1' = \dfrac{1}{60} \text{ of a degree} = \left(\dfrac{1}{60}\right)^{\circ}$

$1 \text{ second} = 1'' = \dfrac{1}{60} \text{ of a minute} = \dfrac{1}{3600} \text{ of a degree} = \left(\dfrac{1}{3600}\right)^{\circ}$

$$60' \text{ minutes} = 1° \text{ or } 60' = 1°$$
$$60 \text{ seconds} = 1' \text{ or } 60'' = 1'$$

▶ $27{\cdot}5° = 27° \ 30'$ [Since $0{\cdot}5 = \frac{1}{2}$ of 60 minutes]

▶ $46{\cdot}325° = 46° + 0{\cdot}325 \times 60' = 46° + 19{\cdot}5' = 46° + 19' + 30'' = 46° \ 19' \ 30''$

▶ $57° \ 36' = 57° + \left(\frac{36}{60}\right)° = 57° + 0{\cdot}6° = 57{\cdot}6°$

You can use your calculator to do these conversions.

Radians

KEY TERM

1 **radian** (rad) is the angle subtended at the centre of a circle by an arc of length 1 radius.

If the angle at the centre is 1 rad, the length of the arc is equal to the radius ($1r$).

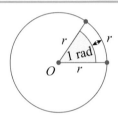

▶ If the angle at the centre is 1 rad, the length of the arc is 6 cm (the same as the radius).

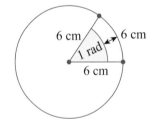

▶ If the angle is 2 rad, the length of the arc is $2r$. The arc shown is 12 cm when the angle at the centre is 2 rad.

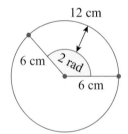

In general, if the angle is θ rad, the length l of the arc is θr.

$l = r\theta$

l = arc length

r = radius

θ = angle in radians

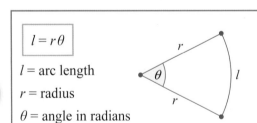

Angle (θ)	Arc length (l)
1 rad	$1r$
2 rad	$2r$
θ rad	θr

Converting between degrees and radians

For a full circle, the length of the arc is the circumference of the circle. Therefore, the length of the arc l in this case is given by:

$l = 2\pi r$ [This is the formula for the length of the circumference of a circle.]

$l = 2\pi r = r\theta \Rightarrow \theta = 2\pi$ rad

Therefore, 2π rad is the angle in radians to go around a full circle.

Measured in degrees, the angle in a full circle is 360°.
Therefore, 2π rad = 360°.

$$\pi \text{ rad} = 180°$$

$$1 \text{ rad} = \frac{180°}{\pi} = 57\cdot3° \text{ (nearly 60°)}$$

$$1° = \frac{\pi}{180} \text{ rad}$$

360° r
2π rad

TIP

Converting radians to degrees: multiply the radians by $\dfrac{180°}{\pi}$.

Converting degrees to radians: multiply the degrees by $\dfrac{\pi}{180}$.

▸ $60° = \dfrac{\pi}{180} \times 60 = \dfrac{\pi}{3}$ rad

▸ $-120° = -\dfrac{\pi}{180} \times 120 \text{ rad} = -\dfrac{2\pi}{3}$ rad

▸ $315° = \dfrac{\pi}{180} \times 315 \text{ rad} = \dfrac{63\pi}{36} \text{ rad} = \dfrac{7\pi}{4}$ rad

▸ $-\dfrac{5\pi}{6} \text{ rads} = -\dfrac{5\pi}{6} \times \dfrac{180°}{\pi} = -150°$

▸ $\dfrac{11\pi}{12} \text{ rad} = \dfrac{11\pi}{12} \times \dfrac{180°}{\pi} = 165°$

▸ $2 \text{ rad} = 2 \times \dfrac{180°}{\pi} = \dfrac{360°}{\pi}$

EXAMPLE 10

Find the length of the arc PQ.

Solution

$l = r\theta \Rightarrow l = 10 \times \dfrac{1}{2} = 5$ cm

Q
10 cm
O $\dfrac{1}{2}$ rad l
10 cm
P

WARNING

The angle θ must be in **radians** to use the arc length formula: $l = r\theta$

EXAMPLE 11

Find the length of the minor arc PQ of a circle with radius 15 cm and centre O.

Solution

A minor arc PQ of a circle with centre O is an arc such that $\left|\angle POQ\right| < 180°$.

Draw lines from P and Q to the centre O.

These lines are the radii. There are 2 angles standing on the minor arc PQ, one on the circle (60°) and the other at the centre of the circle. The angle at the centre is twice the angle on the circle.

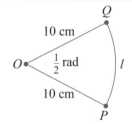

$\theta = 120° = \dfrac{2\pi}{3}$ rad

$l = r\theta = 15 \times \dfrac{2\pi}{3} = 10\pi$ cm

or

$l = \left(\dfrac{120}{360}\right) \times 2\pi r = \dfrac{1}{3} \times 2\pi \times 15 = 10\pi$ cm

Area of a sector of a circle (pie piece)

The area A of a circle is given by the formula: $A = \pi r^2$.

A full circle corresponds to an angle of 2π rad.

This means that an area of $\dfrac{\pi r^2}{2\pi} = \dfrac{1}{2}r^2$

corresponds to an angle of 1 rad.

Area (A)	Angle (θ)
πr^2	2π rad
$\frac{1}{2}r^2$	1 rad
$\frac{1}{2}r^2\theta$	θ rad

The area A of the sector of a circle with radius r subtending an angle θ (rads) at its centre is given by:

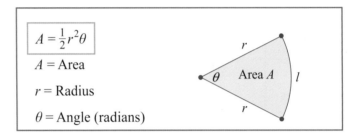

$A = \dfrac{1}{2}r^2\theta$

$A = $ Area

$r = $ Radius

$\theta = $ Angle (radians)

> **WARNING**
> ⚠ The angle θ must be in **radians** to use the formula $A = \frac{1}{2}r^2\theta$ for the area of a sector of a circle.

EXAMPLE 12

Find the area of the sector OPQ of a circle with centre O and radius 10 cm.

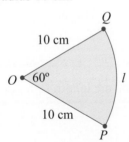

Solution

$\theta = 60° = \dfrac{\pi}{3}$ rad

$A = \dfrac{1}{2}r^2\theta = \dfrac{1}{2} \times 100 \times \dfrac{\pi}{3} = \dfrac{50\pi}{3}$ cm^2

EXAMPLE 13

Find the area of the shaded region $PQRS$ if PS and QR are arcs of a circle with centre O. $|OP| = |PQ| = |OS| = |SR| = 1$ m and $|\angle ROQ| = 1.5$ rad.

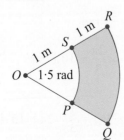

Solution

$A_1 = $ Area $OQR = \frac{1}{2}(2^2) \times 1.5 = 3$ m^2

$A_2 = $ Area $OPS = \frac{1}{2}(1^2) \times 1.5 = 0.75$ m^2

Area $PQRS = A = A_1 - A_2 = 2.25$ m^2

Special angles in radians

Here is the table of the special angles again, this time with the radian measure included. It is on page 13 of the *Formulae and Tables* book.

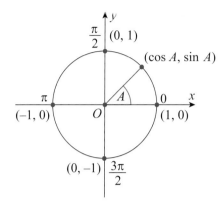

A (degrees)	0°	30°	45°	60°	90°	180°	270°
A (radians)	0	$\dfrac{\pi}{6}$	$\dfrac{\pi}{4}$	$\dfrac{\pi}{3}$	$\dfrac{\pi}{2}$	π	$\dfrac{3\pi}{2}$
cos A	1	$\dfrac{\sqrt{3}}{2}$	$\dfrac{1}{\sqrt{2}}$	$\dfrac{1}{2}$	0	−1	0
sin A	0	$\dfrac{1}{2}$	$\dfrac{1}{\sqrt{2}}$	$\dfrac{\sqrt{3}}{2}$	1	0	−1
tan A	0	$\dfrac{1}{\sqrt{3}}$	1	$\sqrt{3}$	∞	0	∞

ACTIVITY 11

ACTION
Find the trigonometric ratios of angles given in radians

OBJECTIVE
To use your calculator and the Formulae and Tables book to find the trigonometric values of angles in radians

▸ $\cos\left(\dfrac{\pi}{3}\right) = \dfrac{1}{2}$

▸ $\cos\left(\dfrac{\pi}{2}\right) = 0$

You can calculate the trigonometric ratios of angles in radians using the radian mode on your calculator.

▸ $A = 2$ rad $\Rightarrow \sin 2 = 0\cdot91$ [Calculator must be in radian mode.]

▸ $A = -\dfrac{\pi}{12}$ rad $\Rightarrow \tan\left(-\dfrac{\pi}{12}\right) = -2 + \sqrt{3}$

Full revolutions

A full revolution of a circle is 360° or 2π rads.

For A in radians, this means the co-ordinates of a point on the unit circle are the same for A, $A + 2\pi$, $A + 4\pi$, and so on.

$\cos A = \cos(A + 2\pi) = \cos(A + 4\pi) = \ldots = \cos(A + 2n\pi), n \in \mathbb{N}_0 = \{0, 1, 2,\ldots\}$

$\sin A = \sin(A + 2\pi) = \sin(A + 4\pi) = \ldots = \sin(A + 2n\pi), n \in \mathbb{N}_0 = \{0, 1, 2,\ldots\}$

This is an important idea in solving trigonometric equations.

TIP
$\cos(A + \text{even number of } \pi) = \cos A$
$\sin(A + \text{even number of } \pi) = \sin A$

EXAMPLE 14

Evaluate $\cos\left(\dfrac{55\pi}{3}\right)$ using the information in the table on page 13 of the *Formulae and Tables*.

Solution

$\dfrac{55\pi}{3} = 18\tfrac{1}{3}\pi = \dfrac{\pi}{3} + 18\pi$

$\cos\left(\dfrac{55\pi}{3}\right) = \cos\left(\dfrac{\pi}{3} + 18\pi\right) = \cos\left(\dfrac{\pi}{3}\right) = \dfrac{1}{2}$

EXAMPLE 15

A pond is in the form of a sector OPQ of a circle with centre O and radius 10 m with $|\angle OPQ| = 120°$.

(a) Find the length of an arc PQ.

(b) Find the length of the perimeter of the sector OPQ.

(c) Find the area of the sector OPQ.

Give all answers in terms of π.

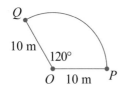

Solution

$$180° = \pi \text{ rad} \implies 120° = \frac{120}{180}\pi = \frac{2}{3}\pi \text{ rad}$$

(a) Length of arc $PQ = l = r\theta = 10 \times \dfrac{2\pi}{3} = \dfrac{20\pi}{3}$ m

(b) Length of perimeter $= \left(\dfrac{20\pi}{3} + 20\right)$ m

(c) Area of the sector $= \dfrac{1}{2}r^2\theta$

$$= \frac{1}{2} \times 100 \times \frac{2\pi}{3}$$

$$= \frac{100\pi}{3} \text{ m}^3$$

EXAMPLE 16

A car B travels along the middle of the outer lane of a motorway from P to Q.

A car C travels along the middle of the inner lane of the motorway from R to S.

B travels 8 m further than C. If the width of each lane is 4 m, find θ in degrees, correct to one decimal place.

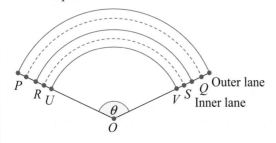

Solution

Let $r = |OU| = |OV|$.

Car B: $l_2 =$ Length of arc $PQ = (r + 6)\theta$

Car C: $l_1 =$ Length of arc $RS = (r + 2)\theta$

$(r + 6)\theta - (r + 2)\theta = 8$

$4\theta = 8 \implies \theta = 2$ rad

π rad $= 180°$

2 rad $= \left(\dfrac{180}{\pi} \times 2\right)^{\circ} = 114\cdot6°$

EXERCISE 2

1. For each of the following, find:

    (a) the length of the arc PQ,

    (b) the length of the perimeter of the sector OPQ,

    (c) the area of each sector OPQ.

Give each answer in terms of π or its exact value.

(i)

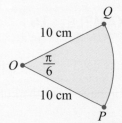

(ii)

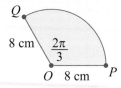

(iii)

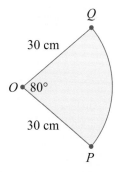

(iv)

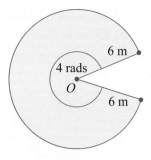

2. The distance between two points P and Q on the Earth is measured along a circle with centre O at the centre of the Earth and radius 6400 km. Find the distance to the nearest kilometre from P to Q if $|\angle POQ| = 60°$.

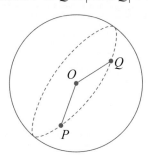

3. Find the angle θ for the sector OPQ of the circles shown given the arc length:

(a)

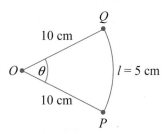

(b)

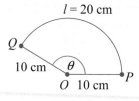

(c)

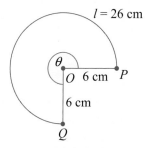

4. Find the area of the shaded region $PQRS$ of the sector of a circle with centre O.

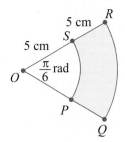

5. Find **(a)** the length of arc PQR and **(b)** the area of the shaded region, in terms of r of the sector of a circle of centre O.

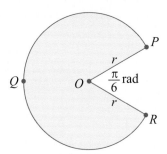

6. Find the length of the major arc and the area of the shaded region of the circle with centre O and radius 1 m.

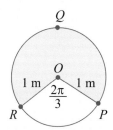

7. Find the length of the minor arc *PQR* of a circle with centre *O* with radius 3 cm and the area of the shaded region.

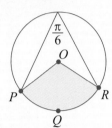

8. Find **(a)** θ, **(b)** length of arc *PS*, **(c)** area of shaded region *PQRS*, if *PS* and *QR* are two arcs of a circle with centre *O*. $\left|OS\right| = \left|OP\right| = 4$ cm and $\left|OR\right| = \left|OQ\right| = 10$ cm.

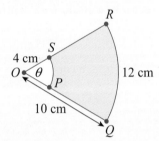

9. Find the area of the following shapes, correct to one decimal place:

   (a) *PQRS* is a square of side 10 cm and *RTS* is a semicircle with diameter [*SR*].

   (b) *PQRS* is a rectangle. *RTS* is a semicircle with diameter [*SR*]. $\left|PQ\right| = 12$ cm and $\left|PS\right| = 6$ cm.

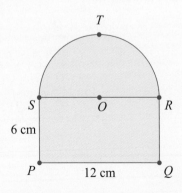

(c) *PQRS* is a rectangle. *RTS* is a semicircle with diameter [*SR*]. *QUR* is a sector of a circle with centre *Q*. $\left|PQ\right| = 10$ cm and $\left|PS\right| = 6$ cm.

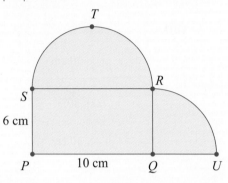

10. Find the area of the shaded region of each of the following, correct to one decimal place:

    (a) s_1 is a circle with radius 3 cm and centre *O*. s_2 is a circle with radius 6 cm and centre *O*.

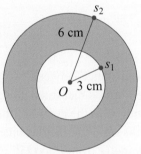

    (b) *PQRT* is a square with a circle *s* with centre *O* of radius 8 cm inscribed in it.

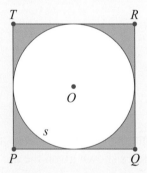

    (c) *s* is a circle with centre *O* and radius 12 cm which circumscribes a square *PQRT*.

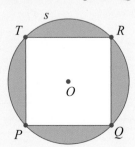

(d) *PQRTUV* is a regular hexagon inscribed in a circle *s* with centre *O* and radius 4 m.

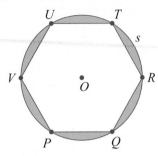

(e) *PQRT* is a square of side 18 cm. Four identical circles touch each other and the sides of the square.

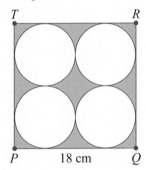

11. Find the area of an equilateral triangle of side 12 cm. s_1, s_2 and s_3 are three identical touching circles, each of radius 6 cm with centres *P*, *Q* and *R* respectively. Find the area of the shaded region, correct to the nearest cm².

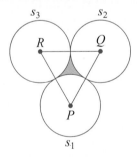

12. (a) *PQRT* is a section of a motorway. *PT* is an arc of a circle with centre *O* and radius 4 m. *QR* is an arc of a circle with centre *O* and radius 8 m. Find the area of the shaded region in terms of π.

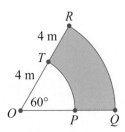

(b) *PUQ* is a semicircular cross-section of a tunnel under a rectangular section *PQRT* of the Earth. If [*PQ*] is the diameter of the semicircle, find the area of the shaded region, correct to two decimal places.

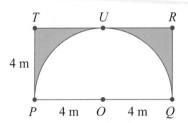

(c) A piece of wood *PQRUT* consists of a rectangle *PQRT* surmounted by a semicircle *RUT* of radius 5 cm and diameter [*TR*]. A circle with centre *O* of diameter 6 cm is removed to insert a clock face. *O* is the midpoint of [*TR*]. Find the area of the wood remaining, correct to the nearest cm², when the circle with centre *O* is removed.

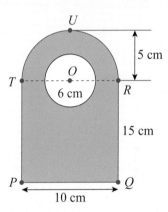

13. A lighthouse *O* emits a beam of radius 30 km and illuminates the area of the shaded sector.

(a) Find the area of the illuminated region, correct to the nearest km².

(b) If a ship travelling along the line *DE* is lit by the lighthouse for 50 km, what is the ship's closest distance to the lighthouse, correct to one decimal place?

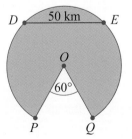

14. A sector of a circle with centre O is used to form the curved surface of a right-circular cone of height 12 cm and base radius 5 cm.

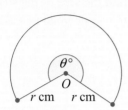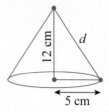

Find:

(a) the slant height d of the cone,

(b) the radius r of the sector of the circle,

(c) the arc length of the sector in terms of π,

(d) the sector angle θ in degrees, correct to two decimal places.

15. (a) A nautical mile is the length on the Earth's surface corresponding to an angle of $1'$ subtended at the centre of the Earth.

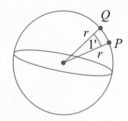

The arc PQ that subtends an angle of $1'$ at the centre of the Earth is shown. If the radius of the Earth is 6380 km, show that 1 nautical mile is approximately $1\cdot856$ km.

(b) A knot is 1 nautical mile per hour. Find the time it takes a plane to fly from New York to Dublin at 500 knots, if the distance from New York to Dublin is 5130 km. Give your answer correct to two decimal places.

16. The sprocket assembly for a bike is shown. If the sprocket of radius r_1 rotates through angle θ, find the angle φ through which the sprocket of radius r_2 rotates, in terms of r_1, r_2 and θ.

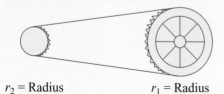

r_2 = Radius $\qquad$ r_1 = Radius

17. A water sprinkler sprays water over a distance of 9 m while rotating through 135° about a point O. Find the area of the lawn that receives water from the sprinkler, giving your answer correct to one decimal place.

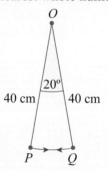

18. A pendulum of length 40 cm swings back and forward through an angle of 20°. Find the length of the arc PQ and the area OPQ traced out by the pendulum, giving your answers correct to the nearest whole number.

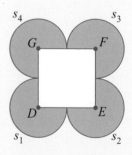

19. A theatre is set out in the shape shown below where $DEFG$ is a square and s_1, s_2, s_3 and s_4 are sectors of circles with centres D, E, F and G respectively. Each circle has a radius equal to half the length of a side of the square. Find the area of the coloured region occupied by the audience if the square has side of length 12 m. Give the answer to the nearest whole number.

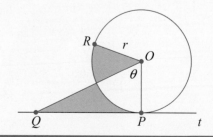

20. t is a tangent at P to a circle with centre O and radius r. If $|PQ|$ is equal to the length of arc PR, show that the area of the two shaded regions is the same.

7.3 Solving right-angled triangles 1

A review of triangle facts

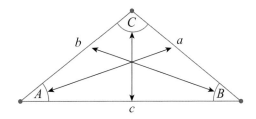

1. Every triangle has six quantities: three sides and their three corresponding opposite angles.

2. All the angles add up to $180°$.

3. The sum of the lengths of any two sides is always greater than the length of the third side.

4. The longest side is always the side opposite the biggest angle.

> **TIP**
>
> If you are given the length of one side of a triangle and two other quantities, you can work out the lengths of all other sides and the measures of all other angles.

Triangles can be divided into two types:

- **Right-angled triangles (RATs):** One angle is $90°$.

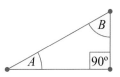

- **Oblique or non right-angled triangles (non-RATs):** No angle is $90°$.

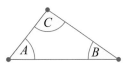

Solving triangles involves finding the length of all sides and the size of all angles, given certain information.

Right-angled triangle facts

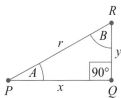

1. $A + B = 90°$

2. Theorem of Pythagoras: if ΔPQR is a right-angled triangle, $r^2 = x^2 + y^2$.

3. The converse of the theorem: if $r^2 = x^2 + y^2$, then ΔPQR is a right-angled triangle.

Trigonometric ratios

In any right-angled triangle:

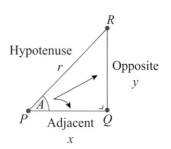

ACTION
Finding trigonometric values using a calculator

OBJECTIVE
To review Junior Cycle work where students use their calculator to find the cos, sin and tan of various angles

1.   Cosine (cos for short): $\cos A = \dfrac{\text{Length of the adjacent side to } A}{\text{Length of the hypotenuse}} = \dfrac{\text{ADJ}}{\text{HYP}} = \dfrac{x}{r}$

2.   Sine (sin for short): $\sin A = \dfrac{\text{Length of opposite side to } A}{\text{Length of hypotenuse}} = \dfrac{\text{OPP}}{\text{HYP}} = \dfrac{y}{r}$

3.   Tangent (tan for short): $\tan A = \dfrac{\text{Length of the opposite side to } A}{\text{Length of the adjacent side to } A} = \dfrac{\text{OPP}}{\text{ADJ}} = \dfrac{y}{x}$

ACTIVITY 16

ACTION
Solving right-angled triangles

OBJECTIVE
To review Junior Cycle work where students use their calculator to solve right-angled triangles

> **TIP**
> Given the length of one side of a right-angled triangle and the size of one angle not equal to 90°, you can find the lengths of all other sides and the measures of all other angles.

Steps for solving right-angled triangles

Use the following steps to solve problems involving right-angled triangles:

1.   Draw a clear picture of the right-angled triangle.

2.   Identify the right angle (90°) and the hypotenuse.

3.   Mark in the measures of all angles you know with letters.

4.   Mark in the lengths of all sides you know.

5.   Write down the trigonometric function (sin, cos or tan) based on what is known and what is to be found.

6.   Solve for the unknown.

> **TIP**
> Remember that you can always use the theorem of Pythagoras.

EXAMPLE 17

In the right-angled triangle *PQR*, find **(a)** *B*, **(b)** *x*, **(c)** *r*, **(d)** the area of the triangle.

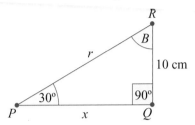

Solution

(a) $B = 90° - 30° = 60°$

(b) For $A = 30°$: OPP = 10 cm, ADJ = x

Only tan connects these three quantities.

$$\therefore \tan 30° = \frac{10}{x} \Rightarrow x = \frac{10}{\tan 30°} = 10\sqrt{3} \text{ cm}$$

(c) $r = \sqrt{x^2 + (10)^2} = \sqrt{300 + 100} = 20 \text{ cm}$

(d) Area $= \frac{1}{2} \times$ Base $\times$ Perpendicular height

$$= \frac{1}{2}(10\sqrt{3})(10)$$

$$= 50\sqrt{3} \text{ cm}^2$$

Right-angled triangles in geometry

You have met many right-angled triangles in geometry.

1. Square

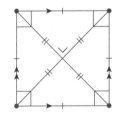

3. Rectangle

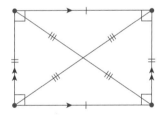

2. Rhombus

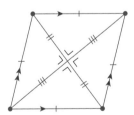

4. Isosceles and equilateral triangles

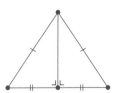

5. Circles

(a) The angle in a semicircle at the circle $= |\angle PRQ| = 90°$.

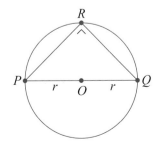

(b) If *PQ* is a tangent at *P* to a circle with centre *O* and radius *r* then:

$$|\angle OPQ| = 90° \text{ and } |OP| = r.$$

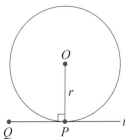

(c) If $[PR]$ is a **chord** of a circle with centre O and radius r and if $|\angle OQP| = 90°$ then: $|OP| = |OR| = r$ and $|PQ| = |QR|$.

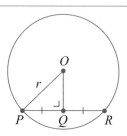

EXAMPLE 18

A rhombus has sides of length 5 cm. One of its diagonals is 8 cm long. Find the length of the other diagonal.

Solution

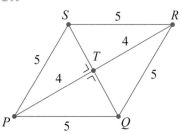

$|PT| = \dfrac{1}{2}|PR| = 4$ cm

$|QT| = \sqrt{25 - 16} = 3$ cm

$|QS| = 2|QT| = 6$ cm

EXAMPLE 19

Taipei 101 in Taiwan is one of the tallest buildings in the world. The indoor observation deck is 438 m above the ground. If the radius of the Earth is 6400 km, how far away is the furthest points on the Earth's surface that a person can see with the aid of a telescope? Give your answer correct to two decimal places.

Solution

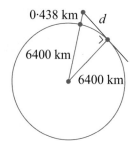

$d^2 + (6400)^2 = (6400 + 0·438)^2$

$d^2 = 5606·6$

$d = 74·88$ km

EXAMPLE 20

A ship travels due south from O to P, a distance of 8 km. At P it turns due east and travels 6 km to Q.

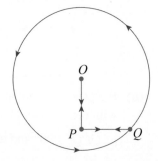

From there, it traces out a circle with centre O until it reaches Q again.

It continues due west back to P and then turns due north back to O. Find the length of the journey to the nearest kilometre.

Solution

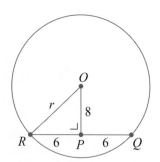

$|RP| = |PQ| = 6$

$|OR| = r = \sqrt{8^2 + 6^2} = 10$

Total distance $= 8 + 6 + 2\pi \times 10 + 6 + 8$

$= 28 + 20\pi$

$\simeq 91$ km

EXAMPLE 21

s is a circle with centre *O* and radius 6 cm. Find the angles *A* and *B*, correct to two decimal places.

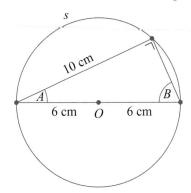

Solution

The angle in a semicircle is 90°.

$$\left.\begin{array}{l} \text{Angle} = A \\ \text{ADJ} = 10 \\ \text{HYP} = 12 \end{array}\right] \Rightarrow \cos A$$

$$\cos A = \frac{10}{12} = \frac{5}{6}$$

$$A = \cos^{-1}\left(\frac{5}{6}\right) = 33{\cdot}56°$$

$$B = 90° - A$$
$$= 90° - 33{\cdot}56°$$
$$= 56{\cdot}44°$$

EXAMPLE 22

An oil tank has a circular cross-section of radius 2·5 metres. It is filled to a depth of 4 m. Calculate the width 2*x*, in metres, of the surface of the oil.

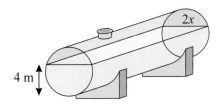

Solution

The tank's cross-sectional area is drawn.

In triangle *OPQ*:

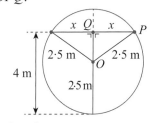

$$(2{\cdot}5)^2 = (1{\cdot}5)^2 + x^2$$
$$x = 2$$
$$2x = 4$$

Width = 4 m

EXERCISE 3

Diagrams are not drawn to scale. Leave answers in surd form when this applies.

1. (a) *PQRS* is a rectangle. Find the length of the diagonal $|QS|$.

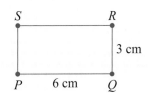

(b) Find the area of $\triangle PQR$.

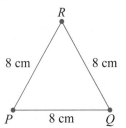

(c) *PQRS* is a square with a circle with centre *O* and radius 6 cm inscribed in it. Find $|QS|$.

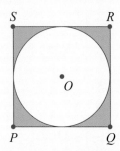

(d) *PQRS* is a square of side 5 cm inscribed in a circle with centre *O* and radius *r*. Find *r*.

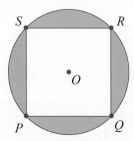

(e) An equilateral triangle has an area of $9\sqrt{3}$ cm². Find the length of each side.

(f) *PQRS* is a quadrilateral in which the diagonals intersect at *T* at right angles. Show that $a^2 + b^2 = c^2 + d^2$ using the theorem of Pythagoras on $\triangle PTS$, $\triangle TQR$, $\triangle STR$ and $\triangle PQT$.

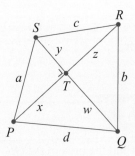

2. **(a)** $[PR]$ is the diameter of a circle with centre *O* and radius *r*. If $|PQ| = |QR| = 8$ cm, find *r*.

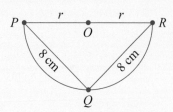

(b) *s* is a circle with centre *O* and radius 5 cm. *PQ* is a tangent to *s* at *Q*. If $|PQ| = 12$ cm, find $|PO|$.

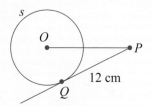

(c) A circular table of radius 0·5 m with centre *O* touches two perpendicular walls. Find the shortest distance from the corner *P* to the rim of the table, correct to two decimal places.

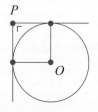

(d) A shelter has a segment of a circle as its cross-section. Find the radius of the circle.

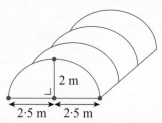

(e) The figure shows the cross-section of a tunnel with a horizontal floor *PQ*. The radius of the circle is 5 m and its centre is *O*. Find the height of the tunnel, giving your answer correct to three decimal places.

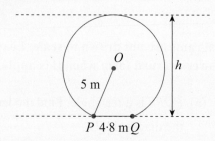

(f) A field *PQRS* is laid out as shown. Find $|SQ|$. Show that $|\angle SPQ| = 90°$.

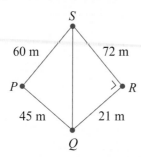

3. Meteorologists use an instrument called a ceilometer to find the height of a cloud above the ground.

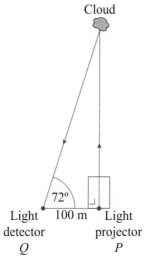

A beam of light from a light projector *P* is directed vertically upwards to strike the base of the cloud. Light scattered by the cloud is detected by a light detector on the ground. Using the information in the diagram above, find the height of the cloud to the nearest metre.

4. The Eiffel Tower was completed on 31 March 1889. If $|PR| = 301\cdot5$ m and $|\angle RPQ| = 85°\ 21'\ 40''$, find the height of the Eiffel Tower, correct to one decimal place.

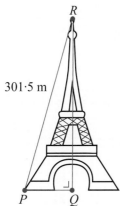

5. To measure the width of a river between two points, a surveyor takes a sighting of a point *Q* on the opposite bank from a point *O* and sets up a marker at *O*. She turns through 90° and walks 220 m to *P* and measures the angle $|\angle OPQ|$. If this angle is 23°, find the width *d* of the river, correct to one decimal place.

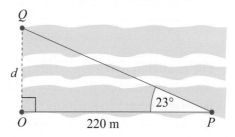

6. In the $\triangle PQR$, find:

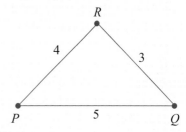

(a) $|\angle PRQ|$

(b) $|\angle RPQ|$, correct to two decimal places

(c) $|\angle RQP|$, correct to two decimal places

7. The top of a hill is 42 m higher than a nearby airport runway. An aeroplane takes off 330 m from a point on the ground vertically below the top of the hill in the direction of the hill. At what angle *A* must the plane take off if it must clear the top of the hill by 42 m, correct to one decimal place?

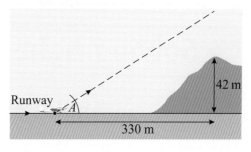

8. Commercial aircraft fly at a height of between 9 km and 11 km. Aircraft begin their gradual descents a long distance away from the airport. A plane starts its descent at a height of 10 km and descends at an angle of 2°. Assuming a straight line path of descent, find correct to two decimal places, the distance from the touchdown point on the runway to the point where the plane begins its descent.

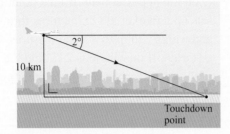

For an aircraft flying at a height of 9·5 km, what must the angle of descent be to touch down at a point 250 km away? Give your answer correct to one decimal place.

9. A piece of jewellery consists of a large semicircle s with centre O and diameter $[PQ]$ of length 12 cm embellished by a set of smaller circles, $s_1, s_2,...,$ of radius 0·6 cm on the ends of metal bars $[QR]$, $[UT]$, etc. which are all perpendicular to $[PQ]$ and equally spaced at 1·2 cm to each other where R is the centre of s_1, is the centre of s_2, etc.

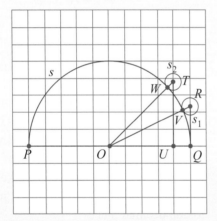

Find:

(a) $|\angle ROQ|$

(b) $|\angle TOQ|$

(c) $|\angle TOR|$

(d) the length of the arc VW

Give all answers correct to two decimal places.

10. If $\sin A = \frac{1}{4}$, find $\sin B$ without using a calculator. O is the centre of the circle and PQ is a diameter.

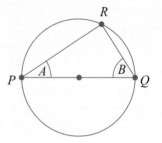

7.4 Solving right-angled triangles 2

Angles of elevation and depression

KEY TERM

An **angle of elevation** (E) is the angle the line of sight (flight/rise) to a point vertically above a horizontal line makes with the horizontal line.

Lift your head (elevate) and look up.

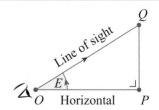

KEY TERM

An **angle of depression** (*D*) is the angle the line of sight (flight, rise) to a point vertically below a horizontal line makes with the horizontal line.

Lower your head (depress) and look down.

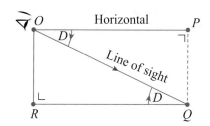

EXAMPLE 23

The angle of depression of a ship as observed from a point *O* on a 20 m vertical cliff is 20·8° at a certain instant. How far is the ship from the base of the cliff at this instant, correct to the nearest metre?

Solution

$$\left.\begin{array}{l} \text{Angle} = 32\cdot8° \\ \text{OPP} = 20 \\ \text{ADJ} = x \end{array}\right] \Rightarrow \tan 32\cdot8°$$

$$\tan 32\cdot8° = \frac{20}{x}$$

$$x = \frac{20}{\tan 32\cdot8°}$$

$$x = 31 \text{ m}$$

EXAMPLE 24

A man's eyes are 1·7 m above the ground at *P*. He observes the top *R* of the head of a window cleaner standing in a cradle whose base *S* is 10 m above the ground. The angle of elevation of the top of the cleaner's head from *P* is 40·5°. If the observer's feet *T* are 12 m from the base of the building *UV*, find the height of the window cleaner, correct to two decimal places.

Solution

For $\triangle PQR$: $\left.\begin{array}{l} \text{Angle} = 40\cdot5° \\ \text{ADJ} = 12 \\ \text{OPP} = |QR| \end{array}\right] \Rightarrow \tan 40\cdot5°$

$$\tan 40\cdot5° = \frac{|QR|}{12}$$

$$|QR| = 12 \tan 40\cdot5° = 10\cdot249$$

$$|SR| = |QR| - |QS|$$

$$= 10\cdot249 - (10 - 1\cdot7)$$

$$= 1\cdot95 \text{ m}$$

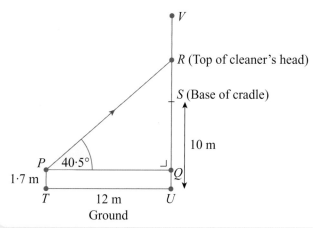

Compass bearings

The cardinal points

On a compass, north (N), south (S), east (E) and west (W) are known as the four cardinal points.

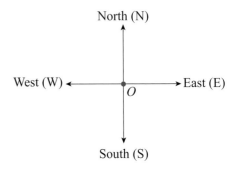

▸ 50 km due west from O brings you to P where $|OP|$ = 50 km.

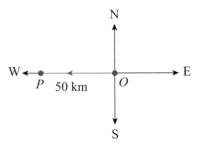

▸ 50 km NE from O brings you to P where $|OP|$ = 50 km, at 45° to both north (N) and east (E).

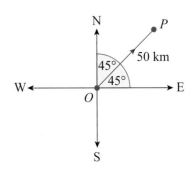

Other directions

▸ 50 km at 70° S of W tells you to move 50 km from O at an angle of 70° traced (rotated) out from W towards S.

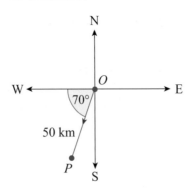

▸ 50 km W 40° N tells you to move 50 km from O at an angle of 40° traced out from W towards N.

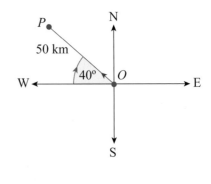

EXAMPLE 25

A ship sailed from a port O at W 37° S and dropped anchor at P, 3 km from the coast as shown. How far did the ship travel, to the nearest kilometre?

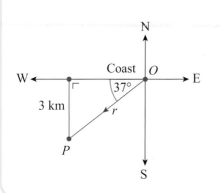

Solution

Angle = 37°
OPP = 3 $\Bigg\} \Rightarrow$ sin 37°
HYP = r

$\sin 37° = \dfrac{3}{r}$

$r = \dfrac{3}{\sin 37°} = 4·98$ km

$r = 5$ km to the nearest kilometre

EXAMPLE 26

A ship travels 20 km due north from Port Lairge (P) to a marker M. It then travels due east for 40 km to an oil rig B. On its return journey, it travels SW from B a certain distance to a point C 20 km due east of P. Draw a diagram to represent this information. Find the total distance travelled, correct to two decimal places.

Solution

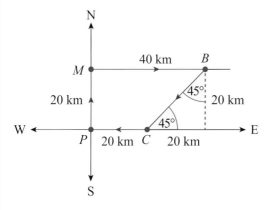

$|BC| = \sqrt{20^2 + 20^2} = 20\sqrt{2}$ km

Total distance $= 20 + 40 + 20\sqrt{2} + 20$

$= 80 + 20\sqrt{2}$

$= 20(4 + \sqrt{2})$ km

$= 108·28$ km

EXAMPLE 27

A fan belt in an engine is stretched around two circular wheels. The distance between the centres, O and C of the wheels, is 16 cm. The radius of the bigger wheel, $|OD|$, is 10 cm and the radius of the smaller wheel, $|CE|$, is 2 cm. Find **(a)** $\theta = |\angle COD|$, **(b)** $\varphi = |\angle FCE|$, **(c)** the length of the fan belt.

The diagram is not drawn to scale.

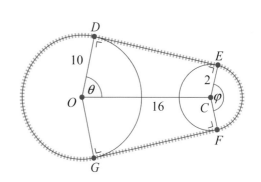

Solution

Draw line segments [CH] and [CK] from the centre, C, of the smaller wheel perpendicular to [OD] and [OG].

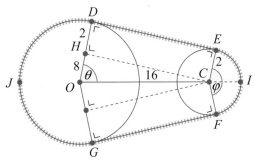

(a) $\cos \theta = \dfrac{8}{16} = \dfrac{1}{2} \Rightarrow \theta = 60° = \dfrac{\pi}{3}$

(b) $|\angle FCE| = \varphi = 2\theta = 120° = \dfrac{2\pi}{3}$

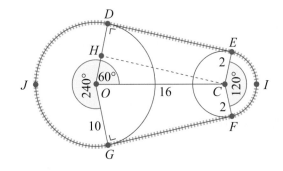

(c) Length of belt:

$$L = |DE| + |\text{arc } EIF| + |FG| + |\text{arc } GJD|$$

$$\sin 60° = \frac{|CH|}{|OC|} \Rightarrow |CH| = 16 \sin 60° = 8\sqrt{3}$$

$$|CH| = |DE| = |GF|$$

$$|\text{arc } EIF| = r\theta = 2 \times \frac{2\pi}{3} = \frac{4\pi}{3}$$

$$|\text{arc } GJD| = r\theta = 10 \times \frac{4\pi}{3} = \frac{40\pi}{3}$$

$$L = \left(\frac{44\pi}{3} + 16\sqrt{3} \right) \text{ cm}$$

Connected right-angled triangles

Use the following steps to solve problems involving connected right-angled triangles:

1. Fill in the values of the measures of all angles you know.
2. Fill in the values of the measures of the lengths of all sides you know.
3. Mark and label any common sides.
4. Separate out the triangles.
5. Start with the triangle for which the most information is given.
6. Using sin, cos or tan, find the measures of the unknown angles and the lengths of the unknown sides.
7. Move on to the next triangle and continue until you are finished.

EXAMPLE 28

The angle of elevation of the top R of the Dublin Spire is 32° from a point P on horizontal ground 194 m from its base.

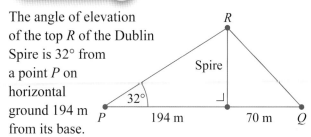

Find the height of the Spire, correct to two decimal places. Find the angle of elevation of the top of the Spire from a point Q on the ground 70 m from the base to the nearest degree.

Solution

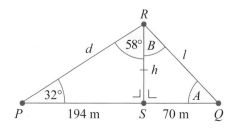

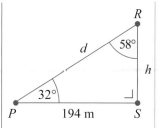

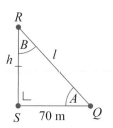

Angle = 32°

OPP = h

ADJ = 194

$$\tan 32° = \frac{h}{194}$$

$$\Rightarrow h = 194 \tan 32°$$

$$= 121·22 \text{ m}$$

Angle = A

OPP = 121·22

ADJ = 70

$$\tan A = \frac{121·22}{70}$$

$$\Rightarrow A = \tan^{-1}\left(\frac{121·22}{70}\right) \simeq 60°$$

EXAMPLE 29

When the top of a mountain is viewed from a point Q, 2200 m above the ground, the angle of depression is 14°. When it is viewed from a point P on the ground directly below Q, the angle of elevation of the top of the mountain is 12°. If Q and P are in the same vertical line, find the height h of the mountain correct to the nearest metre.

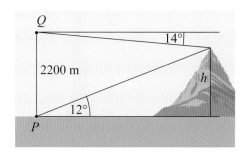

Solution

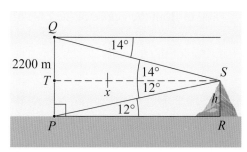

Triangle TSQ:

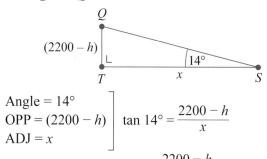

Angle = 14°
OPP = $(2200 - h)$
ADJ = x

$$\tan 14° = \frac{2200 - h}{x}$$

$$\Rightarrow x = \frac{2200 - h}{\tan 14°}$$

Triangle PST:

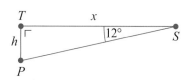

Angle = 12°
ADJ = x
OPP = h

$$\tan 12° = \frac{h}{x} \Rightarrow x = \frac{h}{\tan 12°}$$

$$\frac{2200 - h}{\tan 14°} = \frac{h}{\tan 12°}$$

$$(2200 - h) \tan 12° = h \tan 14°$$

$$2200 \tan 12° = h(\tan 14° + \tan 12°)$$

$$h = \frac{2200 \tan 12°}{\tan 14° + \tan 12°} = 1012 \text{ m}$$

EXAMPLE 30

Two point loudspeakers P and Q send sound waves to a receiver at R.

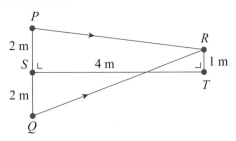

The waves from P travel along the path PR and the waves from Q travel along the path QR as shown. $|PS| = |SQ| = 2$ m, $|ST| = 4$ m and $|RT| = 1$ m.

Find:

(a) $|PR|$ in surd form

(b) $|QR|$

(c) $|QR| - |PR|$, correct to three decimal places

Solution

(a) Draw a perpendicular line from R to PQ to meet it at U.

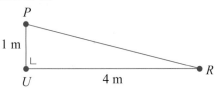

$|PR| = \sqrt{16 + 1} = \sqrt{17}$ m

(b) Draw a perpendicular line from Q to RT to meet it at V.

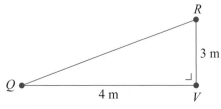

$|QR| = \sqrt{16 + 9} = 5$ m

(c) $|QR| - |PR| = \left(5 - \sqrt{17}\right)$ m $= 0.877$ m

EXERCISE 4

Diagrams are not drawn to scale.

1. A man climbs 8·2 m up a ladder to the roof of a house. When he looks down from the roof along the ladder, the angle of depression is 38°. How far is the foot of the ladder from the base of the wall of the house, correct to two decimal places?

    Find the height of the roof, correct to the nearest metre.

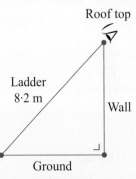

2. A vertical flagpole casts a shadow 17 m long on horizontal ground. What is the angle E of elevation of the sun from O, correct to one decimal place, if the distance from the tip of the shadow to the top of the pole is 20 m? Find the height of the pole, correct to one decimal place.

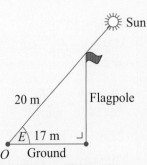

3. The CN tower in Toronto is one of the tallest structures in the world.

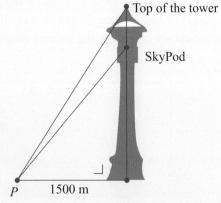

    The angle of elevation of the top of the SkyPod from a point P on horizontal ground, 1500 m from the centre of the base of the tower, is 16·56° and the angle of elevation to the top of the tower is 20·25°.

    Find:

    (a) the height of the tower, correct to two decimal places,

    (b) the height of the top of the tower above the top of the SkyPod, correct to two decimal places.

4. A child P flying a kite originally lets out 76 m of string. At this point the angle of elevation of the kite is $50°$. The child then lets out more string so that the length of string is 102 m. At this point the angle of elevation is $56°$.

   (a) Find the initial height of the kite, correct to two decimal places.

   (b) Find the final height of the kite, correct to two decimal places.

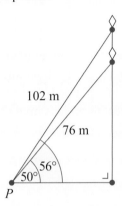

5. A helicopter is flying at 117 m vertically above a motorway PQ along a path parallel to the motorway. Two motorists are driving on the motorway. From the helicopter, the angle of depression to one car is $35°$ and the angle of depression to the other car is $55°$. Find how far apart the cars are, correct to the nearest metre.

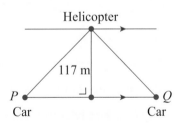

6. A woman swims across a river from P to Q at $41°$ to the bank PR a distance of 25 m. She returns along the line QR as shown.

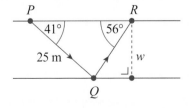

Find:

   (a) the width w of the river, correct to one decimal place,

   (b) $|RQ|$, correct to one decimal place,

   (c) $|PR|$, correct to the nearest metre.

7. After a hot air balloon has ascended 500 m, its angle of elevation from a point P on horizontal ground is $30°$ and its angle of elevation from the top of a vertical building PS is $20°$.

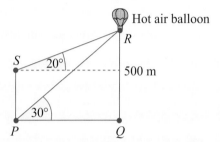

   (a) Find the distance of the base P of the building from the launch point Q of the balloon, correct to the nearest metre.

   (b) Find the height $|PS|$ of the building, correct to the nearest metre.

8. A disc with centre O is placed in front of a light source P so that $|PQ| = 10$ cm, where Q is on the line segment $[PO]$.

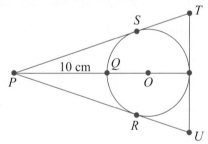

PS is a tangent to the circle at S and PR is a tangent to the circle at R. If $|\angle SPR| = 25°$, find the radius of the circle correct to two decimal places. Find the length of the tangent TU where TU is perpendicular to PO, correct to one decimal place.

9. An aeroplane is flying at a constant altitude h parallel to horizontal ground PQ.

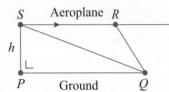

At 9:00 a.m., its angle of elevation from a point Q on the ground is 21°. At 9:01 a.m., its angle of elevation from Q is 58°. What is its altitude if its speed is 780 km/h? Give your answer, correct to three decimal places.

10. A surveyor finds that the angle of elevation of the top of a building is 37° when she is standing 20 m from its base. It is 25° when she walks a certain distance further away on horizontal ground.

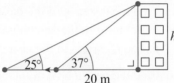

Find:

(a) the height of the building, correct to two decimal places,

(b) the distance the surveyor walked, correct to one decimal place.

11. The angle of elevation of the top of a vertical tree $[RS]$ from a point P on horizontal ground is 28°, where P is 20 m from the base of the tree. Find the height of the tree, correct to two decimal places.

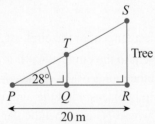

The angle of elevation of the top T of a 2 m vertical wall $[QT]$ from P is also 28°. Find $|PQ|$ and $|QR|$, correct to two decimal places.

12. A boat leaves a harbour H on a course S 55° E at a speed of 25 km/h. Two hours later, it reaches a point K. How far is K from a point P, which is north of K and due east of H, correct to one decimal place?

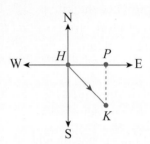

13. Two ships H and K leave port P at the same time. H sails due north and K sails due west. After 1 hour, H has travelled 16 km and K has travelled 25 km. Find the distance between H and K after 1 hour and the angle θ of the line of sight of H from K. Give each answer correct to one decimal place.

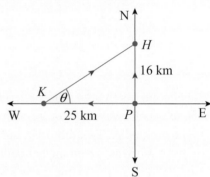

14. A tugboat T leaves a port P and sails NW at 30 km/hr. A second tugboat U leaves the port at the same time as T and sails NE. Two hours later T is due west of U. Find:

(a) the speed of U,

(b) the distance between the tugs after 2 hours, correct to the nearest kilometre.

15. In $\triangle PQR$, S is on $[PQ]$. If $|PR| = 10$ m, $|PS| = 2$ m and $|\angle RPQ| = 53 \cdot 2°$, find:

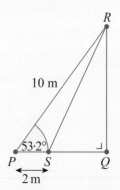

(a) $|QR|$, correct to the nearest metre

(b) $|\angle RSQ|$, correct to the nearest degree

16. $\triangle PQS$ and $\triangle QRS$ are two right-angled triangles.

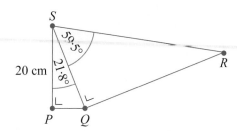

Find each of the following, correct to two decimal places:

(a) $|PQ|$

(b) $|SQ|$

(c) $|SR|$

17. $PQRS$ is a cyclic quadrilateral of a circle with centre O. $[PR]$ is a diameter of the circle and $|SR| = 12$ cm.

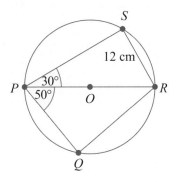

Find:

(a) $|\angle SRP|$

(b) $|\angle PRQ|$

(c) the radius of the circle

(d) $|PS|$

(e) $|PQ|$, correct to one decimal place

(f) $|QR|$, correct to one decimal place

18. From the top of a building, an observer watches a boat sailing directly towards the building. If the observer is 200 m above sea level and if the angle of depression of the boat changes from 30° to 60°, show that the distance that the boat moved is $\dfrac{400\sqrt{3}}{3}$ m.

19. From a point P that is 8 m above level ground, the angle of elevation of the top of a building is 30° and the angle of depression of the base

of the building is 15°. Find the height of the building to the nearest metre.

20. From a point P on horizontal ground, the angle of elevation of the top of a tower is 25°. From a point 25 m closer to the tower, the angle of elevation is 54°. Find the height of the tower, correct to one decimal place.

21. O is the centre of a semicircle with diameter $[PQ]$. Express the radius of the circle in terms of k and θ where $k = |PS|$. Hence, express h in terms of k and θ where $h = |QR|$, if $[RQ]$ is perpendicular to $[PQ]$.

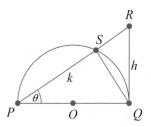

22. $PQRS$ is a square of side l. If $k = |TR|$ and RT is perpendicular to QT, express l in terms of k and θ. Express the area of the square in terms of θ and k.

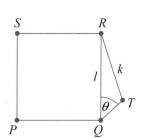

23. OPQ is a right-angled triangle with $|\angle OPQ| = 90°$. PR is the arc of a circle, centre O and radius $k = |OP|$ and $\theta = |\angle QOP|$ is in radians.

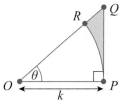

Express:

(a) $|PQ|$ in terms of k and θ,

(b) the area of $\triangle OPQ$ in terms of k and θ,

(c) the area of sector OPR in terms of k and θ,

(d) the area of the shaded region in terms of k and θ.

24. From a point h metres above level ground, the angle of elevation of the top of a house is E and the angle of depression of the foot of the house is D. Show that the height H of the house is given by: $H = \dfrac{h(\tan E + \tan D)}{\tan D}$.

In the following 5 questions, each circle represents circular wheels connected by a belt (broken blue line):

25. (a) Find the length of the belt if O is the centre of s_1 and C is the centre of s_2.

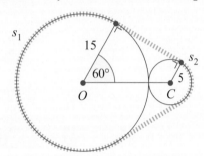

(b) Find θ and hence the length of the belt, if O is the centre of s_1 and C is the centre of s_2. $15\sqrt{3}$ is the radius of s_1, $5\sqrt{3}$ is the radius if s_2 and $|PQ| = 30$. Find the area of the yellow shaded region, correct to one decimal place.

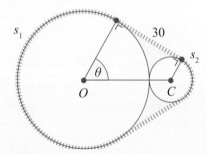

(c) Find the length of the belt if O is the centre of s_1, B is the centre of s_2 and C is

the centre of s_3. 18 is the radius of s_1, 6 is the radius of s_2 and 2 is the radius of s_3.

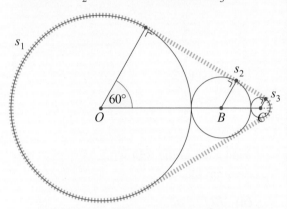

(d) Two wheels of radii 7 units and 2 units are 1 unit apart. Calculate the length of the belt. O is the centre of s_1 and C is the centre of s_2.

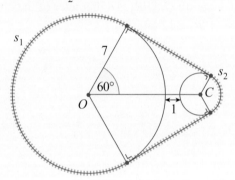

(e) The centre to centre distance, $|OC|$, of two circles is 18 m. Calculate the length of the belt. O is the centre of s_1 and C is the centre of s_2. 10 is the radius of s_1 and 1 is the radius of s_2.

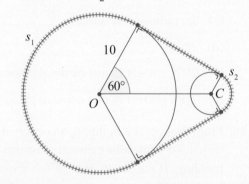

Trigonometry 2

CHAPTER 8

Learning Outcomes

- To use trigonometry to find the area of a triangle.
- To use the sine rule and cosine rule to solve oblique triangles.
- To solve connected triangles and three-dimensional triangles.

Oblique triangles

An **oblique** triangle is a triangle in which no angle measures 90°.
It is a non-right-angled triangle.

An oblique triangle will either have:

1. Three acute angles

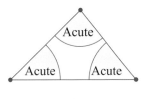

or

2. Two acute angles and one obtuse angle

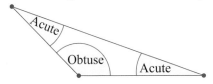

To solve an oblique triangle, you need to find the lengths of all of its sides and the measures of all of its angles.

Every oblique triangle has three angles of measures A, B and C, and their three corresponding opposite sides of lengths a, b and c.

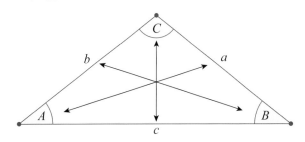

There are six quantities in all in any triangle: A, B, C, a, b, c with $A + B + C = 180°$.

Given a certain combination of three of these six quantities A, B, C, a, b, c, the three unknown quantities can be found using two rules: the **sine rule** and the **cosine rule**.

8.1 The area of triangles and parallelograms

ACTIVITY 18

ACTION
Finding the area of a triangle using trigonometry

OBJECTIVE
To discover how to find the area of a triangle using trigonometry

1. Triangles

From geometry, the area of a triangle $= \frac{1}{2} \times$ Base $\times$ Perpendicular height

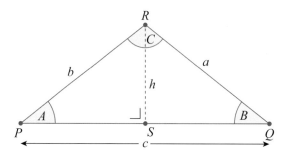

Area $\Delta PQR = \frac{1}{2} \times c \times h$

However, from the right-angled triangle PSR, $\sin A = \dfrac{h}{b} \Rightarrow h = b \sin A$.

Area of the triangle $PQR = \frac{1}{2} \times c \times b \sin A = \frac{1}{2}(bc) \sin A$

There are three versions of this formula:

Area $= \frac{1}{2}(bc) \sin A = \frac{1}{2}(ac) \sin B = \frac{1}{2}(ab) \sin C$

$$\boxed{\text{Area of triangle} = \tfrac{1}{2}bc \sin A = \tfrac{1}{2}ac \sin B = \tfrac{1}{2}ab \sin C}$$

TIP

Remember this area formula as:

$\frac{1}{2}$ (Product of the lengths of any two sides) × sin (Angle between these sides)

The angle between two sides is called their **included** angle.

2. Parallelograms

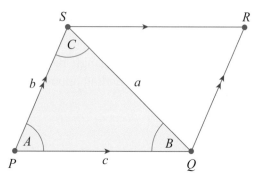

The area of parallelogram $PQRS = 2 \times$ Area of the shaded triangle PQS
$$= bc \sin A = ac \sin B = ab \sin C$$

$$\boxed{\text{Area of parallelogram} = bc \sin A = ac \sin B = ab \sin C}$$

▶ The area of the triangle
$$PQR = \frac{1}{2}(30 \times 14) \sin 35°$$
$$\approx 120.45 \text{ cm}^2$$

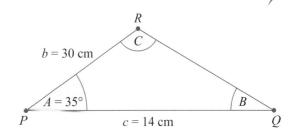

ACTIVITY 19

ACTION
Discover that
$\sin(180° - \theta) = \sin\theta$

OBJECTIVE
To discover that
$\sin(\text{Angle}) = q$, $0 \le q \le 1$,
$q \in \mathbb{R}$, has two solutions
for the angle

TIP

You should always give both answers when finding the angle from $\sin(\text{Angle}) = q$,
$0 \le q \le 1$, $q \in \mathbb{R}$.

▶ If the area of the triangle PQR shown is 76 cm², find c correct to one decimal place.

$$\text{Area} = \frac{1}{2}(15c)\sin 73° = 76$$

$$c = \frac{152}{15\sin 73°} = 10.6 \text{ cm}$$

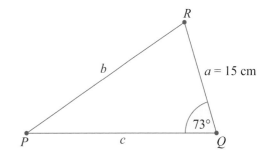

WARNING

A problem arises if you are asked to find an angle in a triangle given its area.

This is because if θ is an acute angle, $(180° - \theta)$ is an obtuse angle and $\sin(180° - \theta) = \sin\theta$ means $\sin\theta$ and $\sin(180° - \theta)$ have the same value. If you enter $\sin^{-1}\left(\frac{1}{2}\right)$ into a calculator, it gives the acute angle $\theta = 30°$ only. But the angle could also be $180° - 30° = 150°$. You must get the other angle yourself by subtracting 30° from 180°, as it could be the required angle.

▶ $\sin\theta = 0.4848 \Rightarrow \theta = \sin^{-1}(0.4848) = 29°$ is the acute angle.
The obtuse angle $= 180° - 29° = 151°$

EXAMPLE 1

If the area of the triangle PQR is 75 cm², find the angle B.

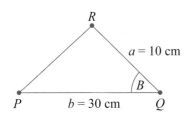

Solution

$$\text{Area} = \frac{1}{2}(10 \times 30)\sin B = 75$$

$$\sin B = \frac{1}{2}$$

$$B = \sin^{-1}\frac{1}{2} = 30° \quad \text{[Acute]}$$

or

$$B = 180° - 30° = 150° \quad \text{[Obtuse]}$$

Always give both answers for the angle.

EXAMPLE 2

$PQRS$ is a quadrilateral with
$|\angle SPQ| = 90°$,
$|SP| = 3$ cm,
$|PQ| = 4$ cm
and $|SQ| = |QR|$.
If the area of the quadrilateral $PQRS$ is 14 cm², find the acute angle D, correct to one decimal place.

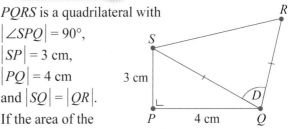

Solution

$$|SQ| = \sqrt{3^2 + 4^2} = 5$$

$$\text{Area } \triangle SPQ = \frac{1}{2} \times 4 \times 3 = 6 \text{ cm}^2$$

$$\text{Area } \triangle SQR = (14 - 6) \text{ cm}^2 = 8 \text{ cm}^2$$

$$\frac{1}{2} \times 5 \times 5 \times \sin D = 8 \Rightarrow \sin D = \frac{16}{25}$$

$$D = \sin^{-1}\left(\frac{16}{25}\right) = 39.8°, 140.2° \quad \text{[Obtuse angle]}$$

However, since D is an acute angle, $D = 39.8°$.

EXAMPLE **3**

OPQ is a sector of a circle of centre *O* and radius 20 cm. $\left|\angle POR\right| = 30°$ and $\left|\angle ORP\right| = 90°$. Find the area of the shaded region *PQR*.

Solution

$30° = \frac{\pi}{6}$ rad

Area of sector $OPQ = \frac{1}{2}r^2\theta = \frac{1}{2} \times 400 \times \frac{\pi}{6} = \frac{100\pi}{3}$ cm$^2 = A_1$

$\cos 30° = \frac{\left|OR\right|}{20} = \frac{\sqrt{3}}{2} \Rightarrow \left|OR\right| = 10\sqrt{3}$ cm

Area of $\triangle OPR = \frac{1}{2} \times 20 \times 10\sqrt{3} \times \sin 30° = 50\sqrt{3}$ cm$^2 = A_2$

$\therefore$ Area of shaded region $A_1 - A_2 = 50\left(\frac{2\pi}{3} - \sqrt{3}\right)$ cm^2

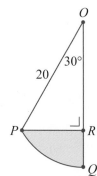

EXERCISE 5

Diagrams are not drawn to scale.

1. Find the area of each polygon, correct to two decimal places.

   (a)

   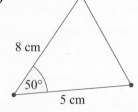

   8 cm
   50°
   5 cm

   (b)

   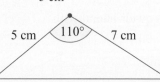

   5 cm 110° 7 cm

   (c)

   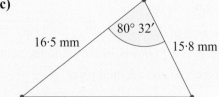

   16·5 mm 80° 32′ 15·8 mm

   (d)

   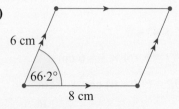

   6 cm
   66·2°
   8 cm

   (e)

   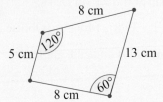

   8 cm
   120°
   5 cm 13 cm
   8 cm 60°

2. Find the exact areas of the following triangles:

   (a)

   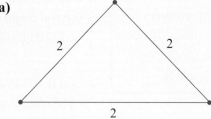

   2   2
   2

   (b)

   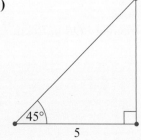

   45°
   5

   (c)

   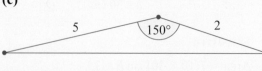

   5 150° 2

   (d)

   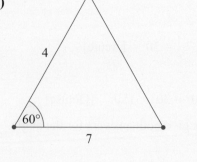

   4
   60°
   7

3. **(a)** Find x, correct to one decimal place, if the area of the triangle shown is 16·3 cm².

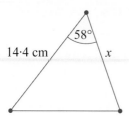

(b) Find x, correct to one decimal place, if the area of the triangle shown is 200 m².

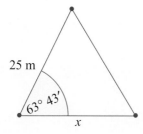

(c) Find x, correct to one decimal place, if the area of the triangle shown is 6·53 cm².

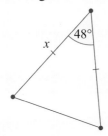

(d) Find x, if the area of the triangle shown is $4\sqrt{3}$ cm².

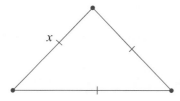

(e) Find x, if the area of the parallelogram shown is $10\sqrt{2}$ cm².

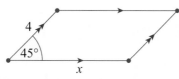

(f) Find x, if the area of the rhombus shown is 4·5 cm².

(g) Find x, if the area of the polygon shown is $9\sqrt{3}$ cm².

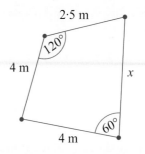

(h) Find x, if the area of the parallelogram shown is 74·17 cm².

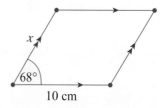

4. **(a)** Find the angle A if the area of the triangle is 12 cm².

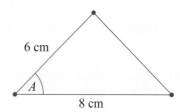

(b) Find the angle A, correct to the nearest degree, if the area of the triangle is 90 cm². Give two answers.

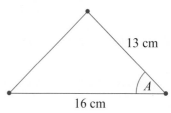

(c) Find the acute angle A, correct to one decimal place, if the area of the triangle is 10 cm².

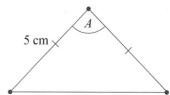

(d) Find the angle A, correct to one decimal place, if the area of the parallelogram is 42 cm². Give two answers.

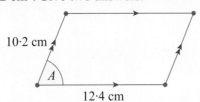

10·2 cm

12·4 cm

5. (a) Find the area of the triangle shown if:

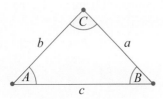

(i) $a = 5$ cm, $b = 6$ cm, $C = 50°$, correct to one decimal place

(ii) $c = 2·4$ cm, $b = 5·2$ cm, $A = 17·4°$, correct to one decimal place

(iii) $c = 8$ cm, $a = 5$ cm, $B = 120°$ in surd form

(iv) $a = 38$ km, $c = 60$ km, $B = 150°$

(b) In a triangle of area 10 cm², $a = 3$ cm and $C = 48°$. Find b correct to one decimal place.

(c) In a triangle, $a = 5$ cm, $b = 10$ cm and its area is 10 cm². Find C if C is acute, correct to one decimal place.

6. OPQ is a sector of a circle with radius r. Show that the area of the shaded region is given by $A = \frac{1}{2}r^2(\theta - \sin \theta)$.

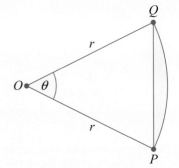

8.2 The sine rule

The sine rule is one of two rules used to solve oblique triangles.

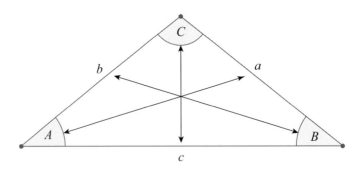

The **sine rule** states that, for any triangle:

$$\frac{\sin A}{a} = \frac{\sin B}{b} = \frac{\sin C}{c} \quad or \quad \frac{a}{\sin A} = \frac{b}{\sin B} = \frac{c}{\sin C}$$

PROOF OF THE SINE RULE

Situation 1: All angles are acute

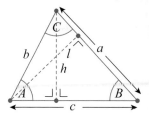

Using the right-angled triangles of height *h*:

$$\sin A = \frac{h}{b} \Rightarrow h = b \sin A$$

$$\sin B = \frac{h}{a} \Rightarrow h = a \sin B$$

$$\therefore b \sin A = a \sin B$$

$$\Rightarrow \frac{\sin A}{a} = \frac{\sin B}{b} \quad ...\textbf{(1)}$$

Using right-angled triangles of height *l*:

$$\sin B = \frac{l}{c} \Rightarrow l = c \sin B$$

$$\sin C = \frac{l}{b} \Rightarrow l = b \sin C$$

$$\therefore c \sin B = b \sin C$$

$$\Rightarrow \frac{\sin B}{b} = \frac{\sin C}{c} \quad ...\textbf{(2)}$$

$$\textbf{(1)} + \textbf{(2)} \Rightarrow \frac{\sin A}{a} = \frac{\sin B}{b} = \frac{\sin C}{c}$$

Situation 2: One angle is obtuse (*A* is obtuse)

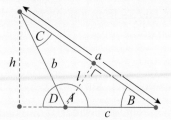

Using the right-angled triangles of height *h*:

$$\sin D = \sin(180° - A) = \frac{h}{b} \Rightarrow h = b \sin A$$

$$\sin B = \frac{h}{a} \Rightarrow h = a \sin B$$

$$\therefore b \sin A = a \sin B$$

$$\Rightarrow \frac{\sin A}{a} = \frac{\sin B}{b} \quad ...\textbf{(1)}$$

Using right-angled triangles of side *l*:

$$\sin B = \frac{l}{c} \Rightarrow l = c \sin B$$

$$\sin C = \frac{l}{b} \Rightarrow l = b \sin C$$

$$\therefore c \sin B = b \sin C$$

$$\Rightarrow \frac{\sin B}{b} = \frac{\sin C}{c} \quad ...\textbf{(2)}$$

$$\textbf{(1)} + \textbf{(2)} \Rightarrow \frac{\sin A}{a} = \frac{\sin B}{b} = \frac{\sin C}{c}$$

When to use the sine rule

Use the sine rule when you are:

1. Given the measures of two angles and the length of one side. (This means you have all three angles as the angles must add to 180°.)

2. Given the length of two sides and the measure of an angle which is not included between the given sides.

Steps for using the sine rule

1. Draw a clear picture of the triangle.

2. Mark on the picture the lengths of all sides you know and the measures of all angles you know.

3. Draw arrows from the angles to their opposite sides.

4. Apply the sine rule to get the required quantity.

5. You can apply the rule again if necessary.

TIP

Remember the sine rule as:
$$\frac{\sin(\text{angle})}{\text{Length of opposite side}} = \frac{\sin(\text{another angle})}{\text{Length of opposite side}}$$

EXAMPLE 4

A.cable car carries passengers from a point P which is 2 km from a point Q at the base of a mountain. The angles of elevation of the top R of the mountain from P and Q are $20°$ and $63°$ respectively.

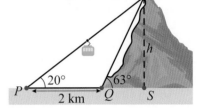

Find:

(a) the length of the cable $|PR|$, correct to two decimal places,

(b) the height h of the mountain, correct to one decimal place.

Solution

Use the sine rule, as you are given two angles and one side.

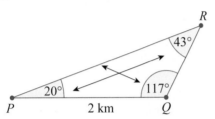

(a) $\dfrac{|PR|}{\sin 117°} = \dfrac{2}{\sin 43°} \Rightarrow |PR| = \dfrac{2 \sin 117°}{\sin 43°} = 2\cdot 61$ km

(b)

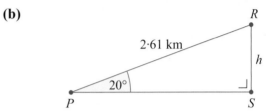

$\sin 20° = \dfrac{h}{2\cdot 61}$

$h = 2\cdot 61 \sin 20° = 0\cdot 9$ km

> **TIP**
>
> Always give both angles when using the sine rule.

All angles in a triangle are less than $180°$. Each angle is either acute or obtuse. This means that the sine of each angle in a triangle is always positive. If the sine of an angle is positive, there are two possible answers for the angle: one in the first quadrant (acute) and one in the second quadrant (obtuse).

EXAMPLE 5

If S is the Sun, E is the Earth and M is Mercury, find:

(a) $|\angle SME|$, correct to one decimal place,

(b) $|EM|$, correct to four significant figures, if $|SM| = 5\cdot 791 \times 10^7$ km and $|SE| = 1\cdot 496 \times 10^8$ km.

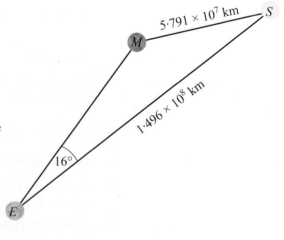

Solution

Use the sine rule, as you are given two sides and one angle not between the sides.

(a) $\dfrac{\sin |\angle SME|}{1\cdot 496 \times 10^8} = \dfrac{\sin 16°}{5\cdot 791 \times 10^7}$

$\sin |\angle SME| = \dfrac{1\cdot 496 \times 10^8 \times \sin 16°}{5\cdot 791 \times 10^7}$

$\sin |\angle SME| = +0\cdot 712059$

$\|\angle SME\| = 45\cdot 4°$ [Acute]	$\|\angle SME\| = 134\cdot 6°$ [Obtuse]
(b) $\|\angle MSE\| = 180° - 45\cdot 4° - 16° = 118\cdot 6°$	$\|\angle MSE\| = 180° - 134\cdot 6° - 16° = 29\cdot 4°$
$\dfrac{\|EM\|}{\sin 118\cdot 6°} = \dfrac{5\cdot 791 \times 10^7}{\sin 16°}$	$\dfrac{\|EM\|}{\sin 29\cdot 4} = \dfrac{5\cdot 791 \times 10^7}{\sin 16°}$
$\|EM\| = 1\cdot 845 \times 10^8$ km	$\|EM\| = 1\cdot 031 \times 10^8$ km

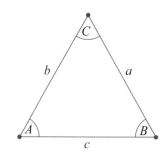

Sine rule identities

The sine rule can be used to prove many results which are true for any triangle.

To prove sine rule identities, use:
$$\frac{\sin A}{a} = \frac{\sin B}{b} = \frac{\sin C}{c} = k \text{ (constant).}$$

This triple equation produces three simultaneous equations:

$\sin A = ak$, $\sin B = bk$, $\sin C = ck$.

These three equations are an alternative way of expressing the sine rule: simply replace $\sin A$ by ak, $\sin B$ by bk and $\sin C$ by ck.

TIP

To prove an identity involving the sine rule put $\sin A = ak$, $\sin B = bk$ and $\sin C = ck$.

EXAMPLE 6

Use the sine rule to show the following for any ΔPQR:

(a) $\dfrac{\sin A - \sin B}{\sin C} = \dfrac{a - b}{c}$

(b) $\dfrac{\sin B + \sin C}{b + c} - \dfrac{\sin A - \sin B}{a - b} = 0$

(c) $a(\sin B - \sin C) + b(\sin C - \sin A) + c(\sin A - \sin B) = 0$

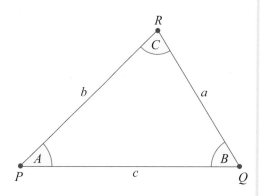

Solution

Sine rule: $\dfrac{\sin A}{a} = \dfrac{\sin B}{b} = \dfrac{\sin C}{c} = k$

$\sin A = ak$, $\sin B = bk$, $\sin C = ck$

(a) $\dfrac{\sin A - \sin B}{\sin C} = \dfrac{ak - bk}{ck} = \dfrac{k(a - b)}{ck} = \dfrac{a - b}{c}$

(b) $\dfrac{\sin B + \sin C}{b + c} - \dfrac{\sin A - \sin B}{a - b} = \dfrac{bk + ck}{b + c} - \dfrac{ak - bk}{a - b} = \dfrac{k(b + c)}{(b + c)} - \dfrac{k(a - b)}{(a - b)} = k - k = 0$

(c) $a(\sin B - \sin C) + b(\sin C - \sin A) + c(\sin A - \sin B)$
$= a(bk - ck) + b(ck - ak) + c(ak - bk)$
$= abk - ack + bck - bak + cak - cbk = 0$

EXERCISE 6

Diagrams are not drawn to scale.

1. Find x or A as applicable in the given triangles, giving all answers correct to one decimal place.

   (a)

   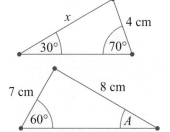

   (b)

   (c)

   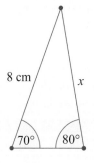

(d)

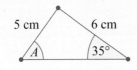

(e)

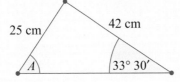

2. In a triangle:

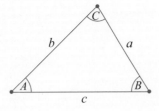

(a) $a = 20$ m, $A = 38°$ and $b = 28$ m. Find **(i)** B, **(ii)** C. Give your answers correct to one decimal place.

(b) $c = 12·5$ cm, $a = 10$ cm and $C = 108°$. Find A and B, correct to one decimal place.

(c) $a = 5$, $b = 4$ and $B = 44°$. Find:

   (i) A **(ii)** C **(iii)** c

Give your answers correct to one decimal place.

3. In the triangle shown, find two possible values for C. Show that for one value of C the triangle is a right-angled triangle and for the other value it is an isosceles triangle.

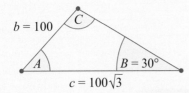

4. When the angle of elevation of the sun is 60° a lamp post $[PQ]$, tilted at 10° from the vertical, casts a shadow of 6 m on level horizontal ground. Find the length of the lamp post, correct to two decimal places.

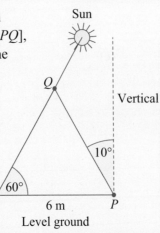

5. The angles of elevation of a balloon R from two points P and Q on the ground are 26° 8′ and 48° 48′ respectively. If $|PQ| = 14$ km, find:

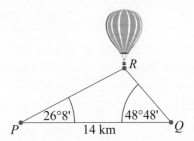

(a) $|PR|$, correct to one decimal place,

(b) $|QR|$ correct to one decimal place,

(c) the height of the balloon above the ground, correct to one decimal place.

6. Coast guard station F is 180 km due east of coast guard station G. A mayday call is received by each station from a ship S in distress. The ship gives its location at E 35° N from G and W 45° N from F.

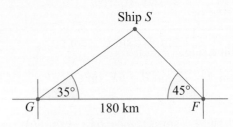

(a) Find how far the ship is from each station, correct to one decimal place.

(b) Find how long it would take a helicopter dispatched from the nearest station to arrive at the ship if its speed is 300 km/h. Give your answer, correct to the nearest minute.

7. R and Q are two points 400 m apart. Q is due north of R. From R, a buoy P is N 48° E. From Q, the buoy is in the direction N 68° E.

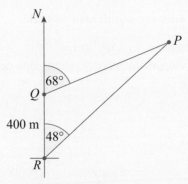

Show that $|PQ| = 869$ m, correct to the nearest metre.

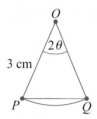

8. For the triangle shown:

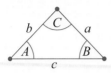

(a) find b if $A = 26°$, $B = 39°$ and $a = 16$ cm,

(b) find b if $A = 50°$, $B = 80°$ and $c = 2$ cm,

(c) find b and c if $A = 124°$, $B = 44°$ and $a = 9$ cm,

(d) find B if $A = 112°$, $b = 2 \cdot 8$ cm and $a = 3 \cdot 8$ cm,

(e) find C if $A = 130°$, $b = 1 \cdot 2$ cm and $a = 4 \cdot 6$ cm.

Give all answers correct to one decimal place.

9. In a $\triangle PQR$: $|QR| = 6$ cm, $|PR| = 8$ cm and $|\angle RPQ| = 40°$. Show that two triangles can be drawn satisfying these conditions and solve them, giving angles correct to the nearest degree and lengths correct to one decimal place.

10. The circle shown has centre O and a radius of 1 m. Find the area of the shaded region.

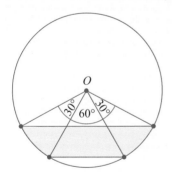

11. O is the centre of circle s with radius r.

Show that the shaded region has an area $A = (\theta - \frac{1}{2} \sin 2\theta)r^2$. If $r = \sqrt{7}$ and $\theta = 60°$, find this area.

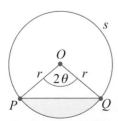

12. O is the centre of circle of radius 3 cm.

(a) Find the area of sector OPQ.

(b) Find the area of $\triangle OPQ$.

(c) If the area of triangle OPQ is $\frac{2}{3}$ of the area of sector OPQ, show that $3\sin 2\theta = 4\theta$.

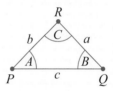

13. In $\triangle PQR$, $|PQ| = 23 \cdot 4$ cm and $|PR| = 37 \cdot 1$ cm. If the area of the triangle is $322 \cdot 58$ cm^2, find $|\angle QPR|$, correct to the nearest degree.

14. In $\triangle PQR$, $a = 2$, $b = 4$ and $c = 5$. Show that $\sin C = \frac{5}{2} \sin A = \frac{5}{4} \sin B$ using the sine rule.

15. Using the sine rule, show that the area of a triangle is $\dfrac{a^2 \sin B \sin C}{2 \sin A}$.

16. Using the sine rule prove that:

(a) $\dfrac{\sin A - \sin B}{a - b} - \dfrac{\sin A + \sin C}{a + c} = 0$

(b) $\dfrac{\sin^2 A - \sin^2 B}{\sin C(\sin A - \sin B)} = \dfrac{(\sin A + \sin B)\sin C}{\sin^2 C}$

(c) $\dfrac{\sin A + \sin B}{\sin C} = \dfrac{a + b}{c}$

(d) $\dfrac{\sin C}{\sin C + c} = \dfrac{\sin B}{\sin B + b}$

(e) $\dfrac{\sin A + \sin B + \sin C}{a + b + c} = \dfrac{\sin A - \sin B + \sin C}{a - b + c}$

(f) $\dfrac{\tan A}{\tan B} = \dfrac{a \cos B}{b \cos A}$

8.3 The cosine rule

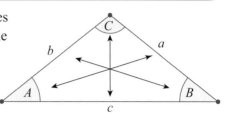

The cosine rule is the second of the two rules needed to solve oblique triangles. The cosine rule may be thought of as an extended version of the theorem of Pythagoras that applies to all triangles.

The cosine rule for any triangle states:

$$a^2 = b^2 + c^2 - 2bc \cos A \dots A \text{ version}$$
$$b^2 = c^2 + a^2 - 2ac \cos B \dots B \text{ version}$$
$$c^2 = a^2 + b^2 - 2ab \cos C \dots C \text{ version}$$

PROOF OF THE COSINE RULE

In triangle OPQ:

$$a = \left| PQ \right| \Rightarrow a = \sqrt{(b \cos A - c)^2 + (b \sin A - 0)^2}$$
$$a^2 = (b^2 \cos^2 A - 2bc \cos A + c^2) + b^2 \sin^2 A$$
$$a^2 = b^2 (\cos^2 A + \sin^2 A) + c^2 - 2bc \cos A$$
$$a^2 = b^2 + c^2 - 2bc \cos A$$

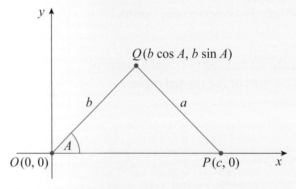

The other versions can be proved in the same way.

When to use the cosine rule

Use the cosine rule when you are:

1. Given the lengths of two sides and the measures of the angles between them (the included angle).

2. Given the lengths of three sides.

EXAMPLE 7

In $\triangle PQR$, $\left| PR \right| = 8$ cm, $\left| PQ \right| = 10$ cm and $\left| \angle RPQ \right| = 53°$. Find $\left| RQ \right|$, correct to one decimal place.

Solution

Use the A version to find $a = \left| RQ \right|$.

$$a^2 = b^2 + c^2 - 2bc \cos A$$
$$a^2 = 64 + 100 - 2(8)(10) \cos 53°$$
$$\therefore a = 8 \cdot 2 \text{ cm}$$

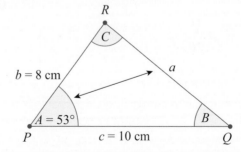

If the cosine of an angle in a triangle is positive, the angle is always acute and the $\cos^{-1}$ calculator button gives you this answer.

If the cosine of an angle in a triangle is negative, the angle is obtuse and the $\cos^{-1}$ calculator button gives you this answer.

EXAMPLE 8

Find the biggest angle in the triangle shown, correct to two decimal places.

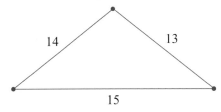

Solution

The biggest angle C is the angle opposite the longest side.

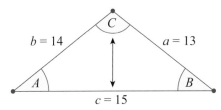

Use the C version to get C.

$$c^2 = a^2 + b^2 - 2ab\cos C$$
$$15^2 = 14^2 + 13^2 - 2(13)(14)\cos C$$
$$225 = 196 + 169 - 364\cos C$$
$$364\cos C = 140$$
$$\cos C = \frac{140}{364}$$
$$C = \cos^{-1}\left(\frac{140}{364}\right) = 67\cdot38°$$

ACTIVITY 20

ACTION
Using the sine and cosine rules

OBJECTIVE
To learn which of the two rules should be used to solve a given triangle

EXAMPLE 9

A ship H leaves port O at 3 p.m. and travels S 20° W at 30 km/h. Another ship K leaves the same port O at 3:30 p.m. and travels at 40 km/h in a direction S 35° E. How far are the ships apart at 5 p.m., correct to one decimal place?

Solution

After 2 hours, H has travelled 60 km.

After 1·5 hours, K has travelled 60 km.

Use the cosine rule, as you have two sides and one angle between these sides.

$$|HK|^2 = 60^2 + 60^2 - 2 \times 60 \times 60\cos 55°$$
$$|HK| = 55\cdot4 \text{ km}$$

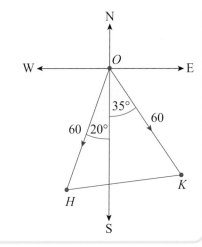

TIP
You may be asked to solve a problem that requires you to use both the sine and cosine rules or one of these rules a number of times. Start with the sine rule or the cosine rule as appropriate. From then on, use the cosine rule exclusively.

EXAMPLE 10

In the triangle PQR: $A = 37°$, $a = 9\cdot2$ cm and $b = 7\cdot9$ cm.

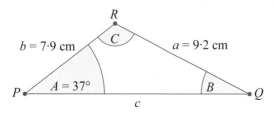

Find:

(a) B **(b)** C **(c)** c

Give all answers correct to one decimal place.

Solution

(a) Since two sides and a non-included angle are given, use the sine rule.

$$\frac{\sin B}{7\cdot9} = \frac{\sin 37°}{9\cdot2} \Rightarrow \sin B = \frac{7\cdot9 \sin 37°}{9\cdot2}$$

$$\sin B = 0\cdot51678$$

$$B = 31\cdot1° \text{ or } B = 148\cdot9°$$

[The obtuse angle is impossible because when it is added to A, it exceeds $180°$.]

(b) $C = 180° - 37° - 31\cdot1° = 111\cdot9°$

(c) Now use the cosine rule.

$$c^2 = 7\cdot9^2 + 9\cdot2^2 - 2 \times 7\cdot9 \times 9\cdot2 \times \cos 111\cdot9°$$

$$c = 14\cdot2 \text{ cm}$$

EXAMPLE 11

A mass is supported by two strings of lengths 70 cm and 80 cm attached to points R and Q, 120 cm apart on a horizontal beam.

(a) Find $\left|\angle RPQ\right|$, correct to the nearest degree.

(b) Find $\left|\angle RQP\right|$, correct to the nearest degree.

(c) Find $\left|\angle QRP\right|$, correct to the nearest degree.

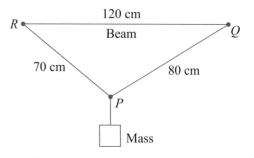

Solution

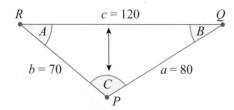

(a) $c^2 = a^2 + b^2 - 2ab \cos C$

$$120^2 = 70^2 + 80^2 - 2(70)(80) \cos C$$

$$11\,200 \cos C = -3100$$

$$\cos C = -\frac{31}{112}$$

$$C = \cos^{-1}\left(-\frac{31}{112}\right) = 106°$$

(b) $b^2 = a^2 + c^2 - 2ac \cos B$

$$70^2 = 80^2 + 120^2 - 2(80)(120) \cos B$$

$$19\,200 \cos B = 15\,900$$

$$\cos B = \frac{159}{192}$$

$$B = \cos^{-1}\left(\frac{159}{192}\right) = 34°$$

(c) $\left|\angle QRP\right| = 180° - 106° - 34° = 40°$

Cosine rule identities

The cosine rule can be used to prove many results which are true for any triangle.

To prove cosine rule identities:

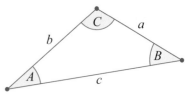

1. Write down two or three versions of the cosine rule under one another.

2. Add or subtract as indicated by the question (the clue will be in the question).

EXAMPLE 12

Use the cosine rule to prove that in any triangle $c = a \cos B + b \cos A$.

Solution

Prove that $c = a \cos \underline{B} \oplus b \cos \underline{A}$

Write down:

B version: $b^2 = a^2 + c^2 - 2ac \cos B$ ... **(1)**

A version: $a^2 = b^2 + c^2 - 2bc \cos A$ ... **(2)**

Adding **(1)** and **(2)**:

$a^2 + b^2 = a^2 + b^2 + 2c^2 - 2ac \cos B - 2bc \cos A$

We add because of $\oplus$.

$2ac \cos B + 2bc \cos A = 2c^2$ [Divide by $2c$.]

$a \cos B + b \cos A = c$

$\therefore c = a \cos B + b \cos A$

EXERCISE 7

Diagrams are not drawn to scale.

1. Find x or A as appropriate in each of the following triangles, correct to one decimal place.

   (a)

   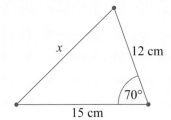

   (b)

   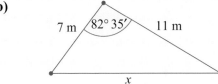

   (c)

   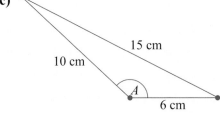

   (d)

   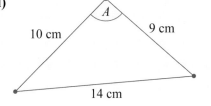

2. In the triangle:

   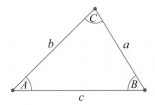

   (a) find the biggest angle if $a = 8$ cm, $b = 15$ cm and $c = 11$ cm,

   (b) find the smallest angle if $a = 12$ cm, $b = 6$ cm and $c = 11$ cm.

   Give both answers correct to the nearest degree.

3. The diagram shows part of a golf course.

   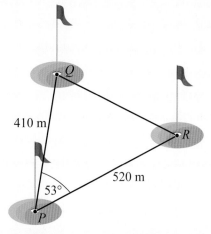

   Find $|QR|$, correct to the nearest metre, and $|\angle PQR|$, correct to the nearest degree.

4. A rhombus has sides of length 10 cm and an angle of $63°$ at one vertex. Find the lengths of the diagonals correct to two decimal places.

   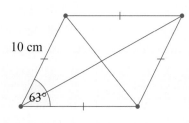

5. Two cars leave from the same location *P* and travel along two different motorways with an angle of 80° between them. If their average speeds are 80 km/h and 100 km/h, what is the distance between them after 30 minutes, correct to the nearest kilometre?

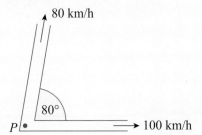

6. For Δ*PQR*:

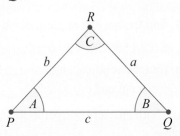

   (a) If $a = 5$ cm, $b = 7$ cm, $C = 70°$, find c.

   (b) If $a = 2·8$ m, $c = 3·2$ m, $B = 78°$, find b.

   (c) If $c = 80$ m, $b = 40$ m, $A = 140°$, find a.

   (d) If $a = 3$, $b = 4$, $c = 2$, find A.

   (e) If $a = 6$, $b = 3$, $c = 5$, find B.

   Give all angles correct to the nearest degree and the length of all sides correct to one decimal place.

7. A surveyor is asked to carry out a survey of a triangular field *PQR*.

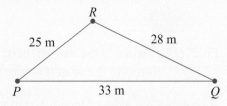

She draws a diagram of the field with the lengths of each side shown.

She calculates the measures of the angles ∠*PRQ*, ∠*RPQ* and ∠*PQR*, correct to three decimal places to check them against her theodolite (an instrument used to measure angles) readings. She then calculates the area of the field, correct to one decimal place.

What angles and area did she calculate?

8. If *EFGH* is a parallelogram, use the cosine rule on Δ*EFH* and Δ*EFG* to show that $p^2 + q^2 = 2x^2 + 2y^2$, where $|HF| = q$, $|EG| = p$, $|EF| = |HG| = y$, $|EH| = |FG| = x$ and $|\angle HEF| = \theta$.

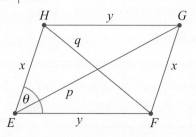

9. The lengths of the sides of a Δ*PQR* are $|PR| = \sqrt{3}$, $|RQ| = \sqrt{12}$ and $|PQ| = \sqrt{21}$. Find all angles correct to the nearest degree.

10. Solve by finding the measures of all the unknown angles correct to the nearest degree and the lengths of all unknown sides correct to one decimal place.

   (a)   **(b)**

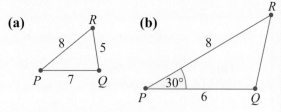

11. The lengths of the sides of a triangle are 13, 14 and 15. The smallest angle is θ. Show that $\cos \theta = \frac{3}{5}$. Find $\sin \theta$ and the area of the triangle.

12. Find the length of each diagonal in the parallelogram *EFGH*, correct to one decimal place.

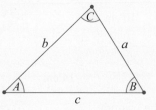

13. For any triangle use the cosine rule to show that:

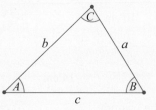

   (a) $c = a \cos B + b \cos A$

   (b) $a = b \cos C + c \cos B$

   (c) $b = a \cos C + c \cos A$

   Deduce that $a + b + c =$
$(a + b) \cos C + (a + c) \cos B + (b + c) \cos A$.

14. For any triangle use the cosine rule to show that:

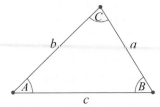

(a) $\dfrac{a^2 - b^2}{c} = a \cos B - b \cos A$

(b) $\dfrac{b^2 - a^2}{abc} = \dfrac{\cos A}{a} - \dfrac{\cos B}{b}$

(c) $bc \cos A + ac \cos B + ab \cos C = \dfrac{1}{2}(a^2 + b^2 + c^2)$

(d) $\dfrac{\cos A}{a} + \dfrac{a}{bc} = \dfrac{\cos B}{b} + \dfrac{b}{ca}$

15. Two cars A and B travel away from O as shown. How far are they apart after t hours?

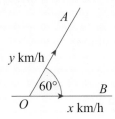

16. In $\triangle PQR$, $|PQ| = 5x$, $|PR| = 3x$ and $|\angle RPS| = |\angle QPS| = 60°$.

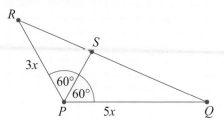

Show that $|QR| = 7x$ using the cosine rule.

Use the sine rule to show that $\dfrac{|RS|}{|QS|} = \dfrac{3}{5}$.

Hence, show that $|SR| = \dfrac{21x}{8}$.

17. Use the sine rule and the cosine rule to prove the following in any triangle:

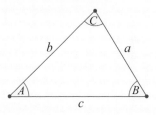

(a) $a \sin A + b \sin B - c \sin C = 2a \sin B \cos C$

(b) $\dfrac{a \cos B - b \cos A}{c} = \dfrac{\sin^2 A - \sin^2 B}{\sin^2 C}$

18. The lengths of the three sides of a triangle are consecutively in an arithmetic progression. The biggest angle is 120°. Use the cosine and sine rules to show that the smallest angle is $\sin^{-1}\left(\dfrac{3\sqrt{3}}{14}\right)$.

8.4 Connected triangles

If you are given two connected triangles, use the following steps to solve them:

1. Mark in the lengths of all sides and the measures of all angles you know.
2. Identify right-angled triangles and oblique triangles.
3. Mark the common sides.
4. Separate out the triangles.
5. Start with the triangle for which the most information is known.
6. Use sine/cosine/tangent for right-angled triangles.
7. Use the sine rule/cosine rule for oblique triangles.

EXAMPLE 13

The diagram shows a school playing field.

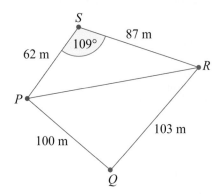

Find:

(a) $|PR|$, correct to the nearest metre,

(b) $|\angle PQR|$, correct to the nearest degree,

(c) the area of the field, correct to three significant figures.

Solution

PQ is a common side. Mark it and call it l.

Let $L = |\angle PQR|$.

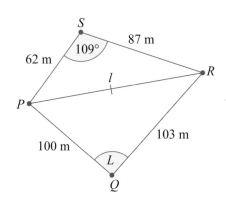

Oblique triangle		Oblique triangle

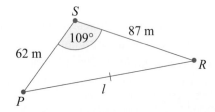

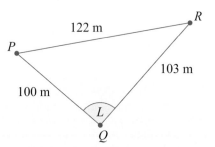

(a) **Cosine rule:**

$$l^2 = 62^2 + 87^2 - 2 \times 62 \times 87 \times \cos 109°$$

$$l = 122 \text{ m} = |PR|$$

(b) **Cosine rule:**

$$122^2 = 100^2 + 103^3 - 2 \times 100 \times 103 \times \cos L$$

$$\cos L = \frac{5725}{20\,600}$$

$$L = |\angle PQR| = \cos^{-1}\left(\frac{5725}{20\,600}\right) \simeq 74°$$

(c) Area $= \frac{1}{2} \times 62 \times 87 \times \sin 109° + \frac{1}{2} \times 100 \times 103 \times \sin 74° \simeq 7500 \text{ m}^2$

EXERCISE 8

Diagrams are not drawn to scale.

1. In the quadrilateral *PQRS*, find:

   (a) $|QS|$, correct to one decimal place

   (b) $|\angle SRQ|$, correct to the nearest degree

   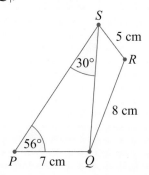

2. In $\triangle PQR$: $|PS| = |SQ|$, $|PQ| = 9.4$ and $|\angle SPQ| = 34°\,45'$.

   (a) Find $|SP|$, correct to one decimal place.

   (b) If $|RP| = 25.7$, find $|RQ|$ correct to one decimal place.

   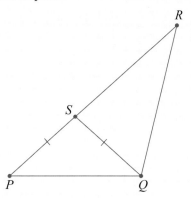

3. $\triangle QRS$ is a right-angled triangle, $|SP| = |SQ|$, $|SR| = 6$ m, $|RQ| = 8$ m and $SP \parallel RQ$.

   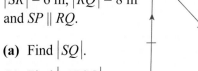
   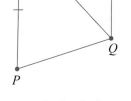

   (a) Find $|SQ|$.

   (b) Find $|\angle RSQ|$, correct to two decimal places.

   (c) Find $|PQ|$, correct to one decimal place.

4. *PRS* is a triangle with *Q* on $[PR]$, $|PQ| = 3$ cm, $|RS| = 5$ cm, $|\angle PRS| = 62°$ and $|\angle RSQ| = 75°$.

   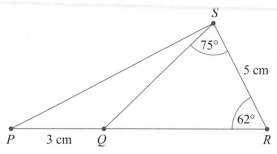

   Find:

   (a) $|QR|$, correct to the nearest centimetre

   (b) the area of $\triangle PRS$, correct to the nearest square centimetre

5. *PQR* is a triangle with *S* on $[PQ]$ and $[RS]$ perpendicular to $[PQ]$.

   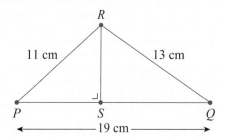

   Find:

   (a) $|\angle RPQ|$, correct to one decimal place

   (b) $|RS|$, correct to one decimal place

6. In $\triangle PQR$, *S* is on $[PQ]$ and $|RP| = |RS|$.

   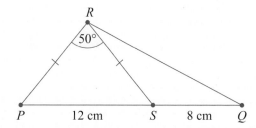

   Find:

   (a) $|RS|$, correct to one decimal place

   (b) $|RQ|$, correct to the nearest centimetre

7. In $\triangle PQR$, S is on $[PQ]$.

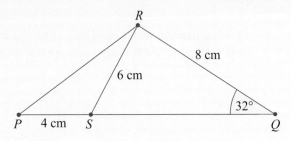

Find:

(a) $|\angle RSQ|$, correct to the nearest degree

(b) $|PR|$, correct to one decimal place

8. $PQRS$ is a quadrilateral with $|PQ| = 5$ cm, $|SQ| = 6$ cm and $|\angle SRQ| = 28°$.

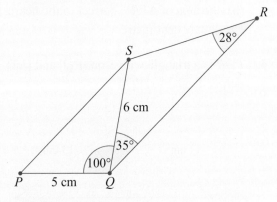

Find:

(a) $|SP|$, correct to two decimal places

(b) $|QR|$, correct to two decimal places

(c) the area of the quadrilateral, correct to one decimal place

9. Three ships Q, R and S are in a straight line. P is a port.

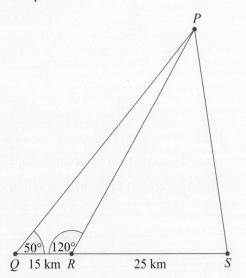

Find how far:

(a) R is from the port, correct to the nearest km,

(b) S is from the port, correct to the nearest km.

10. A vertical mast $[RS]$ is supported by two straight cables $[SP]$ and $[SQ]$ tied to points P and Q on level horizontal ground.

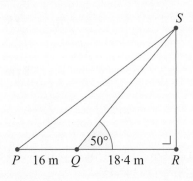

(a) Find $|SQ|$, correct to one decimal place.

(b) Find $|PS|$, correct to one decimal place.

11. $PQRS$ is a quadrilateral.

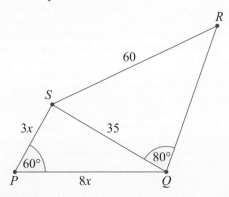

(a) Find x.

(b) Find $|\angle QRS|$, correct to the nearest degree.

12. (a) For the triangle shown, find:

(i) $|RS|$

(ii) $|RQ|$

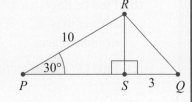

(b) For the triangle PQR shown, $[PS]$ is perpendicular to $[PQ]$.

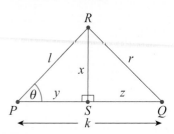

Express:

(i) x in terms of l and θ,

(ii) y in terms of l and θ,

(iii) z in terms of l, θ, k,

(iv) r in terms of l, θ, k.

13. For the triangle PQR shown, S is on $[PQ]$.

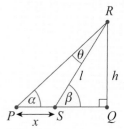

Express:

(a) θ in terms of α and β,

(b) l in terms of h and β,

(c) x in terms of α and β.

14. In the right-angled triangle PQR, S is on $[QR]$.

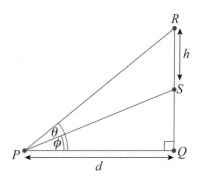

Express h in terms of d, θ and ϕ where $\left|\angle SPQ\right| = \phi$ and $\left|\angle RPQ\right| = \theta$.

15. If $\triangle PQR$, $\triangle PRS$ and $\triangle PST$ are three right-angled triangles, find $\left|QR\right|$, correct to two decimal places where $\left|\angle SPR\right| = 30°$ and $\left|\angle SPT\right| = 45°$.

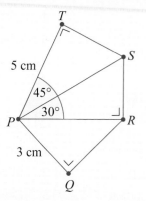

16. In the triangles shown, $\left|\angle SPQ\right| = \left|\angle QRS\right| = \left|\angle QTR\right| = 90°$, $\left|\angle SQR\right| = 30°$ and $\left|\angle RQT\right| = 60°$.

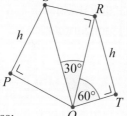

If $\left|SP\right| = \left|RT\right| = h$, express:

(a) $\left|QR\right|$ in terms of h,

(b) $\left|SQ\right|$ in terms of h.

Find $\left|\angle PQS\right|$, correct to one decimal place.

17. In $\triangle PQR$, $[RS]$ is perpendicular to $[PQ]$, $\left|RP\right| = \left|RQ\right| = r$, $\left|RS\right| = h$ and $\left|PQ\right| = x$.

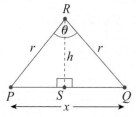

Show that:

(a) $h = r \cos\left(\dfrac{\theta}{2}\right)$

(b) $x = 2r \sin\left(\dfrac{\theta}{2}\right)$

(c) area of $\triangle PQR$ is $r^2 \sin\left(\dfrac{\theta}{2}\right) \cos\left(\dfrac{\theta}{2}\right)$

8.5 3D trigonometry

ACTIVITY 21

ACTION
Working with 3D
trigonometry

OBJECTIVE
*To learn to spot
right-angled triangles
in 3D space*

TIP

A vertical pole is
**perpendicular to any
line** through it in a
horizontal plane.

To solve three-dimensional (3D) trigonometric
problems, it is important to be able to identify all
the right-angled triangles in a figure.

If $[ST]$ is a vertical pole and P, Q, R and
S are points in a horizontal plane, then
$[ST] \perp [SR]$, $[ST] \perp [SP]$ and $[ST] \perp [SQ]$.

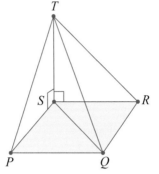

Steps for solving 3D figures

1. Draw a diagram.

2. Identify all right-angled and oblique triangles.

3. Label all vertices and put in the measures of any angles and the lengths of
    any sides you know.

4. Separate out the triangles and solve using the theorem of Pythagoras,
    trigonometric ratios, the sine rule and/or the cosine rule.

EXAMPLE 14

ST is a vertical pole and P, Q, R and S are the four
vertices of a square $PQRS$ in a horizontal plane.
If $|\angle SRT| = 60°$ and $|RT| = 20$ m, find:

(a) $|SR|$ **(b)** $|ST|$ **(c)** $|SQ|$ **(d)** $|QT|$

Solution

1. There are five right-angled triangles: $\triangle SRT$,
    $\triangle SPT$, $\triangle SQT$, $\triangle SQR$ and $\triangle SQP$ because $PQRS$
    is a square.

2. Separate out the triangles.

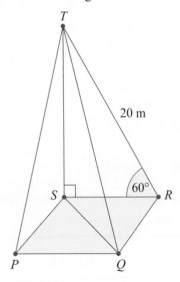

(a) $\triangle SRT$ (RAT):

$$\cos 60° = \frac{|SR|}{20} = \frac{1}{2}$$

$$\Rightarrow |SR| = 10 \text{ m}$$

(b) $\sin 60° = \dfrac{|ST|}{20} = \dfrac{\sqrt{3}}{2}$

$$\Rightarrow |ST| = 10\sqrt{3} \text{ m}$$

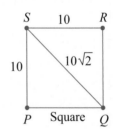

(c) Square $PQRS$:

$$|SQ| = \sqrt{100 + 100}$$

$$= 10\sqrt{2} \quad \text{[Pythagoras]}$$

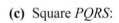

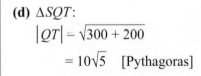

(d) $\triangle SQT$:

$$|QT| = \sqrt{300 + 200}$$

$$= 10\sqrt{5} \quad \text{[Pythagoras]}$$

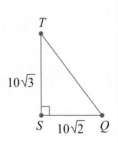

EXAMPLE 15

Romeo is serenading Juliet on her balcony in Verona. From Romeo's position on horizontal level ground *PRQ*, the angle of elevation to Juliet's eyes is 30°. A few hours later another suitor, Pietro, arrives to woo Juliet. His position is 13 m from where Romeo stood as shown. From his position, the angle of elevation to Juliet's eyes is 60°.

(a) Express $|RQ|$ in terms of h.

(b) Express $|PQ|$ in terms of h.

(c) Find h, correct to two decimal places, where h is the height of Juliet's eyes above the ground.

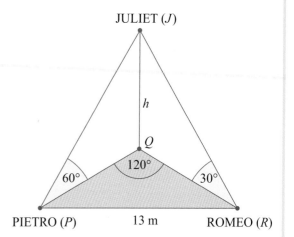

Solution

(a) ΔQRJ (RAT):

$$\tan 30° = \frac{h}{|RQ|}$$

$$|RQ| = \frac{h}{\tan 30°} = h\sqrt{3}$$

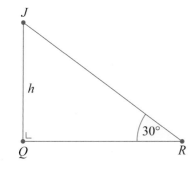

(b) ΔPQJ (RAT):

$$\tan 60° = \frac{h}{|PQ|}$$

$$|PQ| = \frac{h}{\tan 60°} = \frac{h}{\sqrt{3}}$$

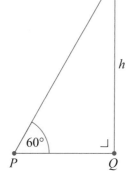

(c) ΔPRQ (Oblique):

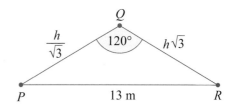

The cosine rule gives:

$$13^2 = \left(\frac{h}{\sqrt{3}}\right)^2 + (h\sqrt{3})^2 - \frac{2h}{\sqrt{3}}(h\sqrt{3})\cos 120°$$

$$169 = \frac{h^2}{3} + 3h^2 + h^2$$

$$169 = \frac{13h^2}{3}$$

$$h^2 = 39$$

$$h = \sqrt{39} = 6·24 \text{ m}$$

EXERCISE 9

Diagrams are not drawn to scale.

1. PR is vertical. R, Q and S are on horizontal level ground with $|PR| = 25$ m, $|\angle PQR| = 20°$ and $|\angle PSR| = 30°$. Find $|PQ|$ and $|PS|$, giving your answers correct to one decimal place.

2. SR is vertical. P, Q and R are in a horizontal plane where $\beta = |\angle SQR| = 30°$ and $\alpha = |\angle SPR| = 60°$. Express $|PR|$ and $|QR|$ in terms of h. Find $|PQ|$ if $\tan|\angle PRQ| = \sqrt{8}$.

3. RS is vertical. P, Q and S are on horizontal ground. $|\angle PSQ| = 90°$. Show that

$$|PQ|^2 = \frac{h\sqrt{\tan^2\alpha + \tan^2\beta}}{\tan\alpha\tan\beta} \text{ where } \alpha = |\angle RPS|$$

and $\beta = |\angle RQS|$.

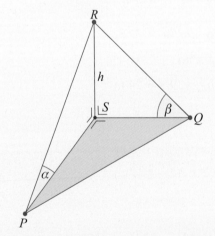

4. $PQRT$ is a rectangle in a horizontal plane. SR is a vertical pole. $|\angle STR| = 30°$, $|TP| = 5$ m and $|PQ| = 10$ m. Find:

   (a) $|SR|$

   (b) $|\angle RQS|$, correct to the nearest degree

(c) $|PR|$

(d) $|\angle SPR|$, correct to one decimal place

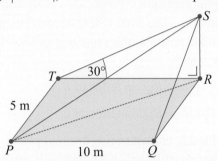

5. $PQTU$ is a rectangle in a horizontal plane. $[ST]$ and $[RQ]$ are two equal vertical poles. $|\angle RPQ| = 30°$, $|US| = 50$ cm and $|UP| = 90$ cm.

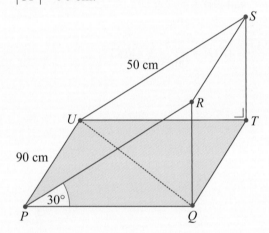

Find:

(a) $|PQ|$

(b) $|RQ|$

(c) $|UQ|$, correct to two decimal places

(d) $|\angle RUQ|$, correct to the nearest degree

6. Find θ in the cuboid shown, correct to one decimal place.

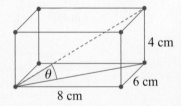

7. A parallelogram *PQST* is propped up at 60° to the horizontal by a vertical post *SR*. $|\angle TPQ| = 80°$, $|SR| = 2$ m and $|PQ| = 3$ m. Find $|SQ|$ if $|\angle SQR| = 60°$. Find $|SP|$, correct to one decimal place.

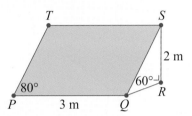

8. *PRST* is a rectangle in a horizontal plane as shown. $|PR| = 15$ m, $|RS| = 8$ m and [*PQ*] is a vertical post with $|PQ| = 6\sqrt{2}$. Find $|PS|$. Find $|SQ|$ and $|TQ|$.

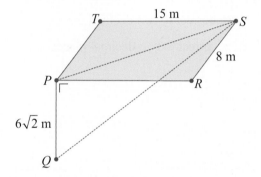

9. *PRS* is a triangle in a horizontal plane and *PQ* is a vertical. Find $|PS|$, if $|QS| = 5$ m and $|\angle PQS| = 30°$. If $|\angle PSR| = 90°$ and $|\angle PRS| = 55°$, find $|PR|$, giving your answer correct to one decimal place.

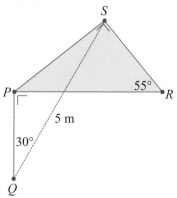

10. *PQRS* is a square in a horizontal plane. *TS* is a vertical pole. If $|ST| = 10$ and $|\angle SRT| = 30°$, find:

(a) $|SR|$

(b) $|SQ|$

(c) $|TQ|$

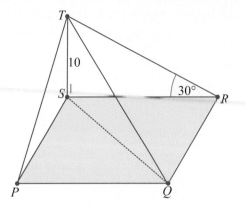

11. *PQR* is a right-angled triangle in a horizontal plane. *RS* is a vertical pole. $|PQ| = 5$, $|PR| = 4$ and $|\angle RQS| = 30°$. Find:

(a) $|RQ|$

(b) $|RS|$

(c) $|PS|$

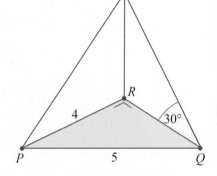

12. A surveyor standing at point *P* on horizontal ground observes two vertical masts, *ST* and *RQ*, of different heights. *P, Q* and *T* are all in the same horizontal plane. From *P*, the angles of elevation of the tops of the poles are 24° and 19° respectively. The surveyor is 20 m from the base of *ST* and the height of *RQ* is 8 m.

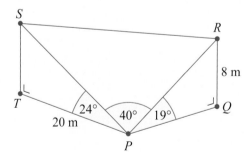

Find:

(a) $|PR|$, correct to two decimal places,

(b) $|SP|$, correct to two decimal places,

(c) $|SR|$, correct to one decimal place if $|\angle SPR| = 40°$.

13. *PQTS* is a rectangle in a horizontal plane with $|PQ| = 6$ and $|QT| = 15$ m, [*PR*], [*SV*], [*TU*] and [*QW*] are vertical and $|PR| = |SV| = |TU| = |QW| = 8$ m.

Find:

(a) $|RQ|$

(b) $|RU|$

(c) $|QU|$

(d) $|\angle URQ|$, correct to the nearest degree

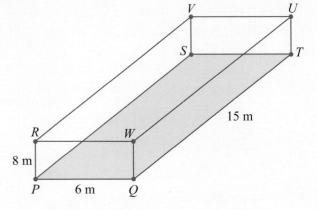

14. The diagram shows a ridge tent pitched on a horizontal section of ground *PQTS* with [*RV*] perpendicular to [*PQ*], $|RV| = 1·3$ m, $|PQ| = 1·5$ m and $|QT| = 2·2$ m.

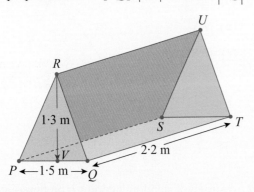

Find:

(a) $|QR|$, correct to two decimal places

(b) $|RT|$, correct to two decimal places

15. A tetrahedron consists of an equilateral triangle *PQR* as base and three faces which are isosceles triangles.

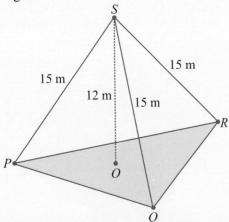

The length of each equal side of the isosceles triangles is 15 cm and the height of the tetrahedron is 12 cm. Find the length of each side of the equilateral triangle.

16. *TS* is a vertical mast on level horizontal ground containing points *P*, *Q* and *R*. It is supported by three cables that join the top *S* of the mast to each

point *P*, *Q* and *R* on the ground. The foot of the mast *T* lies inside $\triangle PQR$. Each cable is 52 m long.

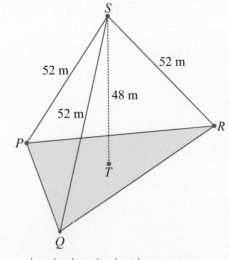

(a) If $|TP| = |TQ| = |TR|$, find these lengths.

(b) If $|PQ| = 34$ m and $|PR| = 38$ m, find $|\angle PTQ|$, $|\angle PTR|$ and $|\angle QTR|$, correct to two decimal places.

(c) Find $|QR|$, correct to one decimal place.

17. P, Q and R are three points on horizontal ground. S is vertically above P. Find $|PR|$ and $|\angle PQR|$.

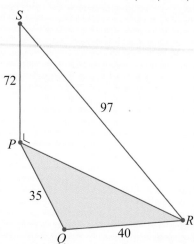

18. A rectangular box is shown. Find $|UP|$ and $|UQ|$. Find the angle between $[UQ]$ and $[TP]$, giving your answer correct to two decimal places.

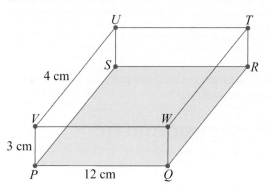

19. $QRST$ is a vertical rectangular wall of height h. P is a point on level horizontal ground in front of the wall. The angle of elevation of R from P is θ and the angle of elevation of S from P is 2θ.

If $|PQ| = 3|PT|$, find θ using

$$\tan 2\theta = \frac{2\tan\theta}{1 - \tan^2\theta}.$$

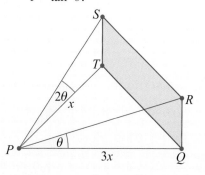

20. P, Q and R are three points on horizontal ground. $[RS]$ is a vertical pole. If $3c^2 = 13h^2$, find $|\angle PRQ|$ where $|RS| = h$ and $|PQ| = c$.

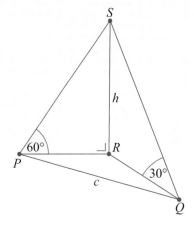

Learning Outcomes

- To prove trigonometric identities.
- To solve trigonometric equations.
- To understand trigonometric graphs.
- To understand inverse trigonometric functions.

9.1 Trigonometric identities

There are numerous results in trigonometry which are **true for all angles.**
These are known as **trigonometric identities.**

The fundamental trigonometric identity

In Chapter 7, the fundamental trigonometric identity was proved:

$$\cos^2 A + \sin^2 A = 1$$

This is one of the two most important trigonometric identities.
It leads to two further identities:

$$\cos^2 A = 1 - \sin^2 A \quad [\text{You can replace } \cos^2 A \text{ by } 1 - \sin^2 A.]$$
$$\sin^2 A = 1 - \cos^2 A \quad [\text{You can replace } \sin^2 A \text{ by } 1 - \cos^2 A.]$$

Compound angle identities

KEY TERM

A **compound angle** is an angle which can be written as a sum or difference of two or more angles: $A + B$, $A - B$, $2A + B$, $A + B - C$, etc.

All trigonometric identities in the tables come from the compound angle formula:

$\cos(A - B) = \cos A \cos B + \sin A \sin B$, which you need to prove.

PROOF

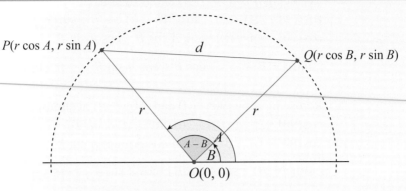

P and Q are two points on a circle with centre O and radius r. The line OQ makes an angle B with the positive x-axis. The line OP makes an angle A with the positive x-axis.

$d = |PQ| = \sqrt{(r\cos A - r\cos B)^2 + (r\sin A - r\sin B)^2}$ [Using the distance formula]

$d = |PQ| = \sqrt{r^2 + r^2 - 2(r)(r)\cos(A - B)} = \sqrt{2r^2 - 2r^2\cos(A - B)}$ [Using the cosine rule]

$\therefore \sqrt{(r\cos A - r\cos B)^2 + (r\sin A - r\sin B)^2} = \sqrt{2r^2 - 2r^2\cos(A - B)}$

$(r\cos A - r\cos B)^2 + (r\sin A - r\sin B)^2 = 2r^2 - 2r^2\cos(A - B)$

$r^2\cos^2 A - 2r^2\cos A\cos B + r^2\cos^2 B + r^2\sin^2 A - 2r^2\sin A\sin B + r^2\sin^2 B = 2r^2 - 2r^2\cos(A - B)$

$r^2(\cos^2 A + \sin^2 A) + r^2(\cos^2 B + \sin^2 B) - 2r^2(\cos A\cos B + \sin A\sin B) = 2r^2 - 2r^2\cos(A - B)$

$r^2(1) + r^2(1) - 2r^2(\cos A\cos B + \sin A\sin B) = 2r^2 - 2r^2\cos(A - B)$

$2r^2 - 2r^2(\cos A\cos B + \sin A\sin B) = 2r^2 - 2r^2\cos(A - B)$

$-2r^2(\cos A\cos B + \sin A\sin B) = -2r^2\cos(A - B)$

$\therefore \cos(A - B) = \cos A\cos B + \sin A\sin B$

TIP

This result is true for all angles A and B. A and B can have **any** values.

$\boxed{\cos(A - B) = \cos A\cos B + \sin A\sin B}$ **[Compound angle 1]**

Many other trigonometric formulae can be deduced from **compound angle 1**.

EXAMPLE 1

(a) Using $\cos(A - B) = \cos A\cos B + \sin A\sin B$, show that $\cos(90° - A) = \sin A$ for any angle A.

(b) Using $\cos(A - B) = \cos A\cos B + \sin A\sin B$ on $\cos(90° - (90° - A))$, show that $\sin(90° - A) = \cos A$ for any angle A.

Solution

(a) $\cos(90° - A) = \cos 90°\cos A + \sin 90°\sin A$
$\qquad\qquad = 0 \times \cos A + 1 \times \sin A$
$\qquad\qquad = \sin A$

(b) $\cos(90° - (90° - A)) = \cos A$

Using **compound angle 1**: $\cos(90° - (90° - A))$
$= \cos 90°\cos(90° - A) + \sin 90°\sin(90° - A)$
$= 0 \times \cos(90° - A) + 1 \times \sin(90° - A)$
$= \sin(90° - A)$
$\therefore \sin(90° - A) = \cos A$

TIP

$\cos(90° - A) = \sin A$ and $\sin(90° - A) = \cos A$ for all angles A

Deductions

$\boxed{\cos(A + B)}$

1. Replacing A by A and B by $-B$ in **compound angle 1** gives:
$\cos(A - (-B)) = \cos A\cos(-B) + \sin A\sin(-B)$

$\boxed{\cos(A + B) = \cos A\cos B - \sin A\sin B}$ **[Compound angle 2]**

$\boxed{\sin(A+B)}$

2. Replacing A by $(90° − A)$ and B by B in **compound angle 1** gives:

$\cos((90° − A) − B) = \cos(90° − A)\cos B + \sin(90° − A)\sin B$

$\cos(90° − (A + B)) = \sin A \cos B + \cos A \sin B$

$$\boxed{\sin(A + B) = \sin A \cos B + \cos A \sin B}$$ **[Compound angle 3]**

$\boxed{\sin(A-B)}$

3. Replacing A by $(90° − A)$ and B by $(−B)$ in **compound angle 1** gives:

$\cos(90° − A − (−B)) = \cos(90° − A)\cos(−B) + \sin(90° − A)\sin(−B)$

$\cos(90° − (A − B)) = \sin A \cos B − \cos A \sin B$

$$\boxed{\sin(A − B) = \sin A \cos B − \cos A \sin B}$$ **[Compound angle 4]**

$\boxed{\tan(A+B)}$

4. $\tan(A+B) = \dfrac{\sin(A+B)}{\cos(A+B)} = \dfrac{\sin A \cos B + \cos A \sin B}{\cos A \cos B − \sin A \sin B}$

$= \dfrac{\dfrac{\sin A \cos B}{\cos A \cos B} + \dfrac{\cos A \sin B}{\cos A \cos B}}{\dfrac{\cos A \cos B}{\cos A \cos B} − \left(\dfrac{\sin A}{\cos A}\right)\left(\dfrac{\sin B}{\cos B}\right)}$ [Dividing above and below by $\cos A \cos B$]

> **TIP**
> ▲ You can replace A and B by any angle.

$= \dfrac{\tan A + \tan B}{1 − \tan A \tan B}$

$$\boxed{\tan(A + B) = \dfrac{\tan A + \tan B}{1 − \tan A \tan B}}$$ **[Compound angle 5]**

$\boxed{\tan(A-B)}$

5. If you replace A by A and B by $−B$ in **compound angle 5** gives:

$$\boxed{\tan(A − B) = \dfrac{\tan A − \tan B}{1 + \tan A \tan B}}$$ **[Compound angle 6]**

The six compound angle formulae are in the *Formulae and Tables* book.

EXAMPLE 2

If $\sin A = \frac{12}{13}$, A acute and $\cos B = \frac{4}{5}$, B acute, find:

(a) $\cos(A − B)$ **(b)** $\tan(A + B)$

Solution

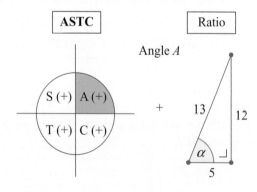

α is the reference angle for A and is equal to A as A is acute.

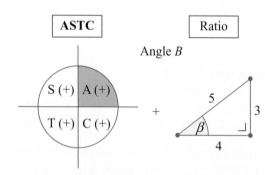

β is the reference angle for B and is equal to B.

(a) $\cos(A − B) = \cos A \cos B + \sin A \sin B$

$= \left(\dfrac{5}{13}\right)\left(\dfrac{4}{5}\right) + \left(\dfrac{12}{13}\right)\left(\dfrac{3}{5}\right) = \dfrac{20}{65} + \dfrac{36}{65} = \dfrac{56}{65}$

(b) $\tan(A + B) = \dfrac{\tan A + \tan B}{1 − \tan A \tan B}$

$= \dfrac{\dfrac{12}{5} + \dfrac{3}{4}}{1 − \dfrac{12}{5} × \dfrac{3}{4}}$ [Multiply above and below by 20.]

$= \dfrac{48 + 15}{20 − 36} = −\dfrac{63}{16}$

The negative sign in this answer means $(A + B)$ is obtuse.

EXAMPLE 3

If $\sin A = \frac{3}{5}$, A obtuse, and $\cos B = -\frac{8}{17}$, B obtuse, find:

(a) $\sin(A + B)$ (b) $\cos(A - B)$

Solution

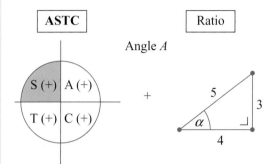

α is the reference angle for A.

(a) $\sin(A + B)$

$= \sin A \cos B + \cos A \sin B$

$= \left(\frac{3}{5}\right)\left(-\frac{8}{17}\right) + \left(-\frac{4}{5}\right)\left(\frac{15}{17}\right) = -\frac{24}{85} - \frac{60}{85} = -\frac{84}{85}$

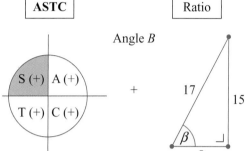

β is the reference angle for B.

(b) $\cos(A - B)$

$= \cos A \cos B + \sin A \sin B$

$= \left(-\frac{4}{5}\right)\left(-\frac{8}{17}\right) + \left(\frac{3}{5}\right)\left(\frac{15}{17}\right) = \frac{32}{85} + \frac{45}{85} = \frac{77}{85}$

EXAMPLE 4

Simplify the following:

(a) $\cos 47° \cos 23° + \sin 47° \sin 23°$ (b) $\cos(x - 30°) - \cos(x + 30°)$

Solution

(a) $\cos 47° \cos 23° + \sin 47° \sin 23°$

$= \cos(47° - 23°)$ [Using $\cos(A - B)$]

$= \cos 24°$

(b) $\cos(x - 30°) - \cos(x + 30°)$

$= (\cos x \cos 30° + \sin x \sin 30°) - (\cos x \cos 30° - \sin x \sin 30°)$

$= \left[(\cos x)\frac{\sqrt{3}}{2} + (\sin x)\frac{1}{2}\right] - \left[(\cos x)\frac{\sqrt{3}}{2} - (\sin x)\frac{1}{2}\right]$

$= \frac{\sqrt{3}}{2}\cos x + \frac{1}{2}\sin x - \frac{\sqrt{3}}{2}\cos x + \frac{1}{2}\sin x$

$= \sin x$

EXAMPLE 5

Show that $\tan 15° = 2 - \sqrt{3}$ without using your calculator.

Solution

$\tan 15° = \tan(60° - 45°)$

$= \frac{\tan 60° - \tan 45°}{1 + \tan 60° \tan 45°}$

$= \frac{\sqrt{3} - 1}{1 + \sqrt{3}} = \frac{(\sqrt{3} - 1)}{(1 + \sqrt{3})} \times \frac{(1 - \sqrt{3})}{(1 - \sqrt{3})}$

$= \frac{\sqrt{3} - 1 - 3 + \sqrt{3}}{-2} = \frac{2\sqrt{3} - 4}{-2}$

$= 2 - \sqrt{3}$

Multiple angle identities

Multiple angles are angles such as $2A$, $3A$, $4A$, etc.

There are seven identities involving $2A$ in the *Formulae and Tables* book. They can all be derived from the compound angle formulae and the fundamental trigonometric identity.

EXAMPLE 6

Prove the following:

(a) $\cos 2A = \cos^2 A - \sin^2 A$ **(b)** $\sin 2A = 2 \sin A \cos A$ **(c)** $\tan 2A = \dfrac{2 \tan A}{1 - \tan^2 A}$

Solution

(a) In the identity $\cos(A + B) = \cos A \cos B - \sin A \sin B$, replacing B by A and A by A gives:

$$\cos(A + A) = \cos A \cos A - \sin A \sin A$$
$$\cos 2A = \cos^2 A - \sin^2 A$$

(b) In the identity $\sin(A + B) = \sin A \cos B + \cos A \sin B$, replacing A by A and B by A gives:

$$\sin(A + A) = \sin A \cos A + \cos A \sin A$$
$$\sin 2A = 2 \sin A \cos A$$

(c) $\tan 2A = \dfrac{\sin 2A}{\cos 2A} = \dfrac{2 \sin A \cos A}{\cos^2 A - \sin^2 A}$ [Divide above and below by $\cos^2 A$.]

$$= \dfrac{\dfrac{2 \sin A \cos A}{\cos^2 A}}{\dfrac{\cos^2 A}{\cos^2 A} - \dfrac{\sin^2 A}{\cos^2 A}} = \dfrac{2\left(\dfrac{\sin A}{\cos A}\right)}{1 - \left(\dfrac{\sin A}{\cos A}\right)^2}$$

$$= \dfrac{2 \tan}{1 - \tan^2 A}$$

The seven multiple angle formulae are in the *Formulae and Tables* book.

$\cos 2A = \cos^2 A - \sin^2 A = (\cos A)^2 - (\sin A)^2$ **[Multiple angle 1]**

$\sin 2A = 2 \sin A \cos A$ **[Multiple angle 2]**

$\cos^2 A = \frac{1}{2}(1 + \cos 2A)$ **[Multiple angle 3]**

$\sin^2 A = \frac{1}{2}(1 - \cos 2A)$ **[Multiple angle 4]**

$\tan 2A = \dfrac{2 \tan A}{1 - \tan^2 A}$ **[Multiple angle 5]**

$\cos 2A = \dfrac{1 - \tan^2 A}{1 + \tan^2 A}$ **[Multiple angle 6]**

$\sin 2A = \dfrac{2 \tan A}{1 + \tan^2 A}$ **[Multiple angle 7]**

TIP

You can replace A by any angle in these seven multiple angle formulae.

You should know how to derive multiple angle formulae 3, 4, 5, 6 and 7 from multiple angle formulae 1 and 2.

EXAMPLE 7

If $\tan A = \frac{4}{3}$, A acute, find:

(a) $\sin 2A$ **(b)** $\cos 2A$ **(c)** $\tan 2A$

Solution

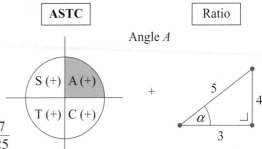

(a) $\sin 2A = 2 \sin A \cos A = 2\left(\frac{4}{5}\right)\left(\frac{3}{5}\right) = \frac{24}{25}$

(b) $\cos 2A = (\cos A)^2 - (\sin A)^2 = \left(\frac{3}{5}\right)^2 - \left(\frac{4}{5}\right)^2 = \frac{9}{25} - \frac{16}{25} = -\frac{7}{25}$

(c) $\tan 2A = \dfrac{2 \tan A}{1 - \tan^2 A} = \dfrac{2 \times \frac{4}{3}}{1 - \left(\frac{4}{3}\right)^2} = \dfrac{\frac{8}{3}}{1 - \frac{16}{9}} = -\dfrac{24}{7}$

α is the reference angle for A and is equal to A as A is acute.

EXAMPLE 8

If $\cos A = \frac{4}{5}$, A acute, find:

(a) $\cos\left(\frac{A}{2}\right)$ **(b)** $\sin\left(\frac{A}{2}\right)$ **(c)** $\tan\left(\frac{A}{2}\right)$

Solution

(a) In $\cos^2 A = \frac{1}{2}(1 + \cos 2A)$

replacing A by $\frac{A}{2}$ gives: $\cos^2\left(\frac{A}{2}\right) = \frac{1}{2}(1 + \cos A)$

$$= \frac{1}{2}\left(1 + \frac{4}{5}\right) = \frac{9}{10}$$

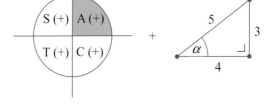

$\cos\left(\frac{A}{2}\right) = \dfrac{3}{\sqrt{10}}$ $\left[A \text{ acute} \Rightarrow \frac{A}{2} \text{ acute}\right]$

a is the reference angle for A and is equal to A as A is acute.

(b) In $\sin^2 A = \frac{1}{2}(1 - \cos 2A)$

replacing A by $\frac{A}{2}$ gives: $\sin^2\left(\frac{A}{2}\right) = \frac{1}{2}(1 - \cos A) = \frac{1}{2}\left(1 - \frac{4}{5}\right) = \frac{1}{10}$

$\sin\left(\frac{A}{2}\right) = \dfrac{1}{\sqrt{10}}$

(c) Using $\tan\left(\frac{A}{2}\right) = \dfrac{\sin\left(\frac{A}{2}\right)}{\cos\left(\frac{A}{2}\right)} = \dfrac{\frac{1}{\sqrt{10}}}{\frac{3}{\sqrt{10}}} = \dfrac{1}{3}$

Trigonometric conversions

There are elegant methods for converting products of trigonometric functions into sums of trigonometric functions and vice versa.

Products to sums

There are four product-to-sum formulae in the *Formulae and Tables*. These enable you to convert products of sines and cosines into sums of sines and cosines.

$$2 \cos A \cos B = \cos(A + B) + \cos(A - B) \quad \textbf{[Product-to-sum formula 1]}$$

$$2 \sin A \cos B = \sin(A + B) + \sin(A - B) \quad \textbf{[Product-to-sum formula 2]}$$

$$2 \sin A \sin B = \cos(A - B) - \cos(A + B) \quad \textbf{[Product-to-sum formula 3]}$$

$$2 \cos A \sin B = \sin(A + B) - \sin(A - B) \quad \textbf{[Product-to-sum formula 4]}$$

TIP

You can replace A and B by any angle in the four product-to-sum formulae.

These formulae are derived from the compound angle formulae by adding and subtracting them in pairs.

EXAMPLE 9

Use $\sin(A + B) = \sin A \cos B + \cos A \sin B$ and $\sin(A - B) = \sin A \cos B - \cos A \sin B$ to derive $2 \sin A \cos B = \sin(A + B) + \sin(A - B)$.

Solution

$\sin(A + B) = \sin A \cos B + \cos A \sin B ... \textbf{(1)}$

$\sin(A - B) = \sin A \cos B - \cos A \sin B ... \textbf{(2)}$

$\sin(A + B) + \sin(A - B) = 2 \sin A \cos B ... \textbf{(1)} + \textbf{(2)}$

$\therefore 2 \sin A \cos B = \sin(A + B) + \sin(A - B)$

Try to derive the other three product-to-sum formulae in the same way.

▸ $2 \sin x \cos 2x = \sin(x + 2x) + \sin(x - 2x) \quad \textbf{[Product-to-sum formula 2]}$

$$= \sin 3x + \sin(-x)$$

$$= \sin 3x - \sin x \quad \text{[Negative sign filters out]}$$

▸ $2 \cos 15° \sin 35° = \sin(15° + 35°) - \sin(15° - 35°) \quad \textbf{[Product-to-sum formula 4]}$

$$= \sin 50° - \sin(-20°)$$

$$= \sin 50° + \sin 20°$$

▸ $\sin 3B \sin 5B = \frac{1}{2} \times (2 \sin 3B \sin 5B) \quad \text{[You need a 2 to operate the formulae.]}$

$$= \frac{1}{2} \times (\cos(3B - 5B) - \cos(3B + 5B))$$

$$= \frac{1}{2}(\cos(-2B) - \cos(8B))$$

$$= \frac{1}{2}(\cos 2B - \cos 8B)$$

▸ $2 \cos(A + B) \cos(A - B) = \cos((A + B) + (A - B)) + \cos((A + B) - (A - B))$

$$= \cos 2A + \cos 2B$$

TIP

The product-to-sum formulae are used to convert products into sums. These conversions are very useful when differentiating and integrating products of trigonometric functions.

Sums to products

There are four sum-to-product formulae in the *Formulae and Tables* book. These enable you to convert sums of sines and cosines into products of sines and cosines.

$$\cos A + \cos B = 2 \cos\left(\frac{A+B}{2}\right)\cos\left(\frac{A-B}{2}\right) \quad \textbf{[Sum-to-product formula 1]}$$

$$\cos A - \cos B = -2 \sin\left(\frac{A+B}{2}\right)\sin\left(\frac{A-B}{2}\right) \quad \textbf{[Sum-to-product formula 2]}$$

$$\sin A + \sin B = 2 \sin\left(\frac{A+B}{2}\right)\cos\left(\frac{A-B}{2}\right) \quad \textbf{[Sum-to-product formula 3]}$$

$$\sin A - \sin B = 2 \cos\left(\frac{A+B}{2}\right)\sin\left(\frac{A-B}{2}\right) \quad \textbf{[Sum-to-product formula 4]}$$

TIP — You can replace A and B by any angle in the four sum-to-product formulae.

These formulae are derived from the four product-to-sum formulae by replacing A by $\left(\frac{A+B}{2}\right)$ and B by $\left(\frac{A-B}{2}\right)$.

EXAMPLE 10

Show that $2 \sin\left(\frac{A+B}{2}\right)\cos\left(\frac{A-B}{2}\right) = \sin A + \sin B$.

Solution

$$2 \sin\left(\frac{A+B}{2}\right)\cos\left(\frac{A-B}{2}\right) = \sin\left(\left(\frac{A+B}{2}\right)+\left(\frac{A-B}{2}\right)\right) + \sin\left(\left(\frac{A+B}{2}\right)-\left(\frac{A-B}{2}\right)\right) \quad \text{[Using \textbf{product-to-sum formula 1}]}$$

A B

$$= \sin A + \sin B$$
$$\therefore \sin A + \sin B = 2 \sin\left(\frac{A+B}{2}\right)\cos\left(\frac{A-B}{2}\right)$$

Try to derive the other three product-to-sum formulae.

▸ $\sin 3A + \sin 5A = 2 \sin\left(\frac{3A+5A}{2}\right)\cos\left(\frac{3A-5A}{2}\right)$
$$= 2 \sin 4A \cos A$$

▸ $\sin 75° - \sin 15° = 2 \cos\left(\frac{75°+15°}{2}\right)\sin\left(\frac{75°-15°}{2}\right)$
$$= 2 \cos 45° \sin 30°$$
$$= 2 \times \frac{1}{\sqrt{2}} \times \frac{1}{2} = \frac{\sqrt{2}}{2}$$

▸ $\cos(3A-B) - \cos(A+B) = -2 \sin\left(\frac{(3A-B)+(A+B)}{2}\right)\sin\left(\frac{(3A-B)-(A+B)}{2}\right)$
$$= -2 \sin 2A \sin(A-B)$$

TIP — The sum-to-product formulae are used to convert sums into products. These conversions are very useful for solving trigonometric equations.

Proving trigonometric identities

A trigonometric identity is a result which is true for **all** values of the angle(s).

Technique

To prove a trigonometric identity, you must show that the left-hand side (LHS) of the identity is equal to the right-hand side (RHS) by simplifying each side until they are identical.

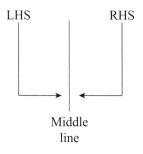

Middle line

Steps for proving trigonometric identities

1. Look at the **angles** in the identity and decide if you are dealing with single, compound or multiple angles.

2. Change all trigonometric functions into sine and cosine and do not change back.

3. Simplify each side using the trigonometric formulae in the tables.

4. If you see an expression on the LHS that is on the RHS or vice versa do not change it. (Hold onto it for dear life!)

5. Never cross over the middle line. Never do the same operation to both sides. These are not equations.

6. Use algebra throughout (factorising, tidying up) on each side of the identity.

EXAMPLE 11

Prove that $\dfrac{1 + \cos A}{\sin A} + \dfrac{\sin A}{1 + \cos A} = \dfrac{2}{\sin A}$.

Solution

All angles are single angles A (no multiple or compound angles).

LHS	RHS
$\dfrac{(1 + \cos A)}{\sin A} + \dfrac{\sin A}{(1 + \cos A)}$	$\dfrac{2}{\sin A}$
$= \dfrac{(1 + \cos A)^2 + \sin^2 A}{\sin A (1 + \cos A)}$	
$= \dfrac{1 + 2\cos A + \cos^2 A + \sin^2 A}{\sin A(1 + \cos A)}$	
$= \dfrac{2 + 2\cos A}{\sin A(1 + \cos A)}$	
$= \dfrac{2(1 + \cos A)}{\sin A(1 + \cos A)}$	
$= \dfrac{2}{\sin A}$	

$$\therefore \text{LHS} = \text{RHS}$$

EXAMPLE 12

Prove that $\cos(A + B)\cos(A - B) = \cos^2 A - \sin^2 B$.

Solution

There are compound angles on the LHS and single angles on the RHS.

LHS	**RHS**
$\cos(A + B)\cos(A - B)$	$\cos^2 A - \sin^2 B$
$= (\cos A \cos B - \sin A \sin B)(\cos A \cos B + \sin A \sin B)$	
$= \cos^2 A \cos^2 B - \sin^2 A \sin^2 B \quad [\text{Keep } \cos^2 A \text{ and } \sin^2 B.]$	
$= \cos^2 A(1 - \sin^2 B) - (1 - \cos^2 A)\sin^2 B$	
$= \cos^2 A - \cos^2 A \sin^2 B - \sin^2 B + \cos^2 A \sin^2 B$	
$= \cos^2 A - \sin^2 B$	

$$\therefore \text{LHS} = \text{RHS}$$

Can you think of an alternative method?

EXAMPLE 13

Prove that $\cos 2A = \dfrac{1 - \tan^2 A}{1 + \tan^2 A}$.

Solution

There is a multiple angle on the LHS and a single angle on the RHS.

LHS	**RHS**
$\cos 2A$	$\dfrac{1 - \tan^2 A}{1 + \tan^2 A}$
$= \cos^2 A - \sin^2 A$	$= 1 - \dfrac{\dfrac{\sin^2 A}{\cos^2 A}}{1 + \dfrac{\sin^2 A}{\cos^2 A}} \quad [\text{Multiply above and below by } \cos^2 A.]$
	$= \dfrac{\cos^2 A - \sin^2 A}{\cos^2 A + \sin^2 A}$
	$= \dfrac{\cos^2 A - \sin^2 A}{1}$

$$\therefore \text{LHS} = \text{RHS}$$

EXAMPLE 14

Prove that $\sin 3A = 3 \sin A - 4 \sin^3 A$.

Solution

There is a multiple angle on the LHS and a single angle on the RHS.

LHS

$\sin(3A)$

$= \sin(A + 2A)$ [This is a compound angle.]

$= \sin A \cos 2A + \cos A \sin 2A$

$= \sin A (\cos^2 A - \sin^2 A) + \cos A (2 \sin A \cos A)$

$= \sin A \cos^2 A - \sin^3 A + 2 \sin A \cos^2 A$

$= 3 \sin A \cos^2 A - \sin^3 A$

$= 3 \sin A (1 - \sin^2 A) - \sin^3 A$ [Keep $\sin A$ and $\sin^3 A$.]

$= 3 \sin A - 3 \sin^3 A - \sin^3 A$

$= 3 \sin A - 4 \sin^3 A$

RHS

$3 \sin A - 4 \sin^3 A$

$\therefore$ LHS = RHS

EXERCISE 10

1. If $\sin A = \frac{4}{5}$ and $\cos B = \frac{5}{13}$, A, B acute, find:

   (a) $\sin(A + B)$
   (b) $\sin(A - B)$
   (c) $\cos(A + B)$
   (d) $\cos(A - B)$
   (e) $\tan(A + B)$
   (f) $\tan(A - B)$

2. If $\sin A = \frac{3}{5}$ and $\tan B = \frac{8}{15}$, A, B acute, find:

   (a) $\sin(A + B)$
   (b) $\sin(A - B)$
   (c) $\cos(A + B)$
   (d) $\cos(A - B)$
   (e) $\tan(A + B)$
   (f) $\tan(A - B)$

3. If $\sin A = \frac{15}{17}$ and $\cos B = -\frac{3}{5}$, A and B obtuse, find:

   (a) $\sin(A + B)$
   (b) $\cos(A - B)$
   (c) $\tan(A + B)$

4. Simplify the following as the sine or cosine of a single angle:

   (a) $\cos 48° \cos 20° + \sin 48° \sin 20°$
   (b) $\cos 25° \cos 50° - \sin 25° \sin 50°$
   (c) $\sin(-5) \cos 3 + \cos 5 \sin(-3)$
   (d) $\cos 10° \sin 15° - \sin 10° \cos 15°$
   (e) $\sin 56° \cos 4° + \cos 56° \sin 4°$

5. Simplify the following:

   (a) $\cos(x - 30°) + \cos(x + 30°)$
   (b) $\sin(45° + x) - \sin(45° - x)$
   (c) $\cos(45° - A) - \sin(45° - A)$
   (d) $\sin(60° + x) + \sin(60° - x)$

6. Show that:

   (a) $\cos 15° = \dfrac{\sqrt{2} + \sqrt{6}}{4}$

   (b) $\sin\left(\dfrac{7\pi}{12}\right) = \dfrac{\sqrt{2} + \sqrt{6}}{4}$

   (c) $\tan 75° = 2 + \sqrt{3}$

   (d) $\tan 105° = -2 - \sqrt{3}$

7. If $\sin A = \dfrac{5}{13}$ and $\cos B = \dfrac{4}{5}$, A, B and $(A + B)$ acute, find:

   (a) $\sin(A + B)$

   (b) $\cos(180° - A)$

   (c) $\sin(270° + B)$

   (d) $\cos(90° - (A + B))$

   (e) $\sin(180° + (A + B))$

8. If A, B and C are the angles of a triangle, where $\sin(A + B) = \dfrac{3}{5}$, $(A + B)$ acute, find $\sin C$ and $\cos C$.

9. If $\tan(A + B) = \dfrac{1}{7}$ and $\tan A = 3$, find $\tan B$.

10. If $\cos A = \dfrac{15}{17}$, A acute, find:

    (a) $\cos 2A$ (c) $\tan 2A$

    (b) $\sin 2A$

    In what quadrant is $2A$?

11. If $\cos A = -\dfrac{3}{5}$, A obtuse, find:

    (a) $\cos 2A$ (c) $\tan 2A$

    (b) $\sin 2A$

    In what quadrant is $2A$?

12. (a) If $\sin A = \dfrac{12}{13}$, A acute, find $\cos\left(\dfrac{A}{2}\right)$, $\sin\left(\dfrac{A}{2}\right)$ and $\tan\left(\dfrac{A}{2}\right)$.

    (b) If $\cos A = \dfrac{2}{3}$, A acute, find $\cos\left(\dfrac{A}{2}\right)$, $\sin\left(\dfrac{A}{2}\right)$ and $\tan\left(\dfrac{A}{2}\right)$.

    (c) If $\tan A = \dfrac{3}{4}$, A acute, find $\cos\left(\dfrac{A}{2}\right)$, $\sin\left(\dfrac{A}{2}\right)$ and $\tan\left(\dfrac{A}{2}\right)$.

13. If $\sin A = \dfrac{3}{5}$, A and $2A$ acute, find:

    (a) $\sin 2A$ (c) $\sin 3A$

    (b) $\cos 2A$ (d) $\sin 4A$

14. If $\cos A = \dfrac{5}{13}$, A acute, find:

    (a) $\cos 2A$ (b) $\sin 2A$ (c) $\cos 4A$

15. If $\tan A = \dfrac{1}{2}$, A acute, find:

    (a) $\tan 2A$ (b) $\tan 3A$ (c) $\tan 4A$

16. Find $\tan 2\alpha$ if $\sin \alpha = \dfrac{3}{5}$, α acute, without using a calculator or tables.

17. If $\cos A = \dfrac{7}{25}$, find $\tan\left(\dfrac{A}{2}\right)$, A acute, without using a calculator.

18. Express the following as sums:

    (a) $2 \sin 3\alpha \cos 5\alpha$

    (b) $2 \cos 4A \cos A$

    (c) $2 \cos 4x \sin 6x$

    (d) $2 \sin(A + B) \sin(A - B)$

    (e) $2 \cos 3A \sin 4A$

    (f) $2 \sin(4A + 2B) \sin(2A - 4B)$

    (g) $\cos(2A + B) \cos(B - 2A)$

    (h) $\cos 3x \cos 5x$

    (i) $2 \sin\left(\dfrac{t}{2}\right) \cos\left(\dfrac{t}{2}\right)$

    (j) $\sin A \sin A$

19. Express the following as products:

    (a) $\sin 7B + \sin 2B$

    (b) $\sin 5\theta - \sin 3\theta$

    (c) $\cos 2x + \cos x$

    (d) $\cos 7x - \cos x$

    (e) $3 \cos 5A - 3 \cos 2A$

    (f) $\dfrac{1}{4} \cos 7A - \dfrac{1}{4} \cos 5A$

    (g) $\sin 50° - \sin 30°$

    (h) $\cos 60° - \cos 20°$

    (i) $\sin(A + B) - \sin(A - B)$

    (j) $\sin(x - 60°) + \sin(x + 60°)$

20. Prove that $\dfrac{\sin A + \sin 3A}{\cos A + \cos 3A} = \tan 2A$.

21. Prove that $\dfrac{\sin 5A + \sin 3A + \sin A}{\cos 5A + \cos 3A + \cos A} = \tan 3A$.

22. Prove that $\sin^2 5A - \sin^2 2A = \sin 7A \sin 3A$.

23. Prove that $\cos 70° + \cos 50° - \cos 10° = 0$.

24. Prove that $\sin A \sin(60° - A) \sin(60° + A)$
$= \dfrac{1}{4}\sin 3A$.

25. Prove the following identities:

(a) $2\cos^2 A - 1 = 1 - 2\sin^2 A$

(b) $\left(\dfrac{\cos A}{\sin A} + \dfrac{1}{\sin A}\right)^2 = \dfrac{1 + \cos A}{1 - \cos A}$

(c) $\cos^4 A - \sin^4 A = \cos^2 A - \sin^2 A$

(d) $\dfrac{2\tan A}{1 + \tan^2 A} = 2\sin A \cos A$

(e) $\dfrac{1 - \tan^2 A}{1 + \tan^2 A} = 1 - 2\sin^2 A$

(f) $\dfrac{\cos^3 A - \sin^3 A}{\cos A - \sin A} = 1 + \sin A \cos A$

(g) $\dfrac{1 + \sin A}{1 - \sin A} - \dfrac{1 - \sin A}{1 + \sin A} = \dfrac{4\sin A}{\cos^2 A}$

26. Prove the following identities:

(a) $2\cos(45° + A)\cos(45° - A) = \cos^2 A - \sin^2 A$

(b) $\sin^2(A + B) - \sin^2(A - B) = \sin 2A \sin 2B$

27. Prove the following identities:

(a) $\tan A + \dfrac{1}{\tan A} = \dfrac{2}{\sin 2A}$

(b) $\dfrac{1}{\cos 2A} = \dfrac{1}{2\cos^2 A - 1}$

(c) $(\sin A + \cos A)^2 = 1 + \sin 2A$

(d) $\dfrac{\sin A}{\cos A - \sin A} + \dfrac{\cos A}{\cos A + \sin A} = \dfrac{1}{\cos 2A}$

(e) $\cos 3A = 4\cos^3 A - 3\cos A$

(f) $\cos 4A = 8\cos^4 A - 8\cos^2 A + 1$

9.2 Trigonometric equations

The graphs of $y = \sin x$ and $y = \dfrac{1}{2}$ intersect at an infinite number of points for $x \geq 0$, $x \in \mathbb{R}$.

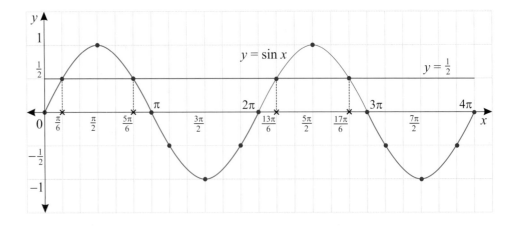

There is one solution $\alpha_1 = \dfrac{\pi}{6}$ in the first quadrant of the unit circle and another solution $\beta_1 = \dfrac{5\pi}{6}$ in the second quadrant of the unit circle. There are no solutions in the other two quadrants.

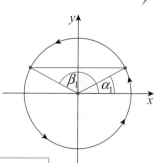

These two so-called **basic solutions** are then replicated by adding multiples of 2π rad to them.

This means that there is an infinite number of solutions to the equation $\sin x = \frac{1}{2}$ for $x \geq 0$, $x \in \mathbb{R}$.

Basic solution: $\dfrac{\pi}{6}$
α_1: $\sin \dfrac{\pi}{6} = \dfrac{1}{2}$
α_2: $\sin \dfrac{13\pi}{6} = \dfrac{1}{2}$
α_3: $\sin \dfrac{25\pi}{6} = \dfrac{1}{2}$
$\vdots$

Basic solution: $\dfrac{5\pi}{6}$
β_1: $\sin \dfrac{5\pi}{6} = \dfrac{1}{2}$
β_2: $\sin \dfrac{17\pi}{6} = \dfrac{1}{2}$
β_3: $\sin \dfrac{29\pi}{6} = \dfrac{1}{2}$
$\vdots$

$$\therefore \sin\left(\frac{\pi}{6} + 2n\pi\right) = \frac{1}{2}, \; n \in \mathbb{N}_0 \qquad \therefore \sin\left(\frac{5\pi}{6} + 2n\pi\right) = \frac{1}{2}, \; n \in \mathbb{N}_0$$

This is because $\sin x$ is a function which replicates itself in steps of 2π:
$\sin x = \sin(x + 2\pi) = \sin(x + 4\pi) = \ldots = \sin(x + 2n\pi)$, $n \in \mathbb{N}_0$ for all $x \in \mathbb{R}$.
$\sin x$ is a periodic function. We will examine periodic functions in Section 9.3.

Steps for solving trigonometric equations

Use the following steps to solve trigonometric equations of the form
$r \sin kx = p$ and $r \cos kx = p$:

1. Isolate the trigonometric function on one side: $\sin kx = \dfrac{p}{r}$ or $\cos kx = \dfrac{p}{r}$.

2. Using **ASTC** and the sign of $\dfrac{p}{r}$, mark the two quadrants which contain the two **basic** angles.

3. To find the reference angle θ in the first quadrant for the basic angles, find $\sin^{-1}\left|\dfrac{p}{r}\right|$ or $\cos^{-1}\left|\dfrac{p}{r}\right|$ on your calculator.

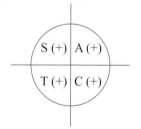

4. Hence, find the two basic angles from the following possibilities, depending on what quadrant they are in:

$$kx = \begin{cases} \theta \; \text{(First)} \\ 180° - \theta \; \text{(Second)} \\ 180° + \theta \; \text{(Third)} \\ 360° - \theta \; \text{(Fourth)} \end{cases}$$

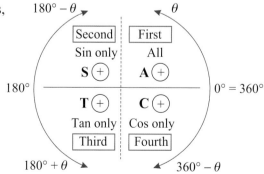

5. Add $360°$ or 2π to each one of these basic angle solutions as many times as required so that when you divide by k the answers are within the given range.

6. If asked to get the **general solution**, add $2n\pi$, $n \in \mathbb{N}_0$, to each of these basic angles and divide by k.

EXAMPLE 15

Find the general solution of the equation $\sin 2x = -\frac{1}{2}$.

Solution

$\sin 2x = -\frac{1}{2}$

The solutions lie in the third and fourth quadrants where sin is negative.

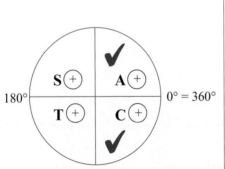

Reference angle: $\theta = \sin^{-1}\left|-\frac{1}{2}\right| = 30° = \frac{\pi}{6}$

$$2x = \begin{cases} 180° + 30° = \mathbf{210°} \; or \; \pi + \dfrac{\pi}{6} = \dfrac{\mathbf{7\pi}}{\mathbf{6}} & \text{[Basic angle]} \\[3mm] 360° - 30° = \mathbf{330°} \; or \; 2\pi - \dfrac{\pi}{6} = \dfrac{\mathbf{11\pi}}{\mathbf{6}} & \text{[Basic angle]} \end{cases}$$

$$2x = \begin{cases} \dfrac{7\pi}{6} + 2n\pi, \; n \in \mathbb{N}_0 \\[3mm] \dfrac{11\pi}{6} + 2n\pi, \; n \in \mathbb{N}_0 \end{cases}$$

$$x = \begin{cases} \dfrac{7\pi}{12} + n\pi, \; n \in \mathbb{N}_0 \\[3mm] \dfrac{11\pi}{12} + n\pi, \; n \in \mathbb{N}_0 \end{cases}$$

For negative solutions as well as positive ones, just say $n \in \mathbb{Z}$.

EXAMPLE 16

Solve $2\cos 3x = \sqrt{3}$, $0° \leq x \leq 360°$.

Solution

$\cos 3x = +\dfrac{\sqrt{3}}{2}$

The solutions lie in the first and fourth quadrants where cos is positive.

$\theta = \cos^{-1}\left|\dfrac{\sqrt{3}}{2}\right| = 30°$

$$3x = \begin{cases} \mathbf{30°}, \, 390°, \, 750°, \, 1110°... \text{[30° and 330° are the} \\ \mathbf{330°}, \, 690°, \, 1050°,... \quad \text{two basic angles.]} \end{cases}$$

$$x = \begin{cases} 10°, \, 130°, \, 250°, \, 370° \\ 110°, \, 230°, \, 350° \end{cases}$$

$x = 10°, \, 110°, \, 130°, \, 230°, \, 250°, \, 350°$

Products to sums

The solutions of $f(x) \times g(x) = 0$, where $f(x)$ and $g(x)$ are functions of x, are also the solutions of $f(x) = 0$ and $g(x) = 0$. This is known as the zero rule: $f(x) \times g(x) = 0$ $\Rightarrow f(x) = 0$ or $g(x) = 0$

▸ Solve $x^2 - 5x + 6 = 0$

To solve this equation, convert the sum of the left-hand side of the equation to a product.

Sum: $x^2 - 5x + 6 = 0$

Product: $(x - 3)(x - 2) = 0$

$\Rightarrow (x - 3) = 0$ or $(x - 2) = 0$

$x = 2, 3$

To solve equations involving sums of trigonometric functions, convert them into a product first using the formulae in the *Formulae and Tables* book.

EXAMPLE 17

Solve $\sin 8x + \sin 4x = 0$, $0 \le x \le \pi$.

Solution

Using the formula:

$$\sin A + \sin B = 2 \sin\left(\frac{A+B}{2}\right) \cos\left(\frac{A-B}{2}\right)$$

$\sin 8x + \sin 4x = 2 \sin 6x \cos 2x$

$\therefore \sin 8x + \sin 4x = 0$

$\Rightarrow 2 \sin 6x \cos 2x = 0$

$\Rightarrow \sin 6x = 0$ or $\cos 2x = 0$

$\sin 6x = 0$ $\qquad$ $\cos 2x = 0$

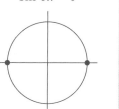

$6x = \begin{cases} \mathbf{0}, 2\pi, 4\pi, 6\pi \\ \boldsymbol{\pi}, 3\pi, 5\pi,\dots \end{cases}$ $\qquad$ $2x = \begin{cases} \dfrac{\boldsymbol{\pi}}{\mathbf{2}}, \dfrac{5\pi}{2} \\[2mm] \dfrac{\mathbf{3\pi}}{\mathbf{2}}, \dfrac{7\pi}{2} \end{cases}$

$x = \begin{cases} 0, \dfrac{\pi}{3}, \dfrac{2\pi}{3}, \pi \\[2mm] \dfrac{\pi}{6}, \dfrac{\pi}{2}, \dfrac{5\pi}{6} \end{cases}$ $\qquad$ $x = \begin{cases} \dfrac{\pi}{4}, \dfrac{5\pi}{4} \\[2mm] \dfrac{3\pi}{4}, \dfrac{7\pi}{4} \end{cases}$

The solutions in ascending order of size are:

$$x = 0, \frac{\pi}{6}, \frac{\pi}{4}, \frac{\pi}{3}, \frac{\pi}{2}, \frac{2\pi}{3}, \frac{3\pi}{4}, \frac{5\pi}{6}, \pi$$

EXERCISE 11

1. Solve for x.

   (a) $\cos x = -\dfrac{1}{2}$, $0 \le x \le 2\pi$

   (b) $\sin 2x = -\dfrac{\sqrt{3}}{2}$, $0° \le x \le 180°$

   (c) $\cos 3x = 0.5$, $0° \le x \le 180°$

   (d) $\sin\left(\dfrac{x}{2}\right) = 0.5$, $0 \le x \le 6\pi$

   (e) $4 \cos 2x = 1$, $0 \le x \le 360°$, to the nearest degree

   (f) $\cos 2x = -0.5592$, $0° \le x \le 360°$, to the nearest degree

   (g) $\sin(2x + 46°) = 0.9272$, $0° \le x \le 360°$, to the nearest degree

   (h) $\cos(3x + 360°) = 1$, $0° \le x \le 360°$

   (i) $\sin^2 x = 1$, $0 \le x \le 2\pi$

   (j) $2 \cos 4x = -\sqrt{2}$, $0 < x < 180°$

2. Find the general solution, in terms of π, of the following:

   (a) $\sin 3x = \dfrac{1}{2}$, $x > 0$, $x \in \mathbb{R}$

   (b) $\cos 2x = -\dfrac{1}{\sqrt{2}}$, $x > 0$, $x \in \mathbb{R}$

   (c) $\cos 4x = 0$, $x > 0$, $x \in \mathbb{R}$

   (d) $\sin 5x = 0$, $x > 0$, $x \in \mathbb{R}$

   (e) $\cos 3x = -1$, $x > 0$, $x \in \mathbb{R}$

3. Solve the following by changing into products:

   (a) $\cos x = \cos 3x$, $0° \le x \le 180°$

   (b) $\sin x - \sin 5x = 0$, $0° \le x \le 180°$

   (c) $\cos 2x + \cos 4x = 0$, $0 \le x \le \pi$

   (d) $\sin 2x + \sin 5x = 0$, $0 \le x \le \pi$

4. (a) By factorising $6 \sin^2 x + \sin x - 1$, solve $6 \sin^2 x + \sin x - 1 = 0$, $0° \le x \le 360°$, giving your answer correct to one decimal place.

   (b) Using $\cos^2 x = 1 - \sin^2 x$, write $3 \cos^2 x + 4 \sin x$ as a quadratic in $\sin x$. Hence, solve $3 \cos^2 x + 4 \sin x = 4$, $0 \le x \le 180°$, giving your answer correct to one decimal place.

   (c) Using $\cos 2x = \cos^2 x - \sin^2 x$, write $\cos 2x + \sin x$ as a quadratic in $\sin x$. Hence, solve $\cos 2x + \sin x = 0$, $0° \le x \le 360°$.

   (d) Express $\sin 3x - \sin x$ as a product. Hence, solve $\sin 3x + \cos 2x - \sin x = 0$, $0° \le x \le 360°$.

   (e) For the graph of $y = \sin 4x - \sin x$, find all x intercepts in the interval $[0, 360°]$.

   (f) This is the graph of $y = \sin 3x \cos 2x$. Find P, Q and R in terms of π.

   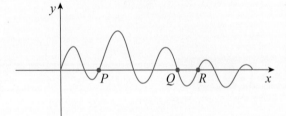

5. A golfer hits a ball with an initial speed $u = 70$ m/s from O. It lands at P.

   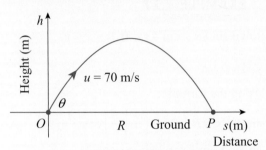

   The distance $R = |OP|$ the ball travels parallel to the ground depends on the angle θ of launch and is given by $R = \dfrac{u^2 \sin 2\theta}{g}$, where $g = 9 \cdot 8$ m/s². If the golfer wants the ball to travel 250 m, at what angles must she strike the ball?
   The maximum height H the ball reaches above the ground is given by $H = \dfrac{u^2 \sin^2 \theta}{g}$. Find at what angle the ball must be hit to reach a maximum height of 375 m.

9.3 Periodic trigonometric functions

Periodic phenomena repeat themselves regularly. They occur widely in the real world.

Examples

- The number of daylight hours at a certain location
- The depth of water in a harbour due to the tides
- The phases of the moon
- The height of a swing
- The flowering of plants

WORKED EXAMPLE Periodic functions in action

The depth d of water in metres at a harbour entrance was recorded every hour for 15 hours.

The data collected is shown below:

Time t (h)	0	1	2	3	4	5	6	7	8	9	10	11	12	13	14	15
Depth d (m)	4	4·5	4·86	5·0	4·86	4·5	4	3·5	3·13	3	3·13	3·5	4	4·5	4·86	5

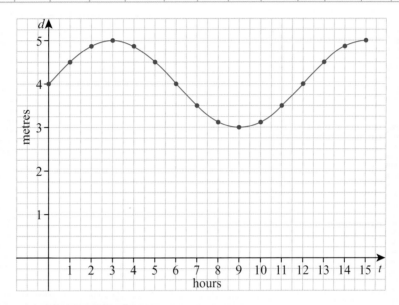

Clearly, this function starts to replicate (repeat) itself after 12 hours. One full cycle (wave) is 12 hours long. This is known as the **period** of the function.

The maximum value of d is 5 m and the minimum value of d is 3 m and all values of d are between 3 m and 5 m. These values are in the interval [3, 5] which is known as the **range** of the function.

Consider the following function: $y = f(x), x \in \mathbb{R}$

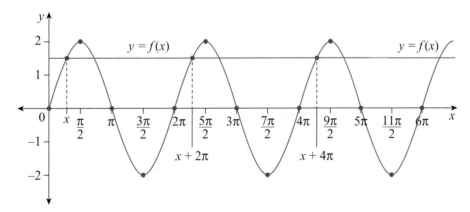

$f(x) = f(x + 2\pi) = f(x + 4\pi) \ldots$ for **all** $x \in \mathbb{R}$.

The period P is the length of one cycle (wave).

$\therefore P = 2\pi$, because $f(x) = f(x + 2\pi)$ for **all** $x \in \mathbb{R}$.

It is true that $f(0) = f(0 + \pi) = f(0 + 2\pi) = f(0 + 3\pi) = \ldots = 0$. This might lead you to think that π is the period of this function.

But π is not the period, as this is **not true for all** $x \in \mathbb{R}$. For example, $f\left(\frac{\pi}{2}\right) \neq f\left(\frac{\pi}{2} + \pi\right)$.

A function $y = f(x)$ is periodic if $f(x) = f(x + P)$ for all values of x in the domain of the function. The smallest non-zero value of P for which $f(x) = f(x + P)$ for all values of x in the domain of the function is the **period** of the function.

The range of the three trigonometric functions

WORKED EXAMPLE

Range of the cosine and sine functions

The range of values of $\cos A$ and $\sin A$ can be calculated by reference to the unit circle:

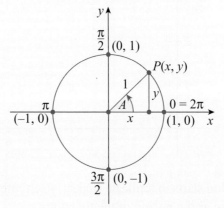

$$\cos A = \frac{x}{1} = x \qquad \text{and} \qquad \sin A = \frac{y}{1} = y.$$

As the point $P(x, y)$ moves around the circle in an anticlockwise direction, x takes on all values between -1 and $+1$.

As the point $P(x, y)$ moves around the circle in an anticlockwise direction, y takes on all values between -1 and $+1$.

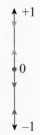

$-1 \leq x \leq 1 \Rightarrow -1 \leq \cos A \leq 1$

This means if $b > 0$, $-b \leq b \cos A \leq b$

and $a - b \leq a + b \cos A \leq a + b$.

$-1 \leq y \leq 1 \Rightarrow -1 \leq \sin A \leq 1$

This means if $b > 0$, $-b \leq b \sin A \leq b$

and $a - b \leq a + b \sin A \leq a + b$.

The range of a periodic function is the interval of values the function can have.

The maximum value of both $a + b\cos A$ and $a + b\sin A$ is $(a + b)$ if $b > 0$ and $(a - b)$ if $b < 0$.

The minimum value of both $a + b\cos A$ and $a + b\sin A$ is $(a - b)$ if $b > 0$ and $(a + b)$ if $b < 0$.

The range of $a + b\cos A$ and $a + b\sin A$ is always written as the interval [Min, Max] with the minimum value on the left and the maximum value on the right in the square brackets.

The angle A has no influence on the range.

> For $a + b\cos A$ and $a + b\sin A$:
>
> Range $= [a - b, a + b]$, if $b > 0$
>
> **but**
>
> Range $= [a + b, a - b]$, if $b < 0$

▸ The range of $3\cos 2x = [-3, 3]$.

▸ The range of $5 + 3\cos(45° - \theta) = [5 - 3, 5 + 3] = [2, 8]$.

▸ The range of $5 - 3\cos\left(\dfrac{x}{4}\right) = [5 + (-3), 5 - (-3)] = [2, 8]$.

▸ The range of $-3 + \dfrac{2}{5}\cos 5B = \left[-3 - \dfrac{2}{5}, -3 + \dfrac{2}{5}\right] = \left[-\dfrac{17}{5}, -\dfrac{13}{5}\right]$.

EXAMPLE 18

If the range of $f(x) = a + b\cos 4x$, $x \in \mathbb{R}$, is $[2, 8]$, find a, b if $b > 0$.

Solution

Range $= [a - b, a + b]$

$a - b = 2$

$a + b = 8$

$2a = 10$

$\therefore a = 5$

$b = 3$

$a + b\cos 4x = 5 + 3\cos 4x$

EXAMPLE 19

If the range of $f(x) = a + b\sin 2x$, $x \in \mathbb{R}$, is $[-5, 7]$, find a and b if $b < 0$.

Solution

Range $= [a + b, a - b]$

$a + b = -5$

$a - b = 7$

$2a = 2$

$a = 1$

$b = -6$

$a + b\sin 2x = 1 - 6\sin 2x$

WORKED EXAMPLE Range of the tan function

The range of values of tan A can be calculated by reference to the unit circle:

$$\tan A = \frac{\sin A}{\cos A} = \frac{y}{x}$$

As the point $P(x, y)$ moves around the circle in an anticlockwise

direction, x varies between -1 and $+1$ but $\frac{y}{x}$ varies between $-\infty$ and $+\infty$.

As A goes from 0 to $\frac{\pi}{2}$, x goes from 1 to 0 and y goes from 0 to 1.

Therefore, $\frac{y}{x}$ goes from 0 to $+\infty$.

As A goes from $\frac{\pi}{2}$ to π, x goes from 0 to -1 and y goes from 1 to 0.

Therefore, $\frac{y}{x}$ goes from $-\infty$ to 0.

As A goes from π to $\frac{3\pi}{2}$, x goes from -1 to 0 and y goes from 0 to -1. Therefore, $\frac{y}{x}$ goes from 0 to $+\infty$.

As A goes from $\frac{3\pi}{2}$ to 2π, x goes from 0 to 1 and y goes from -1 to 0. Therefore, $\frac{y}{x}$ goes from $-\infty$ to 0.

$\therefore$ Range of tan A is $[-\infty, \infty]$.

The range of $a + b \tan A$ is $[-\infty, \infty]$.

The period of the three trigonometric functions

1. $y = \cos x$

The graph of $y = \cos x$, $0° \leq x \leq 720°$ is shown below.

0	0°	90°	180°	270°	360°	450°	540°	630°	720°
cos x	1	0	−1	0	1	0	−1	0	1

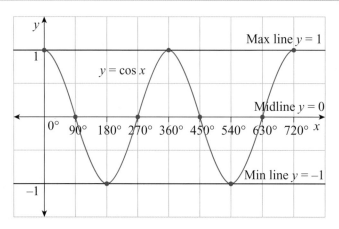

You might think that 180° is the period as clearly

$$\cos(90°) = \cos(90° + 180°) = \cos(90° + 360°) = \ldots = 0.$$

This is not true for all values of $x \in \mathbb{R}$ as it is not true for $x = 0°$: $\cos(0°) \neq \cos(0° + 180°)$

The period is 360° as $\cos x = \cos(x + 360°)$ **for all** $x \in \mathbb{R}$.

The curve is continuous with range $[-1, 1]$.

It has a maximum value of 1.

It has a minimum value of -1.

The midline is the line halfway between the maximum and minimum values.

The midline has the equation $y = \dfrac{\text{Max} + \text{Min}}{2} = \dfrac{1 + (-1)}{2} = 0$

KEY TERM

The **amplitude** r is the distance between the maximum line and the midline.

Amplitude $r = \left|\text{Maximum value} - \text{Midline value}\right| = 1 - 0 = 1$

For $y = \cos x$: Period = 360° = 2π rad, range $[-1, 1]$, midline $y = 0$, amplitude $r = 1$

WORKED EXAMPLE Calculating the period 1

What is the period of $y = \cos 3x$?

$\cos 3x = \cos(3x + 2\pi) = \cos(3x + 4\pi) = \ldots$ for all $x \in \mathbb{R}$.

$\Rightarrow \cos 3x = \cos 3\left(x + \dfrac{2\pi}{3}\right) = \cos 3\left(x + \dfrac{4\pi}{3}\right) = \ldots$

$\cos 3x$ has the same value at x, $x + \dfrac{2\pi}{3}$, $x + \dfrac{4\pi}{3}$, ... for all $x \in \mathbb{R}$.

$\dfrac{2\pi}{3}$ is the smallest value of x at which the function repeats itself.

Period $P = \dfrac{2\pi}{3}$

As $3x$ goes from 0 to 2π through a full cycle, x goes from 0 to $\dfrac{2\pi}{3}$.

TIP

The period of $y = \cos(kx + \alpha)$ is still $\dfrac{2\pi}{k}$. α has no influence on the period.

In general, for $y = \cos kx$ the period $P = \dfrac{2\pi}{k} = \dfrac{360°}{k}$.

▸ $y = 2\cos x$: Period $P = \dfrac{2\pi}{1} = 2\pi$, Range = $[-2, 2]$

▸ $y = -3\cos 2x$: Period $P = \dfrac{2\pi}{2} = \pi$, Range = $[-3, 3]$

▸ $y = 4 + 2\cos 5x$, Period $P = \dfrac{2\pi}{5}$, Range = $[2, 6]$

▸ $y = -3 - 5\cos\left(\dfrac{\pi x}{50}\right)$, Period $P = \dfrac{2\pi}{\left(\dfrac{\pi}{50}\right)} = 100$, Range = $[-8, 2]$

2. $y = \sin x$

The graph of $y = \sin x$, $0 \le x \le 4\pi$ is shown below.

x	0	$\dfrac{\pi}{2}$	π	$\dfrac{3\pi}{2}$	2π	$\dfrac{5\pi}{2}$	3π	$\dfrac{7\pi}{2}$	4π
$\sin x$	0	1	0	−1	0	1	0	−1	0

ACTIVITY 23

ACTION
Finding the range and period of certain trigonometric functions

OBJECTIVE
To find the range and period of $a + b\cos kx$ and $a + b\sin kx$

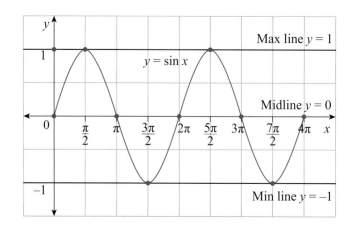

For $y = \sin x$: Period $P = 360° = 2\pi$ rad, range $[-1, 1]$, midline $y = 0$, amplitude $r = 1$

WORKED EXAMPLE Calculating the period 2

What is the period of $y = \sin 4x$?

$\sin 4x = \sin(4x + 2\pi) = \sin(4x + 4\pi) = \sin(4x + 6\pi) = \ldots$ for all $x \in \mathbb{R}$.

$\Rightarrow \sin 4x = \sin 4\left(x + \dfrac{2\pi}{4}\right) = \sin 4\left(x + \dfrac{4\pi}{4}\right) = \sin 4\left(x + \dfrac{6\pi}{4}\right) = \ldots$

$= \sin 4\left(x + \dfrac{\pi}{2}\right) = \sin 4(x + \pi) = \sin 4\left(x + \dfrac{3\pi}{2}\right) = \ldots$

$\sin 4x$ has the same value at x, $x + \dfrac{\pi}{2}$, $x + \pi$, $\ldots$ for all $x \in \mathbb{R}$.

$\dfrac{2\pi}{4} = \dfrac{\pi}{2}$ is the smallest value of x at which the function repeats itself.

Period $P = \dfrac{2\pi}{4} = \dfrac{\pi}{2}$

As $4x$ goes 0 to 2π through a full cycle, x goes from 0 to $\dfrac{\pi}{2}$.

TIP
The period of $y = \sin(kx + \alpha)$ is still $\dfrac{2\pi}{k}$. The addition of α to the angle has no influence on the period.

In general, for $y = \sin kx$ the period $P = \dfrac{2\pi}{k} = \dfrac{360°}{k}$.

Conclusion

For $y = a + b\sin(kx + \alpha)$ and $y = a + b\cos(kx + \alpha)$:

Period $P = \dfrac{2\pi}{k}$, Range $[a - b, a + b]$, $b > 0$ and $[a + b, a - b]$, $b < 0$

EXAMPLE 20

Find the period, range, equation of the midline and amplitude of the following functions:

(a) $y = \frac{1}{2} \sin 3x$

(b) $y = 4 - \frac{3}{2} \sin \left(\frac{1}{2} x\right)$

Solution

(a) $y = \frac{1}{2} \sin 3x$

Period $= \dfrac{2\pi}{3}$

Range $= \left[-\dfrac{1}{2}, \dfrac{1}{2}\right]$

Midline: $y = \dfrac{-\frac{1}{2} + \frac{1}{2}}{2} = 0$

Amplitude $r = \dfrac{1}{2}$

(b) $y = 4 - \frac{3}{2} \sin \left(\frac{1}{2} x\right)$

Period $P = \dfrac{2\pi}{\frac{1}{2}} = 4\pi$

Range $= \left[\dfrac{5}{2}, \dfrac{11}{2}\right]$

Midline: $y = \dfrac{\frac{5}{2} + \frac{11}{2}}{2} = 4$

Amplitude: $r = \dfrac{11}{2} - 4 = \dfrac{3}{2}$

EXAMPLE 21

Construct a function of the form $y = a + b \cos kx$ that describes the graph below:

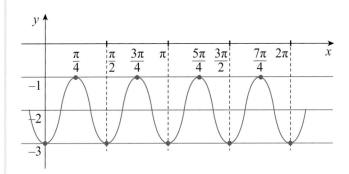

Solution

1 full wave $= \dfrac{\pi}{2}$

Period $P = \dfrac{2\pi}{k} = \dfrac{\pi}{2}$

$\therefore k = 4$

$y = a + b \cos 4x$

$x = 0, y = -3$: $a + b \cos 0 = -3$

$a + b = -3 \ ...(1)$

$x = \dfrac{\pi}{4}, y = -1$: $a + b \cos \pi = -1$

$a - b = -1 \ ...(2)$

$(1) + (2)$: $a = -2, b = -1$

$y = -2 - \cos 4x$

EXAMPLE 22

The amount A in tonnes of garden waste processed by a waste company during time t is modelled by the equation $A = 230 - 150 \sin(30t + 60)°$, $0 \le t \le 12$, where $t = 1$ stands for January, $t = 2$ stands for February and so on.

(a) What is the maximum amount of garden waste processed during 1 month?

(b) During which month is the maximum waste processed?

(c) What is the minimum amount of garden waste processed during 1 month?

(d) During which month is the minimum waste processed?

(e) In which months does the model predict a waste amount of 155 tonnes?

(f) What is the value of A for the amount of garden waste in June, correct to the nearest tonne?

Solution

$A = 230 - 150 \sin(30t + 60)°$

(a) A_{max} occurs when $\sin(30t + 60)° = -1$.

$A_{max} = 230 + 150 = 380$ tonnes

(b) $(30t + 60)° = 270°$

$30t + 60° = 270°$

$30t = 210°$

$t = 7$

Therefore, the maximum waste occurs in July.

(c) $A_{min} = 230 - 150 = 80$ tonnes

(d) $(30t + 60°) = 90°$

$30t = 30°$

$t = 1$

Therefore, the minimum waste occurs in January.

(e) $155 = 230 - 150 \sin(30t + 60)°$

$150 \sin(30t + 60)° = 75$

$\sin(30t + 60)° = 0.5$

$30t + 60 = \begin{cases} 30° & 390° \\ 150° & 510° \end{cases}$

$30t = \begin{cases} -30° & 330° \\ 90° & 450° \end{cases}$

$t = \begin{cases} -1 & 11 \\ 3 & 15 \end{cases}$

$\therefore t = 3, 11$ [March and November]

(f) $t = 6 \Rightarrow A = 230 - 150 \sin(180 + 60)°$

$= 230 - 150 \sin 240° = 360$ tonnes

EXAMPLE 23

A wrecking ball moves backwards and forwards along the arc AB of a circle with centre O.

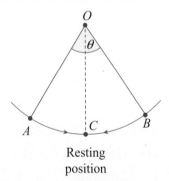

Resting position

Its displacement in metres from its resting position C along the arc AB at any time t in seconds is described by the graph below:

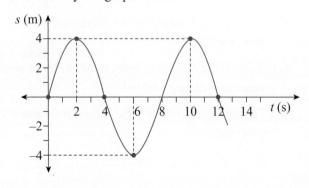

(a) What is the period of the wrecking ball?

(b) What is the amplitude of the ball's motion?

(c) Find θ if $|OA| = |OB| = 5$ m.

(d) What is the frequency of the wrecking ball (how many complete swings are there in 1 second)?

(e) Where is the ball after 16 s if it starts at C?

(f) How many complete swings does the ball describe in 6 minutes?

Solution

(a) Period = 8 seconds

It takes 8 seconds to return to C starting from C.

(b) Amplitude = 4 m = length of arc CB

= length of arc CA

(c)

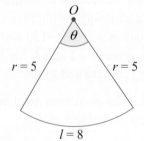

$l = r\theta \Rightarrow \theta = \dfrac{8}{5} = 1.6$ rad

(d) One complete swing in 8 seconds means $\frac{1}{8}$ of a swing in one second.

∴ Frequency $f = \frac{1}{8}$ s^{-1}

(e) After 16 s, the ball is at C.

(f) 6 minutes = 360 seconds

$$\therefore \frac{360}{8} = 45$$

45 swings occur in 6 minutes.

---

3. $y = \tan x$

The graph of $y = \tan x$, $0 \le x \le \frac{7\pi}{2}$, $x \in \mathbb{R}$, is shown below.

x	0	$\frac{\pi}{4}$	$\frac{\pi}{2}$	$\frac{3\pi}{4}$	π	$\frac{5\pi}{4}$	$\frac{3\pi}{2}$	$\frac{7\pi}{4}$	2π	$\frac{9\pi}{4}$	$\frac{5\pi}{2}$	$\frac{11\pi}{4}$	3π	$\frac{13\pi}{4}$	$\frac{7\pi}{2}$
$\tan x$	0	1	$-\infty$	-1	0	1	∞	-1	0	1	$-\infty$	-1	0	1	∞

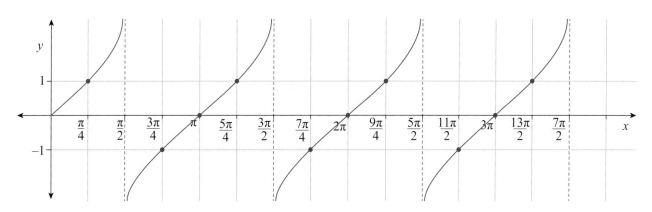

The period of $y = \tan x$ is π.

The function is not continuous for $x \in \mathbb{R}$.

The range is $[-\infty, \infty]$.

The equation of the midline is always $y = 0$.

For $y = \tan x$: Period = π, range: $[-\infty, \infty]$, midline: $y = 0$

In general, for $y = a + b \tan kx$: Period $P = \frac{\pi}{k}$, range = $[-\infty, \infty]$.

▸ $3 \tan 4x$: Period $P = \frac{\pi}{4}$ and range $[-\infty, \infty]$.

▸ $4 - \frac{1}{2} \tan 5x$: Period $P = \frac{\pi}{5}$ and range $[-\infty, \infty]$.

Steps for plotting periodic graphs

Use the following steps for plotting graphs of $y = a + b \cos kx$ and $y = a + b \sin kx$:

1. Find the range.

2. Find the period $P = \dfrac{2\pi}{k}$.

3. Divide the period by 4 and use this value as your spacing for the x values in the given domain.

4. Draw up a table as follows:

x				
kx				
$\cos kx$ or $\sin kx$				
$a + b \cos kx$ or $a + b \sin kx$				

5. Find the equations of the following:

   The maximum line: $y = $ maximum value

   The minimum line: $y = $ minimum value

   Midline $y = \dfrac{\text{Maximum value} + \text{Minimum value}}{2}$

6. Find the number of cycles (waves).

   Number of cycles (waves) $= \dfrac{\text{Length of the domain}}{\text{Period}}$

7. Plot the graph on graph paper by drawing one complete wave and replicating it for the number of cycles (waves) required.

EXAMPLE 24

Plot the graph of $y = 2 \cos 3x$, $0 \le x \le \pi$, $x \in \mathbb{R}$.

Solution

$y = 2 \cos 3x$

1. Range $= [-2, 2]$

2. Period $P = \dfrac{2\pi}{3}$

3. Spacing $= \dfrac{1}{4} \times \dfrac{2\pi}{3} = \dfrac{\pi}{6}$

   Go up in steps of $\dfrac{\pi}{6}$ in your table for the x values.

4. Draw up a table.

x	0	$\dfrac{\pi}{6}$	$\dfrac{\pi}{3}$	$\dfrac{\pi}{2}$	$\dfrac{2\pi}{3}$	$\dfrac{5\pi}{6}$	π
$3x$	0	$\dfrac{\pi}{2}$	π	$\dfrac{3\pi}{2}$	2π	$\dfrac{5\pi}{2}$	3π
$\cos 3x$	1	0	-1	0	1	0	-1
$2 \cos 3x$	2	0	-2	0	2	0	-2

5. Equations of lines:

Maximum line: $y = 2$

Minimum line: $y = -2$

Midline: $y = \dfrac{-2+2}{2} = 0$ (*x*-axis)

6. Number of waves $= \dfrac{\pi}{\frac{2\pi}{3}} = 1\frac{1}{2}$

7. Plot the graph:

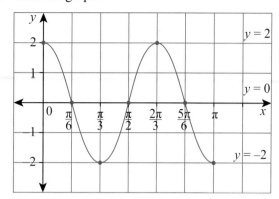

EXAMPLE 25

A ferris wheel rotates in an anticlockwise direction. The height h in metres of a person's feet on the wheel above the ground at a time t in minutes is given by $h = 24 - 20\cos\left(\dfrac{3t}{4}\right)$.

Plot a graph of the person's height for $0 \le t \le 8\pi$, $t \in \mathbb{R}$. How long does it take for one revolution of the wheel?

Solution

$h = 24 - 20\cos\left(\dfrac{3t}{4}\right)$

1. Range = [4, 44]

2. Period $P = \dfrac{2\pi}{k} = \dfrac{2\pi}{\frac{3}{4}} = \dfrac{8\pi}{3}$

3. Spacing $= \dfrac{1}{4} \times \dfrac{8\pi}{3} = \dfrac{2\pi}{3}$

4. Draw up the table:

t	0	$\frac{2\pi}{3}$	$\frac{4\pi}{3}$	2π	$\frac{8\pi}{3}$	$\frac{10\pi}{3}$	4π	$\frac{14\pi}{3}$	$\frac{16\pi}{3}$	6π	$\frac{20\pi}{3}$	$\frac{22\pi}{3}$	8π
$\frac{3t}{4}$	0	$\frac{\pi}{2}$	π	$\frac{3\pi}{2}$	2π	$\frac{5\pi}{2}$	3π	$\frac{7\pi}{2}$	4π	$\frac{9\pi}{2}$	5π	$\frac{11\pi}{2}$	6π
$\cos\frac{3t}{4}$	1	0	−1	0	1	0	−1	0	1	0	−1	0	1
$24 - 20\cos\frac{3t}{4}$	4	24	44	24	4	24	44	24	4	24	44	24	4

5. Equations of lines:

Maximum line: $h = 44$

Minimum line: $h = 4$

Midline: $h = \dfrac{4+44}{2} = 24$

6. Number of waves $= \dfrac{8\pi}{\frac{8\pi}{3}} = 3$

7. Plot the graph:

The highest point of the person's feet above the ground is 44 m.

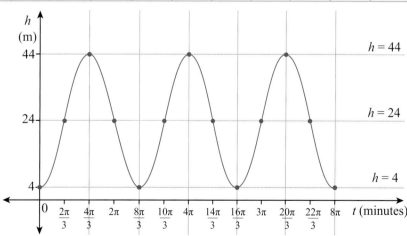

The wheel completes one revolution in $\dfrac{8\pi}{3}$ minutes.

$\therefore$ 1 revolution takes $\dfrac{8\pi}{3}$ minutes.

EXAMPLE 26

Plot $f(x) = \cos 2x$ and $g(x) = \sin x$ on the same diagram for $0° \leq x \leq 360°$, $x \in \mathbb{R}$. Use your graphs to solve $\cos 2x = \sin x$, $0° \leq x \leq 360°$, $x \in \mathbb{R}$.

Find the exact solutions by solving $\cos 2x = \sin x$.

Solution

$\boxed{f(x) = \cos 2x}$

1. Range = $[-1, 1]$

2. Period $P = 180°$

3. Spacing = $45°$

4. Draw up the table:

x	$2x$	$\cos 2x$
0	0	1
45°	90°	0
90°	180°	−1
135°	270°	0
180°	360°	1
225°	450°	0
270°	540°	−1
315°	630°	0
360°	720°	1

5. Equations of lines:

   Maximum line: $y = 1$

   Minimum line: $y = -1$

   Midline $y = 0$

6. Number of cycles (waves) = 2

$\boxed{g(x) = \sin x}$

1. Range = $[-1, 1]$

2. Period $P = 360°$

3. Spacing = $90°$

4. Draw up the table:

x	$\sin x$
0	0
90°	1
180°	0
270°	−1
360°	0

5. Equation of lines:

   Maximum line: $y = 1$

   Minimum line: $y = -1$

   Midline: $y = 0$

6. Number of cycles (waves) = 1

7. Plot the graphs:

Solutions to $f(x) = g(x)$ from the graph:

$x = 30°, 150°, 270°$

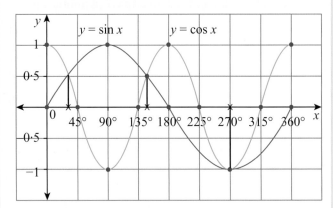

By calculation: $\cos 2x = \sin x$

$\cos^2 x - \sin^2 x = \sin x$

$1 - \sin^2 x - \sin^2 x = \sin x$

$2 \sin^2 x + \sin x - 1 = 0$

$(2 \sin x - 1)(\sin x + 1) = 0$

$\sin x = \dfrac{1}{2}$

$x = \begin{cases} 30° \\ 150° \end{cases}$

$\sin x = -1$

$x = 270°$

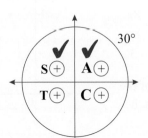

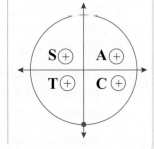

EXERCISE 12

1. Write down the period and range of the following functions defined for $x \in \mathbb{R}$:

   (a) $y = 3\cos x$

   (b) $y = \cos 4x$

   (c) $y = p\sin x$

   (d) $y = -2\cos(2x + 45°)$

   (e) $y = 5\sin\left(\dfrac{x}{2} + 30°\right)$

   (f) $y = 7\sin(2x + 13)$

   (g) $y = 8\tan 9x$

   (h) $y = 11\tan(5x - 6)$

   (i) $y = 2 + 3\sin 4x$

   (j) $y = 4 - 5\cos 7x$

   (k) $y = 3 + 2\tan 4x$

   (l) $y = p + q\sin kx, \; q > 0$

   (m) $y = p + q\cos kx, \; q < 0$

   (n) $y = \dfrac{1}{2} + 3\sin\left(\dfrac{x}{2}\right)$

   (o) $y = 4\sin 2x - 1$

2. Write down a function of the form $y = a + b\cos x$ with the following ranges:

   (a) $[-1, 1], \; b > 0$ **(d)** $[-5, 3], \; b < 0$

   (b) $[-3, 3], \; b > 0$ **(e)** $[-7, 2], \; b < 0$

   (c) $\left[\tfrac{1}{2}, 2\right], \; b > 0$

3. Find a and b for the following functions, given their ranges:

   (a) $a + b\cos 2x$ is $[-5, 5], \; b > 0$

   (b) $y = a + b\sin(7x + \alpha)$ is $[-7, 7], \; b > 0$

   (c) $a + b\cos 2x$ is $[-4, 2], \; b > 0$

   (d) $a + b\sin 3x$ is $[-4, 2], \; b < 0$

   (e) $y = a + b\sin\left(\dfrac{x}{2}\right)$ is $[-7, 4], \; b > 0$

4. Find the period P and range of the periodic function $y = f(x)$ shown. Write down $f(0), f(5)$ and $f(7)$.

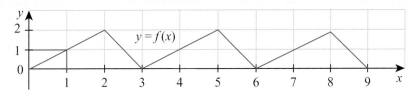

5. State the period P and range of the following periodic function $y = f(x), \; x \in \mathbb{R}$:

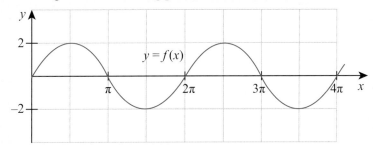

   Evaluate $f(\pi), f\left(\dfrac{\pi}{2}\right), f(4\pi), f(10\pi)$.

6. What is the period P and range of the following periodic function $y = f(x), \; x \in \mathbb{R}$?

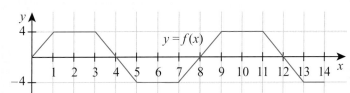

   Find $f(2), f(4), f(7), f(10), f(19)$.

7. Write down the period P and range of the following periodic function $y = f(x)$, $x \in \mathbb{R}$:

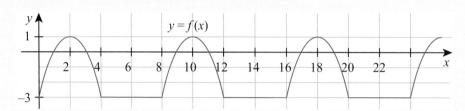

   Find $f(2), f(4), f(8), f(34)$. What is the minimum value of $f(x)$?

8. Write down the period P and range of the periodic function $y = f(x)$, $x \in \mathbb{R}$.

   Evaluate $f(0), f(\pi), f\left(-\dfrac{\pi}{2}\right), f\left(\dfrac{3\pi}{4}\right), f(10\pi), f\left(\dfrac{31\pi}{4}\right)$. What is the minimum value of $f(x)$?

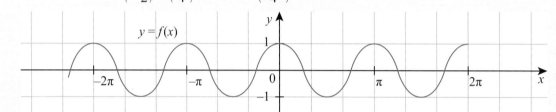

9. The graph of $y = r \sin (kx)°$, $0° \le x \le 120°$, $x \in \mathbb{R}$, is shown. Find k and r if $(30°, 4)$ is a maximum point.

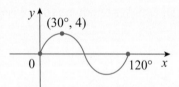

10. The graph of $y = r \cos kx$, $x \in \mathbb{R}$, is shown. Find r and k.

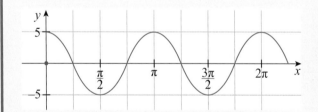

11. The graph of $y = f(x) = r \sin kx$, $x \in \mathbb{R}$, is shown. $P(90°, 1·5)$ is the maximum point.

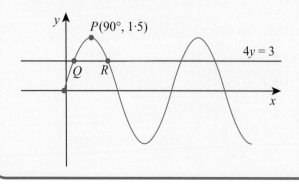

   (a) Find r and k.

   (b) Find the co-ordinates of Q and R, the points at which the line $4y = 3$ intersects $y = f(x)$.

12. For $y = f(x) = a + b \sin kx$, $b > 0$, find a, b and k, $x \in \mathbb{R}$.

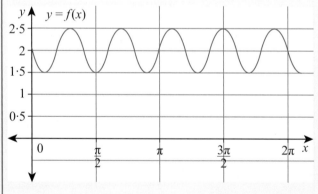

13. For $y = f(x) = a + b \cos kx$, find a, b and k, $x \in \mathbb{R}$.

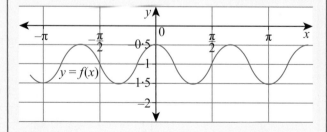

14. Draw graphs of the following on separate diagrams:

(a) $y = 3\cos 2x$, $0 \le x \le 2\pi$, $x \in \mathbb{R}$

(b) $y = 4\sin\left(\dfrac{x}{2}\right)$, $0 \le x \le 8\pi$, $x \in \mathbb{R}$

(c) $y = 3 + 2\sin 3x$, $0° \le x \le 360°$, $x \in \mathbb{R}$

(d) $y = 4 - 3\cos 4x$, $0° \le x \le 360°$, $x \in \mathbb{R}$

15. Find the period and range of $f(x) = 4\cos 2x$ and $g(x) = 3\cos x$ and plot them on the same diagram using the same axes and same scales in the domain $0° \le x \le 360°$, $x \in \mathbb{R}$.

16. Draw graphs of $f(x) = \sin x$ and $g(x) = \cos x$ for $0 \le x \le 360°$, $x \in \mathbb{R}$, on the same diagram using the same axes and scales.

Use your graphs to estimate the value of x for which $\sin x = \cos x$, $0° \le x \le 360°$.

Compare these values with the exact solutions of $\sin x = \cos x$, $0° \le x \le 360°$, by solving this equation by calculation.

17. Draw graphs of $f(x) = \tan x$ and $g(x) = \cos x$, $0° \le x \le 180°$, $x \in \mathbb{R}$, using the table below:

x	0°	30°	45°	60°	90°	120°	135°	150°	180°
tan x									
cos x									

Use your graphs to estimate the solutions of $\cos x = \tan x$, $0° \le x \le 180°$, correct to the nearest degree.

18. Plot $y = 3\sin x$, $0° \le x \le 360°$, $x \in \mathbb{R}$. Use your graph to estimate the solution of $3\sin x = 1\cdot5$.

19. The graphs shown below are of the three functions $2\sin 4x$, $\sin 4x$ and $4\sin 2x$.

Identify which of these three functions is
(a) $f(x)$, (b) $g(x)$, (c) $h(x)$.

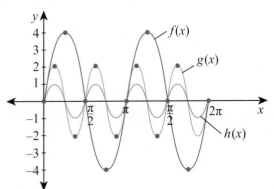

20. The graph below shows $y = f(x) = b\sin kx$, $x \in \mathbb{R}$.

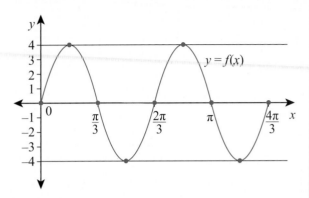

Find:

(a) the period

(b) the range

(c) b, $b > 0$

(d) k

21. The graph of $y = f(x) = 7\cos 2x$, $x \in \mathbb{R}$, is shown below.

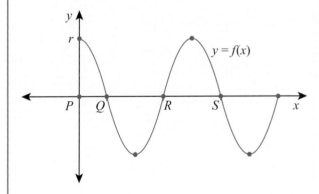

Find:

(a) the amplitude r

(b) the period

(c) P, Q, R and S

22. If $f(x)$ and $g(x)$ are functions of the form $b\sin kx$, find b and k for each function.

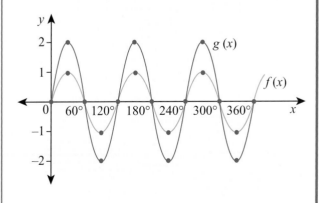

23. The graph shows a function $f(x) = b \tan x$, $x \in \mathbb{R}$. Find b.

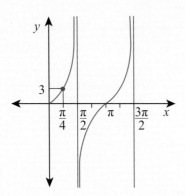

24. Molly is swinging on a garden swing. The distance h in metres of the seat below the point O of suspension can be modelled by the equation $h = 2 + 0 \cdot 18 \cos\left(\dfrac{3\pi t}{2}\right)$, where t is the time in seconds after Molly is at the lowest point.

  (a) Find the distance the seat is below O when $t = 2 \, s$ and $t = \dfrac{8}{3} \, s$.

  (b) What is the value h when the seat is at:

      (i) its highest point,

      (ii) its lowest point above the ground?

  (c) Find the interval between the times when the seat is at its lowest point.

25. The height h in metres above the ground of the end of a spring hanging from the ceiling is given by $h = 2 + 0 \cdot 35 \cos (30t)^\circ$, t seconds after it begins to move.

  Find:

  (a) the maximum value of h,

  (b) the height of the spring above the floor after 4 s,

  (c) when the height of the spring is first at $2 \cdot 175$ m above the floor.

26. At a certain latitude the number N of daylight hours each day in every 365 days is given by $N = a + b \sin (kt)^\circ$, where t is the time in days after the spring equinox.

Assume the number of daylight hours follow an annual cycle, with a period of 365 days.

  (a) Find k correct to three decimal places.

  (b) If the shortest and longest days have 6 and 18 hours of daylight respectively, find a and b.

  (c) Find in hours and minutes, correct to the nearest minute, the number of daylight hours 60 days after the spring equinox.

  (d) Find the two days after the spring equinox that a town at the specified latitude has exactly 8 hours of daylight.

27. The depth h of water in a harbour continually varies between a minimum of $2 \cdot 5$ m below a watermark and a maximum of $1 \cdot 5$ m above it over a 12-hour period.

Construct a trigonometric function of the form $h = a + b \sin kt$ describing the relation between the height h in metres and time t in hours if $h = 2$ m at $t = 0$, where $t = 0$ is 8 a.m.

Use the function to find:

  (a) the height of the water at 2 p.m.,

  (b) the times at which the height is $2 \cdot 25$ m during the 12-hour period.

28. A buoy in the ocean oscillates up and down in periodic motion above sea level. At $t = 0$, the buoy is at the highest point of its motion and returns to that high point every 10 seconds. The buoy moves $1 \cdot 5$ m from its highest point to its lowest point above sea level.

  (a) Using a trigonometric function of the form $h = b \cos kt$, create a function to model the motion of the buoy.

  (b) How high is the buoy above sea level at $t = 2 \cdot 5$ s?

  (c) By finding its velocity show that it is moving down at $t = 2 \cdot 5$ s and show that it is rising at $t = 7 \cdot 5$ s.

  (d) How many times in 2 minutes will it be at sea level?

29. The height h in metres of the foot of a 110 m hurdler above the ground between nine equally spaced hurdles can be modelled by the equation $h = 0.535 + 0.535\cos(300t)^\circ$, where t is the time after his foot is at the top of the first hurdle.

(a) Find the height of each hurdle.

(b) Find the time it takes him to travel between two hurdles.

(c) Find his average speed between hurdles if they are spaced 9·14 m apart, correct to one decimal place.

(d) Using this average speed, how long does he take to complete the race, correct to one decimal place?

9.4 Inverse trigonometry

TIP

Your calculator can calculate inverse trigonometric functions.

Doing inverse trigonometry (IT) is the opposite process to doing trigonometry. There are three inverse trigonometric functions to be considered: $\sin^{-1} x$, $\cos^{-1} x$ and $\tan^{-1} x$.

Inverse sine

$\sin^{-1} x$ means the angle whose sine is x.

▶ $\sin^{-1} \frac{1}{2}$ is the angle whose sine is $\frac{1}{2}$. The answer is 30°.

$$\therefore \sin^{-1}\left(\frac{1}{2}\right) = 30°$$

Escaping from inverse sine

$$y = \sin^{-1} x \Leftrightarrow \sin y = x = \frac{x}{1} = \frac{OPP}{HYP}$$

Now you can find the other trigonometric ratios.

$$\cos y = \sqrt{1 - x^2}$$

$$\tan y = \frac{x}{\sqrt{1 - x^2}}$$

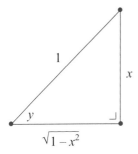

Inverse cosine

$\cos^{-1} x$ is the angle whose cos is x.

▶ $\cos^{-1}\left(\frac{\sqrt{3}}{2}\right)$ is the angle whose cos is $\frac{\sqrt{3}}{2}$. The answer is 30°.

$$\therefore \cos^{-1}\left(\frac{\sqrt{3}}{2}\right) = 30°$$

Escaping from inverse cosine

$$y = \cos^{-1} x \Leftrightarrow \cos y = x = \frac{x}{1} = \frac{ADJ}{HYP}$$

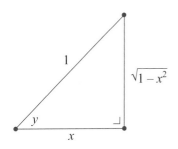

Inverse tangent

$\tan^{-1} x$ means the angle whose tan is x.

▶ $\tan^{-1}(-1)$ is the angle whose tan is -1.

The answer is $-45°$.

∴ $\tan^{-1}(-1) = -45°$

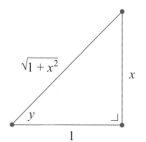

Escaping from inverse sine

$y = \tan^{-1} x \Leftrightarrow \tan y = x = \dfrac{x}{1} = \dfrac{\text{OPP}}{\text{ADJ}}$

$$y = \sin^{-1} x \Leftrightarrow \sin y = x$$
$$y = \cos^{-1} x \Leftrightarrow \cos y = x$$
$$y = \tan^{-1} x \Leftrightarrow \tan y = x$$

EXAMPLE 27

If $y = \sin^{-1} \frac{2}{3}$, show that $\tan y = \dfrac{2}{\sqrt{5}}$.

Solution

$y = \sin^{-1} \dfrac{2}{3} \Rightarrow \sin y = \dfrac{2}{3}$

$\tan y = \dfrac{2}{\sqrt{5}}$

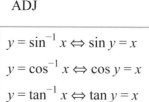

EXAMPLE 28

Evaluate $\tan\left(\cos^{-1}\left(\frac{2}{5}\right)\right)$ exactly.

Solution

Let $\theta = \cos^{-1}\left(\dfrac{2}{5}\right) \Rightarrow \cos\theta = \left(\dfrac{2}{5}\right)$.

$\tan\left(\cos^{-1}\left(\dfrac{2}{5}\right)\right) = \tan\theta = \dfrac{\sqrt{21}}{5}$

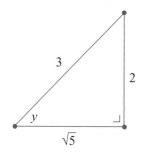

EXAMPLE 29

Show that $\tan(\sin^{-1} x) = \dfrac{x}{\sqrt{1-x^2}}$.

Solution

$\theta = \sin^{-1} x \Rightarrow \sin\theta = x$

$\tan(\sin^{-1} x) = \tan\theta = \dfrac{x}{\sqrt{1-x^2}}$

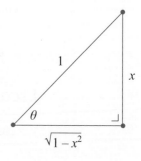

EXERCISE 13

1. Evaluate the following exactly using your calculator or in your head:

   (a) $\sin^{-1}\left(\dfrac{\sqrt{2}}{2}\right)$

   (b) $\sin^{-1}\left(\dfrac{\sqrt{3}}{2}\right)$

   (c) $\sin^{-1}(-1)$

   (d) $\sin\left(\sin^{-1}\left(\dfrac{1}{2}\right)\right)$

   (e) $\sin^{-1}\left(\sin\dfrac{\pi}{4}\right)$

   (f) $\sin^{-1}\left(\sin\dfrac{2\pi}{3}\right)$

   (g) $\cos(\tan^{-1}1)$

   (h) $\tan^{-1}\left(\dfrac{1}{\sqrt{3}}\right)$

   (i) $\tan^{-1}\left(-\dfrac{\sqrt{3}}{3}\right)$

   (j) $\cos(\sin^{-1}1)$

2. Evaluate the following exactly:

   (a) $\sin(\tan^{-1}\sqrt{3})$

   (b) $\tan\left(\tan^{-1}\dfrac{2}{3}\right)$

   (c) $\cos(\tan^{-1}3)$

   (d) $\tan\left(2\tan^{-1}\left(\dfrac{3}{4}\right)\right)$

   (e) $\cos\left(2\sin^{-1}\left(\dfrac{15}{17}\right)\right)$

3. Show the following:

   (a) $\cos(\sin^{-1}x)=\sqrt{1-x^2},\ -1\le x\le1$ (Let $\theta=\sin^{-1}x$)

   (b) $\sin(\tan^{-1}x)=\dfrac{x}{\sqrt{1+x^2}}$ (Let $\theta=\tan^{-1}x$)

   (c) $\sin(2\sin^{-1}x)=2x\sqrt{1-x^2}$ (Let $\theta=\sin^{-1}x$)

   (d) $\sin^{-1}x=\tan^{-1}\left(\dfrac{x}{\sqrt{1-x^2}}\right)$ (Let $\theta=\sin^{-1}x$ or $\tan^{-1}x$)

4. (a) Solve $\tan^{-1}(2x-1)=\dfrac{\pi}{4}$.

   (b) Solve $2\sin^{-1}(3x-2)=\dfrac{\pi}{3}$.

REVISION QUESTIONS

1. A hospital patient had an illness in which his temperature T in °C t days after he first became ill varied according to the formula: $T = a + b\sin kt$. His highest temperature was 40·2 °C and his lowest temperature was 37·2 °C.

    The length of time between successive high temperatures was 12 days.

    (a) Find the period and range of this sine function.

    (b) Find k, a and b.

    (c) Find the patient's original temperature.

    (d) What is the patient's temperature on day 3 of his illness?

    (e) When did the first lowest temperature occur?

2. The power output P in terawatts (TW) from all nuclear reactors in the world every year since 1950 can be described by the equation $P = 2800 \sin\left(\dfrac{3t}{2}\right)^\circ$, where t is the year after 1950, $0 \le t \le 60$.

    (a) Find the power output in 1950.

    (b) Find the power output in 1980, correct to the nearest TW.

    (c) Find the maximum yearly power output.

    (d) Find the year in which the maximum power output occurred.

    (e) Find the year in which the power output was 1400 TW.

    (f) Draw a graph of power output from $0 \le t \le 60$ using the table below.

t (years)	0	10	20	30	40	50	60
P (TW)							

    (g) If the model is to be believed beyond 60 years, in what year in the future will the power output be zero?

3. (a) Solve $\sin x = 0\cdot7$, $0° \le x \le 360°$, $x \in \mathbb{R}$, giving all answers correct to one decimal place.

    (b) The diagram shows the curve $y = \sin x$, $0 \le x \le 2\pi$, $x \in \mathbb{R}$, and the lines $y = k$ and $y = -k$.

    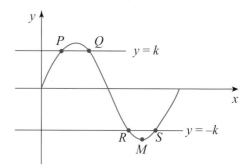

    The line $y = k$ intersects the curve at P and Q and $y = -k$ intersects it at R and S.

    M is the minimum point of the curve.

    (i) Write down the co-ordinates of M.

    (ii) The x co-ordinate of P is θ. Write down the co-ordinates of Q in terms of π and θ.

    (iii) Find $|RS|$ in terms of π and θ.

    (c) Sketch the graph of $y = \sin 3x$, $0 \le x \le \dfrac{4\pi}{3}$, $x \in \mathbb{R}$.

4. The distance x in centimetres (cm) of a mass below O on a spring is described by the equation $y = 10 + 4\cos\left(\dfrac{\pi}{2}t\right)$, where t is the number of seconds after the mass was set in motion.

    (a) (i) When $t = 2$ s, show that $y = 6$ cm.

    (ii) Find the maximum value of y.

    (iii) Find the minimum value of y, during the motion.

    (iv) Find the period of the function.

    (v) If the period is the time to complete a full oscillation, find the number of oscillations per second (frequency).

    (vi) Find the velocity $v = \dfrac{dy}{dt}$ at $t = \dfrac{4}{3}$ s.

(b) The graph of $y = \cos x$, $0 \le x \le 360°$, $x \in \mathbb{R}$, is shown.

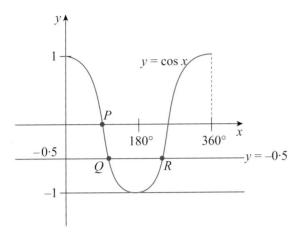

Find the co-ordinates of P, Q and R.

5. (a) $PQRS$ is a parallelogram, where $|SQ| = 12$ cm and $|PR| = 10$ cm.

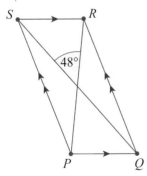

Find $|PQ|$ and $|PS|$, giving your answer correct to three decimal places.

(b) Two circles s_1 and s_2 intersect at two points R and T. Find the distance between the centres of P and Q of the circles if t_1 is the tangent to s_1 at R and t_2 is the tangent to s_2 at R.

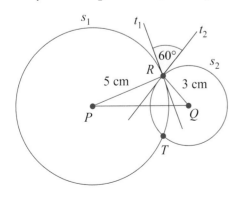

(c) Prove that:

(i) $\dfrac{\cos^2 A}{1 + \sin A} = 1 - \sin A$

(ii) $\dfrac{\tan \theta}{\sqrt{1 + \tan^2 \theta}} = \sin \theta$

6. (a) Using $\sin^2 x = 1 - \cos^2 x$, write $6 \sin^2 x + \cos x - 4 = 0$ as a quadratic equation in $\cos x$. Hence, find x, $0° \le x \le 360°$, correct to the nearest degree.

(b) $|PQ|$ is the distance between two points on opposite parallel banks PV and QU of a river.

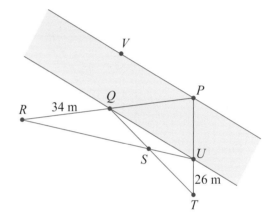

(i) If $|QU| = 60$ m and $|RU| = 80$ m, find $|\angle RQU|$ and $|\angle PQU|$, correct to two decimal places, using $\triangle RQU$.

(ii) If $|QT| = 72$ m, find $|\angle QUT|$ and $|\angle QUP|$, correct to two decimal places, using $\triangle QUT$.

(iii) Using $\triangle QUP$, find $|PQ|$ and $|PU|$, correct to the nearest metre.

(iv) Find the shortest distance across the river, correct to the nearest metre.

7. (a) Solve $\cos 2x = -\dfrac{\sqrt{3}}{2}$, $0° \le x \le 360°$, $x \in \mathbb{R}$.

(b) Snell's law for the refraction of light states that $a \sin \theta = b \sin \varphi$.

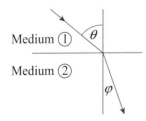

The Fresnel coefficient P for polarisation is given by $P = \dfrac{a \cos \theta - b \cos \varphi}{a \cos \theta + b \cos \varphi}$.

Show that $P = \dfrac{\sin (\varphi - \theta)}{\sin (\varphi + \theta)}$.

(c) A rope $PQRST$ is fixed at P and T on a wall $[PT]$. It is guided around a circular pulley of radius 8 cm fixed at its centre O and touching the wall at U such that $|PU| = |UT| = 8\sqrt{3}$ cm.

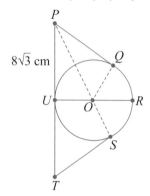

Find: **(i)** $|\angle POU|$

(ii) $|PO|$

(iii) $|\angle POQ|$

(vi) $|PQ|$

(v) $|\angle QOR|$

(vi) $|\angle QOS|$

(vii) the length of the rope

8. (a) (i) Find the period and range of the function $y = -3 + 4 \sin 2t$, $t \in \mathbb{R}$.

(ii) If the period of $y = a + b \cos kx$ is $\dfrac{\pi}{3}$ and its range is $[-2, 3]$, find a, b and k if $b < 0$.

(b) A person OB of height $1\cdot 7$ m stands x m from the base of a wall of a church and looks at a stained glass window PQ of height 3 m on a vertical wall PR.

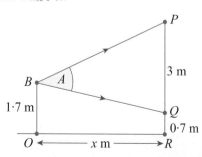

(i) If $|\angle PBQ| = A$, show that $\tan A = \dfrac{3x}{x^2 - 2}$.

(ii) Find x if $A = 40\cdot 6°$ correct to the nearest metre.

(c) A perfect triangle is a triangle in which the lengths of all sides are natural numbers and the perimeter is equal to the area.

For the triangle shown find $\cos \theta$, where $\theta = |\angle RPQ|$ and hence show that PQR is a perfect triangle.

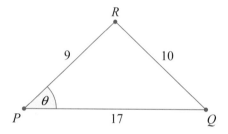

9. (a) A spy satellite S circles the Earth at a height h kilometres (km) above the Earth's surface whose centre is O.

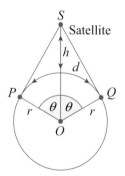

d is the distance of the minor arc PQ in kilometres (km) on the Earth that can be observed by the satellite.

(i) Write down an equation relating h to θ, in terms of the radius r of the Earth.

(ii) Express d in terms r and θ.

(iii) If $d = 4000$ km and $r = 6400$ km find h, giving your answer correct to two decimal places.

(iv) If the height of the satellite is 500 km, what distance d of the Earth's surface can be observed by the satellite? Give your answer to two significant figures. The radius of the Earth is 6400 km.

(b) A drone D flying at 2000 m above a point E on the Earth spots a vehicle A approaching its base B.

The angle of depression of the base is 20° and the angle of depression of the vehicle is 30°.

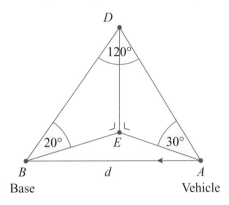

Base d Vehicle

(i) Find, correct to the nearest metre, how far the vehicle is from the base if $|\angle BDA| = 120°$.

(ii) If the vehicle is travelling at 90 km/h, how many minutes will it take to get to the base? Give your answer correct to one decimal place.

10. A window in the form of an isosceles triangle ABC has two circular stained glass panels s_1 and s_2 with centres at E and D on $[AF]$ where $[AF]$ is perpendicular to $[BC]$. s_1 and s_2 touch each other and the sides of $\triangle ABC$. The radii of s_1 and s_2 are 2 m and 1 m respectively. The remaining parts of the window are made of plain glass.

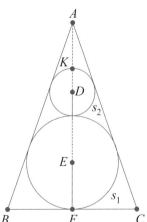

(a) Using similar triangles, find $|AK|$.

(b) Find $\sin x$ where $x = |\angle FAC|$.

(c) Find $\tan x$.

(d) Find $|FC|$.

(e) Find the area of the plain glass in the form $(a\sqrt{b} - c\pi)$ m^2, $a, b, c \in \mathbb{N}$.

11. Four houses P, Q, R and S are arranged on a square. They are joined by a pipe system consisting of five pipes $[PF]$, $[QG]$, $[FG]$, $[SF]$ and $[GR]$ with $|PF| = |QG| = |FS| = |GR|$ as shown.

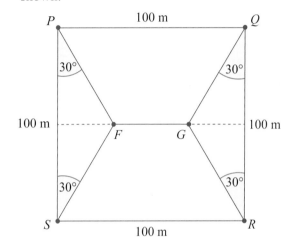

(a) Find the total length of this pipe system.

(b) Show that this length is less than $|PR| + |SQ|$.

12. (a) If $\cos x = \dfrac{1}{\sqrt{5}}$, x acute, find $\tan 2x$. What can you say about the angle $2x$?

(b) (i) Write $\sin x + \sin 3x$ as a product.

(ii) Hence, solve $\sin x + \sin 3x = \sin 2x$, $0 \le x \le 2\pi$, $x \in \mathbb{R}$.

(c) s_1 and s_2 are two circles with centres P and Q and radii r_1 and r_2 respectively which touch at R. $[EF]$ is parallel to $[PQ]$. $|\angle EPR| = \dfrac{\pi}{4}$ and $|\angle FQR| = \dfrac{\pi}{3}$.

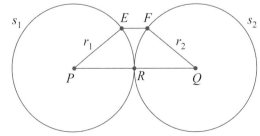

Show that $\dfrac{r_1}{r_2} = \dfrac{\sqrt{6}}{2}$.

13. In $\triangle PQR$, $\tan \theta = \dfrac{4\sqrt{3}}{11}$ where $\theta = \left|\angle RPQ\right|$.

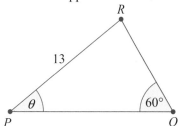

(a) Show that $\sin \theta = \dfrac{4\sqrt{3}}{13}$.

(b) Find $\left|QR\right|$.

(c) Show that $\sin(120° - \theta) = \dfrac{15\sqrt{3}}{26}$.

(d) Find the area of $\triangle PQR$.

14. (a) $PQRS$ is a quadrilateral.

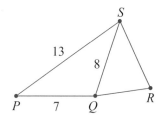

(i) Show that $\left|\angle PQS\right| = 120°$.

(ii) If the area of $PQRS = \dfrac{35\sqrt{3}}{2}$,

show that $\dfrac{\text{Area } \triangle PQS}{\text{Area } \triangle QRS} = 4$.

(b) A company's logo consists of the region enclosed by the sector OPQ of a circle s_1 with centre O and radius 15 cm and a semicircle s_2 of diameter $[PQ]$ where $\left|PQ\right| = 24$ cm.

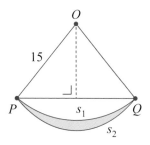

Find:

(i) $\left|\angle POQ\right|$ correct to the nearest degree,

(ii) the area $\triangle POQ$, correct to the nearest cm^2,

(iii) the area of shaded region, correct to the nearest cm^2.

15. Three identical circular pulleys each of radius r touch each other as shown. A belt $PQRSTU$ (coloured blue) is guided around the pulley system as shown and is taut. The centres of the circles are D, E, F.

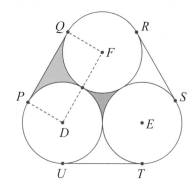

Find:

(a) the area of the rectangle $PDFQ$,

(b) the area of the region coloured green,

(c) the area of the region coloured pink,

(d) the total area enclosed by the belt.

Trigonometry

1. **(a)** The three basic trigonometric ratios

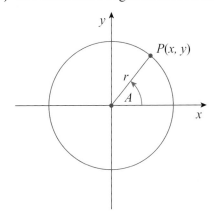

$$\cos A = \frac{x \text{ co-ordinate}}{\text{Radius}}$$

$$\sin A = \frac{y \text{ co-ordinate}}{\text{Radius}}$$

$$\tan A = \frac{y \text{ co-ordinate}}{x \text{ co-ordinate}} = \frac{\cos A}{\sin A}$$

(b) Dealing with angles not in the first quadrant

ASTC	Location

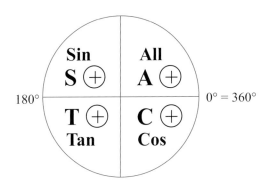

Always locate angles using the $(0° – 180°)$ line:

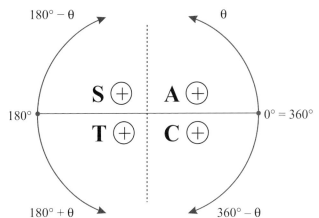

(c) Negative angles
$\cos (-A) = \cos A$
$\sin (-A) = -\sin A$
$\tan (-A) = -\tan A$

θ is the reference angle in the first quadrant.

2. Degrees versus radians:

(a) Conversion: π rads $= 180°$

(b) Arc length of circle

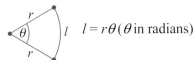

$l = r\theta \,(\theta \text{ in radians})$

(c) Area of sector of circle

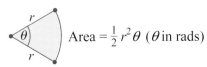

Area $= \frac{1}{2} r^2 \theta \, (\theta \text{ in rads})$

3. Solving triangles:

(a) RATs (right-angled triangles):

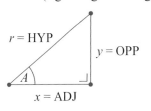

$$\cos A = \frac{\text{ADJ}}{\text{HYP}}$$

$$\sin A = \frac{\text{OPP}}{\text{HYP}}$$

$$\tan A = \frac{\text{OPP}}{\text{ADJ}}$$

Pythagoras: $r^2 = x^2 + y^2$

(b) Area of a triangle

Area $= \frac{1}{2} bc \sin A = \frac{1}{2} ac \sin B = \frac{1}{2} ab \sin C$

(c) Sine rule (proof required)

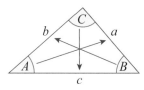

$$\frac{a}{\sin A} = \frac{b}{\sin B} = \frac{c}{\sin C}$$

or

$$\frac{\sin A}{a} = \frac{\sin B}{b} = \frac{\sin C}{c}$$

(d) Cosine rule (proof required)

$a^2 = b^2 + c^2 - 2bc \cos A \ldots A$ version

$b^2 = c^2 + a^2 - 2ac \cos B \ldots B$ version

$c^2 = a^2 + b^2 - 2ab \cos C \ldots C$ version

4. Trigonometric conversions:

(a) Products to sums:

$2 \sin A \cos B = \sin(A + B) + \sin(A - B)$

$2 \cos A \sin B = \sin(A + B) - \sin(A - B)$

$2 \cos A \cos B = \cos(A + B) + \cos(A - B)$

$2 \sin A \sin B = \cos(A - B) - \cos(A + B)$

(b) Sums to products:

$$\sin A + \sin B = 2 \sin \left(\frac{A + B}{2} \right) \cos \left(\frac{A - B}{2} \right)$$

$$\sin A - \sin B = 2 \cos \left(\frac{A + B}{2} \right) \sin \left(\frac{A - B}{2} \right)$$

$$\cos A + \cos B = 2 \cos \left(\frac{A + B}{2} \right) \cos \left(\frac{A - B}{2} \right)$$

$$\cos A - \cos B = -2 \sin \left(\frac{A + B}{2} \right) \sin \left(\frac{A - B}{2} \right)$$

5. Trigonometric equations:

(a) Isolate the trigonometric function on one side.

(b) Use ASTC to locate the two quadrants the basic angles are in.

(c) Find the reference angle θ in the first quadrant.

(d) Find the two basic angles.

(e) Find all angles in the range of values specified.

(f) Find the general solution if required.

Change a sum into a product to solve an equation involving a sum of sines and cosines.

6. Trigonometric graphs:

(a) $y = a + b \cos kx$ and $y = a + b \sin kx$:

Period $P = \dfrac{2\pi}{k}$

Range $[a - b, a + b]$ if $b > 0$

$[a + b, a - b]$ if $b < 0$

(b) $y = a + b \tan kx$:

Period $P = \dfrac{\pi}{k}$

Range $[-\infty, \infty]$

7. Inverse trigonomery:

(a) $y = \cos^{-1} x \Leftrightarrow \cos y = x$

(b) $y = \sin^{-1} x \Leftrightarrow \sin y = x$

(c) $y = \tan^{-1} x \Leftrightarrow \tan y = x$

SECTION 4

Co-ordinate Geometry

There are many applications of co-ordinate geometry. Computer programmers use co-ordinate geometry because most of the programs they write generate PDF files. In a PDF file, the printed page is a co-ordinated plane. PDF files contain text and images that are placed in position using (x, y) co-ordinates and simple trigonometry. Other applications of co-ordinate geometry are in imaging, scanning, positioning (GPS) and surveying.

CHAPTER 10

Line 1

Learning Outcomes

- To understand how to plot points (ordered pairs) in the Cartesian plane.
- To understand and apply the formulae for finding the distance between points, the midpoint of a line segment, the area of a triangle, the slope of a straight line and the equation of a straight line.
- To use your knowledge of dilations from geometry and to apply it to dilations on the Cartesian plane.

10.1 The Cartesian plane

One way to locate the position of a point in two-dimensional space is to use an **ordered** pair of letters (x, y) known as its co-ordinates. Starting with a reference point O called the **origin**, two perpendicular number lines are drawn. The horizontal number line is labelled as the x-axis and the vertical number line is labelled as the y-axis.

KEY TERM

The **Cartesian plane** is a flat two-dimensional surface made up of an x-axis (horizontal line) and a y-axis (vertical line) intersecting at right angles at a point O called the origin.

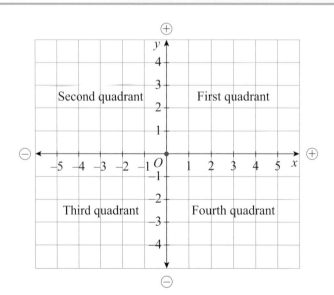

Descartes

Numbers to the right of O on the x-axis are always positive and numbers to the left of O are always negative. Numbers up from O along the y-axis are always positive, while numbers down from O along the y-axis are always negative.

Features of the Cartesian plane

1. The x-axis to the right of O is called the $+x$-axis. The x-axis to the left of O is called the $-x$-axis.

2. The y-axis up from O is called the $+y$-axis. The y-axis down from O is called the $-y$-axis.

3. The axes divide the plane into four quadrants, starting from the $+x$-axis and rotating anticlockwise. They are called the first, second, third and fourth quadrants, respectively.

4. The spacing of the numbers on the x-axis is equal. The spacing of the numbers on the y-axis is also equal.

5. The Cartesian plane is called after French philosopher and mathematician René Descartes, who devised it.

EXERCISE 1

1. Plot the following points on graph paper:

   (a) $P(-1, 0)$, $Q(3, 0)$, $R(0, -3)$, $S(0, 3)$.
   Find $|PQ|$ and $|RS|$.

   (b) $P(-3, -4)$, $Q(4, 3)$, $R(4, -3)$, $S(-3, 4)$.
   Find $|PS|$ and $|QR|$.

2. (a) What do the points $P(1, 0)$, $Q(-5, 0)$, $R(110, 0)$ and $S(-4.5, 0)$ have in common?

   (b) What do the points $P(-2, 3)$, $Q(-2, 4)$, $R(-2, 11)$ and $S(-2, 55.6)$ have in common?

   (c) What do the points $P(x_1, -7)$, $Q(x_2, -7)$, $R(x_3, -7)$ and $S(x_4, -7)$ have in common?

3. (a) A woman moves from $P(4, 7)$ to $Q(4, 15)$. How many steps has she moved? If 1 step = 10 m, how far has she moved?

   (b) O is the control tower on an airfield. An aeroplane moves from P to Q and then from Q to R. How far does it travel if 1 step = 50 m on each axis?

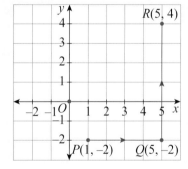

4. State in which quadrant or on which axis the following points are:
   $P(2, -7)$, $Q(-5, -6)$, $R(-110, 42)$,
   $S(0, -32.4)$, $T\left(\dfrac{20}{3}, \sqrt{2}\right)$, $U(20, 0)$

5. On the Cartesian plane, plot all the points with:

   (a) x co-ordinate of 0

   (b) $y = 4$

   (c) $x = -2$

   (d) $y = 0$

   (e) $y = -8$

   What conclusions can you make?

10.2 The distance between points

The distance formula

WORKED EXAMPLE

Finding the distance between two points

If $P(2, 3)$ and $R(5, 8)$ are two points, find $|PR|$.

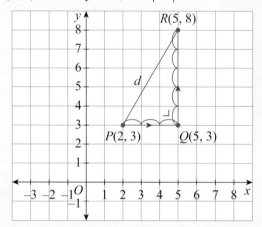

Draw a horizontal line through P and a vertical line through R to meet at Q. Q has co-ordinates $(5, 3)$.

$|PQ| = |5 - 2| = 3$ and $|QR| = |8 - 3| = 5$.

$|PR|$ can be found using Pythagoras' theorem:

$$d = |PR| = \sqrt{|PQ|^2 + |QR|^2} = \sqrt{3^2 + 5^2} = \sqrt{34}$$

If $P(x_1, y_1)$ and $Q(x_2, y_2)$ are two points, find an expression for the distance d between them.

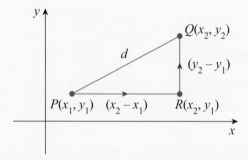

$|PR| = (x_2 - x_1)$ steps

$|RQ| = (y_2 - y_1)$ steps

Pythagoras' theorem: $d = |PQ| = \sqrt{(x_2 - x_1)^2 + (y_2 - y_1)^2}$

The distance d between two points $P(x_1, y_1)$ and $Q(x_2, y_2)$ is given by:

$$d = |PQ| = \sqrt{(x_2 - x_1)^2 + (y_2 - y_1)^2}$$

TIP

Remember as:

$d = \sqrt{(\text{Difference of } x \text{ co-ordinates})^2 + (\text{Difference of } y \text{ co-ordinates})^2}$

Some points to note on the distance formula

1. This formula works for all points.

2. It does not matter if the differences are positive or negative because when squared they will always be positive: $(5 - 2)^2 = (2 - 5)^2 = 9$

3. It does not matter in which order you find the differences because $(x_2 - x_1)^2 = (x_1 - x_2)^2$.

4. Distance is always positive.

5. For two points on a line parallel to the x-axis:

    $d = $ Absolute value of the difference of the x co-ordinates
    $\quad = |\text{Difference in } x \text{ values}|$

6. For two points on a line parallel to the y-axis:

    $d = $ Absolute value of the difference of the y co-ordinates
    $\quad = |\text{Difference in the } y \text{ values}|$

EXAMPLE 1

$A(-1, 5)$, $B(2, 3)$ and $C(0, 0)$ form $\triangle ABC$. Find:

(a) $|AB|$ **(b)** $|BC|$ **(c)** $|AC|$

(d) Say whether the triangle is scalene, isosceles or equilateral.

(e) Show that $|AC|^2 = |AB|^2 + |BC|^2$.

(f) Find $|\angle ABC|$, $|\angle BAC|$ and $|\angle CAB|$.

(g) Find the area of $\triangle ABC$.

Solution

Points: $A(-1, 5)$, $B(2, 3)$, $C(0, 0)$

(a) Points: $A(-1, 5)$, $B(2, 3)$

$$|AB| = \sqrt{(-1 - 2)^2 + (5 - 3)^2} = \sqrt{9 + 4} = \sqrt{13}$$

(b) Points: $B(2, 3)$, $C(0, 0)$

$$|BC| = \sqrt{(2 - 0)^2 + (3 - 0)^2} = \sqrt{4 + 9} = \sqrt{13}$$

(c) Points: $A(-1, 5)$, $C(0, 0)$

$$|AC| = \sqrt{(-1 - 0)^2 + (5 - 0)^2} = \sqrt{1 + 25} = \sqrt{26}$$

(d) The triangle is isosceles because $|AB| = |BC|$.

(e) $|AC|^2 = 26 = 13 + 13 = |AB|^2 + |BC|^2$

Therefore, Pythagoras' theorem holds in $\triangle ABC$ with $[AC]$ as the hypotenuse:

$$\therefore |\angle ABC| = 90°$$

(f) $\left|\angle ABC\right| = 90° \Rightarrow \left|\angle BAC\right| = \left|\angle ACB\right| = 45°$

The triangle is isosceles.

(g) Area $= \frac{1}{2}\left|BC\right| \times \left|AB\right| = \frac{1}{2} \times \sqrt{13} \times \sqrt{13} = \frac{13}{2}$

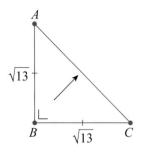

EXAMPLE 2

A sailing course is marked out as shown. A buoy B_1 is placed at $(-2, 3)$. Another buoy B_2 is placed at $(1, z)$, $z > 0$, such that $\left|B_1B_2\right| = 1000$ m. $O(0, 0)$ is the starting line for the race and one circuit of the course is the triangle OB_1B_2. If 1 unit in the Cartesian plane is 200 m, find:

(a) the value of z,

(b) how far B_2 is from O in metres, correct to the nearest metre.

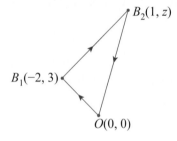

Solution

(a) 1 unit = 200 m $\Rightarrow \left|B_1B_2\right| = 1000$ m = 5 units

$$\boxed{\begin{array}{c} B_1(-2, 3) \\ \downarrow \downarrow \\ B_2(1, z) \end{array}}$$

$\left|B_1B_2\right| = \sqrt{(-2-1)^2 + (3-z)^2} = 5$

$\sqrt{9 + (3-z)^2} = 5$

$9 + (3-z)^2 = 25$

$(3-z)^2 = 16$

$3 - z = \pm 4$

$z = 7, z = -1$

$z = 7$ since $z > 0$

(b)
$$\boxed{\begin{array}{c} O(0, 0) \\ \downarrow \downarrow \\ B_2(1, 7) \end{array}}$$

$\left|OB_2\right| = \sqrt{(0-1)^2 + (0-7)^2}$

$= \sqrt{1 + 49}$

$= \sqrt{50}$

$= 5\sqrt{2}$ units

Distance $= 5\sqrt{2} \times 200$ m $= 1000\sqrt{2}$ m $\simeq 1414$ m

EXERCISE 2

1. For each of the following pairs of points, find $\left|AB\right|$.

   (a) $A(0, 0), B(4, 2)$

   (b) $A(-1, 4), B(3, 7)$

   (c) $A(4, -3), B(5, 1)$

   (d) $A(-5, 3), B(-2, 1)$

   (e) $A(-3, -2), B(-7, -3)$

   (f) $A\left(\frac{1}{2}, 1\right), B\left(\frac{3}{2}, 2\right)$

   (g) $A(\sqrt{2}, 2\sqrt{3}), B(3\sqrt{2}, \sqrt{3})$

   (h) $A(-z, 4z), B(5z, z)$

2. (a) If $A(-1, 2)$, $B(3, 5)$ and $C(11, 11)$ are three points, find:

(i) $|AC|$ **(ii)** $|BC|$

Show that $|AC| : |BC| = 3 : 2$.

(b) If $A(-2, -1)$, $B(0, 2)$ and $C(4, -4)$ are three points, find:

(i) $|AB|$ **(ii)** $|BC|$

Show that $\dfrac{|AB|}{|BC|} = \dfrac{1}{2}$.

3. Use the distance formula to classify each $\triangle ABC$ below as scalene, isosceles or equilateral.

(a) $A(1, 2)$, $B(0, 5)$, $C(-3, 6)$

(b) $A(2, 2)$, $B(5, 10)$, $C(6, 3)$

(c) $A(0, 6)$, $B(-2\sqrt{3}, 0)$, $C(2\sqrt{3}, 0)$

(d) $A(1, -\sqrt{3})$, $B(6, 0)$, $C(0, 2\sqrt{3})$

4. $A(2, -3)$, $B(5, 1)$ and $C(1, 4)$ form $\triangle ABC$.

(a) Find $|AB|$.

(b) Find $|BC|$.

(c) Find $|AC|$.

(d) Say why $\triangle ABC$ is isosceles.

(e) Show that $|AC|^2 = |AB|^2 + |BC|^2$.

(f) Find $|\angle ABC|$, $|\angle BAC|$ and $|\angle ACB|$.

(g) Find the area of $\triangle ABC$.

5. An air traffic controller sees two aeroplanes P and Q on his computer screen. Both aeroplanes are heading for the airport O at 11:15 a.m.

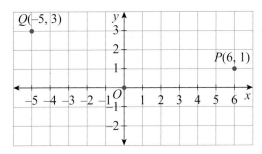

(a) If the scale on each axis is 1 unit = 1 km, find:

(i) the distance of P from the airport O at 11:15 a.m., correct to one decimal place,

(ii) the distance of Q from the airport O at 11:15 a.m., correct to one decimal place,

(iii) the distance of P from Q at 11:15 a.m., correct to one decimal place.

(b) If P is travelling at 200 km/h, what is its estimated time of arrival, correct to the nearest minute?

6. (a) Find z if $A(3, 1)$ and $B(0, z)$ are 5 units apart.

(b) Find z if $|AB| = \sqrt{106}$, where $A(2, 6)$ and $B(7, z)$ are two points.

(c) Find z if $|OA| = \sqrt{32}$, where $A(z, z)$ and $O(0, 0)$ are two points.

(d) Find z if $A(-1, 2)$ and $B(z, 0)$ are equidistant from $C(2, 3)$.

(e) $A(z, 2z)$, $B(z + 2, 3z)$ and $C(2z, 3z + 1)$ are three points. Find z if $|AB| = |AC|$.

7. Find the circumcentre of $\triangle ABC$, where $A(0, 3)$, $B(3, -1)$ and $C(3, 4)$.

8. Show that $A(-6, -4)$, $B(-6, 4)$ and $C(2, 4)$ are three vertices of a square $ABCD$. Find the fourth vertex D and the area of the square.

9. The co-ordinates of three Garda stations P, Q and R relative to Garda Headquarters at $O(0, 0)$ are $P(3, 8)$, $Q(-5, 2)$ and $R(1, -6)$. (Scale: 1 unit = 1 km)

(a) Find:

(i) $|PQ|$ **(ii)** $|QR|$ **(iii)** $|PR|$

(b) Show that $|\angle PQR| = 90°$.

(c) A communications mast is to be placed equidistant from all three stations. Where must it be placed?

(d) How far is this mast from each station?

10.3 The midpoint of a line segment

ACTIVITY 3

ACTION
Understanding the midpoint of a line segment

OBJECTIVE
To understand and work with the formula for finding the midpoint of a line segment

Given a line segment with end points $P(x_1, y_1)$ and $Q(x_2, y_2)$, it is possible to find a point R that is exactly halfway between P and Q. In other words, you can find a point $R(x, y)$ such that $|PR| = |RQ|$ or $|PR| : |RQ| = 1 : 1$.

To go from P to Q, you can go directly from P to Q, or in two steps from P to R and then from R to Q.

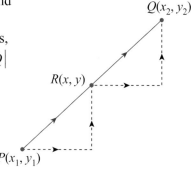

From x_1 to x_2: One step of $x_2 - x_1$ or two steps each of $\dfrac{x_2 - x_1}{2}$

$$\Rightarrow x = x_1 + \frac{x_2 - x_1}{2} = \frac{x_1 + x_2}{2}$$

From y_1 to y_2: One step of $y_2 - y_1$ or two steps each of $\dfrac{y_2 - y_1}{2}$

$$\Rightarrow y = y_1 + \frac{y_2 - y_1}{2} = \frac{y_1 + y_2}{2}$$

KEY TERM
The **midpoint** of a line segment is the point that is exactly halfway between the end points of the line segment.

The midpoint formula

The midpoint of $[PQ]$, where the points are $P(x_1, y_1)$ and $Q(x_2, y_2)$, is $R(x, y)$, where $x = \dfrac{x_1 + x_2}{2}$ and $y = \dfrac{y_1 + y_2}{2}$.

The midpoint of $[PQ]$ is $R\left(\dfrac{x_1 + x_2}{2}, \dfrac{y_1 + y_2}{2}\right)$

$Q(x_2, y_2)$
$R(x, y)$
$P(x_1, y_1)$

TIP
Remember as: $R\left(\dfrac{\text{Add the } x \text{ values}}{2}, \dfrac{\text{Add the } y \text{ values}}{2}\right)$

or $R(\text{Average of } x \text{ values, Average of } y \text{ values})$

EXAMPLE 3

Find the co-ordinates of the midpoint of $[AB]$, where $A(6, -5)$ and $B(-4, -3)$, using **(a)** the midpoint formula and **(b)** equal steps.

Solution

Points: $A(6, -5)$, $B(-4, -3)$

(a) $x = \dfrac{6 + (-4)}{2} = 1$, $y = \dfrac{-5 + (-3)}{2} = -4$

Midpoint of $[AB] = (1, -4)$

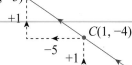

(b) x: The change in x from A to B is one step of $-4 - 6 = -10$ or two steps each of -5.

∴ x co-ordinate of the midpoint of $[AB]$ is $= 6 + (-5) = 1$

y: The change in y from A to B is one step of $-3 - (-5) = +2$ or two steps each of $+1$.

∴ y co-ordinate of the midpoint of $[AB]$ is $= -5 + 1 = -4$

∴ The midpoint of $[AB]$ is $C(1, -4)$

EXAMPLE 4

$C(-4, 7)$ is the midpoint of $[AB]$ where $A(-6, 3)$. Find the co-ordinates of B.

Solution

Method 1:

By two steps (translations):

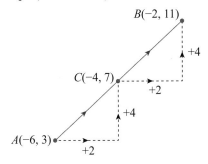

Method 2:

Use the midpoint formula: $A(-6, 3)$, $B(x, y)$

Midpoint: $C(-4, 7)$

$$\frac{-6 + x}{2} = -4 \qquad \frac{3 + y}{2} = 7$$

$$-6 + x = -8 \qquad 3 + y = 14$$

$$x = -2 \qquad y = 11$$

∴ $B(-2, 11)$

Finding the midpoint is just like going up or down stairs in one or two steps.

EXAMPLE 5

Three aeroplanes P, Q and R appear on an air traffic controller's screen with co-ordinates $P(-5, 6)$, $Q(5, 8)$ and $R(3, 2)$. The controller tells P to proceed to a point T halfway between P and R and then to turn to S so that T is halfway between S and Q. The controller goes off air before he gives P the co-ordinates of T and S. The pilot in aeroplane P is able to work out these co-ordinates. Find the total distance travelled by P to S, correct to the nearest km, if 1 unit = 1 km.

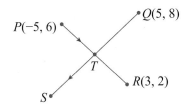

Solution

The midpoint T of $[PR] = \left(\dfrac{-5 + 3}{2}, \dfrac{6 + 2}{2}\right) = (-1, 4)$

Find the co-ordinates of S:

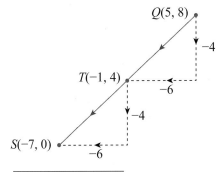

$$|PT| = \sqrt{(-5 + 1)^2 + (6 - 4)^2} = \sqrt{16 + 4} = \sqrt{20}$$

$$|TS| = \sqrt{(-1 + 7)^2 + (4 - 0)^2} = \sqrt{36 + 16} = \sqrt{52}$$

Distance travelled $= \sqrt{20} + \sqrt{52} \approx 12$ km

EXERCISE 3

Diagrams are not drawn to scale.

1. Find the midpoint C of the line segment $[AB]$, if given the following points:

   (a) $A(-1, 2)$ and $B(3, 4)$

   (b) $A(2, 0)$ and $B(4, 8)$

   (c) $A(-5, 3)$ and $B(4, -7)$

   (d) $A(1, 1)$ and $B(-1, 3)$

   (e) $A(-1, -4)$ and $B(-7, -6)$

   (f) $A\left(\frac{1}{2}, 1\right)$ and $B\left(1, -\frac{1}{2}\right)$

   (g) $A(2\sqrt{2}, -\sqrt{3})$ and $B(4\sqrt{2}, 7\sqrt{3})$

   (h) $A(2z, 0)$ and $B(0, 2z)$

   (i) $A(z + 1, z + 2)$ and $B(z - 1, 4z - 2)$

   (j) $A(x_1, y_1)$ and $B(x_2, y_2)$

2. (a) If $C(-1, 2)$ is the midpoint of $[AB]$, find $A(x, y)$ given $B(2, 1)$. Verify $|AC| = |CB|$.

   (b) If $C(-2, 3)$ is the midpoint of $[AB]$ and $A(0, 2)$, find $B(x, y)$.

   (c) A woman drives a car from A to B, takes a right turn along $[BD]$ and stops halfway at C. She then proceeds to D, turns left and ends up at E.

      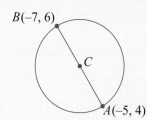

      (i) Find D.

      (ii) Find the total distance travelled if 1 unit = 1 km.

3. (a) $[AB]$ is the diameter of a circle with centre C. Find C and the radius of the circle if $A(-5, 4)$ and $B(-7, 6)$ are two points.

   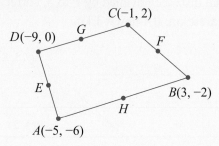

   (b) $[AB]$ is the diameter of a circle with centre C. Find the radius and the co-ordinates of B.

   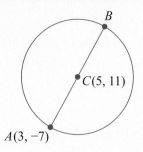

   (c) $ABCD$ is a parallelogram. Find E and hence the co-ordinates of D.

   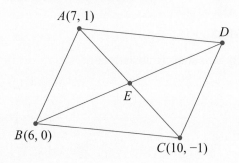

4. (a) $\triangle ACB$ is a triangle.

   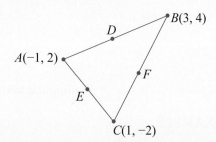

   Find:

   (i) D, the midpoint of $[AB]$,

   (ii) E, the midpoint of $[AC]$,

   (iii) F, the midpoint of $[BC]$.

   Show that $|BC| = 2|DE|$.

   Is $|AC| = 2|DF|$? Why?

   (b) $ABCD$ is a quadrilateral.

Find:

(i) E, the midpoint of $[AD]$,

(iii) G, the midpoint of $[DC]$,

(ii) F, the midpoint of $[BC]$,

(iv) H, the midpoint of $[AB]$.

Show that $|EG| = |HF|$.

(c) Find the points D, C and E that divide $[AB]$ into four equal parts, where $A(3, 7)$ and $B(19, 19)$ are two points.

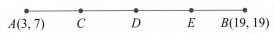

$A(3, 7) \qquad C \qquad D \qquad E \qquad B(19, 19)$

(d) $[AB]$ is a chord of the circle with centre C, where $A(-1, 3)$, $B(5, 1)$ and $C(3, 5)$ are three points.

(i) If $CP \perp AB$, find $P \in [AB]$.

(ii) Find $|AB|$.

(iii) Find the radius of the circle.

(iv) Find D on the circle.

(v) Find $|DB|$.

(vi) Show that $|\angle ABD| = 90°$.

(e) The co-ordinates of a binary asteroid are plotted from a point $O(0, 0)$ on the surface of the Earth.

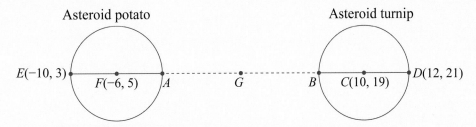

Asteroid potato

Asteroid turnip

$E(-10, 3)$ $\quad F(-6, 5) \quad A \qquad G \qquad B \quad C(10, 19) \quad D(12, 21)$

The asteroids are approximate spheres, as shown, and their centres, F and C, line up on the line $[ED]$. The centre of gravity G of the system is halfway between A and B. Find G. Find $|OG|$ in kilometres if 1 unit = 12 000 000 km, correct to the nearest km.

---

5. A teacher in a Maths class draws five points A, B, C, D and E on the board, such that $[AC]$ and $[BD]$ intersect at E. The teacher asks them to find the midpoints of $[AC]$ and $[BD]$ and then asks them what can be concluded about the points A, B, C and D.

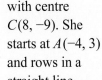

$A(-3, 4)$ $\qquad B(1, 3)$

E

$D(-4, -1)$ $\qquad C(0, -2)$

The teacher then asks the class to find:

(a) $|EB|$

(c) $|AD|$

(b) $|EC|$

(d) $|AB|$

(Hint: The diagonals of a parallelogram bisect each other.)

She then asks them to write down:

(e) $|ED|$

(g) $|BC|$

(f) $|EA|$

(h) $|DC|$

6. A woman rows a boat across an artificial circular lake with centre $C(8, -9)$. She starts at $A(-4, 3)$ and rows in a straight line through C. She ends up at B. She rows back to A via D along $[BD]$ and $[DA]$.

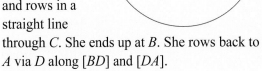

(a) Find the co-ordinates of B.

(b) Find the radius of the lake, correct to nearest metre if 1 unit = 20 m.

(c) Find the area of the lake, correct to the nearest square metre.

(d) If $|BD| = 200$ m, find $|AD|$, correct to the nearest metre.

10.4 The area of a triangle

Two expressions for the area of a triangle have been demonstrated previously:

1. Geometry

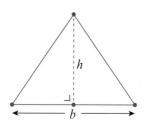

$$\text{Area} = \tfrac{1}{2}\, b \times h$$

2. Trigonometry

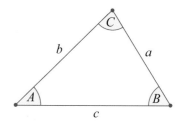

$$\text{Area} = \tfrac{1}{2}\, ab \sin C$$

Area of a triangle by vertex co-ordinates

There is a third co-ordinate geometry version for the area of a triangle, with vertices $O(0, 0)$, $P(x_1, y_1)$ and $Q(x_2, y_2)$.

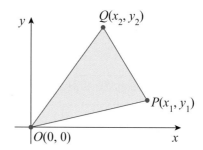

The area of a triangle with vertices $O(0, 0)$, $P(x_1, y_1)$ and $Q(x_2, y_2)$ is given by the vertex co-ordinate formula:

$$\text{Area} = \tfrac{1}{2}\left| x_1\, y_2 - x_2\, y_1 \right|$$

EXAMPLE 6

Find the area of $\triangle OPQ$, with vertices $O(0, 0)$, $P(1, 5)$ and $Q(3, 4)$.

Solution

$O(0, 0) = (\cancel{0}, \cancel{0})$ [$(0, 0)$ plays no part in calculating the area.]

$P(1, 5) = (x_1, y_1)$

$Q(3, 4) = (x_2, y_2)$

$\text{Area} = \tfrac{1}{2}\left| x_1\, y_2 - x_2\, y_1 \right|$

$\text{Area of } \triangle OPQ = \tfrac{1}{2}\left| (1)(4) - (3)(5) \right| = \tfrac{1}{2}\left| 4 - 15 \right| = \tfrac{1}{2}\left| -11 \right| = \tfrac{11}{2} = 5{\cdot}5$

Finding the area of a triangle

Find the area of $\triangle ABC$ with vertices $A(0, 0)$, $B(-1, 3)$ and $C(4, -7)$.

Quick method

1. Cross out $A(0, 0)$.

2. Write points B and C underneath each other with the arrows as shown.

$$
\begin{array}{c}
\cancel{A(0,0)} \\
B(-1, 3) \\
\text{S} \diagdown\diagup \text{F} \\
C(4, -7)
\end{array}
$$

3. Find the area from area $= \frac{1}{2}|\mathbf{F} - \mathbf{S}|$ by cross multiplying the numbers connected by the arrows.

Area $\triangle ABC = \frac{1}{2}|\mathbf{F} - \mathbf{S}|$

$= \frac{1}{2}|(-1)(-7) - (4)(3)|$

$= \frac{1}{2}|7 - 12| = \frac{1}{2}|-5|$

$= \frac{5}{2} = 2{\cdot}5$

What if one vertex is not $(0, 0)$? In this case, translate one vertex to $(0, 0)$ and let the other two vertices follow under the same translation.

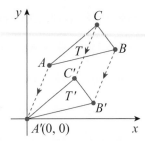

$A \to A'(0, 0)$

$B \to B'$

$C \to C'$

Remember that translating a triangle does not change its area. Find the area of T' by using the co-ordinate area formula. The area of T' is equal to the area of T.

Steps for finding the area of a triangle

1. Translate one point to $(0, 0)$.

2. Apply the same translation on the other two points.

3. Write the resulting points under one another.

$$
\begin{array}{c}
\cancel{O(0,0)} \\
P(x_1, y_1) \\
\text{S} \diagdown\diagup \text{F} \\
Q(x_2, y_2)
\end{array}
$$

Area $= \frac{1}{2}|\mathbf{F} - \mathbf{S}| = \frac{1}{2}|(x_1)(y_2) - (x_2)(y_1)|$

EXAMPLE 7

Find the area of $\triangle ABC$ with vertices $A(-1, 5)$, $B(7, -8)$ and $C(2, 7)$.

Solution

$A(-1, 5) \to A'(0, 0)$

Add $+1$ to each x co-ordinate and add -5 to each y co-ordinate.

$B(7, -8) \to B'(8, -13)$

$C(2, 7) \to C'(3, 2)$

Now find the area of $\triangle A'B'C'$ as before.

$$
\begin{array}{c}
\cancel{A'(0,0)} \\
B'(8, -13) \\
\text{S} \diagdown\diagup \text{F} \\
C'(3, 2)
\end{array}
$$

Area $\triangle ABC = \frac{1}{2}|\mathbf{F} - \mathbf{S}|$

$= \frac{1}{2}|(8)(2) - (3)(-13)|$

$= \frac{1}{2}|16 + 39|$

$= \frac{55}{2}$

$= 27{\cdot}5$

1. You can now find the area of any polygon given its vertices, as it can be split into triangles.

2. The area of a parallelogram $ABCD = 2 \times$ area of $\triangle ABC$.

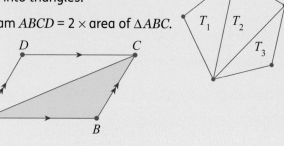

EXAMPLE 8

Find the area of a parallelogram $ABCD$ if the vertices are $A(2, -1)$, $B(4, 0)$, $C(5, 3)$ and $D(3, 2)$.

Solution

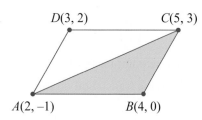

For $\triangle ABC$:

$A(2, -1) \rightarrow$ $A'(0, 0)$

$B(4, 0) \rightarrow$ $B'(2, 1)$

$C(5, 3) \rightarrow$ $C'(3, 4)$

Area $\triangle A'B'C' = \frac{1}{2}\left|(2)(4) - (3)(1)\right| = \frac{1}{2}\left|5\right| = 2{\cdot}5$

Area $ABCD = 2 \times 2{\cdot}5 = 5$

EXAMPLE 9

Find the area of the triangle formed by $A(0, 0)$, $B(2, 1)$ and $C(4, z)$ in terms of z.

(a) Find z if the area of $\triangle ABC$ is 6.

(b) Find z if A, B, C are collinear.

Solution

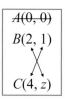

Area $\triangle ABC = \frac{1}{2}\left|(2)(z) - (4)(1)\right| = \frac{1}{2}\left|2z - 4\right| = \left|z - 2\right|$

(a) $\left|z - 2\right| = 6 \Rightarrow z - 2 = \pm 6$

$z = 8, -4$

(b) A, B, C are collinear, which means the area of $\triangle ABC = 0$.

$\left|z - 2\right| = 0 \Rightarrow z - 2 = 0 \Rightarrow z = 2$

EXAMPLE 10

Three marine researchers wish to map out a triangular area ADB of the seabed. A takes up a position on the shore and B takes up a position on a headland perpendicular to the shore. C rows out from a point on the shore and moves parallel to the headland until she reaches D, such that the area of the $\triangle ADB$ is $250\,000$ m^2.

Find how far C rows out to sea, if $A(6, 0)$, $B(0, 5)$, $D(4, z)$ and 1 unit on each scale is 100 m.

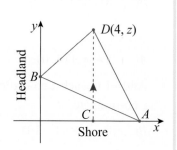

Solution

Area of $\triangle ADB$

$A(6, 0) \rightarrow A'(0, 0)$

$D(4, z) \rightarrow \boxed{(-2, z)}$

$B(0, 5) \rightarrow \boxed{(-6, 5)}$

Area $\triangle ADB = \frac{1}{2}\left|(-2)(5) - (-6)(z)\right| = \frac{1}{2}\left|-10 + 6z\right| = \left|3z - 5\right|$

$250\,000$ m^2 = 25 units squared

$\left|3z - 5\right| = 25 \Rightarrow 3z - 5 = \pm\, 25$

$3z = 30$ or $3z = -20$

$z = 10$ or $z = -\frac{20}{3}$

Clearly, $z = 10$ from the diagram.

Distance C rows out = $10 \times 100 = 1000$ m
= 1 km

EXERCISE 4

Diagrams are not drawn to scale.

1. Find the area of $\triangle ABC$ if given the following points:

   (a) $A(0, 0)$, $B(3, 5)$, $C(2, 8)$

   (b) $A(0, 0)$, $B(-4, 6)$, $C(3, 6)$

   (c) $A(0,0)$, $B\left(\frac{3}{2}, \frac{2}{3}\right)$, $C\left(3, \frac{8}{3}\right)$

   (d) $A(0, 0)$, $B(a, b)$, $C(-b, a)$

   (e) $A(1, -3)$, $B(-4, 1)$, $C(2, 5)$

   (f) $A(z, z + 2)$, $B(z + 3, z - 1)$, $C(z + 2, z + 3)$

2. Find the area of $\triangle ABC$.

   (a)

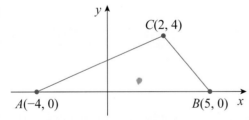

   (b)

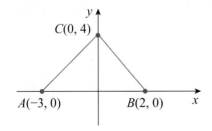

(c)

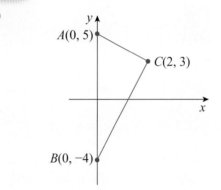

3. Show that $ABCD$ is a parallelogram by finding the midpoints of $[AC]$ and $[BD]$. In each case, find the area of the parallelogram:

   (a) $A(0, 0)$, $B(4, 1)$, $C(5, 4)$, $D(1, 3)$

   (b) $A(4, -3)$, $B(-2, -5)$, $C(-3, 4)$, $D(3, 6)$

4. Find the area of the quadrilateral $OBCD$, where the vertices are $O(0, 0)$, $B(7, 1)$, $C(5, 5)$ and $D(1, 6)$.

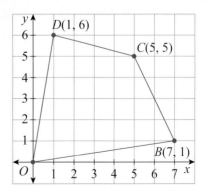

5. A rectangular field $OABC$ has a triangular section $\triangle DEF$ roped off for planting. A path FG runs through this triangular section at right angles to DE.

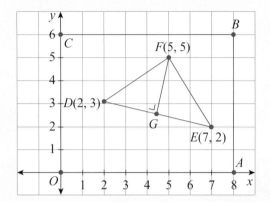

Find:

(a) the area of $\triangle DEF$ in m^2,

(b) the area of the unplanted section in m^2,

(c) the length of the path $[FG]$, correct to one decimal place.
(1 unit on each axis = 10 m)

6. (a) Find z, if 17 is the area of the triangle $\triangle ABC$, with vertices $A(0, 0)$, $B(3, z)$ and $C(-1, 4)$.

(b) Find z, if 9·5 is the area of the triangle $\triangle ABC$, with vertices $A(0, 0)$, $B(z, 2)$ and $C(3, z)$.

(c) Find z, if 7 is the area of the triangle $\triangle ABC$, with vertices $A(-1, 2)$, $B(2, 3)$ and $C(z, 5)$.

(d) Find z, if the points $A(2, 1)$, $B(z + 1, z + 3)$ and $C(z + 3, z)$ are collinear.

(e) If $A(-3, 4)$, $B(5, 8)$ and $C(x, y)$ are three points such that the area of $\triangle ABC = 2$, show that C can be on either of two parallel lines.

7. A ship sails from port $P(0, 0)$ to $A(3, 4)$ to begin laying a triangular boom around an oil slick. The slick is in the form of a triangle $\triangle ABD$ with vertices $A(3, 4)$, $B(12, 3)$ and $D(7, 8)$. The scale of each axis is 1 unit = 100 m.

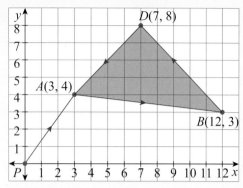

(a) Find the distance the ship travels from port P to the starting point A of its boom-laying operation.

(b) Find the area of the oil slick.

(c) If the ship is moving at 8 km/h, find the time it takes the ship to complete the operation (that is, the time to return to P), correct to the nearest minute.

8. A circular lake is constructed inside a triangular-paved area in a shopping centre. The co-ordinates of the vertices of the triangle are relative to the centre of the lake $O(0, 0)$. The scale on this diagram is 1 unit = 10 m. If the radius of the circle is 1 unit, find the area of the paved area correct to the nearest m^2.

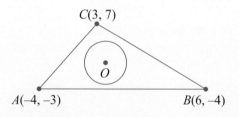

9. Prove that the area of $\triangle ABC = \frac{1}{2}|x_1 y_2 - x_2 y_1|$ by subtracting the areas of the triangles $T_1 (\triangle ADB)$, $T_2 (\triangle BEC)$, $T_3 (\triangle ACF)$ from the area of the rectangle $ADEF$.

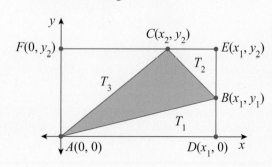

10. (a) **(i)** Show that the length of the radius r of the incircle of any triangle ABC is given by:

$$r = \frac{2 \text{ (Area of } \triangle ABC)}{\text{Perimeter of } \triangle ABC}$$

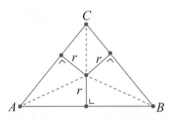

(ii) For $\triangle ABC$ with $A(7, 0)$, $B(3, -2)$ and $C(5, 4)$, find its radius, correct to two decimal places.

(b) **(i)** A perfect triangle is a triangle in which the area is numerically equal to the length of the perimeter. Show that the radius of the incircle of a perfect triangle must be 2.

(ii) Use the cosine rule to find $\cos \theta$. Hence, write down $\sin \theta$. Show that the area of this triangle = 36. Is this a perfect triangle?

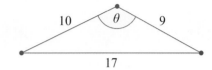

10.5 Slope of a straight line

Which of the two lines l_1 or l_2 is steeper? Which is harder to climb up or, alternatively, which gives you the best thrill sliding down?

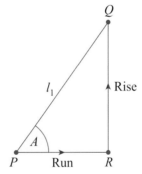

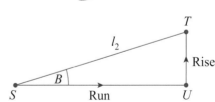

Line l_1 is steeper of course. It has a bigger slope than line l_2 because the angle A is bigger than B.

The **slope** of a line is a measure of its steepness.

Measurement of slope

l_1 has a big slope because the length of the rise (vertical or y step) of l_1 is much bigger than the length of its run (horizontal or x step). However, the length of the rise of l_2 is much less than the length of its run and so its slope is small. This leads to the idea of how to measure the slope of a line.

The slope m of a line is how much the length of the rise is bigger or smaller than the length of its run.

$$\text{Slope } m \text{ of a line} = \frac{\text{Rise}}{\text{Run}} = \frac{\text{Vertical step}}{\text{Horizontal step}}$$

For more advanced work, the precise definition below is needed.

> **KEY TERM**
>
> The slope m of a line is the tan of the angle measured to the line from the $+x$-axis in an anticlockwise direction:
>
> $m = \tan A$

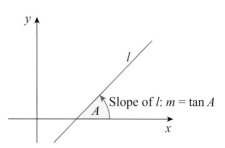

Slope of l: $m = \tan A$

Examples of slopes

▶ **1.**

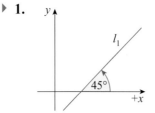

$m_1 = \tan 45° = +1$

▶ **2.**

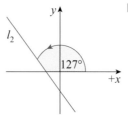

$m_2 = \tan 127° = -1 \cdot 33$

▶ **3.**

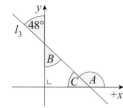

$B = 48° \Rightarrow C = 42°$

$A = 180° - 42° = 138°$

$m_3 = \tan 138° \simeq 0 \cdot 9$

1. Acute vs obtuse angles

(a) Acute angle

If A is acute, $m = \tan A > 0$ (m is positive). If $m > 0$, the line rises as you go from left to right.

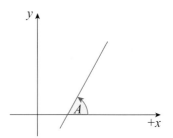

(b) Obtuse angle

If A is obtuse, $m = \tan A < 0$ (m is negative). If $m < 0$, the line falls as you go from left to right.

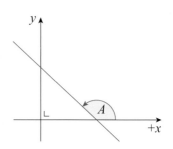

2. Horizontal and vertical lines

(a) Horizontal lines (lines parallel to the x-axis)

All horizontal lines make an angle of $0°$ with the $+x$-axis: $m = \tan 0° = 0$

They all have zero slope – they are dead flat.

> The slope of every horizontal line is 0.

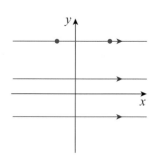

(b) Vertical lines (lines parallel to the y-axis)

All vertical lines make an angle of 90°
with the +y-axis: $m = \tan 90° = \infty$

They all have infinite slopes – they
are dead steep.

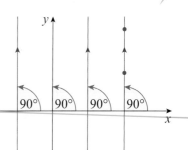

> The slope of every vertical line is ∞.

EXAMPLE 11

Find the slopes of the lines l_1, l_2 and l_3 in the
diagram below.

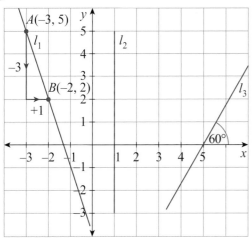

Solution

$l_1: m_1 = \dfrac{\text{Rise}}{\text{Run}} = \dfrac{-3}{+1} = -3$

$l_2: m_2 = \tan 90° = \infty$

$l_3: m_3 = \tan 60° = \sqrt{3}$

EXAMPLE 12

Find the slope of the Leaning Tower of Pisa and
the angle of tilt ϕ to the vertical.

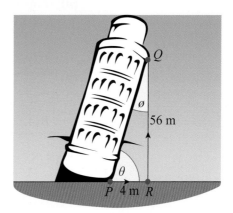

Solution

$m = \tan \theta = \dfrac{56}{4} = 14$

$\theta = \tan^{-1}(14) = 85\cdot9°$

$\phi = 90° - 85\cdot9° = 4\cdot1°$

The slope formula

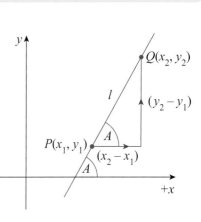

Consider the two points $P(x_1, y_1)$ and $Q(x_2, y_2)$
which are any two points on the line l.

$$m = \tan A = \frac{(y_2 - y_1)}{(x_2 - x_1)}$$

The slope of a line given any two points
$P(x_1, y_1)$ and $Q(x_2, y_2)$ on the line is
given by the slope formula:

$$m = \frac{(y_2 - y_1)}{(x_2 - x_1)} = \frac{\text{Difference in } y \text{ co-ordinates}}{\text{Difference in } x \text{ co-ordinates}}$$

Some points to note on the slope formula

1. The difference in the y co-ordinates is always on the top in this formula, while the difference in the x co-ordinates is always on the bottom.

2. The differences in the above formula **must** always be calculated in the same order for the y co-ordinates and the x co-ordinates.

   If $(y_2 - y_1)$ is on the top, $(x_2 - x_1)$ must be on the bottom. However, if $(y_1 - y_2)$ is on the top, $(x_1 - x_2)$ must be on the bottom.

3. $0° \leq A \leq 180°$ always.

EXAMPLE 13

(a) Find the slope of the line AB if $A(3, -1)$ and $B(4, 5)$.

(b) If the slope of the line AB is $-\frac{2}{3}$, find z, where $A(2, 3)$ and $B(z, -2)$.

Solution

(a)
$$
\boxed{\begin{array}{cc} A(3, & -1) \\ \downarrow & \downarrow \\ B(4, & 5) \end{array}}
$$

Slope $m = \dfrac{-1 - 5}{3 - 4} = 6$

(b)
$$
\boxed{\begin{array}{cc} A(2, & 3) \\ \downarrow & \downarrow \\ B(z, & -2) \end{array}}
$$

$$
m = \frac{3 - (-2)}{2 - z} = -\frac{2}{3}
$$

$$
\frac{5}{2 - z} = -\frac{2}{3}
$$

$$
15 = -2(2 - z)
$$

$$
15 = -4 + 2z
$$

$$
2z = 19
$$

$$
z = \frac{19}{2}
$$

EXAMPLE 14

Find the slope of line PQ, where $P(-1, 2)$ and $Q(-7, 7)$. State whether the angle the line makes with the $+x$-axis is acute or obtuse. Find this angle, correct to one decimal place.

Solution

$$
\boxed{\begin{array}{c} P(-1, 2) \\ \downarrow \downarrow \\ Q(-7, 7) \end{array}}
$$

$$
m = \frac{2 - 7}{-1 - (-7)} = -\frac{5}{6} = \tan A
$$

$m < 0 \Rightarrow$ angle A is obtuse.

Solve $\tan A = -\frac{5}{6}$.

The reference angle $\theta = \tan^{-1}\left(\frac{5}{6}\right)$

$$
= 39 \cdot 8°
$$

$$
A = \begin{cases} 180° - 39 \cdot 8° = 140 \cdot 2° \\ 360° - 39 \cdot 8° = 320 \cdot 2° \end{cases}
$$

$A = 140 \cdot 2°$ (obtuse)

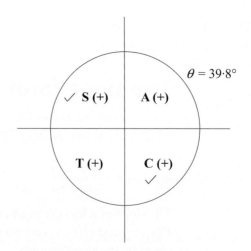

Parallel and perpendicular lines

1. Parallel lines

Parallel lines all make the same angle with the $+x$-axis. (The x-axis is a transversal.)

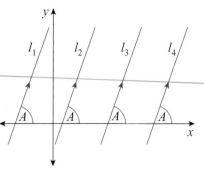

Conversely, all lines that have the same slope $m = \tan A$ must make the same angle A with the $+x$-axis and so are parallel. Parallel lines are all equally steep; they are just in different places.

> **Parallel lines**
>
> For any two lines l_1 and l_2 with slopes m_1 and m_2, respectively: $l_1 \parallel l_2 \Leftrightarrow m_1 = m_2$
>
> 1. Parallel lines have equal slopes.
>
> 2. Lines with equal slopes are parallel.

▶ $m_1 = 2{\cdot}8 = \tan 70{\cdot}3°$

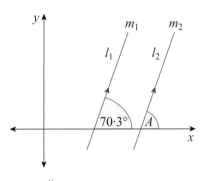

$$l_1 \parallel l_2 \Rightarrow m_2 = 2{\cdot}8$$
$$m_1 = m_2 \Leftrightarrow A = 70{\cdot}3°$$

▶ $m_1 = m_2 = 3{\cdot}3$

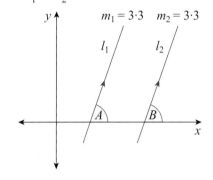

$$\Rightarrow \tan A = \tan B = 3{\cdot}3$$
$$\therefore A = B = 73°$$
$$\therefore l_1 \parallel l_2$$

EXAMPLE **15**

(a) Show that the line AB is parallel to the line CD, if $A(-1, 2)$, $B(3, 5)$, $C(-2, -3)$ and $D(2, 0)$.

(b) If PQ is parallel to RS, find z, where the points are $P(1, 3)$, $Q(4, 5)$, $R(z, 2)$ and $S(2, -8)$.

Solution

(a)
$$\begin{array}{c} A(-1, 2) \\ \downarrow\ \downarrow \\ B(3, 5) \end{array}$$

Slope of AB: $m_1 = \dfrac{2 - 5}{-1 - 3} = \dfrac{3}{4}$

$$\begin{array}{c} C(-2, -3) \\ \downarrow\ \downarrow \\ D(2,\ 0) \end{array}$$

Slope of $CD = m_2 = \dfrac{-3 - 0}{-2 - 2} = \dfrac{3}{4}$

$$m_1 = m_2 \Rightarrow AB \parallel CD$$

(b)
$$\begin{array}{c} P(1, 3) \\ \downarrow\ \downarrow \\ Q(4, 5) \end{array}$$

Slope of PQ: $m_1 = \dfrac{3 - 5}{1 - 4} = \dfrac{2}{3}$

$$\begin{array}{c} R(z,\ 2) \\ \downarrow\ \downarrow \\ S(2, -8) \end{array}$$

Slope of RS: $m_2 = \dfrac{2 - (-8)}{z - 2} = \dfrac{10}{z - 2}$

$$PQ \parallel RS \Rightarrow m_1 = m_2$$
$$\therefore \frac{2}{3} = \frac{10}{(z - 2)}$$
$$2(z - 2) = 30$$
$$2z - 4 = 30$$
$$2z = 34$$
$$z = 17$$

2. Perpendicular lines

Consider the anticlockwise rotation of a line through 90°.

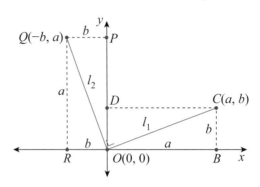

Rotate a rectangular piece of cardboard $OBCD$ anticlockwise through 90° by sticking a pin into it at $O(0, 0)$. It rotates into the rectangle $OPQR$. Horizontal lines in $OBCD$ become vertical lines in $OPQR$ and vertical lines in $OBCD$ become horizontal lines in $OPQR$.

$[OB] \rightarrow [OP]$, $[BC] \rightarrow [PQ]$, $[CD] \rightarrow [QR]$, $[DO] \rightarrow [RO]$, $l_1 \rightarrow l_2$ and $C(a, b) \rightarrow Q(-b, a)$

The slope of $l_1 = m_1 = \dfrac{b - 0}{a - 0} = \dfrac{b}{a}$

The slope of $l_2 = m_2 = \dfrac{a - 0}{-b - 0} = -\dfrac{a}{b}$

The slope of $l_2 = -\dfrac{1}{\text{Slope of } l_1}$

This means $m_2 = -\dfrac{1}{m_1}$ or $m_1 m_2 = -1$.

Perpendicular lines

For any two lines l_1 and l_2 with slopes m_1 and m_2, respectively:
$l_1 \perp l_2 \Leftrightarrow m_1 m_2 = -1$

1. If two lines are perpendicular, the product of their slopes is -1.

2. If the product of the slopes of two lines is -1, the lines are perpendicular:
$$m_1 \times m_2 = -1 \Leftrightarrow m_2 = -\frac{1}{m_1} \Leftrightarrow l_1 \perp l_2$$

EXAMPLE 16

Show the line AB is perpendicular to the line CD, if $A(-1, 2)$, $B(3, 4)$, $C(4, -2)$ and $D(3, 0)$.

Solution

$A(-1, 2)$
↓ ↓
$B(3, 4)$

Slope of AB: $m_1 = \dfrac{2 - 4}{-1 - 3} = \dfrac{1}{2}$

$C(4, -2)$
↓ ↓
$D(3, 0)$

Slope of CD: $m_2 = \dfrac{-2 - 0}{4 - 3} = -\dfrac{2}{1}$

$m_1 m_2 = \dfrac{1}{2} \times -\dfrac{2}{1} = -1 \Rightarrow AB \perp CD$

EXAMPLE 17

(a) Find the slope of a line perpendicular to AB, if $A(5, -7)$ and $B(-2, -3)$.

(b) If the line PQ is perpendicular to the line RS, find z, if $P(-1, 3)$, $Q(-3, 7)$, $R(2, z)$ and $S(0, 1)$ are four points.

Solution

(a)
$$\begin{array}{c} A(5, -7) \\ \downarrow \quad \downarrow \\ B(-2, -3) \end{array}$$

Slope of AB: $m = \dfrac{-7 - (-3)}{5 - (-2)} = -\dfrac{4}{7}$

The slope of a line perpendicular to $AB = \dfrac{-1}{-\dfrac{4}{7}}$

$$= \dfrac{7}{4}$$

(b)
$$\begin{array}{c} P(-1, 3) \\ \downarrow \quad \downarrow \\ Q(-3, 7) \end{array}$$

Slope of PQ: $m_1 = \dfrac{3 - 7}{-1 - (-3)} = \dfrac{-4}{2} = -2$

$$\begin{array}{c} R(2, z) \\ \downarrow \quad \downarrow \\ S(0, 1) \end{array}$$

Slope of RS: $m_2 = \dfrac{(z - 1)}{2 - 0} = \dfrac{(z - 1)}{2}$

$PQ \perp RS \Rightarrow m_1 m_2 = -1$

$$(-2)\left(\dfrac{z - 1}{2}\right) = -1$$

$$z - 1 = 1$$

$$z = 2$$

Collinear points

If the line AB is parallel to the line BC, then the lines AB and BC must be one and the same line because B has to be on both lines.

The three points A, B and C are on the same straight line. These points are said to be collinear.

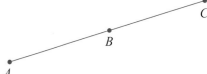

KEY TERM

Three points are **collinear** if they are on the same straight line.

This means that the slope of AB = slope of BC = slope of AC = the unique slope of the line.

TIP

To show that three points are collinear, you must show that the slope calculated from any pair of points is the same as the slope calculated from any other pair of points.

EXAMPLE 18

Show that the points $A(-1, 2)$, $B(2, 5)$ and $C(4, 7)$ are collinear.

Solution

$$\begin{array}{c} A(-1, 2) \\ \downarrow \quad \downarrow \\ B(2, 5) \end{array}$$
Slope of AB: $m_1 = \dfrac{2 - 5}{-1 - 2} = 1$

$$\begin{array}{c} B(2, 5) \\ \downarrow \quad \downarrow \\ C(4, 7) \end{array}$$

Slope of BC: $m_2 = \dfrac{5 - 7}{2 - 4} = 1$

$m_1 = m_2 = 1$

$\Rightarrow$ slope of AB = slope of BC = 1

= slope of the line through A, B and C

$\therefore A$, B and C are collinear.

EXAMPLE 19

For the points $A(-2, 6)$, $B(4, -3)$ and $C(z, 1)$, find z, if A, B and C are collinear.

Solution

$$A(-2, \quad 6)$$
$$\downarrow \quad \downarrow$$
$$B(4, -3)$$

Slope of AB: $m_1 = \dfrac{6 - (-3)}{-2 - 4} = -\dfrac{3}{2}$

$$B(4, \quad -3)$$
$$\downarrow \quad \downarrow$$
$$C(z, \quad 1)$$

Slope of BC: $m_2 = \dfrac{-3 - 1}{4 - z} = \dfrac{-4}{4 - z}$

A, B, C are collinear $\Rightarrow m_1 = m_2 \Rightarrow -\dfrac{3}{2} = \dfrac{-4}{(4 - z)}$

$3(4 - z) = 8$

$12 - 3z = 8$

$3z = 4$

$z = \dfrac{4}{3}$

Average rate of change

We see slopes in everyday life, whether climbing up the stairs or driving down a hill. However, there is another way to look at slopes.

The formula: $m = \dfrac{\text{Change in } y}{\text{Change in } x} = \dfrac{y_2 - y_1}{x_2 - x_1}$ enables us to view the slope m as a measure of how fast y changes on average by comparison to x.

The slope m of a line joining two points is a measure of the average rate of change of y with respect to x between those two points.

▸ If the slope of a line is 2, the y co-ordinate is changing twice as fast as the x co-ordinate. So if x changes by $+4$, y changes by $+8$ (y increases as x increases).

▸ $m = -\dfrac{1}{2} \Rightarrow \dfrac{\text{Change in } y}{\text{Change in } x} = -\dfrac{1}{2}$

If x changes by $+4$, y changes by -2 (y decreases as x increases).

TIP

Graphs in mathematics are always read from left to right in the direction of increasing values of x. The change in x is always positive when working out the change in y. This means that a positive value for the change in y means y is increasing and that a negative value means y is decreasing.

WORKED EXAMPLE Exploring average rate of change

A greyhound trainer timed the distance s in metres travelled by a young greyhound every second. He plotted the greyhound's performance on a graph, as shown.

Slope $m = \dfrac{s_2 - s_1}{t_2 - t_1} = \dfrac{60 - 15}{4 - 1} = \dfrac{45}{3} = +15$ m/s $= \dfrac{\text{Change in distance}}{\text{Change in time}}$

The greyhound's distance increases 15 times faster than the time increases. For every 1 second increase in time, the greyhound's distance increases by 15 m. The average rate of change of distance with respect to time = slope of the distance against time graph = 15 m/s

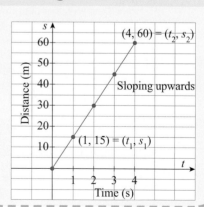

EXERCISE 5

Diagrams are not drawn to scale.

1. **(a)** Find the slope of *l* in surd form.

    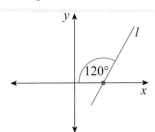

    (b) Find the slope of *l* in surd form.

    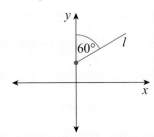

    (c) Find the slope of *l* correct to three decimal places.

    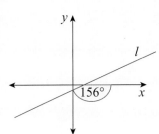

    (d) Find the slope of *l* as an integer.

    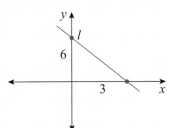

2. **(a)** Find the slope of *AB*.

    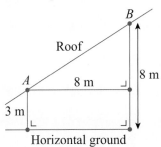

    (b) Find the slope of the ramp *AB*.

    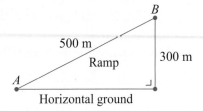

    (c) A category 3 climb on one stage of the Tour de France has a slope of 10%. If the length of the climb is 1 km, find the rise and the run, correct to one decimal place.

    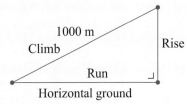

    (Hint: Let rise = *h*)

3. Find the slopes of the following:

    (a) A line *AB* where $A(0, 0)$ and $B(-1, 4)$

    (b) A line passing through the points $A(2, -1)$ and $B(4, 7)$

    (c) A line with points $A\left(\frac{1}{2}, -1\right)$ and $B\left(2, \frac{1}{3}\right)$ on it

    (d) A line through $(1, 2)$ parallel to the *x*-axis

    (e) A line through $(-1, 4)$ parallel to the *y*-axis

    (f) A line making an angle of $150°$ with the $+x$-axis

    (g) A line making an angle of $\tan^{-1}\left(\frac{3}{2}\right)$ with the $+x$-axis

    (h) A line making an angle of $\tan^{-1}(-2)$ with the $+x$-axis

    (i) The *x*-axis

    (j) A line making $60°$ with $+y$-axis

4. Find *z* if the slope of *AB* is:

    (a) $\frac{1}{3}$, where the points are $A(z, 1)$ and $B(0, 0)$,

    (b) -2, where the points are $A(z, 3)$ and $B(2, 1)$,

    (c) $-\frac{5}{4}$, where the points are $A(z, -2)$ and $B(4, z + 1)$.

273

5. (a) Find the slope of the line AB, if $A(-2, 3)$ and $B(4, 7)$. State whether the line makes an acute or obtuse angle with the $+x$-axis, and find this angle, correct to one decimal place.

(b) Find the slope of the line AB, if $A(7, -1)$ and $B(5, 3)$. State whether or not the line makes an acute or obtuse angle with the $+x$-axis, and find this angle, correct to one decimal place.

6. (a) Write down the slope of a line parallel to the line AB, if $A(3, -5)$ and $B(4, 11)$.

(b) Show that the line AB is parallel to the line CD, where $A(1, 3)$, $B(4, 7)$, $C(5, 3)$ and $D(11, 11)$.

(c) Show that the line AB is not parallel to the line CD, where $A(2, -3)$, $B(1, 2)$, $C(3, 7)$ and $D(-4, -1)$ are four points.

(d) If the line AB is parallel to the line BC, what can you say about these lines?

(e) Find z if the line AB is parallel to the line CD, where $A(z, -2)$, $B(3, 6)$, $C(-1, -3)$ and $D(-2, 1)$ are four points.

7. (a) Test whether or not the line AB is perpendicular to the line CD, given the following points:

    (i) $A(-1, 4)$, $B(3, 2)$, $C(0, 3)$ $D(1, 5)$

    (ii) $A(3, 7)$, $B(4, 2)$, $C(-6, -3)$ $D(0, 1)$

    (iii) $A(z, z + 2)$, $B(z - 6, z - 3)$, $C(z + 1, z)$, $D(z - 4, z + 6)$

(b) Write down the slope of a line perpendicular to the line AB, given the following points:

    (i) $A(3, 2)$, $B(5, 7)$

    (ii) $A(-1, 4)$, $B(2, -6)$

    (iii) $A(2, 4)$, $B(-8, 4)$

    (iv) $A(-9, 3)$, $B(-7, 11)$

(c) Find z if the line AB is perpendicular to CD, given the following points:

    (i) $A(z, -1)$, $B(3, 4)$, $C(-1, 0)$, $D(4, 2)$

    (ii) $A(-3, 5)$, $B(4, 1)$, $C(2, -3)$, $D(6, z)$

(d) Find z if the line AB is perpendicular to a line of slope $-\frac{5}{2}$, where $A(3, 2)$ and $B(z, -3)$ are two points.

(e) Given the points $A(1, 4)$, $B(-2, 0)$, $C(5, -2)$ and $D(3, z)$, find z, if:

    (i) the line AB is parallel to the line CD,

    (ii) the line AD is perpendicular to the line BC.

8. In $\triangle ABC$ the vertices are $A(-1, 2)$, $B(3, 7)$ and $C(-2, 11)$. By finding the slopes of the lines AB, AC and BC, show that $\triangle ABC$ is a right-angled triangle. Which angle is the right angle?

9. (a) Show that the points A, B and C are collinear, given $A(-5, -3)$, $B(4, -2)$ and $C(22, 0)$.

(b) Show that the points A, B and C are non-collinear, given $A(-2, 3)$, $B(4, 1)$ and $C(6, 2)$.

(c) Find z if the points $A(1, 2)$, $B(z, 3)$ and $C(5, 4)$ are collinear.

10. A man wants to build a drain in a straight line running from $R(2, 3)$ to $P(8, 11)$ in his garden. He wants to put a marker at $Q(5, y)$ so that Q is on the line RP.

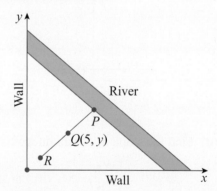

(a) Find y.

(b) Find $\left|RQ\right|$ in metres.

(c) Find $\left|QP\right|$ in metres.
(Scale: 1 unit on each axis is 2 m)
What can you conclude?

11. The slope of a line p_1 is $\frac{5}{8}$ and the slope of a line q_1 is $-\frac{8}{5}$.

(a) What is the angle between the lines?

If p_1 is rotated through 90° to the line p_2 and q_1 is rotated through 90° to the line q_2:

(b) what is the slope of p_2,

(c) what is the slope of q_2,

(d) what is the angle between p_2 and q_2?

12. A line p has slope -3. It makes an acute angle of θ with the $+y$-axis. The line p is rotated clockwise through $90°$ to a line q.

   (a) What is the slope of q?

   (b) The y-axis is rotated clockwise through $90°$ to a line l. What is this line l called?

   (c) Find θ correct to one decimal place.

13. $C(4, 3)$ is a point on the line AB. The area of $\triangle AOB$ is 24, where $O(0, 0)$. Write down two equations in a and b and hence find a and b. (Hint: B, C and A are collinear.)

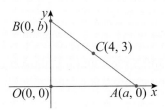

14. The height h in metres of an aeroplane above the ground is plotted against the distance s in metres travelled down the runway.

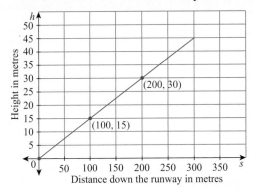

   (a) Find the average rate of change of the height of the aeroplane with respect to its distance down the runway.

   (b) For a change of 70 m along the runway, what is the change in height?

15. The population P of a country in millions is recorded against time t in years, where $t = 0$ is the year that records began.

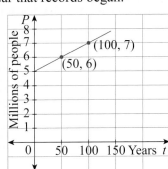

   (a) Has the population increased or decreased since records began?

   (b) What is the average rate of change of the population?

   (c) What was the population in the year that records began?

16. A car's distance s in kilometres is plotted against time t in hours for a journey of 9 hours.

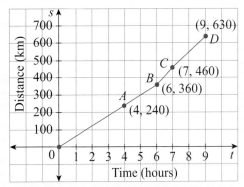

   (a) Find the average speed of the car:

     (i) from O to A,   **(iii)** from B to C,

     (ii) from A to B,   **(iv)** from C to D.

   (b) Find the total distance and total time for the journey and the average speed for the whole journey.

17. The graph below shows the number of grams m of a substance that can be dissolved in a fixed quantity of water when the temperature of the water is $T\,°C$.

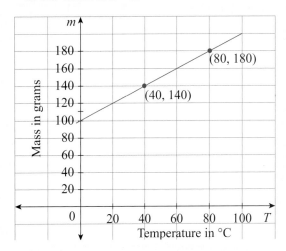

Find:

   (a) the average rate at which the mass of the substance dissolves per $°C$,

   (b) the mass that can be dissolved at $0\,°C$.

10.6 The equation of a straight line

WORKED EXAMPLE

Exploring a linear relationship 1

Consider the diagrams as shown below.

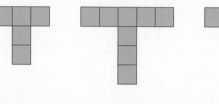 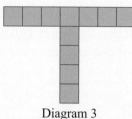

Diagram 1   Diagram 2   Diagram 3

Let n represent the diagram number and S represent the number of squares in each diagram. The table below shows how S is related to n for these three diagrams.

Diagram number (n)	1	2	3
Number of squares (S)	5	8	11

To find a general formula connecting S to n, the values of S are plotted on the vertical (y) axis against the values n on the horizontal (x) axis.

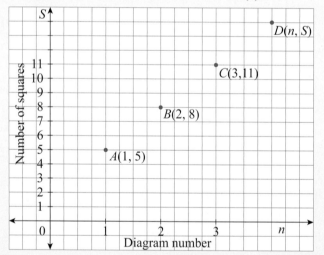

The three points A, B and C are collinear. This means there is a **linear relationship** between S and n. If the point $D(n, S)$ is collinear with the other three points, then:

Slope of AD = Slope of AB

$$\Rightarrow \frac{(S-5)}{(n-1)} = \frac{8-5}{2-1} = 3$$

$$(S-5) = 3(n-1)$$

$$S - 5 = 3n - 3$$

$$S = 3n + 2$$

This equation is the **equation of the straight line** that would pass through A, B and C. This equation is very powerful as it enables you to predict the number of squares in any diagram without having to draw the diagram. For example, the number of squares in diagram 20 is obtained by putting $n = 20$ into this equation.

$n = 20 \Rightarrow S = 3(20) + 2 = 62$

There are 62 squares in diagram 20.

Notes

1. Since the number of squares S **depends** on the diagram number n, S is known as the dependent variable and n the independent variable.

2. The dependent variable is always plotted on the y-axis and the independent variable on the x-axis.

3. Strictly speaking, the points should not be joined by a straight line as n is a discrete variable. It can only take on certain discrete values $n = 1, 2, 3, \ldots$ For example, the 3·5th diagram does not exist.

Now consider an example of a linear relationship involving a continuous variable. This is a variable that can have any real number value, e.g. temperature.

KEY TERM

A **continuous variable** is a variable that can have any real number value.

WORKED EXAMPLE Exploring a linear relationship 2

Joe and his family are going to Disneyland in Florida for a two-week summer vacation. He has learned in Science class that Americans use a different temperature scale called the Fahrenheit scale. He wants to get an equation connecting degrees Celsius (C) to degrees Fahrenheit (F) so that he can convert Fahrenheit to Celsius. He knows:

Freezing point of water	Boiling point of water
32 °F	212 °F
0 °C	100 °C

He also knows that there is a linear relationship between C and F.

Using this information, he plots a straight-line graph with F as the independent variable and C as the dependent variable. He has two points, $A(32, 0)$ and $B(212, 100)$, and there is a linear relationship between C and F. He plots these two points and joins them with a straight line. All other points connecting C and F lie on this line.

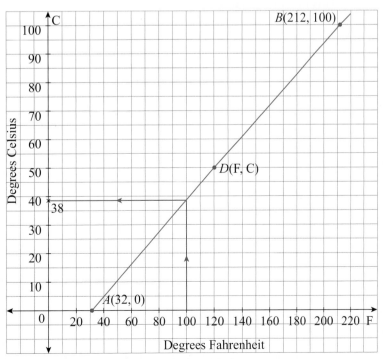

The points A, D and B are collinear.

$\Rightarrow$ slope of AD = slope of AB

$$\frac{C - 0}{(F - 32)} = \frac{100 - 0}{212 - 32}$$

$$C = \frac{100(F - 32)}{180}$$

$$C = \frac{5}{9}(F - 32) = \frac{5F}{9} - \frac{160}{9}$$

Again, this is a very powerful result. It enables Joe to convert any Fahrenheit temperature to the corresponding Celsius temperature with which he is familiar, using the calculator on his phone.

For example, F = 100: $C = \frac{5}{9}(100 - 32)$

$$= \frac{5}{9} \times 68 \simeq 38\ °C$$

He could equally well have used his graph to get a direct reading for F = 100, as shown on the graph. Clearly, given two points on a straight line, it is always possible to get a general formula connecting any dependent variable y on this straight line with its corresponding independent variable x. This formula is known as the equation of the straight line.

Finding the equation of a straight line

Given a point $P(3, 2)$, there is an infinite number of lines you can draw through it. They all have different slopes.

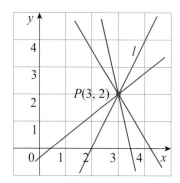 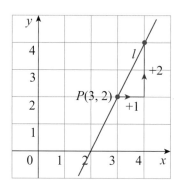

However, given a point $P(3, 2)$, there is only one line that can be drawn through it with slope 2.

This line l is unique.

In general, given a point (x_1, y_1) and a slope m, there is one and only one line that can be drawn through (x_1, y_1) with this slope. (x_1, y_1) and m completely determine a unique straight line.

Finding the equation of a straight line

Consider a line l of slope m passing through the point (x_1, y_1). If (x, y) is any other point on l, we can find a formula connecting x and y as follows:

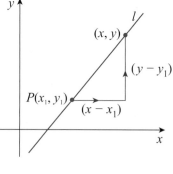

$$\text{Slope of } l = m = \frac{\text{Rise}}{\text{Run}} = \frac{y - y_1}{(x - x_1)} \Rightarrow m = \frac{(y - y_1)}{(x - x_1)}$$

$$\Rightarrow (y - y_1) = m(x - x_1)$$

This is a formula connecting the y co-ordinate with the x co-ordinate for every other point (x, y) on the line.

The equation of a straight line of slope m passing through (x_1, y_1) is given by:

$$(y - y_1) = m(x - x_1)$$

Using the equation of a straight line

To find the equation of a straight line you need two things: a fixed point (x_1, y_1) on the line and the slope m of the line.

Steps for finding the equation of a straight line

1. Find m.
2. Write down (x_1, y_1).
3. Put into the formula: $(y - y_1) = m(x - x_1)$
4. Tidy up the formula into an equation of the form $ax + by + c = 0$, known as standard form.

TIP
The slope of a line can be read directly from its equation given in standard form $ax + by + c = 0$.

EXAMPLE 20

Find the equation of the line AB, where $A(-1, 3)$ and $B(4, 5)$.

Solution

$A(-1, 3)$
$\downarrow \quad \downarrow$
$B(4, \quad 5)$

$m = $ slope of AB
$= \dfrac{3 - 5}{-1 - 4} = \dfrac{2}{5}$

Which point do you choose as (x_1, y_1)? You can choose whichever one you like, as both points are on the line.

$(x_1, y_1) = (4, 5)$

$(y - 5) = \dfrac{2}{5}(x - 4)$ [Multiply across by 5.]

$5(y - 5) = 2(x - 4)$

$5y - 25 = 2x - 8$

$2x - 5y + 17 = 0$

This equation is in standard form with $a = 2$, $b = -5$ and $c = 17$.

WORKED EXAMPLE

Reading the slope of a line from the equation of a line

The equation of a line of slope $m = -\dfrac{3}{2}$ passing through the point $(x_1, y_1) = (4, 2)$ is given by:

$(y - 2) = -\dfrac{3}{2}(x - 4)$

$2(y - 2) = -3(x - 4)$

$2y - 4 = -3x + 12$

$3x + 2y - 16 = 0$

Working backwards:

$3x + 2y - 16 = 0$
$\downarrow \quad \downarrow$
$ax + by + c = 0$

$a = 3, b = 2$

$m = -\dfrac{3}{2} = -\dfrac{a}{b}$

The slope m of a straight line with equation $ax + by + c = 0$ is given by

$$m = -\frac{a}{b} = -\frac{\text{(Number in front of } x)}{\text{(Number in front of } y)}.$$

ACTIVITY 7

ACTION
Finding the equation of a line

OBJECTIVE
To find the equation of a line given certain information

The constant c in the equation $ax + by + c = 0$ has no part in finding the slope of a line.

▸ $3x - 4y + 7 = 0$: $m = -\dfrac{(3)}{(-4)} = \dfrac{3}{4}$

▸ $-4x + 7y = 11 \Rightarrow 4x - 7y + 11 = 0$: $m = -\dfrac{(4)}{(-7)} = \dfrac{4}{7}$

▸ $x = -3y + 1 \Rightarrow 1x + 3y - 1 = 0$: $m = -\dfrac{(1)}{(3)} = -\dfrac{1}{3}$

▸ $4x - 1 = 0 \Rightarrow 4x + 0y - 1 = 0$: $m = -\dfrac{(4)}{(0)} = \infty$

▸ $3y - 2 = 0 \Rightarrow 0x + 3y - 2 = 0$: $m = -\dfrac{(0)}{3} = 0$

▸ $y = \dfrac{2x + 1}{3} \Rightarrow 3y = 2x + 1 \Rightarrow 2x - 3y + 1 = 0$: $m = \dfrac{2}{3}$

TIP

The equation of a line can be written down directly from its slope by noticing a pattern.

WORKED EXAMPLE Writing down the equation of a line from its slope

Equation → Slope

$2x - 3y + 11 = 0 \rightarrow m = +\dfrac{2}{3}$

$4x + 5y - 7 = 0 \rightarrow m = -\dfrac{4}{5}$

$4x + 0y + 3 = 0 \rightarrow m = -\dfrac{4}{0} = \infty$

$0x + 2y - 3 = 0 \rightarrow m = -\dfrac{0}{2} = 0$

Slope → Equation

$m = +\dfrac{5}{6} \rightarrow 5x - 6y + c = 0$

$m = -\dfrac{2}{7} \rightarrow 2x + 7y + c = 0$

$m = +\dfrac{1}{0} = \infty \rightarrow 1x - 0y + c = 0 \Rightarrow x + c = 0$

$m = +\dfrac{0}{1} = 0 \rightarrow 0x - 1y + c = 0 \Rightarrow y - c = 0$

To find c you need to be given a point on the line.

Testing if a point is on a line

The equation of a straight line is a formula connecting the y co-ordinate of any point **on the line** with its x co-ordinate. If a point satisfies this equation (requirement), it is on the line. If it does not, it is not on the line. It is rather like the requirements for getting into college. If you satisfy them, you get in. If you do not satisfy the requirements, you do not get in.

To test whether or not a point P is on a line with equation $ax + by + c = 0$, substitute the co-ordinates of P into the expression $ax + by + c$ on the left-hand side of the equation. If you get 0 (the right-hand side), then it is on the line. If you do not get 0, it is not on the line.

EXAMPLE 21

A straight road passes through the points $A(4, 1)$ and $B(9, 11)$. Find its equation.

(a) Is $D(-2, 8)$ on this road?

(b) Is $E(2, -3)$ on this road?

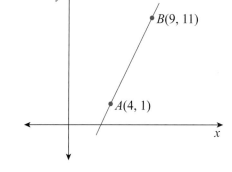

Solution

$$
\boxed{\begin{array}{c} A(4, 1) \\ \downarrow\ \downarrow \\ B(9, 11) \end{array}}
$$

Slope $m = \dfrac{1 - 11}{4 - 9} = \dfrac{-10}{-5} = \dfrac{2}{1}$

Slope = 2	*or* Slope = 2, $(x_1, y_1) = (4, 1)$
Equation: $2x - 1y + c = 0$	Equation: $(y - y_1) = m(x - x_1)$
(4, 1): $8 - 1 + c = 0 \Rightarrow c = -7$	$y - 1 = 2(x - 4)$
$2x - y - 7 = 0$	$y - 1 = 2x - 8$
	$2x - y - 7 = 0$

(a) Substitute $D(-2, 8)$ into the left-hand side of the equation.

LHS	RHS
$2x - y - 7 = 0$	0
(−2, 8): $2(-2) - 8 - 7$	
$\qquad = -19$	

$$\therefore \text{LHS} \neq \text{RHS}$$

$(-2, 8)$ is not on this road.

(b) Substitute $E(2, -3)$ into the left-hand side of the equation.

LHS	RHS
$2x - y - 7 = 0$	0
(2, −3): $2(2) - (-3) - 7$	
$\qquad = 4 + 3 - 7$	
$\qquad = 0$	

$$\therefore \text{LHS} = \text{RHS}$$

$(2, -3)$ is on this road.

EXAMPLE 22

(a) Find c if $(-5, 7)$ lies on the straight line with equation $5x - 3y + c = 0$.

(b) Find z if $(z, -2)$ lies on the line with equation $3x + 7y + 5 = 0$.

Solution

(a) $(-5, 7)$ is on $5x - 3y + c = 0$

$$5(-5) - 3(7) + c = 0$$

$$c = 46$$

(b) $(z, -2)$ is on $3x + 7y + 5 = 0$

$$3z - 14 + 5 = 0$$

$$3z = 9$$

$$z = 3$$

TIP

If $(0, 0)$ is on a straight line with equation $ax + by + c = 0$, then $c = 0$ because $a(0) + b(0) + c = 0 \Rightarrow c = 0$.

Conversely, if there is no constant in the equation of a straight line, the line passes through $(0, 0)$.

▶ $3x - 2y = 0$ passes through $(0, 0)$.

The slope intercept form of the equation of a line: $y = mx + c$

Two variables x and y are also said to be linearly related if y can be written in terms of x as $y = mx + c$, where m is the slope of the line and c is the y-intercept (the y co-ordinate of the point where $x = 0$).

WORKED EXAMPLE
Slope intercept form of the equation of a line

(a) Find the equation of the line of slope 2 that crosses the y-axis at $(0, 3)$.

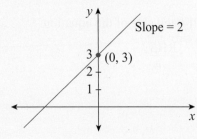

$m = 2$, $(x_1, y_1) = (0, 3)$ [y-intercept $= +3$]

Equation: $(y - 3) = 2(x - 0)$

$$y - 3 = 2x$$

$$y = 2x + 3$$

This is the slope intercept form of the equation of the line.

(b) Find the equation of the line of slope m that crosses the y-axis at $(0, c)$.

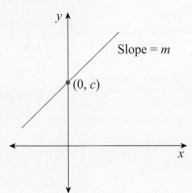

Slope $= m$, $(x_1, y_1) = (0, c)$ [y-intercept $= +c$]

$$y - c = m(x - 0)$$

$$y = mx + c$$

TIP

For a relationship between two variables x and y to be linear, you must be able to write it in the form $y = mx + c$, where m and c are constants.

- The equation of the line l is $y = -\frac{1}{3}x + 7$, since $m = -\frac{1}{3}$ and $c = 7$.

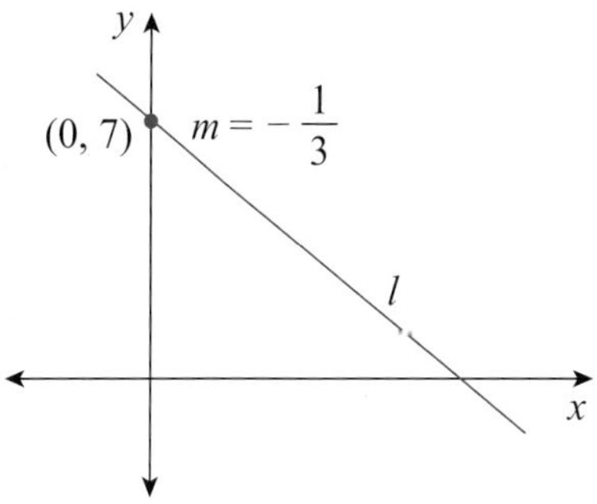

You can always write the equation of a line given in standard form in the form $y = mx + c$.

- $3x - 2y + 6 = 0$

$$-2y = -3x - 6$$
$$y = \frac{3}{2}x + 3$$
$$\therefore\ m = \frac{3}{2} \text{ and } c = 3$$

WORKED EXAMPLE

Linear relationship between temperature and resistance

The electrical resistance R in ohms (Ω) for a pure metal wire is related to its temperature T in degrees Celsius (°C) by the following formula:

$R = R_0 + \alpha T$, where R_0 and α are constants.

$R = R_0 + \alpha T \Rightarrow R = \alpha T + R_0\ (y = mx + c)$

This is a linear relationship, as α and R_0 are constants. The slope is α and the y-intercept is R_0. For copper, $R_0 = 2$ Ω and $\alpha = 0{\cdot}004$ Ω/°C.

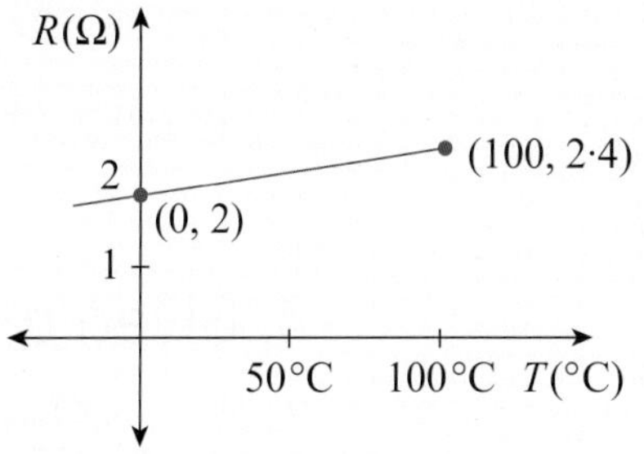

$R = 0{\cdot}004T + 2$

At $T = 0$ °C: $R = 2$ Ω

At $T = 100$ °C: $R = 2{\cdot}4$ Ω

Finding the equation of a line given certain information

1. Given its slope and a point on the line

EXAMPLE 23

Find the equation of the line of slope −2 that passes through the point (−1, 4).

Solution

$m = -2$ *or* $m = -\frac{2}{1}$

$(x_1, y_1) = (-1, 4)$	Equation: $2x + y + c = 0$
$(y - 4) = -2(x - (-1))$	**(−1, 4):** $-2 + 4 + c = 0$
$y - 4 = -2(x + 1)$	$c = -2$
$y - 4 = -2x - 2$	$2x + y - 2 = 0$
$2x + y - 2 = 0$	

2. Given two points on the line

EXAMPLE 24

Find the equation of the straight-line road PQ if $P(-4, 3)$ and $Q(1, 5)$ are two points on the road.

Solution

Points: $P(-4, 3)$, $Q(1, 5)$

$$m = \frac{3 - 5}{-4 - 1} = \frac{-2}{-5} = \frac{2}{5} \qquad or \qquad m = \frac{2}{5}$$

$(x_1, y_1) = (1, 5)$	Equation: $2x - 5y + c = 0$
$(y - 5) = \frac{2}{5}(x - 1)$	**(1, 5):** $2 - 25 + c = 0$
$5(y - 5) = 2(x - 1)$	$c = 23$
$5y - 25 = 2x - 2$	$2x + 5y + 23 = 0$
$2x - 5y + 23 = 0$	

3. Given a point on the line and a parallel line

Parallel lines have the same slope.

EXAMPLE 25

Find the equation of the straight-line runway q through the point $(2, -1)$, which is parallel to the straight-line runway with equation $p: 2x - 3y + 1 = 0$.

Solution

Slope of $p = \frac{2}{3}$ and slope of $q = \frac{2}{3}$ since $q \parallel p$.

$$m = \frac{2}{3} \qquad or \qquad m = \frac{2}{3}$$

$(x_1, y_1) = (2, -1)$	Equation: $2x - 3y + c = 0$
$(y - (-1)) = \frac{2}{3}(x - 2)$	**(2, -1):** $4 + 3 + c = 0$
$3(y + 1) = 2(x - 2)$	$c = -7$
$3y + 3 = 2x - 4$	$2x - 3y - 7 = 0$
$2x - 3y - 7 = 0$	

$p: 2x - 3y + 1 = 0$

q $(2, -1)$

4. Given a point on the line and a perpendicular line

EXAMPLE 26

Find the equation of the straight-line path of red light emanating from a laser source at the point $(-3, 5)$ that strikes a straight line with equation $p: 3x + 7y - 1 = 0$ at right angles on a screen.

Solution

$p: 3x + 7y - 1 = 0$

Slope of $p = -\frac{3}{7} \Rightarrow$ slope of $q = \frac{7}{3}$ since $q \perp p$.

$m = \frac{7}{3}$ *or* $m = \frac{7}{3}$

$(x_1, y_1) = (-3, 5)$ Equation: $7x - 3y + c = 0$

$(y - 5) = \frac{7}{3}(x - (-3))$ $(-3, 5):\ -21 - 15 + c = 0$

$3(y - 5) = 7(x + 3)$ $c = 36$

$3y - 15 = 7x + 21$ $7x - 3y + 36 = 0$

$7x - 3y + 36 = 0$

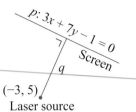

5. Given the line is horizontal or vertical

WORKED EXAMPLE   Equations of horizontal and vertical lines

(a) Horizontal lines (lines parallel to the x-axis)

All horizontal lines have a slope equal to 0 and all the points on horizontal lines have the same y co-ordinate.
Find the equation of horizontal lines l_1, l_2 and l_3, as shown.

Line l_1: All the points on l_1 have $y = 5$. This is the equation of l_1.

Line l_2: All the points on l_2 have $y = 0$. This is the equation of the x-axis.

Line l_3: All the points on l_3 have $y = -4$. This is the equation of l_3.

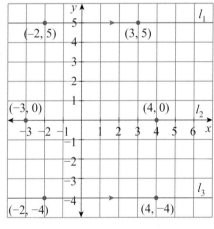

> All horizontal lines have slope 0, are parallel to the x-axis and have equation $y = c$, where c is the y co-ordinate of any point on the line.

▸ A woman walks along the sixth floor of a hotel in a straight line.
She passes points $P(50, 6)$ and $Q(23, 6)$. What is the equation of her path?
Points: $P(50, 6)$, $Q(23, 6) \Rightarrow y = 6 \Rightarrow y - 6 = 0$

(b) Vertical lines (lines parallel to the y-axis)

All vertical lines have slope ∞ and all points on vertical lines have the same x co-ordinate.
Find the equation of the vertical lines l_1, l_2 and l_3, as shown.

Line l_1: All the points on l_1 have $x = -2$. This is the equation of l_1.

Line l_2: All the points on l_2 have $x = 0$. This is the equation of the y-axis.

Line l_3: All the points on l_3 have $x = 4$. This is the equation of l_3.

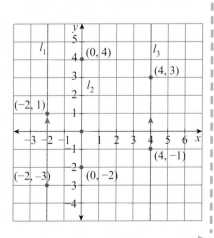

> All vertical lines have slope ∞, are parallel to the y-axis and have equation $x = c$, where c is the x co-ordinate of any point on the line.

> ▸ A bottle falls from a balloon in a straight line. $A(15, 40)$ and $B(15, 32)$ are points on this line. What is the equation of the line AB?
>
> Points: $A(15, 40)$, $B(15, 32) \Rightarrow x = 15 \Rightarrow x - 15 = 0$

6. Given the graph of the straight line

EXAMPLE 27

A ship sails along a straight line course AB from $A(7, 8)$ to a point B such that the y-intercept of B is 3. Find the equation of the course.

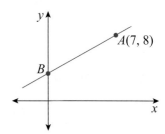

Solution

A y-intercept of 3 means the line AB crosses the y-axis at $(0, 3)$.
There are two points on AB: $A(7, 8)$ and $B(0, 3)$

$m = \dfrac{5}{7}$ *or* $m = \dfrac{5}{7}$ *or* $m = \dfrac{5}{7}, c = 3$

$(x_1, y_1) = (0, 3)$	Equation: $5x - 7y + c = 0$	$y = \dfrac{5}{7}x + 3$ $(y = mx + c)$
$(y - 3) = \dfrac{5}{7}(x - 0)$	**(7, 8):** $35 - 56 + c = 0$	$7y = 5x + 21$
$7(y - 3) = 5x$	$c = 21$	$5x - 7y + 21 = 0$
$7y - 21 = 5x$	$5x - 7y + 21 = 0$	
$5x - 7y + 21 = 0$		

7. Given a point on the line and the angle the line makes with +x-axis

Remember the slope m of a line is the tan of the angle it makes with the +x-axis.

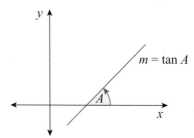

EXAMPLE 28

A skateboarder rides along a straight line on a ramp passing through the point $(-2, 10)$ and making an angle of $135°$ with the +x-axis. Find the equation of this path.

Solution

Slope $m = \tan 135° = -1$

$m = -1$ *or* $m = -1$

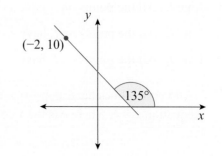

$(x_1, y_1) = (-2, 10)$	Equation: $x + y + c = 0$
$(y - 10) = -1(x + 2)$	**(-2, 10):** $-2 + 10 + c = 0$
$y - 10 = -x - 2$	$c = -8$
$x + y - 8 = 0$	$x + y - 8 = 0$

EXAMPLE 29

Find the equation of the line making an angle of $\tan^{-1}\left(-\frac{3}{4}\right)$ with the $+x$-axis and passing through $(-5, 3)$.

Solution

Slope of the line $m = \tan A$

However, $A = \tan^{-1}\left(-\frac{3}{4}\right) \Rightarrow \tan A = -\frac{3}{4}$

$m = -\frac{3}{4}$ *or* $m = -\frac{3}{4}$

$(x_1, y_1) = (-5, 3)$ Equation: $3x + 4y + c = 0$

$(y - 3) = -\frac{3}{4}(x + 5)$ $(\mathbf{-5, 3})$: $-15 + 12 + c = 0$

$4(y - 3) = -3(x + 5)$ $c = 3$

$4y - 12 = -3x - 15$ $3x + 4y + 3 = 0$

$3x + 4y + 3 = 0$

Plotting lines

To plot a straight-line graph all you need are two points on it.

(a) Steps for plotting a straight line given its equation

1. Choose two points on the line by picking any suitable value for x and working out the corresponding value of y or vice versa.

2. Plot these two points in the Cartesian plane.

3. Draw the straight line through them.

EXAMPLE 30

Plot the straight line with equation
$l: 3x + 5y - 18 = 0$.

(a) What is the slope of l?

(b) Is the point $(0, 3\cdot5)$ on l?

Solution

$3x + 5y - 18 = 0$

$3x + 5y = 18$

$y = 0$: $3x = 18 \Rightarrow x = 6$

$\therefore (6, 0)$ is one point.

$x = 1$: $3 + 5y = 18$

$5y = 15$

$y = 3$

$\therefore (1, 3)$ is another point.

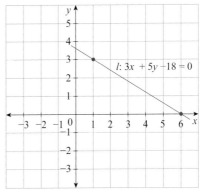

(a) Slope $= -\dfrac{(3)}{(5)} = -\dfrac{3}{5}$ [Sloping downwards]

(b) $(0, 3\cdot5)$: $3x + 5y - 18 = 0$

LHS	RHS
$17\cdot5 - 18$	0
$= -0\cdot5$	

LHS $\neq$ RHS

$\therefore (0, 3\cdot5)$ is not on the line.

When choosing points on a straight line, the best points to choose are:

(a) the point at which $x = 0$ (where it crosses the y-axis) and

(b) the point at which $y = 0$ (where it crosses the x-axis).

(b) Steps for plotting a straight line given its slope and a point on it

1. Find its equation and proceed as in part **(a)**.

   or

2. Plot the given point and draw the run and the rise starting from the given point.

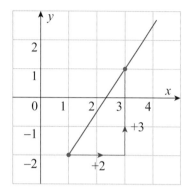

▸ A gun mounted at the point $(1, -2)$ fires a shell along a line with slope $\frac{3}{2}$. Plot the path of the shell.

Starting at $(1, 2)$, $m = \frac{3}{2}$:

Change in $x = +2$, change in $y = +3$

Finding where lines meet (intersecting lines)

If two lines are drawn on the same set of axes, there are three possible situations that can occur:

1. The lines never meet. $l_1 \cap l_2 = \{\}$ This means the lines are parallel and so their slopes are equal.

▸ Consider the pair of lines: $l_1: 2x - 3y + 7 = 0$, $l_2: 4x - 6y + 12 = 0$

$l_1: 2x - 3y + 7 = 0$ has slope $\frac{2}{3}$

$l_2: 4x - 6y + 12 = 0 \Rightarrow 2x - 3y + 6 = 0$ has slope $\frac{2}{3}$

The lines are parallel but not identical. Therefore, there are no points of intersection.

2. The lines meet at an infinite number of points.   This means the lines are coincident (identical). 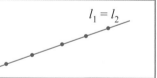

▸ Consider the pair of lines: $l_1: 4x - 3y + 2 = 0$, $l_2: 6y - 8x - 4 = 0$

$l_1: 4x - 3y + 2 = 0$ has slope $\frac{4}{3}$

$l_2: 6y - 8x - 4 = 0 \Rightarrow 8x - 6y + 4 = 0 \Rightarrow 4x - 3y + 2 = 0$ has slope $\frac{4}{3}$

The lines are identical. Therefore, there is an infinite number of points of intersection.

3. The lines meet at a single point. $l_1 \cap l_2 = \{P\}$ This means the lines have different slopes. 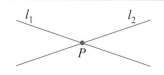

▸ Consider the pair of lines: $l_1 : 4x + y - 3 = 0$, $l_2 : 7x - 3y + 2 = 0$

$l_1 : 4x + y - 3 = 0$ has slope -4

$l_2 : 7x - 3y + 2 = 0$ has slope $\frac{7}{3}$

The lines are not parallel. Therefore, there is one and only one point of intersection.

The point of intersection of two lines with different slopes can be found by:

(a) Graphing the lines on a co-ordinated set of axes and reading off this point.

or

(b) Solving their equations simultaneously.

EXAMPLE 31

Find the point of intersection of the straight-line paths of a proton and antiproton moving in the Large Hadron Collider along the straight line with equations $l_1 : 3x - 2y + 1 = 0$ and $l_2 : 4x + 3y - 10 = 0$, respectively just before collision.

Solution

The lines l_1 and l_2 have different slopes and so have only one point of intersection.

$3x - 2y = -1$ ... **(1)**

$4x + 3y = 10$ ... **(2)**

$9x - 6y = -3$ ... **(1)** $\times 3$

$8x + 6y = 20$ ... **(2)** $\times 2$

$17x = 17 \Rightarrow x = 1$

Substituting back into **(1)**:

$3 - 2y = -1$

$-2y = -4$

$y = 2$

The point of intersection is $(1, 2)$.

EXERCISE 6

Diagrams are not drawn to scale.

1. A sales assistant in a mobile phone shop receives a basic salary of €220 per week. He also receives €5 for each phone insurance policy sold in 1 week.

   (a) Construct a table of weekly salary P against the number n of phone insurance policies sold in 1 week.

n	0	1	2	3	4	5	6
P(€)							

   (b) What are the independent and dependent variables?

   (c) Plot the points on a co-ordinated set of axes.

   (d) Is the relationship between P and n linear?

   (e) Find a formula for the relationship between P and n.

   (f) Is it sensible to join the points in this case?

2. A tank contains 140 litres of water. When the tap is opened, water flows out at a steady rate of 0·8 litres per minute.

   (a) Copy and complete the table below for the volume V of water in the tank against time t in minutes, where t is the time after the tap is opened.

t (mins)	0	10	20	30	40	50
V (litres)						

(b) What are the dependent and independent variables?

(c) Plot the points in the table on a co-ordinated set of axes.

(d) Is the relationship between V and t linear?

(e) Is it sensible to join the points in this case?

(f) Find a formula for the relationship between V and t.

(g) Find how many litres of water are in the tank after 37 minutes.

3. Test whether or not the given point P is on the given line l:

(a) $P(3, 2)$, l: $2x - y - 4 = 0$

(b) $P(1, 2)$, l: $4x + 7y - 18 = 0$

(c) $P(-2, 1)$, l: $3x - 4y - 2 = 0$

(d) $P(-1, -4)$, l: $3x - 2y - 5 = 0$

(e) $P(5, -2)$, l: $y - x = -7$

(f) $P(7, -11)$, l: $x = 3y + 1$

(g) $P\left(5, -\frac{1}{2}\right)$, l: $2y + 1 = 0$

(h) $P(0, 0)$, l: $7x + 11y = 0$

4. Find the unknown letter given the following information:

(a) $(2, z)$ is on the line $3x - y + 1 = 0$

(b) $(z, 2)$ is on the line $x - 3y + 7 = 0$

(c) $(-z, 1)$ is on the line $3x - 2y - 4 = 0$

(d) $(z, 3z)$ is on the line $2x - 5y + 26 = 0$

(e) $(2, -3)$ is on the line $5x - 2y + c = 0$

(f) $(-1, 5)$ is on the line $ax - 3y + 2 = 0$

(g) $\left(\frac{1}{2}, \frac{3}{2}\right)$ is on the line $3x + by - 15 = 0$

(h) $(0, 0)$ is on the line $2x + 5y + c = 0$

5. Write down the slope of the line l, given its equation:

(a) l: $3x - y + 7 = 0$

(b) l: $5x + 11y - 7 = 0$

(c) l: $y = 4 - 5x$

(d) l: $x = 2y - 3$

(e) l: $3y = 2$

(f) l: $4x = 7$

(g) l: $2y - 3x + 1 = 0$

(h) l: $-3y + 2 = 7x$

6. State which of the following relationships are linear. In the case of any linear relationships, draw a rough graph stating the slope and the y-intercept, given that the variable on the left-hand side of each equation is the dependent variable and the variable on the right-hand side is the independent variable.

(a) $y = 2x$

(b) $y = 2x + 3$

(c) $y = x^2$

(d) $y = 2^x$

(e) $2y = x$

(f) $3y = x + 1$

(g) $V = IR$ (R constant)

(h) $F = ma$ (m constant)

(i) $P = \dfrac{k}{V}$ (k constant)

(j) $w = 1{\cdot}5s - 23{\cdot}5$

(k) $V = V_0 + \dfrac{T}{273{\cdot}15}$ (V_0 constant)

(l) $H = I^2Rt$ (I, R constants)

7. From the following graphs, write down a linear relationship between the dependent and independent variables in slope intercept form:

(a)

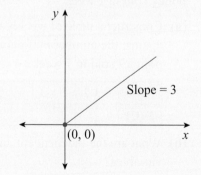

(b)

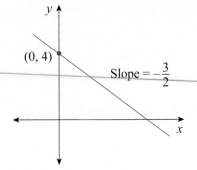

(0, 4)

Slope $= -\dfrac{3}{2}$

(c)

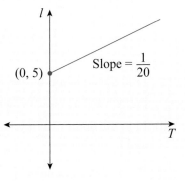

(0, 5) Slope $= \dfrac{1}{20}$

T

(d)

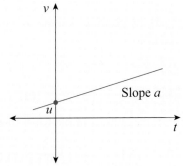

Slope a

u

t

8. Find the equation of the straight line in each case, given the following information:

- **(a)** Slope 3 passing through the point $(1, 2)$
- **(b)** Slope -5 passing through the point $(-3, 4)$
- **(c)** Slope $\dfrac{4}{7}$ passing through the point $(-6, -1)$
- **(d)** Slope $-\dfrac{3}{5}$ passing through the point $\left(\dfrac{1}{2}, -2\right)$
- **(e)** Slope $\dfrac{1}{2}$ passing through the point $(0, 0)$

9. Find the equation of the line AB if given the following points:

- **(a)** $A(0, 0)$, $B(2, 4)$
- **(b)** $A(3, 4)$, $B(5, 7)$
- **(c)** $A(-1, 1)$, $B(3, -2)$
- **(d)** $A(-3, 1)$, $B(4, -3)$
- **(e)** $A\left(-\dfrac{1}{4}, -1\right)$, $B\left(\dfrac{3}{4}, -2\right)$
- **(f)** $A(z, -z)$, $B(3z, 4z)$ in terms of z

10. Find the equation of the line passing through the point P and parallel to the line l, if:

- **(a)** $P(1, 3)$ and $l: x - 2y + 1 = 0$
- **(b)** $P(4, 4)$ and $l: 2x + y - 3 = 0$
- **(c)** $P(-3, 2)$ and $l: 2x - y + 11 = 0$
- **(d)** $P(0, 0)$ and $l: 3x - 6y + 4 = 0$
- **(e)** $P\left(-\dfrac{2}{3}, \dfrac{4}{5}\right)$ and $l: 6x - 5y + 9 = 0$

11. Find the equation of the line passing through the point P and perpendicular to the line l, if:

- **(a)** $P(6, 1)$ and $l: x - 2y + 3 = 0$
- **(b)** $P(2, 0)$ and $l: 2x + y - 1 = 0$
- **(c)** $P(-5, 1)$ and $l: 4x - 3y + 7 = 0$
- **(d)** $P(-3, -11)$ and $l: 3y = -4x + 7$
- **(e)** $P\left(\dfrac{3}{4}, -\dfrac{4}{7}\right)$ and $l: 7x - 8y + 1 = 0$

12. Find the equation of the line in each case:

- **(a)** Passing through $A(-1, 2)$ and $B(11, 2)$
- **(b)** Passing through $A(-6, -3)$ and $B(-6, 4)$
- **(c)** Parallel to the x-axis and passing through $(5, 11)$
- **(d)** Parallel to the y-axis and passing through $(-1, 4)$
- **(e)** Perpendicular to the x-axis and passing through $(3, -2)$
- **(f)** Perpendicular to the y-axis and passing through $(7, -7)$

13. Find the equation of the straight line l described or illustrated in each case:

- **(a)** The line l making an intercept of $+8$ on the x-axis and -6 on the y-axis
- **(b)**

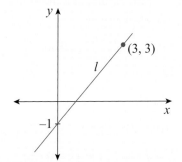

(3, 3)

l

-1

(c)

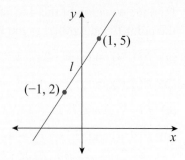

(d)

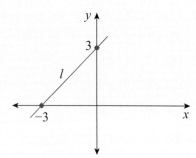

(e)

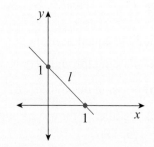

(f) The line l making equal intercepts on the $+x$ and $+y$ axes and passing through $(2, 5)$

(g)

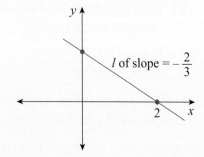

14. Find the points of intersection of the lines l_1 and l_2, if any, where:

(a) $l_1: x - y + 1 = 0$ and $l_2: x + y - 5 = 0$

(b) $l_1: 3x + 5y = 17$ and $l_2: y = 2 - 2x$

(c) $l_1: \dfrac{x}{2} + \dfrac{y}{3} = 2$ and $l_2: 3x - 3 = -5y$

(d) $l_1: 4x - 3y + 7 = 0$ and $l_2: 6y - 8x - 1 = 0$

(e) $l_1: x - 5y + 11 = 0$ and $l_2: 4x - 20y = -44$

(f) $l_1: 7x + 3y = 1$ and $l_2: 5x + 2y = 0$

15. The point B is on the line $x - 3y - 2 = 0$. The line AB is inclined at $\tan^{-1}\left(\frac{3}{4}\right)$ to the $+x$-axis where $A(3, 2)$.

(a) Find the equation of AB.   **(b)** Find B.

16. $A(5, -2)$ is a point on the line AB.

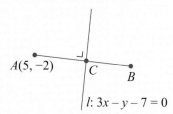

(a) Find the equation of the line AB if it is perpendicular to $l: 3x - y - 7 = 0$.

(b) Find the point C of intersection of AB and l.

(c) If C is the midpoint of $[AB]$, find B.

17. Find the point where the line l crosses the axes if:

(a) $l: x - 2y - 6 = 0$ **(c)** $l: x + 4y = 8$

(b) $l: 2x - 3y + 12 = 0$ **(d)** $l: 2x - 3y - 18 = 0$

Plot these lines in the Cartesian plane.

18. Two candles A and B are lit at the same time.

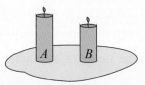

A is 25 cm long when lit and burns at a rate of 3 mm per hour. B is 15 cm long when lit and burns at 1 mm per hour.

(a) Copy and complete the tables below for the height h (mm) of each candle t hours after it is lit.

Candle A:

t(hours)	0	25	50	75
h(mm)	250			

Candle B:

t(hours)	0	25	50	75
h(mm)				

(b) Copy the grid below and draw a graph of h against t on this grid for each candle.

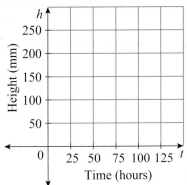

(c) Find an equation connecting h and t for each candle.

(d) After how many hours will the candles have the same height?

(e) Which one burns out first? How long after it goes out does the second one burn out?

19. Find the equation of a line l:

(a) Passing through $P(-1, 2)$ and making an angle of $45°$ with the $+x$-axis

(b) Passing through $P(5, 2)$ and making an angle of $135°$ with the $+x$-axis

(c) Passing through $P(-1, 1)$ and making an angle of $\tan^{-1}\left(\frac{5}{3}\right)$ with the $+x$-axis

(d)

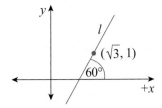

(e) Passing through $P(-1, 7)$ and making an angle of $\tan^{-1}\left(-\frac{7}{2}\right)$ with the $+x$-axis

20. Find the equation of the following:

(a) The line parallel to the x-axis making an intercept of $+10$ on the y-axis

(b) The y-axis

(c) The line of slope $-\frac{1}{4}$ passing through the point $(0, 0)$

(d) The line of slope -3 with a y-intercept of $+2$

(e) The line making intercepts of $+5$ on the axes

(f) The line that bisects the line segment $[AB]$ at right angles, where $A(-7, 5)$ and $B(13, -11)$ are two points

(g) The line that is parallel to the line $4x - 6y + 9 = 0$ and which passes through the point $(2, 4)$

(h) The line that is perpendicular to the line $2x + 5y - 8 = 0$ and which passes through the point $(4, -3)$

21. Find the equation of the line making an angle of $\tan^{-1}\left(\frac{1}{5}\right)$ with the $+x$-axis and which cuts the y-axis at $(0, 5)$. Show that $(-15, 2)$ is on this line.

22. The line q is the image of the line p under the translation $A(1, 4) \rightarrow B(3, 2)$. If the equation of p is $x - 2y + 7 = 0$, show that $A(1, 4)$ is on p. Find the equation of q.

10.7 Dilations

ACTION
Understanding dilations

OBJECTIVE
To use your knowledge of dilations from geometry and to apply this knowledge to dilations on the Cartesian plane

KEY TERM

A **dilation** (enlargement or reduction) is a geometrical transformation that changes the size but not the shape of an object.

The triangle $\triangle P'Q'R'$ is the image of $\triangle PQR$ under an enlargement with centre O and scale factor k. This means that $\dfrac{|OP'|}{|OP|} = \dfrac{|OQ'|}{|OQ|} = \dfrac{|OR'|}{|OR|} = k$.

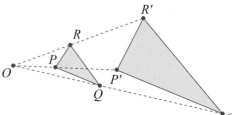

The important idea of performing dilations in the co-ordinate plane is illustrated in the following example.

EXAMPLE 32

Show that $(0, 0)$, $A(-3,7)$ and $A'(-6,14)$ are collinear and that $|OA'| = 2|OA|$.

Solution

Points: $(0, 0)$, $A(-3,7)$ and $A'(-6,14)$

Slope of $OA = -\dfrac{7}{3}$

Slope of $OA' = \dfrac{-14}{6} = -\dfrac{7}{3}$

$\therefore O, A$ and A' are collinear.

$|OA| = \sqrt{(-3 - 0)^2 + (7 - 0)^2} = \sqrt{58}$

$|OA'| = \sqrt{(-6 - 0)^2 + (14 - 0)^2}$

$\qquad = \sqrt{232} = \sqrt{4 \times 58} = 2\sqrt{58} \Rightarrow |OA'| = 2|OA|$

To find the image A' of a point A under an enlargement of scale factor 2 with centre $O(0, 0)$, you simply multiply each co-ordinate of A by 2.

EXAMPLE 33

Plot the image $\triangle A'B'C'$ of $\triangle ABC$ under the enlargement with centre $O(0, 0)$ of scale factor $\frac{3}{2}$, where $A(2, 0)$, $B(-2, 2)$ and $C(0, -2)$.

(a) Show that $|A'B'| = \frac{3}{2}|AB|$.

(b) Show that the area of $\triangle A'B'C' = \frac{9}{4}$(Area $\triangle ABC$).

Solution

Scale factor $k = \frac{3}{2}$

$A(2, 0) \rightarrow A'(3, 0)$

$B(-2, 2) \rightarrow B'(-3, 3)$

$C(0, -2) \rightarrow C'(0, -3)$

(a) $|A'B'| = \sqrt{36 + 9} = \sqrt{45} = 3\sqrt{5}$

$|AB| = \sqrt{16 + 4} = \sqrt{20} = 2\sqrt{5}$

$\dfrac{|A'B'|}{|AB|} = \dfrac{3}{2}$

$\therefore |A'B'| = \frac{3}{2}|AB|$

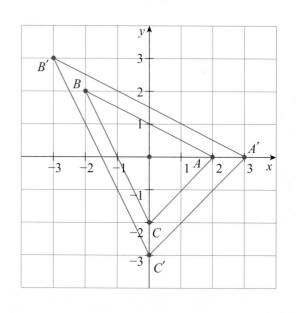

(b) ΔABC

$A(2, 0) \to \cancel{(0, 0)}$

$B(-2, 2) \to (-4, 2)$

$C(0, -2) \to (-2, -2)$

Area $\Delta ABC = \frac{1}{2}|8 - (-4)|$

$= 6$

$\Delta A'B'C'$

$A'(3, 0) \to (0, 0)$

$B'(-3, 3) \to (-6, 3)$

$C'(0, -3) \to (-3, -3)$

Area $\Delta A'B'C' = \frac{1}{2}|18 - (-9)|$

$= \frac{27}{2}$

$$\therefore \frac{\text{Area }\Delta A'B'C'}{\text{Area }\Delta ABC} = \frac{\frac{27}{2}}{6} = \frac{27}{12} = \frac{9}{4} = \left(\frac{3}{2}\right)^2$$

TIP

In general, the image A' of a point $A(x, y)$ under a dilation with centre $O(0, 0)$ and scale factor k is $A'(kx, ky)$.

If $k > 1$, the dilation is an enlargement. If $0 < k < 1$, the dilation is a reduction.

Dilation formulae

1. If the line segment $[A'B']$ is the image of the line segment $[AB]$ under a dilation with centre $O(0, 0)$ and scale factor k, then $\frac{|A'B'|}{|AB|} = k$.

2. If shape S' is the image of shape S under a dilation with centre $O(0, 0)$ and scale factor k, then $\frac{\text{Area }S'}{\text{Area }S} = k^2$.

EXAMPLE 34

Plot the image $A'B'C'D'$ of the quadrilateral $ABCD$ shown under the dilation with centre $O(0, 0)$ and scale factor $\frac{1}{2}$, where $A(-4, 6)$, $B(12, 8)$, $C(8, 14)$ and $D(-6, 14)$. Show that $|B'D'| = \frac{1}{2}|BD|$.

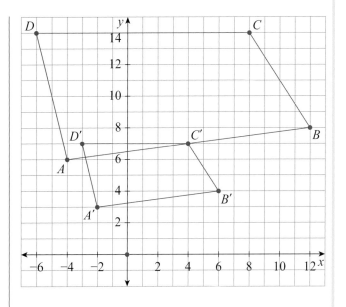

Solution

$A(-4, 6) \to A'(-2, 3)$

$B(12, 8) \to B'(6, 4)$

$C(8, 14) \to C'(4, 7)$

$D(-6, 14) \to D'(-3, 7)$

$|BD| = \sqrt{18^2 + 6^2} = 6\sqrt{10}$

$|B'D'| = \sqrt{9^2 + (-3)^2} = \sqrt{81 + 9} = \sqrt{90} = 3\sqrt{10}$

$\frac{|B'D'|}{|BD|} = \frac{3\sqrt{10}}{6\sqrt{10}} = \frac{1}{2}$

$|B'D'| = \frac{1}{2}|BD|$

EXERCISE 7

1. What is the scale factor of the dilation with centre $O(0, 0)$ for the following?:

   (a) $(x, y) \rightarrow (3x, 3y)$ **(c)** $(x, y) \rightarrow \left(\frac{2}{3}x, \frac{2}{3}y\right)$

   (b) $(x, y) \rightarrow \left(\frac{x}{2}, \frac{y}{2}\right)$ **(d)** $(x, y) \rightarrow (7x, 7y)$

2. $A'B'C'D'E'$ is the image of the diagram $ABCDE$ below under the reduction $(x, y) \rightarrow \left(\frac{1}{2}x, \frac{1}{2}y\right)$ with centre $O(0, 0)$.

   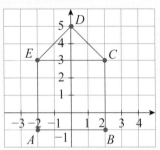

   (a) List the co-ordinates of A, B, C, D and E.

   (b) List the co-ordinates of A', B', C', D' and E'.

3. Copy the diagram below onto graph paper and draw the image of the square $ABCD$ under the enlargement with centre $O(0, 0)$ and scale factor 2.

   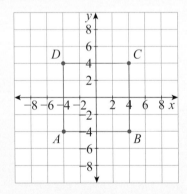

4. Copy the diagram below onto graph paper and draw the image of the rectangle $ABCD$ under the reduction with centre $O(0, 0)$ and scale factor $\frac{1}{2}$.

   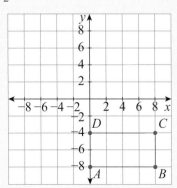

5. $A'B'C'D'$ is the image of $ABCD$ under an enlargement with centre $(0, 0)$.

   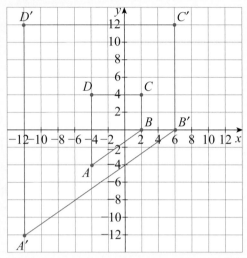

   (a) What is the scale factor k of the enlargement?

   (b) Find the $\dfrac{\text{Area } A'B'C'D'}{\text{Area } ABCD}$ and show it is equal to k^2.

   (c) Find the equation of AB and show that $P(-1, -2)$ is on AB.

   (d) What is the image P' of P under the enlargement above?

   (e) Show that P' is on $A'B'$.

6. If $O(0, 0)$, $A(x, y)$ and $A'(kx, ky)$ are three points, show that:

   (a) the slope of OA = the slope of OA',

   (b) $|OA'| = k|OA|$.

7. Copy the diagram below onto graph paper and draw the enlargement of the rectangle $ABCD$ under a scale factor of 2 using $(3, 2)$ as the centre of the enlargement.

   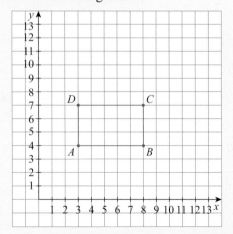

Line 2

CHAPTER 11

Learning Outcomes

• To learn how to divide a line segment in a given ratio.

• To find the acute and obtuse angles between intersecting lines.

• To learn how to find the perpendicular distance from a point to a line.

11.1 Division of a line segment in a given ratio

Given a line segment with end points $A(x_1, y_1)$ and $B(x_2, y_2)$, is it possible to find a point $C(x, y)$ that divides $[AB]$ into two parts so that $|AC| : |CB| = m : n$?

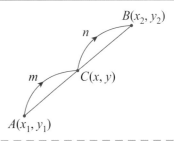

WORKED EXAMPLE Division of a line segment in a given ratio

Given $A(1, 2)$ and $B(6, 7)$ are end points of a line segment $[AB]$, find $C(x, y)$ between A and B that divides $[AB]$ in the ratio 3:2.

1. Draw a line through A parallel to the x-axis and a line through B parallel to the y-axis. These lines intersect at $D(6, 2)$.

2. Draw a line through C parallel to the x-axis to intersect BD at $E(6, y)$.

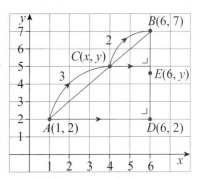

As $\triangle CEB$ and $\triangle ADB$ are similar triangles:

$$\frac{|CE|}{|AD|} = \frac{|CB|}{|AB|} \Rightarrow \frac{6-x}{5} = \frac{2}{5} \ \dots (1)$$

$$6 - x = 2$$
$$x = 4$$

and

$$\frac{|EB|}{|DB|} = \frac{|CB|}{|AB|} \Rightarrow \frac{7-y}{5} = \frac{2}{5} \ \dots (2)$$

$$7 - y = 2$$
$$y = 5$$

$$\therefore C \text{ is } (4, 5).$$

This process can be generalised for finding a point (x, y) that divides a line segment $[AB]$ internally in the ratio $m:n$, where $A(x_1, y_1)$ and $B(x_2, y_2)$.

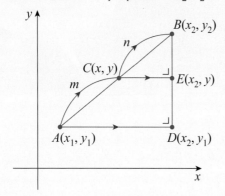

As $\triangle CEB$ and $\triangle ADB$ are similar:

$$\frac{|CE|}{|AD|} = \frac{|CB|}{|AB|} \Rightarrow \frac{(x_2 - x)}{(x_2 - x_1)} = \frac{n}{(m + n)} \ \dots \text{(1)}$$

$$(m + n)(x_2 - x) = n(x_2 - x_1)$$

$$mx_2 - mx + nx_2 - nx = nx_2 - nx_1$$

$$mx_2 + nx_1 = mx + nx$$

$$mx_2 + nx_1 = (m + n)x$$

$$\therefore x = \frac{mx_2 + nx_1}{m + n}$$

and

$$\frac{|EB|}{|DB|} = \frac{|CB|}{|AB|} \Rightarrow \frac{(y_2 - y)}{(y_2 - y_1)} = \frac{n}{(m + n)} \ \dots \text{(2)}$$

$$(m + n)(y_2 - y) = n(y_2 - y_1)$$

$$my_2 - my + ny_2 - ny = ny_2 - ny_1$$

$$my_2 + ny_1 = my + ny$$

$$my_2 + ny_1 = (m + n)y$$

$$\therefore y = \frac{my_2 + ny_1}{m + n}$$

The internal and external division formula

1. Internal division

The point between $A(x_1, y_1)$ and $B(x_2, y_2)$ that divides $[AB]$ in the ratio $m:n$ is given by $C(x, y)$, where:

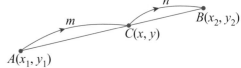

$$x = \frac{mx_2 + nx_1}{m + n}, y = \frac{my_2 + ny_1}{m + n}$$

2. External division

If the point $C(x, y)$ is outside $[AB]$, you get the external division formula:

$$x = \frac{mx_2 - nx_1}{m - n}, y = \frac{my_2 - ny_1}{m - n}$$

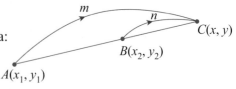

TIP
The external division formula is the same as the internal division formula with all the plus (+) signs replaced by minus (−) signs.

Applying the internal division formula

Find the point that divides $[AB]$ internally in the ratio $3:1$, where $A(-2, 1)$ and $B(4, -3)$.

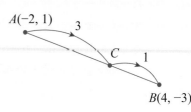

Method 1: Formula

$m = 3$	$n = 1$
$x_1 = -2$	$x_2 = 4$
$y_1 = 1$	$y_2 = -3$

$$x = \frac{3x_2 + 1x_1}{3 + 1}$$

$$= \frac{3(4) + 1(-2)}{3 + 1} = \frac{10}{4} = \frac{5}{2}$$

$$y = \frac{3y_2 + 1y_1}{3 + 1}$$

$$= \frac{3(-3) + 1(1)}{3 + 1} = \frac{-8}{4} = -2$$

$$C\left(\tfrac{5}{2}, -2\right)$$

Method 2: Cross-multiplication (a quick way of using the formula)

Step 1: Write down the given points side by side in the order given in the question, and put the ratios over the points in the same order.

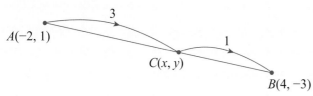

Step 2: Cross-multiply and divide by the sum of the ratios.

$$x = \frac{3(4) + 1(-2)}{3 + 1} = \frac{10}{4} = \frac{5}{2}$$

$$y = \frac{3(-3) + 1(1)}{3 + 1} = \frac{-8}{4} = -2$$

$$C\left(\tfrac{5}{2}, -2\right)$$

Method 3: Steps

A to B is 4 steps (3 and then 1). So 4 steps for x and 4 steps for y.

x: 4 steps $= 4 - (-2) = 6$.   [Divide by 4 to get the length of 1 step.]

1 step $= \frac{3}{2} \Rightarrow$ 3 steps $= \frac{9}{2}$

Add $\frac{9}{2}$ to -2 to get $\frac{5}{2}$.

y: 4 steps $= -3 - 1 = -4$

1 step $= -1 \Rightarrow$ 3 steps $= -3$

Add -3 to 1 to get -2.

$$C\left(\tfrac{5}{2}, -2\right)$$

EXAMPLE **1**

Find the points of trisection (three equal parts) of the line segment $[AB]$, where $A(-1, 3)$ and $B(4, -7)$ are end points.

Solution

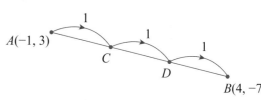

D divides $[AB]$ internally in the ratio $2:1$

$$x = \frac{2(4) + 1(-1)}{2 + 1} = \frac{7}{3}$$

$$y = \frac{2(-7) + 1(3)}{2 + 1} = -\frac{11}{3}$$

$D\left(\frac{7}{3}, -\frac{11}{3}\right)$

C is the midpoint of $[AD]$: $x = \dfrac{-1 + \frac{7}{3}}{2} = \dfrac{2}{3}, y = \dfrac{3 - \frac{11}{3}}{2} = -\dfrac{1}{3}$

$C\left(\frac{2}{3}, -\frac{1}{3}\right)$

EXAMPLE 2

If $A(-1, 2)$ and $B(4, 7)$, find a point $C(x, y)$ outside $[AB]$ such that $|AC| : |BC| = 3 : 2$.

Solution

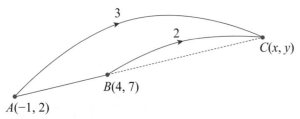

This means that $|AB| : |BC| = 1 : 2$ or $B(4, 7)$ divides $[AC]$ internally in the ratio $1 : 2$.

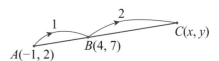

①	②
$(-1, 2)$	(x, y)

$\dfrac{1x + 2(-1)}{1 + 2} = 4$ $\dfrac{1y + 2(2)}{1 + 2} = 7$

$x - 2 = 12$ $y + 4 = 21$

$x = 14$ $y = 17$

$C(14, 17)$

Because C is outside the line segment $[AB]$, this division is an example of an external division of the line segment $[AB]$. C can be found directly using the external division formula.

EXAMPLE 3

Find the point $C(x, y)$ that divides $[AB]$ externally in the ratio $3 : 1$, where $A(-1, -4)$ and $B(5, 2)$.

Solution

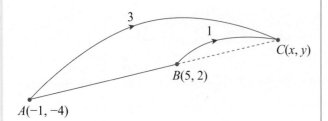

External division formula:

③	①
$(-1, -4)$	$(5, 2)$

$x = \dfrac{3(5) - 1(-1)}{3 - 1} = 8$ $y = \dfrac{3(2) - 1(-4)}{3 - 1} = 5$

$C(8, 5)$

EXERCISE 8

Diagrams are not drawn to scale.

1. Find the point that:

    (a) divides $[AB]$ internally in the ratio $5:3$, where $A(7, 6)$ and $B(-1, 6)$ are end points,

    (b) divides $[AB]$ internally in the ratio $3:2$, where $A(5, 1)$ and $B(0, -4)$ are end points,

    (c) divides $[AB]$ internally in the ratio $1:2$, where $A(-5, 7)$ and $B(-2, 13)$ are end points,

    (d) divides $[AB]$ internally in the ratio $1:1$, where $A(x_1, y_1)$ and $B(x_2, y_2)$ are end points.
    What can you conclude from this result?

2. $\triangle ACB$ is a triangle with vertices $A(-1, 4)$, $B(3, 8)$ and $C(7, -3)$.

    (a) Find D, the midpoint of $[AC]$. What do you call the line segment $[BD]$?

    (b) If G is a point on $[BD]$ such that $|BG|:|GD| = 2:1$, find G.

    (c) Find E, the midpoint of $[AB]$.

    (d) Find the point that divides $[CE]$ in the ratio $2:1$.

    (e) What is G called?

    (f) Can you make a conclusion?

    (g) Show that $G = \left(\dfrac{\text{Sum of } x \text{ co-ordinates}}{3}, \dfrac{\text{Sum of } y \text{ co-ordinates}}{3} \right)$.

3. A solar panel $[CB]$ is to be positioned on the roof of a house $ODBA$ with its lower edge at C, as shown, and its upper edge at B, such that $|AC|:|CB| = 3:2$.

    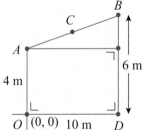

    Find:

    (a) the co-ordinates of A and B,

    (b) the co-ordinates of C,

    (c) the height of C above the ground,

    (d) the length $|CB|$ of the panel, correct to the nearest metre.

4. Find the points of trisection of the line segment $[AB]$, if $A(-2, 3)$ and $B(13, 9)$.

5. **(a)** In $\triangle ABC$, find D, if D is the midpoint of $[AB]$.

    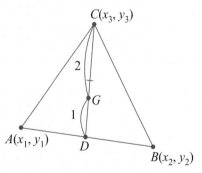

    (b) The centroid G of $\triangle ABC$ is a point that divides a median in the ratio $2:1$. Show that the centroid is

    $$G\left(\frac{x_1 + x_2 + x_3}{3}, \frac{y_1 + y_2 + y_3}{3} \right).$$

6. Town planners are given the job of drawing up a plan for a new road *q*. They are told that it must be perpendicular to an existing road *l* with equation *l*: $2x - 5y + 3 = 0$. It must also intersect a road joining two towns *A* and *B*, with co-ordinates $A(-1, -2)$ and $B(9, -12)$, at *C* such at $|AC| = 1\cdot5|CB|$. What is the equation of *q*?

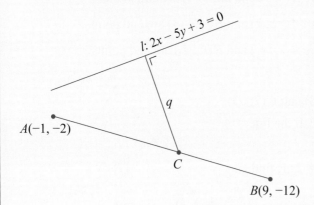

7. Find the equation of the line *l* with slope -3 that divides $[AB]$ in the ratio $2:1$.

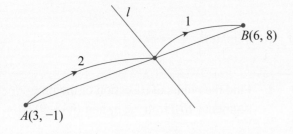

8. For $\triangle ABD$:

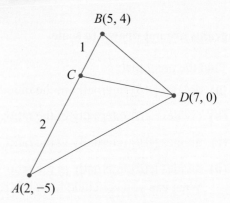

(a) Find *C*, if *C* divides $[AB]$ in the ratio $2:1$.

(b) Show that $[DC]$ is perpendicular to $[AB]$.

(c) Find the area of $\triangle ADB$.

(d) Find $|DC|$.

9. Find $C(x, y)$, which divides $[AB]$ externally in the ratio:

(a) $2:1$, if $A(2, -3)$ and $B(1, -5)$,

(b) $5:3$, if $A(-2, 1)$ and $B(3, 6)$.

11.2 The angle between lines

Given the equations of two lines l_1 and l_2, you can find the measures of the angles between them from their slopes.

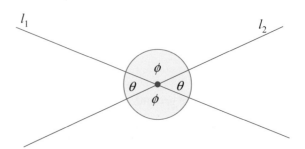

θ is the acute angle and ϕ is the obtuse angle.

ACTIVITY 10

ACTION
Understanding the angle between lines

OBJECTIVE
To understand and work with the formula for finding the angle between lines

SYLLABUS NOTE
The proof of the formula for the angle between lines is not required.

WORKED EXAMPLE　Finding the angle between lines

Find the acute angle θ between the lines $l_1: 3x + 2y - 12 = 0$ and $l_2: x - y - 1 = 0$.

Draw the lines by finding the points where they cut the axes.

$l_1: 3x + 2y - 12 = 0: (0, 6), (4, 0)$

$l_2: x - y - 1 = 0: (0, -1), (1, 0)$

Find the angle A: Slope of $l_1 = -\dfrac{3}{2}$

$\therefore A = 180° - \tan^{-1}\left(-\dfrac{3}{2}\right) = 123 \cdot 7°$

Find the angle B: Slope of $l_2 = 1$

$\therefore B = \tan^{-1}(1) = 45°$

$A = B + \theta \Rightarrow \theta = A - B$

$\theta = 123 \cdot 7° - 45° = 78 \cdot 7°$　[Acute angle]

$\phi = 180° - 78 \cdot 7° = 101 \cdot 3°$　[Obtuse angle]

The angle between lines formula

Slope of $l_1 = m_1 = \tan A$

Slope of $l_2 = m_2 = \tan B$

$A = B + \theta \Rightarrow \theta = (A - B)$

$\tan \theta = \tan(A - B)$

$\tan \theta = \dfrac{\tan A - \tan B}{1 + \tan A \tan B}$

$\tan \theta = \dfrac{m_1 - m_2}{1 + m_1 m_2}$

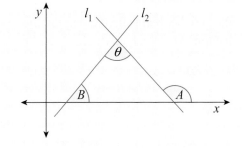

This is the **tan θ formula** for finding the angle θ between two lines.

$$\tan \theta = \dfrac{m_1 - m_2}{1 + m_1 m_2}$$

TIPS

1. There are two angles between intersecting lines.

2. Always find the acute angle θ first by taking the absolute value of tan θ.

   $\tan \theta = \left| \dfrac{m_1 - m_2}{1 + m_1 m_2} \right|$ will always give you the

   acute angle between intersecting lines.

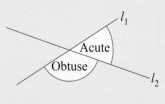

3. To find the obtuse angle ϕ, subtract the acute angle from 180°: $\phi = 180° - \theta$

Some notes on the tan θ formula

1. Parallel lines: $m_1 = m_2 \Leftrightarrow \tan\theta = 0 \Leftrightarrow \theta = 0° \Leftrightarrow l_1 \parallel l_2$

   Do not use the formula if the slopes are the same because $\theta = 0°$ in this case.

2. Perpendicular lines: $m_1 m_2 = -1 \Leftrightarrow \tan\theta = \infty \Leftrightarrow \theta = 90° \Leftrightarrow l_1 \perp l_2$

   Do not use the formula if $m_1 m_2 = -1$ because $\theta = 90°$ in this case.

3. $m_1 = 0 \Leftrightarrow \tan\theta = |m_2|$

   Do not use the formula if one slope is zero, as $\tan\theta$ is just the modulus of the other slope.

EXAMPLE 4

Find the acute and obtuse angles between the lines $l_1 : 2x + y - 3 = 0$ and $l_2 : 4x - 7y + 1 = 0$, correct to the nearest degree.

Solution

$l_1 : 2x + y - 3 = 0 \Rightarrow$ slope of $l_1 : m_1 = -2$

$l_2 : 4x - 7y + 1 = 0 \Rightarrow$ slope of $l_2 : m_2 = \dfrac{4}{7}$

$$\tan\theta = \left| \frac{-2 - \frac{4}{7}}{1 + (-2)\left(\frac{4}{7}\right)} \right| = \left| \frac{-14 - 4}{7 - 8} \right| = \left| \frac{-18}{1} \right| = 18$$

$\theta = \tan^{-1} 18 = 87°$ is the acute angle.

$\phi = 180° - 87° = 93°$ is the obtuse angle.

EXAMPLE 5

A white snooker ball is fired along the line p to hit the cushion. At A it rebounds along the line q.

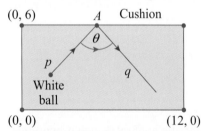

If the equations of p and q are $p : 2x - y = 0$ and $q : x + y - 9 = 0$, find:

(a) the acute angle through which the white ball is deflected, correct to the nearest degree,

(b) the point A at which the white ball strikes the cushion.

Solution

(a) $p : 2x - y = 0 \Rightarrow$ slope of p is $m_1 = 2$

$q : x + y - 9 = 0 \Rightarrow$ slope of q is $m_2 = -1$

$$\tan\theta = \left| \frac{2 - (-1)}{1 + 2(-1)} \right| = \left| \frac{3}{-1} \right| = 3$$

$\theta = \tan^{-1} 3 = 71 \cdot 565° \simeq 72°$

(b) $2x - y = 0$ ... **(1)**

$\underline{x + y = 9}$ ... **(2)**

$3x = 9 \Rightarrow x = 3$

Substituting back into **(1)** gives:

$6 - y = 0 \Rightarrow y = 6$

$\therefore A(3, 6)$

Working backwards – finding the slope

A much more difficult problem is to find the slopes of the lines making a given angle θ with a line whose equation is given.

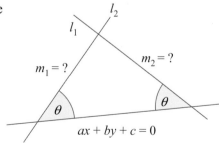

EXAMPLE 6

Find the slopes of the lines that make equal acute angles of 45° with the line $4x + y - 3 = 0$.

Solution

Let q be one of the lines and let its slope be m.

Slope of q: $m_1 = m$

Slope of p: $m_2 = -4$

$\theta = 45°$

Using the tan θ formula: $\tan 45° = \left|\dfrac{m - (-4)}{1 + m(-4)}\right| \Rightarrow 1 = \left|\dfrac{m + 4}{1 - 4m}\right|$

$\therefore \pm 1 = \dfrac{m + 4}{1 - 4m}$ [When you remove the bars from a modulus equation, you put $\pm$ on one side or the other.]

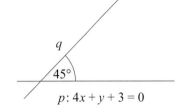

$\oplus$

$1 = \dfrac{m + 4}{1 - 4m}$

$1 - 4m = m + 4$

$5m = -3$

$m = -\dfrac{3}{5}$

$\ominus$

$-1 = \dfrac{m + 4}{1 - 4m}$

$-1 + 4m = m + 4$

$3m = 5$

$m = \dfrac{5}{3}$

You should get two slopes, one for each line. The tan θ formula automatically works out both answers for you.

EXAMPLE 7

A ship moving along the line AB with equation $x + y - 12 = 0$ is only visible from a lighthouse $L(0, 0)$ when the angles $\angle LAB$ and $\angle LBA$ are greater than $\theta = \tan^{-1}\dfrac{3}{2}$.

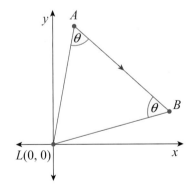

(a) Find the equations of the lines AL and BL.

(b) Find A and B.

(c) Find $|AB|$, if 1 unit = 1 km.

Solution

(a) Let the slope m_1 of AL be m.

$m_1 = m$

Slope of AB: $m_2 = -1$

$\theta = \tan^{-1}\dfrac{3}{2} \Rightarrow \tan \theta = \dfrac{3}{2}$

Using the tan θ formula:

$\tan \theta = \dfrac{3}{2} = \left|\dfrac{m - (-1)}{1 + m(-1)}\right| \Rightarrow \pm\dfrac{3}{2} = \dfrac{m + 1}{1 - m}$

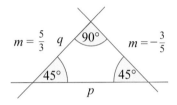

$\oplus$

$\dfrac{3}{2} = \dfrac{m + 1}{1 - m}$

$3 - 3m = 2m + 2$

$5m = 1$

$m = \dfrac{1}{5}$

$\ominus$

$-\dfrac{3}{2} = \dfrac{m + 1}{1 - m}$

$-3 + 3m = 2m + 2$

$m = 5$

Equation of LB:

$y - 0 = \dfrac{1}{5}(x - 0)$

$x - 5y = 0$

Equation of LA:

$y - 0 = 5(x - 0)$

$5x - y = 0$

(b)

A	B

A

$$5x - y = 0 \quad ... \textbf{(1)}$$
$$\underline{x + y = 12 \ ... \ \textbf{(2)}}$$
$$6x = 12$$
$$x = 2$$

Substituting back into **(2)**:

$$y = 10$$
$$A(2, 10)$$

B

$$x - 5y = 0 \ ... \ \textbf{(1)}$$
$$\underline{x + y = 12 \ ... \ \textbf{(2)}}$$
$$-6y = -12 \ ... \ \textbf{(1)} - \textbf{(2)}$$
$$y = 2$$

Substituting back into **(2)**:

$$x = 10$$
$$B(10, 2)$$

(c) $|AB| = \sqrt{64 + 64} = 8\sqrt{2}$ km

EXERCISE 9

Diagrams are not drawn to scale.

1. Find the acute angle θ and the obtuse angle φ between the given lines, correct to the nearest degree:

   (a) $y = 0$, $\sqrt{3}\,x - y + 7 = 0$

   (b) $2x + 3y = 17$, $3x - 7y + 5 = 0$

   (c) $5x + y - 4 = 0$, $3x + y - 8 = 0$

   (d) $3x - 4y = 10$, $4x + 3y = 8$

   (e) $x = 5$, $y = -3$

   (f) $2x + y = 7$, $3x - y - 9 = 0$

   (g) $4x - y + 5 = 0$, $3x - 2y + 7 = 0$

   (h) $x + 2y + 3 = 0$, $2x - 5y = -3$

2. **(a)** Find the acute angle between the lines $l_1 : 3x - 11y + 5 = 0$ and $l_2 : 3x - 1 = 0$, correct to one decimal place.
   (Hint: A line at right angles to a line of slope ∞ has a slope of 0.)

   (b) Find the acute angle between the lines $l_1 : ax + by + c = 0$ and $l_2 : (a - b)x + (a + b)y + d = 0$.

3. In $\triangle ACB$, show that the acute angle $|\angle ABC|$ equals the acute angle $|\angle ACB|$. Verify $|AB| = |AC|$.

   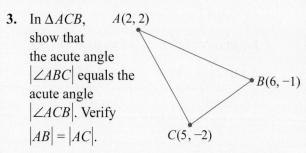

4. Show that $A(-2, 3)$, $B(4, 1)$, $C(6, 4)$ and $D(0, 6)$ are the vertices of the parallelogram $ABCD$. Find the acute angle between the diagonals, correct to the nearest degree.

   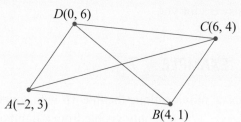

5. Find the slopes of the lines:

   (a) making angles of 45° with the line $x + 3y - 4 = 0$,

   (b) making angles of 60° with the line $\sqrt{3}x - y = 5$.

6. **(a) (i)** A ship moves from A to B. Find the slope of this line.

   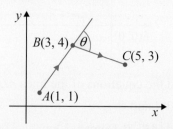

   (ii) It changes direction at B and moves along BC. Find the slope of BC.

   (iii) Find the acute angle θ through which it turns at B, correct to the nearest degree.

(b) A cross-country course is set out in the form of the triangle $\triangle ABC$. The course starts at $A(0, 0)$ and finishes at $A(0, 0)$.

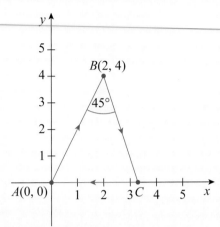

(i) Find the slope of AB.

(ii) Find the slope of BC.

(iii) Find the equation of BC.

(iv) Find the point C.

(v) Find the total length of the course, correct to the nearest metre, if 1 unit = 200 m on each axis.

(c) A camera placed at $A(1, 1)$ scans along a line l with equation $5x - y + 9 = 0$ through $90°$ from B to C.

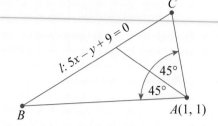

Find:

(i) the slopes of AB and AC, if AB has a positive slope,

(ii) the equation of AB and AC,

(iii) B and C,

(iv) $|BC|$.

11.3 The perpendicular distance from a point to a line

Given the equation of a line $l: ax + by + c = 0$ and a point $P(x_1, y_1)$, it is possible to find the perpendicular distance d from P to l using what you already know about similar triangles.

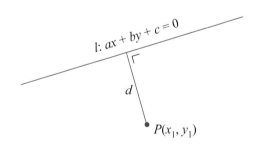

WORKED EXAMPLE

WORKED EXAMPLE

Perpendicular distance from a point to a line

Find the distance from $P(2, 1)$ to $l: x + 2y - 8 = 0$.

Draw the line by finding the points where it cuts the axes.

$l: x + 2y - 8 = 0$: $(0, 4)$, $(8, 0)$

Draw $x = 2$ through P to meet l at R.
Substituting $x = 2$ into l:

$2 + 2y - 8 = 0$

$\qquad 2y = 6$

$\qquad y = 3$

$R(2, 3)$

Draw $y = 1$ through P to meet l at Q.
Substituting $y = 1$ into l:

$x + 2 - 8 = 0$

$\qquad x = 6$

$Q(6, 1)$

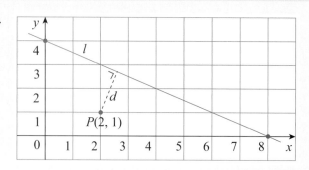

$|QR| = \sqrt{(6 - 2)^2 + (1 - 3)^2} = \sqrt{16 + 4} = \sqrt{20} = 2\sqrt{5}$

Triangles $\triangle PRS$ and $\triangle PRQ$ are similar:

$\therefore \dfrac{d}{2} = \dfrac{4}{2\sqrt{5}} \Rightarrow d = \dfrac{8}{2\sqrt{5}} = \dfrac{4}{\sqrt{5}}$

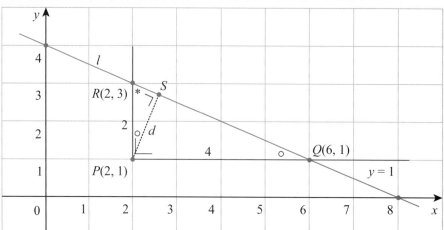

The process outlined in the Worked Example to obtain the perpendicular distance from a point P to a line l is very long and tedious.

However, it can be generalised to give the perpendicular distance formula for the distance d from any point $P(x_1, y_1)$ and any line l with equation $ax + by + c = 0$:

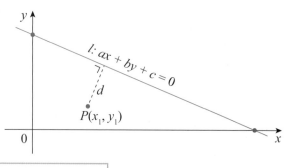

$$d = \frac{\left|ax_1 + by_1 + c\right|}{\sqrt{a^2 + b^2}}$$

TIP

Remember the formula as: $d = \dfrac{\left|ax_1 + by_1 + c\right|}{\sqrt{a^2 + b^2}} = \dfrac{\left|\text{Point in line}\right|}{\text{Pythagoras}}$

Some points on using the perpendicular distance formula

1. Point in line: If the point is $P(x_1, y_1)$ and the line is $l: ax + by + c = 0$, substitute (x_1, y_1) into $ax + by + c$ to obtain $ax_1 + by_1 + c$.

2. Pythagoras: $\sqrt{a^2 + b^2}$ from $\boldsymbol{a}x + \boldsymbol{b}y + c = 0$

1. Finding the perpendicular distance from a point to a line

EXAMPLE 8

Find the perpendicular distance from **(a)** $P(2, -3)$ and **(b)** $Q(4, -2)$ to the line $3x + 4y - 4 = 0$.

Solution

$l: 3x + 4y - 4 = 0 \Rightarrow a = 3, b = 4$

(a) $P(2, -3): d = \dfrac{|3(2) + 4(-3) - 4|}{\sqrt{3^2 + 4^2}} = \dfrac{|-10|}{5} = \dfrac{10}{5} = 2$

(b) $Q(4, -2): d = \dfrac{|3(4) + 4(-2) - 4|}{\sqrt{3^2 + 4^2}} = \dfrac{0}{5} = 0$

$d = 0$ means the point Q is on the line $l: 3x + 4y - 4 = 0$.

2. Finding the distance of closest approach

EXAMPLE 9

A boat sails from a point P, 16 km due North of a port $O(0, 0)$, to a point Q, 20 km due East of O, as shown.

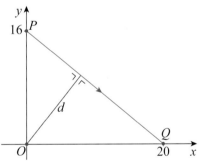

(a) Find the equation of the line PQ.

(b) Find the distance d of closest approach of the boat to O, correct to one decimal place.

(c) If the boat is visible when 14 km or less away from O, find the distance the boat travels while visible from O, correct to one decimal place.

Solution

(a) $P(0, 16), Q(20, 0)$

Slope of $PQ = \dfrac{16 - 0}{0 - 20} = \dfrac{-16}{20} = -\dfrac{4}{5}$

Equation of PQ: $(y - 16) = -\dfrac{4}{5}(x - 0)$

$5(y - 16) = -4x$

$4x + 5y - 80 = 0$

(b) To find the distance d of closest approach, use the perpendicular distance formula for the point $O(0, 0)$ and the line PQ.

$O(0, 0), PQ: 4x + 5y - 80 = 0$

$\therefore d = \dfrac{|4(0) + 5(0) - 80|}{\sqrt{4^2 + 5^2}} = \dfrac{80}{\sqrt{41}}$ km $\approx 12 \cdot 5$ km

(c) Draw lines from O to PQ of length 14 km.

$|AC| = \sqrt{14^2 - d^2}$

$= 6 \cdot 3$ km

$|AB| = 12 \cdot 6$ km

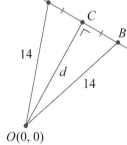

The boat is visible for the distance $|AB|$.

3. Finding the perpendicular distance between parallel lines given their equations

EXAMPLE 10

Find the perpendicular distance between the parallel lines $l_1: 2x - 3y + 1 = 0$ and $l_2: 4x - 6y - 5 = 0$.

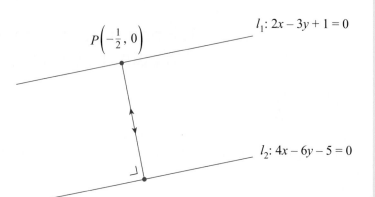

$P\left(-\frac{1}{2}, 0\right)$

$l_1: 2x - 3y + 1 = 0$

$l_2: 4x - 6y - 5 = 0$

Solution

Choose a point on one line and find the perpendicular distance from this point to the other line.

Choose **any** point P on one line, say l_1.

$l_1: y = 0 \Rightarrow 2x + 1 = 0$

$\qquad x = -\frac{1}{2}$

$\therefore P\left(-\frac{1}{2}, 0\right)$

Find the perpendicular distance from P to l_2: $d = \dfrac{\left|4\left(-\frac{1}{2}\right) - 6(0) - 5\right|}{\sqrt{4^2 + (-6)^2}} = \dfrac{7}{\sqrt{52}} = \dfrac{7\sqrt{13}}{26}$

EXAMPLE 11

Two parallel runways p and q are shown on an airfield.

(a) Find the equation of p.

(b) Find the equation of q.

(c) Find the distance apart of the runways, correct to one decimal place.

(1 unit = 1 km)

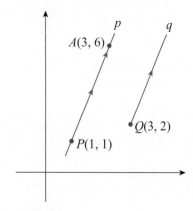

Solution

(a) $p: A(3, 6), P(1, 1)$

Slope of $p = \dfrac{6 - 1}{3 - 1} = \dfrac{5}{2}$

Equation of $p: (y - 1) = \frac{5}{2}(x - 1)$

$2(y - 1) = 5(x - 1)$

$2y - 2 = 5x - 5$

$5x - 2y - 3 = 0$

(b) Equation of $q: m = \frac{5}{2}, Q(3, 2)$

$(y - 2) = \frac{5}{2}(x - 3)$

$2(y - 2) = 5(x - 3)$

$2y - 4 = 5x - 15$

$5x - 2y - 11 = 0$

(c) Distance from $Q(3, 2)$ to $p: 5x - 2y - 3 = 0$:

$d = \dfrac{\left|5(3) - 2(2) - 3\right|}{\sqrt{5^2 + (-2)^2}} = \dfrac{\left|15 - 4 - 3\right|}{\sqrt{25 + 4}}$

$= \dfrac{8}{\sqrt{29}} \approx 1\cdot5 \text{ km}$

4. Finding the equations of lines with a given slope which are a given distance from a given point

EXAMPLE 12

Find the equations of the tangents of slope $\frac{1}{2}$ to the circle with centre $C(4, -2)$ and radius $\sqrt{20}$.

Solution

If t is a tangent to the circle, the perpendicular distance from the centre of the circle to the tangent is equal to the radius.

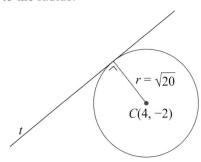

$r = \sqrt{20}$

$C(4, -2)$

t

Slope of $t = \frac{1}{2}$

Equation of t: $x - 2y + c = 0$

Find the perpendicular distance from the point $(4, -2)$ to the tangent t, and then put the distance equal to $\sqrt{20}$.

$$\therefore d = \frac{|4 + 4 + c|}{\sqrt{(1)^2 + (-2)^2}} = \sqrt{20}$$

$$|8 + c| = \sqrt{20} \times \sqrt{5}$$

$$|8 + c| = 10$$

$$8 + c = \pm 10$$

$$c = 2, -18$$

The equations of the tangents are: $x - 2y + 2 = 0$ and $x - 2y - 18 = 0$.

EXERCISE 10

Diagrams are not drawn to scale.

1. Find the perpendicular distance from:

   (a) point $P(2, 1)$ to the line l: $3x - 4y + 4 = 0$,

   (b) point $P(-3, 2)$ to the line l: $x - y + 3 = 0$,

   (c) point $P\left(-\frac{1}{2}, \frac{2}{3}\right)$ to the line l: $4x - 3y + 7 = 0$,

   (d) point $P(-1, 4)$ to the line l: $\frac{x}{3} + \frac{y}{4} = 1$,

   (e) point $P(c, d)$ to the line l:
   $x \cos \alpha + y \sin \alpha - a = 0$.

2. Find the distance between the parallel lines:

   (a) l_1: $3x + 4y - 7 = 0$ and l_2: $3x + 4y = 13$

   (b) l_1: $4x - 5y + 5 = 0$ and l_2: $8x - 10y - 1 = 0$

   (c) l_1: $ax + by + c = 0$ and l_2: $ax + by + d = 0$

3. Show that the point $A(1, 1)$ is equidistant from the lines:

   l_1: $3x - 4y + 6 = 0$

   l_2: $5x + 12y - 4 = 0$

   l_3: $4x + 3y - 2 = 0$

4. Find the equation(s) of the following:

   (a) The lines of slope -2 and $3\sqrt{5}$ units from the point $(6, 2)$

   (b) The lines parallel to the line
   l: $3x + 4y - 5 = 0$ and 3 units from the point $P(1, 2)$

   (c) The lines perpendicular to the line
   l: $x + 7y - 5 = 0$ and $\sqrt{2}$ units from $(-1, 1)$

   (d) The lines parallel to the line
   l: $12x + 5y - 3 = 0$ at a distance of 3 units from it

   (e) The line parallel to the line
   l: $x - 2y - 6 = 0$ and at the same distance from the point $P(3, 2)$

   (f) The lines making angles of 60° with the $+x$-axis and 4 units from the point $(\sqrt{3}, 5)$

   (g) The lines making angles of $\tan^{-1}\left(\frac{2}{3}\right)$ with the $+x$-axis and $2\sqrt{13}$ units from the point $(1, 6)$

(h) The lines making equal intercepts on the axes and $3\sqrt{2}$ units from $(2, 3)$.
(Hint: Equal intercepts on the axes means the slope $= \pm1$)

5. A ship sails from a port $P(0, 5)$ at a heading of E $\tan^{-1} 2$ N. It sails between two buoys $A(6, 3)$ and $B(2, 8)$.
(Scale : 1 unit = 1 km on each axis)

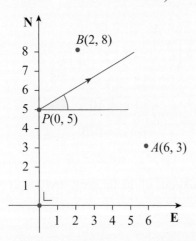

(a) Find the equation of the ship's path.

(b) Find its distance of closest approach to buoys A and B, correct to two decimal places.

6. Two swimmers A and B enter a river at $A(0, 0)$ and $B(0, -3)$, respectively. They swim along parallel paths over to the other bank DC.

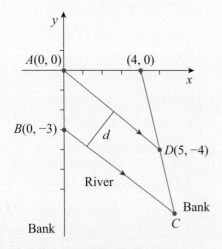

(a) Find the equation of AD.

(b) Find the equation of BC.

(c) Find their closest possible distance apart d, correct to one decimal place.

(d) Find the co-ordinates of C, the point where B lands on the opposite bank.
(1 unit on each axis = 10 m)

7. $p : x - y = 0$ and $q : 7x + y = 8$ intersect at A. $B(x, y)$ is a point on the bisector of the angle $\angle DAE$ between p and q.

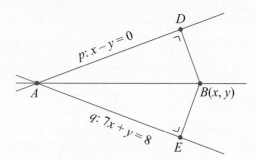

(a) Prove $|BD| = |BE|$, where $|\angle BDA| = |\angle BEA| = 90°$.

(b) Find A.

(c) Show by putting $|BD| = |BE|$ that (x, y) can lie on two perpendicular lines.

(d) Can you explain part **(c)**?

8. A ray of light from a point source P on the x-axis casts a shadow of a circular object with centre $C(4, 0)$ and radius 5 on a vertical wall.

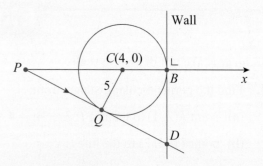

Find the co-ordinates of B. If the slope of the tangent PQ to the circle at Q is $-\frac{3}{4}$, find:

(a) the equation of PQ,

(b) $|BD|$,

(c) the co-ordinates of P.

9. Find the co-ordinates of the points $P(a, b)$ which are on the line $p : x + 5y + 6 = 0$ and which are 2 units from the line $q : 12x - 5y + 7 = 0$.

(Hint: If $P(a, b)$ is on the line p, its co-ordinates (a, b) satisfy the equation of p.)

Circle 1

CHAPTER 12

Learning Outcomes

- To know the three ways in which the equation of a circle can be written.
- To consider different situations where a line and a circle intersect, involving tangents and chords.

Circles are curves

ACTIVITY 12

ACTION
Understanding curves and points on curves

OBJECTIVE
To describe the equations of curves in words and to investigate whether or not points lie on curves

We meet terms like ring, hoop, disc and orbit regularly in our daily lives. These terms have all one thing in common. They are all circular in nature.

Just as a straight line can be described by an equation, many curves can be similarly described by an equation that is satisfied by every point (x, y) on the curve. This equation is a formula connecting the x and y co-ordinates for every point on the curve.

The equation $y = x^2$ of a curve simply means that every y co-ordinate on the curve is obtained by squaring its x co-ordinate.

▸ $(3, 1)$ is on the straight line with equation $4x - 7y - 5 = 0$
   because $4(3) - 7(1) - 5 = 0$. $(3, 1)$ satisfies the equation $4x - 7y - 5 = 0$.

▸ $(2, 4)$ is on the curve $y = x^2$ because $4 = (2)^2$. However, $(4, 7)$ is not on the curve $y = x^2$ because $7 \neq 4^2$.

12.1 The three equations of a circle

KEY TERM

A **circle** is a set of points such that **every** point (x, y) of the set is the same distance r (radius) from a fixed point called the centre C.

$$\left|CP_1\right| = \left|CP_2\right| = \left|CP_3\right| = \left|CP_4\right| = r$$

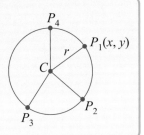

TIP

Once you know the centre C and radius r, then there is only one circle you can draw with these specifications.

▸ A circle with centre $C(3, 4)$ and radius 2 is unique.

$P(5, 4)$ is on this circle because
$$|CP| = \sqrt{(5-3)^2 + (4-4)^2}$$
$$= \sqrt{4} = 2 = r$$

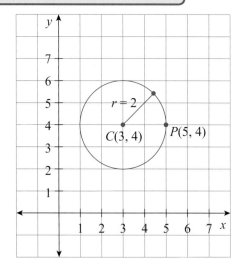

Writing the equation of a circle

There are three ways in which to write the equation of a circle, depending on how the centre C is given.

ACTIVITY 13

ACTION
Deriving the equations of circles

OBJECTIVE
To derive the equations of circles using a general point (x, y) on the circle and Pythagoras' theorem

1. Equation of a circle with centre $C(0, 0)$ and radius r.
2. Equation of a circle with centre $C(h, k)$ and radius r.
3. Equation of a circle with centre $C(-g, -f)$ and radius r.

1. Equation of a circle with centre $C(0, 0)$ and radius r

For every point $P(x, y)$:
$$|CP| = \sqrt{(x-0)^2 + (y-0)^2} = r$$
$$\sqrt{x^2 + y^2} = r$$
$$x^2 + y^2 = r^2$$

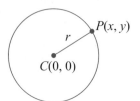

$x^2 + y^2 = r^2$ is the equation of a circle with centre $C(0, 0)$ and radius r.

EXAMPLE 1

Find the equation of a circle with centre $C(0, 0)$ with:

(a) radius 5

(b) radius $\sqrt{7}$

(c) radius $\frac{1}{2}$

Solution

(a) $r = 5$

Equation of the circle:

$x^2 + y^2 = (5)^2$

$x^2 + y^2 = 25$

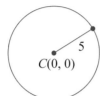

(b) $r = \sqrt{7}$

Equation of the circle:

$x^2 + y^2 = (\sqrt{7})^2$

$x^2 + y^2 = 7$

(c) $r = \frac{1}{2}$

Equation of the circle:

$x^2 + y^2 = \left(\frac{1}{2}\right)^2$

$x^2 + y^2 = \frac{1}{4}$

$4x^2 + 4y^2 = 1$

2. Equation of a circle with centre $C(h, k)$ and radius r

For every point $P(x, y)$:

$|CP| = \sqrt{(x - h)^2 + (y - k)^2} = r$

$(x - h)^2 + (y - k)^2 = r^2$

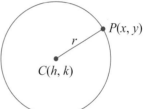

$(x - h)^2 + (y - k)^2 = r^2$ is the equation of a circle with centre $C(h, k)$ and radius r.

EXAMPLE 2

Find the equation of a circle with:

(a) centre $C(-1, 5)$ and radius 3

(b) centre $C(1, 0)$ and radius $\frac{2}{3}$

Solution

(a) $C(-1, 5) = (h, k)$

$h = -1, k = 5$

Radius: $r = 3$

Equation of the circle:

$(x - (-1))^2 + (y - 5)^2 = (3)^2$

$(x + 1)^2 + (y - 5)^2 = 9$

Multiplying out the brackets gives:

$x^2 + 2x + 1 + y^2 - 10y + 25 = 9$

$x^2 + y^2 + 2x - 10y + 17 = 0$

The equation of a circle is normally written in the above form with the terms in that exact order.

(b) $C(1, 0) = (h, k), r = \frac{2}{3}$

Equation of the circle:

$(x - 1)^2 + (y - 0)^2 = \left(\frac{2}{3}\right)^2$

$x^2 - 2x + 1 + y^2 = \frac{4}{9}$

$9x^2 - 18x + 9 + 9y^2 = 4$

$9x^2 + 9y^2 - 18x + 5 = 0$

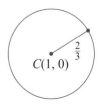

3. Equation of a circle with centre $C(-g, -f)$ and radius r

For every point $P(x, y)$:

$$\left|CP\right| = \sqrt{(x - (-g))^2 + (y - (-f))^2} = r$$

$$\sqrt{(x + g)^2 + (y + f)^2} = r$$

$$(x + g)^2 + (y + f)^2 = r^2$$

$$x^2 + 2gx + g^2 + y^2 + 2fy + f^2 = r^2$$

$$x^2 + y^2 + 2gx + 2fy + (g^2 + f^2 - r^2) = 0$$

$$x^2 + y^2 + 2gx + 2fy + c = 0, \text{ where } c = g^2 + f^2 - r^2.$$

or $x^2 + y^2 + 2gx + 2fy + c = 0$ where $r = \sqrt{g^2 + f^2 - c}$

> $x^2 + y^2 + 2gx + 2fy + c = 0$ is the equation of a circle with centre $C(-g, -f)$ and radius r, where $r = \sqrt{g^2 + f^2 - c}$.

ACTIVITY 14

ACTION
Writing the equation of a circle by finding g, f and c

OBJECTIVE
To write the values of g, f and c, given certain information about the circle, and to hence write the equation of the circle

EXAMPLE 3

Find the equation of a circle with centre $C(-2, 3)$ and radius 4.

Solution

$C(-2, 3) = (-g, -f)$

$g = 2, f = -3$

$r = 3 = \sqrt{(2)^2 + (-3)^2 - c}$

$9 = 4 + 9 - c$

$c = 4$

The equation of the circle is $x^2 + y^2 + 2(2)x + 2(-3)y + (4) = 0$

$$x^2 + y^2 + 4x - 6y + 4 = 0$$

TIP
Once you know the g, f and c values for a circle, you can find out everything else about the circle.

EXAMPLE 4

Find the equation of the circle with centre $C\left(-\frac{1}{2}, -2\right)$ and radius 1.

Solution

$C\left(-\frac{1}{2}, -2\right) = (-g, -f)$

$g = \frac{1}{2}, f = 2, r = 1$

$r = 1 = \sqrt{\left(\frac{1}{2}\right)^2 + (2)^2 - c}$

$1 = \frac{1}{4} + 4 - c$

$c = \frac{13}{4}$

The equation of the circle is:

$$x^2 + y^2 + 2\left(\frac{1}{2}\right)x + 2(2)y + \frac{13}{4} = 0$$

$$4x^2 + 4y^2 + 4x + 16y + 13 = 0$$

It is important to get used to writing the equation of a circle in the above form with the terms in exactly that order.

Reducing three versions to one

There are three versions of the equation of a circle, depending on how the centre C is given:

- $x^2 + y^2 = r^2$, centre $(0, 0)$, radius r … **Version 1**
- $(x - h)^2 + (y - k)^2 = r^2$, centre (h, k), radius r … **Version 2**
- $x^2 + y^2 + 2gx + 2fy + c = 0$, centre $(-g, -f)$, radius $r = \sqrt{g^2 + f^2 - c}$ … **Version 3**

However, you can find the equation of any circle using version **(3)** exclusively.

Notes on the equation of a circle

1. The equation of every circle can be put into the form:
   $$x^2 + y^2 + 2gx + 2fy + c = 0$$

2. There **must always** be an x^2 term and a y^2 term and their coefficients (numbers in front of them) must be equal.
   $2x^2 + 2y^2 + 8x - 7y - 4 = 0$ is the equation of a circle.
   $3x^2 + y^2 - 8x - 7y - 4 = 0$ is not the equation of a circle.

3. Some values of g, f and c can be 0, but they cannot all be 0.

4. There is no xy term in the equation of a circle.

ACTIVITY 15

ACTION
Writing the centre and radius of a circle from the equation in the form $x^2+y^2+2gx+2fy+c=0$

OBJECTIVE
To find the centre and radius of a circle by inspecting equations in the form $x^2+y^2+2gx+2fy+c=0$

Reading off the centre and radius of a circle from its equation

Reading off the centre or radius from an equation written in **version 1** or **2** is easy. To read off the centre and radius of a circle from its equation in **version 3**, follow the steps below:

1. Put the equation into the form $x^2 + y^2 + 2gx + 2fy + c = 0$, making sure you have $1x^2$ and $1y^2$ before you start.

2. Multiply the coefficients of x and y by $\frac{1}{2}$ to read off the g and f values, respectively.

3. Read off the c value.

4. Find the radius from $r = \sqrt{g^2 + f^2 - c}$.

5. Write down the centre $(-g, -f)$.

EXAMPLE 5

Find the centre and radius of the circle with the following equations:

(a) $5x^2 + 5y^2 = 15$ **(b)** $(x - 5)^2 + (y + 2)^2 = 5$ **(c)** $x^2 + y^2 + 4x - 2y + 1 = 0$ **(d)** $(2x - 3)^2 + 4y^2 - 8y = 1$

Solution

(a) $5x^2 + 5y^2 = 15$
   $x^2 + y^2 = 3$

   This is **version 1** of the equation of the circle.

   Centre $(0, 0)$, $r = \sqrt{3}$

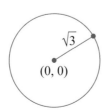

(b) $(x - 5)^2 + (y + 2)^2 = 5$

   This is **version 2** of the equation of the circle.

   Centre $(h, k) = (5, -2)$, $r = \sqrt{5}$

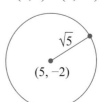

(c) $x^2 + y^2 + 4x - 2y + 1 = 0$

Compare this circle equation to the general circle equation: $x^2 + y^2 + 2gx + 2fy + c = 0$

$x^2 + y^2 + 4x - 2y + 1 = 0$

$2g = 4, 2f = -2, c = 1$

$g = \frac{1}{2}(4) = 2; f = \frac{1}{2}(-2) = -1; c = 1$

$r = \sqrt{g^2 + f^2 - c} = \sqrt{4 + 1 - 1} = 2$

Centre: $(-g, -f) = (-2, 1)$

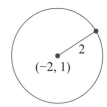

(d) $(2x - 3)^2 + 4y^2 - 8y = 1$

Multiply out first:

$4x^2 - 12x + 9 + 4y^2 - 8y - 1 = 0$

$\quad 4x^2 + 4y^2 - 12x - 8y + 8 = 0$

Divide by 4 to get $1x^2$ and $1y^2$:

$x^2 + y^2 - 3x - 2y + 2 = 0$

$g = -\frac{3}{2}, f = -1, c = 2$

$r = \sqrt{\frac{9}{4} + 1 - 2} = \frac{\sqrt{5}}{2}$

Centre: $\left(\frac{3}{2}, 1\right)$

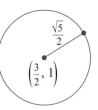

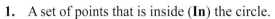

ACTIVITY 16 — Points inside, outside or on the circle

ACTION
Establishing if a point is inside, on or outside a circle

OBJECTIVE
To investigate the position of a point in relation to a circle

When you draw a circle in a plane, the plane is divided into three regions:

1. A set of points that is inside (**In**) the circle.

2. A set of points that is outside (**Out**) the circle.

3. A set of points that is on (**On**) the circle.

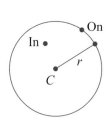

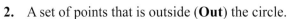

EXAMPLE 6

Is the point $P(-2, -4)$ inside, outside or on the circle with equation $x^2 + y^2 - 4x + 8y - 5 = 0$?

Solution

$x^2 + y^2 - 4x + 8y - 5 = 0$

$g = -2, f = 4, c = -5$

Centre $C(2, -4)$

$r = \sqrt{4 + 16 + 5} = 5$

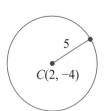

The distance from C to P is:

$|CP| = \sqrt{(4)^2 + (0)^2} = 4 < 5$

$|CP| < r$ means $(-2, -4)$ is inside the circle.

In general, if C is the centre of a circle of radius r and P is any point:

1. $|CP| < r$ means P is **In**.

2. $|CP| > r$ means P is **Out**.

3. $|CP| = r$ means P is **On**.

EXAMPLE 7

Show that $P(-1, 2)$ is on the circle with the equation $x^2 + y^2 + 6x + 11y - 21 = 0$.

Solution

You could find the distance from the centre of the circle to P and compare it with the radius of the circle as in Example 6 or just substitute the co-ordinates of P into the equation of the circle.

LHS	RHS
$x^2 + y^2 + 6x + 11y - 21$	0
(−1, 2): $(-1)^2 + (2)^2 + 6(-1) + 11(2) - 21$	
$\quad = 1 + 4 - 6 + 22 - 21$	
$\quad = 0$	

LHS = RHS

$(-1, 2)$ satisfies the equation of the circle. Therefore, $(-1, 2)$ is on the circle.

TIP

You can use this method of substitution to test **In/Out/On** for any point P by substituting P into the left-hand side (LHS) of the equation:

If $x^2 + y^2 + 2gx + 2fy + c = 0$, then

LHS $< 0 \Rightarrow P$ is **In**. $\qquad$ LHS $> 0 \Rightarrow P$ is **Out**. $\qquad$ LHS $= 0 \Rightarrow P$ is **On**.

EXAMPLE 8

The equation of the circle described by the blades of a wind turbine is $x^2 + y^2 - 100y + 1875 = 0$. A bird flies to a point $P(22, 40)$. Is the bird in danger?

Blade

Solution

The bird is in danger if it is inside or on the circle.

Substitute $P(22, 40)$ into LHS of $x^2 + y^2 - 100y + 1875 = 0$.

(22, 40): $22^2 + 40^2 - 100(40) + 1875 = -41$

As $-41 < 0$, the bird is inside the circle and is therefore in danger.

EXERCISE 11

Diagrams are not drawn to scale.

1. Find the equation of the circle with centre C and radius r, in the form $x^2 + y^2 + 2gx + 2fy + c = 0$ for:

   (a) $C(0, 0)$, $r = 4$

   (b) $C(0, 2)$, $r = 3$

   (c) $C(-1, 4)$, $r = 7$

   (d) $C(-5, -2)$, $r = \sqrt{2}$

   (e) $C(3, 0)$, $r = \frac{3}{4}$

   (f) $C(-5, -8)$, $r = 5$

   (g) $C(-a, a)$, $r = a$

   (h) $C(-a, -a)$, $r = 2a$

   (i) $C\left(\frac{3}{2}, \frac{1}{2}\right)$, $r = 2$

   (j) $C\left(-\frac{5}{4}, \frac{3}{4}\right)$, $r = \sqrt{3}$

2. The London Eye is the tallest Ferris wheel in Europe. It has a maximum height above the ground of 135 m and its diameter is 120 m.

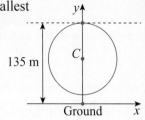

135 m

C

Ground   x

(a) Find the co-ordinates of its centre above the ground.

(b) Find the equation of the circle it traces out.

(c) If it takes 30 minutes for the wheel to do a complete circle, find its speed in km/h, correct to two decimal places.

3. Say which of the following equations describe the equation of a circle. Give a reason for saying why an equation does not describe a circle.

(a) $x - y = 0$

(b) $y = 3x$

(c) $x^2 + y^2 - 2x = 0$

(d) $x^2 + y^2 + 2xy = 3$

(e) $y^2 = 2x$

(f) $y = x^2$

(g) $3x + 2y - 7 = 0$

(h) $x^2 + y^2 + 5y - 7 = 0$

(i) $3x^2 + 4y^2 - 2x + 3y - 7 = 0$

(j) $x^2 + y^2 - 2x + 4y - 6 = 0$

4. A CD for PlayStation 4 has a diameter of 0·12 m. If the centre of the disc is (0, 0), find the equation of the rim of the circle of the disc. (Use the scale: 1 unit = 1 m)

5. The Physics teacher in a school wants to demonstrate the idea of centripetal force to her class. She whirls a bucket full of water from a point 1·5 m above the ground on the end of a string of radius 0·5 m. Find the equation of the circle described by the knot K. (Use the scale: 1 unit = 1 m)

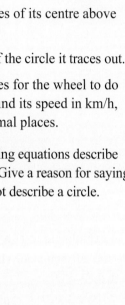

y

K

(0, 1·5) 0·5

(0, 0)   x

6. The centres C_1 and C_2, respectively, of the front and rear wheels of a car sitting in a driveway are separated by 2·6 m. If the diameter of each tyre is 0·6 m, find the equation of each circle. (Use the scale: 1 unit = 1 m)

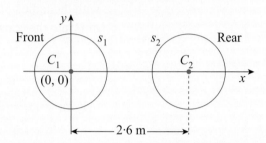

y

Front s_1 s_2 Rear

C_1 C_2

(0, 0)   x

2·6 m

7. A swimmer in a 25-metre pool swims the freestyle stroke down the length of the pool by moving his arms in circles around his shoulder joint. The depth of the pool is 1·2 m and the length of his arm is 0·6 m.

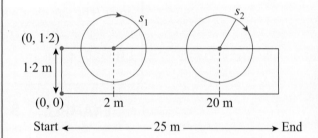

s_1 s_2

(0, 1·2)

1·2 m

(0, 0)   2 m   20 m

Start ← ———— 25 m ———— → End

Find the equation of the circle his arm is describing when his shoulder joint is:

(a) 2 m from the start of the pool (circle s_1),

(b) 20 m from the start of the pool (circle s_2). (Use the scale: 1 unit = 1 m)

8. Find the centre C and radius r of each circle given its equation:

(a) $x^2 + y^2 = 10$

(b) $4x^2 = 1 - 4y^2$

(c) $(x - 3)^2 + (y + 1)^2 = 2$

(d) $(x - 2)^2 + y^2 + 2y = 6$

(e) $x^2 + y^2 + 4x - 6y - 4 = 0$

(f) $(3x - 1)^2 + (3y - 4)^2 = 9$

(g) $x^2 + y^2 - 3x - 3y - 3 = 0$

(h) $8x^2 + 8y^2 - 20y - 12x = 0$

(i) $3x^2 + 3y^2 - 6x - 2 = 0$

(j) $3(x^2 + y^2) - 2x - 3y = 0$

9. A circle s_1 has equation $x^2 + y^2 = 1$. A circle s_2 has equation $(x - 5)^2 + (y - 8)^2 = 4$. Find the centre and radius of each circle and the distance between their centres. Draw these circles on graph paper and hence show they do not overlap.

10. Investigate if the point P is inside, outside or on the circle with equation s:

(a) $P(-1, 3), s : x^2 + y^2 = 7$

(b) $P(2, -4), s : 4x^2 + 4y^2 = 11$

(c) $P(7, -3), s : (x - 3)^2 + (y + 4)^2 = 22$

(d) $P(-1, 1), s : x^2 + y^2 - 3x - 2y - 1 = 0$

(e) $P(0, 0), s : x^2 + y^2 - 6x = 0$

(f) $P(4, 1), s : 2x^2 + 2y^2 + 5x + 4y - 1 = 0$

12.2 Line and circle: tangents and chords

When you draw a line and a circle in a plane, three possibilities exist regarding the point(s) of contact.

1. Touch

In the diagram, the line t touches the circle s at one and only one point P. This line t is called the **tangent** to the circle at P. The point P is called the **point of contact**.

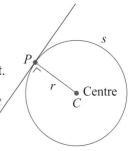

> **KEY TERM**
> ▲ A **tangent** to a circle is a straight line that touches the circle at one and only one point.

2. Cut

In the diagram, the line l cuts the circle s at two points B and D. The line segment $[BD]$ is called a **chord** of the circle s.

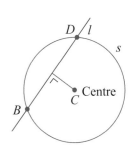

> **KEY TERM**
> ▲ A **chord** is a line segment that cuts a circle at exactly two points.

3. Miss

In the diagram, the line q completely misses the circle s. This is of no interest to us here. There are no points of intersection of s and q.

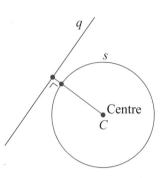

Problem-solving technique for a line and a circle

Problems involving a line and a circle are basically straight line questions all over again. Once you know the centre and radius of the circle (by being given them directly) or its equation, the circle plays no further part in the question.

Remember, there are two versions of the equation of a line:

1. $(y - y_1) = m(x - x_2)$ [Point and slope version.]

You should use this version when you are given both the point (x_1, y_1) and the slope m of the line, or when given just a point (x_1, y_1) on the line.

2. $y = mx + c$ [Intercept and slope version.]

You should use this version when you are given just the slope m of the line. (You are not given a point on the line.)

Both versions can then be put into the standard form $ax + by + c = 0$.

Tangents

What you know about tangents from geometry:

1. A tangent t is a line that touches a circle s at one and only one point P called the **point of contact**.

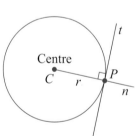

2. The line n (n for normal) drawn from the centre C of the circle to the point of contact P is **always at right angles** to the tangent t.
(Drawing the normal line n is always a clever thing to do in all tangent questions.)

$$\therefore \text{ Slope of } t = -\frac{1}{\text{Slope of } n}$$

3. P is on both t and n.

4. P is the point of intersection of t and n.

5. If you solve the equation of the circle s with the equation of the tangent t, you get only one solution, the point P.

6. The perpendicular distance from the centre C to the tangent t is equal to the radius r.

Tangent 1: The point of contact is given

> **TIP**
> A question that says 'tangent at' means the point of contact is given.

EXAMPLE 9

Find the equation of the tangent to the circle $s : x^2 + y^2 - 8x + 10y + 1 = 0$ at (2, 1).

Solution

First find the centre C and radius of s:
$x^2 + y^2 - 8x + 10y + 1 = 0$.

$g = -4, f = 5, c = 1$

Radius: $r = \sqrt{16 + 25 - 1} = \sqrt{40}$

Centre: $C(4, -5)$

Draw a clear picture putting in all the information:

Slope of normal $n = \dfrac{-5 - 1}{4 - 2} = \dfrac{-6}{2} = -3$

Slope of tangent $t = m = \dfrac{1}{3}$

Equation of t: $m = \dfrac{1}{3}$, $(x_1, y_1) = (2, 1)$

$(y - 1) = \dfrac{1}{3}(x - 2)$

$3y - 3 = x - 2$

$t : x - 3y + 1 = 0$

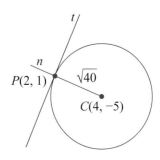

Tangent 2: The slope of the tangent is given directly or indirectly

> **TIP**
> To solve tangent problems where only the slope and either $ax + by + c = 0$ or $y = mx + c$ forms of the equation of a straight line are given, use the perpendicular distance formula.

EXAMPLE 10

Find the equations of the tangents to the circle $s : x^2 + y^2 - 8x + 6y + 20 = 0$, which has a slope of 2.

Solution

$s : x^2 + y^2 - 8x + 6y + 20 = 0$

$g = -4, f = 3, c = 20$

Radius: $r = \sqrt{16 + 9 - 20} = \sqrt{5}$

Centre: $C(4, -3)$

A line of slope 2 has equation: $2x - y + c = 0$

or

You can find the equation of the tangent using $y = mx + c$:

$\qquad y = 2x + c$

$2x - y + c = 0$

The perpendicular distance from C to t is equal to the radius r:

$\dfrac{\left| 2(4) - (-3) + c \right|}{\sqrt{4 + 1}} = \sqrt{5}$

$\left| 11 + c \right| = 5$

$11 + c = \pm 5$

$c = -6, -16$

$t_1 : 2x - y - 6 = 0$ and $t_2 : 2x - y - 16 = 0$

The maths automatically gives both tangents.

EXAMPLE 11

Find the equations of the tangents to the circle $s: x^2 + y^2 - 4x + 6y + 3 = 0$
which are parallel to the line $l: x + 3y - 5 = 0$.

Solution

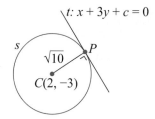

$s: x^2 + y^2 - 4x + 6y + 3 = 0$.

$g = -2, f = 3, c = 3$

Radius $r = \sqrt{4 + 9 - 3} = \sqrt{10}$

Centre $C(2, -3)$

A line parallel to $l: x + 3y - 5 = 0$ has equation $t: x + 3y + c = 0$.

The perpendicular distance from C to $t = \sqrt{10}$:

$$\frac{|2 - 9 + c|}{\sqrt{1 + 9}} = \sqrt{10}$$

$$|c - 7| = 10$$

$$c - 7 = \pm 10$$

$$c = -3, 17$$

$t_1: x + 3y - 3 = 0$ and $t_2: x + 3y + 17 = 0$

EXAMPLE 12

A hammer thrower whirls the hammer in a circle with equation $s: x^2 + y^2 - 4x + 6y + 3 = 0$.
When the hammer is released, its path is tangential to s. It hits a wall l, which
has equation $3x - y + 7 = 0$, at right angles.

(a) Find the co-ordinates of the centre of the circle s and its radius r.

(b) Find the slope of the wall and hence the slope of the path.

(c) Using $y = mx + c$, show that the equation of the path is $x + 3y - 3c = 0$.

(d) Using the perpendicular distance from a point to a line formula, find $c > 0$.

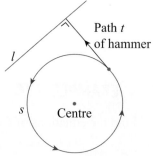

Solution

(a) $x^2 + y^2 - 4x + 6y + 3 = 0$

$\quad g = -2, f = 3, c = 3$

$\quad$ Radius: $r = \sqrt{4 + 9 - 3} = \sqrt{10}$

$\quad$ Centre: $(2, -3)$

(b) Slope of wall $l = 3$

$\quad$ Slope of path $= m = -\frac{1}{3}$

(c) Equation of path t:

$\quad y = mx + c$

$\quad y = -\frac{1}{3}x + c$

$\quad t: x + 3y - 3c = 0$

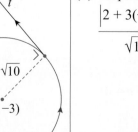

(d) Perpendicular distance from $(2, -3)$ to t is $\sqrt{10}$:

$$\frac{|2 + 3(-3) - 3c|}{\sqrt{1 + 9}} = \sqrt{10}$$

$$|-7 - 3c| = 10$$

$$-7 - 3c = \pm 10$$

$3c = -17$	$3c = 3$
$c = -\frac{17}{3}$	$c = 1$

Answer: $c = 1$ as $c > 0$

EXAMPLE 13

s is the circle with equation $s: x^2 + y^2 - 6x - 2y + 1 = 0$.

(a) Show that $5x + 12y + 12 = 0$ is a tangent to s.

(b) If $t: 5x + 12y = 0$ is a tangent to the circle $s: x^2 + y^2 - 6x - 4y + c = 0$, find c.

Solution

$s: x^2 + y^2 - 6x - 2y + 1 = 0$

$g = -3, f = -1, c = 1$

$r = \sqrt{9 + 1 - 1} = 3$

Centre $(3, 1)$

(a) If $5x + 12y + 12 = 0$ is a tangent to s, then the perpendicular distance from $(3, 1)$ to this line should be 3.

$$\text{Perpendicular distance} = \frac{|15 + 12 + 12|}{\sqrt{25 + 144}} = 3$$

The line is a tangent.

(b) $s: x^2 + y^2 - 6x - 4y + c = 0$

$g = -3, f = -2$

Radius: $r = \sqrt{9 + 4 - c}$

$\qquad = \sqrt{13 - c}$

Centre: $(3, 2)$

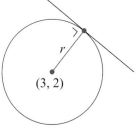

$r = $ perpendicular distance from the centre to t

$$r = \frac{|15 + 24|}{\sqrt{25 + 144}} = 3$$

$\therefore r = 3 = \sqrt{13 - c}$

$\qquad 9 = 13 - c$

$\qquad c = 4$

Tangent 3: The tangent is drawn from a point outside a circle to the circle

> **TIP**
>
> Call the slope of the tangent m and use $(y - y_1) = m(x - x_1)$ to write the equation of the tangent in the form $ax + by + c = 0$ and then use the
>
> perpendicular distance formula $d = \dfrac{|ax_1 + by_1 + c|}{\sqrt{a^2 + b^2}}$ to find m.

EXAMPLE 14

Two tangents are drawn from the point $Q(-4, 0)$ outside the circle $s: x^2 + y^2 - 4x - 8y - 30 = 0$ to the circle.

(a) Find the co-ordinates of the centre C of the circle and its radius r.

(b) If the slope of either tangent is m, use $(y - y_1) = m(x - x_1)$ to show that the equation of a tangent from $(-4, 0)$ to the circle s is $mx - y + 4m = 0$.

(c) Using the perpendicular distance formula, show that $m = -\dfrac{17}{7}$, or -1.

(d) Hence, find the equations of both tangents.

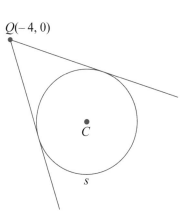

Solution

(a) $s : x^2 + y^2 - 4x - 8y - 30 = 0$

$g = -2, f = -4, c = -30$

Radius: $r = \sqrt{4 + 16 + 30} = \sqrt{50}$

Centre: $C(2, 4)$

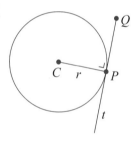

(b) 'From' means the point $(-4, 0)$ is outside the circle. If m is the slope of the tangent t, its equation is:

$y - 0 = m(x + 4)$

$mx - y + 4m = 0 \ldots$ **(1)**

(c) The perpendicular distance from C to t is equal to the radius r:

$$\dfrac{\left|2m - 4 + 4m\right|}{\sqrt{m^2 + 1}} = \sqrt{50}$$

$\left|6m - 4\right| = \sqrt{50}\,\sqrt{m^2 + 1}$ [Square both sides.]

$36m^2 - 48m + 16 = 50(m^2 + 1)$

$36m^2 - 48m + 16 = 50m^2 + 50$

$14m^2 + 48m + 34 = 0$

$7m^2 + 24m + 17 = 0$

$(7m + 17)(m + 1) = 0$

$m = -\dfrac{17}{7}, -1$

(d) Substitute these values of m into equation **(1)**:

$t_1 : -\dfrac{17}{7}x - y - \dfrac{68}{7} = 0$

$17x + 7y + 68 = 0$

$t_2 : -x - y - 4 = 0$

$x + y + 4 = 0$

Tangent 4: Length of the tangent

The length of a tangent from a point Q **outside** a circle to the circle is just the distance from Q to the point of contact P of the tangent t to the circle from Q.

Length of the tangent $= \left|QP\right|$

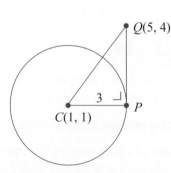

EXAMPLE 15

Find the length of the tangent from the point $(5, 4)$ to the circle $s : x^2 + y^2 - 2x - 2y - 7 = 0$.

Solution

$s : x^2 + y^2 - 2x - 2y - 7 = 0$

$g = -1, f = -1, c = -7$

Radius: $r = \sqrt{1 + 1 + 7} = 3$

Centre: $C(1, 1)$

$\left|CQ\right| = \sqrt{16 + 9} = 5$

$\left|CP\right| = r = 3$

$\left|QP\right| = \sqrt{25 - 9} = 4$ [Using Pythagoras' theorem.]

TIP

For the circle $s : x^2 + y^2 + 2gx + 2fy + c = 0$, the length of the tangent from (x_1, y_1) is given by $\sqrt{x_1^2 + y_1^2 + 2gx_1 + 2fy_1 + c}$. Try this formula on the previous example.

Chords

What you know about chords from geometry:

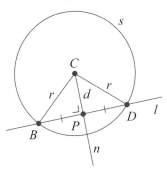

> **TIP**
> ↑ Always draw the perpendicular line *n* from the centre of a circle to a chord.

1. A chord $[BD]$ is a line segment that cuts a circle *s* at two points *B* and *D*.
2. The perpendicular line *n* drawn from the centre *C* to the chord $[BD]$ bisects it: $|BP| = |PD|$.
3. *P* is the midpoint of $[BD]$.
4. $\triangle CBP$ and $\triangle CPD$ are congruent triangles that are both right-angled.
5. You can apply Pythagoras' theorem to $\triangle CBP$ and $\triangle CPD$ to find $d = |CP|$.
6. The perpendicular distance from *C* to $[BD]$ is equal to *d*.
7. If you solve the equation of the circle *s* with the equation of the chord *l*, you get exactly two solutions (the points *B* and *D*).

Chord 1: The midpoint of the chord is given

EXAMPLE 16

Find the equation of the chord of the circle
$s : x^2 + y^2 - 4x + 2y - 3 = 0$ whose midpoint is
$(3, 1)$. Find also the length of this chord.

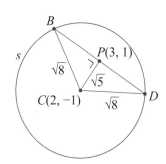

Solution

$s : x^2 + y^2 - 4x + 2y - 3 = 0$

$g = -2, f = 1, c = -3$

Radius: $r = \sqrt{4 + 1 + 3} = \sqrt{8}$

Centre: $C(2, -1)$

$P(3, 1)$ is the midpoint of the chord $[BD]$.

Therefore, $CP \perp BD$

Slope of $CP = \dfrac{-1 - 1}{2 - 3} = 2$

Slope of $BD = -\dfrac{1}{2}$

Equation of $[BD]$: $P(3, 1) = (x_1, y_1)$, $m = -\dfrac{1}{2}$

$(y - 1) = -\dfrac{1}{2}(x - 3)$

$2(y - 1) = -(x - 3)$

$2y - 2 = -x + 3$

$x + 2y - 5 = 0$

$|CP| = \sqrt{(2 - 3)^2 + (-1 - 1)^2} = \sqrt{1 + 4} = \sqrt{5}$

$|BP| = \sqrt{8 - 5} = \sqrt{3}$ [Using Pythagoras' theorem.]

Length of chord $|BD| = 2\sqrt{3}$

Chord 2: The slope of the chord is given directly or indirectly

> **TIP**
>
> Write down the equation of the chord in the form $ax + by + c = 0$ from its slope $m = -\dfrac{a}{b}$ and then use the perpendicular distance formula
>
> $$d = \frac{|ax_1 + by_1 + c|}{\sqrt{a^2 + b^2}}$$ to find c.

EXAMPLE 17

Part of a cross-country course involves running along a path $l_1 : x + 3y + 15 = 0$ until the point $D(-3, -4)$ is reached and then turning onto a road l_2 at right angles to l_1. l_2 crosses a circular lake s with equation $x^2 + y^2 - 4x - 2y - 15 = 0$ at B and E. The length of the bridge $[BE]$ is $2\sqrt{10}$.

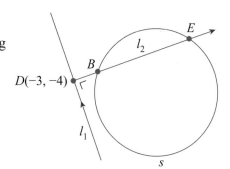

Find:

(a) the centre and radius of the circle s,

(b) the perpendicular distance from the centre of s to l_2,

(c) the slope of l_2,

(d) the equation of l_2.

Solution

(a) $s : x^2 + y^2 - 4x - 2y - 15 = 0$

$g = -2, f = -1, c = -15$

Radius: $r = \sqrt{4 + 1 + 15} = \sqrt{20}$

Centre: $C(2, 1)$

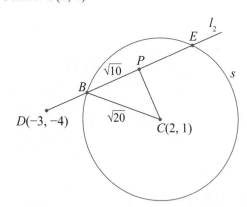

(b) $|CP| = \sqrt{20 - 10} = \sqrt{10}$

(c) Slope of $l_1 = -\dfrac{1}{3}$

Slope of $l_2 = 3$

Equation of $l_2 : 3x - y + c = 0$

(d) Perpendicular distance from C to $l_2 = \sqrt{10}$

$$\frac{|6 - 1 + c|}{\sqrt{10}} = \sqrt{10}$$

$|5 + c| = 10$

$5 + c = \pm 10$

$c = 5, -15$

Equation of $l_2 : 3x - y + 5 = 0$ or $3x - y - 15 = 0$

Since $(-3, -4)$ satisfies $3x - y + 5 = 0$ only, the equation of l_2 is $3x - y + 5 = 0$.

Chord 3: The chord is drawn from a point outside a circle to the circle

> **TIP**
>
> Call the slope of the chord m. Use $(y - y_1) = m(x - x_1)$ to write the equation of the chord in the form $ax + by + c = 0$ and then use the perpendicular distance
>
> formula $d = \dfrac{|ax_1 + by_1 + c|}{\sqrt{a^2 + b^2}}$ to find m.

EXAMPLE **18**

(a) Find the centre and radius of the circle
$s: x^2 + y^2 - 6x + 2y - 15 = 0$.

(b) A line l drawn from $Q(-5, -2)$ cuts off a chord of length 6 units on s. Find the perpendicular distance from the centre of the circle s to l.

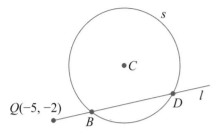

(c) Hence, find the equations of such chords.

Solution

(a) $s: x^2 + y^2 - 6x + 2y - 15 = 0$

$g = -3, f = 1, c = -15$

Radius: $r = \sqrt{9 + 1 + 15} = 5$

Centre: $C(3, -1)$

(b)

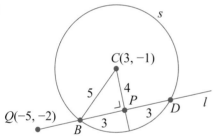

$|CP| = \sqrt{25 - 9} = 4$

(c) Equation of l of slope m: $(y + 2) = m(x + 5)$
$l: mx - y + (5m - 2) = 0 \ldots$ **(1)**

The perpendicular distance from C to $l = 4$

$$\frac{|3m + 1 + 5m - 2|}{\sqrt{m^2 + 1}} = 4$$

$|8m - 1| = 4\sqrt{m^2 + 1}$ [Square both sides.]

$64m^2 - 16m + 1 = 16(m^2 + 1)$

$48m^2 - 16m - 15 = 0$

$(12m + 5)(4m - 3) = 0$

$m = -\dfrac{5}{12}, \dfrac{3}{4}$

Substituting these values of m into **(1)** to give the equations of the chords:

$l_1: -\dfrac{5}{12}x - y - \dfrac{49}{12} = 0$

$\qquad 5x + 12y + 49 = 0$

$l_2: \dfrac{3}{4}x - y + \dfrac{7}{4} = 0$

$\qquad 3x - 4y + 7 = 0$

The point(s) of intersection of a line and a circle

To find the point(s) of intersection of a line and a circle, solve the equation of the line (tangent or chord) with the equation of the circle.

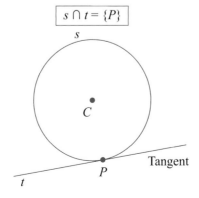

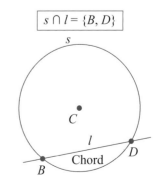

EXAMPLE 19

Find the points of intersection of the line
$l : x + y - 6 = 0$ and the circle
$s : x^2 + y^2 - 4x + 2y - 20 = 0$.

Solution

$l : x + y - 6 = 0 \Rightarrow y = (6 - x) \dots \textbf{(1)}$

$s : x^2 + y^2 - 4x + 2y - 20 = 0 \dots \textbf{(2)}$

Substitute equation **(1)** into **(2)**:

$x^2 + (6 - x)^2 - 4x + 2(6 - x) - 20 = 0$

$x^2 + 36 - 12x + x^2 - 4x + 12 - 2x - 20 = 0$

$2x^2 - 18x + 28 = 0$

$x^2 - 9x + 14 = 0$

$(x - 2)(x - 7) = 0$

$x = 2, 7$

Substituting these values of x into equation **(1)**:
$y = 4, -1$

Therefore, the points of intersection are $(2, 4)$ and $(7, -1)$.

EXAMPLE 20

Find the point of contact of the tangent
$t : 2x + 2y - 3 = 0$ and the circle
$s : 4x^2 + 4y^2 + 8x + 4y - 13 = 0$.

Solution

$t : 2x + 2y - 3 = 0$

$2y = 3 - 2x$

$y = \dfrac{(3 - 2x)}{2} \dots \textbf{(1)}$

$s : 4x^2 + 4y^2 + 8x + 4y - 13 = 0 \dots \textbf{(2)}$

Substituting y from **(1)** into **(2)**:

$4x^2 + \dfrac{4(3 - 2x)^2}{4} + 8x + \dfrac{4(3 - 2x)}{2} - 13 = 0$

$4x^2 + (3 - 2x)^2 + 8x + 2(3 - 2x) - 13 = 0$

$4x^2 + 9 - 12x + 4x^2 + 8x + 6 - 4x - 13 = 0$

$8x^2 - 8x + 2 = 0$

$4x^2 - 4x + 1 = 0$

$(2x - 1)(2x - 1) = 0$

$x = \dfrac{1}{2}$

Substituting this value of x into equation **(1)**:

$y = \dfrac{3 - 1}{2} = 1$

Therefore, the point of contact is $\left(\dfrac{1}{2}, 1 \right)$.

EXAMPLE 21

Find the co-ordinates of the points where the circle $s : x^2 + y^2 - 4x - 2y - 15 = 0$ cuts the y-axis. Find the length of the chord the circle s cuts off on the y-axis.

Solution

$s : x^2 + y^2 - 4x - 2y - 15 = 0 \dots \textbf{(1)}$

y-axis: $x = 0 \dots \textbf{(2)}$

Solving: $y^2 - 2y - 15 = 0$

$(y + 3)(y - 5) = 0$

$y = -3, 5$

The points are $(0, -3)$ and $(0, 5)$.

Therefore, the length of the chord is 8 units.

EXERCISE 12

Diagrams are not drawn to scale.

1. Find the equation of the tangent to the circle s at the point P in each case:

   (a) $s : x^2 + y^2 + 6x - 2y = 0$ at $P(0, 0)$

   (b) $s : x^2 + y^2 - 8x - 2y = 0$ at $P(3, 5)$

   (c) $s : x^2 + y^2 + 4x + 2y - 12 = 0$ at $P(-1, 3)$

   (d) $s : (x - 2)^2 + (y - 3)^2 = 1$ at $P(2, 2)$

   (e) $s : 2x^2 + 2y^2 + 5x + 8y - 1 = 0$ at $P(1, -1)$

2. **(a)** Find the equations of the tangents to the circle $s : x^2 + y^2 - 4x - 2y - 11 = 0$ with slope $\frac{4}{3}$.

   (b) Find the equations of the tangents to the circle $s : x^2 + y^2 - 6x - 4y - 3 = 0$ that make an angle of $\tan^{-1} \frac{5}{12}$ with the +x-axis.

   (c) Find the equations of the tangents to the circle $s : x^2 + y^2 - 2x - 4y + 1 = 0$ that are parallel to the line $l : 3x - 4y + 1 = 0$.

   (d) Find the equations of the tangents to the circle $s : x^2 + y^2 - 8x + 5y + 4 = 0$ that are perpendicular to the line $l : 3x + 8y - 11 = 0$.

   (e) Find the equations of the tangents to the circle $s : x^2 + y^2 - 2x + 4y + 3 = 0$ that make equal intercepts on the +x and +y axis.

3. Find the equations of the tangents from the point Q to the circle s in each case:

   (a) $Q(0, 0), s : x^2 + y^2 - 2x - 4y + 1 = 0$

   (b) $Q(0, -2), s : x^2 + y^2 - 6x + 2y + 5 = 0$

   (c) $Q(5, -1), s : x^2 + y^2 = 13$

   (d) $Q(7, -1), s : x^2 + y^2 - 8x + 4y + 12 = 0$

4. **(a)** Find the length of the tangent from the point Q to the circle s in each case:

   (i) $Q(4, 2), s : x^2 + y^2 = 9$

   (ii) $Q(-4, -5), s : (x + 1)^2 + (y + 1)^2 = 1$

   (iii) $Q(-6, 7), s : x^2 + y^2 - 2y - 6x - 7 = 0$

   (b) (i) If the length of the tangent from $Q(7, 5)$ to $s : x^2 + y^2 - 4x - 6y + c = 0$ is 1, find c.

   (ii) If the length of the tangent from $(b, 8)$ to $s : x^2 + y^2 - 8x - 4y - 5 = 0$ is $\sqrt{15}$, find b.

(c) Find c if the line $t : 4x + 3y + c = 0$ is a tangent to the circle $s : x^2 + y^2 - 2x - 2y - 7 = 0$.

(d) Prove that the line $t : 2x + 2y - 3 = 0$ touches the circle $s : 4x^2 + 4y^2 + 8x + 4y - 13 = 0$.

(e) Test whether or not the line $t : x + y - 2 = 0$ is a tangent to the circle $s : 2x^2 + 2y^2 - 3x + 5y - 2 = 0$.

5. **(a)** Find the equation of the chord of the circle $s : x^2 + y^2 = 81$ whose midpoint is $(2, -3)$. Find the length of the chord.

   (b) Find the equation of the chord of the circle $s : x^2 + y^2 + 2x - 8y - 15 = 0$ whose midpoint is $(2, 6)$. Find the length of the chord.

   (c) Find the equations of the chords of the circle $s : x^2 + y^2 - 4x + 6y - 12 = 0$ of slope -1 and length $2\sqrt{23}$.

   (d) Through $Q(3, 4)$ on $s : 4x^2 + 4y^2 - 24x - 7y = 0$, two chords of length 5 are drawn.

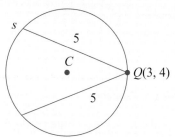

   (i) Find the centre C and radius r of the circle.

   (ii) Find the perpendicular distance from C to either chord.

   (iii) If m is the slope of either chord, show that the equation of this chord is $mx - y + (4 - 3m) = 0$.

   (iv) Find m.

6. Find the point(s) of intersection of the line l and the circle s in each case:

   (a) $l : y = 0, s : x^2 + y^2 - 4x + 2y + 4 = 0$

   (b) $l : x - 5y + 4 = 0,$ $s : x^2 + y^2 - 6x - 8y + 12 = 0$

   (c) $l : 3x - 2y - 5 = 0, s : x^2 + y^2 - 2x = 7$

7. Find where the circle s cuts each axis and find the lengths of the chords the circle s cuts off on each axis:

(a) $s: x^2 + y^2 - 6x - 4y - 12 = 0$

(b) $s: x^2 + y^2 - 8x - 10y + 12 = 0$

8. An asteroid originating from the point $P(7, 1)$ in space approaches a planet and is captured by the gravitational field of the planet so that it moves in a circular orbit s with equation $s: x^2 + y^2 + 4x + 2y - 12 = 0$.

(a) Find the equations of the two possible straight-line paths from P to the points of tangency to the orbit.

(b) Find the acute angle θ between these paths, correct to the nearest degree.

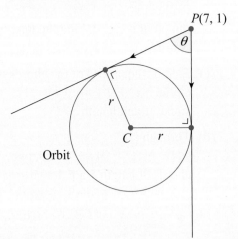

(c) Find the distance travelled from P to each point of tangency.

9. A ring s slides down a chute made from two parallel metal bars l_1 and l_2, where each bar makes equal intercepts on the axes.

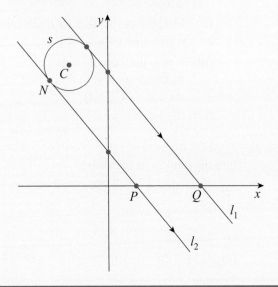

At one instant, the centre C of the ring is at $C(-3, 8)$. The radius of the ring is $\dfrac{3\sqrt{2}}{2}$.

Find:

(a) the equations of l_1 and l_2,

(b) the points where l_1 and l_2 cross the x-axis,

(c) the equation of the ring at the instant shown,

(d) the point N where the ring touches l_2, when its centre is at C.

10. A circle $s: x^2 + y^2 + 2gx + 2fy + c = 0$ touches both axes in the first quadrant.

(a) Show that:

(i) $c = g^2 = f^2$

(ii) its centre C has co-ordinates $C(-g, -g)$.

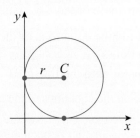

(b) t_1 and t_2 are tangents to circle $s: x^2 + y^2 + 2gx + 2fy + c = 0$, which touches both axes in the first quadrant.

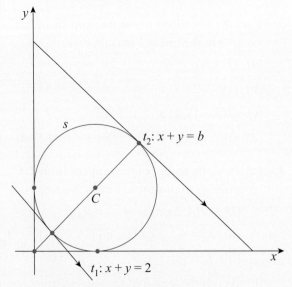

(i) Show that $b = -4g - 2$.

(ii) By finding the perpendicular distance, or otherwise, from C to t_2, show that $g = -2 \pm \sqrt{2}$.

(iii) Show that $b = 6 \pm 4\sqrt{2}$.

Circle 2

CHAPTER 13

Learning Outcomes

- To find the equation of a circle given certain information.
- To handle different situations involving intersecting circles.

13.1 Finding the equation of a circle given certain information

One of the most challenging types of problems on the circle is to find its equation given certain information. Sometimes the information can be difficult to understand as well as tricky to handle.

What you know:

The equation of a circle s with centre $(-g, -f)$ and radius r is given by:

$x^2 + y^2 + 2gx + 2fy + c = 0$, where $r = \sqrt{g^2 + f^2 - c}$

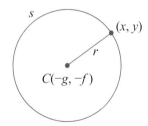

The values of g, f and c distinguish one circle from another.

> TIP
> To find the equation of a circle, you need to find the values of g, f and c for that circle.

Notes

1. Do not confuse (x, y), which is a point **on** the circle with $(-g, -f)$, which is the centre of the circle.

2. If a point (x, y) is on a circle, it satisfies the equation of the circle.

3. To find the equation of a circle, first find the g, f and c values and then substitute them into $x^2 + y^2 + 2gx + 2fy + c = 0$.

Type 1: Centre and radius

EXAMPLE 1

Find the equation of the circle with centre $C(-2, 3)$ and radius 4.

Solution

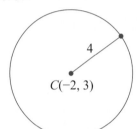

$C(-2, 3) = (-g, -f)$

$g = 2, f = -3$

$r = 4 = \sqrt{4 + 9 - c}$

$16 = 13 - c$

$c = -3$

Equation of the circle:

$x^2 + y^2 + 4x - 6y - 3 = 0$

or

$C(h, k) = C(-2, 3), r = 4$

$(x - h)^2 + (y - k)^2 = r^2$

$(x + 2)^2 + (y - 3)^2 = 16$

Type 2: Two points on the ends of a diameter

EXAMPLE 2

Find the equation of the circle with diameter $[PQ]$, if $P(-1, 2)$ and $Q(3, -4)$.

Solution

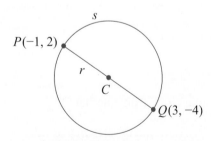

The centre C is the midpoint of

$[PQ] = \left(\dfrac{-1 + 3}{2}, \dfrac{2 + (-4)}{2}\right) = (1, -1)$

$C(1, -1) = (-g, -f)$

$g = -1, f = 1$

$r = |CP| = \sqrt{(2)^2 + (-3)^2} = \sqrt{13}$

$r = \sqrt{13} = \sqrt{1 + 1 - c}$

$13 = 2 - c$

$c = -11$

The equation of s: $x^2 + y^2 - 2x + 2y - 11 = 0$

or

$C(h, k) = C(1, -1), r = \sqrt{13}$

$(x - h)^2 + (y - k)^2 = r^2$

$(x - 1)^2 + (y + 1)^2 = 13$

Type 3: Three points on the circle

EXAMPLE 3

Emer the postwoman begins her round at the post office C. Her delivery route is a circle with C as centre. She makes deliveries at three points $P(6, 2)$, $Q(5, 3)$ and $R(3, -1)$, respectively, and returns to C.

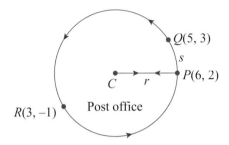

Find:

(a) the equation of the circle,

(b) the radius of the circle,

(c) the total length of her journey, correct to one decimal place, if 1 unit = 1 km.

Solution

(a) Substitute each point P, Q and R in turn into the general equation of a circle and solve the three equations simultaneously to get g, f and c.

$$x^2 + y^2 + 2gx + 2fy + c = 0$$

$P(6, 2)$: $36 + 4 + 12g + 4f + c = 0$

$$12g + 4f + c = -40 \dots \textbf{(1)}$$

$Q(5, 3)$: $25 + 9 + 10g + 6f + c = 0$

$$10g + 6f + c = -34 \dots \textbf{(2)}$$

$R(3, -1)$: $9 + 1 + 6g - 2f + c = 0$

$$6g - 2f + c = -10 \dots \textbf{(3)}$$

Solving these equations:

$\textbf{(1)} - \textbf{(2)}$: $2g - 2f = -6 \Rightarrow g - f = -3 \dots \textbf{(4)}$

$\textbf{(2)} - \textbf{(3)}$: $4g + 8f = -24 \Rightarrow g + 2f = -6 \dots \textbf{(5)}$

$\textbf{(5)} - \textbf{(4)}$: $3f = -3 \Rightarrow f = -1$

Substituting this value of f back into equation $\textbf{(4)}$: $g + 1 = -3$

$$g = -4$$

Substituting these values of g and f back into equation $\textbf{(1)}$: $-48 - 4 + c = -40$

$$c = 12$$

The equation of the circle is

$$x^2 + y^2 - 8x - 2y + 12 = 0.$$

(b) Radius: $r = \sqrt{16 + 1 - 12} = \sqrt{5}$

(c) Total distance $= 2\pi r + 2r = 2r(\pi + 1)$

$$= 2\sqrt{5}(\pi + 1) = 18{\cdot}5 \text{ km}$$

TIP

The circle s: $x^2 + y^2 + 2gx + 2fy + c = 0$ passes through $(0, 0) \Rightarrow c = 0$

Alternative method

The perpendicular bisectors of the chords pass through the centre C of the circle. Find the equations of SC and TC and then solve them simultaneously to find C, the co-ordinates of the centre. The radius of the circle is the distance from C to any of the points P, Q and R. You can now find the equation of the circle. Try it for the question in Example 3.

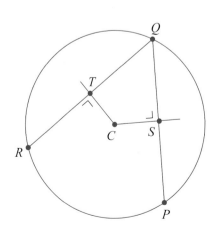

Type 4: The centre is on a line

1. The centre $C(-g, -f)$ is on the x-axis: $f = 0$

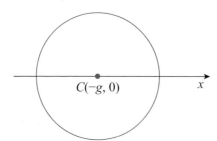

$C(-g, 0)$

2. The centre $C(-g, -f)$ is on the y-axis: $g = 0$

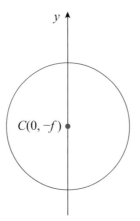

$C(0, -f)$

3. The centre $C(-g, -f)$ is on the line $ax + by + c = 0$:

$$(-g, -f) \in ax + by + c = 0$$
$$-ag - bf + c = 0$$

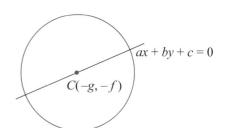

$ax + by + c = 0$

$C(-g, -f)$

EXAMPLE 4

Find the equations of the circles of radius 2 with centre on the y-axis that pass through the point $(0, 1)$.

Solution

Centre is on y-axis: $g = 0$

$$r = 2 = \sqrt{0 + f^2 - c}$$
$$4 = f^2 - c$$
$$c = f^2 - 4$$

$(0, 1)$ is on the circle: $(0, 1)$ satisfies:

$$x^2 + y^2 + 2fy + (f^2 - 4) = 0$$
$$0 + 1 + 2f + f^2 - 4 = 0$$
$$f^2 + 2f - 3 = 0$$
$$(f - 1)(f + 3) = 0$$
$$f = 1, -3$$

Substituting into $c = f^2 - 4$:

$f = 1$: $c = -3$
$f = -3$: $c = 5$

The equations of the circles are:

$$x^2 + y^2 + 2y - 3 = 0 \text{ and } x^2 + y^2 - 6y + 5 = 0$$

EXAMPLE 5

Find the equations of the circles of radius 5 with centre on the line $x - y = 0$ that pass through $(2, 1)$.

Solution

Centre $(-g, -f)$ is on line $x - y = 0$: $-g + f = 0$.

$f = g$

$r = 5 = \sqrt{g^2 + g^2 - c}$

$25 = 2g^2 - c$

$c = 2g^2 - 25$

$(2, 1)$ satisfies the circle equation:

$x^2 + y^2 + 2gx + 2gy + 2g^2 - 25 = 0$

$4 + 1 + 4g + 2g + 2g^2 - 25 = 0$

$2g^2 + 6g - 20 = 0$

$g^2 + 3g - 10 = 0$

$(g - 2)(g + 5) = 0$

$g = 2, -5$

Substituting into $c = 2g^2 - 25$:

$g = 2$: $f = 2$, $c = -17$

$g = -5$: $f = -5$, $c = 25$

The equations of the circles are:

$x^2 + y^2 + 4x + 4y - 17 = 0$ and

$x^2 + y^2 - 10x - 10y + 25 = 0$

EXAMPLE 6

Find the equation of the circle with centre on the line l: $2x + y + 4 = 0$ that passes through the points $(2, -6)$ and $(4, -2)$.

Solution

Call the circle s: $x^2 + y^2 + 2gx + 2fy + c = 0$.

$(2, -6)$ is on s: $4 + 36 + 4g - 12f + c = 0$

$4g - 12f + c = -40$ ... **(1)**

$(4, -2)$ is on s: $16 + 4 + 8g - 4f + c = 0$

$8g - 4f + c = -20$ ... **(2)**

$C(-g, -f)$ is on l: $-2g - f + 4 = 0 \Rightarrow 2g + f = 4$ ... **(3)**

(2) − **(1)**: $4g + 8f = 20 \Rightarrow 2g + 4f = 10$ ... **(4)**

(4) − **(3)**: $3f = 6 \Rightarrow f = 2$

$\therefore g = 1$, $c = -20$

s: $x^2 + y^2 + 2x + 4y - 20 = 0$

Alternative method

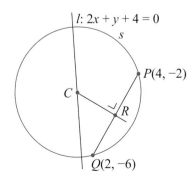

The perpendicular bisector of the chord PQ passes through the centre C. Solve the equations of this bisector and l simultaneously to find C, the co-ordinates of the centre.

Equation of bisector of $[PQ]$:

$R(3, -4)$ is the midpoint of chord $[PQ]$.

Slope of PQ: $m = \dfrac{-2 - (-6)}{4 - 2} = 2$

Slope of bisector $= -\dfrac{1}{2}$

Equation of bisector: $(y - (-4)) = -\dfrac{1}{2}(x - 3)$

$x + 2y + 5 = 0$

Solving the equation of the perpendicular bisector and l simultaneously gives $x = -1$ and $y = -2$.

Therefore, centre $C(-1, -2)$.

The radius is the distance from the centre to any point on the circle.

$r = |CP| = \sqrt{(4 - (-1))^2 + (-2 - (-2))^2} = 5$

Equation of the circle:

$(x - (-1))^2 + (y - (-2))^2 = (5)^2$

$(x + 1)^2 + (y + 2)^2 = 25$

Type 5: The circle touches a line

Two situations arise when a circle touches a line:

1. The circle touches the line $ax + by + c = 0$.

2. The circle touches one or both axes.

1. The circle touches the line $t: ax + by + c = 0$

As t is a tangent to the circle s, this means:

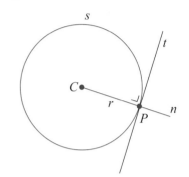

(a) The line n joining the centre C to the point of contact P of the tangent is at right angles to the tangent.

(b) C is on the line n.

(c) P is on t and on n and s.

(d) $|CP| = r$

(e) The perpendicular distance from C to t is equal to r.

EXAMPLE 7

Find the equations of the circles of radius 5, if $t: 4x - 3y - 15 = 0$ is a tangent at the point $(6, 3)$.

Solution

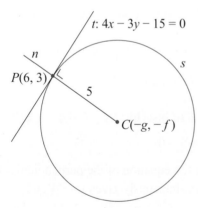

Slope of $t = \dfrac{4}{3}$

Slope of $CP = \dfrac{(3+f)}{(6+g)} = -\dfrac{3}{4}$

$(3 + f) = -\dfrac{3}{4}(6 + g) \ldots$ **(1)**

$|CP| = 5$

$\sqrt{(6+g)^2 + (3+f)^2} = 5$

$(6 + g)^2 + (3 + f)^2 = 25 \ldots$ **(2)**

Substituting $(3 + f)$ from equation **(1)** into **(2)**:

$(6 + g)^2 + \dfrac{9}{16}(6 + g)^2 = 25$

$16(6 + g)^2 + 9(6 + g)^2 = 16 \times 25$

$25(6 + g)^2 = 16 \times 25$

$(6 + g)^2 = 16$

$6 + g = \pm 4 \Rightarrow g = -2, -10$

Substituting into **(1)**:

$g = -2: 3 + f = -3 \Rightarrow f = -6$

$g = -10: 3 + f = 3 \Rightarrow f = 0$

$r = \sqrt{g^2 + f^2 - c} = 5 \Rightarrow c = g^2 + f^2 - 25 \ldots$ **(3)**

Substituting into **(3)**:

$g = -2, f = -6: c = 4 + 36 - 25 = 15$

$g = -10, f = 0: c = 100 + 0 - 25 = 75$

The circles are $x^2 + y^2 - 4x - 12y + 15 = 0$ and $x^2 + y^2 - 20x + 75 = 0$.

2. The circle touches one or both axes

(i) The circle touches the *x*-axis:

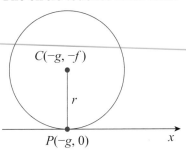

The point of contact *P* is $(-g, 0)$.

$$r = |-f| = \sqrt{g^2 + f^2 - c}$$

$$f^2 = g^2 + f^2 - c$$

$$\boxed{c = g^2}$$

(ii) The circle touches the *y*-axis:

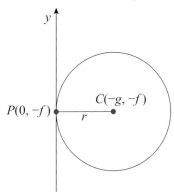

The point of contact *P* is $(0, -f)$.

$$r = |-g| = \sqrt{g^2 + f^2 - c}$$

$$g^2 = g^2 + f^2 - c$$

$$\boxed{c = f^2}$$

(iii) The circle touches both axes:

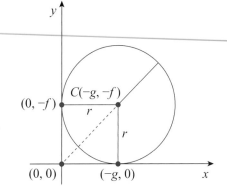

From the results in **(i)** and **(ii)**:

$$c = g^2 = f^2 \Rightarrow \boxed{f = \pm g}$$

- $f = +g$ is true if the circle is in the first or third quadrants.

- $f = -g$ is true if the curve is in the second or fourth quadrants.

If the centre is in the first quadrant, $f = g$ and so the line joining the centre to $(0, 0)$ has equation $x = y$.

EXAMPLE 8

Find the equation of the circle that touches the *x*-axis at the point $(3, 0)$ and whose centre is on the line $2x - y + 3 = 0$.

Solution

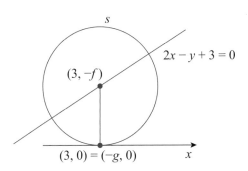

$(-g, 0) = (3, 0)$

$g = -3$

$c = g^2$ [Touches the *x*-axis.]

$c = 9$

$(3, -f)$ is on $2x - y + 3 = 0$.

$6 + f + 3 = 0$

$f = -9$

The equation of *s* is $x^2 + y^2 - 6x - 18y + 9 = 0$.

EXAMPLE 9

A teacher draws a grid on the board and asks the class if any student would like to draw a circle s through the point (2, 4) touching both axes.
A student comes up and draws a circle without any problem. The teacher then asks what about the other circle. Is another circle possible?

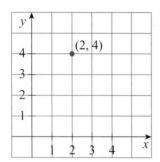

Solution

s touches both axes: $c = g^2 = f^2$

The centre is in the first quadrant: $f = g$

The equation of s: $x^2 + y^2 + 2gx + 2gy + g^2 = 0$.

(2, 4) is on s: $4 + 16 + 4g + 8g + g^2 = 0$

$$g^2 + 12g + 20 = 0$$

$$(g + 2)(g + 10) = 0$$

$g = -2$: $f = -2, c = 4$

$g = -10$: $f = -10, c = 100$

There are two circles:

A little circle: $x^2 + y^2 - 4x - 4y + 4 = 0$ with radius $r = \sqrt{4 + 4 - 4} = 2$.

A big circle: $x^2 + y^2 - 20x - 20y + 100 = 0$ with radius $r = \sqrt{100 + 100 - 100} = 10$.

The circle cuts the axes

EXAMPLE 10

Find the equation of the circle passing through the origin and making intercepts of +6 units on the x-axis and +8 units on the y-axis, respectively.

Solution

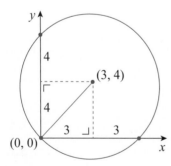

(0, 0) on the circle: $c = 0$

Centre is (3, 4) = $(-g, -f)$

$g = -3, f = -4$

The equation of the circle is $x^2 + y^2 - 6x - 8y = 0$.

EXERCISE 13

Diagrams are not drawn to scale.

1. Find the equation of the circle s with the following properties:

   (a) Centre $C(-1, 3)$, radius 4

   (b) Centre $C\left(\frac{1}{3}, -\frac{1}{2}\right)$, radius $\sqrt{7}$

   (c) $P(-1, 2), Q(3, 4)$ on the ends of a diameter

   (d) $P(-5, 7), Q(4, -5)$ on the ends of a diameter

   (e) Passing through $P(0, 0), Q(-3, 1)$ and $R(-3, 9)$

   (f) Passing through $P(0, 1), Q(1, 2)$ and $R(1, 0)$

   (g) Passing through $P(5, 1), Q(4, 2)$ and $R(2, -2)$

2. Find the equation(s) of the circle s with the following properties:

   (a) Centre on x-axis, $(0, 0)$ on s and radius 6

   (b) Centre on y-axis, radius 5 and $(3, 1)$ on s

   (c) Centre on the line $x - y - 1 = 0$, radius 3 and $(7, 3)$ on s

3. Find the equation(s) of the circle(s) s with the following properties:

   (a) Centre $(2, -5)$ and touches the x-axis

   (b) Touches the y-axis, radius 5, and passes through $(8, 0)$ on s

   (c) Touches both axes and centre on the line $2x - y + 2 = 0$ in the first quadrant

   (d) Passes through $(4, 2)$ and touches both axes in the first quadrant

   (e) Radius 5 and touches the line $3x + 4y + 9 = 0$ at $(1, -3)$

4. A circular cycle track passes through three checkpoints $P(5, 5)$, $Q(4, 8)$ and $R(-7, -3)$.

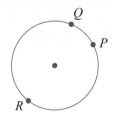

   (a) Find the equation of the circle.

   (b) Find the centre of the circle.

   (c) Find the radius of the circle.

   (d) Find the length of the track correct to two decimal places, if 1 unit = 1 m.

   (e) Does the track pass through $(3, -2)$?

5. An aeroplane is about to touch down at the point $(3, 0)$. It is told to go around just before it hits the runway. Find the equation of the circular path if it starts its descent at the point $(0, 1)$.

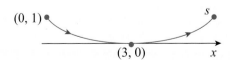

6. An electron in a cyclotron travels in a circle and passes through the point $B(4, -2)$. When it reaches the point $D(2, 4)$, it leaves the

circle along the tangent line at this point. If the equation of the tangent line t at D is $2x - y = 0$, find the equation of the circle. Does the electron pass through the point $(8, 0)$?

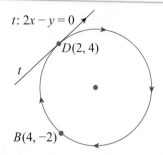

Find the radius of the circle correct to two decimal places, if 1 unit = 1 m. Find the speed of the electron in the cyclotron if it traces out $5\,400\,000$ revolutions in 1 second, correct to three significant figures.

7. A garden is laid out in the form of a sector of a circle with centre C, as shown. A path with equation $2x - 3y - 7 = 0$ passes through C.

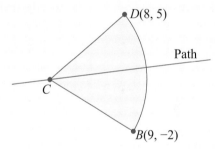

   (a) Find the equation of the circle with centre C that passes through $B(9, -2)$ and $D(8, 5)$.

   (b) Find C.

   (c) Show that $\left| \angle BCD \right| = 90°$.

8. The x-axis is a road that is a tangent to a circular roundabout at the point $(5, 0)$.

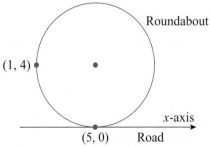

If $(1, 4)$ is a point on the roundabout, find:

   (a) the equation of the roundabout,

   (b) the radius of the roundabout, if 1 unit = 1 m.

13.2 Intersecting circles

When two circles s_1 and s_2 are drawn in the plane, there are three possibilities regarding their intersection:

Steps for dealing with two circles s_1 and s_2

1. First find their centres C_1 and C_2 and their radii to see which has the bigger radius.

2. Find $\left| C_1 C_2 \right|$.

3. Draw the circles and join their centres with a straight line $C_1 C_2$. This line is called the **line of centres** (LC).

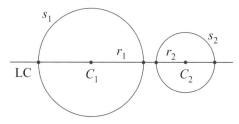

Situation 1: External touch $s_1 \cap s_2 = \{P\}$

Always draw the line of centres (LC) and the line perpendicular to the line of centres at the point of contact P of the circles.

This line is called the **common tangent** (CT) at the point of contact P.

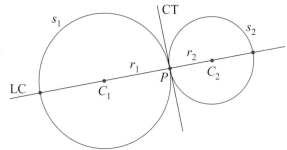

> The condition for two circles to touch externally is that the distance between the centres is equal to the sum of the radii: $\left| C_1 C_2 \right| = r_1 + r_2$.

EXAMPLE 11

Show that the circles with equations
$s_1 : x^2 + y^2 - 6x - 4y + 11 = 0$ and
$s_2 : x^2 + y^2 + 4x + 6y - 19 = 0$ touch externally.

Find:

(a) the slope and equation of their line of centres,

(b) the point of contact P,

(c) the equation of the tangent at the point of contact.

Solution

$s_1 : x^2 + y^2 - 6x - 4y + 11 = 0$

Centre: $C_1(3, 2)$

Radius: $r_1 = \sqrt{9 + 4 - 11} = \sqrt{2}$

$s_2 : x^2 + y^2 + 4x + 6y - 19 = 0$

Centre: $C_2(-2, -3)$

Radius: $r_2 = \sqrt{4 + 9 + 19} = 4\sqrt{2}$

$|C_1 C_2| = \sqrt{25 + 25} = \sqrt{50} = 5\sqrt{2}$

$r_1 + r_2 = \sqrt{2} + 4\sqrt{2} = 5\sqrt{2}$

$\therefore s_1$ and s_2 touch externally.

Having found the centres and the radii, we can now draw the circles. s_2 has the bigger radius.

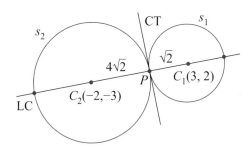

(a) Slope of LC $= \dfrac{-3 - 2}{-2 - 3} = 1$

Equation of LC: $(y - 2) = 1(x - 3)$

Equation of LC: $x - y - 1 = 0$

(b) The point of contact P divides $[C_1 C_2]$ in the ratio 1:4.

①		④
(3, 2)		(−2, −3)

$x = \dfrac{1(-2) + 4(3)}{1 + 4} = 2, \quad y = \dfrac{1(-3) + 4(2)}{1 + 4} = 1$

$\therefore P(2, 1)$

(c) The equation of the common tangent at the point of contact can be done in two ways.

Conventional method

Since CT $\perp$ LC, the slope of the CT $= -1$.

$P(2, 1)$ is on the CT so its equation is

$y - 1 = -1(x - 2)$.

Equation of the common tangent: $x + y - 3 = 0$

Trick method

The equation of the CT is obtained by subtracting the equation of one circle from the other.

$s_1 : x^2 + y^2 - 6x - 4y + 11 = 0$

$s_2 : x^2 + y^2 + 4x + 6y - 19 = 0$

$s_1 - s_2 : \quad -10x - 10y + 30 = 0$

Equation of the common tangent: $x + y - 3 = 0$

Situation 2: Internal touch $s_1 \cap s_2 = \{P\}$

Again always draw the line of centres and the common tangent at the point of contact P.

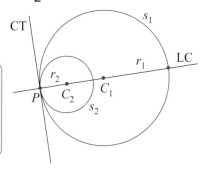

> The condition for which two circles to touch internally is that the distance between the centres is the bigger radius minus the smaller radius: $|C_1 C_2| = r_1 - r_2$.

EXAMPLE 12

An electron is accelerated in a cyclotron s_1 with equation s_1:
$x^2 + y^2 - 10x - 24y + 167 = 0$ before being injected into the synchrotron
s_2 with equation $s_2 : x^2 + y^2 + 8x - 6y - 175 = 0$ at the point of contact P
of the two circles.

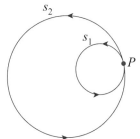

(a) Show that s_1 touches s_2 internally.

(b) Find the slope and equation of the line joining the centres of s_1 and s_2.

(c) Find the point of contact P of s_1 and s_2.

(d) Find the equation of the common tangent to s_1 and s_2 at P.

Solution

(a) $s_1 : x^2 + y^2 - 10x - 24y + 167 = 0$

Centre: $C_1(5, 12)$

Radius: $r_1 = \sqrt{25 + 144 - 167} = \sqrt{2}$

$s_2 : x^2 + y^2 + 8x - 6y - 175 = 0$

Centre: $C_2(-4, 3)$

Radius: $r_2 = \sqrt{16 + 9 + 175} = \sqrt{200} = 10\sqrt{2}$

$|C_1 C_2| = \sqrt{81 + 81} = 9\sqrt{2}$

$r_2 - r_1 = 10\sqrt{2} - \sqrt{2} = 9\sqrt{2}$

Therefore, s_1 touches s_2 internally.

(b) Slope of line of centres (LC) $= \dfrac{3 - 12}{-4 - 5} = 1$

Equation of LC:

$y - 3 = 1(x + 4)$

$x - y + 7 = 0$

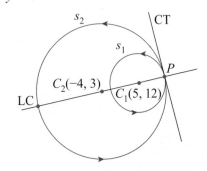

(c) C_1 divides $[C_2 P]$ in the ratio 9:1.

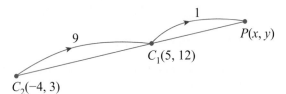

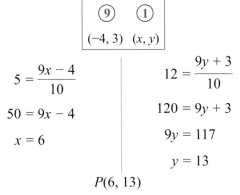

$5 = \dfrac{9x - 4}{10}$

$50 = 9x - 4$

$x = 6$

$12 = \dfrac{9y + 3}{10}$

$120 = 9y + 3$

$9y = 117$

$y = 13$

$P(6, 13)$

(d) Method 1: Slope of common tangent at the point of contact $= -1$, $P(6, 13)$

Equation of CT: $y - 13 = -1(x - 6)$

$x + y - 19 = 0$

Method 2

$s_1 : x^2 + y^2 - 10x - 24x + 167 = 0$

$s_2 : \quad x^2 + y^2 + 8x - 6y - 175 = 0$

$s_1 - s_2 : \quad -18x - 18y + 342 = 0$

Equation of CT: $x + y - 19 = 0$

Situation 3: A cut $s_1 \cap s_2 = \{B, D\}$

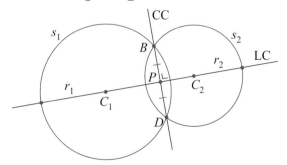

TIP

Always draw the line of centres (LC) and the line perpendicular to the line of centres through the points of intersection of the circles. This line through the points of intersection is known as the common chord (CC) and is bisected by the line of centres.

EXAMPLE **13**

The circles $s_1 : x^2 + y^2 - 8x - 4y - 5 = 0$ and $s_2 : x^2 + y^2 - 4x - 2y - 5 = 0$ intersect at two points. Find the co-ordinates of their centres and their radii.

(a) If $l : 2x + y = 0$ is the common chord of s_1 and s_2, through the points of intersection of s_1 and s_2, find these points.

(b) Show that the equation of the common chord can be obtained from $s_1 - s_2$ and is perpendicular to the line of centres of s_1 and s_2.

(c) Show that the midpoint of the points of intersection of s_1 and s_2 is also the point of intersection of the line of centres and common chord of s_1 and s_2.

Solution

$s_1 : x^2 + y^2 - 8x - 4y - 5 = 0$

Centre: $C_1(4, 2)$

Radius: $r_1 = \sqrt{16 + 4 + 5} = 5$

$s_2 : x^2 + y^2 - 4x - 2y - 5 = 0$

Centre: $C_2(2, 1)$

Radius: $r_2 = \sqrt{4 + 1 + 5} = \sqrt{10}$

(a) l intersects s_1.

$l : 2x + y = 0 \Rightarrow y = -2x$ ... **(1)**

$s_1 : x^2 + y^2 - 8x - 4y - 5 = 0$ ... **(2)**

Substitute **(1)** into **(2)**:

$x^2 + 4x^2 - 8x + 8x - 5 = 0$

$5x^2 - 5 = 0$

$x^2 = 1$

$x = \pm 1$

Substituting these values of x back into equation **(1)**: $y = \mp 2$

The points of intersection of l and s_1 are $P(1, -2)$ and $Q(-1, 2)$.

Show that these points are also on s_2.

$s_2 : x^2 + y^2 - 4x - 2y - 5 = 0$

$P(1, -2) : 1 + 4 - 4 + 4 - 5 = 0$ [$P(1, -2)$ is on s_2 as it satisfies the equation of s_2.]

$Q(-1, 2) : 1 + 4 + 4 - 4 - 5 = 0$ [$Q(-1, 2)$ is on s_2 as it satisfies the equation of s_2.]

(b) $s_1 : x^2 + y^2 - 8x - 4y - 5 = 0$

$s_2 : x^2 + y^2 - 4x - 2y - 5 = 0$

$s_1 - s_2 : \quad -4x - 2y = 0 \Rightarrow 2x + y = 0$, which is the equation of the given common chord.

The slope of the common chord (CC) $= -2 = m_1$

The slope of the line of centres (LC) $= \dfrac{1 - 2}{2 - 4} = \dfrac{1}{2} = m_2$

$m_1 m_2 = -1 \Rightarrow CC \perp LC$

(c) Midpoint of $[PQ] = \left(\dfrac{-1 + 1}{2}, \dfrac{2 - 2}{2}\right) = (0, 0)$

Equation of LC: $(y - 2) = \dfrac{1}{2}(x - 4)$

$2y - 4 = x - 4$

$x - 2y = 0$

Equation of CC: $2x + y = 0$

Solving these equations simultaneously gives $(0, 0)$, which is the midpoint of $[PQ]$.

Situation 4: A miss $s_1 \cap s_2 = \{\}$

EXAMPLE 14

The effective broadcast area of a radio station is bounded by the circle: $s_1 : x^2 + y^2 = 900$. Another radio station's broadcast area is bounded by the circle $s_2 : x^2 + y^2 - 240x - 240y + 26\,300 = 0$. Find the centre and radius of each circle and the distance between the centres. Investigate by drawing a diagram to check if there is any location that can receive both stations. Both x and y are measured in kilometres.

Solution

$s_1 : x^2 + y^2 = 900$

Radius: $r_1 = 30$

Centre: $C_1(0, 0)$

$s_2 : x^2 + y^2 - 240x - 240y + 26\,300 = 0$

$g = -120, f = -120, c = 26\,300$

Radius: $r_2 = \sqrt{120^2 + 120^2 - 26\,300} = 50$

Centre: $C_2(120, 120)$

$\left| C_1 C_2 \right| = \sqrt{120^2 + 120^2}$

$\qquad = 120\sqrt{2}$ km

$r_1 + r_2 = 30 + 50 = 80$ km

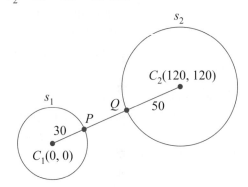

No location can receive both stations because s_1 and s_2 do not intersect anywhere.

EXERCISE 14

1. Show that the circles with equations
    $s_1 : x^2 + y^2 - 8y - 4 = 0$ and
    $s_2 : x^2 + y^2 + 6x + 4y + 8 = 0$ touch externally.
    Find their point of contact and the equation of the common tangent at the point of contact.

2. Show that the circles with equations
    $s_1 : x^2 + y^2 - 8x - 2y + 7 = 0$ and
    $s_2 : x^2 + y^2 - 9x + y - 2 = 0$ touch internally.
    Find their point of contact and the equation of the common tangent at this point.

3. If the circles with equations
    $s_1 : x^2 + y^2 - 2x - 8y + 1 = 0$ and
    $s_2 : x^2 + y^2 + 6x - 2y + c = 0$ touch internally, find c.

4. If the circles with equations
    $s_1 : x^2 + y^2 + 2x + 4y + c = 0$ and
    $s_2 : x^2 + y^2 - 10x - 5y + 25 = 0$ touch externally, find c.

5. Show that the circles with equations
    $s_1 : x^2 + y^2 + 2x - 4y - 4 = 0$ and
    $s_2 : x^2 + y^2 - 4x - 12y + 36 = 0$ touch externally. Find the equation of the circle s_3 that is touched by s_2 and s_1 internally, as shown.

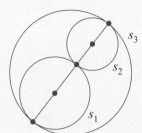

6. A watch face has a circular minute–hour dial with equation $s_1: x^2 + y^2 - 4x - 6y + 5 = 0$. It also has a second hand dial with equation $s_2: x^2 + y^2 - 6x - 8y + 23 = 0$. Show that these two dials touch and find the point of contact D.

7. A necklace consists of a chain with two silver rings attached to it at B and attached to each other at D. s_1 has centre $(8, 5)$ and radius 6. s_2 has a centre $(2, -3)$. Find the radius of s_2.

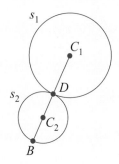

8. Two circular ring roads s_1 and s_2 intersect at D and E. Their equations are
$s_1: x^2 + y^2 - 8x + 2y - 23 = 0$ and
$s_2: x^2 + y^2 + 6x + 4y + 3 = 0$, respectively.

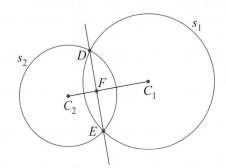

(a) Find the co-ordinates of the centres C_1 and C_2 of each circle and the radius of each circle.

A road DE intersects the road C_2C_1 at F and E.

(b) Find the equation of the road DE if $D(-2, 1)$.

(c) Find the co-ordinates of F and E.

9. The two windscreen wipers W_1 and W_2 on a Ford C-Max describe circles s_1 and s_2 with centres C_1 and C_2, respectively. The equations of the circles are:

$$s_1 : (x - 0{\cdot}25)^2 + y^2 = \frac{1}{16}$$

$$s_2 : (x - 0{\cdot}6)^2 + y^2 = \frac{9}{25}$$

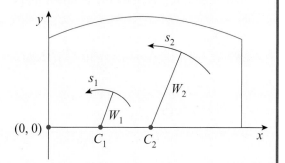

Find:

(a) C_1, the centre of s_1

(b) C_2, the centre of s_2

(c) $|C_1C_2|$

(d) r_1, the radius of s_1

(e) r_2, the radius of s_2

Do the circles overlap?
(Use the scale: 1 unit = 1 m)

REVISION QUESTIONS

1. l is the line $3x + by = 11$. If $A(1, 2)$ is on this line, find b. Find where l cuts the y-axis.

2. $l_1: 2x - 3y = 15$ and $l_2: 5x - y - 5 = 0$ are the equations of two straight lines. Find their point of intersection.

3. (a) Show that the line p is perpendicular to the line q, where $p: 5x + 2y = 10$ and $q: 2x - 5y + 8 = 0$.

   (b) If the line p is perpendicular to the line q, find $b \in \mathbb{R}$, where $p: 4x + by - 12 = 0$ and $q: 8x - y = 7$.

4. A water pipe $[AB]$ runs between two buildings that are represented by the points A and B.

   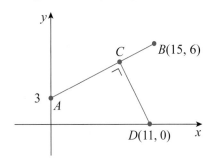

   (a) Show that the equation of the line AB is $x - 5y + 15 = 0$.

   (b) An overflow pipe CD, perpendicular to AB, is built at C. Find the equation of CD.

   (c) Find C.

5. Two towns $A(-3, -5)$ and $B(7, 9)$ are connected by a road AB. A motorway CD is to be constructed at right angles to CD and exactly halfway between A and B.

   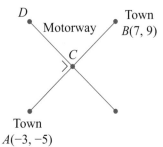

   (a) Find C, the midpoint of $[AB]$.

   (b) Find the slope of AB.

   (c) Find the slope of CD.

   (d) Find the equation of CD.

6. Copy and complete the following table. Plot **(b)** on graph paper or on a co-ordinated rectangular grid.

Equation of line	Slope	x-intercept	y-intercept
(a) $3x - 2y - 12 = 0$			
(b) $4x + y - 4 = 0$			
(c) $y = -2x + 3$			
(d) $y = -3$			
(e) $x = 4$			

7. $ABCD$ is a parallelogram with $A(-3, -4)$ and $B(-2, -10)$ as two vertices. The equation of DC is $6x + y - 3 = 0$. The slope of BC is $\frac{7}{3}$.

   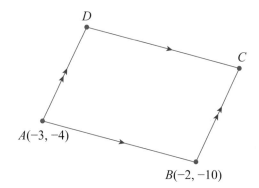

   Find:

   (a) the equation of AD,

   (b) the point D,

   (c) the point C,

   (d) the area of the parallelogram $ABCD$.

8. s is a circle with centre $C(2, 5)$ and radius 5.

   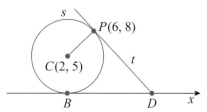

   (a) The x-axis is a tangent at B. Find B.

   (b) Verify that $P(6, 8)$ is on this circle.

   (c) Find the equation of PC.

   (d) Find the equation of the tangent t to the circle at P.

   (e) Find the point D where the tangent t crosses the x-axis.

9. $\triangle ABC$ has vertices $A(2, 4)$, $B(0, -2)$ and $C(6, 0)$. The line p bisects $[AB]$ at right angles at D. The line q bisects AC at right angles at E.

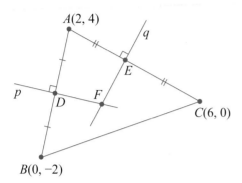

(a) Find D.

(b) Find the equation of p.

(c) Find E.

(d) Find the equation of q.

(e) Find the circumcentre of $\triangle ABC$ (that is, the point of intersection of p and q).

10. A ship A leaves port $O(0, 0)$ and sails along the path OQ to Q. Another ship B sails along the path shown at $45°$ to A's path.

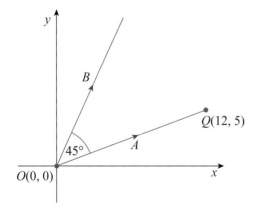

Find:

(a) the equation of A's path,

(b) the equation of B's path,

(c) the distance of closest approach of B's path to Q. (Scale: 1 unit = 1 km)

11. A spacecraft is moving in a circular orbit s with equation $x^2 + y^2 - 8x - 4y + 15 = 0$. Its path is tracked by an observer at $Q(0, 0)$.

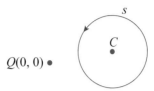

Find:

(a) the co-ordinates of the centre C of the circle s,

(b) the radius of the circle,

(c) $|QC|$,

(d) the point on s where the spaceship is nearest to Q,

(e) the point on s where the spaceship is farthest from Q.

12. A bicycle is hung from a ceiling by a rope PQ. The equation of wheel s_1 is $x^2 + y^2 + 2x - 4y - 20 = 0$ and the equation of wheel s_2 is $x^2 + y^2 - 16x + 20y + 139 = 0$. The bar t is a tangent to both wheels at H and G, respectively, and makes a positive intercept on the y-axis.

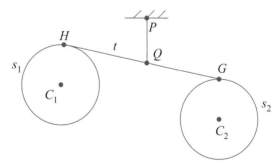

Find:

(a) the centre C_1 and radius of s_1,

(b) the centre C_2 and radius of s_2,

(c) $|C_1C_2|$,

(d) the slope of C_1C_2,

(e) the equation of t,

(f) the co-ordinates of H,

(g) the co-ordinates of G.

13. A section of a machine consists of a rectangle *EFGH* with two equal circular metal-reinforcing hoops, s_1 and s_2, touching each other and the sides of the rectangle.

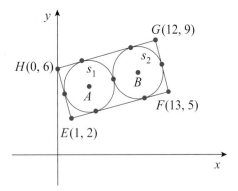

Find:

(a) the midpoint of $[EH]$,

(b) the midpoint of $[GF]$,

(c) the point of contact of the circles,

(d) the centre C_1 of s_1,

(e) the centre C_2 of s_2,

(f) the radius of s_1,

(g) the equation of s_1.

14. A circle *s* touches the *y*-axis at $B(0, 4)$ and passes through the point $D(4, 8)$.

(a) Find the equation of *s*.

(b) Find the equation of the perpendicular bisector *l* of the chord $[BD]$.

(c) Show that the centre of the circle *s* lies on *l*.

(d) Find the equation of the tangents to *s* parallel to *l*.

15. The pendulum of a clock swings through three points, $A(-4, 8)$, $B(0, 4)$ and $D(2, 6)$ on a circle *s*.

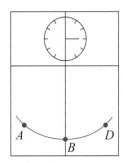

Find:

(a) the equation of the circle *s*,

(b) its centre and radius,

(c) the equation of the tangent at *D*.

16. Ballyderoe (*B*) is located 12 km East and 18 km North of Passagenorth (*P*). A mobile mast (*M*) is to be positioned so that the distance from the mast $M(x, y)$ to *B* is twice its distance to $P(0, 0)$.

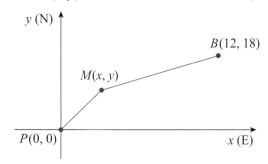

(a) Show that the mast must lie on a circle *s* and find the equation of *s*.

(b) Find the centre and radius of this circle.

(c) What is the furthest distance the mast can be from *P*?

(d) What are the co-ordinates of *M* so that *M* is farthest from *P*?

17. A reflecting telescope mirror is an arc of a circle with centre $C(5, -1)$ and radius 5. The axis of symmetry of the mirror passes through the point $B(9, 2)$.

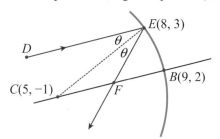

(a) Find the equation of the circle of which the mirror is an arc.

(b) Show that $E(8, 3)$ is on the circle.

(c) A ray of light *DE* is parallel to the axis *CB* of the mirror. Find the slope of *DE*.

(d) Find the slope of *CE*.

(e) If θ is the acute angle between DE and CE, find $\tan \theta$.

According to the law of reflection, the reflected ray EF makes an equal angle with CE.

(f) Find the slope of EF.

(g) Find the equation of EF.

(h) Find the co-ordinates of the point F where EF crosses the axis of symmetry.

18. A beam of electrons travels along the line $l: 3x - 4y = 0$. At the point B, it is drawn into a circular orbit s.

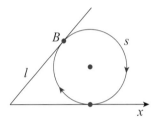

(a) If the circle s touches the x-axis and has centre (h, k), show that $h = 3k$, if $h > 0$ and $k > 0$.

(b) Find the equation of the circle in terms of k, if $h > 0$ and $k > 0$.

19. To measure the distance between two planets s_1 and s_2, a laser beam is fired from $P(6, 8)$ on s_1 with equation $x^2 + y^2 = 100$ to strike a mirror at Q on s_2 with equation $x^2 + y^2 - 42x - 6y + 425 = 0$. PQ is a tangent to both circles.

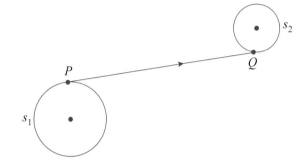

Find:

(a) the centre C_1 and radius r_1 of s_1,

(b) the equation of the tangent to s_1 at P,

(c) the centre C_2 and radius r_2 of s_2,

(d) the equation of $C_2 Q$,

(e) the co-ordinates of Q,

(f) $|PQ|$.

SUMMARY

Co-ordinate Geometry

1. The distance between two points:

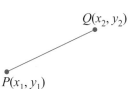

$$\left|PQ\right| = \sqrt{(x_2 - x_1)^2 + (y_2 - y_1)^2}$$

Remember as: $\sqrt{(\text{Difference in } x \text{ co-ordinates})^2 + (\text{Difference in } y \text{ co-ordinates})^2}$

2. The midpoint formula:

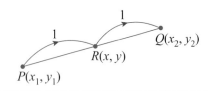

$$\text{Midpoint of } [PQ] = R\left(\frac{x_1 + x_2}{2}, \frac{y_1 + y_2}{2}\right)$$

Remember as:

$$\frac{\text{Add the } x \text{ values}}{2}, \frac{\text{Add the } y \text{ values}}{2},$$

3. The area of a triangle:

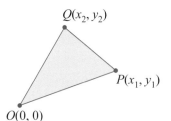

$$\text{Area} = \frac{1}{2}\left|x_1 y_2 - x_2 y_1\right|$$

4. The slope of a line:

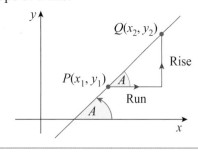

$$\text{Slope} = m = \tan A = \frac{\text{Rise}}{\text{Run}} = \frac{(y_2 - y_1)}{(x_2 - x_1)}$$

Remember as: $\dfrac{\text{Difference in } y \text{ co-ordinates}}{\text{Difference in } x \text{ co-ordinates}}$

Slope = average rate of change of y with respect to x

5. **(a)** Parallel lines have the same slope:

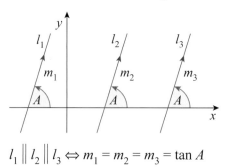

$$l_1 \parallel l_2 \parallel l_3 \Leftrightarrow m_1 = m_2 = m_3 = \tan A$$

(b) Perpendicular lines:

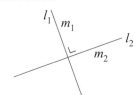

$$l_1 \perp l_2 \Leftrightarrow m_1 m_2 = -1 \Leftrightarrow m_2 = -\frac{1}{m_1}$$

(c) All horizontal lines have slope 0:

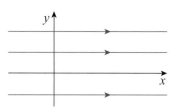

$$m = \tan 0° = 0$$

(d) All vertical lines have slope ∞:

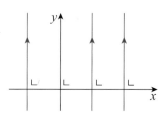

$$m = \tan 90° = \infty$$

(e) Lines making equal intercepts on the axes have a slope of ± 1:

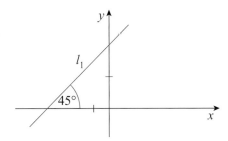

Slope of $l_1 = m = \tan 45° = +1$

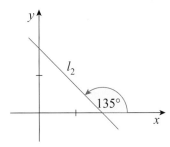

Slope of $l_2 = \tan 135° = -1$

(f) Collinear points:

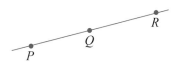

Slope of PQ = slope of PR = slope of QR

6. The equation of a straight line:

(a) To find the equation of a straight line, you need two things:

(i) Slope m

(ii) Point $P(x_1, y_1)$ on the line

$$(y - y_1) = m(x - x_1)$$

(b) The slope intercept form of the equation of a straight line:

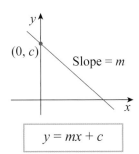

$$y = mx + c$$

(c) The slope m of the straight line with equation $ax + by + c = 0$ is:

$$m = -\frac{a}{b} = -\frac{(\text{Coefficient of } x)}{(\text{Coefficient of } y)}$$

7. Intersecting lines $l_1 \cap l_2 = \{P\}$:

P is found by solving the equations of l_1 and l_2 simultaneously.

8. Division of a line segment:

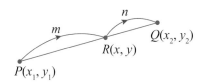

$$x = \frac{mx_2 \pm nx_1}{m \pm n}, \quad y = \frac{my_2 \pm ny_1}{m \pm n}$$

9. Angle between lines:

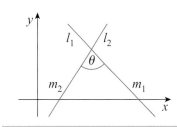

$$\tan \theta = \left| \frac{m_1 - m_2}{1 + m_1 m_2} \right|, \text{ for } \theta \text{ acute}$$

10. The perpendicular distance from a point to a line:

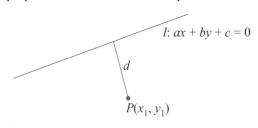

$$d = \frac{|ax_1 + by_1 + c|}{\sqrt{a^2 + b^2}} = \frac{|\text{Point into line}|}{\text{Pythagoras}}$$

11. The equation of a circle:

(a) Centre $C(0, 0)$, radius r:

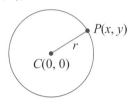

$$x^2 + y^2 = r^2$$

(b) Centre $C(h, k)$, radius r:

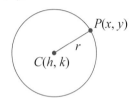

$$(x - h)^2 + (y - k)^2 = r^2$$

(c) Centre $C(-g, -f)$, radius r:

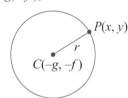

$$x^2 + y^2 + 2gx + 2fy + c = 0$$

$$r = \sqrt{g^2 + f^2 - c}$$

12. Tangents:

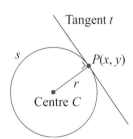

- t is perpendicular to CP at the point of contact P.
- $r = |CP|$
- $s \cap t = \{P\}$

Circle with axes as tangents:

(a) x-axis as a tangent:

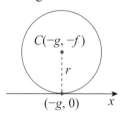

$$r = |-f|, \ c = g^2$$

(b) y-axis as a tangent:

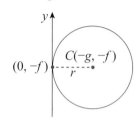

$$r = |-g|, \ c = f^2$$

(c) Both axes as tangent:

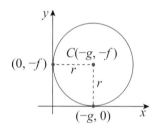

$$r = |-g| = |-f|$$

$$c = g^2 = f^2$$

$$f = \pm g$$

13. Chords:

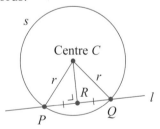

- $s \cap l = \{P, Q\}$
- A perpendicular line drawn from the centre C to a chord $[PQ]$ bisects the chord $[PQ]$:
  $$|PR| = |RQ|$$
- $\triangle CPR \equiv \triangle CQR$ are both right-angled triangles. You can apply Pythagoras' theorem to both triangles.

14. Intersecting circles:

(a) Touching circles:

External:

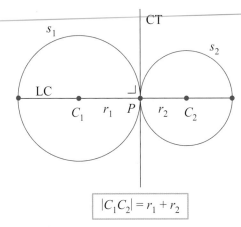

$$\boxed{|C_1C_2| = r_1 + r_2}$$

Internal:

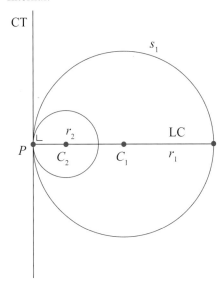

$$\boxed{|C_1C_2| = r_1 - r_2}$$

- $[C_1C_2]$ is the line of centres (LC).
- The common tangent (CT) at the point of contact P is perpendicular to $[C_1C_2]$.
- LC $\cap$ CT = $\{P\}$
- $|C_1P| : |C_2P| = r_1 : r_2$
- CT: $s_1 - s_2 = 0$

(b) Cutting circles:

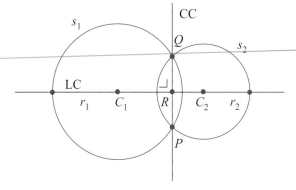

- $[C_1C_2]$ is the line of centres (LC).
- The common chord (CC) through the points of intersection of P and Q of s_1 and s_2 is perpendicular to $[C_1C_2]$.
- $s_1 \cap$ CC = $\{P, Q\}$
  $s_2 \cap$ CC = $\{P, Q\}$
- LC $\cap$ CC = $\{R\}$
  R is the midpoint of $[PQ]$.
- $|QR| = |RP|$

(c) Good habits:

- Find the centres C_1 and C_2 and the radii r_1 and r_2 of the circles s_1 and s_2 before you draw them.
- Draw the LC.
- Find $|C_1C_2|$.

SECTION 5

Probability

Probability has widespread applications in weather forecasting, sports strategy, game theory, gambling and calculating insurance premiums.

The **Kelly criterion** is a famous probability formula that enables investors to maximise long-term growth. It is a formula that gives the borderline between aggressive and foolish investments!

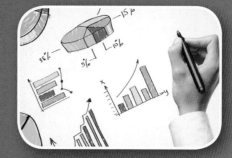

Counting

CHAPTER 14

Learning Outcomes

- To understand the fundamental principle of counting using tree diagrams and tables.
- To work with arrangements (permutations) where the order matters.
- To work with selections (combinations) where the order does not matter.

14.1 Fundamental principle of counting

Tree diagrams and tables

It can be difficult to count the number of ways that one or more operations can be carried out when conducting a trial of an experiment such as rolling a fair die twice. Tree diagrams and tables are very useful tools for counting the number of results of a trial of an experiment.

Each of the individual results of a trial of an experiment is called an **outcome.** The set of all possible outcomes of a trial listed together is called the **sample space** of the experiment.

ACTIVITY 1

ACTION
Understanding the multiplication principle

OBJECTIVE
To learn the fundamental principle of counting using the multiplication principle, and to use tree diagrams and tables to aid your understanding

EXAMPLE 1

There are three bridges leading from the north side of a city (Amiens Bridge (A), Binns Bridge (B) and Connell Bridge (C)) to the south side and then two roads (N1 and N2) leading to the National Stadium. List in a set all the routes from the north side of the city to the stadium:

(a) by constructing a tree diagram,

(b) by drawing up a table.

Solution

(a)

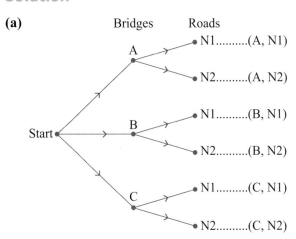

$S = \{(A, N1), (A, N2), (B, N1), (B, N2), (C, N1), (C, N2)\}$
There are 6 possible ways in total of completing the journey.

357

(b)

Bridges	Roads	
	N1	**N2**
A	(A, N1)	(A, N2)
B	(B, N1)	(B, N2)
C	(C, N1)	(C, N2)

The set S of all possible outcomes of this experiment is:

$S = \{(A, N1), (A, N2), (B, N1),$
$(B, N2), (C, N1), (C, N2)\}$

The total number of outcomes
$= 3 \times 2 = 6$

EXAMPLE 2

A student tosses a fair coin twice. This means that she tosses the coin and then she tosses the coin again. Draw a tree diagram and a table to determine all possible outcomes of this experiment. Write out the sample space.

Solution

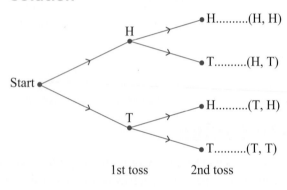

1st toss   2nd toss

First toss	Second toss	
	H	**T**
H	(H, H)	(H, T)
T	(T, H)	(T, T)

The sample space is given by:

$S = \{(H, H), (H, T), (T, H), (T, T)\}$

The total number of outcomes $= 2 \times 2 = 4$

WORKED EXAMPLE — The fundamental principle of counting

A fair coin is tossed **and then** a fair die is rolled. Draw a tree diagram and table for this trial.

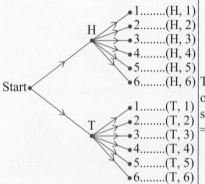

Coin   Die $2 \times 6 = 12$

The total number of elements in this sample space $= 2 \times 6 = 12$

	Die					
Coin	**1**	**2**	**3**	**4**	**5**	**6**
H	(H, 1)	(H, 2)	(H, 3)	(H, 4)	(H, 5)	(H, 6)
T	(T, 1)	(T, 2)	(T, 3)	(T, 4)	(T, 5)	(T, 6)

The sample space is given by:

$S = \{(H, 1), (H, 2), (H, 3), (H, 4), (H, 5), (H, 6),$
$(T, 1), (T, 2), (T, 3), (T, 4), (T, 5), (T, 6)\}$

The elements are in the order in which the operations are done. There are $= 2 \times 6 = 12$ outcomes in all.

There are two outcomes to tossing a coin: head (H), tail (T). Then for each of these outcomes, there are six outcomes to rolling a die: 1, 2, 3, 4, 5, 6.

So if there are two outcomes to one operation and then six outcomes to a second operation, the total number of outcomes to the first **and then** the second $= 2 \times 6 = 12$.

This is the idea behind the multiplication principle, which is the fundamental principle of counting.

It is possible to work out the number of outcomes of two or more consecutive operations without drawing a tree diagram or a table, as tree diagrams and tables become very large for a trial of an experiment with large numbers of outcomes.

MULTIPLICATION PRINCIPLE

If there are a ways (outcomes) to do one operation **and then** b ways to do a second operation **and then** c ways to do a third operation, etc. then the number of ways of doing the first operation **and then** doing the second operation **and then** doing the third operation, etc. is given by $a \times b \times c \times \ldots$.

The multiplication principle is also known as the **'and then'** rule as it gives the elements of the sample space in the order asked.

Steps for using the multiplication principle

1. Draw a box for each operation. Put a description of the operation over the box.
2. Put the number of outcomes for each operation under the box, not in it.
3. Only put numbers/objects in the box that are specified by conditions.

▸ A restaurant menu has five starters, six main courses and four desserts. The number of ways you can have a three-course meal is:

Starter   Main course   Dessert

☐ and then ☐ and then ☐

5 × 6 × 4 = 120

▸ A bicycle lock has two letter wheels and three digit wheels. The number of possible opening configurations is:

Letter   Letter   Digit   Digit   Digit

☐ and then ☐ and then ☐ and then ☐ and then ☐

26 × 26 × 10 × 10 × 10 = 676 000

▸ When a die is thrown four times, the number of possible outcomes is:

1st throw   2nd throw   3rd throw   4th throw

☐ and then ☐ and then ☐ and then ☐

6 × 6 × 6 × 6 = 1296

▸ Throwing four dice at the same time has the same number of outcomes as throwing them consecutively.

Die 1   Die 2   Die 3   Die 4

☐ and then ☐ and then ☐ and then ☐

6 × 6 × 6 × 6 = 1296

More challenging problems

As already mentioned, the multiplication principle rule is also known as the 'and then' rule. This means that if each box is filled from different sets, the sample space consists of elements in the order the boxes are filled. The multiplication principle gives the number of outcomes in the order specified.

EXAMPLE 3

How many exam grades can be made from a letter chosen from {A, B, C, D} followed by a digit chosen from {1, 2}?

Solution

There are two sets: {A, B, C, D} **and then** {1, 2}

Letter   Digit

$\square$ and then $\square$

4   ×   2 = 8

The sample space S = {A1, A2, B1, B2, C1, C2, D1, D2}

The elements in the sample space are in the order the multiplication principle is carried out: a letter followed by a digit A1, A2, B1,.... It does not give 1A, 2A, 1B,... as well.

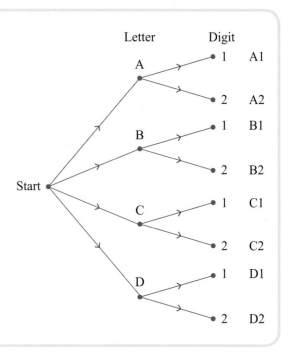

If the boxes are filled from a single set and no object is repeated, the sample space consists of all possible arrangements of the objects in the set. The multiplication principle gives the number of all possible arrangements of these objects.

EXAMPLE 4

How many ways can the symbols in the set {B, A, 5} be placed in order if no symbol is repeated?

Solution

Single set: {B, A, 5}

1st symbol   2nd symbol   3rd symbol

$\square$ and then $\square$ and then $\square$

3   ×   2   ×   1 = 6

There are only two choices for the second box because you cannot use what is in the first box as no symbol can be repeated.

S = {BA5, B5A, AB5, A5B, 5AB, 5BA}

This is the set of all possible arrangements of the symbols B, A, 5.

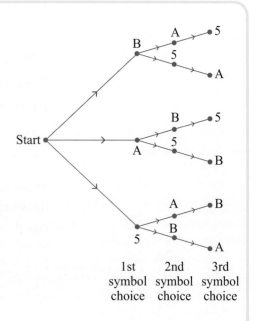

If there are restrictions or conditions on making choices, make sure to build them in first.

▶ How many four-digit numbers are there?

A four-digit number cannot start with a zero as it would then be a three-digit number.

Choose the first digit and then the second and then the third and then the fourth.

There are nine ways to fill the first digit. There are 10 ways to fill the second digit. There are 10 ways to fill the third digit. There are 10 ways to fill the fourth digit.

1st digit		2nd digit		3rd digit		4th digit
☐	and then	☐	and then	☐	and then	☐
9	×	10	×	10	×	10 = 9000

▶ How many of these four-digit numbers end in 3?

Put 3 in the last box and write the number of choices underneath it as 1.

Sometimes restrictions have to be taken into account as you go along.
This means later outcomes are **dependent** on earlier ones.

1st digit		2nd digit		3rd digit		4th digit
☐	and then	☐	and then	☐	and then	3
9	×	10	×	10	×	1 = 900

▶ How many four-digit numbers are there in which no digit is repeated?

First digit: Cannot have a zero (9 possibilities).

Second digit: Can have a zero but cannot be the same as the first digit (9 possibilities).

Third digit: Can have a zero but cannot be the same as the first two digits (8 possibilities).

Fourth digit: Can have a zero but cannot be the same as the first three digits (7 possibilities).

1st digit		2nd digit		3rd digit		4th digit
☐	and then	☐	and then	☐	and then	☐
9	×	9	×	8	×	7 = 4536

▶ How many four-digit numbers end in 3 with no repeated digits?

First digit: Cannot have a zero or a 3 (8 possibilities).

Second digit: Can have a zero but not a 3 and cannot be the same as the first digit (8 possibilities).

Third digit: Cannot be the same as the first two digits or have a 3 (7 possibilities).

Fourth digit: Has to be a 3 (1 possibility).

1st digit		2nd digit		3rd digit		4th digit
☐	and then	☐	and then	☐	and then	3
8	×	8	×	7	×	1 = 448

NOTE

A palindromic number reads the same backwards as forwards. For example, 1221 is a four-digit palindromic number.

▸ How many four-digit palindromic numbers are there?

First digit: Cannot have a zero (9 possibilities).

Second digit: Can have a zero and can also have what is in the first box as repeats are allowed (10 possibilities).

Third digit: Has to be the same as the second digit (1 possibility).

Fourth digit: Has to be the same as the first digit (1 possibility).

1st digit		2nd digit		3rd digit		4th digit
□	and then	□	and then	□	and then	□
9	×	10	×	1	×	1 = 90

EXAMPLE 5

How many three-letter arrangements can be made from the first six letters of the alphabet if:

(a) letters can be repeated,

(b) no letters can be repeated,

(c) adjacent letters cannot be alike?

Solution

(a)

1st letter		2nd letter		3rd letter
□	and then	□	and then	□
6	×	6	×	6 = 216

(b)

1st letter		2nd letter		3rd letter
□	and then	□	and then	□
6	×	5	×	4 = 120

(c)

1st letter		2nd letter		3rd letter
□	and then	□	and then	□
6	×	5	×	5 = 150

First letter: This box can be filled with any one of six letters (6 possibilities).

Second letter: This box can be filled with any one of five letters. It cannot be filled with what is in the first box as adjacent letters cannot be alike (5 possibilities).

Third letter: This box can be filled with any one of five letters. It cannot be filled with what is in the second box as adjacent letters cannot be alike (5 possibilities)

Look out for the word **replacement** in problems.

EXAMPLE 6

How many ways can a card be picked from a pack of cards **and then** another card be picked from the same pack without replacement?

Solution

1st card		2nd card
□	and then	□
52	×	51 = 2652

First card: This box can be filled with any one of 52 cards (52 possibilities).

Second card: This box can be filled with any one of 51 cards. The first card picked was not replaced (51 possibilities).

'And then' versus 'and'

WORKED EXAMPLE — 'And then' is the same as 'and'

How many outcomes are there to tossing a fair coin **and then** throwing a fair die?

Coin   Die

[   ]   and then   [   ]

2   ×   6 = 12

How many outcomes are there to tossing a fair coin **and** throwing a fair die at the same time?

Coin   Die

[   ]   and   [   ]

2   ×   6 = 12

It does not matter whether you toss the coin first and then roll the die or vice versa or do both operations at the same time. In all cases, you get the same number of outcomes.

However, sometimes 'and' and 'and then' are not the same.

WORKED EXAMPLE — 'And then' is not the same as 'and'

A code is formed from one digit and one letter. How many possible codes can be formed from:

(a) a digit **and then** a letter,

(b) a letter **and then** a digit,

(c) a digit **and** a letter?

(a)   D   L

[   ]   and then   [   ]

10   ×   26 = 260

(b)   L   D

[   ]   and then   [   ]

26   ×   10 = 260

(c) 'and' here means a digit and a letter in any order. Therefore, there are 520 possible codes.

EXERCISE 1

1. A bag A contains four balls coloured green (G), pink (P), red (R) and yellow (Y). Another bag B has three balls marked 1, 2 and 3. Copy and complete the table and write out the sample space of all possible outcomes of picking one ball from each bag.

		Bag B		
		1	2	3
Bag A	G	(G, 1)		
	P			
	R			(R, 3)
	Y		(Y, 2)	

2. A fair die is thrown and then a spinner with three equal sectors (A, B and C) is spun. Copy and complete the tree diagram for all possible outcomes and write out the sample space S of one trial of this experiment.

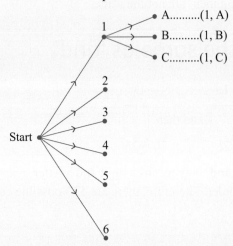

3. A student does a multiple-choice test consisting of five questions with two answers A or B for each question. Copy and complete the tree diagram and list all possible outcomes in the sample space S.

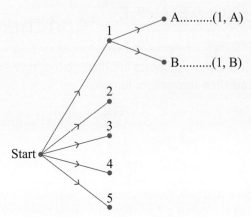

4. A student has to choose either French (F) or German (G) from Option X and one Science subject (Biology (B), Physics (P), Chemistry (C)) from option Y. Copy and complete the tree diagram. List all possible outcomes in a set S.

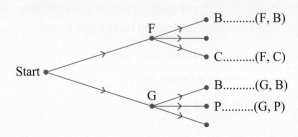

5. A girl tosses a fair coin three times. Copy and complete the tree diagram and list all possible outcomes in a set S (H = Head and T = Tail).

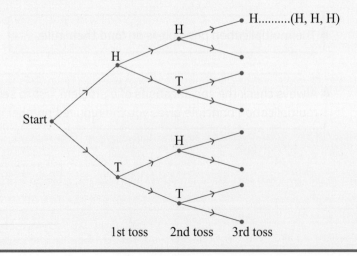

6. A girl can afford three different coloured tops (red, green, blue) and two different styles of dress (long and short). How many ways can she purchase one of each?

7. In a certain restaurant there are two starters (soup and paté), three main courses (lamb, beef, chicken) and two desserts (ice cream and trifle). How many ways can you have a three-course meal?

8. A student has a four-digit ATM card number. He knows the first two digits but is not sure of the second two. However, he knows that the third digit is a 5 or 6 and the fourth digit is a 1 or 9. How many ways can he guess the ATM number?

9. An ice cream shop has five flavours of ice cream (vanilla, chocolate, banana, strawberry and mint) and two toppings (nuts and flake). How many ways can you order a single flavour ice cream with a topping?

10. A man wishes to travel from Dublin to Peru. He knows he can connect to Peru by flying Aer Lingus to London Heathrow or Manchester from Dublin and then flying on to Peru via Paris or Berlin or Amsterdam. How many ways can he fly from Dublin to Peru?

11. A man throws a fair die with outcomes 1, 2, 3, 4, 5, 6 and then tosses a coin with outcomes head (H), tail (T). How many possible outcomes are there?

12. A woman wants to bet on a double by first picking a winner from a six-horse race (A, B, C, D, E, F) and then predicting the result of a match (win, loss, draw) for a team. How many ways can she pick one horse and predict a match result?

13. A dress designer has the seven colours of the rainbow to choose from (red, orange, yellow, green, blue, indigo, violet) and three designs (stripy, polka dot and flowery). How many different types of dress can he design?

14. A girl rolls two different fair dice once. How many outcomes are there?

15. ATM card numbers have four digits. How many possible ATM numbers are there?

16. A new car is available in five colours, three choices of interior and four engine sizes. How many options are there for choosing the car?

17. In a five-horse race, how many ways can the first three places be filled if there are no dead heats?

18. A year group has 100 pupils. How many ways can a president, a vice president, a treasurer and a secretary be chosen, given that no student can hold more than one post?

19. Two different fair dice and a fair coin are tossed together. How many possible outcomes are there?

20. A team of 15 has a captain and a vice captain. In how many ways can these positions be chosen?

21. A student has to choose Irish, English and Maths for the Leaving Certificate and four option subjects, one from each group X, Y, Z and W.

    Option X: French, German, Spanish

    Option Y: Physics, Chemistry, Technical Graphics

    Option Z: Art, Biology, Applied Maths

    Option W: Home Economics, Latin, Computer Science

    How many four-subject options are there?

22. How many ways can a red card be selected from one pack of playing cards and then a black card from another pack of playing cards?

NOTE

There are two red suits and two black suits in a normal pack of playing cards. There are 13 cards in each suit. The four suits are spades, clubs, hearts and diamonds.

23. How many ways can a red card be selected from one pack of playing cards and then a club from another pack of playing cards?

24. How many outcomes are there to tossing a fair coin and drawing a card from a normal pack of 52 playing cards?

25. A fair coin is tossed five times. How many possible outcomes are there?

26. How many five-digit numbers can be made from the digits 1, 2, 3, 4, 5 if:

   (a) no digit is repeated,

   (b) the numbers are even, with no repeated digits?

27. In a certain region, car licence plates start with a letter followed by four digits. How many different licences are possible if:

   (a) the first digit cannot be zero,

   (b) the letter cannot be 'F' or 'I' and the first digit cannot be zero?

28. How many:

   (a) three-digit numbers are there,

   (b) three-digit numbers are there with no repeated digits,

   (c) three-digit numbers are there that end in 5,

   (d) three-digit numbers are there that end in 5 with no repeated digits,

   (e) even three-digit numbers are there?

29. How many palindromic numbers are there:

   (a) from 10 to 99,

   (b) from 100 to 999,

   (c) from 1000 to 9999?

30. How many different results can you get when you roll:

   (a) a fair red die and then a fair blue die,

   (b) a fair blue die and then a fair red die,

   (c) a fair blue die and a fair red die at the same time?

31. A code consists of a letter and a digit. How many codes can be produced if the code consists of:

   (a) a letter followed by a digit,

   (b) a digit followed by a letter,

   (c) a digit and a letter?

32. Ten cards numbered 1 to 10 are placed in a box. How many ways can:

   (a) one card and then another card be picked in order,

   (b) two cards be picked at the same time?

33. One box has five red cards numbered 1 to 5 and six blue cards numbered 6 to 11. Another box has six red cards numbered 1 to 6 and five blue cards numbered 6 to 11. Two cards are picked, one from each box. How many ways can:

   (a) a red card be picked from the first box and then a blue card from the second box,

   (b) a blue card be picked from the first box and then a red card from the second box,

   (c) a red card from one box and a blue card from the other box be picked?

34. Four people pick a card from four different packs of 52 playing cards. In how many ways can all have cards of the same suit?

35. How many different results can you get when you:

   (a) roll a fair die and then spin a spinner with four equal sectors A, B, C, D as shown,

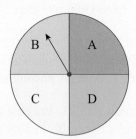

   (b) roll a fair die once and spin the spinner at the same time,

   (c) roll a fair die twice,

   (d) roll a fair die three times,

   (e) toss a fair coin five times?

36. How many five-digit palindromic numbers are there?

14.2 Permutations (arrangements)

> **KEY TERM**
>
> ⬆ A **permutation** of a set of objects is an arrangement with some or all of them in order.

WORKED EXAMPLE Calculating the number of outcomes of an arrangement

How many possible outcomes are there in a three-horse race (with no dead heats)?

This is the same as asking: 'In how many ways can three horses be arranged in order: first, second, third?'

If the horses are A, B and C, then the possible outcomes are ABC, ACB, BAC, BCA, CAB and CBA (six possible outcomes). This problem can be done using the multiplication principle with no repeats as it gives all arrangements of a set of objects.

1st place   2nd place   3rd place

☐   and then   ☐   and then   ☐

3   ×   2   ×   1 = 6 = 3!

3! is pronounced as '3 factorial' or 'factorial 3' and is shorthand notation for $3 \times 2 \times 1$.

Arrangements are concerned with placing objects in order: books on a shelf, people in seats, digits in numbers, letters in words, horses in a race.

EXAMPLE 7

How many ways can four cars be arranged in order in the four spaces of a car park?

Solution

1st place   2nd place   3rd place   4th place

☐   and then   ☐   and then   ☐   and then   ☐

4   ×   3   ×   2   ×   1 = 4! = 24

Permutations of different objects which are all used at the same time but none of which are repeated

The number of arrangements of n different objects in which objects are used and none repeated is given by the multiplication principle:

1st box   2nd box   3rd box nth box

☐   ☐   ☐   ☐

n × $(n-1)$ × $(n-2)$ × ... ×   1

The quantity $n \times (n-1) \times (n-2) \dots \times 1$ is known as $n!$

You can use your calculator to find $n!$

The number of arrangements of *n* different objects all used with no repetition of objects = *n*!

▶ How many arrangements are there of the letters of the word SPRAT if all letters are used and none are repeated?

SPRAT has 5 letters

1st letter	2nd letter	3rd letter	4th letter	5th letter
☐	☐	☐	☐	☐

$5 \times 4 \times 3 \times 2 \times 1 = 5! = 120$

Permutations of different objects which are not all used at the same time and none of which are repeated

The number of ways of arranging a number of different objects not all taken at the same time can also be done using the multiplication principle.

WORKED EXAMPLE
Understanding permutations

How many three-digit numbers can be made from the digits 1, 2, 3, 5, 6, 7, without repeating any digits.

6 digits

You need only three boxes as you are using three letters at a time.

1st digit	2nd digit	3rd digit
☐	☐	☐

$6 \times 5 \times 4 = 120$

The shorthand notation for $6 \times 5 \times 4$ is $^{6}P_{3}$.

$^{6}P_{3}$ is the number of ways of permuting (arranging in order) six different objects taken in groups of three with no repetition.

TIP

$^{n}P_{r}$ = the number of ways of permuting (arranging in order) *n* different objects taken *r* at a time with no repetition. The $^{n}P_{r}$ button on your calculator evaluates this quantity directly.
$^{n}P_{r} = n \times (n-1) \times (n-2) \times \ldots \times (n-r+1)$

▶ $^{7}P_{3} = 7 \times 6 \times 5 = 210$ $[n = 7, r = 3, n - r + 1 = 5]$
$^{7}P_{3} = 210$ [On a calculator]

▶ How many ways can 20 teams be placed 1st, 2nd, 3rd in a league?

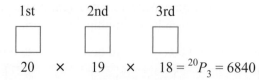

1st	2nd	3rd
☐	☐	☐

$20 \times 19 \times 18 = {}^{20}P_{3} = 6840$

More challenging arrangements questions

More challenging questions involve restrictions or conditions on the number of objects you can place in some or all of the boxes. You should always factor in the conditions/restrictions at the start of any problem.

EXAMPLE 8

How many arrangements are there of the letters of the word TIMBER:

(a) with E first and T last, all letters used and none repeated,

(b) with a vowel first, all letters used and none repeated,

(c) using three letters at a time with R first and no repeated letters?

Solution

TIMBER has 6 letters

(a) E and T are inserted in the first and sixth boxes. This means that there are only 4 letters left to fill the other boxes.

1st	2nd	3rd	4th	5th	6th
E					T
1 ×	4 ×	3 ×	2 ×	1 ×	1

Number of arrangements = 4! = 4 × 3 × 2 × 1 = 24

(b)

1st	2nd	3rd	4th	5th	6th
2 ×	5 ×	4 ×	3 ×	2 ×	1

There are two vowels so the first box has two possibilities.

Number of arrangements = 2 × 5! = 240

(c) 3 letters used at a time means 3 boxes.

1st	2nd	3rd
R		
1 ×	5 ×	4

Number of arrangements = $1 \times {}^5P_2 = 20$

Special cases

1. Togetherness

If some of the objects have to be placed together (adjacent, side by side), treat them as a single unit.

EXAMPLE 9

How many ways can six different books, A, B, C, D, E and F be arranged on a shelf if:

(a) all books are used,   **(b)** books A, B and C are together and all books are used?

Solution

(a) A, B, C, D, E, F

1st place	2nd place	3rd place	4th place	5th place	6th place
6 ×	5 ×	4 ×	3 ×	2 ×	1 = 6! = 720

(b) Put (ABC) together as a single entity to give four different objects: (ABC), D, E, F. Permute the four objects **and then** permute ABC separately.

Number of ways of permuting (ABC), D, E, F:

1st place	2nd place	3rd place	4th place
4 ×	3 ×	2 ×	1 = 4!

Number of ways of permuting ABC among themselves = 3!

Therefore, the total number of ways = 4! × 3! = 144

2. Sets in which not all the objects are different to begin with

EXAMPLE 10

How many ways can all of the letters AABCAAA be arranged among themselves?

Solution

This set has five As: ☐A☐A☐A☐A☐A☐

There are six ways of inserting B into this group of As as there are six available spaces. When B is inserted, there are six letters with seven available spaces. So C can now be inserted in 7 ways.

Number of ways = $6 \times 7 = 42 = \dfrac{7!}{5!} = \dfrac{\text{(Total number of letters)!}}{\text{(Number of letters which are alike)!}}$

TIP

The number of arrangements among themselves of all n objects, p alike of one kind, q alike of another kind $= \dfrac{n!}{p!q!}$

EXAMPLE 11

How many ways can all of the letters of the word MISSISSIPPI be arranged among themselves?

Solution

Number of ways $= \overset{\text{All}}{\dfrac{11!}{\underset{\text{(4S) (2P) (4I)}}{4!\,2!\,4!}}} = 34\,650$

EXAMPLE 12

How many ways can tossing a coin five times give 3 heads (H) and 2 tails (T)?

Solution

This is just the number of arrangements of HHHTT

$= \dfrac{5!}{3!\,2!} = 10$

EXERCISE 2

1. **(a)** How many ways can A, B, C, D, E be arranged in order, if all letters are used and none are repeated?

   (b) How many ways can A, B, C, D, E, F be arranged in order, using four letters at a time with no repetitions?

   (c) How many ways can seven pupils be arranged in order at seven desks in the front row?

   (d) How many ways can the digits 1, 2, 4, 7 be arranged in order, if all digits are used and none are repeated?

   (e) How many ways can 1, 5, 7, 8, 6 be arranged in order, using three at a time with no repetitions?

   (f) How many ways can seven rowers finish a race in first, second and third places (with no dead heats)?

   (g) How many ways can 12 horses finish a race in first, second and third places (with no dead heats)?

   (h) How many ways can 10 different books be arranged in order on a shelf?

   (i) How many ways can nine different DVD titles be arranged on a shelf?

   (j) How many ways can nine different DVD titles be arranged on a shelf if three particular titles are always grouped together?

2. How many ways can eight athletes finish in the first five places in a race (with no dead heats)?

3. The colours of five discs are red (R), blue (B), green (G), white (W) and pink (P). How many ways can these be arranged in groups of four if no colour is repeated?

4. Four people are seated in 8 seats in a row. How many ways can they be arranged in these seats?

5. How many four-digit ATM PINs can be made from the digits 0, 1, 2, 3, 4, 5, 6, 7, 8, 9 if no digit is repeated?

6. How many five-digit numbers can be made from the digits 1, 3, 4, 6, 7, 8, 9 if no digit is repeated?

7. How many six-letter code words can be made from the first ten letters of the alphabet if no letter is repeated?

8. There are 40 horses running in a Grand National. How many ways can the first three places be filled by the horses?

9. How many ways can three cars occupy ten parallel parking spaces?

10. How many ways can six different books be arranged on a shelf if only four are on the shelf at any one time and the other two are beside the bed?

11. **(a)** How many four-digit numbers can be formed from 3, 7, 8, 9 if no digit can be repeated?

    (b) How many of these digits are greater than 5000?

    (c) How many of these digits begin with 8?

    (d) How many of these digits are even?

12. How many arrangements are there of the following groups of letters when all letters are used once?

    (a) ABBA   **(d)** WAGAWAGA

    (b) BUBBLES   **(e)** ROCOCCO

    (c) MASSACHUSETTS

13. How many ways can 10 coins be stacked in a pile if there are four one-cent, three 20-cent and three 50-cent coins?

14. How many ways can six identical green discs, four identical yellow discs and five identical blue discs be stacked in a pile?

15. A coin is tossed four times. How many ways can two heads and two tails result in any order?

16. Six discs of equal size are stacked one on top of the other. There are two identical red discs and one each of yellow, green, white and blue. How many ways can they be stacked if the two red discs must be either at the top or at the bottom of the pile?

17. How many arrangements are there of the letters POLICE:

    (a) if all letters are used and none are repeated,

    (b) if all letters are used and none are repeated with a vowel as the last letter,

    (c) if four letters are used at a time and none are repeated,

    (d) if four letters are used at a time and none are repeated, with L as the last letter?

18. How many arrangements are there of the letters VARIED:

    (a) if all letters are used and none are repeated,

    (b) if all letters are used and none are repeated and with AE side by side, in that order,

    (c) if all letters are used and none are repeated and with AE side by side,

    (d) if all letters are used and none are repeated and with AE not side by side?

19. Four boys and five girls are to be arranged at nine desks in a row. How many arrangements are there if:

    (a) there are no restrictions,

    (b) Mary and Anne are adjacent (side by side),

    (c) Peter and Joe must be separated,

    (d) the order must be alternate boys and girls?

20. How many arrangements are there of the letters of the word TRIANGLE:

  (a) if all letters are used and none are repeated,

  (b) if three letters are used at a time and none are repeated,

  (c) if all letters are used and none are repeated, with the vowels adjacent to each other,

  (d) if all letters are used and none are repeated, with all three vowels not adjacent to each other?

21. A school staff room shelf has five different Maths books, four different English books and three different History books on it. How many ways can these be arranged if:

  (a) there are no restrictions,

  (b) the three History books are side by side?

22. Find the number of ways in which n boys can be arranged in order that:

  (a) Pat and John are adjacent to each other,

  (b) Pat and John are not side by side.

23. How many natural numbers can be formed from the digits 1, 2, 3, 4, 5 if no digit is repeated?

24. How many ways can the letters of the word LEAVING be placed in order with:

  (a) all letters used and none repeated,

  (b) four letters used at a time and none repeated,

  (c) 'A' first, 'L' last, all letters used and none repeated,

  (d) 'A' first, 'L' last, four letters used at a time and none repeated?

25. Let x equal the number of ways A, B, C, D, E can be arranged taken three at a time with no repeated letters. Write down x.

Write out all the ways three letters can be grouped together from A, B, C, D, E. Let y equal the number of these groups.

Show that $x = y \times 3!$

14.3 Combinations (selections)

A combination is a selection of a number of objects from a set of these objects without putting them in order.

> **NOTE**
>
> ↑ **Order** is not important for **selections.**

WORKED EXAMPLE Understanding combinations

Suppose a committee of four people is to be selected from seven people. How many ways can this be done? Unlike arrangements, the order of the people selected is irrelevant. You just need to fill four places. This problem can be solved using the multiplication principle as follows:

Number of arrangements of 7 different objects, taking 4 at a time		Number of ways of selecting 4 different objects from 7	and then	Number of ways of arranging these 4 objects among themselves
$^7P_4$	$=$	x	$\times$	$4!$

$$^7P_4 = x \times 4!$$

$$x = \frac{^7P_4}{4!} = \frac{7 \times 6 \times 5 \times 4}{4 \times 3 \times 2 \times 1} = 35$$

The shorthand notation for $\dfrac{^7P_4}{4!} = \dfrac{7 \times 6 \times 5 \times 4}{4 \times 3 \times 2 \times 1}$ is $^7C_4$.

$^7C_4$ is the number of ways of (combining) selecting seven different objects in groups of four with no regard to the order of the objects in the group.

The ^nC_r button on your calculator evaluates this quantity.

ACTIVITY 4

ACTION
Working with combinations

OBJECTIVE
To learn how to work with combinations with and without your calculator

▸ $^8C_3 = \dfrac{8 \times 7 \times 6}{3 \times 2 \times 1} = 56$

$^8C_3 = 56$ [Using a calculator]

Combinations are used to select groups of objects in which the order of the objects in the group is irrelevant.

Suppose you need to select a team of five basketball players from 11 players. The team ABCDE is the same as the team BDECA.

▸ How many ways can six numbers be selected from 42 numbers in a Lotto draw?

Number of ways to select six numbers from 42 numbers = $^{42}C_6 = 5\,245\,786$.

You do not have to get the six numbers in order. If you did, the number of outcomes would increase dramatically to $^{42}C_6 \times 6! = 3\,776\,965\,920$

Who would ever win the Lotto if you had to get the order right as well?

> The number of ways of selecting r different objects from n different objects is given by: $\dfrac{^nP_r}{r!} = {}^nC_r$

EXAMPLE 13

There are 20 teams in the Premier League. How many matches must be organised if:

(a) each team plays each other team once,

(b) each team plays each other team twice?

Solution

Matches are just selections in groups of two.

(a) 20 teams selected in pairs = Number of matches
= $^{20}C_2 = 190$

(b) $^{20}C_2 \times 2 = 380$

▶ In how many ways can a poker hand of five be selected from a normal pack of 52 playing cards? (Hint: a poker hand consists of five cards.)

$$^{52}C_5 = 2\,598\,960$$

EXAMPLE 14

In a Garda station, three gardaí are chosen for traffic duty daily except on Saturday and Sunday. How many weeks elapse before the same three gardaí are on traffic duty if there are 12 gardaí in the station?

Solution

Three gardaí can be selected from 12 in $^{12}C_3 = 220$ ways.

Five teams of three used weekly $\Rightarrow \dfrac{220}{5} = 44$ weeks before all selections are used up.

More challenging problems on selections

Always build in any obvious restrictions at the start.

EXAMPLE 15

Seven men and six women go up for an election to a five-person committee. How many ways can the members of the committee be made up if:

(a) there are no restrictions,

(b) Ms O'Brien must be on the committee,

(c) Mr Kelly cannot be on the committee due to a conflict of interest,

(d) there must be two men and three women on the committee?

Solution

(a) No restrictions:

7M	6W
5 Places	

Number of ways = $^{13}C_5 = 1287$

(b) One place is reserved for a particular woman so there are only 5 women left from which to choose:

7M	5W
4 Places	

Number of ways = $^{12}C_4 = 495$

(c) A particular man has to be removed from the candidates:

6M	6W
5 Places	

Number of ways = $^{12}C_5 = 792$

(d) There must be two men and three women on the committee:

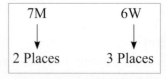

Number of ways = $^{7}C_2 \times {}^{6}C_3 = 420$

TIP

When you come across the term 'at least', you must consider all possibilities.

EXAMPLE 16

How many committees of six can be selected from six men and seven women if there must be at least four women on the committee?

Solution

6M	7W
6 Places	

At least four women: Consider all possibilities.

2 Men and 4 Women = $^6C_2 \times {}^7C_4 = 525$

or

1 Man and 5 Women = $^6C_1 \times {}^7C_5 = 126$

or

0 Men and 6 Women = $^6C_0 \times {}^7C_6 = 7$

Number of committees: 658

TIP

↑ Subgroups: You may have to take account of restrictions as you go along.

EXAMPLE 17

From a class of 13, how many ways can groups of 3, 4 and 6 be formed?

Solution

13
3

and then

10
4

and then

6
6

Group 3   Group 4   Group 6

Number of groups = $^{13}C_3 \times {}^{10}C_4 \times {}^6C_6 = 60\,060$

Geometrical figures

Lines are formed by selecting points in pairs.

Triangles are formed by selecting points in threes.

Quadrilaterals are formed by selecting points in fours.

ACTIVITY 5

ACTION
More counting practice

OBJECTIVE
To master the techniques of counting

EXAMPLE 18

How many triangles can be formed from six points, A, B, C, D, E, F, no three of which are collinear?

Solution

6 points, select groups of 3 where order is irrelevant.

6 points
3

$^6C_3 = 20$

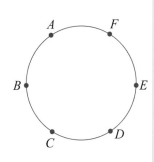

EXERCISE 3

1. (a) How many football teams of 11 can be selected from 15 players?

    (b) How many committees of three can be selected from five boys and five girls?

    (c) How many ways can a student select seven subjects from ten subjects?

    (d) How many committees of seven can be selected from seven men and eight women?

    (e) How many ways can a cabinet of 15 ministers be selected from 70 elected deputies?

    (f) How many ways can a DJ select 20 songs from 50 songs to play at a wedding?

    (g) How many ways can three toppings be chosen from 12 toppings for a pizza in a pizza parlour?

    (h) How many rosters can a supermarket manager organise for his 14 staff if each roster consists of five staff?

    (i) How many ways can a two-card hand be dealt from a normal pack of 52 playing cards?

2. An inter-schools chess competition has 11 teams. How many matches must be organised if each team plays the other once?

3. In how many ways can a student select seven subjects from ten subjects if Irish, English and Maths must be included in the seven?

4. (a) How many subsets of five elements can be made from the set $A = \{E, F, G, H, I, J, K, L\}$?

    (b) How many of these subsets include H and I?

    (c) How many of these subsets do not include F?

5. How many committees of six can be formed from eight men and seven women including Peter O'Brien and Mary Burke:

    (a) if there are no restrictions,

    (b) if Peter O'Brien and Mary Burke are both on the committee,

    (c) if neither Peter O'Brien nor Mary Burke is on the committee,

    (d) if Mary Burke is on but Peter O'Brien is off?

6. How many five-card hands can be dealt from a pack of 52 playing cards? How many of these contain:

    (a) the Ace of hearts

    (b) the Queen of hearts and the Queen of spades

    (c) five hearts?

7. A four-person debating team is selected from a class of ten boys and eight girls. How many teams can be selected if:

    (a) there are no restrictions,

    (b) there must be two boys and two girls on the team

    (c) the team must all be female?

8. A board of six is to be selected from five men and seven women. How many ways can the board be formed if:

    (a) there are no restrictions,

    (b) there must be one man and five women on the board,

    (c) there must be three men and three women on the board,

    (d) there must be more women than men (0 men not allowed) on the board?

9. A bag contains three black discs and four red discs all of different sizes. In how many ways can four discs be selected, if:

   (a) at least one disc is black,

   (b) at least one disc is red?

10. A committee of five is to be selected from five women and six men. How many ways can this be done if there must be at least two women on the committee?

11. How many ways can seven players be split into two teams:

    (a) one of 5 and one of 2,

    (b) one of 4 and one of 3?

12. A soccer team of 11 players is to be selected from 20 girls. Of these, four can only play in goal and ten can only play as midfielders. How many teams can be formed of one goalkeeper, five midfielders and five others?

13. A group of 20 men is to be divided into three groups to undergo drug tests. If there are four men in group A, six men in group B and ten men in group C, how many ways can these groups be formed?

14. How many different 13-card hands of five spades, four hearts, three diamonds and one club can be made from a normal pack of 52 playing cards?

15. How many chords can be drawn using the six points on the circle?

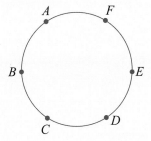

16. How many triangles can be formed from the seven points on the circle shown? How many of these triangles contain the point F?

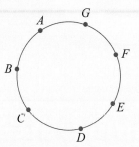

17. How many triangles like [AE] can be formed taking one point from line l_1 and two points from line l_2, which is parallel to l_1?

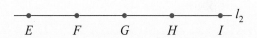

18. There are five points on one line and six points on a parallel line. What is the maximum number of triangles that can be formed from these points?

19. How many diagonals like [AE] does a regular octagon $ABCDEFGH$ have?

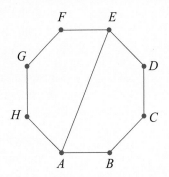

20. How many diagonals does a regular n-sided polygon have?

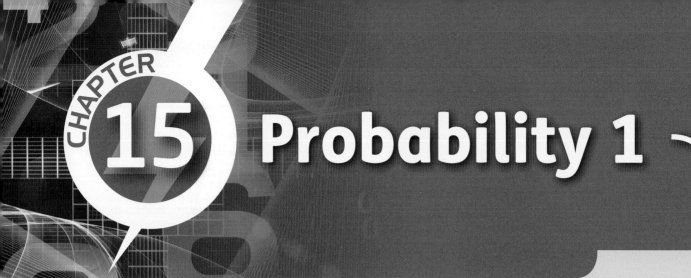

Learning Outcomes

- To become familiar with the language of probability.
- To understand that carrying out many trials (experimental probability) leads to predictable results in the long run (theoretical probability).
- To use Venn diagrams to help you to solve probability problems.
- To understand how to use probability rules to solve more challenging probability problems.

15.1 Experimental probability

The idea of probability

You will have seen statements such as the following:

- The probability of success of a drug treatment is 0·58.
- The chance of living beyond 60 years of age in Yemen is less than 1 in 5.
- The likelihood of rain in Wicklow tomorrow is 28%.

These statements of **chance** or **likelihood** or **probability** are all based on experimental observation.

> **KEY TERM**
>
> **Probability** is the mathematics of chance behaviour and is based on experimental observation.

Probability describes mathematically how likely it is that some event will happen.

Certainty and uncertainty

Can you think of things that are certain to occur?

Can you think of events that are uncertain?

Can you think of events that are certain not to occur?

Here are some examples:

Certain to occur	Uncertain	Certain not to happen
Christmas day will fall on 25 December.	You will get married.	Ireland will host the next Olympics.
The sun will rise tomorrow.	An Icelandic volcano will erupt next week.	The Earth will become flat.
When you toss a fair coin, you will get a head or a tail.	The Wexford hurling team will win its next match.	A triangle exists which has four sides.

Less/more/equally likely

Some results are more likely to occur than others. It is important to be able to decide which results are more likely or less likely to occur than others.

What number is most likely to occur when you throw a fair die once? There is complete randomness in this case, as all outcomes are equally likely.

▸ In the Lotto, are any six numbers equally likely?

Yes. The chances of getting the six numbers 1, 2, 3, 4, 5, 6 are as likely as getting the numbers 3, 17, 21, 35, 40, 41.

> Two results are **equally likely** if they have the same chance of happening.

▸ The chance of landing on **red** on the spinner shown is not the same as the chance of landing on **blue.** Landing on red or landing on blue are not equally likely results of a single trial of the experiment of spinning the arrow.

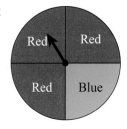

An experiment
Tossing a coin once

As you learned in Chapter 14, when you carry out a trial of an experiment, the set of all possible outcomes (results) is known as the **sample space** S of the experiment.

For tossing a coin once, the sample space is the set $S = \{H, T\}$ where H = head and T = tail.

For the experiment of tossing a coin once, there are only two possible results that can occur in all. The number of elements in the sample space is two.

The results are equally likely because of the symmetry of the coin, assuming it is a fair (unbiased) coin.

Now consider the likelihood (probability) of tossing a head (H) in one toss of a fair coin. This **desired outcome** is put in a set known as an **event** E and, in this case, is given by the set $E = \{H\}$. The number of elements in the event is 1.

As you might expect, the probability of tossing a head in one toss of a fair coin is given by $P(H) = \frac{1}{2}$, because on average 50% of the tosses will result in a head if the coin is tossed many times.

Tossing a coin more than once

Suppose you toss a fair coin many times. This is an experiment consisting of many trials. You cannot predict what will happen at the next toss because each trial is **independent** of the previous one. This means the outcomes of one trial do not influence the outcomes of the next trial.

If you toss a coin many times and plot a graph of the proportion of heads (number of heads divided by the number of tosses) against the number of tosses, the graph will look like the following:

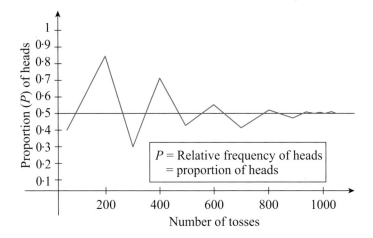

Although chance behaviour is unpredictable in the short run, it is regular and predictable in the long run. This remarkable fact is the basis of probability.

As the number of tosses increases, the proportion of heads (relative frequency) gets closer and closer to $\frac{1}{2}$.

Probability is experimental. It is based on observation. Probability describes what happens in a large number of trials of an experiment.

KEY TERM

The **probability** $P(E)$ of any event E of a random phenomenon occurring is the proportion of times (relative frequency) the outcomes of an event would occur in a very long series of trials (repetitions).

$P(E)$ = Relative frequency of the outcomes of an event as the total frequency becomes very large.

$$\therefore P(E) = \frac{\text{Frequency of outcomes of the event in many trials}}{\text{Total number of trials (total frequency)}}$$

In theoretical probability, the result of such an experiment over many trials is applied to a single trial.

ACTIVITY 9

ACTION
Rolling one die many times

OBJECTIVE
To carry out an experiment of rolling one die many times to find the theoretical probability of finding a particular outcome

WORKED EXAMPLE

Rolling a die many times

In 600 trials of rolling a die the following table was drawn up:

Outcome x	Frequency f	Relative Frequency
1	102	$\dfrac{102}{600}$
2	105	$\dfrac{105}{600}$
3	98	$\dfrac{98}{600}$
4	98	$\dfrac{98}{600}$
5	95	$\dfrac{95}{600}$
6	102	$\dfrac{102}{600}$
	600	

Total frequency = 600 = total number of trials

Probability of rolling a **6** $= \dfrac{102}{600} = 0{\cdot}17 \approx \dfrac{1}{6}$

As total frequency $\to \infty$, $P \to \dfrac{1}{6}$

As the frequency increases, the probability of rolling a 6 approaches $\dfrac{1}{6}$.

Real-life probability

In everyday life, it is important to know the chance or likelihood (probability) of an event occurring in order to make informed decisions.

- A medical procedure with a 95% success rate is worth consideration.
- An investment which gives a profitable return 20% of the time does not sound too attractive.

Banks, insurance companies and investment companies use probabilities to determine loans, premiums and risks.

The probability scale

ACTIVITY 10

ACTION
Understanding real-life probability

OBJECTIVE
To understand how probability applies to real-life situations so you can become a more informed citizen

Since a probability P is a proportion of a total number of trials it is always a **proper fraction**.

$$P = \frac{\text{Number of trials in which the outcomes of an event occur}}{\text{Total number of trials}}$$

TIP

Probability P is always a number between 0 and 1: $0 \leq P \leq 1$

As a percentage: $0\% \leq P\% \leq 100\%$.

All probabilities can be assigned a number between 0 and 1.

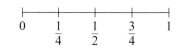

$P = 1$ means complete certainty (certain to happen).

$P = 0$ means impossible (cannot happen).

$P > 0{\cdot}5$ means more likely to happen than not.

ACTIVITY 11

ACTION
Working with probability scales

OBJECTIVE
To work with the probability scale, numbered from 0 to 1

▶ The weather forecast states that there is a 20% chance of rain next Wednesday. This means that on the basis of historical data it rains 1 in every 5 days with similar climate conditions to next Wednesday.

Expected frequency

If a fair coin is tossed 1000 times, you would expect to get about 500 heads because on average you would expect that 1 in 2 tosses would give you a head.

Expected frequency of a head = Probability of a head × Number of trials

$$500 \quad = \quad \frac{1}{2} \quad \times \quad 1000$$

> Expected frequency of an event = Probability of the event × Number of trials

WORKED EXAMPLE

Expected frequency

A spinner has four unequal segments coloured red, blue, green and pink. When the spinner is spun 200 times, the frequency of stopping at each colour is shown in the table.

Colour	Red	Blue	Green	Pink
Frequency	20	40	70	70
Relative frequency	$\frac{20}{200}$	$\frac{40}{200}$	$\frac{70}{200}$	$\frac{70}{200}$
Probability P	0·1	0·2	0·35	0·35

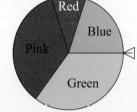

This table is known as a **probability distribution** (relative frequency distribution).

The sum of the probabilities $0·1 + 0·2 + 0·35 + 0·35 = 1$.

This must always be the case as spinning a red or a blue or a green or a pink is a certainty.

If the spinner is spun 520 times, the expected frequency of stopping on a pink is found as follows:

Expected frequency = Probability of stopping on a pink × Number of trials = $0·35 × 520 = 182$

> **TIP**
> In a probability distribution, the sum of the probabilities of all possible outcomes must add to 1.

EXAMPLE 1

A die is biased. The probability it will land on the numbers 1 to 6 is given by the probability distribution table below:

Number	1	2	3	4	5	6
Probability P	0·1	0·3	x	0·1	0·2	0·05

(a) Find x.

(b) Find the probability of rolling a number less than or equal to **5.**

(c) Find the number of times you would expect to roll a **3** in 620 rolls.

Solution

(a) $x = 1 - (0·1 + 0·3 + 0·1 + 0·2 + 0·05) = 0·25$

(b) The probability of a number less than or equal to **5** = $0·1 + 0·3 + 0·25 + 0·1 + 0·2 = 0·95$

(c) The number of times you would expect it to land on a **3** in 620 rolls = $0·25 × 620 = 155$

The language of probability

To explain the terms used in probability, consider the **experiment** of 'tossing two fair coins'.

The single act of tossing two fair coins once is known as a **trial** of the experiment of 'tossing two fair coins'. An experiment consists of one or more trials.

If you were to toss two coins 50 times, the experiment would have 50 trials.

The following table shows all possible **outcomes** of a trial of the experiment of 'tossing two fair coins'.

Coin B

		H	T
Coin A	H	(H, H)	(H, T)
	T	(T, H)	(T, T)

[H = head, T = tail]

KEY TERM

An **outcome** of an experiment is each distinct possible result of one trial of the experiment.

There are four possible outcomes of a trial of the experiment of tossing two fair coins. (T, H) is one possible outcome.

KEY TERM

The set S of all possible distinct outcomes of a single trial of an experiment is known as the **sample space** of the experiment.

$S = \{(H, H), (H, T), (T, H), (T, T)\}$

KEY TERM

An **event** E is a set of desired distinct outcomes of a single trial of an experiment and is a subset of the sample space.

The event of tossing a head and a tail is the set $E = \{(H, T), (T, H)\}$. It is a set consisting of two outcomes of the four outcomes listed in S.

If the two coins were tossed 100 times (100 trials), you might expect to toss a head and a tail in about 50 of these trials.

EXERCISE 4

1. An unbiased coin is tossed.

   (a) How many possible outcomes are there?

   (b) What are the outcomes?

   (c) Write down the sample space S.

   (d) Are the outcomes equally likely?

   (e) Why?

   (f) What is your estimate of the number of heads which would result in 600 tosses of the coin?

   (g) What is the probability of not tossing a head in one throw of a coin?

(h) Can you think of any other real-life situations which would have only two possible outcomes?

(i) What is your estimate of the probability of tossing a tail in one toss of the coin?

2. A spinner has three quadrants of a circle coloured red and one coloured blue. The three red quadrants are labelled RA, RB, RC and the blue quadrant is labelled B.

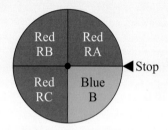

(a) Write out the sample spaces S for stopping on a quadrant.

(b) How many elements are in S?

(c) Write out the event E of stopping on a red.

(d) How many elements are in E?

3. A spinner has three quadrants of a circle coloured red and one coloured blue.

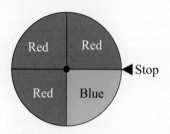

(a) Is stopping on a blue equally as likely as stopping on a red?

(b) What can you say about the spinner in terms of bias?

(c) In 760 spins, how often would the spinner stop on a red?

(d) What is the relative frequency of a red?

(e) What is the probability of stopping on a blue?

4. The table below shows the outcomes of the experiment of rolling two unbiased dice A and B.

Die B

	1	2	3	4	5	6
1	(1, 1)	(1, 2)	(1, 3)	(1, 4)	(1, 5)	(1, 6)
2	(2, 1)	(2, 2)	(2, 3)	(2, 4)	(2, 5)	(2, 6)
3	(3, 1)	(3, 2)	(3, 3)	(3, 4)	(3, 5)	(3, 6)
4	(4, 1)	(4, 2)	(4, 3)	(4, 4)	(4, 5)	(4, 6)
5	(5, 1)	(5, 2)	(5, 3)	(5, 4)	(5, 5)	(5, 6)
6	(6, 1)	(6, 2)	(6, 3)	(6, 4)	(6, 5)	(6, 6)

(Die A labels the rows)

(a) How many elements are in the sample space S of this experiment?

(b) Write out the following events:

    (i) rolling a double (two numbers which are the same),

    (ii) rolling a sum equal to 9,

    (iii) rolling a sum which is prime.

(c) What is your estimate of the probability of rolling a sum less than or equal to 3?

(d) In 180 rolls of the two dice, how many of these rolls would result in a sum less than or equal to 3?

5. Use the multiplication principle to predict the number of outcomes of the following experiments:

    (a) three unbiased coins are tossed,

    (b) three unbiased dice are rolled,

    (c) two coins are tossed and one die is rolled.

6. The table shows all the outcomes of rolling a fair die and tossing a fair coin once.

(a) Write out the sample space *S* of this experiment.

(b) How many outcomes are there in the sample space?

(c) If there are six outcomes to rolling a die and two outcomes to tossing a coin, find the number of outcomes to rolling a die once and then tossing a coin once:

(i) using a tree diagram,

(ii) using the multiplication principle in counting.

	Coin	
	H	**T**
1	(1, H)	(1, T)
2	(2, H)	(2, T)
3	(3, H)	(3, T)
4	(4, H)	(4, T)
5	(5, H)	(5, T)
6	(6, H)	(6, T)

Die

(d) Are all outcomes equally likely?

(e) Write out the event of tossing a head. How many outcomes are in this event?

(f) Write out the event of rolling an even number and tossing a head. How many outcomes are in this event?

(g) Write out the event of rolling a number less than 5 and tossing a tail. How many outcomes are in this event?

(h) The die is rolled and the coin is tossed together 1000 times. How many trials of the experiment of rolling a die and tossing a coin have taken place?

(i) The graphs below are the results of many trials of rolling a die and tossing a coin. Identify each one with a possible event in this experiment.

(i)

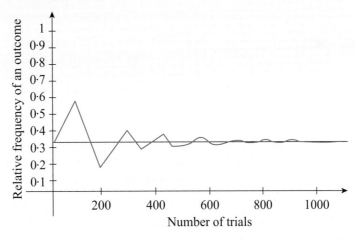

(ii)

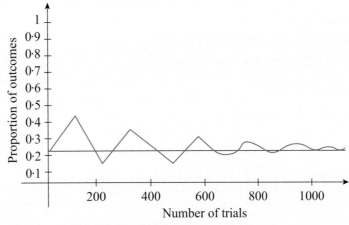

(iii)

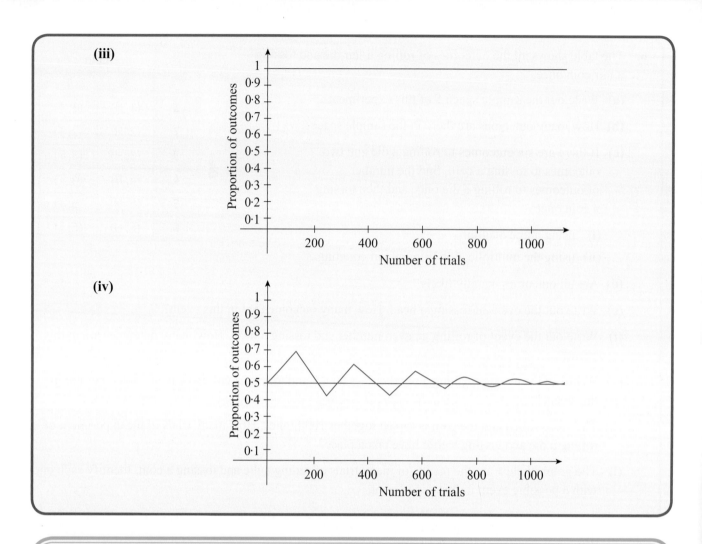

(iv)

15.2 Theoretical probability

ACTIVITY 12

ACTION
Moving from experimental to theoretical probability

OBJECTIVE
To develop a deeper understanding of theoretical probability by answering questions on the outcomes that result from rolling a die

The probability ratio

In experiments such as tossing coins and rolling dice, we carried out many trials and listed the results (outcomes) to estimate the probability of an event. This is known as **experimental** or **empirical probability.**

> **KEY TERM**
> The set S of all possible distinct outcomes of a trial of an experiment is known as the **sample space** of the experiment.

In theoretical probability, rolling a die produces six equally likely outcomes once the die is fair (not loaded). All numbers 1, 2, 3, 4, 5, 6 are equally like because there is no reason to assume any number will appear more often than another.

S = Set of all possible outcomes of a single trial an experiment.

$\therefore S = \{1, 2, 3, 4, 5, 6\}$

> **KEY TERM**
> An **event** E is the set of desired distinct outcomes of a trial of an experiment and is a subset of the sample space.

E = Set of desired outcomes of a trial of an experiment

▶ In rolling a die once, the event of rolling a 6 is $E = \{6\}$ but the event of rolling an odd number is $E = \{1, 3, 5\}$.

Experimental vs theoretical probability

In our experiments, we discovered that in all cases the likelihood (probability) P of an event E is given by:

$P(E)$ = Probability of event E = Relative frequency of the event

$$= \frac{\text{Frequency of the event}}{\text{Total frequency}}$$

We have also discovered that in all our experiments, as the number of trials increases, the relative frequency gets closer and closer to our predicted theoretical probability.

Assuming the outcomes of a trial are equally likely:

$P(E)$ = The value the relative frequency tends to in an infinite number of trials

$$= \frac{\text{Number of times the event occurs}}{\text{Total number of possible outcomes}}$$

$$= \frac{\text{Number of desired outcomes}}{\text{Total number of outcomes}}$$

$$= \frac{\text{Number of elements in the event}}{\text{Number of elements in the sample}} = \frac{\#(E)}{\#(S)}$$

$$\boxed{P(E) = \frac{\text{Number of desired outcomes}}{\text{Total number of outcomes}} = \frac{\#(E)}{\#(S)}}$$

> **TIP**
> ▲ Remember $0 \le P(E) \le 1$ because the minimum value of $\#(E) = 0$ and the maximum value of $\#(E) = \#(S)$.

ACTIVITY 13

ACTION
Knowing your playing cards

OBJECTIVE
To have a knowledge of playing cards, as many probability problems involve cards

EXAMPLE 2

(a) What is the probability P of throwing a 2 or a 6 in one throw of a die?

(b) What is the probability Q of not throwing a 2 or a 6 in one throw of a die?

Solution

(a) $S = \{1, 2, 3, 4, 5, 6\}$

$E = \{2, 6\}$

$\#(S) = 6, \#(E) = 2$

$$P = \frac{\text{Number of desired outcomes}}{\text{Total number of outcomes}} = \frac{2}{6} = \frac{1}{3}$$

(b) $S = \{1, 2, 3, 4, 5, 6\}$

$E = \{1, 3, 4, 5\}$

$\#(S) = 6, \#(E) = 4$

$$Q = \frac{\text{Number of desired outcomes}}{\text{Total number of outcomes}} = \frac{4}{6} = \frac{2}{3} = 1 - \frac{1}{3} = 1 - P$$

ACTIVITY 14

ACTION
Probability with playing cards

OBJECTIVE
To combine your knowledge of playing cards to calculate the probability of drawing certain cards

TIP
When picking out discs, balls, cards, etc. from a container, we assume in all cases that these objects are distinguishable. This means they are not identical.

EXAMPLE 3

From a normal pack of 52 playing cards, what is the probability of picking:

(a) a diamond

(b) a red card

(c) a King

(d) a red picture card

(e) a King or a diamond?

Solution

S = Set of all 52 cards

(a) E = Set of 13 diamonds

$$P(\text{Diamond}) = \frac{13}{52} = \frac{1}{4}$$

(b) E = Set of 26 red cards

$$P(\text{Red}) = \frac{26}{52} = \frac{1}{2}$$

(c) E = Set of 4 Kings

$$P(\text{King}) = \frac{4}{52} = \frac{1}{13}$$

(d) E = Set of 6 red picture cards

$$P(\text{Red picture card}) = \frac{6}{52} = \frac{3}{26}$$

(e) E = Set of 13 diamonds and 3 Kings that are not diamonds

$$P(\text{Diamond or King}) = \frac{16}{52} = \frac{4}{13}$$

EXAMPLE 4

In a class of 25 pupils, there are 15 boys and 10 girls. If a pupil is chosen at random, what is the probability the pupil is a girl?

Solution

S = {B1, B2, B3, B4, B5, B6, B7, B8, B9, B10, B11, B12, B13, B14, B15, G1, G2, G3, G4, G5, G6, G7, G8, G9, G10} where B = boy and G = girl.

There are 25 objects in this sample space.

E = {G1, G2, G3, G4, G5, G6, G7, G8, G9, G10}

$$P = \frac{10}{25} = \frac{2}{5}$$

The following example gives you a trick to help you deal with bias.

EXAMPLE 5

A spinner has eight equal sectors with five red sectors and three green sectors. What is the probability of the spinner stopping at a green sector when spun once?

Solution

You can reflect the bias towards red by labelling each red sector and each green sector with a number as shown: $S = \{R1, R2, R3, R4, R5, G1, G2, G3\}$

$E = \{G1, G2, G3\}$

$P = \dfrac{\text{Number of elements in } E}{\text{Number of elements in } S} = \dfrac{3}{8}$

Outcomes with multiple components

TIP

When dealing with an experiment in which one trial consists of a set of successive actions or a simultaneous set of actions, you should set out the sample space in a tree diagram or a table.

WORKED EXAMPLE Using tables to calculate probabilities

A fair die is rolled and then a fair coin is tossed (two successive actions). The sample space is laid out in a table as shown:

The sample space consists of 12 outcomes each with two components, a digit and a letter.

The event of rolling an even number and then a head is given by $E = \{(2, H), (4, H), (6, H)\}$.

The probability of this event is given by $P = \dfrac{3}{12} = \dfrac{1}{4}$

Sample space Coin second

	H	T
1	(1, H)	(1, T)
2	(2, H)	(2, T)
3	(3, H)	(3, T)
4	(4, H)	(4, T)
5	(5, H)	(5, T)
6	(6, H)	(6, T)

Die first

WORKED EXAMPLE Using tree diagrams to calculate probabilities

A fair coin is tossed three times. The sample space is laid out as a tree diagram where H = head and T = tail.

The sample space consists of eight outcomes each, with three components which are all letters

The event of rolling at least one (one or more) tail start is given by:

$E = \{(H, H, T), (H, T, H), (H, T, T), (T, H, H),$

$\quad (T, H, T), (T, T, H), (T, T, T)\}$

$P(E) = \dfrac{\#(E)}{\#(S)} = \dfrac{7}{8}$

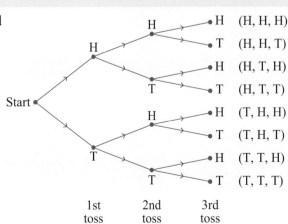

EXERCISE 5

1. What is the probability of a particular person sitting in the middle of a row of seven people?

2. What is the probability of winning a raffle if you buy five of the 200 tickets sold?

3. A fair die is rolled once. Write out the sample space.

   Find the probability of rolling:

   (a) a 6

   (b) a 7

   (c) an even number

   (d) a number greater than or equal to 3

   (e) a prime number

4. A fair spinner with eight sectors of equal area is spun once: Red (R), Green (G) and Blue (B).

   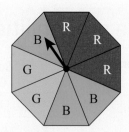

   Find the probability of landing on:

   (a) a red   (c) a blue

   (b) a green   (d) a red or a blue

5. A card is drawn from a set of cards with six red (R) cards, five blue (B) cards, four green (G) cards and five pink (P) cards. Find the probability of drawing:

   (a) a red card

   (b) a blue card

   (c) a green card

   (d) a pink or a green card

6. A biased die has faces marked 1, 2, 3, 4, 5, 5. What is the probability in one roll of rolling:

   (a) a 2   (c) an even number

   (b) a 5   (d) an odd number

7. A bag contains five blue, six green and seven red discs. Two people in succession are to pull out two discs. Joe puts his hand in first and picks out a red and a green disc. Peter then pulls out a red first. What is the probability his second is also a red?

8. The letters MASSACHUSETTS are marked on 13 individual cards and placed in a hat. What is the probability of picking the letter:

   (a) S   (b) T   (c) M?

9. There are six horses in a race A, B, C, D, E, F. What is the probability that:

   (a) A wins

   (b) B wins

   (c) A or E wins?

   Assume there are no dead heats.

10. Leeds United are playing at the weekend. What is the probability you will predict the result of the match (win, lose or draw)?

11. A letter is chosen from the word SYNCHROTRON. Find the probability of choosing a:

    (a) Y   (c) vowel

    (b) O   (d) consonant

12. A fair spinner with eight equal sectors is spun once.

    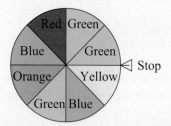

    Find the probability of landing on:

    (a) red   (d) brown

    (b) green   (e) blue or red

    (c) yellow   (f) not red

13. If you randomly choose a classmate, what is the probability that their birthday this year:

(a) falls on a Wednesday,

(b) does not fall on a Sunday,

(c) falls on a weekday,

(d) falls at the weekend?

14. 32 students in a class score the following grades in a test:

Grade	A	B	C	D	E	F
Number of students	5	9	12	4	1	1

If a student is chosen at random, what is the probability he scored:

(a) an A   **(c)** a C or higher

(b) an F   **(d)** a fail (E or F)?

15. There are 12 balls in a bag of two different colours: red and green. The probability of picking a red out is $\frac{1}{3}$.

(a) How many red balls are in the bag?

(b) How many green balls are in the bag?

(c) Two green balls are removed. What is the probability of picking out a red now?

16. In a class of 50 students, each student has to opt for one and only one of three sports. The sports are chosen as follows:

	Boys	Girls
Football	15	3
Swimming	10	9
Athletics	8	5

If a student is selected at random from the group, what is the probability the student is:

(a) a boy

(b) a girl

(c) a student who chooses football

(d) a student who chooses athletics or swimming

(e) a boy who chooses swimming

(f) a girl who chooses football or swimming?

17. A bag contains six red balls, two blue balls and x pink balls. If the probability of picking a pink ball is three times the probability of picking a blue ball, find x.

6 Red balls
2 Blue balls
x Pink balls

18. A box contains nine blue discs and x red discs. Find, in terms of x, the number of discs in the box. Find, in terms of x, the probability of picking out a red disc. If the probability of picking out a red disc is $\frac{2}{5}$, find x.

19. A fair coin is tossed twice. Write out the sample space of this experiment using a tree diagram.

What is the probability of getting:

(a) two heads

(b) a head and a tail

(c) one and only one tail

(d) a head or a tail

(e) at least one tail

(f) no tails?

20. A fair coin is tossed and then a fair die is rolled. Copy and complete the table below to show the sample space of this experiment.

Die

Coin		1	2	3	4	5	6
	H	(H, 1)	(H, 2)				
	T						

What is the probability of getting:

(a) a head and then a 6,

(b) a head and then an even number,

(c) a head and then a prime number,

(d) a tail and then an odd number?

21. Two fair dice are rolled simultaneously. Copy and complete the table below to show the sample space.

Die 2

Die 1	1	2	3	4	5	6
1	(1, 1)	(1, 2)	(1, 3)			
2						
3						
4						
5						
6						

Find the probability of getting:

(a) a double

(b) a sum of 10

(c) two odd numbers

(d) a sum of 7 or 11

22. A fair coin is tossed and a spinner with three equal coloured sectors is then spun. Copy and complete the table to show the sample space of this experiment.

Spinner

Coin	R	G	B
H			
T			

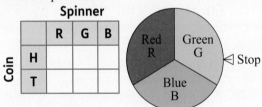

What is the probability of getting:

(a) a head and then a red,

(b) a tail and then a red or a green?

23. Two spinners, each with four equal sectors, are spun simultaneously. Copy and complete the table below to show the sample space of this experiment.

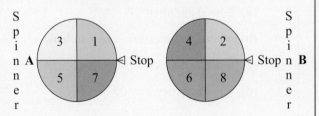

Spinner B

Spinner A	2	4	6	8
1				
3				
5				
7				

When both spinners stop, find the probability that:

(a) both numbers are even,

(b) both numbers add up to an odd number,

(c) both numbers multiply to 12.

24. The two spinners in **Question 23** are used again and the results are added. Complete a new table to show the complete sample space for this experiment.

Use the results to find the probability of a sum:

(a) equal to 9,

(b) that is even,

(c) that is prime.

25. A fair coin is tossed three times. Write out the sample space of this experiment using a tree diagram.

Find the probability of tossing:

(a) a head and then two tails

(b) three heads

(c) one and only one tail

(d) at least one tail

(e) a head and two tails

26. Three fair coins are tossed simultaneously. Write out the sample space of this experiment using a tree diagram. Find the probability of getting:

(a) three heads

(b) two heads and one tail

(c) no heads

15.3 Probability using Venn diagrams

Venn diagrams can be very useful in dealing with two or more events and can be used to do problems using the words **'or'** and **'and'**.

If two events A and B have no outcomes in common, they are said to be **mutually exclusive:** $A \cap B = \{\ \}$

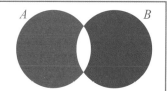

▸ Picking a card which is a King from a deck of playing cards is an event with four possible outcomes. Picking a card which is a Queen from a deck of playing cards is an event with four possible outcomes. Picking a card which is both a King and a Queen from a deck of playing cards is an event with zero outcomes (there is no card called the King of Queens!). Such events which have no outcomes in common are mutually exclusive.

If two events A and B have outcomes in common they are **not mutually exclusive:** $A \cap B \neq \{\ \}$

▸ Picking a card which is a King from a deck of playing cards is an event with four possible outcomes. Picking a card which is a diamond from a deck of playing cards is an event with 13 possible outcomes. Picking a card which is both a King and a diamond from a deck of playing cards is an event with one outcome (the King of diamonds). Such events which have outcomes in common are not mutually exclusive.

EXAMPLE 6

There are 35 students in a class. During the summer, 22 students visited France, 20 visited Germany and 4 visited neither country. Represent this information in a Venn diagram.

Find out how many visited both countries during the summer.

If a student is chosen at random, what is the probability that during the summer the student:

(a) visited France,

(b) visited France only,

(c) visited France or Germany,

(d) visited only one country?

Solution

Let x = number that visited both France and Germany.

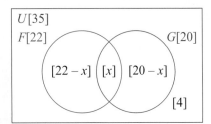

$$22 - x + x + 20 - x + 4 = 35$$
$$-x + 46 = 35$$
$$-x = -11$$
$$x = 11$$

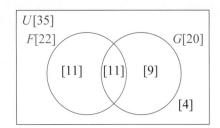

(a) $P(F) = \dfrac{22}{35}$

(b) $P(F \text{ only}) = \dfrac{11}{35}$

(c) **TIP**

↑ In maths, 'or' includes **both**.

So France or Germany means France only and Germany only and **both**.

$$P(F \cup G) = \dfrac{31}{35}$$

(d) $P(\text{Only one country}) = \dfrac{20}{35} = \dfrac{4}{7}$

EXAMPLE 7

In a class, one-third of the students play basketball and half play football. One-tenth of the students play both.

Draw a Venn diagram to represent this information.

If a student is chosen at random, what is the probability that the student plays basketball or football? What is the probability the student plays neither basketball nor football?

Solution

$P(\text{Student plays basketball or football}) = \dfrac{7}{30} + \dfrac{1}{10} + \dfrac{2}{5} = \dfrac{11}{15}$

$P(\text{Neither}) = 1 - \dfrac{11}{15} = \dfrac{4}{15}$

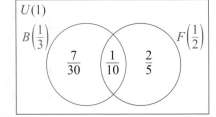

EXERCISE 6

1. A Venn diagram is shown:

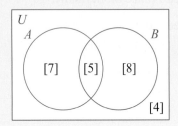

Find:

(a) the number of elements in U

(b) $P(A \cap B)$

(c) $P(A \backslash B)$

(d) $P(B \backslash A)$

(e) $P(A \cup B)$

(f) $P((A \cup B)')$

2. There are 30 students in a class. Eighteen take Physics, 15 take Chemistry and three take neither. Draw a Venn diagram showing this information. Find how many students take both subjects.

If a student is chosen at random find the probability that:

(a) the student takes Physics only,

(b) the student takes Physics or Chemistry,

(c) the student takes Physics and Chemistry.

3. The probability that Joe will be on the school football team is 0·5. The probability that he will be on the hurling team is 0·6. The probability that he will be on both is 0·3.

Draw a Venn diagram showing this information.

What is the probability he will be selected for at least one of these sports?

4. In a certain street $\frac{1}{6}$ of the houses have no newspaper delivered, $\frac{2}{3}$ have a national newspaper delivered and $\frac{1}{4}$ have a local newspaper delivered. Draw a Venn diagram to illustrate this information and use it to find the probability that a house chosen at random has both papers delivered.

5. A fair die is rolled once. List the outcomes in a sample space *S*. The following events are defined:

A = A number greater than 2 but less than 5 is obtained

B = An odd number is obtained

Draw a Venn diagram that depicts the situation. Find:

(a) $P(A)$ **(d)** $P(A \cup B)$

(b) $P(B)$ **(e)** $P(A')$

(c) $P(A \cap B)$

6. A company makes tinned food. The probability of producing a tin with a dent is 0·03 and the probability of producing a tin with a scratch is 0·08. The probability of producing a tin with a scratch and a dent is 0·02.

D = Event of a tin being produced with a dent

S = Event of a tin being produced with a scratch

Are these events mutually exclusive?

Draw a Venn diagram to illustrate the information.

Find the probability of producing a tin with a dent or a scratch.

How many tins out of every 1000 are expected to be dented or scratched?

7. The Venn diagram shows the number of students taking Physics (P), Chemistry (C) and Biology (B) in a class of 35.

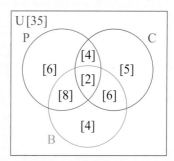

How many students took none of these subjects?

If a student is selected at random find the probability she takes:

(a) Chemistry

(b) Chemistry only

(c) Physics and Chemistry

(d) all three

(e) Physics or Biology

8. Forty students were asked to select sports from football (F), hurling (H) and tennis (T). Each student had to choose at least one. The number of students who selected these sports is shown on the Venn diagram.

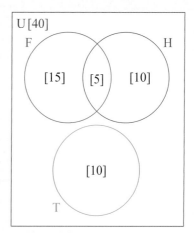

(a) Are the events of selecting football and selecting hurling mutually exclusive? Why?

(b) Are the events of selecting football and selecting tennis mutually exclusive? Why?

(c) What is the probability of selecting football and hurling?

(d) What is the probability of selecting football or hurling?

9. (a) For mutually exclusive events A and B, what can you say about $P(A \text{ and } B)$?

(b) For non-mutually exclusive events A and B, what can you say about $P(A \text{ and } B)$?

10. A survey of 1000 people was carried out to find whether people liked vanilla (V) or chocolate ice cream (C). The probability that a person liked chocolate ice cream was $\frac{7}{20}$ and the probability that a person liked vanilla ice cream was $\frac{13}{20}$. Copy and complete the Venn diagram.

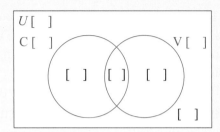

If the probability of a person liking vanilla ice cream, given that they liked chocolate ice cream, was $\frac{2}{5}$, find:

(a) the probability they liked chocolate ice cream and vanilla ice cream,

(b) the probability they liked chocolate ice cream or vanilla ice cream,

(c) the probability they liked neither.

11. The Venn diagram shown has $P(A) = 0\cdot6$, $P(B) = 0\cdot7$ and $P(A \text{ or } B) = 1$. Put the probabilities given in the correct areas of the Venn diagram.

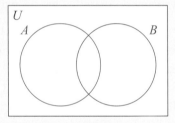

Find $P(A \text{ and } B)$. Show that $P(A \text{ or } B) = P(A) + P(B) - P(A \cap B)$.

Are A and B mutually exclusive?

15.4 Rules of probability

There are two ways to approach theoretical probability problems: the 'all in one go' approach and the 'as you go along approach'.

'All in one go'

The 'all in one go' approach entails writing out the set S of all possible outcomes of the experiment (sample space) and the set E of desired outcomes (the event) and then finding the probability of the event from the formula:

$$P = \frac{\text{Number of elements in } E}{\text{Number of elements in } S}$$

For simple problems, this approach is fine. For more challenging problems, it can be tedious and often impossible as it can be very difficult to list all of the possibilities in E and S.

ACTIVITY 15

ACTION
Practising probability rule 1 – the 'or' rule

OBJECTIVE
To practise using the first probability rule for finding the probability of combined events

'As you go along'

The 'as you go along' approach involves finding the individual probabilities of a series of simple events that are equivalent to carrying out the desired event in one go. These are then combined by the rules of probability to give the final probability for the event.

1. The 'or' rule

To understand the 'or' rule, you have to appreciate the difference between mutually exclusive and non-mutually exclusive events We looked at this idea in the previous section. Here, we look at it in greater detail.

WORKED EXAMPLE Exploring mutually exclusive events

Nine discs are numbered 1 to 9 and placed in a bag.

Consider these two events:

A: Drawing a number greater than **8** = {9}

B: Drawing an even number = {2, 4, 6, 8}

These events are mutually exclusive because they cannot occur together.

They have nothing in common.

There is no even numbered disc that is greater than 8.

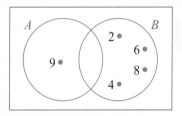

Only one of these two events can happen in one trial of picking a disc: $A \cap B = \{ \}$.

KEY TERM
Mutually exclusive events cannot occur together. They have no common outcomes.

WORKED EXAMPLE Exploring non-mutually exclusive events

A normal pack of playing cards has 52 cards. Consider two events.

A = Drawing a heart = {1H, 2H, 3H, 4H, 5H, 6H, 7H, 8H, 9H, 10H, JH, QH, KH} where H = hearts, 1H = Ace of hearts, J = Jack, Q = Queen, K = King

B = Drawing a Queen = {QH, QC, QS, QD} where C = club, S = spade, D = diamond

These events are not mutually exclusive because they can occur together in one trial of drawing one card from the pack.
They have the Queen of hearts as a common outcome: $A \cap B = \{QH\}$

Both of these events can happen in one trial of drawing a card.

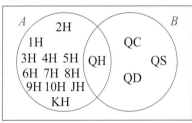

KEY TERM
Non-mutually exclusive events can occur together. They have common outcomes.

For two **mutually exclusive** events
A and B: $A \cap B = \{ \} \Leftrightarrow P(A \cap B) = 0$

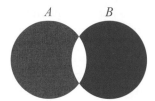

For two **non-mutually** exclusive events
A and B: $A \cap B \neq \{ \} \Leftrightarrow P(A \cap B) \neq 0$

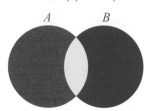

WORKED EXAMPLE Finding the 'or' rule formula

What is the probability of throwing a 5 or a 3 in one roll of a fair die?

All in one go: One event	As you go along: Two single events
$S = \{1, 2, 3, 4, 5, 6\}$	$P(5) = \dfrac{1}{6}$ in one roll
$E = \{5, 3\}$	$P(3) = \dfrac{1}{6}$ in one roll
$P = \dfrac{2}{6} = \dfrac{1}{3}$	If you add $P(5)$ to $P(3)$ you get $\dfrac{1}{3}$.
	$P(5) + P(3) = \dfrac{1}{6} + \dfrac{1}{6} = \dfrac{1}{3}$

This seems to lead to the 'or' rule formula:

$$P(A \text{ or } B) = P(A) + P(B)$$

However, we must be a little bit more careful in using the second approach as the two single events of throwing a 5 and throwing a 3 are **mutually exclusive.** You cannot throw a 5 and a 3 at the same time.

What is the probability of picking either a Queen or a spade from a pack of cards?

All in one go: One event	As you go along: Two single events
S = Set of 52 cards	$P(\text{Spade}) = \dfrac{13}{52}$
E = Set of all spades and 3 Queens	$P(\text{Queen}) = \dfrac{4}{52}$
$P(E) = \dfrac{16}{52} = \dfrac{4}{13}$	When you add these together, you get $\dfrac{17}{52}$. This is because you have counted the Queen of spades twice, once in each event. You must subtract the probability of picking the Queen of spades
	$P(\text{Queen of spades}) = \dfrac{1}{52}$

$$P(\text{Spade}) + P(\text{Queen}) - P(\text{Queen of spades}) = \dfrac{13}{52} + \dfrac{4}{52} - \dfrac{1}{52} = \dfrac{16}{52} = \dfrac{4}{13}$$

The two single events of picking a spade and picking a Queen are **not mutually exclusive.** They can occur at the same time because you can pick the Queen of spades.

Statement of the 'or' rule for two events A and B:

$$\boxed{P(A \text{ or } B) = P(A) + P(B) - P(A \cap B)}$$

1. If A and B are mutually exclusive, then $A \cap B = \{ \}$ and so $P(A \cap B) = 0$.
    The 'or' rule then becomes: $P(A \text{ or } B) = P(A) + P(B)$

2. For more than two mutually exclusive events $E_1, E_2, E_3, \ldots E_n$
    $$P(E_1 \text{ or } E_2 \text{ or } \ldots \text{ or } E_n) = P(E_1) + P(E_2) + \ldots + P(E_n)$$

> **TIP**
>
> ▲ Before using the **'or'** rule, always check whether or not the events involved are mutually exclusive.

EXAMPLE 8

Of 20 balls in a bag, four are red and odd numbered, five are blue and even numbered, six are yellow, with three even numbered and three odd numbered. The remaining five balls are green and not numbered.

A ball is picked at random from the bag.

Find the probability of picking:

(a) a red or a green ball

(b) a yellow or an even ball

(c) a red or a blue or a yellow ball

Solution

4RO (red, odd-numbered), 5BE (blue, even-numbered), 3YE (yellow, even-numbered), 3YO (yellow, odd-numbered), 5G (green)

(a) $\left. \begin{array}{l} P(R) = \dfrac{4}{20} \\[2mm] P(G) = \dfrac{5}{20} \end{array} \right\}$ Mutually exclusive

$$P(R \text{ or } G) = P(R) + P(G) = \frac{4}{20} + \frac{5}{20} = \frac{9}{20}$$

(b) $\left. \begin{array}{l} P(Y) = \dfrac{6}{20} \\[2mm] P(E) = \dfrac{8}{20} \\[2mm] P(Y \cap E) = \dfrac{3}{20} \end{array} \right\}$ Not mutually exclusive

$$P(Y \text{ or } E) = P(Y) + P(E) - P(Y \cap E) = \frac{6}{20} + \frac{8}{20} - \frac{3}{20} = \frac{11}{20}$$

(c) $\left. \begin{array}{l} P(R) = \dfrac{4}{20} \\[2mm] P(B) = \dfrac{5}{20} \\[2mm] P(Y) = \dfrac{6}{20} \end{array} \right\}$ Mutually exclusive

$$P(R \text{ or } B \text{ or } Y) = P(R) + P(B) + P(Y) = \frac{15}{20} = \frac{3}{4}$$

EXAMPLE 9

Non-commercial motor vehicles sold in the US are classified as either light trucks (LT) or cars and as either domestic (D) or imported. In a recent year, 80% of new vehicles sold were domestic, 54% were light trucks and 47% were domestic light trucks. Using a Venn diagram find the probability that a vehicle sold was either domestic or a light truck.

Solution

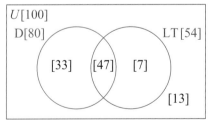

Method 1: 'All in one go'

$$P(D \text{ or } LT) = \frac{33 + 47 + 7}{100} = P(D \cup LT) = 0 \cdot 87$$

Method 2: 'As you go along'

$$P(D \text{ or } LT) = P(D) + P(LT) - P(D \cap LT)$$

$$= \frac{80}{100} + \frac{54}{100} - \frac{47}{100} = \frac{87}{100} = 0 \cdot 87$$

2. The 'and then' rule

To understand the 'and then' rule, you have to know the difference between **independent** and **non-independent** events.

ACTIVITY 16

ACTION
Understanding Probability rule 2: 'and then' vs 'and' rule

OBJECTIVE
To understand the subtle difference of including the word 'then' when calculating the probability of a number of events

WORKED EXAMPLE
Exploring independent events

A fair die is rolled twice.

A: The probability of rolling a **3** on the first roll is $\frac{1}{6}$.

and then

B: The probability of rolling a **3** or a **4** on the second roll is $\frac{1}{3}$.

The two events A and B are independent, as the outcome of the first event A has no influence on the outcome of the second event B.

KEY TERM

Two events A and B are **independent** if the probability of one event occurring does not affect the value of the probability of the other event occurring.

This means that the probability of one event has no influence on the probability of the next event and so on.

WORKED EXAMPLE
Exploring non-independent events

Two cards are drawn from a normal pack of 52 playing cards in succession without replacement.

A: The probability that the first card is a heart $= \frac{13}{52} = \frac{1}{4}$

and then

B: The probability the second card is a heart is influenced by the fact that the first card was a heart. There are only 51 cards left and only 12 hearts left, so the probability of the second card being a heart
$= \frac{12}{51} = \frac{4}{17}$.

The two events A and B are non-independent as the probability of A occurring affects the value of the probability of B occurring.

KEY TERM

Two events A and B are **non-independent** if the probability of one event occurring affects the value of the probability of the other event occurring.

WORKED EXAMPLE
Finding the 'and then' formula

(a) What is the probability of rolling a 6 and then tossing a head when a fair die is rolled and a fair coin tossed?

All in one go: One event

Sample space

	Coin	
	H	T
1	(1, H)	(1, T)
2	(2, H)	(2, T)
3	(3, H)	(3, T)
4	(4, H)	(4, T)
5	(5, H)	(5, T)
6	(6, H)	(6, T)

(Die)

$E = \{(6, H)\}$

$P(6, H) = \frac{1}{12}$

As you go along: Two single events

$P(6) = \frac{1}{6}$

and then

$P(H) = \frac{1}{2}$

If you multiply $P(6)$ by $P(H)$ you get $\frac{1}{12}$:

$P(6) \times P(H) = \frac{1}{6} \times \frac{1}{2} = \frac{1}{12}$

This seems to indicate the 'and then' rule is: $P(A \text{ and then } B) = P(A) \times P(B)$.

However, we must be careful as these events are **independent**.

(b) A bag has three red (R) cards numbered 1 to 3 and two blue (B) cards numbered 4 and 5.

What is the probability of picking a red card **and then** a blue card from the bag?

All in one go: One event	As you go along: Two single events
The number of outcomes in the sample space is the number of ways of picking one card and then another from 5 cards	$P(\text{Red}) = \dfrac{3}{5}$
$= 5 \times 4 = 20$	**and then**
Event: Set of outcomes of picking a red card and then a blue card	$P(\text{Blue given a red has been removed}) = \dfrac{2}{4} = \dfrac{1}{2}$
$= \{R1B4, R1B5, R2B4, R2B5, R3B4, R3B5\}$	$P(\text{Red}) \times P(\text{Blue given a red has been picked})$
$P = \dfrac{6}{20} = \dfrac{3}{10}$	$= \dfrac{3}{5} \times \dfrac{1}{2} = \dfrac{3}{10}$

These events are **non-independent.** Clearly the 'as you go along' method is much simpler than the 'all in one go' method.

TIP

The multiplication rule of probabilities is an **'and then'** rule.

Statement of the 'and then' rule for two events A and B:

1. For two independent events A and B: $P(A \text{ and then } B) = P(A) \times P(B)$

2. For non-independent events:
$P(A \text{ and then } B) = P(A) \times P(B \text{ given } A \text{ has occurred})$

For more than two events, apply the rules above as you go along, taking account of independence or non-independence.

EXAMPLE 10

What is the probability of picking an Ace (A) and then a Jack (J) from a normal pack of 52 playing cards:

(a) if the Ace is replaced,

(b) if the Ace is not replaced?

Solution

(a) Since the Ace is replaced, the two events making up the single desired event are independent.

$\left. \begin{array}{l} P(A) = \dfrac{4}{52} = \dfrac{1}{13} \\[2mm] P(J) = \dfrac{4}{52} = \dfrac{1}{13} \end{array} \right]$ Independent

$P(A \text{ and then } J) = \dfrac{1}{13} \times \dfrac{1}{13} = \dfrac{1}{169}$

(b) Since the Ace is not replaced, the second event is dependent on the first.

$\left. \begin{array}{l} P(A) = \dfrac{4}{52} = \dfrac{1}{13} \\[2mm] P(J \text{ given A is gone}) = \dfrac{4}{51} \end{array} \right]$ Non-independent

$P(A \text{ and then } J) = \dfrac{1}{13} \times \dfrac{4}{51} = \dfrac{4}{663}$

EXAMPLE 11

In a family of three children, what is the probability that the family consists of three boys?

Solution

$P(\text{1st child is a boy}) = \dfrac{1}{2}$

and then

$P(\text{2nd child is a boy}) = \dfrac{1}{2}$ Independent

and then

$P(\text{3rd child is a boy}) = \dfrac{1}{2}$

$P(\text{3 boys}) = \dfrac{1}{2} \times \dfrac{1}{2} \times \dfrac{1}{2} = \dfrac{1}{8}$

EXAMPLE 12

What is the probability of picking three hearts (H) from one pack of cards and then four spades (S) from another pack of cards?

Solution

$P(3H) = \dfrac{^{13}C_3}{^{52}C_3} = \dfrac{11}{850}$ or

$P(3H) = \dfrac{13}{52} \times \dfrac{12}{51} \times \dfrac{11}{50} = \dfrac{11}{850}$

and then

$P(4S) = \dfrac{^{13}C_4}{^{52}C_4} = \dfrac{11}{4165}$ or

$P(4S) = \dfrac{13}{52} \times \dfrac{12}{51} \times \dfrac{11}{50} \times \dfrac{10}{49} = \dfrac{11}{4165}$

$P(3H \text{ and then } 4S) = \dfrac{^{13}C_3}{^{52}C_3} \times \dfrac{^{13}C_4}{^{52}C_4} = \dfrac{121}{3\,540\,250}$

EXAMPLE 13

A bag contains five white (W) discs, four green (G) discs and three red (R) discs. Three discs are picked in succession.

What is the probability of:

(a) picking three white discs if the discs are not replaced each time,

(b) picking a green disc and then a red disc and then another green disc if the discs are not replaced each time?

Solution

There are 12 discs to start with: 5W, 4G, 3R

(a) Picking three white discs means a white **and then** a white **and then** a white.

$P(W) = \dfrac{5}{12}$

and then

$P(W) = \dfrac{4}{11}$ Non-independent

and then

$P(W) = \dfrac{3}{10}$

$\therefore P(WWW) = \dfrac{5}{12} \times \dfrac{4}{11} \times \dfrac{3}{10} = \dfrac{1}{22}$

or

$P(3W) = \dfrac{^{5}C_3}{^{12}C_3} = \dfrac{1}{22}$

(b) $P(G) = \dfrac{4}{12}$

and then

$P(R) = \dfrac{3}{11}$

and then

$P(G) = \dfrac{3}{10}$

$P(GRG) = \dfrac{4}{12} \times \dfrac{3}{11} \times \dfrac{3}{10} = \dfrac{3}{110}$

EXERCISE 7

1. Using the Venn diagram, find:

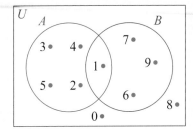

   (a) $P(A)$ **(d)** $P(A \cup B)$

   (b) $P(B)$ **(e)** $P(A$ or $B)$

   (c) $P(A \cap B)$ **(f)** $P(A) + P(B) - P(A \cap B)$

   What can you say about events A and B?

2. Using the Venn diagram, find:

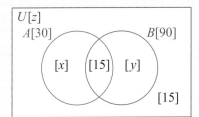

   (a) x **(e)** $P(B)$

   (b) y **(f)** $P(A \cap B)$

   (c) z **(g)** $P(A \cup B)$

   (d) $P(A)$ **(h)** $P(A) + P(B) - P(A \cap B)$

   What can you say about events A and B?

3. Using the Venn diagram, find:

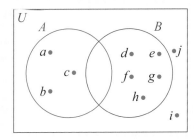

   (a) $P(A)$ **(d)** $P(A \cup B)$

   (b) $P(B)$ **(e)** $P(A) + P(B)$

   (c) $P(A \cap B)$

   What can you say about events A and B?

4. Using the Venn diagram, find:

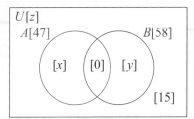

   (a) x **(e)** $P(B)$

   (b) y **(f)** $P(A \cap B)$

   (c) z **(g)** $P(A \cup B)$

   (d) $P(A)$ **(h)** $P(A) + P(B)$

   What can you say about events A and B?

5. In a class of 30 students, 18 study History, 23 study Geography and five study neither. Draw a Venn diagram to find how many study both.

   Find the probability a student chosen at random studies:

   (a) History only

   (b) Geography only

   (c) neither

   (d) both

   (e) History or Geography

6. **(a)** What is the probability of throwing a 5 or an even number in one throw of a fair die?

   (b) What is the probability of selecting a black or a red ball from a bag containing two black, three red, five white and 20 green balls?

   (c) What is the probability of drawing a picture card or a 10 from a normal pack of 52 playing cards?

   (d) What is the probability of drawing a diamond or a picture card from a normal pack of 52 playing cards?

   (e) What is the probability of rolling a number less than 3 or a number greater than 6 in one roll of a fair die?

(f) There are eight chocolate bars in a box, including two Fruit and Nuts and three Turkish Delights. What is the probability that a random pick would result in a Fruit and Nut or a Turkish Delight?

(g) What is the probability of drawing a card numbered 2, 3, 4 or 5 from a pack of 52 playing cards?

(h) What is the probability of choosing a card with a multiple of 2 or 5 written on it from a set of 20 cards numbered 1 to 20?

7. Three people are interviewed for a job. Each has a different combination of degree subjects.

Maeve: Maths/Economics

Paul: Economics/Statistics

Amir: Statistics/Maths

What is the probability the first person interviewed has a degree in Economics or Maths?

8. What is the probability of selecting a number divisible by 3 or 5 from the numbers 1 to 20 inclusive?

9. The spinner shown is spun once.

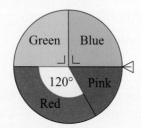

What is the probability:

(a) it stops on a green or a blue,

(b) it stops on a red or a blue,

(c) it does not stop on a red or a green?

10. What is the probability of selecting either a perfect square or a prime number from the numbers 2, 3, 4, 5, 6, 7, 8 and 9?

11. The probability that John will lose a race is $\frac{3}{4}$. The probability that Peter will lose is $\frac{2}{3}$. Find the probability that John or Peter will win the race.

12. In a class of 25 pupils, there are five boys aged 16, seven girls aged 16, seven boys aged 17 and six girls aged 17. One pupil is picked at random. What is the probability that the student is:

(a) a girl or a boy

(b) a boy aged 16 or a girl

(c) a girl aged 17 or a boy aged 16?

13. What is the probability a student was born on a Saturday or a weekday?

14. A number is selected from the following numbers: 1, 2, 3, 4, 5, 6, 7, 8, 9, 10, 11, 12, 13, 14, 15, 16, 17. What is the probability it is odd or prime?

15. (a) How many three-digit numbers are there?

(b) How many three-digit numbers end in 0?

(c) How many three-digit numbers end in 5?

(d) What is the probability that a three-digit number ends in 0?

(e) What is the probability that a three-digit number ends in 5?

(f) What is the probability that a three-digit number is divisible by 5?

16. (a) How many arrangements are there of the letters of the word EQUATION, if all letters are used and none are repeated?

(b) How many of these arrangements end in a vowel?

(c) How many of these arrangements end in T?

(d) What is the probability that the eight letters written in random order will end in a vowel or T?

17. (a) How many four-digit numbers are there?

(b) How many four-digit numbers end in 7?

(c) How many four-digit numbers are even?

(d) If a four-digit number is written down at random, what is the probability it is even or ends in a 7?

18. Four cards are selected from a pack of 52 playing cards. What is the probability the four cards are:

    (a) picture cards

    (b) four Aces

    (c) four picture cards or four Aces?

19. Of 100 tickets sold in a raffle, 40 were red and even numbered, 30 were blue and odd numbered, 30 were green, with 20 of them even numbered and 10 odd numbered. Find the probability that the winning ticket is green or even.

20. When two fair dice are rolled, what is the probability of rolling a sum of less than or equal to 4 or a double?

21. (a) What is the probability of rolling a 2 and then a 5 in two consecutive rolls of a fair die?

    (b) What is the probability of tossing a head using a fair coin and then rolling a 2 using a fair die?

    (c) What is the probability of drawing a King from one pack of 52 playing cards and then drawing a Jack from another pack of 52 playing cards?

    (d) What is the probability of forecasting the results (win, lose, draw) of five football matches correctly?

22. Two cards are drawn from a normal pack of 52 playing cards. Find the probability that both cards are Kings:

    (a) if the first card is replaced,

    (b) if the first card is not replaced.

23. A fair die is rolled twice. Find the probability of rolling a 3, 5 or 6 on the first roll and a 1, 2, 3 or 4 on the second roll.

24. A box contains seven green balls, four white balls and five red balls. What is the probability of picking:

    (a) a green and then a white and then a red in three consecutive picks without replacement,

    (b) a green and then a red and then another red in three consecutive picks without replacement,

    (c) three reds in three consecutive picks without replacement?

25. A bag contains a dozen diamonds all of different sizes but three of them are fake. If you are asked to pick out three diamonds in succession with no replacement, what is the probability you pick out three fakes?

26. There are two men and three women in a doctor's waiting room. What is the probability that the first two people called will be a man and then a woman, in that order?

27. Each letter of the alphabet is written on a separate card and the 26 cards are shuffled. What is the probability of drawing five cards without replacement in the order reading CARDS?

28. A fair coin is tossed and a spinner with three equal coloured sectors, red (R), green (G) and blue (B), is then spun.

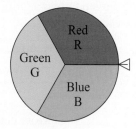

    Find the probability of:

    (a) a head and then a red,

    (b) a tail and then a green or a blue.

29. A fair coin is tossed three times. What is the probability of tossing:

    (a) three heads

    (b) two tails and then a head

    (c) two tails and a head?

30. What is the probability that:

    (a) three boys were born on the same day of the week,

    (b) three boys were born on different days of the week?

31. Sixty-five per cent of all registered voters in a constituency support an independent political candidate. If two voters in the constituency are chosen independently, find the probability that the first voter supports the independent candidate and the second one does not.

32. During World War II, the probability of a British bomber plane being lost in action over Europe in one mission was 0·05. What was the probability the plane returned safely to base after one mission? Assuming all missions were independent, find the probability a particular bomber survived:

  (a) two missions

  (b) three missions

  (c) 20 missions, correct to three decimal places

33. Using two packs of normal playing cards, what is the probability of choosing seven hearts from the first pack and seven picture cards from the second pack? Give your answer in the form $a \times 10^n$, $1 \le a < 10$, $n \in \mathbb{Z}$, where a is given to two significant figures.

34. If $\frac{2}{5}$, $\frac{3}{8}$ and $\frac{3}{4}$ are the probabilities Friar Tuck, the Sheriff of Nottingham and Robin Hood respectively hit a target with an arrow, find the probability that:

  (a) all three hit the target,

  (b) all three miss the target.

35. Three letters are chosen from the name HAMILTON. What is the probability that the first letter is a vowel and the second and third are consonants, if no letters are repeated?

36. A box contains six blue and x green balls. A ball is picked out and then a second one is picked, without replacement. If the probability of picking two green balls is $\frac{4}{13}$, find the number of green balls in the box.

15.5 More challenging probability problems

More challenging probability problems involve non-independent and independent events which require the use of both the 'or' rule and the 'and then' rule.

1. 'And then' vs 'and'

EXAMPLE 14

A bag contains seven green (G) balls and eight red (R) balls. Two balls are picked out in succession.

What is the probability of picking:

(a) a green ball **and then** a red ball

(b) a green ball and a red ball

(c) two green balls?

Solution

There are 7G and 8R balls in the bag.

(a) Using the 'as you go along' approach:
$$P(\text{G and then R}) = \frac{7}{15} \times \frac{8}{14} = \frac{4}{15}$$

(b) The missing word 'then' means we must consider all possibilities.

Using the 'as you go along' approach:
$$P(\text{G and then R}) = \frac{7}{15} \times \frac{8}{14} = \frac{4}{15}$$

or
$$P(\text{R and then G}) = \frac{8}{15} \times \frac{7}{14} = \frac{4}{15}$$

$$\therefore P(\text{G and R}) = \frac{4}{15} + \frac{4}{15} = \frac{8}{15}$$

Using the 'all in one go' approach:
$$P(\text{G and R}) = \frac{{}^7C_1 \times {}^8C_1}{{}^{15}C_2} = \frac{8}{15}$$

(c) Two green balls means a green and then a green.

Using the 'as you go along' approach:
$$P(\text{G and then G}) = \frac{7}{15} \times \frac{6}{14} = \frac{1}{5}$$

Using 'all in one go' approach:
$$P(2\text{G}) = \frac{{}^7C_2}{{}^{15}C_2} = \frac{1}{5}$$

EXAMPLE 15

In five consecutive tosses of a fair coin, what is the probability of throwing:

(a) three heads (H) and then two tails (T)

(b) three heads and two tails?

Solution

All simple events that make up the single desired event are independent.

(a) This is very clear. You need to throw exactly HHHTT in this order.

P(HHHTT) = P(H and then H and then H and then T and then T) = $\frac{1}{2} \times \frac{1}{2} \times \frac{1}{2} \times \frac{1}{2} \times \frac{1}{2} = \frac{1}{32}$

(b) This is difficult because we must find the probability of all permutations of HHHTT and add them all together.

The number of permutations of HHHTT

$= \frac{5!}{3! \times 2!} = {}^5C_3 = 10$

$\therefore P$(3H and 2T) = P(HHHTT) $\times$ 10

$= {}^5C_3 \times \left(\frac{1}{2}\right)^3 \times \left(\frac{1}{2}\right)^2 = \frac{5}{16}$

This formula, together with the idea that the outcomes of tossing five coins simultaneously are the same as tossing one coin five times, lead to the Bernoulli approach to this type of problem, which we will cover in Chapter 16.

Simultaneous	Successively
1st coin H	1st toss H
2nd coin H	2nd toss H
3rd coin H	3rd toss H
4th coin T	4th toss T
5th coin T	5th toss T

When the simple events that make up the single desired event come from different types of sample spaces, 'and' and 'and then' are equivalent.

EXAMPLE 16

What is the probability of picking a heart from a normal pack of cards and rolling an even number on a fair die?

Solution

The sample space for picking a heart is all 52 playing cards. The sample space for rolling an even number on a fair die is {1, 2, 3, 4, 5, 6}. These are sample spaces of completely different types.

P(Heart **and** an even number)

$= P$(Heart **and then** an even number)

$= P$(Heart) $\times$ P(Even) $= \frac{13}{52} \times \frac{3}{6} = \frac{1}{8}$

2. 'One and only one' vs 'at least one'

EXAMPLE 17

Three students Anne, Peter and Muiris attempt to solve a Maths problem. Their respective probabilities of success (S) are: Anne $\frac{3}{7}$, Peter $\frac{2}{5}$, and Muiris $\frac{1}{2}$.

Find the probability that:

(a) one and only one student solves the problem,

(b) at least one student solves the problem, i.e. the problem is solved.

Solution

	Anne	Peter	Muiris
Probability of success (S) P	$\frac{3}{7}$	$\frac{2}{5}$	$\frac{1}{2}$
Probability of failure (F) Q	$\frac{4}{7}$	$\frac{3}{5}$	$\frac{1}{2}$

(a) 'One and only one': Consider all possibilities.

P(Anne succeeds **and then** Peter fails **and then** Muiris fails) $= \dfrac{3}{7} \times \dfrac{3}{5} \times \dfrac{1}{2} = \dfrac{9}{70}$

or

P(Anne fails **and then** Peter succeeds **and then** Muiris fails) $= \dfrac{4}{7} \times \dfrac{2}{5} \times \dfrac{1}{2} = \dfrac{8}{70}$

or

P(Anne fails **and then** Peter fails **and then** Muiris succeeds) $= \dfrac{4}{7} \times \dfrac{3}{5} \times \dfrac{1}{2} = \dfrac{12}{70}$

$\therefore P$(one and only one succeeds) $= \dfrac{9}{70} + \dfrac{8}{70} + \dfrac{12}{70} = \dfrac{29}{70} = \dfrac{29}{70}$

(b) 'At least one':

P(At least one succeeds) $= P$(Only one succeeds) or P(Two succeed) or P(All three succeed)

$\therefore P$(At least one succeeds) $= 1 - P$(None succeed) $= 1 - P$(All three fail)

P(Anne fails **and then** Peter fails **and then** Muiris fails) $= \dfrac{4}{7} \times \dfrac{3}{5} \times \dfrac{1}{2} = \dfrac{12}{70} = \dfrac{6}{35}$

$\therefore P$(Problem is solved) $- 1 - \dfrac{6}{35} = \dfrac{29}{35}$

EXAMPLE 18

There are five blue (B) balls, six green (G) balls and nine red (R) balls in a box. Three balls are picked out.

What is the probability of:

(a) picking out one and only one red ball,

(b) picking out no red balls,

(c) picking out at least two red balls?

Solution

There are 5B, 6G and 9R balls in the box.

(a) One and only one red:

P(R and then not R and then not R) $= \dfrac{9}{20} \times \dfrac{11}{19} \times \dfrac{10}{18} = \dfrac{11}{76}$

or

P(Not R and then R and then not R) $= \dfrac{11}{20} \times \dfrac{9}{19} \times \dfrac{10}{18} = \dfrac{11}{76}$

or

P(Not R and then not R and then R) $= \dfrac{11}{20} \times \dfrac{10}{19} \times \dfrac{9}{18} = \dfrac{11}{76}$

$\therefore P$(One and only one R) $= 3 \times \dfrac{11}{76} = \dfrac{33}{76}$

(b) No red

P(Not R and then Not R and then Not R) $= \dfrac{11}{20} \times \dfrac{10}{19} \times \dfrac{9}{18} = \dfrac{11}{76}$

(c) At least two reds:

P(At least 2R) $= 1 - P$(no R or 1 R) $= 1 - \left(\dfrac{11}{76} + \dfrac{33}{76} \right) = \dfrac{32}{76} = \dfrac{8}{19}$

EXERCISE 8

1. A bucket contains three white and five black balls. Two balls are picked out in succession without replacement. What is the probability of picking:

   (a) a white and then a black

   (b) a black and then a white

   (c) two whites

   (d) two blacks

   (e) a black and a white

   (f) two blacks or two whites?

2. What is the probability of getting one head and two tails in three consecutive tosses of a fair coin?

3. What is the probability of rolling a 2 and a 3 in two consecutive rolls of a fair die?

4. What is the probability of rolling exactly two 6s in five consecutive rolls of a fair die?

5. A school bicycle shed has 20 bicycles, six of which have faulty brakes. If three bicycles are selected at random, what is the probability of one and only one having faulty brakes?

6. Three darts players A, B and C take part in a charity competition called 'hitting the bull'. Their respective probabilities for hitting the bull are: $\frac{2}{5}$, $\frac{1}{2}$ and $\frac{1}{4}$.

Find the probability that:

   (a) one and only one player hits the bull,

   (b) exactly two hit the bull,

   (c) all three hit the bull,

   (d) at least one hits the bull.

7. An actuarial firm calculates the probability of a certain woman being alive in 30 years as $\frac{2}{3}$ and of her husband being alive in 30 years as $\frac{3}{8}$. What is the probability that at least one will be alive in 30 years?

8. A gambling game consists of tossing a coin three times. You win if all three tosses give the same result (three heads or three tails). Calculate the probability of losing.

9. A fair die is rolled three times. What is the probability of throwing:

   (a) exactly two 6s

   (b) at least two 6s?

10. A bag contains three blue balls, four red balls and x green balls. A ball is drawn, not replaced and then another is drawn. If the probability that at least one is green is $\frac{8}{15}$, how many green balls are in the bag?

Probability 2

Learning Outcomes

- To apply the Bernoulli formula to solve probability problems involving success and failure.
- To understand how to carry out conditional probability where the probability of an event is determined by an event that has already happened.
- To use expected value to determine if games are fair and to assess real-life risks.

16.1 Bernoulli trials

The following worked example introduces the idea of a Bernoulli experiment and trials.

WORKED EXAMPLE — Explaining Bernoulli trials

A student answers three multiple-choice questions, each with five possible answers. The student knows none of the answers and guesses each time. What is the probability that he will guess two out of three correctly?

The probability p he will guess the correct answer to one question is $p = \frac{1}{5}$ (success S) and the probability q he will not guess correctly to one question is $q = \frac{4}{5}$ (failure F).

Two out of three correct guesses can be achieved in three ways: SSF or SFS or FSS

$P(\text{SSF})$ = The probability of success on first **and then** success on the second **and then** failure on the third

$= p \times p \times q = \frac{1}{5} \times \frac{1}{5} \times \frac{4}{5} = \frac{4}{125}$

or

$P(\text{SFS})$ = The probability of success on the first **and then** failure on the second **and then** success on the third

$= p \times q \times p = \frac{1}{5} \times \frac{4}{5} \times \frac{1}{5} = \frac{4}{125}$

or

$P(\text{FSS})$ = The probability of failure on the first **and then** success on the second **and then** success on the third

$= q \times p \times p = \frac{4}{5} \times \frac{1}{5} \times \frac{1}{5} = \frac{4}{125}$

$P(\text{SSF}) \text{ or } P(\text{SFS}) \text{ or } P(\text{FSS}) = \frac{4}{125} + \frac{4}{125} + \frac{4}{125} = \frac{12}{125}$

$P(2S \text{ and } 1F) = \left(\frac{1}{5}\right) \times \left(\frac{1}{5}\right) \times \left(\frac{4}{5}\right) \times \left(\frac{3!}{2!}\right) = {}^3C_2 \times \left(\frac{1}{5}\right)^2 \times \left(\frac{4}{5}\right)$

Instead of writing out all these possibilities and using the 'and then' and 'or' rules of probability, there is a much quicker way of doing this problem by using **binomial coefficients** ${}^nC_r$.

Consider this experiment as three independent trials of answering right or wrong to three multiple-choice questions.

$P(\text{Success}) = \frac{1}{5}$ in one trial

$P(\text{Failure}) = \frac{4}{5}$ in one trial

$n = 3 = $ Number of trials

The probability of two successes and one failure $= {}^3C_2\left(\frac{1}{5}\right)^2\left(\frac{4}{5}\right)^1 = 3 \times \frac{1}{25} \times \frac{4}{5} = \frac{12}{125}$

However, this formula can be used only in an experiment which obeys very restrictive rules. These rules were set out by the mathematician Bernoulli.

ACTIVITY 17

ACTION
Carrying out Bernoulli trials

OBJECTIVE
To use the binomial theorem to calculate the probabilities of situations involving success and failure

The Bernoulli rules

A Bernoulli experiment is an experiment in which the following restrictions apply:

- There is a fixed number of trials n.
- There are only two possible outcomes to each trial (success or failure).
- Each trial is independent of any previous one.
- The probabilities of success p and failure q are fixed from trial to trial.

If an experiment consisting of n trials obeys all of the Bernoulli rules, the probability of r successes in n trials is given by:

$$P(r) = {}^nC_r(p)^r(q)^{n-r}$$

where $p = $ probability of success in one trial and $q = $ probability of failure in one trial.

Types of problem

1. Straightforward problems

EXAMPLE 1

If a coin is tossed five times, what is the probability of tossing three heads?

Solution

$n = 5$ (Number of trials)

$p = \frac{1}{2}$ (Success)

$q = \frac{1}{2}$ (Failure)

$P(3H) = {}^5C_3\left(\frac{1}{2}\right)^3\left(\frac{1}{2}\right)^2 = \frac{5}{16}$

2. Problems with 'or' and problems with 'at least'

EXAMPLE 2

There is a fault in a machine manufacturing batteries with the result that only 85% of them work.
A random sample of 10 batteries is tested. What is the probability that:

(a) exactly six work, correct to two decimal places,

(b) six or seven work, correct to two decimal places,

(c) more than seven work, correct to two decimal places,

(d) at least three work, correct to five decimal places?

Solution

$n = 10$ (Number of trials)

$p = 0\cdot85$ (Success)

$q = 0\cdot15$ (Failure)

(a) Exactly six successes:

$$P(6) = {}^{10}C_6(0\cdot85)^6(0\cdot15)^4 = 0\cdot04$$

(b) Six or seven work:

$$P(6 \text{ or } 7) = P(6) + P(7) = {}^{10}C_6(0\cdot85)^6(0\cdot15)^4 + {}^{10}C_7(0\cdot85)^7(0\cdot15)^3 = 0\cdot17$$

(c) $P(8 \text{ or } 9 \text{ or } 10) = P(8) + P(9) + P(10)$

$$= {}^{10}C_8(0\cdot85)^8(0\cdot15)^2 + {}^{10}C_9(0\cdot85)^9(0\cdot15)^1 + {}^{10}C_{10}(0\cdot85)^{10}(0\cdot15)^0 = 0\cdot82$$

$\therefore P(\text{More than } 7) = 0\cdot82$

(d) $P(\text{At least } 3) = P(3 \text{ or } 4 \text{ or } 5 \text{ or } 6 \text{ or } 7 \text{ or } 8 \text{ or } 9 \text{ or } 10)$

$$= 1 - P(0 \text{ or } 1 \text{ or } 2)$$

$$= 1 - [P(0) + P(1) + P(2)]$$

$$= 1 - [{}^{10}C_0(0\cdot85)^0(0\cdot15)^{10} + {}^{10}C_1(0\cdot85)^1(0\cdot15)^9 + {}^{10}C_2(0\cdot85)^2(0\cdot15)^8] = 0\cdot99999$$

3. Problems in which the kth success occurs on the nth (last) Bernoulli trial in n trials

EXAMPLE 3

A fair die is rolled five times in a game. A successful roll is a 4 or a 6. What is the probability that the third success occurs on the fifth roll?

Solution

$p = \frac{2}{6} = \frac{1}{3}$ (4 or a 6)

$q = \frac{4}{6} = \frac{2}{3}$ (not a 4 or a 6)

Third success on the fifth roll means: two successes from the first 4 rolls **and then** one success from the last roll.

$P(\text{3rd success on the 5th roll})$

$= [\text{Bernoulli: } n = 4, P(2 \text{ Successes})] \times \frac{1}{3}$

$= {}^4C_2\left(\frac{1}{3}\right)^2\left(\frac{2}{3}\right)^2 \times \frac{1}{3} = \frac{8}{81}$

4. Problems in which the kth success occurs on the rth Bernoulli trial in n trials

EXAMPLE 4

A fair die is rolled 5 times in a game. A successful roll is a 4 or a 6. What is the probability the third success occurs on the fourth roll?

Solution

$p = \frac{1}{3}$ (4 or 6)

$q = \frac{2}{3}$ (not 4 or 6)

Third success on the fourth roll means: two successes from the first three rolls **and then** a success on the fourth **and then** either a success or a failure on the last roll. The probability is 1 for the last roll as it is a certainty that it is either a success or a failure.

$P(\text{3rd success on the 4th roll means})$

$= [\text{Bernoulli: } n = 3, P(2 \text{ Successes})] \times \frac{1}{3} \times 1$

$= {}^3C_2\left(\frac{1}{3}\right)^2\left(\frac{2}{3}\right)^1 \times \frac{1}{3} \times 1 = \frac{2}{27}$

EXERCISE 9

1. A fair coin is tossed ten times. Find the probability of getting:

   (a) exactly five heads

   (b) exactly eight heads

   (c) three or four heads

   (d) at most one head

   (e) at least eight heads

   (f) at least two heads

2. In Home Economics, one out of five soufflés Joe makes collapses. Joe prepares six soufflés to serve at a party. What is the probability that exactly four soufflés do not collapse?

3. In a colon cancer screening programme, the probability of a misdiagnosis is $\frac{1}{30}$. In a sample of 100, what is the probability that five cases were misdiagnosed, correct to four decimal places?

4. A stockbroker is researching 12 independent stocks for investment. A stock either makes money or loses money. The probability a stock will make money is $\frac{3}{4}$. What is the probability that only nine stocks make money, correct to three decimal places?

5. In a computer manufacturing plant, 2% of the components are defective. If the probability that no components in a sample are defective is 0·6, find the size of the biggest sample.

6. A gas exploration company estimates that only one well in 50 will yield commercial quantities of gas. If 15 wells were drilled, find the probability of getting a well with commercial quantities, correct to three decimal places:

   (a) exactly once   **(c)** at most twice

   (b) no times

7. Ten standard decks of cards are shuffled in front of you. You draw one card from each deck. What is the probability of drawing three hearts, correct to two decimal places?

8. In a game of chess, the probability Boris wins is $\frac{5}{6}$. He plays six games against this opponent. What is the probability:

   (a) he wins exactly five games,

   (b) he wins at least five games,

   (c) his first loss is on the sixth game?

   Give all answers to three decimal places.

9. A rugby team's placekicker has an 80% success rate. In a match he takes five place kicks. What is the probability:

   (a) he has his third success in his fifth kick in a match,

   (b) he has his first success on his fifth kick,

   (c) he has three successes in five kicks,

   (d) he starts off with a score in his first kick and then alternately misses and scores on the next four kicks?

10. A basketball player has a success rate of 72% from the free throw line. In a game, she has 15 free throws. If her first success occurs on the sixth throw, what is the probability she has six successful free throws in all? Give all your answers correct to four significant figures.

11. **(a)** Seven fair coins are tossed. Find the probability of getting four heads and three tails.

    (b) The seven coins are tossed eight times. Find the probability of getting four heads and three tails exactly four times, correct to three decimal places.

12. An American roulette wheel has 38 slots, of which 18 are red, 18 are black and 2 are green. A gambler plays roulette 15 times by spinning the wheel 15 times and bets on red each time.

    (a) Do the 15 spins form a sequence of Bernoulli trials? Why?

    (b) What is the probability he wins:

    (i) only once, correct to three significant figures

    (ii) five times, correct to three decimal places?

13. An insurance company sells life insurance policies to six women all of the same age and all in good health. The actuarial department worked out the probability of a woman of this age being alive in 20 years as 0·63. Find the probability, correct to four decimal places, that the number of these women still alive in 20 years' time will be:

(a) 6

(c) exactly 3

(b) at least 4

(d) none

16.2 Conditional probability

ACTIVITY 18

ACTION
Calculating conditional probability

OBJECTIVE
To calculate the probability of one event given another event has already occurred

Given a man's fingerprints were found on a murder weapon, what is the likelihood he committed the murder?

Conditional (Bayesian) statistics tries to answer such questions.

In a two-horse race between Arkle and Bigfoot, past form shows that in the last 12 races Arkle won eight and Bigfoot won four. It looks like Arkle is a good bet. However, imagine you were told that Bigfoot won his four races on days when it rained heavily and so the going was heavy. This might affect how you bet if it rained for a day or two before the race.

The probability that Bigfoot wins, given the going is heavy, is really the number you need to know.

Conditional probability is a probability given a certain condition already holds.

The probability we assign to an event can change if we know that some other event has occurred beforehand to influence this probability. This idea is central to many applications of probability.

WORKED EXAMPLE Calculating the probability of being dealt an Ace

The probability of being dealt an Ace from a pack of 52 playing cards is:

$$P(\text{Ace}) = \frac{4}{52} = \frac{1}{13}$$

This is because there are four Aces in a pack of 52 cards and each is equally likely to be dealt.

Now suppose you have four cards in your hand already, one of which is an Ace. The probability of now being dealt an Ace as your fifth card, given what you know, is:

$$P(\text{Ace given that you already have an Ace}) = \frac{3}{48} = \frac{1}{16}$$

Knowing that there is an Ace among four cards changes the probability that the next card dealt is an Ace.

KEY TERM

Conditional probability is the probability that an event B will occur under the condition that we know another event A has occurred that influences B.

$P(B|A)$ = Probability that B occurs given that A has occurred already.

NOTES

1. The bar means 'given'. This is read as 'The probability of B given that A has occurred'.

2. $P(B|A)$ makes no sense if the event A can never occur. So $P(B|A)$ requires that $P(A) > 0$.

3. Be sure to keep in mind the distinct roles of events B and A in $P(B|A)$. Event A represents the event that has already occurred and B is the event whose probability you are calculating.

4. If events are independent, then $P(B|A) = P(B)$ and $P(A|B) = P(A)$ because the given event has no influence on the subsequent event. Two events are not independent if one event affects the outcome of the other.

WORKED EXAMPLE Formula for conditional probability

Two cards are picked without replacement from a normal pack of 52 playing cards.

A card is drawn from a pack of 52 and not replaced. A second card is then drawn. What is the probability that the first card is a club and the second is a black card?

These two events are not independent as the probability of drawing the second card is affected by the probability of drawing the first card, which was not replaced.

P(Club (C) and then a Black card (B)) $= P(C) \times P$(Second B given first card was C)

$$= P(C) \times P(B|C)$$
$$= \frac{13}{52} \times \frac{25}{51} = \frac{25}{204}$$

In general: $P(A \text{ and then } B) = P(A \cap B) = P(A) \times P(B|A)$

In terms of sets:

$P(B|A) = $ Probability of B given the sample space is set A

$\therefore P(B|A) = \dfrac{\text{Number of elements in } B \text{ given they are in } A}{\text{Number of elements in } A}$

$$= \frac{\#(A \cap B)}{\#(A)} = \frac{P(A \cap B)}{P(A)}$$

This gives us the following formula:

$$P(B|A) = \frac{P(A \cap B)}{P(A)}$$

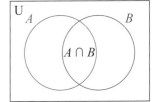

EXAMPLE 5

A bag contains nine identical discs numbered 1 to 9. One disc is drawn from the bag.

Let A = Event that an odd number is drawn.

Let B = Event that a number less than 5 is drawn.

(a) What is $P(B|A)$?

(b) What is $P(A|B)$?

(c) Are events A and B independent?

Solution

①②③④⑤⑥⑦⑧⑨

(a) $P(B|A)$ is the probability of a
number less than 5, given it is odd:
Sample space = {1, 3, 5, 7, 9}
Event = {1, 3}
$\therefore P(B|A) = \frac{2}{5}$.

(b) $P(A|B)$ is the probability of an odd
number, given it is less than 5:
Sample space = {1, 2, 3, 4}
Event = {1, 3}
$\therefore P(A|B) = \frac{2}{4} = \frac{1}{2}$

(c) If the events are independent then
$P(B|A) = P(B)$ and $P(A|B) = P(A)$.
$\frac{2}{5} \neq \frac{4}{9} \Rightarrow P(B|A) \neq P(B)$
$\frac{1}{2} \neq \frac{5}{9} \Rightarrow P(A|B) \neq P(A)$

The events are not independent.

Now, we will do the same problem using a Venn diagram:

(a) $P(B|A) = \dfrac{\#(A \cap B)}{\#(A)} = \dfrac{2}{5}$

(b) $P(B|A) = \dfrac{\#(A \cap B)}{\#(B)} = \dfrac{2}{4} = \dfrac{1}{2}$

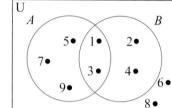

EXAMPLE 6

A game is played with 12 cards numbered 1 to 12
with cards numbered 1, 7, 8, 11 and 12 coloured
red and the others coloured yellow. Let R = Set of
red cards, E = Set of even cards and O = Set of odd
cards.

One card is chosen.

(a) Given it is red, what is the probability it is even?

(b) Given it is red, what is the probability it is odd?

(c) Given it is even, what is the probability it is red?

(d) Is $P(E|R) = P(R|E)$?

(e) Is $P(E|R) = P(E)$?

What does the answer to part **(e)** tell you about the
events of being red and being even?

Solution

| 1 | 2 | 3 | 4 | 5 | 6 | 7 | 8 | 9 | 10 | 11 | 12 |

R = {1, 7, 8, 11, 12}, E = {2, 4, 6, 8, 10, 12},
O = {1, 3, 5, 7, 9, 11}

(a) $P(E|R) = \frac{2}{5}$

(b) $P(O|R) = \frac{3}{5}$

(c) $P(R|E) = \frac{2}{6} = \frac{1}{3}$

(d) $P(R|E) \neq P(E|R)$

(e) $P(E) = \frac{6}{12} = \frac{1}{2}$
$\therefore P(E|R) \neq P(E)$

Therefore, E and R are not independent.

Using a Venn diagram:

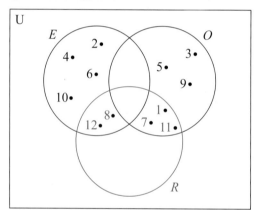

(a) $P(E|R) = \dfrac{\#(E \cap R)}{\#(R)} = \dfrac{2}{5}$

(b) $P(O|R) = \dfrac{\#(O \cap R)}{\#(R)} = \dfrac{3}{5}$

(c) $P(R|E) = \dfrac{\#(R \cap E)}{\#(E)} = \dfrac{2}{6} = \dfrac{1}{3}$

(d) $P(E|R) \neq P(R|E)$

(e) $P(E) = \dfrac{6}{12} = \dfrac{1}{2}$

Some general points on conditional probability

1. $P(A \text{ and then } B) = P(A \cap B) = P(A) \times P(B|A)$

   This is a general multiplication rule. It says that the probability of one event and then another is equal to the probability of the first event multiplied by the probability of the second event, given the first event has already occurred.

2. $P(A|B) \neq P(B|A)$: However, $P(A \cap B) = P(A) \times P(B|A)$ and
$$P(B \cap A) = P(B) \times P(A|B)$$
   $\therefore P(A) \times P(B|A) = P(B) \times P(A|B)$

   $\therefore P(A|B) = \dfrac{P(A) \times P(B|A)}{P(B)}$

3. In general, $P(B|A) \neq P(B)$: The conditional probability $P(B|A)$ is generally not equal to the unconditional probability $P(B)$. This is because the occurrence of A generally gives us some additional information about whether or not B occurs.

   If knowing that A occurs gives no additional information about B, then A and B are independent.

   So $P(B|A) = P(B) \Leftrightarrow B$ and A are independent

   and $P(B|A) \neq P(B) \Leftrightarrow B$ and A are not independent.

EXAMPLE 7

There are six red (R) numbered discs, four blue (B) numbered discs and ten green (G) numbered discs in a box. Two discs are picked one after the other.

Find:

(a) $P(R \cap G)$ **(b)** $P(G \cap R)$

where R is the set of red discs, B is the set of blue discs and G is the set of green discs.

Show that $P(G|R) \neq P(R|G)$ and $P(G|R) \neq P(G)$.

Solution

(a) $P(G|R) =$ Probability a green disc is picked given that a red disc has already been picked

$$P(R \cap G) = P(R) \times P(G|R) = \frac{6}{20} \times \frac{10}{19} = \frac{3}{19}$$

(b) $P(G \cap R) = P(G) \times P(R|G) = \frac{10}{20} \times \frac{6}{19} = \frac{3}{19}$

$$P(G|R) = \frac{10}{19} \neq \frac{6}{19} = P(R|G)$$

$$P(G|R) = \frac{10}{19} \neq \frac{10}{20} = P(G)$$

Therefore, they are not independent.

Types of problems on the general multiplication rule

1. Straightforward problems

Use the following formula for doing straightforward problems on the general multiplication rule:

$$P(A \cap B) = P(A) \times P(B|A) \text{ or } P(B|A) = \frac{P(A \cap B)}{P(A)}$$

EXAMPLE 8

A Maths teacher gave her class two tests. 25% of the class passed both tests and 42% passed the first test. What percentage of those who passed the first test also passed the second test?

Solution

F = Set of students who passed the first set

S = Set of students who passed the second set

$P(F \text{ and } S) = P(F \cap S) = 0 \cdot 25$

$P(F) = 0 \cdot 42$

$P(S|F) = \dfrac{P(F \cap S)}{P(F)} = \dfrac{0 \cdot 25}{0 \cdot 42} \approx 0 \cdot 6 = 60\%$

EXAMPLE 9

In 2003 in the US, approximately $58 \cdot 2\%$ of adults had both a landline (L) and a mobile phone (M), $2 \cdot 8\%$ had a mobile only but no landline and $1 \cdot 6\%$ had no phone service at all.

(a) What percentage of the population could be reached by a landline call in 2003?

(b) Were having a landline and having a mobile phone independent events in 2003? Why?

Solution

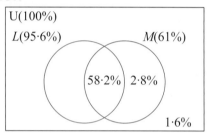

(a) Landline: $100\% - 2 \cdot 8\% - 1 \cdot 6\% = 95 \cdot 6\%$

$\therefore P(L) = 0 \cdot 956$

(b) $P(L|M) = \dfrac{P(L \cap M)}{P(M)} = \dfrac{0 \cdot 582}{0 \cdot 61} = 0 \cdot 954$

$\therefore P(L|M) \approx P(L)$

Therefore, the events are independent.

2. Problems involving tables

EXAMPLE 10

The following table shows the grades obtained by college students in certain subjects:

Grade	A	B	Below B	Total
Arts	2142	1890	2268	6300
Engineering	368	432	800	1600
Health	882	630	588	2100
Totals	3392	2952	3656	10000

E = Set of students in the engineering school

F = Set of students in the college who were awarded a grade below B

Find:

(a) $P(E)$

(b) $P(F)$

(c) $P(F|E)$

(d) $P(E|F)$

(e) $P(E \text{ and } F)$

(f) $P(F \text{ and } E)$

Show that:

(g) $P(E|F) \neq P(B|F)$

(h) $P(E \cap F) = P(E) \times P(F|E)$

(i) $P(F \cap E) = P(F) \times P(E|F)$

Solution

(a) $P(E) = \dfrac{1600}{10\,000} = 0\cdot16$

(b) $P(F) = \dfrac{3656}{10\,000} - 0\cdot3656$

(c) $P(F|E) = $ Probability a student got a grade below B given he studied Engineering $= \dfrac{800}{1600} = 0\cdot5$

(d) $P(E|F) = $ Probability a student studies Engineering given he got a grade below B $= \dfrac{800}{3656} = 0\cdot2188$

(e) $P(E \text{ and } F) = \dfrac{800}{10\,000} = 0\cdot08$

(f) $P(F \text{ and } E) = \dfrac{800}{10\,000} = 0\cdot08$

(g) $P(E|F) = \dfrac{800}{3656} = 0\cdot2188 \neq P(F|E) = \dfrac{800}{1600} = 0\cdot5$

(h) $P(E \cap F) = \dfrac{800}{10\,000} = 0\cdot08 = P(E) \times P(F|E) = \dfrac{1600}{10\,000} \times \dfrac{800}{1600} = 0\cdot08$

(i) $P(F \cap E) = 0\cdot08 = P(F) \times P(E|F) = \dfrac{3656}{10\,000} \times \dfrac{800}{3656} = 0\cdot08$

3. Problems using tree diagrams

Probability problems often require you to combine several of the basic rules of probability into a more elaborate calculation. Tree diagrams are very useful in laying these out.

EXAMPLE 11

One in every 250 people is infected by a virus. A test is used to determine whether a person is infected. If a person is infected, the test is positive 78% of the time and if the person is not infected the test is still positive 6% of the time (false positive).

(a) If a person tests positive, what is the probability that the person is infected?

(b) If a person tests negative, what is the probability that the person is not infected?

Solution

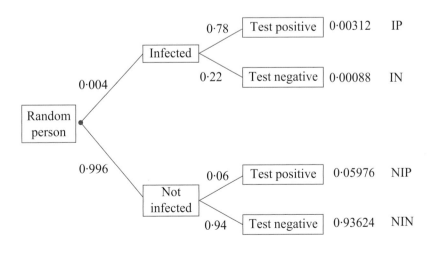

$P(\text{Infected and testing positive [IP]}) = 0.004 \times 0.78 = 0.00312$

$P(\text{Infected and testing negative [IN]}) = 0.004 \times 0.22 = 0.00088$

$P(\text{Not infected and testing positive [NIP]}) = 0.996 \times 0.06 = 0.05976$

$P(\text{Not infected and testing negative [NIN]}) = 0.996 \times 0.94 = 0.93624$

(a) $P(I|P) = \dfrac{P(I \text{ and then } P)}{P(P)} = \dfrac{0.00312}{(0.00312 + 0.05976)} = 0.0496$

(b) $P(NI|N) = \dfrac{P(NI \text{ and then } N)}{P(N)} = \dfrac{0.93624}{(0.00088 + 0.93624)} = 0.999$

EXAMPLE 12

Liam and Joe are playing a tennis match. The winner is the first person to win two sets. Liam is the better player and the probability he wins a set when he plays Joe is $\frac{3}{4}$.

(a) What is the probability Liam wins the match?

(b) What is the probability Joe wins the match?

(c) Given that Liam wins the first set, what is the probability he wins the match?

(d) What is the probability Liam won the first set, given he wins the match?

(e) What is the probability the match lasts for three sets?

Solution

This is a difficult problem so lay it out in a tree diagram.

L = Probability Liam wins a set

J = Probability Joe wins a set

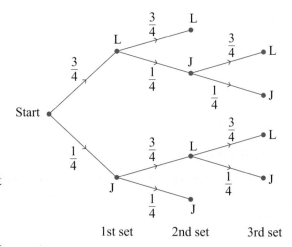

(a) Liam wins the match:

$P(\text{Liam wins the first set \textbf{and then} wins the second set (LL)}) = \frac{3}{4} \times \frac{3}{4} = \frac{9}{16}$

or

$P(\text{Liam wins the first set \textbf{and then} loses the second set \textbf{and then} wins the third set (LJL)}) = \frac{3}{4} \times \frac{1}{4} \times \frac{3}{4} = \frac{9}{64}$

or

$P(\text{Liam loses the first set \textbf{and then} wins the second set \textbf{and then} wins the third set (JLL)}) = \frac{1}{4} \times \frac{3}{4} \times \frac{3}{4} = \frac{9}{64}$

$P(\text{Liam wins}) = \dfrac{9}{16} + \dfrac{9}{64} + \dfrac{9}{64} = \dfrac{36 + 18}{64} = \dfrac{54}{64} = \dfrac{27}{32}$

(b) Joe wins the match:

$P(\text{Joe wins the first set \textbf{and then} wins the second set (JJ)}) = \frac{1}{4} \times \frac{1}{4} = \frac{1}{16}$

or

$P(\text{Joe wins the first set \textbf{and then} loses the second set \textbf{and then} wins the third set (JLJ)}) = \frac{1}{4} \times \frac{3}{4} \times \frac{1}{4} = \frac{3}{64}$

or

$P(\text{Joe loses the first set \textbf{and then} wins the second set \textbf{and then} wins the third set (LJJ)}) = \frac{3}{4} \times \frac{1}{4} \times \frac{1}{4} = \frac{3}{64}$

$P(\text{Joe wins}) = \dfrac{1}{16} + \dfrac{3}{64} + \dfrac{3}{64} = \dfrac{10}{64} = \dfrac{5}{32}$

(c) $P(\text{Liam wins}|\text{he wins the first set}) = \dfrac{P(\text{Liam wins the first set and then the match})}{P(\text{Liam wins first set})}$

$$= \dfrac{\frac{9}{16} + \frac{9}{64}}{\frac{3}{4}} = \dfrac{\frac{45}{64}}{\frac{3}{4}} = \frac{45}{48} = \frac{15}{16} \text{ or just } \frac{3}{4} + \frac{3}{16} = \frac{15}{16}$$

(d) $P(\text{Liam wins first set}|\text{he wins the match}) = \dfrac{P(\text{Liam wins the first set and then the match})}{P(\text{Liam wins match})}$

$$= \dfrac{\frac{9}{16} + \frac{9}{64}}{\frac{27}{32}} = \frac{5}{6}$$

(e) Probability the match last three sets $= \dfrac{9}{64} + \dfrac{9}{64} + \dfrac{3}{64} + \dfrac{3}{64} = \dfrac{24}{64} = \dfrac{3}{8}$

EXERCISE 10

1. A jar contains black and white marbles. Two marbles are picked out in succession without being replaced. The probability of selecting a black marble and then a white marble is 0·32. The probability of selecting a black marble on the first draw is 0·45. What is the probability of selecting a white marble on the second draw, given the first marble drawn was black?

2. At a certain school, the probability that a student takes Technology and Spanish is 0·086. The probability that a student takes Technology is 0·64. What is the probability that a student takes Spanish, given that he is taking Technology?

3. In a Dublin school, 46% of all teenagers own a skateboard and 38% own a skateboard and roller blades. What is the probability that a teenager owns roller blades, given that she owns a skateboard?

4. In a school, 20% of all students play football and basketball. 35% of all students play football. What is the probability a student plays basketball, given that he plays football?

5. In the US, 55% of all children get pocket money and 43% of all children get pocket money and do household chores. What is the probability that a child does chores, given she gets pocket money?

6. In Europe, 85% of all households have a TV. 50% of all households have a TV and a tablet. What is the probability that a household has a tablet, given it has a TV?

7. In Galway, 52% of houses have a garage and 25% have a back garden and a garage. What is the probability that a house has a back garden, given it has a garage?

8. In a school, 64% of all students play Gaelic football and 56% play hurling. If 32% of those who play football also play hurling, find the percentage who play both. Find the percentage of those who play hurling and also play football, correct to two decimal places. Use a Venn diagram.

9. For the Venn diagram shown, find:

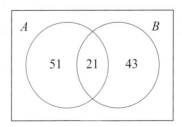

(a) $P(B|A)$ **(b)** $P(A|B)$

10. A check of college students' accommodation revealed that 90% had internet access, 29% had games consoles and 20% had both internet access and games consoles. Draw a Venn diagram to represent this information. What is the probability that a randomly selected student accommodation has:

  (a) a games console but no internet access,

  (b) a games console or internet access but not both,

  (c) neither a game console nor internet access,

  (d) a games console, given it has internet acccss?

11. Real estate advertisements suggest 64% of homes in the US have garages and 21% have swimming pools and 17% have both. Draw a Venn diagram to illustrate this information.

  (a) What is the probability that a home has a pool or a garage?

  (b) What is the probability that a home has neither a pool nor a garage?

  (c) What is the probability that a home has a pool but no garage?

  (d) If a home has a garage, what is the probability it also has a pool?

  (e) Are having a garage and a pool independent? Why?

  (f) Are having a pool and a garage mutually exclusive? Why?

12. A consumer body estimates that 29% of new cars have a cosmetic defect such as a scratch or a dent when they are delivered to dealers. They also believe that 7% have a functional defect and that 2% have both kinds of problems. Illustrate this information using a Venn diagram.

  (a) If you buy a new car, what is the probability it has some kind of defect?

  (b) What is the probability it has a cosmetic defect but no functional defect?

  (c) If there is a dent or scratch on a new car, what is the probability it has a functional defect?

  (d) Are the two events mutually exclusive?

  (e) Are the two kinds of defects independent?

13. For two events $P(A) = 0.7$, $P(B) = 0.5$ and $P(A \cap B) = 0.3$.

  (a) Find $P(A \cup B)$.

  (b) Find $P(A|B)$.

  (c) Are A and B independent?

14. The table below shows the percentage of boys and girls in a class and the percentage of each gender who wear glasses.

	Glasses	No glasses	Totals
Boys	36	24	60
Girls	14	26	40
Totals	50	50	100

The teacher chooses a student randomly from a class.

  (a) What is the probability she chooses a boy?

  (b) What is the probability she chooses someone not wearing glasses?

  (c) What is the probability she chooses a boy, given that the person she chooses is not wearing glasses?

  (d) What is the probability that the person chosen is not wearing glasses, given that the person is a boy?

  (e) Is $P(\text{No glasses}|\text{Boy}) = P(\text{Boy}|\text{No glasses})$?

  (f) What is the probability that she chooses a girl, given the person she chooses is wearing glasses?

  (g) Is $P(\text{Girl}|\text{Glasses}) = P(\text{Glasses}|\text{Girl})$?

15. One hundred people were asked the question 'Do you smoke?'. The following responses were given:

	Yes	No	Total
Male	19	41	60
Female	12	28	40
Total	31	69	100

   (a) What is the probability that the person randomly selected is a male who smokes?

   (b) What is the probability that a randomly selected person is a male?

   (c) What is the probability that a randomly selected person smokes?

   (d) What is the probability that a randomly selected male is a smoker?

   (e) What is the probability that a randomly selected smoker is a male?

16. Three major companies make tyres. Abel (A) has a 50% market share, Bull (B) has a 30% market share and Close (C) has a 20% share. However, 5% of A, 7% of B and 10% of C products are defective.

Company	Good (G)	Defective (D)	Total
A	47·5	2·5	50
B	27·9	2·1	30
C	18·0	2·0	20
Total	93·4	6·6	100

   A product is selected at random.

   (a) What is the probability it is defective?

   (b) What is the probability that a product came from B, given it was defective, i.e. $P(B|D)$?

   (c) Are these events, B and D, independent? Why?

   (d) Find $P(D|B)$.

   (e) Show that $P(D|B) = \dfrac{P(B|D) \times P(D)}{P(B)}$.

17. A researcher wants to evaluate how well a diagnostic test for liver disease works in patients with high blood pressure. The test is performed on 150 patients, of whom 70 have liver disease and 80 are healthy. The results are either positive (the patient has the disease) or negative (the patient does not have the disease).

   The results are set out in the table below.

	Positive (P)	Negative (N)	Total
Diseased (D)	50	20	70
Healthy (H)	15	65	80
Total	65	85	150

   (a) What is the probability a person is healthy and tests positive?

   (b) What is the probability that a person is healthy?

   (c) What is the probability that a healthy person tests positive?

   (d) What is the probability that a diseased person tests negative?

18. Susan goes to school by one of two routes A or B. The probability she goes by route A is 30%. If she goes by route A, the probability of being late for school is 5% and if she goes by route B the probability of being late is 10%.

   Draw a tree diagram to illustrate this information.

   If L is the event of being late, find:

   (a) $P(A)$ (c) $P(L|A)$

   (b) $P(B)$ (d) $P(L|B)$

   (e) Find the probability that Susan is late for school.

   (f) Given Susan is late for school, find the probability that she went via route A.

19. Assume there is a test for cancer that is 98% accurate, i.e. if someone has cancer the test will be positive 98% of the time and if someone does not have cancer the test will be negative 98% of the time. Assume further that 0·5% actually have cancer. Imagine someone has taken the test and the doctor informs them they have cancer.

  (a) What is the probability that a person tests positive for cancer?

  (b) What is the probability that a person has cancer, given they tested positive?

20. Enzyme tests are used to screen blood specimens for the presence of antibodies to HIV, the virus that causes Aids. Antibodies indicate the presence of the virus. The test is quite accurate but is not always correct. Here is a table of approximate probabilities of positive and negative test results when the blood tested does and does not contain antibodies to HIV.

	Positive	Negative
Antibodies present	0·9985	0·0015
Antibodies absent	0·006	0·9940

Suppose 1% of a large population carries antibodies to HIV in their blood.

Draw a tree diagram for selecting a person from this population and for testing his/her blood.

  (a) What is the probability that the test is positive for a randomly chosen person?

  (b) What is the probability that the person has the antibody, given the test is positive?

21. A golf player finds that when the day is calm, the probability of him hitting his target is 0·8. When the day is not calm, the probability of him hitting his target is 0·55. According to the local weather forecasters, the probability that any particular day is calm is 0·6. A day is chosen at random. Using a tree diagram, write out all the possible outcomes. Calculate the probability of each outcome and show that the sum of the probabilities is 1.

  (a) Hence, find the probability of him:

   (i) hitting his target,

   (ii) not hitting his target.

  (b) Given that he does not hit his target, what is the probability that the day is calm?

22. Online chat rooms are dominated by young people. Of all adult internet users, 29% are aged between 18 and 29, 47% are aged between 30 and 49 and 24% are over 50.

  • Of 18–29-year-old internet users, 47% use chat rooms.

  • Of 30–49-year-old users, 21% use chat rooms.

  • Of the over 50s, 7% use chat rooms.

Illustrate this information on a tree diagram.

What is the probability a randomly chosen internet user uses a chat room?

16.3 Expected value

In **experimental probability,** you deduced the probability of a set of outcomes of an experiment by performing a large number of trials of the experiment.

In **theoretical probability,** you used experimental values to develop a method of finding the probability of a set of outcomes of a single trial of an experiment. For example, $P = 0.5$ is the probability for tossing a coin once.

In this section on expected values, you are going to use the probability values from a single trial of an experiment to predict the average value of a variable (discrete random) associated with an outcome of a trial of an experiment over a large number of trials. Before you do this, you need to understand the idea of a random variable.

Random variable

If you toss a coin three times, the results can be recorded as a string of heads and tails such a HTH, where H = head and T = tail. In statistics, you are most often interested in numerical outcomes such as the 'number of heads in three tosses'.

To keep count of the number of heads in each outcome of a trial a variable, x is used: x = Number of heads

If the outcome is HTT: $x = 1$ (one head)

But if the outcome is HHT: $x = 2$ (two heads)

The possible values for x are 0, 1, 2 and 3.

Tossing a coin three times will give x one of these values. Tossing three more times will give x another and probably a different one of these values.

KEY TERM

A **random variable** is a variable whose numerical value is associated with the outcome of a random phenomenon.

The value of a random variable will vary from trial to trial in an experiment.

There are two types of random variable: **discrete** and **continuous.** We will examine continuous random variables later in this chapter.

A random variable has a probability distribution (relative frequency) which is the assignment of probabilities to specific values of a discrete random variable or to a range of values of a continuous random variable. This distribution tells us what values x can take and how to assign probabilities to these values.

Discrete random variable

A discrete random variable is a variable x that can have only a finite number of discrete values giving rise to a discrete probability distribution.

Probability distribution of discrete random variable x

	Values				
Outcome variable x	x_1	x_2	x_3	...	x_n
Probability $P(x)$	P_1	P_2	P_3	...	P_n
Product $xP(x)$	x_1P_1	x_2P_2	x_3P_3	...	x_nP_n

Each probability P_i must satisfy two requirements:

$0 \leq P_i \leq 1$ for all $i \in \{1, 2, \ldots, n\}$

$P_1 + P_2 + P_3 + P_4 + \ldots + P_n = 1$ or $\sum P(x) = 1$.

EXAMPLE 13

A certain college posts its grades online. In Geography, its students received the following grades: 20% got an A, 48% got a B, 25% got a C, 5% got a D and 2% got an E.

Grade A is assigned 4 points, B is assigned 3 points, C is assigned 2 points, D is assigned 1 point and E is assigned 0 points.

Draw up a probability distribution where x represents the points value of a grade.

Find the probability a student got a B or above.

What is the average point score of a randomly selected student?

Solution

Grade	E	D	C	B	A
x	0	1	2	3	4
$P(x)$	0·02	0·05	0·25	0·48	0·2
$xP(x)$	0	0·05	0·5	1·44	0·8

$\sum P(x) = 1$

$P(x \geq 3) = 0·48 + 0·2 = 0·68$

Since $P(x)$ is a relative frequency:

$$\text{Mean } \bar{x} = \frac{\sum xP(x)}{\sum P} = \frac{0 + 0·05 + 0·5 + 1·44 + 0·8}{1}$$

$= 2·79$, where $P(x)$ is the relative frequency or probability.

The meaning of expected value

WORKED EXAMPLE — Explaining expected value

In a university entrance test, students are awarded points corresponding to a grade.

Grade	A	B	C	D	N
Points	4	3	2	1	0

A teacher, in preparing her class for this test, gives them a mock trial test.
The results were as follows:

Grade	A	B	C	D	N
Number of students	3	10	4	2	1

Using these results, she decided to predict the **expected** grade point average mark for her class in the real exam by constructing a probability distribution as follows:

Grade	A	B	C	D	N
Value of grade x	4	3	2	1	0
Relative frequency (*RF*) of grade	0·15	0·5	0·2	0·1	0·05
Probability of grade value x: $P(x)$	0·15	0·5	0·2	0·1	0·05

$P(x)$ is the probability of a value x associated with an outcome. It is also the relative frequency of this outcome in a frequency table of all possible outcomes of one trial of an experiment.

Expected grade point average $\mathbf{E} = \dfrac{\sum xP(x)}{\sum P(x)} = \sum xP(x)$

$$= 4 \times 0.15 + 3 \times 0.5 + 2 \times 0.2 + 1 \times 0.1 + 0 \times 0.05$$

$\mathbf{E} = 2.6$ = Sum of all the x values multiplied by the $P(x)$ values

- The probability values $P(x)$ must always add up to 1, as we are dealing with all possible outcomes of a single trial of an experiment. Every student must get one of the grades A, B, C, D or N.

  Sum of probabilities $= 0.15 + 0.5 + 0.2 + 0.1 + 0.05 = 1$

- The expected value does not have to be one of the original outcome values.
  $\mathbf{E} = 2.6$ is not a value of one of the grades.

KEY TERM

The **expected value** $\mathbf{E}$ of a discrete (random) variable is the sum of the probabilities $P(x)$ of each possible outcome of a single trial of an experiment multiplied by the value of the variable that quantifies the outcome.

	Values				
Outcome variable x	x_1	x_2	x_3	...	x_n
Probability $P(x)$	P_1	P_2	P_3	...	P_n
Product $xP(x)$	$x_1 P_1$	$x_2 P_2$	$x_3 P_3$	...	$x_n P_n$

$$\mathbf{E} = \dfrac{\sum xP(x)}{\sum P} = \sum xP(x) = \text{Sum of } xP(x) = x_1 P_1 + x_2 P_2 + x_3 P_3 + ... + x_n P_n,$$

since $\sum P = P_1 + P_2 + ... + P_n = 1$.

$$\boxed{\mathbf{E} = \sum xP(x)}$$

The expected value of an experiment is the weighted average of all possible values of a variable of a single trial of an experiment associated with an outcome.

The expected value of a variable associated with an outcome of a single trial of an experiment is the average value of the variable in the long run (over many trials).

EXAMPLE 14

A fair coin is tossed three times. What is the expected value of getting a head?

Solution

Let x = Number of heads

	No heads	1 head	2 heads	3 heads
x	0	1	2	3
$P(x)$	$\frac{1}{8}$	$\frac{3}{8}$	$\frac{3}{8}$	$\frac{1}{8}$

$$\therefore \mathbf{E} = 0\left(\frac{1}{8}\right) + 1\left(\frac{3}{8}\right) + 2\left(\frac{3}{8}\right) + 3\left(\frac{1}{8}\right) = \frac{12}{8} = 1.5$$

You expect to get a head 1·5 times out of 3.

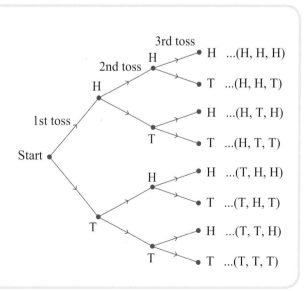

Applications of expected value

1. Fair games

A fair game is a game in which the expected net winnings are zero. A game with negative expected winnings is unfair against the player and vice versa.

Is a game fair?

What is the probability of rolling **(a)** a 6, **(b)** a 1, **(c)** a 2 or a 3 or a 4, **(d)** a 5, in one roll of a fair die?

(a) $P(6) = \frac{1}{6}$

(c) $P(2 \text{ or } 3 \text{ or } 4) = \frac{1}{2}$

(b) $P(1) = \frac{1}{6}$

(d) $P(5) = \frac{1}{6}$

Ann and Barry each have a pile of sweets. They play a game with a fair die. If Barry rolls a 6, Ann gives him four sweets. If he rolls a 1, he gives Ann two sweets. If he rolls a 2 or 3 or 4, he gives Ann one sweet. If he rolls a 5, there is no exchange of sweets.

If x is the number of sweets Barry gets, draw up a probability distribution for this random variable. Find the expected value of the net number of sweets Barry gets.

Probability distribution table:

	Rolls a 6	Rolls 1	Rolls 2 or 3 or 4	Rolls 5
Number of sweets Barry gets x	+4	−2	−1	0
Probability $P(x)$	$\frac{1}{6}$	$\frac{1}{6}$	$\frac{1}{2}$	$\frac{1}{6}$
$xP(x)$	$\frac{2}{3}$	$-\frac{1}{3}$	$-\frac{1}{2}$	0

The sum of $P(x)$ values is 1.

Expected value $\mathbf{E} = \frac{2}{3} - \frac{1}{3} - \frac{1}{2} + 0 = -\frac{1}{6}$

Barry on average will lose $\frac{1}{6}$ of a sweet per game.

This is not a fair game because it favours Ann. If $\mathbf{E}$ were positive, it would favour Barry.

In a fair game, the expected value would be 0.

If Ann were to give Barry one sweet each time he throws a 5 then the game would be fair, as the expected value would be 0.

TIP
A game is fair if the expected value is 0.

EXAMPLE 15

A spinner consists of six sectors all of equal area.

(a) Find the probability the spinner stops on **(i)** €5, **(ii)** €3, **(iii)** €2, **(iv)** €1, **(v)** game over.

(b) A game of 'spin and win' costs €2 per spin. You spin the spinner. Your winnings are whatever amount the spinner stops on. If x denotes your net winnings on a spin, draw up a probability distribution table for x and use it to find the expected value of your winnings per spin. Is this game fair?

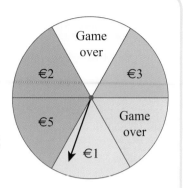

Solution

(a) **(i)** $P(€5) = \frac{1}{6}$ **(iii)** $P(€2) = \frac{1}{6}$ **(v)** $P(€0) = \frac{1}{3}$

    (ii) $P(€3) = \frac{1}{6}$ **(iv)** $P(€1) = \frac{1}{6}$

(b) **Probability distribution table:**

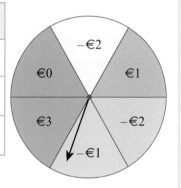

	Stops at €5	Stops at €3	Stops at €2	Stops at €1	Stops at Game over
Net winnings x (euros)	3	1	0	−1	−2
$P(x)$	$\frac{1}{6}$	$\frac{1}{6}$	$\frac{1}{6}$	$\frac{1}{6}$	$\frac{1}{3}$
$xP(x)$	$\frac{1}{2}$	$\frac{1}{6}$	0	$-\frac{1}{6}$	$-\frac{2}{3}$

Sum of the $P(x)$ values is equal to 1.

Expected value $\mathbf{E} = \frac{1}{2} + \frac{1}{6} + 0 - \frac{1}{6} - \frac{2}{3} = -\frac{1}{6}$

This is not a fair game.

If you played 12 times you would lose $\frac{1}{6} \times €12 = €2$.

EXAMPLE 16

(a) The probability of choosing six specified different numbers from 48 different numbers is $\frac{1}{12\,271\,512}$. What is the probability of not selecting the specified six numbers?

(b) A lottery ticket costs €2. If you win €1 000 000 for guessing six numbers correctly from 48 numbers, what is the expected value of your net winnings? Should you play the lottery?

Solution

(a) $P(\text{Not selecting the specified 6 numbers}) = 1 - \frac{1}{12\,271\,512} = \frac{12\,271\,511}{12\,271\,512}$

(b) Let x = Net winnings per game in euros

	Win	Lose
Net winnings x (euros)	999 998	−2
Probability $P(x)$	$\frac{1}{12\,271\,512}$	$\frac{12\,271\,511}{12\,271\,512}$
$xP(x)$	$\frac{999\,998}{12\,271\,512}$	$-\frac{24\,543\,022}{12\,271\,512}$

Expected value $\mathbf{E} = \dfrac{999\,998}{12\,271\,512} - \dfrac{24\,543\,022}{12\,271\,512} = -1\cdot92$

You lose €1·92 on average every time you play, so you should not play the lottery.

2. Risk analysis

Levels of insurance premiums and financial investments are calculated using 'expected value' as one of the criteria.

EXAMPLE 17

A 50-year-old man has a 0·25% chance (risk) of dying in a certain country during the following year. An insurance company charges him a yearly premium of €300 for a life insurance policy that pays €100 000 on death.

(a) Find the probability of the man (i) dying, (ii) not dying, within the year.

(b) What is the expected value of the income from this insurance policy to the man?

Solution

(a) (i) $P(\text{Man dies}) = 0\cdot0025$

   (ii) $P(\text{Man lives}) = 0\cdot9975$

(b) Let x = Net income of the policy to the man

	Dies	Lives
Net income x to man (euros)	€99 700	−€300
Probability $P(x)$	0·0025	0·9975
$xP(x)$	249·25	−299·25

Expected value of income to the man per year

$\mathbf{E} = 249\cdot25 - 299\cdot25 = -€50$

He loses.

The insurance company can afford to offer policies only if, on average, they make money on each policy. They can afford to pay out the occasional claim because those claims are covered by the rest of the insured people.

So why do people buy insurance? Security and peace of mind, of course.

Continuous random variables

Suppose you spin a pointer in a circle graduated from 0 to 1. The pointer can come to rest at any point on the circle and can take any value from 0 to 1.

The sample space $S = \{\text{All numbers } x \mid 0 \leq x \leq 1, x \in \mathbb{R}\}$. How can you assign a probability to an event B such as $B = \{0\cdot3 \leq x \leq 0\cdot8, x \in \mathbb{R}\}$?

There are infinitely many values of x. This means you cannot assign individual probabilities to each value of x and then add up these probabilities to find the probability of B.

Instead, the probability of an event is calculated as an area under a probability (relative frequency) density curve. A density curve has a total area of exactly 1, corresponding to a total probability of 1.

For our example, assuming landing on every point is equally likely, a typical density curve or frequency distribution curve is the straight line shown.

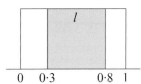

$P(0{\cdot}3 \le x \le 0{\cdot}8) = \big|$Area under the curve l between $0{\cdot}3$ and $0{\cdot}8\big| = 0{\cdot}5$

The idea of probability as an area under a density curve is a second important way of assigning probabilities to events. We will meet this again in Section 6 Statistics.

KEY TERM

A **continuous random variable** x can take on all values in an interval of numbers.

The probability distribution of a continuous random variable x is described by a density curve. The probability $P(B)$ of any event B is the area under the density curve, defined by the range of values of x that make up the event.

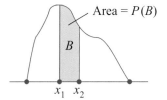

NOTES

The probability density curve for a continuous random variable assigns probabilities to intervals of outcomes rather than to individual outcomes.

In fact, all continuous probability distributions assign a probability 0 to every individual outcome. Only intervals of values have positive probabilities.

EXERCISE 11

1. Copy and complete the following tables. Find the missing value y in each of the following discrete random variable distributions and find $\sum xP(x)$.

   (a)
x	1	3	5	7
$P(x)$	$\frac{1}{5}$	$\frac{1}{5}$	$\frac{1}{5}$	y
$xP(x)$				

   (b)
x	100	200	300	400	500
$P(x)$	0·1	0·2	0·4	y	0·1
$xP(x)$					

   (c)
x	10	15	20	25	30
$P(x)$	0·15	0·2	y	0·25	0·2
$xP(x)$					

2. Suppose x is the number of jobs held during the previous year by students at a school. The following is the probability distribution.

Number of jobs x	0	1	2	3	4
$P(x)$	0·12	0·38	0·25	0·14	y
$xP(x)$					

   (a) Find y.

   (b) Find $P(x \le 2)$.

   (c) Find the probability a student held at least one job.

   (d) Find $\sum xP(x)$.

3. A random variable x has the following probability distribution.

x	−2	0	2
$P(x)$	0·4	0·2	y
$xP(x)$			

   Find:

   (a) y (b) $P(x \le 0)$ (c) $\sum xP(x)$

4. Suppose the probability that you get an A in any test you take is 0·4 and the probability you get a B is 0·6. If an A is worth 4 points and a B, 3 points, find the expected value of your grade point average for this test.

5. A dairy farmer estimates for the next year her cows will produce about 120 000 litres of milk. Because of variation in the market price of milk and the cost of feeding the cows, the profit per litre may vary with the probabilities shown.

Gain per litre (cent)	18	15	10	7	0	−2
Probability $P(x)$	0·3	0·35	0·2	0·05	0·04	0·06
$xP(x)$						

Estimate the expected profit per litre and hence the profit on 120 000 litres.

6. Go Cheap Airlines is planning its staffing levels for the forthcoming year. If a new route is approved, it will hire 1000 new employees. If the new route is not approved, it will hire only 200 new employees. The probability that a new route will be approved is 0·4. Copy and complete the probability distribution table.

	Approved	Not approved
New number of employees x	1000	200
Probability $P(x)$		
$xP(x)$		

Find the expected number of new employees.

7. A lawyer believes his chances of getting a client off a charge are $\frac{3}{4}$. If he loses, he charges the client his expenses of €5000. If he wins, his total fee is €40 000. Find his expected earning at the conclusion of the trial using the probability distribution table.

	Win	Lose
Earning x (€)	40 000	5000
Probability $P(x)$		

8. A company plans to invest in a particular project. There is a 30% chance the company will lose €20 000, a 40% chance it will break even and a 30% chance it will make €50 000. By finding the expected return, what should the company do? Use the table below.

	Lose	Break even	Win
Return €x	−20 000	0	50 000
Probability $P(x)$			
$xP(x)$			

9. A group of fourth-year students were surveyed as to the number x of hours per week they spent playing video games. The probability distribution is given below.

Number of hours per week x	0	1	2	3
Probability $P(x)$	0·35	0·4	0·15	0·1

Verify the sum of probabilities = 1.

Find the expected number of hours a fourth-year student plays video games.

10. You pay €10 to play the following game of chance with a box containing 12 cards, of which five are red, four are blue and the rest are green. You draw one card from the box. You win €15 if you draw a red and €13 if you draw a green.

Find your expected winnings. How much do you expect to win in 100 games?

11. A horse owner estimates the probability his horse will finish first in a race at $\frac{1}{20}$, coming second at $\frac{1}{10}$ and coming third at $\frac{2}{5}$. First place pays €5000, second place pays €3000 and third place pays €1000. If it costs €500 to enter the horse in the race, find the expected net winnings. There is no prize money for being unplaced.

	1st	2nd	3rd	Unplaced
Net winnings (€)	4500	2500	500	−500
Probability	$\frac{1}{20}$	$\frac{1}{10}$	$\frac{2}{5}$	

12. (a) Find the probability of tossing **(i)** zero heads, **(ii)** one head, **(iii)** two heads, **(iv)** three heads when three fair coins are tossed together.

(b) A game at a carnival involves tossing three coins together. You win €2 for each head you throw.

By copying and completing the table below, find the expected value of your winnings.

	0 heads	1 head	2 heads	3 heads
Winning x (€)				
Probability $P(x)$				
$xP(x)$				

(c) (i) What must the carnival owner charge per game to make the game fair?

(ii) If he charges €4 per game, what is his average profit per game?

13. A roulette wheel has 38 different numbers. If you place a ball on one of these numbers, what is the probability:

(a) you will win,

(b) you will lose?

If you bet €1 on a number and you are right, you win €18 and get your €1 back. If you are wrong, you lose your €1. By copying and completing the probability distribution table below, find the expected value of your winnings per game. Is this game fair?

	Win	Lose
Winning x (€)	+18	−1
Probability $P(x)$	$\frac{1}{38}$	
$xP(x)$		

14. (a) Find the probability of rolling **(i)** a 2, **(ii)** a 4, **(iii)** a 6, **(iv)** an odd number, in one throw of a fair die.

(b) A game is played by rolling a single fair die. In this game, a player wins €20 if he rolls a 2 and €40 if he rolls a 4. He loses €30 if he rolls a 6 and neither wins nor loses by rolling any other number. By copying and completing the table below, find the expected value of the winnings of the player.

	Rolls a 2	Rolls a 4	Rolls a 6	Rolls an odd number
Net winnings x(€) of player	+€20	+€40	−€30	€0
Probability $P(x)$				
$xP(x)$				

15. In a raffle, there are 200 prizes of €10, 20 prizes of €50 and 5 prizes of €100. Assume 5000 tickets are sold.

(a) Find the probability of:

(i) winning a €10 prize,

(ii) winning a €50 prize,

(iii) winning a €100 prize,

(iv) winning €0.

(b) Copy and complete the table below and use it to find the expected value of the winnings per ticket.

Winnings x(€) per ticket	+€10	+€50	+€100	€0
Probability $P(x)$				
$xP(x)$				

16. For a particular age group, statistics show that the probability of dying in any one year is 1 in 1000 and the probability of suffering some sort of disability is 3 in 1000.

(a) For this age group, find the probability in the following year that a person:

(i) will die,

(ii) will be disabled,

(iii) will not die or not be disabled.

(b) The Better Life Assurance Company offers a person in this age group a policy with a premium of €100 which pays €20 000 on death and €10 000 for a disability.

By copying and completing the table below, find the expected value of the profit to the company per year from one person.

	Death	Disability	Neither death nor disability
Profit x (€) to company			
Probability $P(x)$			
$xP(x)$			

17. A randomly selected family has three children. Write out the sample space of all possible three-child families using a tree diagram. Let x denote the number of boys in the family. Find the expected value of x, i.e. the average number of boys in a three-child family.

18. The Ryan family wants to have children. A statistical analysis shows that based on families with similar financial status, the probability distribution for the random variable x, where x denotes the number of children they might have, is:

x	0	1	2	3
$P(x)$	0·04	0·62	0·33	0·01

What is the expected value of x?

What does it mean? Is the value a possible outcome for the number of children?

19. The probability that Joe will win a game is 0·02. What is the probability he will not win? If Joe wins, he will get €150 but if he loses he must pay €10. If x denotes the amount of money Joe wins, what is the expected value of x?

20. An insurance company expects 10% of its policy holders to collect claims of €500 this year and the remaining 90% to collect nothing. What is the expected value of the amount they will pay out per claim? If the company wants to make a €10 per year net profit per policy holder how much should they charge each person for insurance?

21. In Ireland in 2000, 80% of children were living with both parents, 12% with their mother only, 5% with their father only and 3% with neither. What is the expected value for the number of parents a randomly selected child was living with in 2000?

22. For a fair coin tossed twice the sample space is $S = \{(H, H), (H, T), (T, H), (T, T)\}$. Let x denote the number of heads. Set up a probability distribution for x and find the expected value of the number of heads when a fair coin is tossed twice.

23. A class of 12 pupils has ten right-handed students and two left-handed students. Two students are chosen from the class. Write out the sample space for this experiment. Draw up a probability distribution for x where x denotes the number of left-handed students. Find the expected value for x.

24. A woman decides to continue having children until she has her first boy or until she has four children, whichever comes first. Let x denote the number of children she has. Assume the probability of a boy is $\frac{1}{2}$ for each birth.

    (a) Write out the sample space using B for boy and G for girl, e.g. GB means she stops after a boy.

    (b) Find the probability of each single event in the sample space.

    (c) Draw up a probability distribution for the discrete random variable x.

    (d) Find the expected number of children the woman will have.

25. Using the information in Question 24, let x denote the number of girls. Draw the probability distribution for x and find the expected number of girls.

26. Find the expected value for x, the sum of the numbers on the faces of two dice when they are thrown together, by copying and completing the table below.

	1	2	3	4	5	6
1	(1, 1)	(1, 2)	(1, 3)	(1, 4)	(1, 5)	(1, 6)
2	(2, 1)	(2, 2)	(2, 3)	(2, 4)	(2, 5)	(2, 6)
3	(3, 1)	(3, 2)	(3, 3)	(3, 4)	(3, 5)	(3, 6)
4	(4, 1)	(4, 2)	(4, 3)	(4, 4)	(4, 5)	(4, 6)
5	(5, 1)	(5, 2)	(5, 3)	(5, 4)	(5, 5)	(5, 6)
6	(6, 1)	(6, 2)	(6, 3)	(6, 4)	(6, 5)	(6, 6)

x	2	3	4	5	6	7	8	9	10	11	12
$P(x)$											

27. A man is deciding to buy travel insurance at €50 for the year. He thinks that the probability he will need it next year is 0·2 and it will cost him €200 if he does not have insurance. Let x denote the cost next year for liabilities and/or insurance.

    (a) If he buys the insurance, what is the value of x? There is only one answer.

    (b) If he does not buy it, x has two values. What are they? Draw a probability distribution.

    (c) Find the expected value of x. Should he buy the insurance?

REVISION QUESTIONS

1. **(a)** State the conditions for an experiment to be a Bernoulli experiment.

    (b) (i) Write down the probability for r successes in a Bernoulli experiment of n trials if p is the probability of success and q the probability of failure in one trial.

    (ii) Two tennis players play a set of six games. Does the set of outcomes of either player in each game form a sequence of Bernoulli trials?

    (c) A type of heart surgery in a certain hospital is unsuccessful in 7% of the cases. The success of all operations is independent of each other in 20 such operations. Find the probability of:

    (i) exactly 17 successful operations, correct to three decimal places,

    (ii) at least 17 successful operations, correct to three decimal places.

2. **(a)** Define expected value of a discrete random variable. Explain what it means in your own words.

    (b) A game consists of rolling a six-sided fair die once. If you roll a 6 you get €3. If you roll a 5 you get nothing. If you roll a number less than 5 you pay €1.

    Draw up a probability distribution using x as the value of your winnings. Find the expected value of your winnings. Should you play this game?

    (c) A company estimates 0·8% of its products fail after a 1-year warranty runs out but within 2 years of purchase. The company offers an extended 2-year warranty for €50. The replacement value of the product is €450. What is the company's expected income on each extended warranty sold? Is it worth its while selling this warranty?

3. **(a)** The probability that Joe will be late for morning assembly is 0·04. The probability that Fiona will be late for assembly is 0·03. The probability that both will be late for assembly is 0·005. Are the events Joe will be late for morning assembly and Fiona will be late for morning assembly independent? Why?

    (b) Felix travels to school by bus every day. The probability that the bus will be late on any day is 0·25. Copy and complete the probability tree diagram for Wednesday and Thursday.

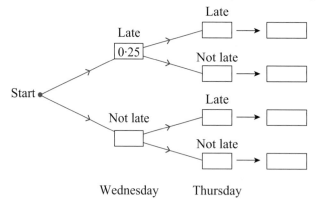

Use the diagram to find the probability that Felix:

    (i) was late on Wednesday and Thursday,

    (ii) was not late on both days,

    (iii) was late on Thursday, given he was not late on Wednesday.

4. (a) Find the probability of tossing four heads and two tails in six tosses of a fair coin.

(b) An insurance company estimates the probability of an earthquake in a region of California in the next year to be 0·0012. The company estimates the average claim per person after an earthquake to be $58 000. The company offers earthquake insurance for $100 per premium to a potential customer. By calculating the expected value of this insurance, advise the customer of the pros and cons of buying this insurance.

(c) A school offers three sports: football (F), basketball (B) and athletics (A) to a year group of 75 students. Every student must take one or more of these sports. The number of students that chooses a sport is shown in the Venn diagram.

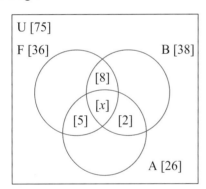

Find x.

If two students are chosen at random find the probability

(i) both play basketball only,

(ii) neither plays football,

(iii) one plays all three sports and the other plays only one sport.

5. (a) The probability of an 18-year-old passing her driving test in any sitting is $\frac{2}{3}$. If she fails she takes it again and again until she passes. Find the probability that:

(i) she passes on the third attempt,

(ii) she passes in less than four attempts.

(b) A gambling game consists of tossing a fair coin three times. You win if you throw three heads or three tails, otherwise you lose. Find the probability that you lose a particular game.

(c) The probability of a man being colour blind is 0·05 and a woman being colour blind is 0·0025. Complete the tree diagram below to find the probability that a person is colour blind in a population with 65% men. Find also the probability a person will be a man given the person is colour blind.

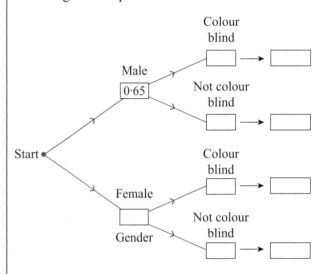

6. (a) A satellite defence system has four satellites which act independently in detecting an incoming missile. If each has a probability of 0·88 of detecting an incoming missile, find the probability of:

(i) exactly three detecting an incoming missile, correct to three decimal places,

(ii) at least one detecting an incoming missile, correct to four decimal places.

Would you feel safe with such a system?

(b) The data below represents the number of traffic fatalities of drivers and passengers in a country over a number of years.

	Male	Female	Total
Driver	20 800	6600	
Passenger			
Total		11 500	38 000

(i) Copy and complete the table.

(ii) What is the probability that a randomly selected traffic fatality who was female was a passenger?

(iii) What is the probability that a randomly selected passenger fatality was female?

(iv) A Garda on his way to a fatal traffic accident is informed on the radio that the victim was the driver. Is the victim more likely to be male or female? Why?

7. (a) A bank alarm system has n detectors covering n zones. The probability that a detector activates when an intruder passes is 0.8. The detectors all operate independently of each other. If an intruder enters the bank and passes through all n zones, what is the smallest number n that is possible so that the probability of at least one detector going off is greater than 0.99?

(b) Seamus is a striker for his school soccer team. The probability of Seamus scoring a number of goals in a game is given by the table shown.

Number of goals x	0	1	2	3
Probability P	0.35	0.35	0.2	0.1

Assuming Seamus's goal-scoring ability in a game is independent of any other game, find the probability that:

(i) he scores in each of three consecutive games, correct to four decimal places,

(ii) he scores a total of seven or more goals in three consecutive games.

Find the expected value of the number of goals Seamus scores per game.

(c) What is the probability that a child in a class of 20 was born on a Monday? What is the probability that:

(i) two children in the class were born on a Monday, correct to three decimal places,

(ii) at most two children in the class were born on a Monday, correct to two decimal places,

(iii) at least two children in the class were born on a Monday, correct to one decimal place?

8. (a) According to a census, 14% of the population of a country lives below the poverty line. What is the probability at least two people in a sample of 25 will be below the poverty line, correct to three decimal places?

(b) In a town, 80% of retirees get the flu jab. The probability of a retiree catching the flu is 0.032 if they got the flu jab but is 0.68 if they did not get the flu jab.

By completing the tree diagram below, find the probability that a retiree picked at random catches the flu.

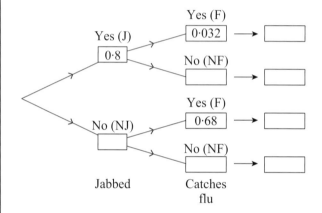

Jabbed   Catches flu

(c) Two darts are thrown at a dartboard. They are equally likely to hit any number between 1 and 20. (Ignore bull's-eye, doubles and trebles.)

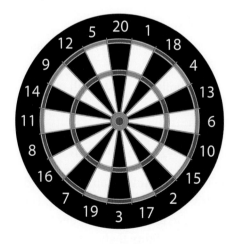

(i) How many different outcomes are there to throwing two darts?

(ii) What is the probability of a total score of 3 from the two darts?

(iii) What is the probability that both darts hit the same number?

(iv) What is the probability of a total score of 17 from the two darts?

9. **(a)** On a road there are four sets of traffic lights which operate independently of each other. The green stays on for 140 seconds and the red for 80 seconds. What is the probability that a random motorist arriving at the lights will have to stop at least once, correct to three decimal places?

(b) A boat has three lifejackets on board. The boat begins to sink. There are two swimmers and three non-swimmers on board. What is the probability that the jackets are grabbed by two non-swimmers and one swimmer?

(c) Airlines regularly overbook flights. An airline sells 120 tickets for a flight with a maximum capacity of 115 seats. If the probability that a passenger does not turn up is $0 \cdot 1$ and all arrive independently for the flight, find the probability that:

(i) every passenger who shows up gets on the flight, correct to two decimal places,

(ii) not every passenger who shows up gets on, correct to four decimal places

10. The Monty Hall problem: You are on a TV game show and you are given a choice of three doors. There is a car behind one door and a goat behind each of the other two doors. You pick a door (Door 1 say). The host Monty knows what is behind each door. He opens another door which has a goat behind it. He asks you if you want to change your mind and switch your choice to Door 2 or Door 3.

Complete the tree diagram below and work out the probability that the car is behind Door 2 given that Monty has opened Door 3. Make a decision about switching your choice.

Remember Monty cannot open Door 1 (your original choice or the door hiding the car).

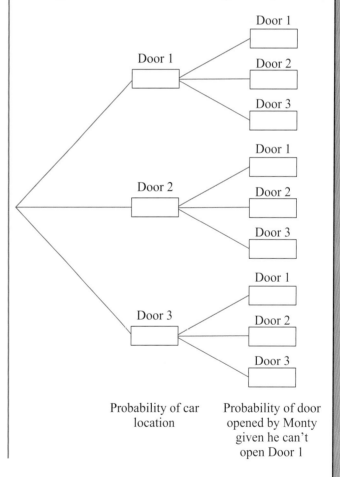

SUMMARY

Probability

1. Counting:

   (a) Multiplication principle: If there are

   a ways to do one operation and

   b ways to do a second operation and

   c ways to do a third operation, etc., the number of ways of doing the first operation and then the second and then the third, etc., is given by:

   $a \times b \times c \times \ldots$

   (b) The number of permutations (arrangements) of n different objects all taken with no repetition $= n! = n \times (n-1) \times (n-2) \times \ldots \times 1$

   (c) The number of permutations (arrangements/ of n different objects taken r at a time with no repetition

   $= {}^nP_r = n \times (n-1) \times \ldots \times (n-r+1)$

   (d) The number of ways of selecting r different objects from n different objects

   $= {}^nC_r = \dfrac{{}^nP_r}{r!} = \dfrac{n!}{r!(n-r)!}$

2. The probability ratio $P(E)$:

   $P(E) = \dfrac{\text{Number of desired outcomes}}{\text{Total number of outcomes}}$

   - $0 \leq P \leq 1$

   - $P(\text{Failure}) = Q = 1 - P(\text{Success})$

3. Rules of probability:

   (a) 'or': $P(A \text{ or } B) = P(A) + P(B) - P(A \cap B)$

   - $A \cap B = \{ \quad \} \Leftrightarrow P(A \cap B) = 0$
     $\Leftrightarrow A$ and B are mutually exclusive

   (b) 'and then': $P(A \text{ and then } B) = P(A) \times P(B)$ once A and B are independent

4. Bernoulli trials:

   (a) The Bernoulli rules

   - The number of trials n is fixed.

   - There are only two possible outcomes to each trial (success or failure).

   - Each trial is independent of any previous one.

   - The probability of success p and failure q are fixed from trial to trial.

   (b) The Bernoulli formula

   The probability of r success in n Bernoulli trials is given by:

   $P(r) = {}^nC_r(p)^r(q)^{n-r}$

5. Conditional probability:

   $P(B|A) = \dfrac{P(A \cap B)}{P(A)}$

   - $P(B|A) = P(B) \Leftrightarrow B$ and A are independent

6. Expected value **E**:

   $\mathbf{E} = \sum x\, P(x)$

Statistics

Statistics has widespread uses in many areas of our daily lives, including:

Actuarial science: The assessment of risk in insurance and finance.

Demography: The study of human populations in space and time.

Econometrics: Financial planning and economic forecasting.

Epidemiology: The study of factors that affect the health and illness of populations.

CHAPTER 17

Statistical Reasoning

Learning Outcomes

- To familiarise yourself with the different types of data collected in statistics.
- To understand how to construct surveys and controlled experiments free of bias in order to answer questions about the world we live in.
- To organise the data you collect by compiling tally frequency tables and stem-and-leaf plots.

Introduction

Every day you are bombarded with facts and figures:

- Support for the Government parties falls by 5%.
- The numbers sitting the Higher Level Leaving Certificate Maths papers have increased every year for the past 3 years.

This information you are receiving is called **data**.

> **KEY TERM**
>
> **Statistics** is a set of tools used to collect, organise and analyse data. This data must be numeric in origin or turned into numbers later on.

Statistics is the science of collecting, organising and interpreting data. It is also the factual data that describes real-life situations.

▷ A survey was carried out on people's work habits

▷ World records in athletics

Purpose of statistics

The main purpose of statistics is to help us make informed decisions about issues that involve uncertainty.

▷ Should we invest more in primary or secondary education?

Statistics is also used to provide us with factual information that has been recorded.

▷ Batting averages in cricket and baseball

▷ CAO points for courses

17.1 Types of data

Raw data and variables

WORKED EXAMPLE Working with data

Suppose you conduct a survey of the heights to the nearest centimetre (cm) of all 20 students in your class and you list the results as follows:

130	123	142	141	133
120	133	130	125	128
132	123	140	136	141
127	122	131	138	139

This is **raw data** because it has not been organised in any way, even though it has been collected. The gender make-up, male (M) or female (F), of this class of 20, corresponding to the heights above, is listed as follows:

M	M	M	F	M
F	F	F	F	F
F	M	F	M	M
F	F	F	M	M

Compare this data list of gender types with the data list of student heights above. Quite clearly, in both sets of raw data, there is a characteristic that varies as you move from one piece of data to the next. This characteristic is known as a **variable.** The variable in the first set is height and in the second case the variable is gender. In each of the examples above, there is only one quantity that is changing. Data in which there is only one variable is called **univariate data**.

Suppose you decide to record the height and the gender together of each pupil in your class, as follows:

130 M	123 M	142 M	141 F	133 M
120 F	133 F	130 F	125 F	128 F
132 F	123 M	140 F	136 M	141 M
127 F	122 F	131 F	138 M	139 M

There are two characteristics that can vary as you move through the data. This data is known as **bivariate data**. It would be interesting to investigate if there is a relationship between the two variables. This will be examined further when you study scatter plots.

KEY TERM

Raw data is information that has not been organised in any way.

KEY TERM

In statistics, a **variable** is a quantity or quality that is characteristic of an item of data whose value changes (varies) from one item to the next.

Categorical and numerical data

Raw data can be subdivided into two general types: categorical (qualitative) data and numerical (quantitative) data.

Categorical data

WORKED EXAMPLE Looking at categorical data

Nominal categorical data

A student conducted a survey of her class and recorded the hand with which each of her classmates wrote, i.e. right-handed (R) or left-handed (L). She listed the results as follows:

R	R	R	R	L	R	R	R
L	R	R	R	R	R	R	R

This non-numerical (qualitative) data captures a characteristic of people and puts them into categories. The variable in the data above is 'writing hand'. There is no natural way to order this variable into its two categories. There is no reason to put R before L or vice versa. This type of categorical data is an example of **nominal** categorical data.

Ordinal categorical data

A set of data is said to be **ordinal** if the values of the variable in the categories can be ranked (put in order) or have a rating scale attached. You can count and order but not measure ordinal data.

Students were surveyed on whether they agreed or disagreed with the following statement: 'School uniforms should be abolished.'

1. Strongly agree..........❑
2. Agree....................❑
3. No opinion..............❑
4. Disagree................❑
5. Strongly disagree.......❑

This is an example of **ordinal** categorical data.

Examples of nominal data:

▶ Race: Caucasian, Asian, African, Native American
▶ Smoking status: Smoker, Non-smoker

KEY TERM

Ordinal data (variable) is data that can be put into categories that can be ranked in order.

Examples of ordinal data:

▶ Satisfaction rating for a restaurant: Very satisfied, Satisfied, No opinion, Dissatisfied, Very dissatisfied

▶ Satisfaction ratings for a social network page: Like, No opinion, Dislike

Numerical data

WORKED EXAMPLE Looking at numerical data

A student carried out a survey of the number of bicycles in the schoolyard each schoolday in a particular week and presented his data as follows:

Monday	Tuesday	Wednesday	Thursday	Friday
26	33	30	28	32

Clearly, the variable here is the 'number of bicycles'. The crucial word is number. Numerical data is data represented by real numbers.

There are two types of numerical data: **discrete** and **continuous**.

Discrete numerical data

The shoe sizes of a class of 10 students are as follows:

$$6 \quad 6\frac{1}{2} \quad 7\frac{1}{2} \quad 7 \quad 7\frac{1}{2} \quad 5\frac{1}{2} \quad 6 \quad 6\frac{1}{2} \quad 7 \quad 8$$

The variable in this set of data is shoe size. Numerical data consists of numbers representing counts (like number of bicycles) or measurements (like shoe sizes). The shoe data and the bicycle data can only take on particular finite values. You cannot have any value you like. For example, you cannot have 24·7 bicycles or a shoe size of 6·2734.

This type of numerical data is called discrete numerical data (variable). The scores when you roll a die is an example of a discrete numerical variable because the only possible values of the variable 'score on a die' are:

$$1 \quad 2 \quad 3 \quad 4 \quad 5 \quad 6$$

The important point is that for discrete numerical data all possible values of the variable can be listed and counted. Discrete numerical data (variables) can have fractional or negative values.

▶ Shirt collar sizes: 15, $15\frac{1}{2}$, 16, $16\frac{3}{4}$, ...

▶ Golf scores with reference to par: −4, −3, −2, −1, 0, 1, 2, 3, ...

▶ Marks taken off for errors in a Maths exam: −1 (slip), −3 (blunder)

Continuous numerical data

Now consider variables like distance, mass and temperature. These variables can take on any real value depending on the accuracy of the measuring instrument. They take on values that do not change in discrete steps. This type of data is said to be **continuous**.

▶ The height h of students in a class between 1·4 m and 1·6 m is an example of a continuous variable because all possible values between the two are possible, e.g. 1·4513 m, 1·562 m.

▶ The speed v of a cosmic ray can take on all possible values between 0 and 3×10^8 m s^{-1}. Speed is a continuous variable.

▶ The time t for a Maths student to solve a problem. This can have any value between 0 and infinity ($0 \leq t < \infty$). This is a continuous variable.

KEY TERM
Numerical data (quantitative) is data with numeric values. Each number represents a measure of a quantity.

KEY TERM
Discrete numerical data is data that can take on only certain countable numeric values.

KEY TERM
Continuous numerical data is data that can assume any value within a finite or infinite interval. It is data that can have infinitely many possible values.

Continuous data can be measured and ordered. Examples include height, weight, time and age. In practice, data for a continuous variable is always given in a rounded form. For example, a temperature T of 25·6 °C that is given to the nearest tenth of a degree could have any value in the range $25{\cdot}55 \leq T < 25{\cdot}65$. Age is an exception, as it is always rounded down. For example, 38 years, 11 months is 38 years, even though age changes continuously.

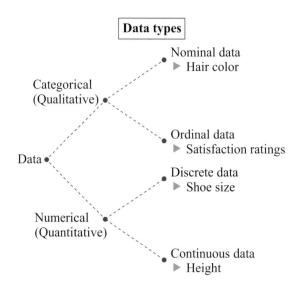

EXERCISE 1

1. The ages of 18 students in a class were recorded as follows:

12	13	12	14	12	13
12	13	14	12	13	12
13	12	13	13	13	13

   (a) What is the variable?

   (b) Is the data univariate? Why?

2. The following univariate data was recorded for 10 pupils:

Fair	Brunette	Black
Fair	Fair	Black
Brunette	Black	Fair
Red		

   (a) What is the variable?

   (b) What percentage of the pupils is (i) fair and (ii) red?

3. The following univariate data was recorded when a die was thrown 24 times:

1	5	4	2	3	6
2	5	5	4	3	6
5	4	3	2	2	1
6	6	4	3	3	3

   What is the variable?

4. The following bivariate data was recorded (H = Head, T = Tail) when a die was thrown and a coin was flipped at the same time:

1H	2T	2H	3T	3H
4H	5T	6T	6H	3H
4T	5H	1H	2H	4H
5T	6H	2H	3H	1T

   What are the two variables?

5. The 19 seats won in five Cork constituencies in the 2011 General Election are listed below with the winning party's name assigned to each seat (FF: Fianna Fáil; FG: Fine Gael; Lab: Labour; SF: Sinn Féin):

SF	Lab	FF	FG
FG	FF	FG	FF
Lab	FG	FG	FF
FG	FG	Lab	Lab
FG	FG	SF	

   (a) What is the variable for this data?

   (b) What percentage of the Cork seats did FG win, correct to the nearest per cent?

6. A survey of 20 people in a class was based on two variables. The results were given in the form of a table:

	Blue	Green	Brown	Black	Total
Blonde	2	0	2	2	6
Red	0	1	2	1	
Brown	1	0	3	3	
Black	2	0	1	0	
Total					

   (a) In this bivariate data, what might the two variables be?

   (b) Copy the table and complete the totals.

   (c) What percentage was blonde and black?

   (d) What percentage was green?

7. The following results were obtained by surveying 10 students in a class (M = Male, F = Female):

M	M	M	M	F
F	M	F	F	M

   (a) What sort of data is this?

   (b) What is/are the variable(s)?

   (c) Is it univariate or bivariate data?

8. In a test for a new drug, scientists can use three categories to assess the outcome of an experiment: Did the patient get Better (B), Worse (W), remain Unchanged (U)? What type of data is this? What is the variable?

9. Joe takes 12 s to complete a 100 m dash. Is 12 s a discrete or continuous variable? Why?

10. A junior infant counts the number of pencils in her pencil case. Is this data discrete or continuous? Why?

11. A group of 10 houses recycles glass bottles. The data below shows the number of bottles each house recycles at the end of a month:

48	52	17	81	54
37	46	97	23	14

Is this data discrete or continuous? Why?

12. Muggsy Bogues was the smallest basketball player ever in the National Basketball Association (NBA) at 1·60 m. Manute Bol and Gheorghe Mureșan were the tallest at 2·31 m.

(a) Is the height of players in the NBA discrete or continuous data? Why?

(b) To what level of accuracy are these heights rounded up?

(c) Describe mathematically the range of heights a 1·73 m tall player falls into, based on this rounding up.

(d) Write down the range of heights of all players in the NBA ever, to this level of accuracy.

13. Six people give their ages as follows:

28   32   47   38   40   39

Explain why this data is continuous, even though it appears discrete.

14. Jean decides to buy a second-hand car. She has a list of priorities:

(a) Mileage – the distance the car has travelled

(b) Year of manufacture

(c) Number of doors

State if each variable is continuous or discrete.

17.2 Carrying out an investigation

When carrying out statistical investigations, two terms appear all the time: **population** and **sample**.

> **KEY TERM**
>
> A **population** is the set of all possible objects about which information is required.

▶ A **census** is a study that obtains data from every member of the population of a country or region.

When carrying out surveys, it is often impossible to question every individual concerned. In these cases, a sample of the population is investigated in the hope that any conclusions arrived at may be applied to the whole population.

> **KEY TERM**
>
> A **sample** is a manageable subset of a population.

▶ In investigating the average industrial wage in Ireland, the population is all Irish employees. A sample of this population would be 1000 employees generated at random from the records of the tax authorities.

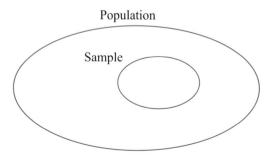

Steps for carrying out a statistical investigation on a sample

Step 1: Ask the question

Clarify the problem to be investigated. Formulate one (or more) questions that need to be answered from the data. What do you want to know?

▸ What are the main causes of unemployment?

▸ Does smoking cause cancer?

▸ Is a new drug more effective than current drugs?

If you do not ask the right questions at this stage, you will miss out on crucial data. If you asked loaded (biased) questions, you will generate misleading information.

Questions can fall into three main categories:

(a) Single piece of data:

▸ What is the average height of a 5-year-old boy?

(b) Comparative data:

▸ Are girls better than boys at learning languages?

(c) Relationship data:

▸ Are taller people better at sport?

Step 2: Explore different ways of collecting data

Some of the methods for collecting data are as follows:

1. Experiments:

▸ Clinical trials to see the effect of a new drug. The group of patients being tested is divided into two groups. One group receives the new drug and the other group, called the control group, is given an inactive substance called a placebo. The groups are compared to see if the drug is effective.

2. Observation and recording:

▸ Counting patients in the Emergency Department of a hospital.

3. Obtaining information from archives in files or on computers.

4. Surveys: In a survey, the interviewer asks questions to another person (the respondent).

▸ Face-to-face, telephone, questionnaires, the internet (for questionnaires and data collection):

Questionnaires should take account of the following:

• Questions should be phrased in simple language with no ambiguity.

• Multiple-choice questions should not be restrictive.

• Questions should not lead or bias the respondent.

Advantages and disadvantages of survey methods

(a) FACE-TO-FACE SURVEYS

Advantages

- The respondent's status can be assessed by the interviewer (age, social class, accuracy of information).
- The interviewer can explain each question.
- There is a higher response rate than telephone or internet due to interviewer persuasion.

Disadvantages

- They can be expensive (training/remuneration of interviewers).
- There may be interviewer bias.
- The respondent might be unwilling to give personal information face-to-face.

(b) TELEPHONE SURVEYS

Advantages

- They are inexpensive.
- They are not time consuming.
- The interviewer can explain the questions.
- The respondent can give spontaneous answers.

Disadvantages

- The respondent finds it easy to refuse the interview.
- There is no assessment of the respondent's status.
- The questionnaire cannot be too long.

(c) INTERNET SURVEYS

Advantages

- There is no interviewer bias.
- It costs very little.
- The respondent has time to consider his or her response.

Disadvantages

- The whole questionnaire can be read by the respondent before answering.
- Only simple questions and instructions can be given.
- Responses are not spontaneous.
- The wrong person may respond.
- There is a poor response rate.
- It is slow. Respondents may take a long time to return the survey.

Step 3: Collect and organise the data

Gather your raw information and start organising it in a meaningful way that other people can make sense of. People have problems trying to digest endless tables of numbers. Present your data with user-friendly charts and graphs.

Step 4: Analyse your data

You may want to find important numbers like mean, mode, standard deviation and correlation coefficient that summarise the data.

Step 5: Form a conclusion

By analysing the sample using statistical methods, you can try to draw **inferences** from the sample about the entire population.

Step 6: Make predictions

You carried out your survey on a small part of the population called a sample. You can now use inferential statistics to apply what you learned from your sample to the general population. You cannot do this with absolute certainty. Your predictions, like all predictions, will be based on probability.

Sampling

To extract the most reliable and significant statistical data from an investigation involving a very large population (all Irish adults for example), a sample is chosen from this population that reflects as closely as possible the characteristics of the entire population relevant to the investigation. The composition of the sample and method of sampling are crucial to the ultimate success of the data in making predictions about the population.

Composition of a sample

1. Representative

A sample must be representative of the population.

▸ In finding the average height of adult Irish males, you should not sample the local senior men's basketball teams.

2. Unbiased (randomisation)

A sample should be free from bias.

▸ In clinical trials, a number of patients is assigned at random to an experimental group (new drug) and an equal number is assigned to a control group (placebo – no new treatment) by tossing a coin to decide to which group each volunteer is assigned. These two groups should be matched as closely as possible.

3. Size

A sample should be as large as possible – the bigger, the better.

▸ A sample of 1000 in a pre-election opinion poll is more reliable than a sample of 100.

WORKED EXAMPLE

WORKED EXAMPLE — Examining selection bias

You get a new job working for a research company. Your job is to survey members of the public to find out their preference for local music stations. You are given a questionnaire that you have to follow exactly when asking your questions. Armed with your questionnaire, you eagerly head off to interview members of the public. Your task is to **randomly** interview 100 members of the public. On leaving the office, you ask your boss what is meant by 'randomly'. Your boss tells you that every person who walks past you on the street has an equal chance of being interviewed by you. You cannot decide to interview just young people who happen to be about the same age as you.

Your eagerness turns to despair after an hour on the street. Everyone is so busy, with most people ignoring you as if you did not exist. Eventually, you are drawn towards people who make eye contact with you or who look like nice people. Once you learn how to spot the right sort of approachable person, the day passes quickly and you get through your quota of 100 people.

Back at the office your boss questions you on your selection of respondents. You assure her that you interviewed young, middle-aged and older people – a good representative sample of the population. Everybody seems happy. However, a week later you get a call from your boss to attend a meeting at the office. Unfortunately for you, the boss is far from happy. The results obtained from your survey are wildly different to the results obtained by the more experienced researchers working in the company. So what went wrong?

The 100 people you interviewed were not randomly selected. Some people (nice, smiling people) had a far better chance of being interviewed by you than other people (grumpy, leave-me-alone types). You were biased in favour of a certain group of people that did not mind being interviewed and perhaps were more sociable than those who did not want to be interviewed. Your sample of 100 people was not representative of the general population. As an interviewer, you were drawn towards a certain group of people and so your sample suffers from **selection bias**.

It is true that your sample is representative of the general population in one respect, in that you managed to interview a wide range of ages. But that is where it ends. You could imagine that nice, smiling people have different tastes in music to the other type of person described in this story. But who really knows? These sweeping generalisations about people may or may not be true. The important point is that we will only find out by interviewing 100 people who have been randomly selected. Our surveys have to be conducted without bias.

Methods of sampling

1. Simple random sampling (SRS)

This is a sampling technique in which a group (sample) is selected from the population so that each member of the sample is chosen entirely by chance and each member of the population has an equal chance of being included in the sample.

▸ A five-card hand selected from a pack of 52 playing cards is a simple random sample, as each five-card hand has an equal chance of being selected as any other hand. Also, every card has an equal chance of being selected.

Advantages of a simple random sample (SRS)

• There is no bias.

• Each object has an equal chance of being selected.

• Every possible sample has an equal chance of being selected.

2. Cluster sampling

This is a sampling technique in which the entire population is divided into groups (clusters) and a random sample of these clusters is selected. Firstly, the population is divided into clusters. A simple random sample of clusters is then selected from all these clusters. Finally, a simple random sample of individual objects is selected from all of these clusters.

▶ To investigate the use of genetically modified (GM) crops in the USA. A cluster could be taken by identifying the states (50) in the US as clusters. A sample of five states would be selected at random and then a simple random sample of farms would be selected from each state.

Advantage of cluster sampling over SRS

- It is much cheaper.

KEY TERM

A **cluster sample** is obtained by taking a simple random sample of a manageable number of similar groups of a population from a large number of groups into which the population can be naturally divided. A simple random sample is then taken from each of the sample groups.

3. Quota sampling

This technique is widely used in opinion polling and market research in which certain numbers (quotas) of members from specified groups that make up the population are sampled.

▶ 30 adult men, 30 adult women, 20 teenage boys and 20 teenage girls are selected to find out their television-viewing habits.

Advantage of quota sampling over SRS

- It is fast and easy to carry out.

KEY TERM

A **quota sample** is obtained by dividing the population into non-overlapping groups in proportion to the size of each group in the population and selecting the members of each group by judgement or convenience but not randomly.

4. Stratified sampling

This is a probability sampling technique where the entire population is divided into non-overlapping subgroups or strata (for example: gender, age) and the final subjects are randomly selected proportionally from the different strata.

▶ Average yield of milk of each breed of cow in a dairy herd. The herd could be divided into breeds of cows: Holstein-Friesian, Jersey, Hereford, etc. and random samples taken from these in proportion to their size in the herd.

Advantage of stratified sampling over SRS

- There is greater precision than using samples of the same size.

KEY TERM

A **stratified random sample** is obtained by dividing the population into subgroups based on a factor that may be influenced by the make-up of the subgroup and then selecting a simple random sample from each subgroup in proportion to the size of the subgroup in the population.

A stratified random sample is very similar to a quota sample; the only difference is that the representatives from each group are chosen at random.

EXAMPLE 1

An international retailer has 8565 employees in 50 shops throughout Europe. The company asks a market research firm to carry out a survey of its employees' job satisfaction by surveying 180 employees.

(a) Explain how the research firm might obtain a simple random sample of size 180 from 8565 employees.

(b) The market research firm selects 5 of the 10 shops that are in France. How many ways could this be done?

   (i) What further steps are required by the research firm to obtain a cluster sample of size 180 from the 8565 employees?

   (ii) Give one reason why a cluster sample might be preferred by the research firm to a simple random sample.

(c) A stratified sample was used by the research firm.

   (i) Suggest two ways in which the sample could be stratified.

   (ii) Why might a stratified sample be preferred to a cluster sample?

(d) How many men and women would there be in a quota sample of 180 based on gender, if there are 5139 female employees altogether?

Solution

(a) The employees are assigned numbers from 0000 to 8564. Select random numbers from 0000 to 8564, ignoring repeats and numbers greater than 8564. Continue this process until 180 different random numbers are obtained. Select the corresponding employees.

(b) $^{10}C_5 = 252$

   (i) From each of the five outlets, a random sample of 36 is selected.

   (ii) The employees interviewed would be geographically localised.

(c) (i) Outlet or length of service.

   (ii) The stratified sample is more representative of the population than the cluster sample.

(d) Female employees: $\frac{5139}{8565} = \frac{3}{5}$

   $\therefore \frac{3}{5}$ of $180 = 108$ women and 72 men

Misuses of statistics

You should be very wary of claims made from statistical data. Often the data is manipulated and sometimes distorted to suit a particular agenda. Always examine the source, sample size and methodology of statistical research before accepting its conclusions. Remember: 'There are three kinds of lies: lies, damned lies and statistics' – Benjamin Disraeli (former British prime minister).

Some abuses and misinterpretations of statistics

- Bad data collection

- Small samples

- Non-representative samples:

   ▸ A survey is carried out in school about the reduction in the voting age from 18 to 16.

- Using an inappropriate variable to suit an agenda:
  - ▸ Using mean salary rather than median salary.
- Designing surveys with loaded questions to influence responses:
  - ▸ 'Do you think the *smiling* Irish are friendlier than the British' in a Dublin vox pop.
- Meaningless claims:
  - ▸ Bromo contains 100% less fat! (Less than what?)
- Misleading causal connection:
  - ▸ Taking Foprin twice a day may reduce your weight by 10 kg in the first few weeks.
- Incomplete information:
  - ▸ 'The number of children in poverty decreased in 1995–1998', not revealing it increased from 1998 to 2003.
- Downright sneakiness:
  - ▸ The first graph gives the impression of a huge gap between the average yearly salary of graduates and non-graduates.

ACTIVITY 2

ACTION
Conducting a survey by means of a questionnaire

OBJECTIVE
To conduct a survey using a questionnaire to answer questions about the world we live in

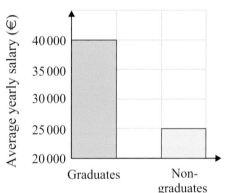

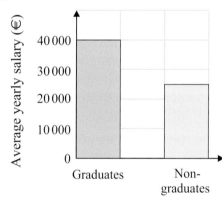

EXERCISE 2

1. Name the population and the sample in each of the following:

   (a) A survey of 2000 Irish households found that 86% had broadband.

   (b) A survey of 1000 American elementary schoolchildren found that 33% were bilingual.

   (c) The average age of every tenth person entering a concert venue was 18.

   (d) Tests on 150 tyres produced in a factory in one week found that 2% were defective.

   (e) A survey of 50 Liverpool season ticket holders found that 80% thought the tickets were too expensive.

   (f) A questionnaire in a school of 240 Leaving Certificate students found that 73% felt that only five subjects should be used in calculating CAO points.

2. The airline safety authority in a country conducted tests on 175 domestic flights on the quality of the air inside the planes in flight.

   (a) What is the population?

   (b) What is the sample?

3. The Road Safety Authority conducts a survey on the proportion of drivers who wear seat belts by observing every fifth driver on a stretch of the M7 between 8:30 a.m. and 9:30 a.m. on 9 September.

 (a) What is the population of interest?

 (b) What is the sample?

 (c) Is the sample a simple random sample?

4. A classical radio station conducts a survey of 100 of its listeners over 30 years of age on what is the most popular type of music in the country for over 30s.

 (a) What is the population?

 (b) What is the sample?

 (c) Explain why the sample is not a simple random sample.

5. You want to know what fifth-year students think about having compulsory Physical Education (PE) classes twice a week in your school. You get the secretary to generate names of 40 fifth-year students from the school database to be surveyed.

 (a) What is the population?

 (b) What is the sample?

 (c) Explain why the sample is a simple random sample.

6. (a) There are 420 boys and 380 girls in a school. A sixth-year student wishes to conduct a survey of 40 students on their opinion of starting school at 8:30 a.m. She interviews 40 boys and girls in her year group in the sixth-year classroom in proportion to the number of boys and girls in the population.

 (i) Is her sample a simple random sample?

 (ii) What would you call this sampling technique? Why?

 (iii) How many boys are in the sample?

 (iv) How many girls are in the sample?

 (b) A government wants to conduct a survey of people's attitudes to same-sex marriage in a country where the ratio of men to women is 4:3. They send out researchers to interview 70 men and women in proportion to the number of men and women in the country. One researcher decides to conduct his interviews outside the local nightclub that is across the street from where he lives.

 (i) What sort of sampling is he conducting? Why? Do you think it is a good survey? Why?

 (ii) How many men did he interview?

 (iii) How many women did he interview?

7. (a) A class consists of 15 girls and 10 boys. Each student is assigned a number.

Girls		Boys	
1.	Lucy	1.	Ben
2.	Sarah	2.	Adam
3.	Mary	3.	Noah
4.	Anne	4.	Jack
5.	Helen	5.	Peter
6.	Emma	6.	Henry
7.	Rachel	7.	Seán
8.	Úna	8.	Fiachra
9.	Maureen	9.	Fred
10.	Siobhán	10.	Haroon
11.	Sinéad		
12.	Fatima		
13.	Natasha		
14.	Gráinne		
15.	Manon		

In a stratified sample of two boys and three girls, the two boys should be selected randomly from the 10 boys and the three girls should be selected randomly from the 15 girls.

 (i) In how many ways can two boys be selected?

 (ii) In how many ways can three girls be selected?

 (iii) How many different stratified samples consist of two boys and three girls?

 (b) A stratified sample of 5 students is taken.

 (i) How many girls are chosen?

 (ii) How many boys are chosen?

     (iii) If a random number generator is used to choose the girls, which girls will be chosen from the numbers: 48, 72, 63, 12, 38, 01, 47, 52, 36, 14?

     (iv) If a random number generator is used to choose the boys, which boys will be chosen from the numbers: 05, 15, 22, 37, 05, 27, 10?

     (v) List the stratified sample.

(c) Find a stratified sample of 5 from the following set of random numbers beginning with the girls: 15, 78, 32, 10, 40, 57, 89, 17, 05, 01, 51, 02, 37, 86, 14.

8. A hospital has 400 employees in the following categories:

Employee	Number
Nurses	180
Doctors	100
Administrative staff	40
Theatre staff	80

How many from each category should be included in a stratified random sample of size 40?

9. Some 48 students were interviewed in a survey on school uniforms. Each student was given a number in the order in which he or she was interviewed, and a list of the interviewees was set out showing their gender, male (M) or female (F):

1M	2M	3M	4F	5M	6M	7F	8F
9F	10F	11F	12F	13M	14F	15M	16M
17F	18F	19M	20M	21M	22F	23M	24F
25F	26F	27M	28F	29F	30M	31F	32M
33M	34M	35F	36F	37F	38F	39F	40M
41M	42M	43F	44F	45F	46F	47M	48F

In a follow-up survey, a stratified sample of 16 was taken.

(a) How many males and females are in the stratified sample?

(b) Using the random numbers below, select the participants in the stratified sample, beginning with the females:

56	32	17	40	11	23	12	50	13	15	16
27	31	80	21	73	58	91	22	04	10	16
51	32	13	81	52	14	05	09	37	20	16

(Hint: Write out the female and male lists in the table above separately.)

10. The Department of Agriculture wishes to carry out a survey of the use of pesticides on farms in Ireland. This is done by randomly selecting 5 counties from the 26 counties, taking a simple random sample of farms from each county.

(a) What name is given to this sort of sampling?

(b) Why would a simple random sample of all the farms in Ireland not be preferable to the sampling technique in part **(a)**?

11. An internet company wants to decide if it is worth their while installing a high-speed fibre-optic cable to 300 households that live in 20 blocks of 15 households by conducting a survey of a sample of 50 households. Describe how the company might conduct such a survey by using:

(a) simple random sampling,

(b) cluster sampling.

12. Identify the sampling technique (random, cluster or stratified) in the following:

(a) At a local community college, five Maths classes are randomly selected out of 20 and 10 students are selected from each of these classes by picking their names from a hat. The students from each class are then interviewed.

(b) A researcher randomly selects and interviews 40 male and 50 female teachers.

(c) A researcher for an airline interviews random groups of 20 passengers on 10 randomly selected flights.

(d) Based on 15 500 responses from 40 000 surveys sent to its alumni, a major university estimated that the annual salary of its alumni was €82 500.

(e) A market researcher randomly selects 300 drivers under 35 years of age and 200 drivers over 35 years of age.

(f) Ten teachers were randomly selected for interview from 85 randomly selected secondary schools in Ireland.

(g) The names of contestants are written on 80 cards. The cards are placed in a bag and three names are picked from the bag.

17.3 Organising data

Tally frequency table

WORKED EXAMPLE Compiling a tally frequency table

A community swimming pool decides to survey its patrons between 9 a.m. and 12 noon one morning to determine the age profile of its swimmers. The survey is being carried out in order to make plans for the future. The ages were recorded as follows:

15	17	25	43	31	57	62	49	4	55	32	41	18	3	93	42
3	6	55	18	13	47	35	48	56	63	41	52	24	57	23	5
15	27	64	57	36	51	18	19	4	7	52	15	31	11	25	59
53	58	52	11	13	29	56	62	64	35	15	18	12	4	12	2
41	33	56	44	31	13	15	28	125	54	38	56	53	51	51	15
36	12	15	17	13											

This is univariate numerical data, as there is only one variable (age) and the data consists of numbers. A tally, in which the data is **grouped** into suitable class intervals, is shown below in a grouped frequency table. 10–20 means greater than or equal to 10 but less than 20.

Age in years (class intervals)	Tally	Frequency (how many?)
0–10	ⅢⅡ ⅠⅠⅠⅠ	9
10–20	ⅢⅡ ⅢⅡ ⅢⅡ ⅢⅡ ⅠⅠⅠ	23
20–30	ⅢⅡ ⅠⅠ	7
30–40	ⅢⅡ ⅢⅡ	10
40–50	ⅢⅡ ⅠⅠⅠⅠ	9
50–60	ⅢⅡ ⅢⅡ ⅢⅡ ⅢⅡ	20
60–70	ⅢⅡ	5
70–80		0
80–90		0
90–100	Ⅰ	1
100–110		0
110–120		0
120–130	Ⅰ	1
		Sum = 85

If you add up the frequencies, you get the total number of people sampled.

This tally immediately shows up a couple of unusual results: 93 and 125. These two values are numerically distant from the others and are known as **outliers**. Before you proceed, you must investigate these outliers to see whether or not they should be ignored. They may be significant or not.

In this case, 125 is not genuine. It is the response of a woman who dislikes being asked her age. The total is now 84. However, 93 is a genuine result. It is the age of Peter Kelly, a well-known former Olympic swimmer, who swims on a daily basis to keep fit.

This information is now presented in a grouped frequency table.

Age in years	Frequency
0–9	9
10–19	23
20–29	7
30–39	10
40–49	9
50–59	20
60–69	5
70–79	0
80–89	0
90–99	1
	84

ACTIVITY 4

ACTION
Using stem-and-leaf plots

OBJECTIVE
To display data using stem-and-leaf plots

KEY TERM

An **outlier** is an item of data that appears to deviate markedly from other members of the sample in which it occurs.

Stem-and-leaf plots

Stem-and-leaf plots are also called stem plots. Stem-and-leaf plots are used to display numerical data, usually from fairly small data sets.

WORKED EXAMPLE

How to construct a stem-and-leaf plot (diagram)

The marks of a class of 30 in a Home Economics test marked out of 50, are shown:

8	35	42	38	28	20	22	18	23	30
15	11	32	19	7	10	12	47	48	50
42	31	26	15	47	35	21	15	11	3

The stem-and-leaf plot is formed by splitting each number into two parts: a **leaf** consisting of the last digit of a data value and a **stem** consisting of the preceding digits of the data value. In our example, the units are the leaves and the tens are the stems.

```
Stem  |              Leaves
  0   | 3  7  8
  1   | 0  1  1  2  5  5   5  8  9
  2   | 0  1  2  3  6  (8) ─────────────►  This number is 28
  3   | 0  1  2  5  5  8
  4   | 2  2  7  7  8
  5   | 0
```

(Key: 3|2 = 32)

The stems are arranged in order of increasing size in the column on the left. For each stem, the leaves are arranged in rows in ascending order of size. The total number of leaves is the total number of data values (points). The key tells you how to read a data value and must always be given with the diagram.

For all stem-and-leaf plots:

1. The stem is the first digit(s) and the leaf is the final digit.

   ▸ For 27, the stem is 2 and the leaf is 7.

   ▸ For 385, the stem is 38 and the leaf is 5.

   ▸ For 6, the stem is 0 and the leaf is 6.

   ▸ For 45·6, the stem is 45 and the leaf is 0·6.

2. Each stem can have many digits, but each leaf must have only one digit.

3. Stem 0 represents the class interval 0–9 inclusive.

4. The stem-and-leaf plot is usually written so that the leaves are arranged in ascending order from left to right. For example: 2 2 3 4 4

5. A whole bunch of leaves of a stem is called a branch.

> **TIP**
>
> There is no need to separate the digits in the leaves with commas.

Reading stem-and-leaf plots

WORKED EXAMPLE Reading a stem-and-leaf diagram

The weights of 25 students were recorded correct to the nearest tenth of a kilogram, as follows:

60·1	61·5	61·2	58·5	58·6	59·4	60·2	60·5	59·4	58·7
56·1	61·3	62·1	65·8	61·4	60·0	61·4	60·2	60·3	59·0
61·7	60·5	61·6	60·7	61·9					

Draw up an appropriate stem-and-leaf plot.

```
56 | 1
57 |
58 | 5  6  7
59 | 0  4  4
60 | 0  1  2  2  3  5  5  7
61 | 2  3  4  4  5  6  7  9
62 | 1
63 |
64 |
65 | 8
```

(Key: 58|6 = 58·6)

As mentioned earlier, an outlier is an extreme value of the data. It is an item of data that is significantly different from the rest of the data. In this case, 56·1 kg and 65·8 kg are outliers. Sometimes outliers may be very significant in the context of the data. Other times they may arise due to recording errors or misinformation and should be ignored.

Advantages and disadvantages of a stem-and-leaf plot

Advantages

1. The plot can be constructed quickly and immediately using pencil and paper.

2. Each individual data value can be read off the diagram.

3. The diagram looks like a histogram when turned on its side. (See Chapter 18: Statistical Graphs and Charts.)

4. It gives a quick, clear picture of the distribution of data and makes it easy to identify clusters of data from the lengths of the branches.

5. Both discrete and continuous data sets can be displayed.

6. Because the data values in each branch are ordered in size from the smallest value to the biggest value, it is very easy to pick out the median, quartiles, maximum and minimum values and to identify any outliers. (See Chapters 19 and 20 for more about these topics.)

7. It shows the shape, centre and spread of data.

Disadvantages

1. It cannot display categorical data.

2. Small data sets with large ranges can be difficult to display on a stem-and-leaf plot without rounding off the values.

Back-to-back stem-and-leaf plots

A back-to-back stem-and-leaf plot is sometimes used to compare two sets of data. In a back-to-back stem-and-leaf plot, the same stem is used for the leaves of both plots.

WORKED EXAMPLE Drawing back-to-back stem-and-leaf plots

Students in two schools, one in County Wexford and one in County Louth, recorded the maximum local daily temperature in degrees Celsius (°C) on the same 10 days in the summer of 2010.

Wexford	18·0	17·0	18·4	25·3	18·1	19·6	19·0	17·8	20·3	20·4
Louth	17·3	17·1	17·6	17·3	16·9	17·4	17·3	17·0	17·8	18·0

(a) Draw a back-to-back stem-and-leaf plot.

(b) State two differences between the distributions of data in each set.

Wexford	Stem	Louth
	16	9
8 0	17	0 1 3 3 3 4 6 8
4 1 0	18	0
6 0	19	
4 3	20	
	21	
	22	
	23	
	24	
3	25	

(Key: 18|1 = 18·1)

The maximum temperatures in Wexford were generally higher. There was a greater range of maximum temperatures in Wexford. Wexford also has an outlier of 25·3 °C, which is probably a faulty device or a bad measurement.

EXERCISE 3

1. A student collected data about the height of pupils in her class, in centimetres correct to the nearest centimetre (cm), as shown:

153	164	157	161	167	173	175	205	168	173	178	154	158	174	165	175	160
171	177	159	173	173	162	155	166	162	137	160	165	167	170	174	167	

   (a) Draw up a tally and a grouped frequency table by copying and completing the table below.

Height (cm)	Tally	Frequency
150–154		
154–158		
158–162		
162–166		
166–170		
170–174		
174–178		

   (Note: 158–162 means greater than or equal to 158 but less than 162.)

   (b) Are there any outliers? Are they significant?

   (c) Is the data numerical or categorical? Why? Which type of numerical/categorical data is it? Why?

2. The following frequency and relative frequency table shows the number of medals won by the first 10 countries at the 2015 World Gymnastics Championships. Copy and complete the table.

Country	Number of medals (frequency)	Relative frequency = Frequency / 40
China	8	
Russia	4	0·1
USA		0·25
Romania	2	0·05
Great Britain	5	
North Korea	2	0·05
Japan	5	0·125
Greece	1	
Cuba		0·05
Netherlands	1	0·025
Total	40	1

3. The following were the scores of a basketball team in a 12-match session:

18	34	19	25	38	29
42	37	28	50	13	19

   (Key: 2|8 = 28)

   Construct a stem-and-leaf plot.

4. The following stem-and-leaf diagram gives the heights of 20 students to the nearest tenth of a centimetre:

```
137 | 3  3  5
138 | 0  4  6
139 | 0  2  2  3  5  7
140 | 0  1  1  3  8
141 | 1  2
142 | 0
```

   (Key: 137|3 = 137·3)

   (a) How many students are 137·3 cm tall?

   (b) How many students are less than 140 cm tall?

(c) How many students have heights in the range 138·0–138·9 cm?

(d) What percentage of students are taller than 140 cm?

5. The following are the ages of all 44 Presidents of the USA on the day of their inauguration:

47	60	42	57	62	51	50
43	46	69	64	58	51	51
57	46	49	54	49	64	65
49	54	54	61	57	55	61
68	51	54	55	55	56	51
52	52	54	55	56	57	61
56	55					

(a) Draw up a stem-and-leaf plot.

(b) What range of ages did most US presidents have? (In what range are the ages clustered: 40–49, 50–59 or 60–69?)

(c) What percentage were aged between 60 and 69, correct to one decimal place?

(d) Who was 69 years old? (Clue: The Berlin Wall – look it up!)

6. The following is the pupil–teacher ratio in Irish second-level schools from 2000 to 2011 in order, reading across the table:

14·8	14·0	13·5	13·2	13·6
13·4	13·1	13·1	12·9	13·0
13·6	13·6			

(a) Draw a stem-and-leaf plot and give the key.

(b) What percentage of ratios are between 13·0 and 13·6 inclusive?

(c) What year had the lowest pupil–teacher ratio?

7. Fasting plasma glucose levels of people with diabetes should be between 90 mg/dl and 130 mg/dl. The following are the fasting plasma glucose levels of 20 people:

140	160	110	149	153	137
98	88	95	150	172	103
220	144	127	380	142	129
75	187				

(a) Construct a stem-and-leaf plot.

(b) Describe the main features of it.

(c) Are there any outliers?

(d) Are these people as a group achieving the required levels in general?

8. The following table shows the number of grams of sugar per serving in 20 breakfast cereals for adults and children:

Adults		Children	
Corn Flakes	4 g	Popcos	10 g
Shreddos	3 g	Chocos	11 g
Minicorn	3 g	Honeyo	13 g
Specials	5 g	Fruitflakes	12 g
Brekki	10 g	Loopos	12 g
Muesli	2 g	Biskies	14 g
Smackos	12 g	Captcorn	12 g
Wheatcrisp	10 g	Flakies	10 g
Crispos	11 g	Wheatbran	3 g
Branos	8 g	Junior Pops	11 g

(a) Draw a back-to-back stem-and-leaf plot.

(b) In general, which cereal eaten by children or adults has the most sugar per serving?

9. The table below shows the voting percentages, to the nearest percentage, obtained by One Direction and Cher Lloyd in the first 10 weeks of *X Factor* 2010.

Week	One Direction	Cher Lloyd
1	10	10
2	10	7
3	11	9
4	12	19
5	12	8
6	14	9
7	13	8
8	12	13
9	17	12
10	18	16

(a) Draw a back-to-back stem-and-leaf plot of these votes.

(b) Which week had the highest percentage score for Cher Lloyd?

(c) Which artist, in your opinion, was consistently more popular with the public?

10. Twenty boys and 20 girls in second year were surveyed on the number of minutes they spent studying on a typical weeknight. The results are shown below:

Boys

90	60	60	75	120
180	90	120	60	75
75	45	150	120	60
75	105	90	105	75

Girls

120	105	120	105	90
120	150	105	90	90
105	120	180	180	150
150	180	120	105	600

(Key: 12|0 = 120)

(a) Draw a back-to-back stem-and-leaf plot.

(b) Are there any surprising results? What is it called? Should it be ignored? Why?

(c) Does it appear that girls study more than boys?

11. The following data is the ages of the best actor and best actress Oscar winners from 1981 to 2010 inclusive.

Actors

76	39	53	45	36	62
43	51	32	42	54	52
37	38	32	45	60	46
40	36	47	29	43	37
38	45	50	48	60	50

Actresses

74	33	49	38	61	21
41	26	81	42	29	33
35	45	49	39	32	26
25	33	35	35	28	30
29	61	33	33	45	29

(Key: 3|0 = 30)

(a) Construct a back-to-back stem-and-leaf plot.

(b) Are actresses justified in claiming that there are fewer good roles for older actresses?

(c) Are there more roles in general for younger actors and actresses?

Statistical Graphs and Charts

CHAPTER 18

Learning Outcomes

- To learn a variety of ways to display statistical data, including pie charts, line plots, bar graphs and trend graphs.
- To understand that histograms are important statistical graphs used to display discrete or continuous numerical data, which is organised in class intervals consisting of touching rectangles.

18.1 Representing data with graphs and charts

There are many ways of displaying statistical data graphically. These include:

1. Pie charts
2. Line (dot) plots
3. Bar graphs
4. Trend graphs
5. Histograms
6. Scatter plots (see Chapter 19)

1. Pie charts

ACTIVITY 5

ACTION
Using pie charts

OBJECTIVE
To use pie charts to display data

Pie charts are used to represent categorical data. A pie chart is a circle divided into sectors, where each sector represents a particular category. The area of each sector is directly proportional to the percentage that the category is of the total set.

KEY TERM

A **pie chart** is a circle divided up into a number of sectors (pie pieces) in which the area of each sector represents a set of data (category) that is a fraction (percentage) of the whole set of data.

A pie chart is a simple, clear way of comparing different categories to each other and each category to the whole set of data, especially if the number of categories is small. Pie charts can be very striking for small numbers of sectors.

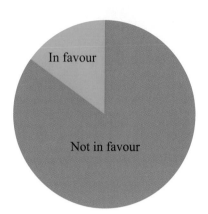

▸ A student survey is carried out in a school to find the number of students who are in favour of wearing a uniform.

As you can see, it is quite easy to compare each sector to the whole. It is immediately obvious that wearing a uniform is unpopular.

EXAMPLE 1

In a class of 30 students a survey was conducted of how students travelled to school. The following pie chart resulted:

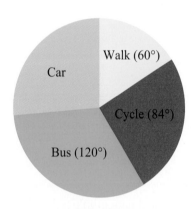

(a) What is the angle in the car sector?

(b) How many students walked to school?

(c) How many students cycled to school?

(d) How many students used the bus?

(e) How many students came to school by car?

Solution

(a) Car: $360° - 60° - 120° - 84° = 96°$

$360° = 30$ students

$1° = \dfrac{30}{360} = \dfrac{1}{12}$ student

(b) Walk: $60° = 60 \times \dfrac{1}{12} = 5$ students

(c) Cycle: $84° = 84 \times \dfrac{1}{12} = 7$ students

(d) Bus: $120° = 120 \times \dfrac{1}{12} = 10$ students

(e) Car: $96° = 96 \times \dfrac{1}{12} = 8$ students

Advantages and disadvantages of pie charts

Advantages

1. They are visually appealing.
2. They are simpler and clearer than many other statistical graphs.
3. They are readily understood because of their widespread use in business and the media.
4. They can be used to summarise a large set of data in visual form.

Disadvantages

1. They do not display raw numerical data values.
2. They should not be used for more than **six** categories.
3. They reveal nothing about the central tendency or dispersion of the data. (See Chapter 19: Central Tendency).
4. They do not reveal any patterns in the data or any causes of the data.
5. They can be easily manipulated to give misleading information.

ACTION
Using line plots

OBJECTIVE
To use line plots to display data

2. Line (dot) plots

Line or dot plots are used to represent numerical data.

KEY TERM

A **line (dot) plot** is a graph that shows the frequency of discrete data as a column of dots on a horizontal graduated line.

WORKED EXAMPLE How to construct a line plot

In a class test out of 20 marks, the following results were obtained:

Score	8	9	10	11	12	13	14	15	16	17	18	19	20
Number of students	1	2	0	5	3	3	4	3	2	2	1	7	1

Draw a line plot by putting the score along the horizontal line in equal intervals and represent each student by a point in a vertical line above its score, as shown.

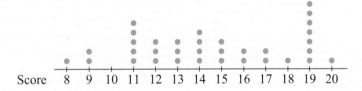

Clearly, there are 34 pupils in the class, which is the total number of dots. The data is also discrete. In this case, the data is discrete numerical data because the variable is the test score: 8, 9, 10, …, 20.

By looking at the graph, you can immediately see:

(a) the minimum score is 8 marks,

(b) the maximum score is 20 marks,

(c) the range of scores is 8–20,

(d) the exact values of the scores,

(e) if outliers are present or not, their values and how many outliers are present,

(f) the clustering of scores (most students scored between 11 and 14),

(g) the most frequent score (19) stands out.

Suppose another class with 34 pupils took the same test and scored as follows:

Score	10	11	12	13	14	15	16	17	18	19	20
Number of students	1	0	1	2	0	5	1	1	1	9	13

You can compare the two classes by doing a back-to-back line plot.

You could infer that maybe some of the students in group 1 did not quite understand the material.

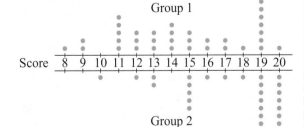

Advantages and disadvantages of line plots

Advantages

1. They give a quick analysis of raw data.

2. They show the data values exactly and their maximum and minimum values, and hence the range of these values clearly.

3. They need a small range of data values.

4. They show clusters and outliers immediately.

Disadvantages

1. They are not very visually appealing.

2. They can only cope with a small range of data.

ACTIVITY 7

ACTION
Using bar graphs

OBJECTIVE
To use bar graphs to display data

3. Bar graphs

Bar graphs are used to represent categorical and numerical data.

KEY TERM

A **bar graph** is a pictorial representation of categorical or numerical data by a number of rectangles of uniform width drawn vertically (columns) or horizontally (bars) with equal spacing between them.

WORKED EXAMPLE

Examining stacked bar graphs

The following stacked bar graph shows the percentage of school-leavers in Ireland in 2001 by their working category. Each subdivision in the bar shows the level of qualification in each category.

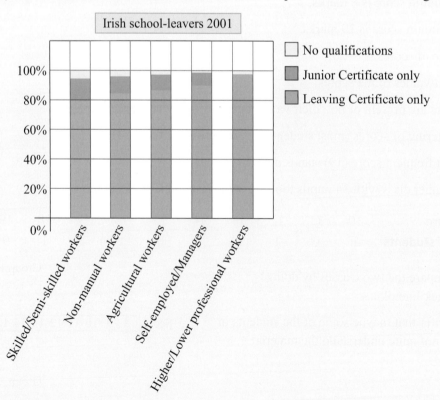

For skilled/semi-skilled workers, 80% had a Leaving Certificate qualification, while 95% of professional workers had a Leaving Certificate qualification.

Advantages and disadvantages of bar graphs

Advantages

1. They give a simple, clear visual representation of a large set of data.

2. They are easy to prepare and update.

3. They show the frequency of each data category.

4. They show trends in categories more clearly than tables.

5. They show relative proportions of different categories.

6. They are widely used in the media because they can communicate data simply.

Disadvantages

1. They only give a visual representation of data. They do not show any relationship between the categories.

2. They can be easily manipulated and hence used to misinform or mislead.

3. They often require explanation.

4. They do not show underlying causes of the data obtained.

ACTIVITY 8

ACTION
Using trend graphs

OBJECTIVE
To use trend graphs to display data

4. Trend graphs

Trend graphs are used to represent numerical data.

KEY TERM

A **trend graph** (time series) is a plot of a series of individual numerical data points at regular time intervals over a fixed period connected by straight lines.

Every day on the business pages of newspapers, you will see the type of graph shown.

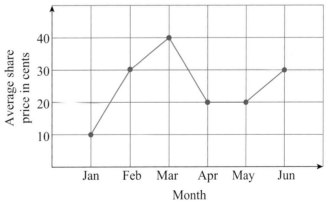

This is an example of a trend graph. It shows the behaviour of numerical data at regular time intervals (every month) over a fixed period of 6 months.

WORKED EXAMPLE

Comparing trend graphs

The following table shows the percentage number of As in Leaving Certificate Maths obtained by girls and boys who took the two Higher Level papers from 2005 to 2011.

Year	2005	2006	2007	2008	2009	2010	2011
Girls (%)	14·3	13·3	14·2	13·1	10·8	12·2	11·3
Boys (%)	16·7	15·0	16·4	15·8	11·0	16·1	14·7

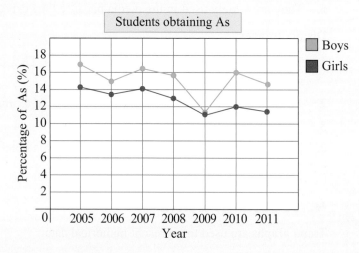

It is quite clear that boys consistently had a larger percentage of As than girls over this period.

Advantages and disadvantages of trend graphs

Advantages

1. They show the values of data at a particular time and their trends very clearly over time.

2. They can help to make predictions about values of data in the future.

3. They can be used to compare the trends of several sets of data of the same kind over the same period.

4. They can be visually simpler than bar graphs or histograms.

5. They are easily understood because they are widely used in business and the media.

Disadvantages

1. They can give misleading information if the time interval is too long.

2. They can give misleading information if the time interval is too short.

3. They do not show trends within each time interval.

4. They reveal little information on spread, dispersion and skew. (See Chapters 19 and 20.)

EXERCISE 4

1. The following table shows the percentage of first preference votes obtained by five parties in a Dublin constituency during an election:

FG	FF	Labour	Greens	SF	Others
35	12	25	3	10	15

Draw up a pie chart with a colour legend.

2. A survey of 900 passengers at Dublin Airport found people going to the following destinations: London, the USA, the Middle East and Europe.

(a) What angle was traced out in the yellow sector?

(b) How many of the 900 passengers were going to the Middle East?

(c) How many were going to the USA?

(d) How many passengers were going to London?

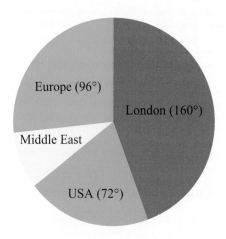

3. The US Federal Budget for 2010 is shown in the following pie chart:

■ Medicaid and Medicare ■ Social Security
■ Defence ■ Discretionary
■ Other mandatory ■ Interest

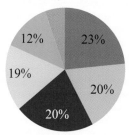

The social security budget was $701 billion.

(a) What percentage of the budget was interest payments?

(b) What was the total budget?

(c) What was the Defence budget?

4. Draw a line plot of the number of absentees in a school year group over a particular week.

Day	M	T	W	Th	F
Number of absentees	12	6	5	4	3

(M = Monday, T = Tuesday, W = Wednesday, Th = Thursday, F = Friday)

(a) Which day has the most absentees?

(b) Assuming no student was absent more than once, what percentages of students in a year group of 100 were absent that week?

(c) Draw a pie chart to illustrate the number of students absent on each day of that week.

5. The following are the shoe sizes of 40 students in a group, taken from a questionnaire:

Shoe size	Number	Shoe size	Number
6	2	$9\frac{1}{2}$	7
$6\frac{1}{2}$	0	10	3
7	3	$10\frac{1}{2}$	2
$7\frac{1}{2}$	1	11	1
8	4	$11\frac{1}{2}$	1
$8\frac{1}{2}$	6	12	1
9	8	20	1

(a) Draw a line plot.

(b) Are there any outliers? Explain.

(c) Is there any clustering of shoe sizes?

(d) What percentage has a shoe size less than or equal to 9?

6. There are two German classes of 25 students each in a school. The following are the results of a German test they were given, out of 10 marks.

Class A		Class B	
Mark	**Number**	**Mark**	**Number**
1	0	1	1
2	0	2	2
3	0	3	1
4	0	4	3
5	0	5	6
6	7	6	8
7	8	7	1
8	5	8	1
9	5	9	1
10	0	10	1

(a) Draw a back-to-back line plot.

(b) Is there an obvious difference between the two classes?

(c) Could you make a deduction about the comprehension of the material between the two classes?

7. In the 2011 Six Nations rugby tournament the following line plot shows the number of tries scored by each country. However, there is a mistake in the plot. There were 51 tries scored in total and three teams scored the same number of tries.

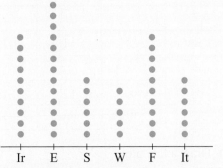

(Ir = Ireland, E = England, S = Scotland, W = Wales, F = France, It = Italy)

(a) Correct the mistake.

(b) Which team scored the most tries? How many did this team score?

(c) Which teams scored the same number of tries? How many tries did these teams score?

(d) What percentage of tries did Ireland score, correct to the nearest tenth of a percentage?

8. Copy and complete the double vertical bar chart of graduates in Maths and Science per 1000 of the population aged 20–29 by gender in 2003 in various European countries.

Country	Female	Male
EU average	7·8	16·8
Belgium	5·6	16·4
Spain	7·8	17·1
Ireland	16·8	31·5
UK	21·0	14·4
Finland	10·4	24·0
France	13·6	30·7

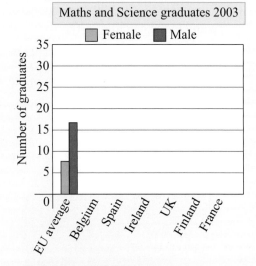

9. The number of nuclear power stations in various countries prior to 1989 is given as follows:

Country	Number
Canada	22
France	52
Japan	43
Russia	73
Spain	10
UK	41
USA	119

Draw a horizontal bar chart of this data with country on the *y*-axis.

10. Copy and complete the following table and stacked bar graph of the following data of successful CAO applicants who qualified for a college degree or diploma.

Year	% Degree	% Diploma
2000	60	
2001		50
2002	30	
2003	70	
2004	80	
2005	70	

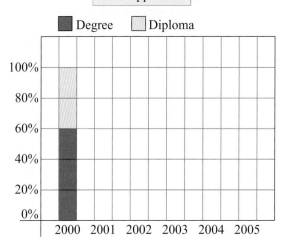

CAO applicants

11. Copy the grid below onto graph paper. Draw two trend graphs for a student's average monthly mark in English and the average number of hours per day of studying over a 6-month period on this grid.

Month	Average English mark	Average study (hours)
Oct	83	5
Nov	80	4·4
Dec	75	3·2
Jan	76	4
Feb	84	5·3
Mar	90	6

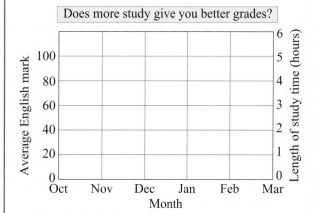

Does more study give you better grades?

Comment on the trend of the graphs and make a conclusion.

18.2 Histograms

ACTIVITY 9

ACTION
Using histograms

OBJECTIVE
To learn how to draw histograms to display data

Histograms play a very important part in our study of statistics. They are used to represent numerical data.

KEY TERM

A **histogram** is a statistical graph consisting of touching rectangles used to display continuous or discrete numerical data organised in class intervals.

The rectangles are drawn so that the area of each rectangle is equal to the frequency of the occurrence of the data in its class interval. Histograms are constructed from frequency tables or from relative frequency tables, which are also known as probability distributions.

Constructing a histogram

WORKED EXAMPLE Constructing a histogram

The following data are the IQ scores of 60 students in a year group:

147	138	134	110	120	132
103	92	125	124	126	107
122	123	113	108	135	134
105	89	102	117	132	101
115	107	102	115	115	114
100	141	111	140	129	100
96	118	133	82	116	130
110	118	112	114	110	125
126	108	122	96	113	83
115	138	104	87	101	102

There are a lot of results shown here. This is raw data that needs to be organised into a frequency distribution table.

1. Divide the set of data into classes of equal width. The data values range from 82 to 147. The class intervals to be used are as follows:

   $75 \leq IQ < 85$, $85 \leq IQ < 95$, $95 \leq IQ < 105$, $105 \leq IQ < 115$, $115 \leq IQ < 125$, $125 \leq IQ < 135$, $135 \leq IQ < 145$ and $145 \leq IQ < 155$

   A class interval of 75–85 means that an IQ of 75 is included but not an IQ of 85. An IQ of 85 will be in the next class interval 85–95.

2. The number of scores in each class is called the **frequency f**.

3. Construct a grouped frequency table, as shown:

IQ score	Frequency
75–85	2
85–95	3
95–105	11
105–115	14
115–125	13
125–135	11
135–145	5
145–155	1
	Sum = 60

KEY TERM

The **frequency** is the number of scores in each class interval.

4. Display this frequency table with rectangles of equal width, putting the classes on the x-axis and the frequency on the y-axis but with no spaces between the rectangles. Each rectangle represents a class. There is no horizontal space between the rectangles unless the frequency of a class is zero, making its height zero.

The class interval 105–115 has a frequency of 14. In other words, 14 students have an IQ between 105 and 115. This is the class interval with the highest frequency and has the tallest rectangle in the histogram. This class interval is called the **modal class**.

The mode is then taken as the mid-interval value of the modal class. In this example, the mode is an IQ of 110.

The **mode** is the most frequent result. It will be described in greater detail in the next chapter.

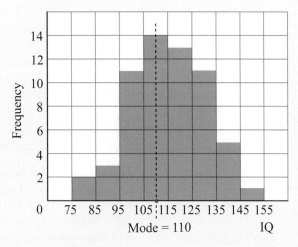

KEY TERM

The **modal class** is the class with the highest frequency.

EXAMPLE 2

The histogram on the right shows the monthly income (in €) of workers in a company.

(a) How many workers are there?

(b) Find the wage range obtained by the maximum number of workers. How many workers received a monthly income in this wage range?

(c) How many were paid less than €3500 per month?

(d) How many were paid €4500 or more per month?

(e) What percentage were paid €3000 or more per month, correct to one decimal place?

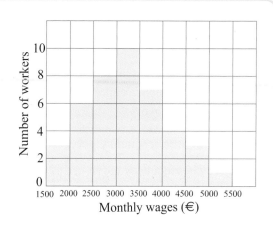

Monthly wages (€)

Solution

(a) Number of workers

$= 3 + 6 + 8 + 10 + 7 + 4 + 3 + 1 = 42$

(b) €3000–€3500: Ten workers earned a monthly income in this range.

(c) Less than €3500: $3 + 6 + 8 + 10 = 27$

(d) €4500 or more: $3 + 1 = 4$

(e) Percentage: $\left(\dfrac{10 + 7 + 4 + 3 + 1}{42}\right) \times 100\% = 59{\cdot}5\%$

Frequency distribution curves

KEY TERM

A **frequency polygon** is a graph obtained by joining the midpoints of the upper horizontal side of each rectangle in a histogram.

WORKED EXAMPLE Producing a frequency polygon from its histogram

The following table gives the blood pressure in millimetres of mercury (mm Hg) of 100 people aged between 45 and 55 in a survey.

Blood pressure (mm Hg)	Number of people
90–95	2
95–100	3
100–105	5
105–110	7
110–115	11
115–120	13
120–125	15
125–130	12
130–135	10
135–140	8
140–145	7
145–150	4
150–155	2
155–160	1

The widths of the class intervals are all the same in this example. Display this information with a histogram and hence draw a frequency polygon.

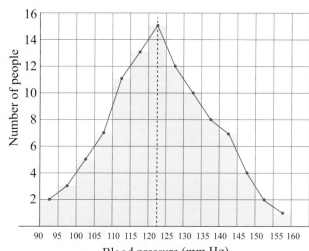

Blood pressure (mm Hg)

If you mark the midpoints of the upper horizontal side of each rectangle and join these dots with straight lines, you get a **frequency polygon**. If the class intervals are made narrower and narrower, the rectangles become closer and closer to straight lines and the frequency polygon becomes a smooth continuous frequency curve. This curve is also known as a **frequency distribution curve**.

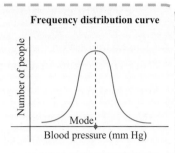

Frequency distribution curve

Describing the frequency polygon

Shape: The frequency curve in this case is more or less bell shaped.

Location: The curve is centred on the mode, which is the middle of the class interval (120–125), with the highest frequency.

Spread: Most values fall between 100 and 145, which means there is a spread of 20 on either side of the 'centre' (mode).

These three properties are important features in describing the distribution of data.

Probability distributions

WORKED EXAMPLE Explaining probability distributions

A relative frequency histogram is shown below for the monthly salaries of 500 workers in a company.

Monthly salary (€)	Number of workers (f)	Relative frequency (f ÷ total)
1500–2000	70	0·14
2000–2500	90	0·18
2500–3000	80	0·16
3000–3500	70	0·14
3500–4000	60	0·12
4000–4500	50	0·10
4500–5000	40	0·08
5000–5500	20	0·04
5500–6000	20	0·04
	Sum = 500	Sum = 1

Joining up the midpoints of the upper horizontal side of each rectangle gives a **relative frequency polygon**. If the class intervals are made narrower, the polygon becomes a smooth continuous relative frequency curve or probability distribution.

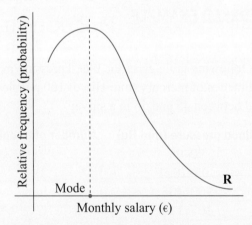

In this distribution, most of the data is to the right of the mode. The right tail **R** extends further from the mode than the left tail. This distribution is said to be positively (right) skewed.

Strictly speaking, you should only draw frequency curves for continuous data. However, drawing them for discrete data in order to interpret the shape of the distribution is fine.

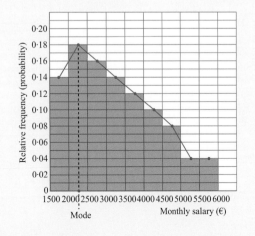

Area is frequency

Histograms are constructed from frequency tables or from relative frequency tables (probability distributions) in which the data is grouped into class intervals.

A histogram consists of touching rectangles. The width w of each rectangle is the width of a class interval. The height h of each rectangle is drawn so that the area of the rectangle is equal to the frequency f of occurrence of the data in that class.

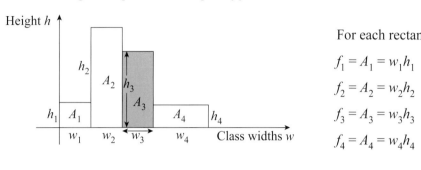

For each rectangle:

$$f_1 = A_1 = w_1 h_1$$
$$f_2 = A_2 = w_2 h_2$$
$$f_3 = A_3 = w_3 h_3$$
$$f_4 = A_4 = w_4 h_4$$

If the widths of all class intervals are equal: $w_1 = w_2 = w_3 = w_4$, then

this width is usually taken as 1 unit. For histograms with equal class intervals, we will take the width of each class interval to be 1.

In this case: $f_1 = h_1, f_2 = h_2, f_3 = h_3, f_4 = h_4$. In other words, the frequency is the height of the rectangle.

WORKED EXAMPLE — Looking at histograms with unequal intervals

Consider a histogram with unequal intervals. Its frequency distribution is as follows:

x	80–83	83–89	89–92	92–95
f	3	15	3	12

Since all class intervals are not the same, the width of the smallest interval is usually taken to be 1 unit. The heights of the rectangles must be adjusted so that the area is equal to the frequency.

$$A = f = w \times h \Rightarrow h = \frac{f}{w}$$

The height is the frequency divided by the width of the class. This is known as the **frequency density**. The heights are plotted on the y-axis as the frequency density.

x	80–83	83–89	89–92	92–95
f	3	15	3	12
Width w	1	2	1	1
Frequency density $h = \dfrac{f}{w}$	3	7·5	3	12

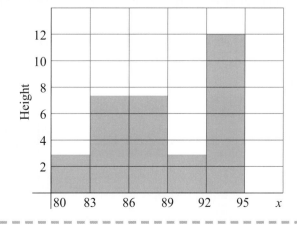

> **TIP**
>
> The area of each rectangle on a class interval in a histogram constructed from a frequency or relative frequency distribution table is equal to the frequency or relative frequency of the data values in that class interval.

If the class intervals in a histogram are made smaller and smaller, the frequency polygon becomes a smooth continuous curve known as a frequency curve (distribution) *or* a relative frequency curve (probability distribution).

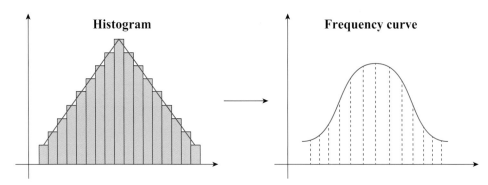

A frequency or relative frequency distribution is a continuous curve representing continuous data in which the y co-ordinates (heights) are plotted in such a way that the area A under the curve and between the lines $x = x_1$, $x = x_2$ and the x-axis is equal to the frequency or proportion (probability), respectively, of the data in the interval $[x_1, x_2]$ occurring.

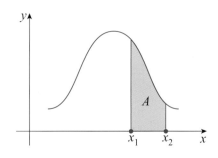

Properties of frequency distributions

1. Shape

Symmetry refers to the degree to which a frequency distribution is a mirror image of itself, relative to the modal line (the line through the point of maximum frequency perpendicular to the horizontal axis).

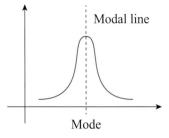

Asymmetrical curves are described by the position of their longer tail relative to the modal line.

*   A frequency distribution curve with a long, skewed right tail is said to be positively skewed.

*   A frequency distribution curve with a long, skewed left tail is said to be negatively skewed.

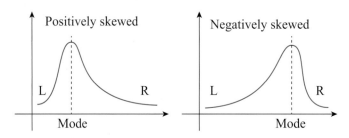

2. Modality

Modality is defined as the number of distinct peaks on the curve.

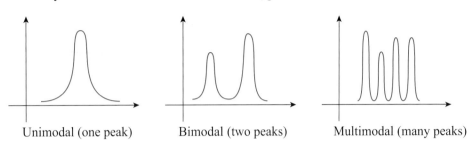

| Unimodal (one peak) | Bimodal (two peaks) | Multimodal (many peaks) |

3. Location

The location of a distribution is usually described in terms of its centre (mean, mode or median). This will be dealt with in Chapter 19: Central Tendency.

4. Spread

The spread of a distribution is a measure of how the data values are dispersed about the centre. Common spread measures are standard deviation and interquartile range. Again, these will be dealt with in Chapter 19: Central Tendency.

Advantages and disadvantages of histograms

Advantages

1. They show a large set of data in a visually strong way.

2. They enable a frequency polygon to be constructed and hence a frequency curve (distribution) to be drawn.

3. They show the central tendency and dispersion of data. (See Chapter 19.)

4. They give a comparison of the data distribution to the normal curve (see later) by drawing the frequency polygon.

5. They give instant visual recognition of the frequency and relative frequency (proportion) of class intervals by associating frequency or relative frequency with the area of the rectangle on the interval.

Disadvantages

1. They cannot be used to read off the frequency of individual data values as the data values in each class interval are assigned the same frequency.

2. They can be easily misread when the class intervals are not equal, as frequency is the area of the rectangle and not its height.

3. They do not reveal trends, causes or patterns.

Note: Scatter plots are another type of statistical graph that will be looked at in Chapter 19. A knowledge of a measure of central tendency called mean is required to study scatter plots fully.

EXERCISE 5

1. The following histogram represents the scores of students in a Chemistry test. Copy and complete the frequency table:

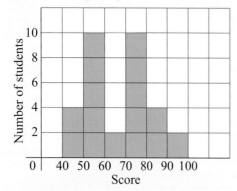

Number of days	Number of employees
0–10	23
10–20	7
20–30	5
30–40	3
40–50	1
50–60	1
60–70	1

Draw a histogram and a frequency polygon and comment on its shape.

Score	Number of students
40–50	
50–60	
60–70	
70–80	
80–90	
90–100	

(a) How many students are in the class?

(b) Draw the frequency polygon and frequency curve. Is the polygon:

    (i) symmetrical or asymmetrical,

    (ii) unimodal or bimodal?

2. The following grouped frequency table shows the number of workdays lost due to illness by 40 employees in a factory over a year.

3. The prime numbers p up to 300 are listed below:

2	3	5	7	11	13	17
19	23	29	31	37	41	43
47	53	59	61	67	71	73
79	83	89	97	101	103	107
109	113	127	131	137	139	149
151	157	163	167	173	179	181
191	193	197	199	211	223	227
229	233	239	241	251	257	263
269	271	277	281	283	293	

(a) Draw a histogram using the intervals: $0 \leq p < 50$, $50 \leq p < 100$, $100 \leq p < 150$, $150 \leq p < 200$, $200 \leq p < 250$ and $250 \leq p < 300$

(b) Draw a frequency polygon. What percentage of these primes are less than 50, correct to the nearest whole number?

4. Two frequency distributions are plotted from histograms:

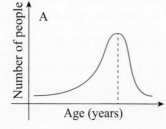

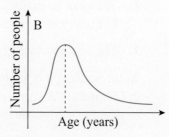

(a) Which one is negatively skewed and which is positively skewed?

(b) One of them shows the distribution of people whose main source of news was the internet against age, while the other shows the distribution of people whose main source of news was radio, TV and newspapers against age. Which is which? Why?

5. The following table gives the heights of 70 plants. All heights were measured to one-tenth of a centimetre and then corrected to the nearest centimetre.

h (cm)	75–80	80–85	85–90	90–95
Number	15	20	20	15

(a) What does the class interval 75–80 mean?

(b) Into which class would a plant that is 84·5 cm tall be placed?

(c) In the class 85–90, what could the height of the tallest plant be, correct to one-tenth of a centimetre?

(d) Draw a histogram and a frequency polygon and sketch the frequency curve. Comment on its shape.

6. The following table shows the number of farm injuries in a given year by age in years:

Age	0–10	10–20	20–30	30–40	40–50	50–60	60–70
Number	8	40	58	42	22	18	212

(a) Draw up a relative frequency table and draw a histogram of this relative frequency table. Comment on the shape of the distribution.

(b) Draw a relative frequency polygon. In what age range are most farm injuries?

(c) What percentage of farm injuries is in the interval 10–40?

7. The following stem-and-leaf plot shows the marks of 30 students in an Irish test marked out of 50.

```
0 | 5
1 | 1  2  7
2 | 3  3  4  7  8
3 | 0  1  1  2  3  4  6  7
4 | 1  1  3  5  5  6  6  8  8  9  9
5 | 0  0
```

(Key: 2|4 = 24)

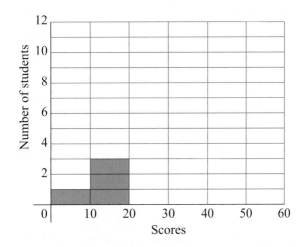

Plot these on graph paper by marking each leaf with one box to generate a histogram, as shown.

Join up the midpoints of the uppermost side of each rectangle in the histogram to generate a frequency polygon. Draw the frequency distribution curve roughly and comment on its shape.

Central Tendency

Learning Outcomes

- To understand the different types of central tendency or averages: mode, mean and median.
- To compare averages and decide which type of average is the best measure for a given situation.
- To display statistical data using scatter plots that show the relationship between two sets of numerical values (bivariate numerical data).

Introduction

A survey is carried out on the age profile of the people entering a computer store. What is the 'typical' age of a person shopping at this store? To answer this question, you need some number that measures a 'representative' age of the people in the survey.

However, there are different ways of coming up with such a number, depending on the data you obtain and what it is you want to derive from it. Such a number is called a measure of **central tendency**.

A central tendency is an average or 'middle value' in a set of data. There are a number of different types of such averages. We will examine three of them: mode, mean and median. You need to choose the right average to make conclusions when analysing data.

> **KEY TERM**
>
> A **central tendency** is an average or middle value of a set of data.

Superstars tend to skew the mean!

In American football, the New York Giants players have a **mean** annual salary of $2·5 million and a **median** annual salary of $850 000. Eli Manning, the superstar quarterback, has an annual salary of $8·5 million. The **mean** salary is obtained by dividing the sum of the salaries of all players by the number of players. The **median** salary is the middle salary, when all salaries are arranged in increasing size.

You need to ask yourself which average is more reflective of the salary that most of the players on the team earn. In this case, the median is probably a better average to use, as Eli Manning gets paid a salary far in excess of the other players. Eli's salary has skewed the results in a particular way. In this chapter, you will become aware of different types of averages and the dangers of jumping to conclusions when interpreting these numbers.

19.1 The mode

KEY TERM

The **mode** of a set of data is the data value that occurs most often or most frequently in the set.

▸ The numbers 5, 6, 8, 9, 9, 11, 12 have a mode of 9, as it is the number that appears most often in the set. This set of data is **unimodal** (one mode).

▸ In a survey of students in a school, 60 had blue eyes, 40 had brown eyes, 10 had green eyes and 5 had grey eyes. The modal eye colour is blue.

▸ The numbers 1, 4, 5, 5, 5, 6, 6, 7, 7, 7, 8 have two modes, 5 and 7, as they both occur most often – three times. This set of data is said to be **bimodal** (two modes).

▸ The numbers 2, 2, 4, 4, 6, 6, 8, 8, 10, 10 have no mode, as all numbers are repeated exactly the same number of times.

WORKED EXAMPLE

How to find the mode of related data sets

This is a technique to quickly find the mode of other sets of data related to a given set. The mode of 2, 3, 4, 5, 5, 5, 6, 7, 8, 8, 9 is 5.

If you multiply each number by 4 and add 10, you get the new set of data 18, 22, 26, 30, 30, 30, 34, 38, 42, 42, 46. This set has a mode of 30. It is the original mode of 5 multiplied by 4 and increased by 10.

TIP

If you have a set of data values and you multiply each data value by k and then increase each value by l, the mode of the new set of data is k times the mode of the old set plus l.

Old mode	Change	New mode
m	Multiply by k and increase by l	$km + l$

EXAMPLE 1

In a 50 km/h speed zone, the Gardaí recorded the speeds of 60 cars to the nearest km/h using a speed detection radar. The results were recorded as follows:

Speed (km/h)	0–10	10–20	20–30	30–40	40–50	50–60	60–70
Number of cars	2	5	6	14	18	10	5

(a) Draw a histogram and frequency polygon.

(b) What is the mode?

(c) What percentage of cars broke the speed limit?

Solution

(a) The histogram and frequency polygon are shown:

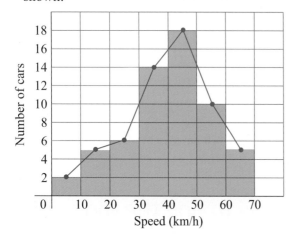

(b) The mode is the mid-interval value of the modal class. The modal class is 40–50, as this class has the highest frequency.

Mid-interval value of the 40–50 modal class
$$= \frac{40 + 50}{2} = \frac{90}{2} = 45$$
$$\text{Mode} = 45 \text{ km/h}$$

> **TIP**
>
> ↑ The mode is the mid-interval value of the class interval of the highest rectangle in a histogram with equal class intervals.

(c) Fifteen cars broke the speed limit.

Percentage: $\frac{15}{60} \times 100\% = 25\%$

Modes of histograms and frequency distributions

A histogram is said to be **unimodal** if its frequency polygon (curve) has a single peak, **bimodal** if it has two distinct peaks, and **multimodal** if it has more than two distinct peaks.

Frequency polygons

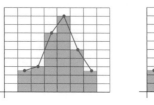 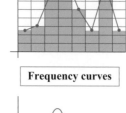 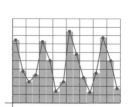

Frequency curves

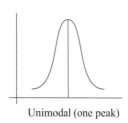 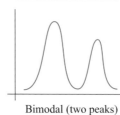 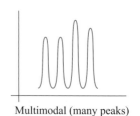

Unimodal (one peak)   Bimodal (two peaks)   Multimodal (many peaks)

Advantages and disadvantages of the mode as a measure of central tendency

Advantages

1. It is the only average that can be used for non-numerical data.
2. It is easily calculated.

Disadvantages

1. There may be more than one mode.
2. There may be no mode.
3. It may not be algebraically defined.
4. It may not accurately represent the data.

EXERCISE 6

1. Find the mode, if it exists, of the following sets of data and say if the set is unimodal, bimodal, multimodal or none of these:

   (a) 3, 5, 6, 6, 6, 7, 8, 9

   (b) 3, 3, 5, 6, 6, 6, 7, 8, 8, 8, 9

   (c) 2, 2, 4, 4, 6, 6, 8, 8

   (d) 1, 1, 1, 2, 3, 3, 3, 3, 4, 5, 5, 5, 5, 6, 7, 7, 7, 7, 8, 9, 10

2. The ages of a class of 20 students in 2015 are: 6, 6, 6, 7, 7, 7, 7, 7, 7, 7, 7, 7, 7, 8, 8, 8, 8, 8, 8, 8.

   (a) What is the modal age?

   (b) If all of the pupils remain in the class in 2016, what will be the modal age in 2016?

3. A teacher does a quick survey of his class and finds that there are more Casio calculators than other models. What is being measured in this survey?

4. For the following frequency distribution, write down the mode(s):

Value x	5	8	9	10
Frequency f	2	3	1	3

5. A set of exam scores is given in a stem-and-leaf plot, as shown:

3	0 4 1
4	1 1 2 2 2 3
5	2 4 6 8 9 9
6	4 5 7
7	2 3 4 4 4 4 5 8
8	1 3 6 6 6 8
9	4 5 7 8

   (Key: 7|3 = 73)

   (a) How many students took the exam?

   (b) What is the mode?

   (c) What is the modal class?

6. The following grouped frequency table shows the daily temperatures recorded in degrees Celsius in a city in Spain for the month of July:

Temperature in °C	Number of days
20–24	6
24–28	8
28–32	12
32–36	5

   (a) Construct a histogram and a frequency polygon.

   (b) Comment on the shape of the polygon.

   (c) Find the mode from the histogram.

19.2 The mean

The **mean** of a set of data is obtained by dividing the sum of the data values by the number of data values.

ACTIVITY 11

ACTION
Using the mean

OBJECTIVE
To appreciate how the mean is used as a measure of central tendency

If you were asked to find the average of the numbers 1, 7, 11, 5, 6, you would add them up and divide by the number of numbers.

$$\text{Average} = \frac{1 + 7 + 11 + 5 + 6}{5} = \frac{30}{5} = 6$$

This number is known technically as the **mean** (or the arithmetic mean) of the numbers. It is obtained by summing each individual value x of the data set and dividing by the number of numbers N in the set. It is usually given the symbol μ.

$$\mu = \frac{\sum x}{N} = \frac{\text{Sum of all the numerical values } x \text{ of a set of data values}}{\text{Number of numbers in the set}}$$

This formula can be rearranged as $\sum x = N \times \mu$.

▶ If the mean age of 30 pupils is 5, the sum of all the ages of the pupils is:
$N \times \mu = 30 \times 5 = 150$

TIP

The sum of the individual values in a data set is equal to the number of numbers in the set multiplied by the mean.

You can only find the mean of numerical data because you must have numbers to add.

WORKED EXAMPLE

Why is the mean a good measure of central tendency?

Consider the data values x: −3, −1, 0, 7, 1, 7, −11, 12, 15

The mean $\mu = \dfrac{-3 - 1 + 0 + 7 + 1 + 7 - 11 + 12 + 15}{9} = \dfrac{27}{9} = 3$

TIP

The deviation d of a data value x from the mean μ is given by $d = (x - \mu)$.

Calculate the sum of the deviations $(x - \mu)$ for numbers less than the mean of 3 first and then for numbers greater than the mean of 3.

Numbers less than 3:

x	$(x - \mu)$
−11	−14
−3	−6
−1	−4
0	−3
1	−2
	$\sum(x - \mu) = -29$

Numbers greater than 3:

x	$(x - \mu)$
7	4
7	4
12	9
15	12
	$\sum(x - \mu) = 29$

If you take the absolute value of $\sum(x - \mu)$ in each case, you get 29.

Numbers < 3: −11, −3, −1, 0, 1	Numbers > 3: 7, 7, 12, 15
|Sum of left deviations| = 29	|Sum of right deviations| = 29

Mean of data set = 3

The mean is a central point where the absolute value of the sum of the deviations of numbers less than the mean and greater than the mean are equal. It is like a centre of gravity (a balance point).

WORKED EXAMPLE

How to find the mean of related data sets

Find the mean of the following numerical data:

A: 8, 4, 11, 7, 5, 1

B: 19, 11, 25, 17, 13, 5

A: Mean $\mu_A = \dfrac{8 + 4 + 11 + 7 + 5 + 1}{6} = \dfrac{36}{6} = 6$

B: Mean $\mu_B = \dfrac{19 + 11 + 25 + 17 + 13 + 5}{6} = \dfrac{90}{6} = 15$

Every value in data set B is each value of data set A multiplied by 2 and increased by 3. The mean of data set B is the mean of data set A multiplied by 2 and increased by 3.

$\therefore \mu_B = 2\mu_A + 3 = 2 \times 6 + 3 = 15$

TIP

If you have a set of data values and multiply each data value by k and then increase this data value by l, the mean of the new set of data values is k times the mean of the old set plus l.

Old mean	Change	New mean
μ	Multiply by k and increase by l	$k\mu + l$

EXAMPLE 2

Show that if the mean of a, b, c is μ, then the mean of $ka + l$, $kb + l$, $kc + l$ is $k\mu + l$.

Solution

Old data set: a, b, c

Old mean: $\mu = \dfrac{a + b + c}{3}$

New data set: $ka + l, kb + l, kc + l$

New mean: $\mu = \dfrac{(ka + l) + (kb + l) + (kc + l)}{3}$

$= \dfrac{k(a + b + c) + 3l}{3}$

$= k\mu + l$

The mean of a frequency distribution

WORKED EXAMPLE Finding the mean and mode of a frequency distribution

The number of goals scored by the 20 FA Premiership teams one weekend during the year was as follows:

3	2	1	0	0	4	3	1	2	1
3	1	2	2	0	1	3	2	1	5

The mean number of goals scored on the weekend:

$$\mu = \frac{3+2+1+0+0+4+3+1+2+1+3+1+2+2+0+1+3+2+1+5}{20} = \frac{37}{20} = 1{\cdot}85$$

$$= \frac{(0+0+0)+(1+1+1+1+1+1)+(2+2+2+2+2)+(3+3+3+3)+(4)+(5)}{20}$$

$$= \frac{(3 \times 0)+(6 \times 1)+(5 \times 2)+(4 \times 3)+(1 \times 4)+(1 \times 5)}{(3+6+5+4+1+1)}$$

$$= \frac{\text{Sum of (frequency } f \times \text{ number of goals } x)}{\text{Sum of frequencies}} = \frac{\Sigma fx}{\Sigma f}$$

Notes

1. $(1+1+1+1+1+1)$ means that 1 appears in the list 6 times. The frequency f of 1 is 6.

2. Three teams scored 0 goals, 6 teams scored 1 goal, 5 teams scored 2 goals, 4 teams scored 3 goals, 1 team scored 4 goals, and 1 team scored 5 goals.

3. Σf = total number of teams = total number of data values = 20

A **frequency table** can be used to find the mean and the mode in a convenient way, as shown:

Number of goals x	Frequency f	fx
0	3	0
1	6	6
2	5	10
3	4	12
4	1	4
5	1	5
	$\Sigma f = 20$	$\Sigma fx = 37$

$\Sigma fx = 37$ = total number of goals scored by all teams

$\Sigma f = 20$ = number of teams

Mean of a frequency distribution:

$$\mu = \frac{\Sigma fx}{\Sigma f} = \frac{37}{20} = 1{\cdot}85$$

TIP

Σf means that you add up all the f-values.
Σfx means that you add up all the fx-values.

Mean of a frequency distribution: $\mu = \dfrac{\Sigma fx}{\Sigma f}$

The mode is 1 goal, as it was scored by most (6) teams.

EXAMPLE 3

A golfer records her weekly golf scores over 20 consecutive weeks on a piece of paper, as follows:

```
6 | 9  9
7 | 0  1  2  2  3  3  3  4  5  6  6  7  7  7  7  8  8  9
```

(Key: 7|3 = 73)

(a) Use this stem-and-leaf plot to draw up a frequency table.

(b) How many weeks were used to record these scores?

(c) Use the table to find the mode and the mean.

Solution

(a)

Score x	Frequency f	fx
69	2	138
70	1	70
71	1	71
72	2	144
73	3	219
74	1	74
75	1	75
76	2	152
77	4	308
78	2	156
79	1	79
	$\sum f = 20$	$\sum fx = 1486$

(b) Number of results = $\sum f$ = 20. Twenty weeks were used to record these results.

(c) Mode = 77
77 was the score for four of her rounds of golf.

$$\text{Mean: } \mu = \frac{\sum fx}{\sum f} = \frac{1486}{20} = 74{\cdot}3$$

You can use your calculator to find the mean directly by inputting the x and f values.

The mean of continuous data

WORKED EXAMPLE Finding the mean of continuous data

Thirty people were surveyed on the distance they travelled to work on a certain day of the week. The results are presented in a grouped frequency table as follows:

Distance (km)	Number of people
3–5	3
5–7	7
7–9	10
9–11	7
11–13	3
	Sum = 30

Is it possible to work out the mean from this grouped frequency table in the same way that we did for discrete data in Example 3? The question arises as to what 'number' in each class interval you multiply the frequency by to get the fx column, as there is an infinite number of numbers in each class interval (3–5, 5–7, etc.). The obvious answer is the mid-interval value. This is the value halfway between the two extreme values of each class.

Mid-interval values

For the 3–5 class, the mid-interval value $= \dfrac{3+5}{2} = 4$.

For the 5–7 class, the mid-interval value $= \dfrac{5+7}{2} = 6$.

Distance (km)	Mid-interval value x	Number of people f	fx
3–5	4	3	12
5–7	6	7	42
7–9	8	10	80
9–11	10	7	70
11–13	12	3	36
		$\sum f = 30$	$\sum fx = 240$

$$\mu = \frac{\sum fx}{\sum f} = \frac{240}{30} = 8$$

TIP

For a grouped frequency table, you can find the mean from your calculator by inputting the mid-interval values x and the frequency values f.

The frequency polygon for this data is obtained by joining the midpoints of the uppermost sides of the rectangles in the histogram by lines. The frequency polygon and frequency distribution curve are shown:

Histogram and frequency polygon

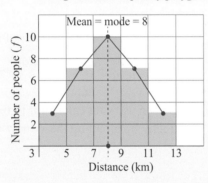

Frequency distribution curve

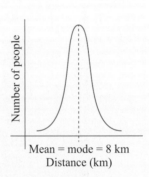

The shape of the frequency curve of this distribution is unimodal and symmetric.

$$\text{Mode} = \text{mid-interval value of (7–9) class} = \frac{7+9}{2} = 8 \text{ km}$$

Mean = 8 km

Therefore, the mean and mode are in the same position in this unimodal symmetric distribution.

EXAMPLE 4

One hundred cars tested in a given month are listed below according to their carbon dioxide (CO_2) emission levels.

Emission level	Number of cars
100–120	22
120–140	48
140–160	20
160–180	5
180–200	3
200–220	2

(a) Find the mean emission level per car.

(b) Find the modal class and the mode.

(c) Draw a histogram, frequency polygon and frequency distribution curve and mark the mean and mode on the frequency distribution curve. Comment on the shape of the curve.

Solution

(a)

Emission level	Mid-interval value x	Number of cars f	fx
100–120	110	22	2420
120–140	130	48	6240
140–160	150	20	3000
160–180	170	5	850
180–200	190	3	570
200–220	210	2	420
		$\sum f = 100$	$\sum fx = 13\,500$

Once you have worked out the mid-interval values, you can use your calculator to find the mean.

$$\mu = \frac{\sum fx}{\sum f} = \frac{13\,500}{100} = 135$$

(b) Modal class: 120–140, mode = 130

(c)

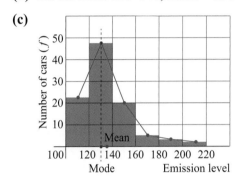

Frequency distribution curve

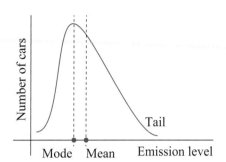

The shape is unimodal, positively skewed with the mean to the right of the mode (mean is greater than mode). There are many more classes with bigger mid-interval values to the right of the mode than to the left of it. This tends to increase the value of the mean, pulling it to the right in the direction of the larger values of the independent variable x.

Advantages and disadvantages of the mean as a measure of central tendency

Advantages

1. It uses all of the data values in a data set.
2. It is the mathematical centre of the distribution.
3. Inferential statistics is based on the mathematical properties of the mean. (See Chapter 22: Inferential Statistics.)
4. It is used in standardising scores from different normal distributions (see Chapter 21: Probability Distributions).

Disadvantages

1. Its value is strongly affected by outliers.
2. Its value does not give any indication of the position of a data value relative to the other data values when the values are arranged in order of increasing size.

EXERCISE 7

1. Find the mean and mode of the following data:

   (a) 1, 2, 5, 7, 10

   (b) −1, 5, −3, 2, 5, 4

   (c) a, b, c, d

   (d) 3, $2\frac{1}{2}$, 4, $5\frac{1}{2}$, 5

   (e) $a, a + d, a + 2d, a + 3d, a + 4d,$
       $a + 5d, a + 6d, a + 7d, a + 8d$

   (f) $x + 1, x + 2, x + 3, x + 4, x + 5,$
       $x + 6, x + 7, x + 8, x + 9$

   (g) 31, 58, 63, 74, 82, 35, 49, 55, 68, 70

   (h) 22·6, 24·7, 25·6, 26·3, 21·8, 29·3, 24·7

   (i) 43, 54, 68, 82, 67, 58, 62, 45, 43

   (j) $\frac{1}{4}, \frac{1}{3}, \frac{1}{2}, \frac{1}{4}, \frac{1}{3}, \frac{1}{2}, \frac{1}{4}, \frac{1}{3}, \frac{1}{2}$

2. Find the mean and mode of the numbers:
   3, 6, 2, 4, 1, 7, 8, 3, 2, 5, 6, 9, 5, 3, 4, 7, 3, 2, 3, 7. Hence, write down the mean and mode of each of the following numbers:

   (a) 2, 5, 1, 3, 0, 6, 7, 2, 1, 4, 5, 8, 4, 2, 3, 6, 2, 1, 2, 6

   (b) 9, 18, 6, 12, 3, 21, 24, 9, 6, 15, 18, 27, 15, 9, 12, 21, 9, 6, 9, 21

   (c) 7, 13, 5, 9, 3, 15, 17, 7, 5, 11, 13, 19, 11, 7, 9, 15, 7, 5, 7, 15

3. (a) If the mean of 2, 7, 9 and x is 5, find x.

   (b) If the mean of 7, 2, x, 1, 5, 11 and 3 is 6, find x.

   (c) If the mean of x, 4·8, x, 6·4 and 2·8 is 5·2, find x.

4. (a) The average price of four items is €2·80. Find the total price of the four items.

   (b) The mean age of a class of 25 pupils is 16. When the teacher walks into the room, the mean age goes up to 17. What is the teacher's age?

   (c) The mean height of 10 people is 1·6 m. A person of height 1·82 m joins them. What is the new mean height?

   (d) The mean earnings of 14 people in a company is €27 000. A new person joins the company. What must he earn to increase the average earnings by €1000?

   (e) Stefan has an average mark of 78·6 on his first five History tests. What must he score on the final sixth test to get an overall average of 80?

   (f) The mean of six numbers is 6. The mean of four numbers is 11. What is the mean of all 10 numbers?

   (g) The mean of nine numbers is 7. If one number is removed, the mean becomes 6. What number is removed?

5. For each of the following, draw up a frequency table and find the mean and mode from it:

   (a) The at-rest pulse rates of 20 swimmers at a meet are:

   55, 54, 57, 58, 54, 54, 58, 56, 55, 54, 54, 58, 58, 54, 53, 53, 54, 55, 55, 56

   (b) A die is thrown 40 times. The outcomes are listed below:

2	3	5	5	1
4	3	2	6	4
3	3	2	1	4
6	4	1	5	2
3	6	2	4	1
4	6	5	4	3
3	2	1	5	6
2	2	1	4	3

(c) The stem leaf diagram gives the scores of a number of students in a test:

2	3				
3	1	2	2		
4	8	8	8	8	8
5	0	4	4	4	4
6	0	0	0	0	
7	5	5			
8	0				
9	4				

(Key: 5|4 = 54)

6. (a) From the frequency table, find the mean.

x	1	2	3	4	5
f	3	1	4	7	5

(b) Find y if the mean is 3.

x	1	2	3	4	5
f	7	y	8	6	7

(c) Find y if the mean is 4.

x	8	7	2	y	5
f	2	3	4	5	6

7. (a) The mean of a, b, c, d is 4. The mean of $a, b, c, 7$ is 2. Find d.

(b) The mean of 5 numbers is a. The mean of 7 numbers is b. Find the mean of all 12 numbers in terms of a and b.

(c) q is the mean of a, b, c, d. Find the mean of $3a + p, 3b + p, 3c + p, 3d + p$ in terms of q and p.

(d) μ is the mean of the n numbers $x_1, x_2, ..., x_n$. Show that $\mu + k$ is the mean of the n numbers $x_1 + k, x_2 + k, ..., x_n + k$.

(e) μ is the mean of the n numbers $x_1, x_2, ..., x_n$. Show that $c\mu$ is the mean of $cx_1, cx_2, ..., cx_n$.

(f) μ is the mean of the n numbers $x_1, x_2, ..., x_n$. Show that $c\mu + k$ is the mean of n numbers $cx_1 + k, cx_2 + k, ..., cx_n + k$.

(g) The mean of x numbers is x^2. The mean of y numbers is y^2. Show that the mean of $x + y$ numbers is $x^2 - xy + y^2$.

(h) If μ is the mean of N numbers: $x_1, x_2, ..., x_N$,

show that $\dfrac{\sum\limits_{r=1}^{N}(x_r \mu)}{N} = \mu^2$.

(i) If the mean of a, b, c is x and the mean of e, f, g, h is also x, show that the mean of the seven numbers is x.

8. (a) Copy and complete the grouped frequency distribution table below:

Class	Mid-interval value	f
0–4		2
4–8		7
8–12		2
12–16		7
16–20		2

(b) Find the mean.

(c) Draw a histogram and its frequency polygon. Mark the mean on the frequency polygon. Comment on the modality of its frequency distribution.

9. Find the mean of the grouped frequency table below:

Class	f
0–5	4
5–10	8
10–15	12
15–20	8
20–25	4

Is it unimodal or bimodal? Mark the mean on a histogram and frequency polygon.

10. A university surveyed 120 final-year students on their expected yearly salaries in the world of work. The results are set out below:

Earnings in €(×1000)	Number of students
0–20	1
20–40	3
40–60	6
60–80	11
80–100	17
100–120	19
120–140	35
140–160	18
160–180	10

(a) Find:

   (i) the mean expected earnings, correct to the nearest euro,

   (ii) the mode.

(b) Plot a histogram and frequency polygon. Comment on the shape of the frequency polygon. Mark the mean and mode on the diagram.

11. If the mean of the grouped frequency distribution below is 36, find y.

Class interval	0–20	20–40	40–60	60–80
Frequency	4	y	3	2

12. One hundred pupils were given an IQ test. The test was tabulated as follows:

Score	Number of pupils
65–70	2
70–75	3
75–80	5
80–85	16
85–90	4
90–95	18
95–100	6
100–105	16
105–110	10
110–115	8
115–120	6
120–125	3
125–130	2
130–135	1

(a) Find the mean.

(b) Draw a histogram and its frequency polygon. Comment on its modality. Mark the mean on the frequency polygon.

(c) What percentage had an IQ greater than or equal to 100?

13. The finishing times of 100 athletes were recorded for a marathon, as follows:

Time (hours)	Number of athletes
2–3	10
3–4	42
4–5	20
5–6	16
6–7	8
7–8	4

(a) Find the mean.

(b) Draw a histogram and frequency polygon.

(c) Use the frequency polygon to find the mode.

(d) Comment on whether the shape of the frequency distribution is:

   (i) unimodal or bimodal,

   (ii) symmetric, positively skewed or negatively skewed.

14. In a survey of 1040 Facebook users, the age in years profile of a sample was investigated.

Age	Number of users
12–18	130
18–24	220
24–30	280
30–36	180
36–42	100
42–48	80
48–54	20
54–60	15
60–66	15

(a) Find the mean age of the sample, correct to the nearest whole number.

(b) Draw up a histogram and comment on the shape of the resulting distribution. Find the mode from the frequency polygon.

15. The weights in pounds (lbs) of the 54 NBA Draft basketball players of 2011 are listed below in a grouped frequency table:

Weight in pounds (lbs)	Frequency
170–180	2
180–190	6
190–200	10
200–210	7
210–220	3
220–230	13
230–240	4
240–250	5
250–260	2
260–270	2

(a) Find the mean weight in pounds (lbs).

(b) Draw a histogram and frequency polygon. Comment on the modality of the histogram.

19.3 The median

KEY TERM

The **median** of a set of numerical data is a number with equal numbers of data values that are less than it as are greater than it, when the data values are arranged in order of increasing size.

WORKED EXAMPLE Finding the median

A class of 17 students takes an Accounting test. The teacher places their marks in increasing order from the smallest to the biggest, as follows:
27, 32, 41, 47, 53, 58, 62, 69, 71, 73, 78, 79, 80, 85, 87, 90, 98

This is an odd number of marks. Clearly, 27 is the smallest mark and 98 is the biggest mark. However, students often want to know whether they are in the bottom half of the class or the top half. To know this, they need to know the median mark. This is the mark that has the same number of marks below it as above it. In this case, the median mark is 71, as there are eight marks below it and eight marks above it.

For a class of 10 students who took the same test, the marks were as follows:
26, 37, 45, 58, 62, 75, 79, 81, 90, 97

This is an even number of marks. There are two marks in the middle, 62 and 75, with as many marks above them as below them. The median is just the arithmetic mean of these two marks.

$$\text{Median} = \frac{62 + 75}{2} = \frac{137}{2} = 68\cdot5$$

Steps for finding the median

1. To find the median of numerical data, all the data values must be ranked in order from the smallest (first number) to the biggest (nth number).

2. If there is an odd number n of data values, the median is the number in the $\left(\dfrac{n+1}{2}\right)^{\text{th}}$ position in the ordered list.

   ▸ 2, 5, 7, 9, 11 ($n = 5$)

   The median is the number in the $\left(\dfrac{5+1}{2}\right)^{\text{rd}}$ position. The median is 7.

3. If there is an even number n of data values, the median is the mean of the values of the numbers in the $\left(\dfrac{n}{2}\right)^{\text{th}}$ and $\left(\dfrac{n}{2}+1\right)^{\text{th}}$ positions.

   ▸ 5, 9, 12, 14, 16, 19 ($n = 6$)

   The median is the mean of the number in the $\left(\dfrac{6}{2}\right)^{\text{rd}} = 3\text{rd}$ and $\left(\dfrac{6}{2}+1\right)^{\text{th}} = 4\text{th}$ positions.

   $$\text{Median} = \frac{12+14}{2} = \frac{26}{2} = 13$$

Median and central tendency

The median is a measure of central tendency because if you group the data values above and below the median, the number of values on each side of it is the same.

▸ 1, 4, 7, 8, 11, 18, 19

Numbers left of 8: 1, 4, 7	Numbers right of 8: 11, 18, 19

Median of sample = 8

8 is the median because there are as many values above it as below it.

WORKED EXAMPLE

How to find the median of related data sets

Find the median of the following data:

(a) *A*: 5, 2, 7, 6, 15, 12, 10

(b) *B*: 17, 8, 23, 20, 47, 38, 32

(a) *A*: 5, 2, 7, 6, 15, 12, 10

In increasing order: 2, 5, 6, 7, 10, 12, 15

Median = 7

(b) *B*: 17, 8, 23, 20, 47, 38, 32

In increasing order: 8, 17, 20, 23, 32, 38, 47

Median = 23 = 7 × 3 + 2

Each number in data set *B* is each number in data set *A* multiplied by 3 and then increased by 2. The median of data set *B* is the median of data set *A* multiplied by 3 and then increased by 2.

TIP

If you have a set of data and you multiply each data value by k and then increase its value by l, the median of the new set of data values is k times the median of the old set of data values plus l.

Old median	Change	New median
c	Multiply by k and increase by l	$kc + l$

EXAMPLE 5

The exam scores of a number of students are laid out below:

```
3 │ 1
4 │ 3  7
5 │ 5  6  8  9
6 │ 2  2  2  7
7 │ 1  8  4  6  8  8
8 │ 3  5  7
9 │ 1  5
```

(Key: 6|2 = 62)

Find the median and the mode.

Solution

There are 22 leaves.

$n = 22$ (even)

The median is the mean of the $\left(\frac{22}{2}\right)^{th} = 11$th and the $\left(\frac{22}{2}+1\right)^{th} = 12$th values, starting from the smallest value.

$$\text{Median} = \frac{67+71}{2} = \frac{138}{2} = 69$$

The mode is 62.

Cumulative frequency (CF) tables

WORKED EXAMPLE Finding the median from cumulative frequency tables

1. Odd number of results

Find the median and mode of the results in the following frequency table by building up a cumulative frequency (CF) table.

x	4·0	4·1	4·2	4·3	4·4	4·5
f	2	6	7	8	7	9

To build up a cumulative frequency (CF) table, produce a running total of results as you go from result to result. Cumulative frequency (CF) is the sum of successive frequencies.

x	f	CF	
4·0	2	2	←2 results to here (= 2)
4·1	6	8	←8 results to here (= 2 + 6)
4·2	7	15	←15 results to here (= 2 + 6 + 7)
4·3 (Median →)	8	23	←23 results to here (= 2 + 6 + 7 + 8)
4·4	7	30	←30 results to here (= 2 + 6 + 7 + 8 + 7)
4·5 (Mode →)	9	39	←39 results to here (= 2 + 6 + 7 + 8 + 7 + 9)
	$\sum f = n = 39$		

$\sum f = n = 39$ = total number of results (odd)

The median value is $\left(\frac{n+1}{2}\right)^{th} = \left(\frac{39+1}{2}\right)^{th} = $ 20th result

Median = 4·3

Mode = 4·5

2. **Even number of results**

Find the median from the frequency table below:

x	25	26	27	28	29	30
f	5	14	4	8	12	3

x	f	CF	
25	5	5	
26	14	19	
27	4	23	← 23rd result is here
28	8	31	← 24th result is in here
29	12	43	
30	3	46	
	$\Sigma f = n = 46$		

$\Sigma f = n = 46 =$ total number of results (even)

The median is the mean of $\left(\frac{n}{2}\right)^{\text{th}}$ and $\left(\frac{n}{2}+1\right)^{\text{th}}$ results, that is, the 23rd and 24th results, starting from the smallest value. Therefore, the median is the average of 27 and 28.

$$\text{Median} = \frac{27+28}{2} = \frac{55}{2} = 27{\cdot}5$$

The median of continuous data

Calculating the median for continuous data given in a grouped frequency distribution can be difficult. You have to find the value of the variable such that one half of the results (observations, measurements) fall below this value and the other half fall above it.

WORKED EXAMPLE Finding the median of continuous data

The time in minutes taken by 80 people to complete a crossword in minutes is given as a grouped frequency distribution.

The median is the result that appears 50% of the way along the set of data from the start.

Time (minutes)	Number of people
0–10	3
10–20	10
20–30	15
30–40	31
40–50	14
50–60	7
	$\Sigma f = 80$

Method 1: Finding the median from a cumulative frequency graph (ogive)

1. Draw up a new cumulative frequency table by adding up the previous frequencies, as follows:

Time t (mins)	Number of people	Time t (mins)	Cumulative number of people (CF)
0–10	3	< 10	3 = 3
10–20	10	< 20	13 = 3 + 10
20–30	15	< 30	28 = 3 + 10 + 15
30–40	31	< 40	59 = 3 + 10 + 15 + 31
40–50	14	< 50	73 = 3 + 10 + 15 + 31 + 14
50–60	7	< 60	80 = 3 + 10 + 15 + 31 + 14 + 7

2. Plot a graph of the cumulative frequency on the y-axis against time t on the x-axis.

3. Join up the points in a continuous curve, giving the cumulative frequency curve (ogive).

4. To find the median, go to the point on the y-axis halfway to the maximum cumulative frequency of 80. This is the cumulative frequency of 40. Draw a horizontal line to intersect the curve at P. Then drop a vertical line down onto the x-axis to read off the median.

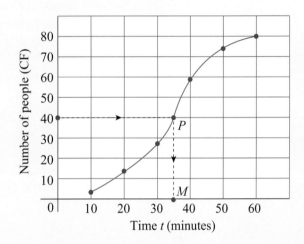

Median $M \approx 34$ minutes

Method 2: Finding the median from a histogram

The median line halves the area of the histogram because the number of results (cumulative frequency) to the left of the median is equal to the number of results (cumulative frequency) to the right of the median. Therefore, the area to the left of the median is equal to the area to the right of the median.

The median time is the time of the person in the 40·5th position. This is in the (30–40) class interval. Take the width of each class interval to be 1 unit (1 unit = 10 minutes).

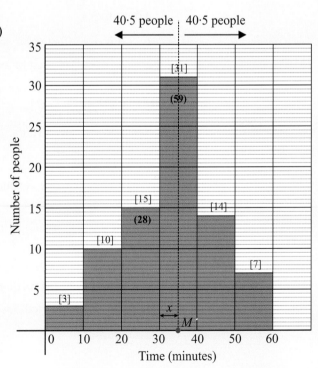

Let x = distance of median M from 30.

Area on left of M = area on right of M

$28 + 31x = 31(1 - x) + 21$

$28 + 31x = 31 - 31x) + 21$

$62x = 24$

$x = \dfrac{12}{31}$

$\therefore M = 30 + \dfrac{12}{31} \times 10 \simeq 34$ minutes

Median and area

For a histogram, frequency curve and relative frequency curve, the frequency of data values in a given class interval (x_1-x_2) is the area A under the curve on that class interval.

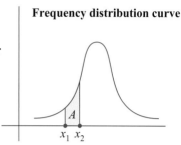

Frequency distribution curve

The cumulative frequency up to the upper extreme value x_2 of a given class interval from the smallest data value is the total number of values less than x_2 and so is equal to the area under the frequency curve up to that point.

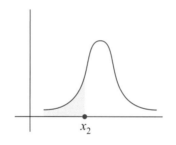

For a histogram, frequency curve and relative frequency curve, the median is the data value that divides the total area under the curve into two equal areas $(A_1 = A_2)$. This is because the total number of results to the left of it is equal to the total number of results to the right of it.

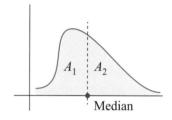

Advantages and disadvantages of the median as a measure of central tendency

Advantages

1. It is not affected by very small and very big values.
2. It is not distorted by outliers or skewed data.
3. It is easy to compute and understand.
4. It is useful for comparing sets of data.
5. It is good for ordinal data.

Disadvantages

1. It does not take account of the precise value of each observation and hence does not use all of the information in the data.
2. Unlike the mean, the median is not amenable to further mathematical calculations and so is not used in many statistical tests.
3. If groups of data are pooled together, the median of the new group cannot be found from the medians of the component groups.
4. The median is tedious to compute for large sets of data.

EXERCISE 8

1. Find the mean, median and mode for each of the following data:

(a) 3, 7, 5, 6, 3, 7, 4

(b) 3, 2, 4, 9, 3, 16, 12

(c) 2·7, 3·4, 7·9, 6·4, 3·2, 0·1, 6·5, 4·3, 4·7, 3·8

(d) 7, 4, 7, 28, 21, 15, 8, 100

(e) −3, −7, −11, −3, 6, −3, −7

(f) $\frac{1}{2}, \frac{1}{3}, \frac{1}{4}, \frac{1}{5}, \frac{1}{6}, \frac{1}{5}, \frac{1}{4}, \frac{1}{4}$

(g) 1, 2, 3, 4, …, 50

(h) 1, 2, 3, 4, …, n, n odd

2. Find the median, mean and mode of the data:

A: 2, 5, 3, 18, 8, 9, 5, 6, 5, 1, 4

Hence, find the median, mean and mode of B, C and D:

B: 6, 9, 7, 22, 12, 13, 9, 10, 9, 5, 8

C: 6, 15, 9, 54, 24, 27, 15, 18, 15, 3, 12

D: 7, 16, 10, 55, 25, 28, 16, 19, 16, 4, 13

3. Find the median, mode and mean (correct to one decimal place) of the following data:

(a)

2	3	5	5	5	7	
3	0	1	1	2	4	
4	2	3	5	6	6	7
5	1	5	6	7	8	9
6	2	8	9	9		

(Key: 4|5 = 4·5)

(b)

x	5	11	20	6	3
f	2	2	7	9	12

(c)

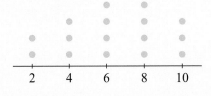

```
              •
          •   •
      •   •   •   •
  •   •   •   •   •
  •   •   •   •   •
  2   4   6   8   10
```

4. A crèche in a shopping centre kept track of the number of babies they cared for over a month using a dot plot.

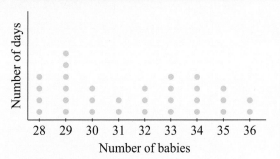

(a) How many days in the month?

(b) Find the median number of babies per day, the mean number (correct to one decimal place) of babies per day, and the modal number of babies per day.

5. Determine the mean, median and mode of 2, 6, 8, 14, 22, 4, 8. If you change the 14 to 17, what are the new mean, median and mode? Comment on anything you notice.

6. The number of goals scored by Wayne Rooney each year in the FA Premiership during his career at Manchester United is presented in the stem-and-leaf diagram below:

1	1	1	2	2	2	2	4	6	7
2	6	7							

(Key: 1|1 = 11)

(a) How many seasons has Rooney played in the Premiership?

(b) Find the median, mode and the mean number (correct to one decimal place) of goals he scored per season.

7. The number of penalty points incurred by drivers in Dublin City in November 2011 is set out in the frequency table below:

Number of points	Number of drivers
1	4295
2	86 752
3	1875
4	18 489
5	1073
6	4236
7	332
8	1064
9	147
10	260
11	39
12	44

Find the modal number of penalty points, the median number of penalty points and the mean number (correct to two decimal places) of penalty points incurred in November 2011 per driver in Dublin City.

8. The drink driving alcohol limits for 27 EU countries are laid out in the frequency table below:

Alcohol limit (mg/ml)	Number of countries
0	6
0·2	2
0·4	1
0·5	16
0·8	2

Find:

(a) the median alcohol level,

(b) the modal level,

(c) the mean alcohol level, correct to one decimal place.

9. The distribution of ages in a sample of 130 people is shown below:

Age (years)	Number of people
0–10	5
10–20	15
20–30	25
30–40	35
40–50	20
50–60	15
60–70	10
70–80	5

(a) Find the mean age of the sample, correct to the nearest whole number.

(b) Draw up a cumulative frequency table.

(c) Use it to draw an ogive and estimate the median, correct to the nearest year.

10. The life of 30 AA batteries was tested in a survey.

Battery life (minutes)	Frequency
360–370	1
370–380	4
380–390	5
390–400	8
400–410	6
410–420	3
420–430	2
430–440	1

(a) Find the mean lifetime of the battery.

(b) What percentage has a lifetime greater than or equal to 400 minutes?

(c) Draw up a cumulative frequency table and use it to draw the ogive.

(d) Use the ogive to estimate the median lifetime, correct to the nearest minute.

11. The frequency table below shows the points obtained by 50 people who took a drugs test:

Points	Number of people
0–20	4
20–40	10
40–60	20
60–80	8
80–100	8

(a) Find the mean number of points.

(b) Draw a histogram.

(c) Find the median correct to the nearest whole number.

(d) Mark the mean, median and mode on the histogram.

(e) If you need 65 points or more to pass the test, find the greatest possible number who could have passed.

12. A concert starts at 8:00 p.m. The cumulative frequency table below gives the number of people in the hall at the times stated. The doors open at 7:00 p.m.

Time (p.m.)	Number of people
< 7:10	0
< 7:20	28
< 7:30	96
< 7:40	154
< 7:50	268
< 8:00	400

(a) Draw up a frequency table by copying and completing the table below.

Time (p.m.)	Number of people
7:10–7:20	
7:20–7:30	
7:30–7:40	
7:40–7:50	
7:50–8:00	

(b) Find the mean time of arrival, correct to the nearest minute.

(c) Draw a histogram.

(d) Find the median time of arrival, correct to the nearest minute and mark the mean and median on the histogram.

13. From the histogram shown, find the median score. Draw up a cumulative frequency table and find the median by putting the area to the left of the dotted line equal to the right of the dotted line.

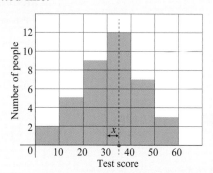

14. The number of decays from a radioactive source was measured in 5-second intervals.

Time (s)	Number of decays
0–5	65
5–10	52
10–15	35
15–20	23
20–25	12
25–30	8
30–35	5

Find the median time for a radioactive decay, correct to the nearest second.

19.4 Comparing averages

ACTION
Comparing averages

OBJECTIVE
To appreciate the advantages and disadvantages of the various types of central tendency

Which is the 'best' average?

Remember that an average is a measure of central tendency. The three numbers – mode, mean and median – may give different values for a set of data. So which is the most suitable? The answer often depends on the context. The best average is the one that best represents the central tendency of the set in the context of the data values.

Guidelines for selection of appropriate measure of central tendency

First of all, the mean and median deal only with numerical data, whereas the mode can handle numerical and categorical data.

- The **mean** is generally considered the best measure of central tendency and the most frequently used.
- The **median** is preferred when there are extreme values (outliers) in the distribution of the data.
- The **mode** is preferred for non-numerical data.

WORKED EXAMPLE

Which measure of central tendency is best?

(a) Mean is best

This is a set of 10 marks of a Biology class in a test marked out of 10: 2, 2, 2, 3, 4, 4, 5, 5, 7, 8

Mode = 2

$\text{Median} = \dfrac{4+4}{2} = 4$

$\text{Mean} = \dfrac{2+2+2+3+4+4+5+5+7+8}{10} = \dfrac{42}{10} = 4 \cdot 2$

Clearly, any of the averages could be taken as a measure of central tendency because the centre of the numbers is around 4 or 5. If you must pick one, then pick the **mean** because all numbers in the list contribute to its calculation.

(b) Median is best

This is a set of 10 marks of a Geography class in a test marked out of 100: 2, 2, 2, 3, 4, 4, 5, 5, 7, 98

These marks are identical to the marks in **(a)**, except that the 8 is changed to 98.

Mode = 2

$\text{Median} = \dfrac{4+4}{2} = 4$

$\text{Mean} = \dfrac{2+2+2+3+4+4+5+5+7+98}{10} = \dfrac{132}{10} = 13 \cdot 2$

These averages are wildly different to each other. The 98 mark is so large by comparison to the other marks that it has skewed the mean. The median, however, is not affected at all by the change of 8 to 98. In this case, the **median** is the best average as it is the most representative of the set, in that it gives a good numerical indication of the ability of the class. The **mean** of $13 \cdot 2$ would be misleading, as only one person in fact scored more than $13 \cdot 2$; the other nine were well below it.

TIP

The mean is sensitive to extreme data values (outliers), while the median is not. The median is unchanged by extreme values (outliers) because it is the number with as many data values less than it as greater than it, when the results are placed in ascending order of size. The biggest and smallest data values do not play a role in calculating the median.

Which measure of central tendency do you use?

Unlike the mean, the median is not influenced by outliers or extreme data values. So the median might be used for statistics involving salaries and house prices, whereas the mean would be used for finding a student's average grade in a number of exams, as all grades must be accounted for. The mode is used for the 'most common' (popular) data.

Mean: Use for numerical data when the frequency distribution is roughly symmetrical (evenly distributed).

Median: Use for numerical data when the frequency distribution is positively or negatively skewed.

Mode: Use for numerical or categorical data when the most frequent data value (result) is required.

When choosing a measure of central tendency for a set of data values, you should always be aware of the context in which it is to be used.

▸ The 'average' income of a family is usually the median income. However, this is not always the number required. If you want, as a government, to find the effect of a tax increase of 2%, you need to use the mean taxable income, so you can multiply it by the number of families to get the increase in revenue.

Economic data often has a positively skewed distribution.

▸ Most US universities had endowments that were much less than $5 billion in 2011. However, a few like Yale ($19 billion), Princeton ($17 billion) and Harvard ($31 billion) skew the distribution to the right. Therefore, the median is the average value that should be quoted here.

▸ For opinion polls, family size, hair colour and other surveys involving categorical data, the mode is the only measure of central tendency that can be used.

Shapes of distributions

In this section, the shapes of frequency distributions are examined in more detail to see what happens to the mode, mean and median in different situations.

1. The mode

The mode is the data value with the highest frequency f. It is simply the value which occurs most often.

(a) Symmetrical distribution

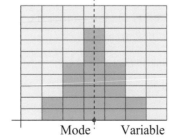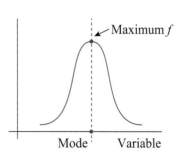

Mode = mid-interval value of class with the tallest rectangle

(b) Skewed right (positively skewed)

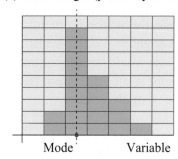 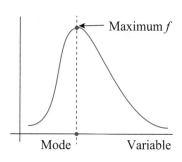

(c) Skewed left (negatively skewed)

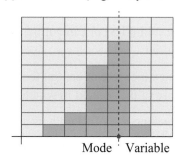 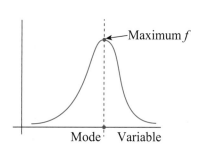

2. The median

The median is the number that is right in the middle of the distribution in that there are as many results less than it as greater than it, when the results are placed in ascending order of size.

> **TIP**
>
> For a frequency distribution, the frequency of the class interval is equal to the area under the curve on that class interval.

Median		
50% of the results are on the left of the median	and	50% of the results are on the right of the median
Sum of the frequencies on left of median	=	Sum of the frequencies on right of median
Total area to the left of the median	=	Total area to the right of the median

For a symmetric distribution, the median is the point where the axis of symmetry crosses the x-axis, as it splits the area under the curve into two equal areas.

For a symmetrical distribution: Mode = Median

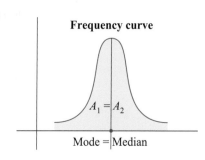

For a positively skewed distribution, there are many little rectangles to the right of the mode. The median must shift slightly to the right of the mode, so that the area on the left of the median is equal to the area on the right of it.

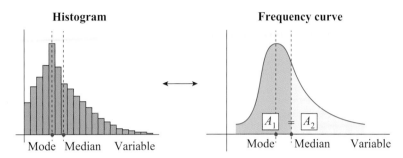

For a negatively skewed distribution, there are many little rectangles to the left of the mode. The median must shift slightly to the left of the mode, so that the area on the left of the median is equal to the area on the right of it.

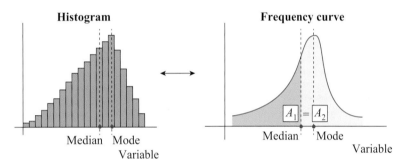

3. The mean

The mean μ of a frequency distribution is given by $\mu = \dfrac{\text{Sum of the } fx \text{ values}}{\text{Sum of the } f \text{ values}}$, where x is the mid-interval value of a class interval and f is the frequency of values in this interval.

$$\therefore \mu = \frac{\text{Sum of the areas of each rectangle multiplied by its mid-interval value}}{\text{Total area}}$$

So, not only does the area of a rectangle contribute to the position of the mean, but its mid-interval value also has a part to play. This means rectangles with large mid-interval values x (those furthest from the y-axis) increase the value of μ, whereas rectangles with small values of x decrease the value of μ.

For a symmetric distribution:

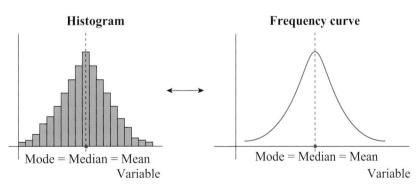

For a positively skewed distribution, the many small rectangles that are far away from the *y*-axis pull the mean to the right of the median.

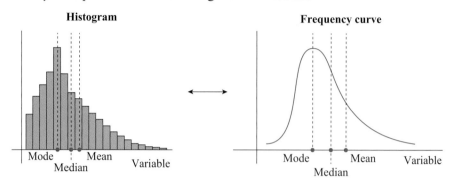

For a negatively skewed distribution, the many small rectangles that are close to the *y*-axis pull the mean to the left of the median.

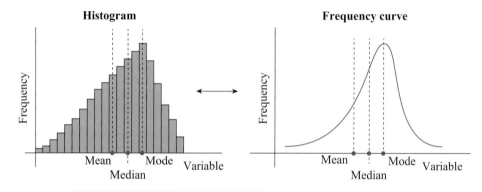

EXERCISE 9

1. Find the mode, mean and median of each of the following data. Then select the 'best' measure of central tendency. Give approximate answers correct to one decimal place.

   (a) 2, 4, 5, 6, 6, 7, 7, 8, 9

   (b) 2·6, 2·4, 2·3, 5·8, 2·7, 3·2, 9·4

   (c) 129, 132, 145, 128, 99, 187, 165, 192, 171, 186, 134, 142

   (d) 23·1, 24·7, 26·2, 25·0, 27·3, 22·4, 26·5, 24·8, 23·9, 25·8

   (e) 41, 47, 55, 48, 72, 58, 48, 65, 56, 42, 57, 60, 71, 43, 49, 0, 0, 61, 74, 62, 64

2. Determine which 'average' (mean, mode or median) is being described in the following situations:

   (a) The average Irish citizen's share of the national debt is €30 000.

   (b) In a recent survey of car colour choices, it was found that most people prefer red.

   (c) Half of the students in a class scored more than 38% in a recent test.

   (d) Town planners in a county council are looking at plans for a new housing estate. They need to know the average size of an Irish family.

   (e) Auctioneers give the average price of houses in Wicklow as €125 000.

   (f) A student has an average score of 81·2 in seven subjects.

   (g) The average income of a player in the English Premiership.

   (h) The average salary for a software programmer in Ireland is €50 786.

   (i) The average household debt in Ireland is €108 311, whereas the average gross income per household is €53 864 based on total debt and total income figures from the OECD.

   (j) The average test scores when results are skewed.

   (k) In an opinion poll, the New Democratic Party got 785 first preference votes in a poll of 1000 people.

3. The median annual income for a household of four in an OECD country was €45 000 in 2007. If the mean per capita annual income in the country for 2007 was €25 000, what was the total annual income for a household of four? Explain this high figure.

4. A solicitor's office advertises for a junior clerk. The office has four senior solicitors, two junior solicitors and one receptionist. The mean annual salary of the practice is €90 000. Can the junior clerk expect to get this salary? Why is the mean so high?

5. Two Irish Government agencies gave the annual household income for a year as €47 000 and €56 000. Explain.

6. An accountant in an electricity supplier in the 26 counties wants to work out the mean electrical consumption per household in a particular year. He gets the mean household consumption for each county, adds them up and divides by 26. Is this right?

7. The ages of students in years in an adult education class are: 18, 18, 19, 19, 20, 20, 21, 21, 22, 22, 22, 23, 51, 58, 64. What would you give as the average age?

8. The median of eight results is 23·5. The results are as follows, in ascending order: 5, 11, 18, 20, x, 29, 33, 52. Find x.

9. The following daily temperatures for a city for a week were listed as:

15 °C, 15·2 °C, 16·3 °C, 27 °C, 15·3 °C, 16·1 °C, 16·0 °C

What would you give as the average daily temperature? Why?

10. Make up seven test marks out of 10 so that the mean is greater than the median.

11. Sarah has a mean mark of 78·9 in five tests. What mark must she score in the sixth test to get an overall mean of 80?

12. One newspaper reports that the average annual salary of a soccer player at Paris Saint-Germain is $9·08 million. Another reports the average as $8 million. Explain.

13. Only four players in the NBA have scored 60 points or more in a game: Michael Jordan (5 times), Kobe Bryant (5 times), Elgin Baylor (4 times) and the great Wilt Chamberlain (32 times). Here is the frequency table of Wilt's 60+ points scores:

Highest scores	Number of games
60	3
61	6
62	6
63	2
65	3
66	1
67	4
68	1
70	1
72	1
73	2
78	1
100	1

(a) Find the mean highest score in a single game for Wilt, correct to the nearest whole number.

(b) Find his median highest score.

(c) Wilt's highest score is an outlier. By dropping it, find the new mean (correct to the nearest whole number) and the new median.

14. The weights in kilograms (kg) of 30 babies at birth is listed below:

3·0	3·4	2·6	4·2	3·3
3·9	3·6	3·2	3·9	3·3
3·2	3·3	2·7	3·6	3·2
3·5	3·3	3·2	3·1	3·7
3·4	3·1	3·6	3·9	2·9
3·3	4·2	3·3	3·1	3·8

(a) Organise this data into a stem-and-leaf plot.

(b) Find the mode, the mean (correct to one decimal place) and the median.

(c) Which is the best average? Why?

(d) Draw a histogram using equal class intervals with the lowest (2·6–2·8) kg. Comment on its shape.

15. For each of the histograms below, find the mean and median, correct to one decimal place. Determine whether the mean is less than, greater than or approximately equal to the median. Describe the shape of each distribution.

(a)

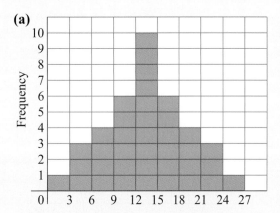

(b)

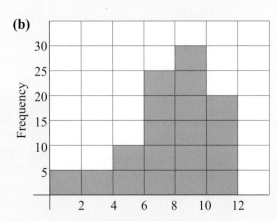

(c)

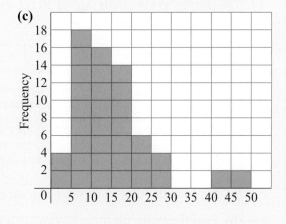

16. A frequency distribution of the test scores for students in three different classes is shown:

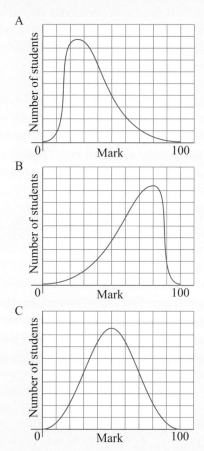

(a) Describe the shape of each distribution.

(b) Mark in the approximate positions of the mode, mean and median on each diagram.

(c) State, in each case, if the percentage that passed was well over 50%, well under 50% or about 50%, if the pass mark was 50.

17. The following two distributions show the marks obtained by two classes in a History test. Distribution *B* is perfectly symmetrical.

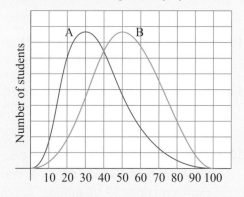

(a) Describe the shape of distribution A.

(b) Find the mode, mean and median marks for distribution B.

(c) Which mark did most students in class A obtain?

(d) In which class did more students get higher marks? Why?

(e) If you were told that the average age of class B was greater than class A, could you conclude that the reason class B did better than class A was because they were older?

18. Mark in the mode and approximate positions of the mean and median on the two frequency distributions shown.

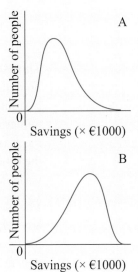

One of these distributions was a survey of 1000 people 50 years or younger. The other was a survey of people over 50 years of age. Which distribution is for which group? Why?

19. The number of deaths per 10 000 of population according to age for two countries is shown in a given year. One country is Japan, the other is Mozambique. Which is which? Why?

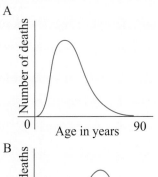

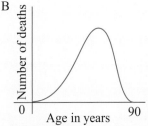

19.5 Scatter plots

Scatter plots show the relationship between two sets of data and help us to decide what type of relationship exists between the two sets.

KEY TERM

A **scatter plot** shows the relationship between two sets of numerical data (bivariate numerical data). One set of values is plotted on the x-axis (independent variable) and the other set on the y-axis (dependent variable).

WORKED EXAMPLE

WORKED EXAMPLE — The concept of a scatter plot

A student carried out a survey on 15 students in her class to see if there was any connection between the mark out of 10 each student got in a Biology test and the number of pets each student owned. The data was recorded in the following table:

Number of pets	Mark
2	3
1	4
3	7
4	6
1	5
2	4
1	3
5	8
3	8
2	9
3	4
2	5
1	6
2	7
1	8

The student plotted a graph with the number of pets on the x-axis and the marks received on the y-axis.

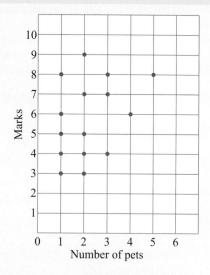

This is an example of a scatter plot. To make a scatter plot, you need two sets of numerical data (bivariate numerical data). One set is plotted on the x-axis (independent variable) and the other on the y-axis (the dependent variable).

The plot shows at a glance if there is any relationship (correlation) between the two sets of data. In this case, the dots are all over the place. There is clearly no correlation between the two sets of data because there is no shape to this pattern.

EXAMPLE 6

An athlete enters a 10 km run and notes his times at certain distances.

	Time x (minutes)	Distance y (km)
Start	0	0
Drink station 1	20	3·2
Marker	25	4·6
Drink station 2	34	5·8
Marker	42	7·0
Drink station 3	50	9·2
Finish	56	10·0

Draw a graph of distance versus time, with time on the x-axis and distance on the y-axis.

Solution

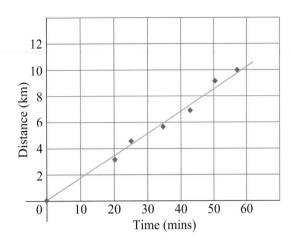

The data points fall very strongly along a straight line. There appears to be a very **strong correlation** between the two sets of data. If the equation of this line can be found, it can be used to predict the time it will take the athlete to cover distances not included in the table.

EXAMPLE 7

The table below shows the price of a bottle of water in euro at certain distances from the Louvre Museum in Paris.

Distance from Louvre (m)	100	200	300	400	500	600	700	800	900
Price (€)	2·00	1·50	1·80	1·10	1·00	1·20	0·60	1·00	5·00

(a) Draw a scatter plot graph with distance along the *x*-axis and price along the *y*-axis.

(b) What conclusion can you make? What type of correlation exists between the data sets?

(c) Are there any outliers?

(d) Draw the line of best fit (LOBF).

Solution

(a)

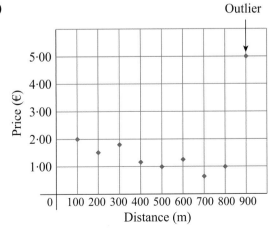

(b) It is clear that the points do not lie exactly on a straight line but seem to be scattered about a straight line. More particularly, the price appears to get lower as you move further away from the Louvre. There appears to be a moderate negative correlation between the two variables because they are scattered about a straight line and as one variable increases (distance), the other decreases (price).

(c) The point marked with the arrow is an outlier – you have walked into the most expensive hotel in Paris!

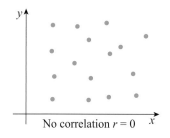

No correlation $r = 0$

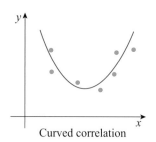

Curved correlation

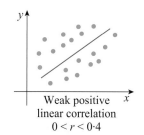

Weak positive
linear correlation
$0 < r < 0.4$

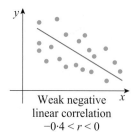

Weak negative
linear correlation
$-0.4 < r < 0$

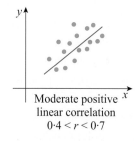

Moderate positive
linear correlation
$0.4 < r < 0.7$

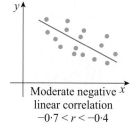

Moderate negative
linear correlation
$-0.7 < r < -0.4$

(d) You can draw the line of best fit (LOBF) using all points except the outlier. This is the line with roughly the same number of points on each side of it and sloping up or down, depending on whether the y values increase or decrease as the x values increase.

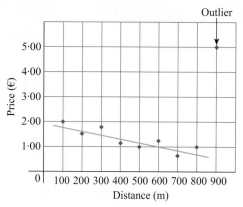

The process of determining the line of best fit is also known as **linear regression**. A line of best fit is an average description of the relationship between the dependent and independent variables in a set of bivariate data.

Describing the pattern of a scatter plot

Remember a scatter plot shows the relationship between two sets of numerical values (bivariate numerical data). One set of values is plotted on the x-axis (independent variable) and the other set on the y-axis (dependent variable).

When describing a scatter plot, you should consider the following:

1. **Form (shape):** linear or curved or none.
2. **Direction:** For linear forms, the direction is positive (positive slope) or negative (negative slope).

    Positive means the value of the dependent variable tends to increase as the value of the independent variable increases. Negative means the value of the dependent variable tends to decrease as the value of the independent variable increases.

3. **Strength:** For linear forms, the strength of the correlation between two sets of data is a measure of how close the points are to the line of best fit. The correlation coefficient r is a number that measures this strength.

    The table below shows how to interpret values of r:

Strong positive correlation	$0.7 < r < 1$
Moderate positive correlation	$0.4 < r < 0.7$
Weak positive correlation	$0 < r < 0.4$
Strong negative correlation	$-1 < r < -0.7$
Moderate negative correlation	$-0.7 < r < -0.4$
Weak negative correlation	$-0.4 < r < 0$

4. **Outliers:** Outliers are any data points that are very far from the overall pattern of the rest of the data.

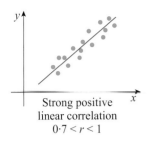

Strong positive
linear correlation
$0 \cdot 7 < r < 1$

Some points to note about r

- r is always a value from -1 to 1:
  $-1 \le r \le 1$
- Perfect correlation: $r = \pm 1$
- No correlation: $r = 0$
- Line of best fit with a positive
  slope: $r = +$

- Line of best fit with a negative
  slope: $r = -$
- r has no unit.
- r is very sensitive to outliers.

If a scatter plot shows a set of data that has a form that is fairly linear, the line of best fit provides a model that enables you to analyse and use this data. The line of best fit can be drawn in two ways:

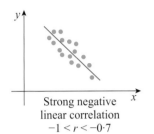

Strong negative
linear correlation
$-1 < r < -0 \cdot 7$

- By eye
- By calculation

Line of best fit (LOBF)

Drawing the line of best fit by eye

1. Construct a scatter plot of the bivariate data.
2. Find the mean $\bar{x}$ of the independent variable values and the mean $\bar{y}$ of the dependent variable values using your calculator, if possible.
3. Plot $(\bar{x}, \bar{y})$ on the scatter diagram.
4. Draw a straight line through $(\bar{x}, \bar{y})$, dividing the data points so that there are as many points on one side of the line as on the other, excluding outliers.
5. Find the equation of the line of best fit using $(\bar{x}, \bar{y})$ and one other data point on the line of best fit.

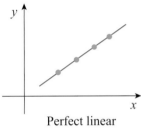

Perfect linear
positive correlation
$r = +1$

> **NOTE**
> The mean of the x values is denoted by $\bar{x}$ (pronounced x bar). The mean of the y values is denoted by $\bar{y}$.

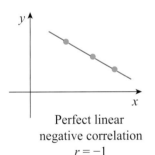

Perfect linear
negative correlation
$r = -1$

Drawing the line of best fit by calculation

1. Construct a scatter plot of the bivariate data.
2. Enter all the data into the STAT MODE of the calculator and find A, B, $\bar{x}$, $\bar{y}$.
3. The equation of the line of best fit is $y = A + Bx$ and $(\bar{x}, \bar{y})$ is on this line.
4. Plot the line of best fit using $(\bar{x}, \bar{y})$ and one other point of your choice on the line $y = A + Bx$.

> **TIP**
> The best way to plot a line of best fit is to enter the data into your calculator and calculate $(\bar{x}, \bar{y})$ and A and B. You can plot the line of best fit using $(\bar{x}, \bar{y})$ as one point and the equation $y = A + Bx$ to find another point.

EXAMPLE 8

The data in the following table shows the weights of 1-year-old children (x) compared to their weights (y) at 30 years of age:

Weight at 1: x (kg)	9·5	10	9·1	10·9	10·5	7·2	6·3	10	8·2	11
Weight at 30: y (kg)	57	58	59	58	60	52	53	59	55	61

(a) Construct a scatter plot.

(b) Draw the line of best fit and find its equation.

(c) Use this line to predict the weight, correct to the nearest kilogram, of a 30-year-old if his weight at 1 year of age was 8·5 kg.

Solution

(a)

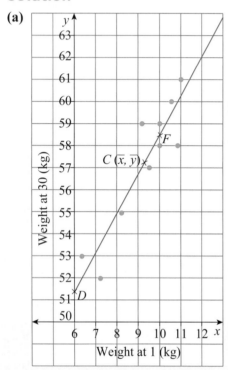

(b) Draw the line of best fit by eye:

1. Plot the points as shown above.
2. $\bar{x} = 9·27$, $\bar{y} = 57·2$
3. Plot $(\bar{x}, \bar{y}) = (9·27, 57·2)$, as shown at C.
4. Draw the line of best fit through C with as many points on one side of this line as on the other.

5. Choose any other point, for example, $D(6·0, 51·5)$.

Slope $CD = m = \dfrac{57·2 - 51·5}{9·27 - 6·0} = 1·74$

Equation of CD: $y - 57·2 = 1·74\,(x - 9·27)$

$y = 1·74x + 41·1$

(c) $x = 8·5$: $y = 1·74(8·5) + 41·1 \approx 56$ kg

(b) Draw the line of best fit using your calculator:

1. Plot the points as shown above.
2. $\bar{x} = 9·27$, $\bar{y} = 57·2$, $A = 41·4$, $B = 1·7$ [By calculator]
3. Equation of the line of best fit: $y = A + Bx$ $\Rightarrow y = 41·4 + 1·7x$
4. Use the equation to find another point F: $x = 10 \Rightarrow y = 58·4$
5. Plot the line of best fit using the points $C(9·27, 57·2)$ and $F(10, 58·4)$.

(c) Using the line of best-fit equation:
$y = 41·4 + 1·7x$ [This equation from the calculator is more accurate than the one obtained by eye.]

$x = 8·5$: $y = 41·4 + 1·7 \times 8·5$

≈ 56 kg

TIP

In general, the line of best fit can go through none, all or some of the points in a scatter plot, but it always goes through $(\bar{x}, \bar{y})$.

ACTIVITY **16**

ACTION
Finding *r* by
calculation

OBJECTIVE
To find r by calculation

Correlation coefficient *r*

Instead of judging visually the amount of spread or scatter of data points about the line of best fit, a number called the correlation coefficient can be calculated to give an exact value for the strength of the correlation between two sets of data.

EXAMPLE 9

The following table shows the household size (number of people that live in the house) and its average weekly water consumption in litres for 10 households recorded by a water meter on the road:

Household size	2	7	9	4	10	6	9	3	2	4
Average weekly water consumption (*l*)	600	1300	1400	400	1500	800	1600	500	800	900

(a) What is the independent variable?

(b) Find the correlation coefficient between water consumption and household size.

(c) What does *r* tell you?

(d) If the average weekly consumption was measured in gallons, would the value of *r* change?

Solution

(a) Household size is the independent variable. The level of consumption depends on the household size.

(b)

x	2	7	9	4	10	6	9	3	2	4
y	600	1300	1400	400	1500	800	1600	500	800	900

Calculator: $r = 0.8846$

(c) $r = +0.8846$: There is a strong positive correlation between water consumption and household size.

(d) No, *r* has no dimensions.

ACTIVITY **17**

ACTION
Understanding
causation versus
correlation

OBJECTIVE
*To understand
what causation and
correlation implies*

Causation versus correlation

Do not confuse correlation with causation and beware of lurking variables. When you get a strong correlation (large value of *r*) between a dependent variable and an independent variable, it is tempting to say that a change in the independent variable **causes** a change in the dependent variable.

WORKED EXAMPLE — Correlation and causation

The scatter plot below shows the population of the Spanish city of Salamanca versus the stork population of Salamanca over a number of years:

The correlation coefficient between human population and stork population is $r = 0.98$. This does not mean an increase in the stork population causes an increase in the human population. Storks don't deliver babies! You cannot say a large stork population causes a large human population.

There are many other (lurking) variables that cause the population of a town to rise: for example, the economy, development, investment, tourism. It is possible for two variables to have a strong correlation but not have one cause the other. Strong correlation does not always imply causation. However, causation always implies strong correlation.

▸ Ocean earthquakes cause tsunamis: This means there is high correlation between the occurrence of tsunamis and the occurrence of earthquakes.

TIP

▲ Strong correlation does not always imply causation but causation always implies strong correlation.

EXAMPLE 10

The following table shows the numbers of cars and televisions sold in a retail park in eight different months:

Number of cars sold (x)	20	36	40	60	8	24	70	24
Number of televisions sold (y)	40	63	78	110	26	38	120	50

Find the correlation coefficient. Does this mean a rise in car sales tends to lead to a rise in the sale of televisions?

Solution

x	20	36	40	60	8	24	70	24
y	40	63	78	110	26	38	120	50

$r = 0{\cdot}989$

There is a very strong correlation here, but it does not imply causation. People normally replace cars and televisions when they break down and are unlikely to do it at the same time. The high correlation is probably due to the 'lurking variable' of a healthy economy.

EXERCISE 10

1. (a) Draw a scatter plot of each of the three tables below, giving all points correct to two decimal places.

   (b) State the type of correlation, if any, by finding the correlation coefficient. Use your calculator to find $(\bar{x}, \bar{y})$ in each case, where $\bar{x}$ is the mean of x and $\bar{y}$ is the mean of y, correct to two decimal places.

   (c) Draw the line of best fit using $(\bar{x}, \bar{y})$ by eye or by finding its equation using your calculator in the form $y = A + Bx$, with A and B correct to two decimal places.

   (i)
x	0	1	2	3	4	5
y	0	2	4	6	8	10

   (ii)
x	0	1	2	3	4	5
y	2	8	3	7	4	10

   (iii)
x	0	1	2	3	4	5
y	9	7	6	4	2	2

2. Draw a scatter plot of the following data:

Year of birth	Life expectancy (years)
1930	59
1940	63
1950	68
1960	70
1970	72
1980	76

(a) State the type of correlation, if any, under two headings:

    (i) Strength   (ii) Direction

(b) Draw the line of best fit by eye and use it to estimate life expectancy in 2020.

3. The equation of the line of best fit for a scatter plot of summer exam results (y) against Christmas exam results (x) in Maths for a class is given by $y = 0{\cdot}8x + 28$.

    (a) If a student scores 78 at Christmas, what does he score in the summer exam?

    (b) If the mean score of the class in the summer exam was 56·5, find the mean score of the class at Christmas, correct to one decimal place.

    (c) Is the correlation positive or negative? Why?

4. The table below shows the average number of hours (x) per day spent by 10 fifth-year students watching television and the average mark (y) they achieved in their summer exams.

x	5	3	0	5	3	6	10	9	8	12
y	27	33	40	35	32	32	20	28	22	23

    (a) Find the correlation coefficient r between the two quantities, correct to two decimal places.

    (b) Interpret the answer.

    (c) Does this result lead to the conclusion that more time spent viewing television causes lower exam grades? Why?

5. The following data shows the fuel consumption of a car in litres of petrol at a given speed in km/h:

Speed (km/h) x	Fuel (litres) y
10	20
20	12
30	9
40	8
50	7
60	5·8
70	6·2
80	7·1
90	7·6
100	8·3

(a) Draw a scatter plot graph.

(b) Comment on the type of correlation under the headings:

    (i) Strong or weak

    (ii) Linear or curved

6. A teacher in a certain county conducted a survey for the Bird Society over an 8-year period on the number of breeding pairs of doves in the school grounds and the percentage of males who returned the next season.

Number of breeding pairs x	Percentage return y
3	80
4	84
4	75
4	62
5	68
6	55
5	40
7	55
7	44

(a) Draw a scatter plot and comment on any correlation between the percentage return and number of breeding pairs by calculating the correlation coefficient, correct to two decimal places.

(b) Find the equation of the line of best fit by drawing or by calculation.

7. A student's project for the Junior Cycle was to measure the length (in cm) of icicles grown in the laboratory at $-10\ {}^{\circ}\text{C}$ in a freezer.

Time t (minutes)	Length l (cm)
10	0·5
20	1·6
30	3·0
40	3·8
50	5·2
60	6·0
70	7·8
80	10·0
90	11·0
100	12·5
110	14·3
120	16·5

(a) Draw a scatter plot of length versus time.

(b) Find the mean time and mean length, correct to two decimal places.

(c) Find the equation of the line of best fit by drawing or by calculation.

(d) Find the correlation coefficient, correct to two decimal places.

8. The following are the results of 10 students in Geography tests, one taken at Christmas and the other in summer:

Test 1 (x)	55	43	54	67	73	85	90	41	62	88
Test 2 (y)	78	65	73	87	91	96	0	68	80	99

(a) Plot a scatter plot with test 1 on the x-axis and test 2 on the y-axis.

(b) Are there any outliers?

(c) Excluding any outliers, find the correlation coefficient, correct to two decimal places, and the equation of the line of best fit by drawing or by calculation.

9. The following results show a possible cause of lung cancer due to smoking in 20 countries:

Average number of cigarettes per person per day (x)	Lung cancer deaths per 10 000 people (y)
17	12
19	16
19	18
22	15
22	17
24	18
24	21
26	21
26	26
30	24
30	26
30	26
33	26
33	24
34	24
27	20
25	23
38	21
41	27
42	28

(a) Draw a scatter plot.

(b) What, if any, is the correlation pattern? Can you conclude that smoking causes cancer?

(c) Find the correlation coefficient r, correct to two decimal places, and draw the line of best fit through $(\bar{x}, \bar{y})$ by eye, where $\bar{x}$ is the mean of x and $\bar{y}$ is the mean of y.

(d) Find the equation of the line of best fit by finding its y-intercept.

10. Probably the most famous scatter plot in astronomy is the Hertzsprung–Russell diagram, which shows the luminosity of stars versus temperature (K). Most stars in the neighbourhood of the Sun fall on a well-defined main sequence. The luminosity of the Sun = 1.

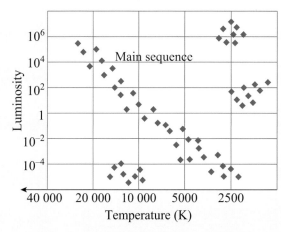

(a) Copy the diagram into your copybook. Draw a line of best fit for the main sequence and state the type of correlation.

(b) There are three groups of outliers:

    (i) A group of very faint hot stars. Label these as WD (White Dwarfs).

    (ii) A group of bright cold stars. Label these as RG (Red Giants).

    (iii) A group of very bright cold stars. Label these as BG (Blue Supergiants).

11. Carbon dioxide levels in the atmosphere are shown for the years 1986–2006, where $x = 0$ is 1986:

Year x	CO_2 parts per million y
0	347·0
1	351·3
2	354·0
3	356·3
4	358·9
5	362·7
6	366·5
7	369·4
8	372·0
9	377·5
10	380·9

(a) Calculate the correlation coefficient between CO_2 levels in the atmosphere and the year, correct to three decimal places.

(b) If the line of best fit is approximated by the equation $y = 3·3x + 347$, find the CO_2 level in 1984.

(c) Use the equation in **(b)** to estimate the CO_2 level in 2018.

12. The following table gives the area of sea ice in the Arctic in millions of square kilometres from 1986 to 2006:

Year x	Ice area y (millions km^2)
1986	7·6
1988	7·5
1990	6·2
1992	7·6
1994	7·1
1996	7·9
1998	6·6
2000	6·3
2002	6·0
2004	6·1
2006	5·7

(a) Make a scatter plot.

(b) Draw the line of best fit by eye. Use it to estimate the ice area in 2010.

13. The owner of a garage surveyed his customers about the number (x) of times they changed the oil in their car per year and their car repair costs per year (y). The results of his survey are shown in the table:

Number of oil changes per year (x)	Costs of repair per year (y)
3	300
5	350
2	500
3	400
1	700
4	250
6	100
4	400
3	450
2	650
0	600
8	0

(a) Find the mean $\bar{x}$ of the number of oil changes per year and the mean $\bar{y}$ of the repair costs per year, correct to two decimal places.

(b) Draw a scatter plot of y against x and draw the line of best fit using $(\bar{x}, \bar{y})$ and using $y = 700$ as the y-intercept.

(c) Find the correlation coefficient r, correct to two decimal places, and interpret it.

(d) Would the data convince a driver to change the oil regularly?

(e) Find the slope of the line of best fit using $(\bar{x}, \bar{y})$ and the y-intercept, correct to two decimal places.

(f) Find the equation of the line of best fit from part **(e)**.

(g) Use the equation to predict how much a customer is likely to spend on repairs if she changes the oil seven times a year, correct to the nearest euro.

(h) Does the data prove that regularly changing the oil in a car's engine reduces repair costs?

14. On 28 January 1986, the space shuttle *Challenger* exploded just after take-off. Richard Feynman, a famous Nobel Laureate physicist, stated after an investigation that two rubber O-rings had failed, allowing the fuel to spill out of the tanks and engulf the shuttle. However, the engineers at Morton Thiokel Inc. had recommended the flight be delayed that day because of the low temperature at launch. They had previously analysed data in the laboratory on the O-ring failure at low temperatures T. The data on O-ring failure is shown:

T (°C) (x)	Failure index F (y)
12	11
14	4
17	2
19	0

(a) Draw a scatter plot of the failure index F against T. Find the correlation coefficient r, correct to two decimal places.

(b) Find the mean $\bar{T}$ of T and the mean $\bar{F}$ of F. Find the equation of the line of best fit

using $(\bar{T}, \bar{F})$ as one point on the line and $(17, 2)$ as another point.

(c) Use the equation of the line of best fit to find the failure index at:

(i) 6 °C,

(ii) −1 °C (temperature at launch).

(d) Would you have launched the shuttle? Why?

15. (a) A line of best fit is plotted in which $\bar{x} = 6\cdot8$ is the mean of the values of the independent variable and $\bar{y} = 8\cdot5$ is the mean of the values of the dependent variable. The line intersects the y-axis at $10\cdot2$. Find the slope and equation of the line of best fit.

(b) (i) A teacher gave a test of 10 questions. If x is the number of questions a student got right and y is the number she got wrong, write down an equation connecting x and y.

(ii) If a scatter plot is constructed of y against x for all students in the class, write down the equation of the line of best fit.

(iii) Find r, the correlation coefficient.

16. (a) 'There is a strong positive correlation between ice-cream sales and air temperature.' Does this mean a high air temperature causes high ice-cream sales?

(b) 'There is a strong positive correlation between the level of homelessness and the crime rate.' Does this mean that increasing levels of crime cause homelessness?

(c) A sociologist claims that there is a strong correlation between the number of people that play a certain video game and the number of car thefts in a city. It is reported by a television station that playing certain video games causes an increase in car theft. Criticise the television station's report.

(d) Research showed a strong positive correlation between the vocabulary of children under 12 and the number of fillings in their teeth. Does this mean that eating more sweets would cause an increase in a 12-year-old's vocabulary? Explain.

Measures of Spread

CHAPTER 20

Learning Outcomes

- To understand the different types of spread: range, interquartile range and standard deviation.

- To make decisions on which type of spread is the best measure for a given situation.

Introduction

In the previous chapter, we looked at central tendency to find a typical value or 'average' to represent a set of data. In this chapter, we look at how data values are spread about the average. We will examine three measures of spread:

- Range (R)

- Interquartile range (IQR)

- Standard deviation (SD)

WORKED EXAMPLE   Why the idea of spread is important

In Class A of 10 students, the Biology test scores at the end of the mid-term were as follows:
4, 4, 5, 5, 5, 5, 5, 6, 6, 7

The mean $\mu_A = \dfrac{4 + 4 + 5 + 5 + 5 + 5 + 5 + 6 + 6 + 7}{10} = \dfrac{52}{10} = 5 \cdot 2$

Class B of 10 students took the same test and the scores were: 1, 1, 1, 2, 2, 8, 8, 9, 10, 10

The mean $\mu_B = \dfrac{1 + 1 + 1 + 2 + 2 + 8 + 8 + 9 + 10 + 10}{10} = \dfrac{52}{10} = 5 \cdot 2$

You might conclude that as they both have the same mean the two classes are exactly the same in ability. This is not the case. Clearly, the results in class A cluster around the mean and do not have very low results or very high results. The lowest score is 4 and the highest is 7, which gives a **range** of values of 3. But the opposite is true of class B. The results do not cluster around the mean. In fact, there are many very low scores and also many very high ones. The lowest score is 1 and the highest is 10, giving a **range** of 9!

20.1 Range

ACTIVITY 18

ACTION
Understanding range

OBJECTIVE
To appreciate how the range is used as a measure of spread

The simplest measure of spread of data is the **range**. It is simply the difference between the largest data value, known as the upper extreme (UE), and the smallest data value, known as the lower extreme (LE), in the data set.

KEY TERM

The **range** R of a set of numerical data values is given by:
R = upper extreme (UE) – lower extreme (LE)

EXAMPLE 1

(a) What is the range of the data values 3, 5, 11, 16, −2, 0, 7, −11, 14, −2, 21?

(b) For the following set of results, find the range:

482	464	475	484	496	468
472	480	476	475	480	

Solution

(a) Arranging the values in ascending order:

−11, −2, −2, 0, 3, 5, 7, 11, 14, 16, 21

Upper extreme (UE) = +21 (largest value)

Lower extreme (LE) = −11 (smallest value)

Range R = +21 − (−11) = 32

(b) Arranging the values in ascending order:

464, 468, 472, 475, 475, 476, 480, 480, 482, 484, 496

Upper extreme (UE) = 496

Lower extreme (LE) = 464

Range R = 496 − 464 = 32

Although the two sets of numbers are completely different, they have the same range.

TIP

The range tells you nothing about the data values between the two extreme data values.

EXAMPLE 2

What is the range of the following data?

482	464	475	484	10	496
468	472	480	476	475	480

Solution

Arranging the values in ascending order:

10, 464, 468, 472, 475, 475, 476, 480, 480, 482, 484, 496

Upper extreme (UE) = 496

Lower extreme (LE) = 10

Range R = 496 − 10 = 486

The value of the range is affected enormously by the outlier 10. Because it is so different to the other values, it has had a huge effect on the range. Although 11 of the values are very close together, the range is 486.

EXAMPLE 3

The line plots below show the frequency distribution of the heights in centimetres (cm) of players on two basketball teams, Meteors and Comets, correct to the nearest centimetre (cm). Find the range of each frequency distribution.

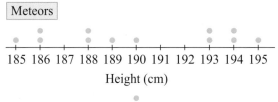

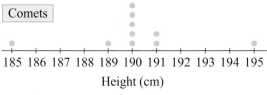

Solution

Meteors:

Upper extreme = 195; Lower extreme = 185

R = 195 − 185 = 10 cm

Comets:

Upper extreme = 195; Upper extreme = 185

R = 195 − 185 = 10 cm

The range is the same for both teams and does not show up the variation in the heights of the two teams. Meteors have heights that are spread out throughout the range, whereas Comets have heights that cluster around 190 cm.

EXAMPLE 4

The grouped frequency distribution of the highest mountains in the world that are at least 7200 m high is given in the table below:

Height (*m*)	Number of mountains
7200–7400	43
7400–7600	31
7600–7800	17
7800–8000	12
8000–8200	9
8200–8400	0
8400–8600	3
8600–8800	1
8800–9000	1

Find the following:

(a) The modal height

(b) The range (not the Himalayas!)

Solution

(a) Modal height = mid-interval value of the (7200–7400) m class interval = 7300 m

(b) For a grouped frequency distribution, the range R is given by:

R = upper extreme of the highest class interval − lower extreme of the lowest class interval

= 9000 − 7200 = 1800 m

Advantages and disadvantages of the range as a measure of data spread

Advantages

1. It is very simple to calculate.

2. It gives a measure of the total spread of the data.

3. It is a good measure of spread for symmetric data with no outliers.

Disadvantages

1. It only measures the spread between the largest and smallest data values.

2. It only relies on two numbers (the two extreme values) and so is affected badly by outliers, whether they are errors in data recording or genuine values.

3. It is dependent on the size of the sample. The more numbers there are, the bigger the range is likely to be.

4. It provides no information on how the remaining data between the two extreme values is distributed.

5. It does not use the concept of deviations (see 20.3 Standard deviation).

6. It might not give a true indication of the spread if there are outliers.

EXERCISE 11

1. Find the range of the following data:

   (a) A: 7, 2, 9, 0, 4, 8, 11, 12

   (b) B: 4, −4, 3, −3, 2, −2, 7, −7

   (c) C: 5, 7, 3, 0, 1, −11, 12

   (d) D: 998, 986, 987, 990, 1009, 1004, 1000

   (e) E: −11, 998, 987, 990, 1009, 1004, 1000

2. (a) Line plot: Find the range, mean, mode and median of the following data.

   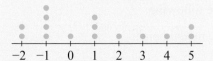

   (b) Stem-and-leaf plot: The following back-to-back stem plot gives the average number of fizzy drinks consumed by 12–20-year-olds in a given 30-day period each year between 1991 and 2005.

Male		Female
	1	5 6 7 7
	2	1 2 4 4 4 4 4 4 7 7 8
9 8 8 6	3	
8 8 6 5 5 4 4 3 1 1	4	
1	5	

(Key: 2|4 = 24)

Find the following:

   (i) The median number of drinks for males

   (ii) The range for males

   (iii) The median number of drinks for females

   (iv) The range for females

   (v) The mode for females

(c) Frequency distribution: The following frequency table gives the number of countries with an under 5 mortality rate (U5MR) of 10 or less in 2001. (U5MR = number of children dying between birth and exactly 5 years of age per 1000 live births.)

U5MR	Number of countries
3	1
4	4
5	11
6	14
7	3
8	3
9	6
10	1

Find the following:

(i) The modal U5MR

(ii) The mean U5MR, correct to one decimal place

(iii) The median U5MR

(iv) The range of the U5MR

3. (a) Find the mean (correct to one decimal place), mode and range of the following grouped frequency distribution:

Variable x	Frequency f
0–5	2
5–10	3
10–15	8
15–20	12
20–25	8
25–30	3
30–35	2

(b) Draw a histogram and comment on its shape. Mark the median on the diagram.

4. A car dealer makes 20 sales in one week. His profit on each sale in euro is recorded in a book when he makes the sale:

350	270	1500	2300	1700
200	150	600	800	2100
1800	1600	1500	2000	1900
100	850	900	1200	1700

(a) Find the following:

(i) The mean profit

(ii) The median profit

(iii) The range

(b) Which is the best average: mean, mode or median? Why?

5. The following set of results gives carbon dioxide (CO_2) emissions per person in metric tonnes in 2008 for the top 20 emitter countries.

53·5	37·3	26·3	21·7	13·6
16·4	21·9	18·9	14·3	17·5
17·2	29·0	19·6	16·4	15·3
31·9	26·3	14·1	13·6	21·7

(a) Find the following:

(i) The mean emission per person

(ii) The median emission per person

(iii) The range of emissions per person

(b) Which average is more important here for the public, mean or median? Why?

20.2 Interquartile range

The **interquartile range** (IQR) is a better measure of spread of data values than the range as it takes into account more than just two values to calculate the spread. It is based on the concept of dividing a set of data, which is ranked in ascending order, into four equal sections, as shown:

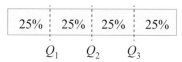

1. The **median** Q_2 (second quartile) has one-half or 50% of the values below it and 50% of the values above it. It is also known as the 50th percentile.

2. The **lower quartile** Q_1 (first quartile) has one-quarter or 25% of the values below it and 75% of the values above it. It is also known as the 25th percentile.

3. The **upper quartile** Q_3 (third quartile) has three-quarters or 75% of the values below it and 25% of the values above it. It is also known as the 75th percentile.

4. The interquartile range (IQR) = $Q_3 - Q_1$ = upper quartile − lower quartile

Finding the interquartile range

WORKED EXAMPLE

Finding the interquartile range for discrete data – odd number of data results

The following 21 results are the marks of a History class in a test:
2, 10, 56, 56, 56, 57, 58, 58, 58, 60, 61, 61, 61, 62, 63, 65, 68, 69, 70, 70, 100

The range $R = 100 - 2 = 98$

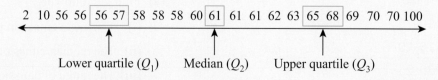

There are 21 results in all. The median is the 11th number in the list: $Q_2 = 61$. The median divides the data into two halves. To divide the data into quarters, you must find the medians of each of these two halves.

TIP

If you have an **odd** number of data values, where the median is an actual data value, then you do not include that value in your quartile computations. To find the upper and lower quartiles, just take the values above and below the median, respectively. Exclude the median itself.

There are 10 results to the left of the median. The lower quartile is the mean of the fifth and sixth of these results.

Lower quartile Q_1 = mean of 56 and 57 = $\dfrac{56 + 57}{2}$ = 56·5

There are 10 results to the right of the median. The upper quartile is the mean of the fifth and sixth of these results.

Upper quartile Q_3 = mean of 65 and 68 = $\dfrac{65 + 68}{2}$ = $\dfrac{133}{2}$ = 66·5

Interquartile range IQR = $Q_3 - Q_1$ = 66·5 − 56·5 = 10

The range does not describe the spread of most of the data and is badly influenced by outliers. Clearly, the interquartile range is a much better description of the spread of most of the values and is not influenced at all by the outliers, 2 and 10.

IQR test for outliers: A data value is a possible outlier, if it falls more than 1·5 times the IQR below the first quartile or 1·5 times the IQR above the third quartile.

So for this example: 1·5 × IQR = 1·5 × 10 = 15

Suspicious outliers:

Numbers < 56·5 − 15 = 41·5

Numbers > 66·5 + 15 = 81·5

Therefore, 2, 10 and 100 are possible outliers.

WORKED EXAMPLE Finding the interquartile range for discrete data – even number of data results

The ages of 20 contestants in a diving competition are given as follows in ascending order:

13, 14, 15, 15, 17, 19, 19, 20, 21, 23, 24, 24, 25, 26, 26, 27, 28, 29, 29, 32

13 14 15 15 | 17 19 | 19 20 21 | 23 24 | 24 25 26 | 26 27 | 28 29 29 32

Lower quartile (Q_1)   Median (Q_2)   Upper quartile (Q_3)

There are 20 results. The median is the mean of the 10th and 11th results.

$Q_2 = \dfrac{23 + 24}{2}$ = 23·5

The median divides the data into two halves. To divide the data into quarters, you must find the medians of each of these halves.

TIP

If you have an even number of data values, where the median is the mean of the two middle values, then you include these middle values in your upper and lower quartile computations.

Lower quartile Q_1: There are 10 results to the left of the median. The lower quartile is the mean of the 5th and 6th of these results.

$Q_1 = \dfrac{17 + 19}{2}$ = 18

Upper quartile Q_3: There are 10 results to the right of the median.
The upper quartile is the mean of the 5th and 6th of these results.

$$Q_3 = \frac{26 + 27}{2} = 26 \cdot 5$$

Interquartile range $= Q_3 - Q_1 = 26 \cdot 5 - 18 = 8 \cdot 5$

TIP

Upper quartile Q_3 = median of the upper half of the data values

Lower quartile Q_1 = median of the lower half of the data values

KEY TERMS

Quartiles divide the data values into four equal parts with 25% of the data in each part.

The **interquartile range** measures the spread of the middle 50% of a set of data values ordered in increasing size.

Steps for finding the IQR for a discrete set of data

1. Arrange the data values in order from the smallest to the largest value (in increasing size).

2. Find the median Q_2 of the data values.

3. Find the median Q_1 of the lower 50% of the data values = lower quartile (*LQ*).

4. Find the median Q_3 of the upper 50% of the data values = upper quartile (*UQ*).

5. Interquartile range IQR $= Q_3 - Q_1 = UQ - LQ$

EXAMPLE 5

A teacher decides to compile a table of the number of absences of the 27 students in his class over one year.

Number of absences	Number of students
0	2
1	2
2	3
3	4
4	6
5	5
6	3
7	0
8	1
9	1

Find the following:

(a) The mean, correct to one decimal place

(b) The mode

(c) The median

(d) The lower quartile

(e) The upper quartile

(f) The interquartile range

Solution

x	f	fx	Cumulative frequency	
0	2	0	2	
1	2	2	4	
2	3	6	7	← LQ is here: 7th result
3	4	12	11	
4	6	24	17	← Median is in here: 14th result
5	5	25	22	← UQ is in here: 21st result
6	3	18	25	
7	0	0	25	
8	1	8	26	
9	1	9	27	
	$\sum f = 27$	$\sum fx = 104$		

(a) Mean $\mu = \dfrac{\sum fx}{\sum f} = \dfrac{104}{27} \approx 3 \cdot 9$

(b) Mode = 4   [4 occurs six times.]

(c) Median Q_2: There are 27 results. Therefore, the median is the value of the 14th result.

$Q_2 = 4$

(d) Lower quartile Q_1: There are 13 results below the 14th result. The median of these is the 7th result below the 14th result.

$Q_1 = 2$

(e) Upper quartile Q_3: There are 13 results above the 14th result. The median of these is the 7th result above the 14th result, which is the 21st result.

$Q_3 = 5$

(f) Interquartile range = $Q_3 - Q_1 = 5 - 2 = 3$

The upper and lower quartiles for continuous data can be found by drawing an ogive in the same way that the median is found.

EXAMPLE 6

A survey was carried out on 80 students in a school on the number of servings of fruit or vegetables they eat per day.

Number of servings	Number of students
0–1	12
1–2	18
2–3	24
3–4	10
4–5	10
5–6	4
6–7	2

From the data given, draw up a cumulative frequency table and the ogive. From it, estimate, correct to one decimal place:

(a) the median,

(b) the lower quartile,

(c) the upper quartile,

(d) the interquartile range,

(e) the range.

Solution

Although the values requested can be calculated from the table, it is easier to estimate them using a cumulative frequency curve (ogive).

Cumulative frequency table:

Number of servings	Number of students
<1	12
<2	30
<3	54
<4	64
<5	74
<6	78
<7	80

Cumulative frequency curve (ogive):

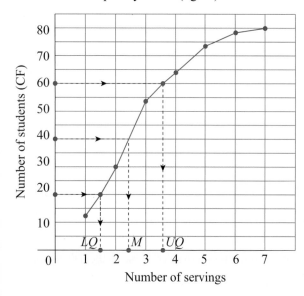

(a) One half of 80 is 40.
Median: Draw a horizontal line from 40 across to the curve. $M = 2·4$

(b) One-quarter of 80 is 20.
Lower quartile: Draw a horizontal line from 20 across to the curve. $LQ = 1·4$

(c) Three-quarters of 80 is 60.
Upper quartile: Draw a horizontal line from 60 across to the curve. $UQ = 3·6$

(d) Interquartile range $= 3·6 - 1·4 = 2·2$

(e) Range $= 7 - 0 = 7$

Advantages and disadvantages of the interquartile range as a measure of data spread

Advantages

1. It is easy to calculate.

2. It ignores extreme values.

3. It is not affected very strongly by outliers.

Disadvantages

1. It is hard to understand.

2. It disregards all values except the lower and upper quartiles.

3. The upper and lower quartiles are not always actual scores and so may turn out to be non-whole numbers, even though the scores themselves are whole numbers. This leads to confusion.

EXERCISE 12

1. The following information is given for a set of data values:

   (i) The values range from 45 to 98

   (ii) The median is 75

   (iii) 25% of the values are less than or equal to 65

   (iv) 75% of the values are less than or equal to 88

   Find the following:

   (a) The range

   (b) The largest value

   (c) The smallest value

   (d) The middle value

   (e) The lower quartile

   (f) The upper quartile

   (g) The interquartile range

2. The at-rest pulse rates of a group of 20 athletes are given as follows:

   65, 68, 55, 53, 60, 52, 54, 55, 55, 56

   58, 54, 56, 57, 65, 66, 64, 60, 58, 59

   Find the following:

   (a) The range

   (b) The median

   (c) The lower quartile

   (d) The upper quartile

   (e) The interquartile range

3. A survey was carried out on the number of text messages sent by a group of 400 students during one schoolday.

Number of texts	Number of students
0	15
1	37
2	48
3	54
4	90
5	55
6	48
7	36
8	17

   Find the following:

   (a) The range

   (b) The median

   (c) The lower quartile

   (d) The upper quartile

   (e) The interquartile range

4. The salaries of the employees in a company were recorded in a grouped frequency table, as follows:

Salary (€ × 1000)	Number of employees
0–20	14
20–40	25
40–60	42
60–80	60
80–100	19

   (Note: 20–40 means $20 \leq x < 40$). Draw the ogive for this data and from it find the following, correct to the nearest thousand euro:

   (a) The median salary

   (b) The lower quartile

   (c) The upper quartile

   (d) The interquartile range

5. The cumulative frequency table below shows the time in minutes in which 80 Olympic athletes completed the marathon after the winner.

Time (mins)	Number of athletes
<2	8
<4	19
<6	28
<8	52
<10	68
<12	80

Draw the ogive and use it to estimate the following, correct to the nearest minute:

(a) The median time

(b) The lower quartile

(c) The upper quartile

(d) The interquartile range

(e) The range

6. In a game, 100 people got the following scores:

Score	Number of people
0–20	5
20–40	24
40–60	31
60–80	28
80–100	12

Draw up a cumulative frequency table and an ogive. Use the ogive to estimate the following, correct to the nearest whole number:

(a) The median score

(b) The range

(c) The lower quartile

(d) The upper quartile

(e) The interquartile range

7. The number of minutes taken by 60 students to travel to school is given in the following stem-and-leaf plot:

```
0 | 5 5 8 8 9 9 9
1 | 0 0 4 4 4 5 5 6 7 7 7 7 8 8 8 9 9
2 | 0 0 0 0 0 0 1 1 2 2 2 3 3 4 4 4 5 6 7 8
3 | 0 0 0 0 1 1 1 2 2 3 4 5 5 5
4 | 0 2
```
(Key: 2|3 = 23)

Find the following:

(a) The range

(b) The median

(c) The lower quartile

(d) The upper quartile

(e) The interquartile range

Use the 1·5 IQR test to see if there are possible outliers.

8. From the histogram shown, construct a grouped frequency table and hence construct a cumulative frequency table and an ogive:

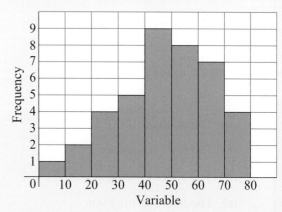

(a) Use your table to find the mean and the mode.

(b) Use your table or ogive to estimate the following, correct to the nearest whole number:

(i) The median

(ii) The lower quartile

(iii) The upper quartile

(iv) The interquartile range

9. A survey was carried out on a number of patients on how long they spent in the Emergency Department of a hospital on a particular day. The cumulative frequency table is given as follows:

Number of hours	Number of patients
<2	8
<4	18
<6	23
<8	74
<10	98
<12	120

(Note: <2 means less than 2 hours)

(a) Estimate the following, correct to one decimal place:

   (i) The median time

   (ii) The lower quartile

   (iii) The upper quartile

   (iv) The interquartile range

(b) Draw up a grouped frequency table and hence find the mean (correct to one decimal place) and the mode.

10. Here are 70 numbers in ascending order:

2	3	3	4	5	5
5	6	7	8	11	12
13	13	13	14	16	17
17	19	22	23	24	24
24	24	26	29	29	29
31	34	35	35	36	37
38	38	39	39	40	41
42	43	44	47	47	47
47	49	50	50	50	52
52	52	53	55	56	56
60	61	65	67	68	68
69	69	105	109		

Find the following:

(a) The median

(b) The lower quartile

(c) The upper quartile

(d) The interquartile range

(e) The range

Use the 1·5 IQR test to see if there are suspicious outliers.

20.3 Standard deviation

The basic drawback in the range and interquartile range in measuring spread is that they only take account of a small number of data values in their calculation. Clearly, a measure of spread that is calculated using all of the data values in a data set is desirable. This measure is known as the **standard deviation**.

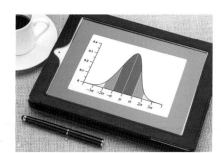

Looking for a spread that takes all of the data into account

Two Leaving Certificate Economics classes undertake a test that is marked out of 10. A line plot of the performance of each class is shown.

1. **Class A**

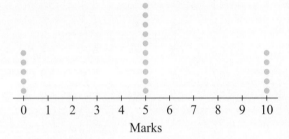

Mean = $\dfrac{100}{20} = 5$

Median = 5

Range = 10

IQR = $7\cdot 5 - 2\cdot 5 = 5$

2. **Class B**

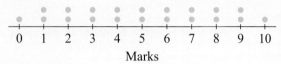

Marks

Mean = $\dfrac{100}{20} = 5$

Median = 5

Range = 10

IQR = $7\cdot 5 - 2\cdot 5 = 5$

Both classes have exactly the same mean, median, range and interquartile range, but obviously the two classes did not perform exactly the same in the test. Class A's results cluster around the 5 mark, whereas class B's results are more or less evenly spread out from 0 to 10. One measure of spread (variability) that takes account of all the data values in a set is the **standard deviation** (σ).

KEY TERM

Standard deviation is a measurement of how individual data values in a set differ (deviate) from the mean of all the data values.

Calculating standard deviation

Steps for calculating standard deviation

Find the standard deviation of the numbers 2, 6, 8, 9, 10.

Step 1: Find the mean μ.

$$\mu = \frac{\sum x}{n} = \frac{2 + 6 + 8 + 9 + 10}{5} = \frac{35}{5} = 7$$

Step 2: Find the deviation d of each data value x from the mean μ.

The deviation $d = (x - \mu)$ is the difference between each data value x and the mean.

For $x = 2$: $d = x - \mu = 2 - 7 = -5$

Step 3: Find the sum of the deviations squared.

x	d	d^2
2	−5	25
6	−1	1
8	1	1
9	2	4
10	3	9
	$\sum d = 0$	$\sum d^2 = 40$

TIP

The sum of the deviations is equal to zero: $\sum d = 0$. This is always true. It is a useful check when you are working out the standard deviation. If you do not get $\sum d = 0$, you have made a mistake.

Step 4: Find the variance:

Variance $= \dfrac{\text{Sum of } d^2}{n}$, where n is the total number of data values.

Variance $= \dfrac{40}{5} = 8$

Step 5: Find the standard deviation σ.

$\sigma = \sqrt{\text{Variance}}$

Standard deviation: $\sigma = \sqrt{8} = 2 \cdot 8$

Standard deviation σ:

$\sigma = \sqrt{\text{Variance}}$

$\quad = \sqrt{\dfrac{\text{Sum of the deviations squared}}{\text{Total number of data values}}}$

$\quad = \sqrt{\dfrac{\text{Sum of } d^2}{n}}$

where $d = (x - \mu)$ and n is the total number of data values.

▸ For seven numbers, $\sum d^2 = 175$.

$\sum d^2 = 175, \ n = 7$

$\sigma = \sqrt{\dfrac{\sum d^2}{n}} = \sqrt{\dfrac{175}{7}} = \sqrt{25} = 5$

TIP

↑ The standard deviation tells you how individual data values differ from the mean. If the data values are clustered around the mean, the variance and standard deviation are small. If the data values are widely scattered around the mean, the variance and standard deviation are large.

EXAMPLE 7

Find the mean, variance and standard deviation (correct to three decimal places) of the following numbers: 3, 6, 7, 9, 11, 12.

Solution

$\mu = \dfrac{3 + 6 + 7 + 9 + 11 + 12}{6} = \dfrac{48}{6} = 8$

Variance $= \dfrac{\sum d^2}{n} = \dfrac{56}{6} = \dfrac{28}{3}$

$\sigma = \sqrt{\dfrac{28}{3}} \approx 3 \cdot 055$

Your calculator can find the mean and standard deviation directly.

x	$d = (x - \mu)$	d^2
3	−5	25
6	−2	4
7	−1	1
9	1	1
11	3	9
12	4	16
	$\Sigma d = 0$	$\Sigma d^2 = 56$

The desirability of a small or a large standard deviation depends on the situation. In quality control in industry, consistency is required. So, although every bag of pasta has a weight printed on it, not every bag has that exact weight. However, all bags should have a weight extremely close to the printed weight. This means that a small standard deviation in weight is required. In IQ tests the value of the standard deviation is usually big.

Standard deviation and related data sets

WORKED EXAMPLE Finding the standard deviation of related sets of data

Find the mean and standard deviation (correct to two decimal places) of the following sets of related data:

(a) A: 4, 7, 8, 10, 11

(b) B: 6, 9, 10, 12, 13

(c) C: 12, 21, 24, 30, 33

(d) D: 11, 17, 19, 23, 25

(a) A: 4, 7, 8, 10, 11

Mean $\mu_A = 8$, standard deviation $\sigma_A = 2 \cdot 45$ [Use your calculator to find these values.]

(b) B: 6, 9, 10, 12, 13

The values in B are the values in A increased by 2.

Mean $\mu_B = 10$, standard deviation $\sigma_B = 2 \cdot 45$ [Use your calculator to find these values.]

$\therefore \sigma_B = \sigma_A$

TIP

> If you increase or decrease each data value in a data set by the same number, the standard deviation of the new data set is the same as the standard deviation of the old data set.

(c) C: 12, 21, 24, 30, 33

The values in C are the values in A multiplied by 3.

Mean $\mu_C = 24 = 3 \times 8$, standard deviation $\sigma_C = 7 \cdot 35 = 3\sigma_A$

TIP

> If you multiply each data value in a data set by the same number, the standard deviation of the new data set is the same as the standard deviation of the old data set multiplied by that number.

(d) D: 11, 17, 19, 23, 25

The values in A are the values in D doubled and then increased by 3.

Mean $\mu_D = 19 = 2 \times 8 + 3$, standard deviation $\sigma_D = 4 \cdot 9 = 2\sigma_A$

So, the doubling of values doubles the standard deviation, but the increase by 3 has no effect on the standard deviation.

TIP

Old SD	Change	New SD
σ	Increase or decrease by l	σ
σ	Multiply by k	$k\sigma$
σ	Multiply by k and then increase or decrease by l	$k\sigma$

EXAMPLE 8

A class of 15 Junior Infants has a mean age of 5·2 years with a standard deviation of 0·6 years.

(a) What is the mean and standard deviation in Senior Infants, assuming the class personnel has not changed in any way?

(b) What is the mean and standard deviation when they enter secondary school 7 years later?

Solution

(a) Senior Infants: Mean = 5·2 + 1 = 6·2 years

Standard deviation = 0·6 years

(b) Secondary school 7 years later:

Mean = 5·2 + 7 = 12·2 years

Standard deviation = 0·6 years

EXAMPLE 9

Six garages have a mean price per litre of petrol at €1·60 with a standard deviation of €0·05. If petrol prices are decreased by 20%, what is the new mean and new standard deviation?

Solution

Mean: €1·60 × 0·8 = €1·28

Standard deviation: €0·05 × 0·8 = €0·04

Standard deviation of a frequency and grouped frequency distribution

EXAMPLE 10

The frequency table below gives the number of apples eaten by a sample of 70 students in a school per week.

Number of apples x	Number of students f
0	16
1	5
2	10
3	15
4	8
5	10
8	1
10	5

Find:

(a) the mean number of apples eaten per week,

(b) the standard deviation, correct to two decimal places.

Solution

(a) Draw up a table, as shown. Find the mean:

$$\mu = \frac{\sum fx}{\sum f} = \frac{210}{70} = 3$$

(b) Now work out the deviation $d = (x - \mu)$ of each result and fill in the other columns, as shown:

x	f	fx	$d = (x - \mu)$	d^2	fd^2
0	16	0	−3	9	144
1	5	5	−2	4	20
2	10	20	−1	1	10
3	15	45	0	0	0
4	8	32	1	1	8
5	10	50	2	4	40
8	1	8	5	25	25
10	5	50	7	49	245
	$\sum f$ = 70	$\sum fx$ = 210			$\sum fd^2$ = 492

Find the standard deviation: $\sigma = \sqrt{\dfrac{\sum fd^2}{\sum f}} = \sqrt{\dfrac{492}{70}} = 2·65$

Your calculator can find the standard deviation directly for you.

EXAMPLE 11

In a botanical experiment, 300 plants were grown and the length of the stems was measured 3 months after planting.

Length of stem (cm)	Number of plants
20–30	20
30–40	99
40–50	79
50–60	50
60–70	52

Find:

(a) the mean length of stem after 3 months,

(b) the standard deviation, correct to two decimal places.

Solution

Draw up a table as shown. The mid-interval value (MIV) represents the value x.

Length of stem (cm)	MIV(x)	f
20–30	25	20
30–40	35	99
40–50	45	79
50–60	55	50
60–70	65	52
		$\Sigma f = 300$

Using the mid-interval value for x, find the mean and standard deviation, employing the same procedure as in Example 10 or just use your calculator.

(a) $\mu = 45\cdot5$ cm

(b) $\sigma = 12\cdot06$ cm

Standard deviation is the measure of spread most commonly used in statistics, whereas the mean is the most common measure of central tendency. Standard deviation measures the spread of data values around the mean. Like the mean, it uses all data values in a data set.

Advantages and disadvantages of standard deviation as a measure of data spread

ACTIVITY 20

ACTION
Understanding standard deviation

OBJECTIVE
To appreciate how the standard deviation is used as a measure of spread

Advantages

1. It measures the deviation from the mean, which is very important in statistics.

2. It is always positive.

3. Its value is very sensitive to outliers and can be used to detect them.

4. It can be used to convert scores calculated on different scales to scores on a standard scale. (See Chapter 21: Probability Distributions for more on z-scores.)

5. It can be used to estimate the accuracy of a sample mean as an estimate of a population mean. (See Chapter 22: Inferential Statistics for more on confidence intervals.)

6. It is useful for comparing two data sets that have approximately the same mean. An item selected at random from a data set with a lower standard deviation has a better chance of being close to the mean than an item from a data set with a higher standard deviation.

Disadvantages

1. Its value can be greatly affected if the mean is a poor measure of central tendency.

2. Its value is influenced by outliers. One outlier could affect its value enormously.

EXERCISE 13

1. In each case below, find the mean and standard deviation exactly or correct to one decimal place:

   (a) 3, 5, 8, 11, 13

   (b) −4, 5, 11, 2, 6, 7, 3, 0, 9, 1

   (c) $a, 2a, 3a$

   (d) 0·5, 3, 7·2, 3·7, 4·8, 7·9, 6·5

   (e) $3x, 11x, 9x, 15x, 7x$

2. Find the mean and standard deviation of data A, correct to two decimal places:

   A: 4, 1, 1, 5, 7, 6, 2

   Hence, deduce the mean and standard deviation of the following data sets:

   (a) B: 7, 4, 4, 8, 10, 9, 5

   (b) C: 8, 2, 2, 10, 14, 12, 4

   (c) D: 14, 5, 5, 17, 23, 20, 8

3. Find the mean and standard deviation (correct to two decimal places) of the following frequency table:

x	1	2	3	4	5
f	4	3	6	3	4

4. The frequency table below gives the number of DVDs bought by 40 students in a class in a year.

x	0	1	2	3	4	5	6
f	3	5	11	y	2	$y - 3$	2

   Find y. Find the mean and standard deviation correct to one decimal place.

5. For seven numbers with value x:
   $\sum(x - \mu)^2 = 112$, find the standard deviation if μ is the mean of these numbers.

6. In one year, the mean mark on Leaving Certificate Higher Level Maths papers was 58 and the standard deviation was 7·2. If the student grades were rounded to whole numbers, what is the range of student scores that lie within 2 standard deviations of the mean?

7. Consider the following two groups of numbers A and B:

   A: 3, 8, 13, 18, 23

   B: 103, 108, 113, 118, 123

   Without doing any calculation, state which set has the greater standard deviation. Do the same for the following two groups of numbers C and D:

   C: 1, 8, 9, 11, 20

   D: 8, 8, 9, 9, 10

8. The annual salaries of three Science teachers in a school in 2011 were €32 000, €42 000 and €52 000.

   (a) If each got an increment (increase) of €1000 the following year, how did this affect their mean salary in 2012? How did it affect the standard deviation?

   (b) If in 2020 they get a 20% rise in their 2011 salaries, how would this affect the mean and standard deviation of the 2011 salaries?

9. Two classes of 12 students take the same Biology test.

   Their marks are shown as follows:

Class A					
20	88	88	89	90	92
92	94	95	96	98	100

Class B					
15	33	45	45	65	66
74	83	87	88	94	95

   Find the range and standard deviation (correct to one decimal place) of each class. Is the range misleading? What does it appear to tell you about the classes? What does the standard deviation tell you? What is your conclusion?

10. Find the mean and standard deviation (correct to one decimal place) of the grouped frequency distribution.

Class interval	0–4	4–8	8–12	12–16	16–20
Frequency	2	4	7	4	2

11. Three classes of 30 students were given a standard Physics test marked out of 50. The results were presented as follows:

Class A

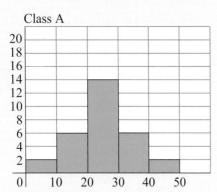

Class B

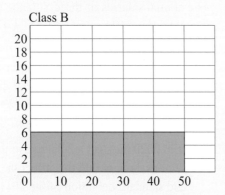

Class C

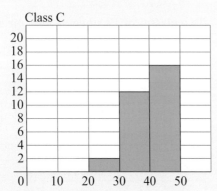

(a) Which distribution has:

    (i) the greatest standard deviation,

    (ii) the smallest standard deviation?

(b) Calculate the mean and standard deviation of each, correct to one decimal place, by constructing a grouped frequency distribution for each.

12. The number of phone calls made in an office each day of a 5-day working week was recorded as follows:

Monday	16
Tuesday	24
Wednesday	18
Thursday	30
Friday	22

(a) Find the mean number μ of phone calls per day.

(b) Find the standard deviation σ, correct to one decimal place.

(c) Calculate **(i)** $\mu + \sigma$ and **(ii)** $\mu - \sigma$.

(d) On how many days is the number of calls within 1 standard deviation of the mean? Write the number of calls on these days as a percentage of the total number of calls, correct to the nearest whole number.

13. The heights of 7000 students were measured and the results recorded as shown. The mean μ is 1·5 m and standard deviation σ is 0·15 m.

Height (m)	Number of students
0·9–1·05	10
1·05–1·20	100
1·20–1·35	1100
1·35–1·50	2200
1·50–1·65	2400
1·65–1·80	1090
1·80–1·95	100

(a) Draw a histogram. Is it symmetric?

(b) Calculate $\mu + \sigma$.

(c) Calculate $\mu - \sigma$.

(d) What is the total number of students whose heights are less than $\mu + \sigma$?

(e) What is the total number of students whose heights are less than $\mu - \sigma$?

(f) Calculate the number of students whose heights are within 2 standard deviations of the mean and write this as a percentage of the total number of students.

Probability Distributions

CHAPTER 21

Learning Outcomes

- To understand that many situations in nature produce bell-shaped symmetrical frequency distribution curves called normal curves.
- To use the empirical rule to deduce properties of the normal distribution curve.
- To understand two measures of position for a data value in a set of values: percentiles and z-scores.
- To understand the difference between percentiles and percentages.
- To understand that any normal curve can be transformed to a standard normal distribution curve, allowing many types of calculations to be carried out.

21.1 Normal curves

ACTIVITY 21

ACTION
Understanding normal curves and the empirical rule

OBJECTIVE
To study normal curves and to use the empirical rule to analyse these curves

Continuous numerical data can be plotted as a histogram, which is a pictorial representation of how often ranges (class intervals) of values occur. The area of each rectangle in a histogram is equal to the frequency of data in the class interval that forms the base of the rectangle. The shape of this histogram reflects what is known as the data's frequency distribution.

Frequency distributions

WORKED EXAMPLE Frequency distribution of a data set

The grouped frequency table below shows the weights of 250 14-year-old boys.

Weight (kg)	30–35	35–40	40–45	45–50	50–55	55–60	60–65	65–70	70–75
Number of boys	5	15	30	45	60	45	30	15	5

The histogram and frequency polygon of this data are drawn, as shown overleaf.

543

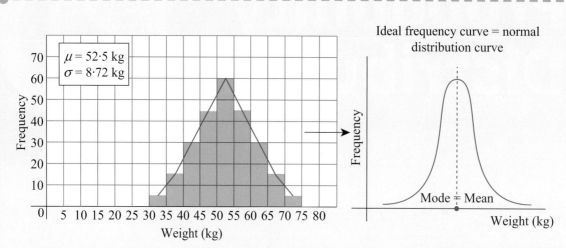

If another group of children were surveyed, the picture might look slightly different, but it is likely that all surveyed groups will follow a common pattern with most data clustered around the centre of the histogram. This pattern is common to many sets of continuous data in that it peaks in the middle and tails at the beginning and end.

Properties of a histogram shape

The histogram in the previous Worked Example has the following properties:

1. There is a single highest rectangle centred on the mean and mode. The mean and the mode are equal. It is unimodal.

2. The sum of the frequencies (areas of the rectangles) to the left of the mean is equal to the sum of the frequencies to the right of the mean.

3. It is symmetric about the line through the mean and mode perpendicular to the x-axis. The left-hand side is a mirror image of the right-hand side.

4. The frequency values get lower as you move further from the mean in a way that produces a bell shape.

A histogram/frequency curve with these characteristics is called a normal distribution curve.

KEY TERM

A **normal distribution curve** is a bell-shaped curve, in which the frequency values in a data set are distributed symmetrically about the mean and the frequency values decrease as you move away from the mean.

To get a perfect model of the weight distribution of all 14-year-old boys, you would take a huge sample, take measurements to an infinite number of decimal places, and have the widths of the rectangles approach zero. This is obviously impossible. However, an approximate model can be created to describe this ideal situation.

This ideal curve is the so-called normal distribution curve. It is unimodal, symmetric and its bell shape is completely determined by its mean μ and its standard deviation σ, according to the equation:

SYLLABUS NOTE

Knowledge of this equation is not required for this course.

$f = \dfrac{1}{\sigma\sqrt{2\pi}} \, e^{-\frac{(x-\mu)^2}{2\sigma^2}}$, where f is the frequency of occurrence of a variable x (weight in our example).

Properties of the normal distribution

1. All normal curves have the same overall shape. Any particular normal distribution is determined by two numbers:

   (a) The mean μ: This is the point at which the axis of symmetry cuts the x-axis.

   (b) The standard deviation σ: This is the distance from the axis of symmetry to the points at which the curvature changes. It is a measure of the spread of the data about the mean.

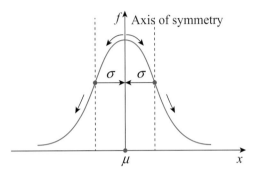

2. Normal distribution curves are all continuous, unimodal and symmetric about the mean. They are bell shaped. The curve never touches the x-axis. The mean, mode and median are all equal and are located at the point where the axis of symmetry crosses the x-axis.

3. Not all bell-shaped symmetrical curves are normal. This is because they do not obey the equation of the normal curve.

4. Just as for any frequency distribution curve, the area under the normal curve in any class interval $(x_1 - x_2)$ on the x-axis is equal to the frequency (or relative frequency/proportion/percentage) of data values between x_1 and x_2. The area A is the frequency of data values between x_1 and x_2.

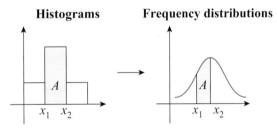

5. Because of the symmetry of the normal curve, the median is equal to the mean, as the area under the normal curve to the left of the mean is equal to the area under the curve to the right of the mean.

6. Changing:

   (a) the mean from μ to $\mu + k$ but keeping the standard deviation the same simply translates the curve parallel to the x-axis:

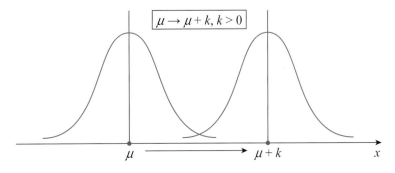

(b) the standard deviation from σ to δ changes the spread but not the position of the axis of symmetry or the value of the mean:

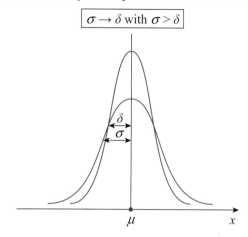

$$\sigma \rightarrow \delta \text{ with } \sigma > \delta$$

(c) both the mean and the standard deviation shifts the mean and changes the spread about the mean:

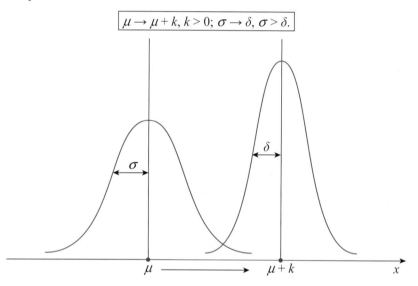

$$\mu \rightarrow \mu + k,\, k > 0;\, \sigma \rightarrow \delta,\, \sigma > \delta.$$

EXAMPLE 1

The monthly share prices of an Irish company over 38 months are listed in euro in ascending order:

10·43	11·32	12·04	12·27	12·31
13·02	13·09	13·40	13·55	13·70
13·88	13·92	14·04	14·12	14·25
14·56	14·63	14·64	14·65	14·76
14·78	14·83	14·84	14·88	14·91
14·97	15·14	15·27	15·32	15·36
15·50	15·64	15·76	16·18	16·50
16·75	17·98	18·03		

(a) Find the mean.

(b) Find the median.

(c) Find the standard deviation.

(d) Show that 100% of the results are within 3 standard deviations of the mean.

(e) What percentage of the results is within 1 standard deviation of the mean?

(f) Using (10–11) as the smallest class interval, draw a histogram and frequency curve with equal class intervals.

Solution

(a) $\mu = 14\cdot506$ [Using your calculator.]

(b) Median = average of 19th and 20th values

$$= \frac{14\cdot65 + 14\cdot76}{2} = 14\cdot705$$

Clearly, $\mu \approx$ median.

(c) Standard deviation $\sigma = 1\cdot575$ [Using your calculator.]

(d) Three standards deviations of mean:

$$\mu + 3\sigma = 19 \cdot 23$$

$$\mu - 3\sigma = 9 \cdot 78$$

∴ 100% of the results lie between these values.

(e) Percentage of share prices between 1 standard deviation of mean:

$$\mu + \sigma = 16 \cdot 08$$

$$\mu - \sigma = 12 \cdot 93$$

Percentage of results between these values:

$$= \frac{28}{38} \times 100\% = 73 \cdot 7\%$$

(f) Histogram and frequency curve:

Share price (€)	10–11	11–12	12–13	13–14	14–15	15–16	16–17	17–18	18–19	
Frequency	1	1	3	7	14	7	3	1	1	Sum = 38

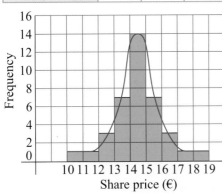

The frequency curve seems to be approximately normal. Although share prices are not usually normally distributed, the frequency distributions of many events in nature are. Many physical, biological and psychological measurements are normally distributed.

Where are normal distributions important in statistics?

1. They are good descriptions of real data, for example, lengths of cats' tails, IQ scores, etc.
2. They are good approximations of the results of many kinds of random (chance) outcomes, as in the proportion (relative frequency) of tails in repeated coin tosses.
3. Many statistical results based on the normal distribution work well for other roughly symmetrical distributions (approximately near normal).

The closer a frequency distribution is to a normal curve, the more probable that the distribution has the same mathematical properties of the normal curve. As a frequency distribution approaches a normal curve, generalisations (inferences) about the data set from which the distribution was derived can be made with greater certainty. Generalisability is the basis of statistical analysis.

Empirical rule

Although normal curves may differ in their mean and standard deviation, they all have common properties because of the mathematical equation that the frequency obeys. In particular, all normal curves obey the 68–95–99·7 rule, known as the **empirical rule**.

> The **empirical rule** states that in any normal distribution with mean μ and standard deviation σ:
>
> 1. 68·26% of the data falls within 1σ of the mean μ.
> 2. 95·46% of the data falls within 2σ of the mean μ.
> 3. 99·74% of the data falls within 3σ of the mean μ.

In fact:

1. 95% of all data values are within $1\cdot96\sigma$ of the mean.

2. Exactly 50% of all data values are on the left of the mean and 50% on the right of it.

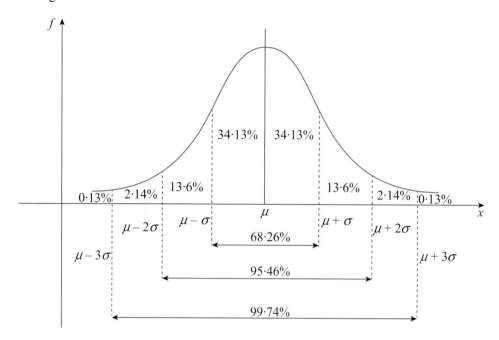

These percentages are based on the amount of area under the normal curve (area is equal to the frequency) between the locations specified. Theoretically, the curve extends to infinity in both directions and the total area is 100% (all results). Because the curve is symmetric, the percentages are evenly split on either side of the mean.

> **TIP**
>
> You can apply this empirical result to data distributions that are normal or near normal.

EXAMPLE 2

A bundle of stocks had a mean cost per share of €21·50 with a standard deviation of €5·23. If the distribution is normal, what interval will contain approximately 95% of the stock prices?

Solution

$\mu = 21\cdot5$, $\sigma = 5\cdot23$

Normal distribution: About 95% lies between $\mu \pm 2\sigma$.

$\mu - 2\sigma = 21\cdot5 - 2 \times 5\cdot23 = 11\cdot04$

$\mu + 2\sigma = 21\cdot5 + 2 \times 5\cdot23 = 31\cdot96$

Therefore, 95% of the prices are between €11·04 and €31·96.

EXAMPLE 3

A set of test results with a mean of 54 and a standard deviation of 5 are normally distributed.

(a) Approximately what percentage of the results is between 44 and 64?

(b) What percentage of the above results lies between 59 and 69?

Solution

(a) $\mu = 54$

$\sigma = 5$

$44 = 54 - 10 = 54 - 2\sigma$

$64 = 54 + 10 = 54 + 2\sigma$

Therefore, approximately 95% lie between 44 and 64.

(b) $59 = 54 + 5 = 54 + \sigma$

$69 = 54 + 15 = 54 + 3\sigma$

Therefore, the percentage between $\mu + 1\sigma$ and $\mu + 3\sigma$:

$$\frac{99 \cdot 74}{2} - \frac{68 \cdot 26}{2} = 15 \cdot 74\%$$

EXAMPLE 4

In a sample of dogs of a certain breed, 84% of their weights lay between 20 kg and 28 kg, as shown in the shaded area of a normal distribution.

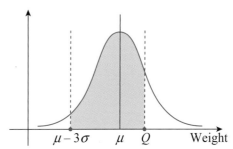

(a) Identify the point Q in terms of standard deviations from the mean μ.

(b) Find σ and μ.

Solution

(a) $\mu - 3\sigma$ to μ contains 49·87% of the weights.

μ to Q contains $84 - 49 \cdot 87\%$ of the weights. This is 34·13% of the weights.

Therefore, Q is 1 standard deviation from the mean.

(b) $20 = \mu - 3\sigma$

$\underline{28 = \mu + \sigma}$

$8 = 4\sigma$

$\sigma = 2$ kg

$\mu = 20 + 6 = 26$ kg

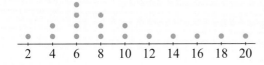

EXERCISE 14

1. Which of the following distributions are normally or approximately normally distributed? Draw each frequency distribution roughly.

(a) Line plot:

```
            •
            •
         •  •
      •  •  •  •
   •  •  •  •  •  •  •  •  •  •
   2  4  6  8  10 12 14 16 18 20
```

(b) Stem-and-leaf:

1	2	3	4					
2	1	2	3	6				
3	2	2	4	4	5	5	6	
4	1	2	5	6				
5	8	4						

(Key: 2|3 = 23)

(c) Stem-and-leaf:

14	1								
15	5	5	6						
16	4	5	8	9					
17	3	3	4	6	7	7	8	9	9
18	1	1	2	4	7	7	3		
19	1	4	5	6	8				
20	2	2	3						
21	4	4							
22	3								
23	2								
24	6								

(Key: 16|4 = 164)

2. Copy and complete the following frequency distributions. Comment on their shape and mark in the position of the mode and approximate positions of the median and mean:

(a)

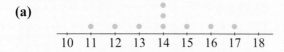

(b)

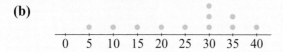

(c)

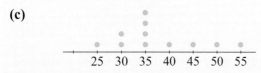

(d)

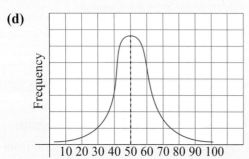

(e)

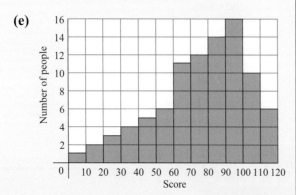

Use the empirical rule for the questions that follow.

3. Light bulbs have a mean lifetime of 850 hours with a standard deviation of 70 hours.

   (a) What percentage last:

      (i) between 850 and 920 hours,

      (ii) between 780 hours and 920 hours,

      (iii) longer than 990 hours?

   (b) If a shop bought 2000 of these bulbs, how many might burn out before 920 hours?

4. In a Business test the mean is 50 and the standard deviation is 4. What percentage of students score between 42 and 62?

5. A class survey shows that students watch an average of 23 hours of television per week with a standard deviation of 2 hours. What approximate percentage of students watch more than 25 hours per week? If a student is selected at random, what is the probability that he or she watches more than 25 hours of television per week?

6. On a normal distribution curve, 68·26% of the survival time of mice distributed symmetrically about the mean were between 8 and 14 days after being infected by a bacterium. Find the following:

   (a) The mean survival time

   (b) The standard deviation in this time

7. The temperatures at a meteorological station in the month of February measured in degrees Celsius are shown in the following table:

4·2	3·8	5·6	8·8	7·1
8·7	7·3	4·4	9·2	9·2
7·9	7·5	8·3	8·8	10·0
10·1	10·4	8·1	6·9	9·1
12·6	14·1	14·1	10·5	9·7
11·9	10·3	11·5	12·3	

   (a) Find the mean temperature and the standard deviation (correct to one decimal place).

   (b) Assuming approximately normal distribution, find what range of temperatures centred on the mean in February will occur 95·46% of the time.

8. The length of human pregnancies from conception to birth varies according to an approximate normal distribution with a mean of 265 days and standard deviation of 16 days.

   (a) Between what values on either side of the mean do the lengths of 95·46% of all pregnancies fall?

   (b) How short is the shortest 2·14% of all pregnancies?

9. The mean quantity of milk produced daily by a cow in a dairy herd is 12 litres. Assuming normal distribution with a standard deviation of 0·5 litres, what is the range of volumes of milk on either side of the mean produced by 99·74% of the herd using the empirical rule? What percentage of the herd produced between 11 litres and 12·5 litres?

21.2 Measures of position 1: Percentiles

ACTIVITY 22

ACTION
Understanding measures of position 1: Percentiles

OBJECTIVE
Working with a set of data, to calculate percentiles, quartiles and deciles

In a class of 50 students, 8% of the students scored a mark less than or equal to 27 in a test. This mark of 27 is known as the eighth percentile and means that 8% of the students scored less than or equal to 27 marks. Therefore, 4 students scored less than or equal to 27.

KEY TERM

The **pth percentile** of a data distribution is the data value that has p% of the data values equal to it or less than it when all data values are ranked in order of increasing size.

A percentile p is a number and its corresponding percentile rank is p%.

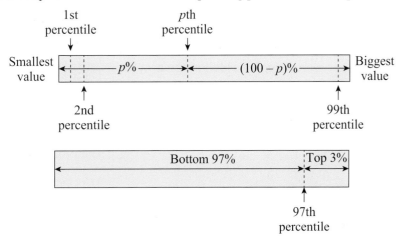

REMEMBER

The **quartiles** of a set of data values are the three points that divide the data set into four equal groups, each group comprising a quarter of the data.

The **deciles** of a data set are the nine points that divide the data set into 10 equal groups, where each set comprises one-tenth of the set.

There are 99 percentiles in a data set.

*   The 50th percentile is the median.
*   The 25th percentile is the lower quartile.
*   The 75th percentile is the upper quartile.

EXAMPLE 5

The marks of 25 students in an Art exam are as follows:

83	91	47	62	44
60	58	52	65	74
75	79	53	68	80
84	34	38	43	57
28	95	50	86	94

(a) Find:

    (i) The 44th percentile

    (ii) The 6th decile

    (iii) The median

(b) (i) What percentile rank is 75?

    (ii) What percentile is 75?

Solution

The numbers written in ascending order of size are:

28, 34, 38, 43, 44, 47, 50, 52, 53, 57, 58, 60, 62, 65, 68, 74, 75, 79, 80, 83, 84, 86, 91, 94, 95

(a) (i) 44th percentile: 44% of 25 = 25 × 0·44 = 11

The number in the 11th position is 58.

(ii) 6th decile = 60th percentile: 60% of 25 = 25 × 0·6 = 15

The number in the 15th position is 68.

(iii) The median is the number in the $\left(\frac{25+1}{2}\right)^{\text{th}}$ position = 13th position = 62

(b) (i) There are 17 numbers less than or equal to 75.

Therefore, 75 has a percentile rank of $\frac{17}{25} \times 100\% = 68\%$.

(ii) 75 is the 68th percentile.

EXAMPLE 6

The speeds in km/h of various cars in a 50 km/h speed limit zone were recorded as follows in a stem-and-leaf diagram over a certain time:

2	0	2			
3	0	2	3	5	7
4	2	3	4	5	6	7
5	1	2	3	4	8
6	0	3			

(Key: 4|4 = 44)

Find the 70th percentile.

Solution

There are 20 results.

70% of 20 = 14

The 70th percentile is the 14th position.

Therefore, the 70th percentile = 51.

51 is a cut-off point in that 70% of the cars had a speed less than or equal to 51 km/h and 30% had a speed higher than 51 km/h.

The percentile value of 51 km/h is a measure of location. The percentile of 70 gives us an idea of the relative position of the data value 51 km/h in the set.

Percentiles and percentages

Percentiles are used extensively in child development tests and IQ tests to show the comparative performance of individuals in a population or sample. Do not confuse it with a percentage. A percentage is related to an individual's own performance. For example, if you scored 79%, you got 79 marks out of 100.

A percentile relates an individual's performance to the performance of others in the sample (class). For example, if your mark was at the 85th percentile, it means that 85% of the students in the sample scored less than or equal to you.

▶ Luke was told by his teacher that he scored 85%. He was not particularly happy but when the teacher told him that that was at the 95th percentile mark, he perked up, as he realised that he scored higher than 95% of the students taking the test. There were 60 students who took the test. So 95% of 60 is 57 students. Therefore, Luke realised that he scored higher than 57 of the students.

▶ Suzanna was told that she was 38th out of a class of 150. What is her percentile position? 38th out of 150 means there are 114 students ranked below her.

$$p\% = \frac{114}{150} \times 100\% = 76\%$$

Suzanna is at the 76th percentile.

Continuous data

For continuous data given as a grouped frequency distribution, percentiles can be estimated by calculation or from an ogive, as shown in the next example.

EXAMPLE 7

The IQ test scores for 200 students are shown below.

Score	40–45	45–50	50–55	55–60	60–65	65–70	70–75	75–80	80–85	85–90	90–95	95–100
Number of students	2	4	7	11	16	24	48	38	30	10	8	2

(a) Draw up an ogive and estimate the 58th percentile IQ.

(b) What percentile is an IQ of 86?

Solution

(a) Draw up a cumulative frequency table first and then an ogive:

Score	<40	<45	<50	<55	<60	<65	<70	<75	<80	<85	<90	<100
Number of students	0	2	6	13	24	40	64	112	150	190	198	200

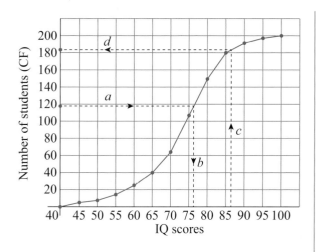

The 58th percentile is the IQ at or below 58% of the students scored: 58% of 200 = 116

Draw a horizontal line a from 116 on the y-axis to the ogive and drop a vertical line b down to the x-axis to get 76. 76 is the 58th percentile IQ score.

(b) Go to 86 on the x-axis. Draw a vertical line c up from 86 to the ogive and draw a horizontal line d across to the y-axis to get 184.

$$p\% = \frac{184}{200} \times 100\% = 92\%$$

Therefore, 86 is the 92nd percentile.

Percentiles and frequency distributions

Percentiles can be applied to all frequency distributions whether or not they are normal. Because the area under a frequency distribution curve to the left of a data value X is equal to the number of data values less than or equal to X, the percentile rank of X is the percentage $p\%$ that this area is of the total area under the curve.

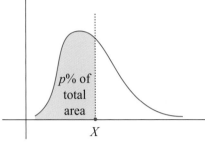

▶ The distribution on the right shows the length in centimetres (cm) of certain plants after 2 weeks. The 25th percentile rank is the length which 25% of plants are at or below. Could this be 30 cm? No, as the area to the left of the 30 cm line is not 25% of the total area (sum of the frequencies). The 25th percentile is much less than 30 cm.

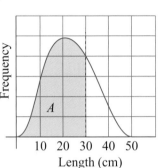

EXERCISE 15

1. Mick scores the top mark in a group of 100 students. What percentile is he in?

2. How many deciles are there?

Smallest value ⟶ 1st decile ... ? decile ⟵ Biggest value

3. What is the 65th percentile score in the following scores? 21, 24, 27, 30, 32, 35, 42, 48, 49, 50, 51, 53, 54, 55, 62, 71, 85, 86, 94, 96

4. What is the sixth decile for the following shoe sizes of a sample of 16?

$11\frac{1}{2}$, 7, 9, 5, 11, 10, $9\frac{1}{2}$, $12\frac{1}{2}$, $6\frac{1}{2}$, 13, 6, 8, 12, $8\frac{1}{2}$, $10\frac{1}{2}$

5. The seventh decile is the same as the 70th percentile. Is this true or false?

6. Copy and complete the following:

   (a) The 50th percentile is the same as the _____.

   (b) The 25th percentile is the same as the _____.

   (c) The 75th percentile is the same as the _____.

7. For the frequency curve shown, find the 20th percentile if the shaded area is 80% of the total area under the curve.

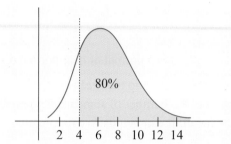

80%

2 4 6 8 10 12 14

8. On the scholastic aptitude test (SAT) in a class of 50 students, how many students had a score greater than 600 on the Maths test, if this score was at the 74th percentile? How many scored greater than 600 on the verbal test, if this score was at the 78th percentile?

9. What value would be affected most by a large valued outlier in a set: the first quartile, the third quartile or the 99th percentile?

10. The grouped frequency table below gives the number of unemployed jobseekers by age group in a certain town.

Age (years)	Number
15–25	350
25–35	280
35–45	150
45–55	100
55–65	40

Draw up an ogive. Use it to find the value of the 68th percentile, correct to the nearest year. Try to calculate the 68th percentile using the same technique for calculating the median from a grouped frequency table.

11. A standard English test is given to two schools, one in Kilanor and one in Ballygan. The 80th percentile for the Kilanor school was 70. The 80th percentile for the Ballygan school was 53. Is this worrying? Why?

21.3 Measures of position 2: z-scores

Another way to compare the relative positions of data values in a **normal or near normal distribution only** is to find their positions relative to the mean in terms of standard deviations.

KEY TERM

A **z-score** (standard score) is the number of standard deviations a particular data value x differs from the mean in a normal distribution.

EXAMPLE 8

The mean score on a test in which the marks were normally distributed was 57 with a standard deviation of 4. How many standard deviations from the mean was a student who scored 69?

Solution

$\mu = 57$, $\sigma = 4$

Score $x = 69$

$x - \mu = 69 - 57 = 12 = 3\sigma$

In terms of σ, this is 3 standard deviations from the mean.

3 is the z-score of 69.

Therefore, $z = 3$.

z-score formula

$$z = \frac{x - \mu}{\sigma}$$

where x is a data value,

μ is the mean of the data values,

σ is the standard deviation of the data values in a normal or near normal distribution.

A z-score gives the position of a score in relation to the mean using the standard deviation as a unit of measurement. It is the number of standard deviations by which a data value departs from the mean. It can be positive or negative.

> **Notes**
>
> 1. z-scores can be positive or negative.
> 2. If $z = 0$, then $x = \mu$.
> 3. If z is positive, the score x is greater than the mean.
> 4. If z is negative, the score x is less than the mean.
> 5. $z = +1 \cdot 5$: This means that the score is $1 \cdot 5 \times$ (standard deviation) greater than the mean.
> 6. 95% of data values in a normal distribution have z-scores that lie between $-1 \cdot 96$ and $+1 \cdot 96$.
> 7. z-scores can be used to compare data values in different normal distributions.

Comparing normal distributions

WORKED EXAMPLE Using z-scores to compare performance

Suppose you took an English course and you scored 74 out of 100 and your friend took a Psychology course and scored 80 out of 100. It looks like your friend has bragging rights, but has he? Maybe his course was easier. Maybe the students in his class were less or more able than those in yours. It is difficult to compare raw scores without more information.

Suppose the mean score on your course was 52 with standard deviation of 20, while in your friend's course the mean was 70 with standard deviation 15, and both sets of marks were normally distributed.

You	Friend
$x = 74$	$x = 80$
$\mu = 52$	$\mu = 70$
$\sigma = 20$	$\sigma = 15$
$z = \dfrac{74 - 52}{20} = \dfrac{22}{20} = 1 \cdot 1$	$z = \dfrac{80 - 70}{15} = \dfrac{10}{15} = 0 \cdot 67$

So you are $1 \cdot 1$ standard deviations above the mean in your course and your friend is only $0 \cdot 67$ standard deviations above the mean in his course. You are more standard deviations above your class mean than your friend is above his. Assuming a normal distribution in both classes, you did better than he did. You are higher up in your class than he is in his class. You could, of course, get a percentile for each score. You did better relative to your group than he did relative to his group.

EXAMPLE 9

A sample following normal distribution has a mean of 80 and standard deviation of 8. What score gives a z-value of $+1\cdot5$?

Solution

$z = +1\cdot5$

$\mu = 80,\ \sigma = 8,\ x = ?$

$1\cdot5 = \dfrac{x - 80}{8}$

$12 = x - 80$

$x = 92$

EXAMPLE 10

A recent survey of students at school surveyed their attitude to authority. Boys had a mean score of 105 and standard deviation of 12. Girls had a mean score of 113 and standard deviation of 11. A score higher than 90 indicates a pro-authority feeling. Relative to his or her gender, who is more pro-authority: a male student who scored 118 or a female student who scored 123? Both sets of scores were normally distributed.

Solution

Boys	**Girls**
$\mu = 105$	$\mu = 113$
$\sigma = 12$	$\sigma = 11$
$x = 118 > 90\ (\therefore\ \text{pro})$	$x = 123 > 90\ (\therefore\ \text{pro})$
$z = \dfrac{x - \mu}{\sigma} = \dfrac{118 - 105}{12} = 1\cdot08$	$z = \dfrac{x - \mu}{\sigma} = \dfrac{123 - 113}{11} = 0\cdot91$

$$1\cdot08 > 0\cdot91$$

Therefore, relative to the boys, this boy is more pro-authority than the girl, because relative to the girls he is further from the mean of the boys than she is from the mean of the girls.

EXERCISE 16

Assume in all of the following questions that all data values are normally distributed.

1. Given a mean test mark of 75 with standard deviation of 5, calculate the z-score for a test mark of 83.

2. In a test with a mean mark of 83 and standard deviation of 6, find the mark corresponding to a z-score of $-1\cdot6$.

3. Given a z-score of 0, what can you say about the actual score?

4. A final exam result for a student is 60. The mean of the results is 70 and the variance is 25. What is his z-score?

5. True or false:
   (a) A negative z-score means a score less than the mean.
   (b) A z-score represents the number of standard deviations that a data value is above or below the mean of the data set.

(c) $z = \dfrac{\mu - x}{\sigma}$

(d) z-values are only worthwhile for normal or approximately normal distributions.

(e) Most z-scores are between -4 and $+4$.

6. A normal distribution of scores has $\sigma = 10$. Find z-scores for the following:

   (a) A score 20 points below the mean

   (b) A score 10 points below the mean

   (c) A score 15 points above the mean

   (d) A score 30 points below the mean

7. In a normal distribution of data values with a mean of 30, the z-score for a data value of 40 is -2. Why is this impossible?

8. In a normal distribution, a score of 82 has $z = +1$ and a score of 85 has $z = +2$. What is the mean and standard deviation?

9. A set of Physics exam marks has a mean of 71 and standard deviation of 9. A set of History exam marks has a mean of 76 and standard deviation of 18. For which exam would a score of 80 have been a higher relative standing?

10. On a statistics exam, you scored 78. If the mean was 70, would you prefer a standard deviation of 8 or 16?

11. A survey was conducted on first-year and sixth-year students on whether or not they were in favour of wearing a uniform. On the attitude scale, a score greater than 50 was judged to be pro-uniform. The mean score for first years was 65 with standard deviation of 8. The mean score for sixth years was 58 with standard deviation of 5. Relative to their own group, which student was more pro-uniform: a first year who scored 68 or a sixth year who scored 60?

12. For 1, 9, 17, 25, 33, 41, 49, find the mean and standard deviation. Find the z-value of each score. Show the mean of z-scores is 0 and the standard deviation of z-scores is 1.

13. A student's test score on the normal curve is at the 98th percentile. Find her z-score using the empirical rule. If her z-score is -1, what is her percentile, correct to the nearest whole number, using the empirical rule?

14. For $x_1, \ldots, x_n$ with mean μ and standard deviation σ, express:

    (a) μ in terms of $x_1, \ldots, x_n$ and n,

    (b) σ in terms of $x_1, \ldots, x_n$, μ and n.

15. If $z_i = \dfrac{x_i - \mu}{\sigma}$, show that the mean of $z_1, z_2, \ldots, z_n$ is 0 and the standard deviation of $z_1, z_2, \ldots, z_n$ is 1.

21.4 Standard normal distribution

ACTIVITY 24

ACTION
Understanding standard normal curves

OBJECTIVE
To analyse the properties of standard normal curves

If you take any normal frequency distribution with mean μ and standard deviation σ, the frequency f is given by: $f = \dfrac{1}{\sigma\sqrt{2\pi}}\, e^{-\frac{(x-\mu)^2}{2\sigma^2}}$, where the area under the curve is the total number of data values.

The shaded area between x_1 and x_2 is the number of data values between x_1 and x_2.

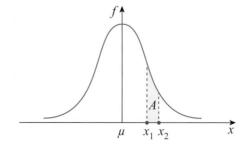

The percentage (proportion) of data values or relative frequency of data values

between x_1 and $x_2 = \dfrac{\text{Area of the shaded region}}{\text{Total area under the curve}}$.

Of course, this is also the probability that a result will fall between x_1 and x_2. Since each normal curve has its own mean and standard deviation, the centre of symmetry and spread of normal curves are all different. It would be very convenient if we could transform every normal curve into a single standard normal curve. We could then work out the percentage of data values between two given values on this standard curve in the same way for any normal distribution. Then we could transform these results back to the original normal curve to give the percentage of data values between two given values for that particular curve.

This can be done using the linear transformation $z = \dfrac{x - \mu}{\sigma}$.

In other words, the standard normal curve is the normal curve with variable z rather than variable x.

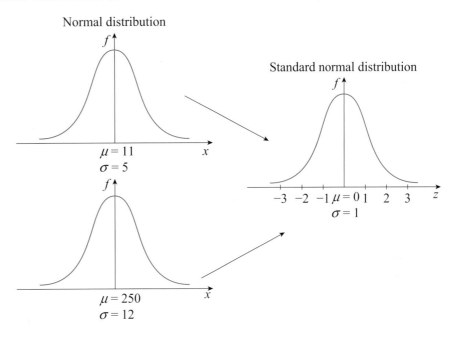

Properties of the standard normal distribution curve

This transformation $z = \dfrac{x - \mu}{\sigma}$ turns all bell-shaped normal distributions with a variable x into a standard normal bell-shaped distribution with variable z. It has the following properties:

1. Mean = 0. [Mean of z-scores = 0]

2. Standard deviation = 1.
    [Standard deviation of z-scores = 1]

3. Total area under curve = 1, with
    $0{\cdot}5$ of the area on the right of the
    mean and $0{\cdot}5$ on the left of it.

4. A common z-scale.

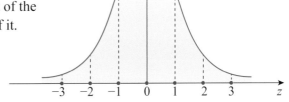

5. Percentage of data values (proportion of observations) between Z_1 and Z_2

= relative frequency of data value between Z_1 and Z_2

$$= \frac{\text{Area between } Z_1 \text{ and } Z_2}{1}$$

= area between Z_1 and Z_2

= probability of a result between Z_1 and Z_2

$= P(Z_1 \leq z \leq Z_2)$

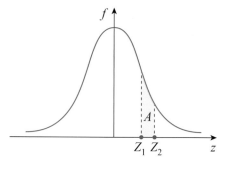

6. The area under the curve to the left of a given value Z

= percentage (proportion) of z-values less than or equal to Z

= probability of a z-value less than or equal to Z

$= P(z \leq Z)$

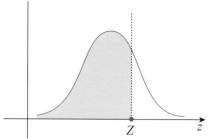

7. Positive values of z give areas greater than 0·5. Negative values of z give areas less than 0·5.

$P(z) > 0{\cdot}5 \Leftrightarrow z > 0; \; P(z) < 0{\cdot}5 \Leftrightarrow z < 0$

8. The area under the curve to the left of $-Z$ is equal to the area of the curve to the right of Z because the curve is symmetric about the mean.

$P(z \leq -Z) = P(z \geq Z)$

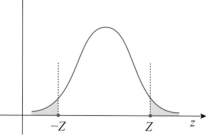

Reading the standard normal distribution area table

The area (probability) under the standard normal distribution curve to the left of a particular value Z of z has been calculated and tabulated in the normal standard distribution table. This table is on pages 36 and 37 of the *Formulae and Tables* book.

The z numbers in the table give you the percentage of data values less than or equal to a particular value Z of z

= probability of a result less than or equal to Z

= proportion of results $\leq Z$

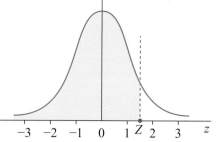

= total cumulative frequency of values $\leq Z$

= shaded area under the curve to the left of Z

Using the standard normal distribution table

1. **The numbers in the table give the area of the region to the left of a given value Z of z.**

   Area of shaded region = $P(-\infty \leq z \leq Z)$

   = percentage of results from $-\infty$ to Z

   ▶ Find $P(z \leq 1\cdot58)$.

   This is the area under the curve from $Z = -\infty$ to $Z = 1\cdot58$.

   $P(z \leq 1\cdot58) = 0\cdot9429 = 94\cdot29\%$
     = percentage of results less than or equal to $Z = 1\cdot58$.

   $1\cdot58$ is the z-value of the 94th percentile.

   ▶ Use the table to estimate the z-value of the 80th percentile.

   You need the value of z such that 80% of results are below it.

   Find Z such that $P(z \leq Z) = 0\cdot8$.

   The nearest value in the table to $0\cdot8$ is $0\cdot7995$, giving a value of $Z = 0\cdot84$.

   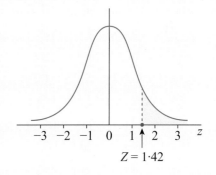

2. **The total area under the curve is 1.**

   ▶ Find the percentage of results
   to the right of $Z = 1\cdot42$.

   In other words, find $P(z > 1\cdot42)$.

   From the table, $P(z \leq 1\cdot42)$ = area from $z = -\infty$ to
   $z = 1\cdot42$, which is $0\cdot9222$.

   $P(z > 1\cdot42) = 1 - P(z \leq 1\cdot42)$

   $\quad = 1 - 0\cdot9222$

   $\quad = 0\cdot0778$

   $\quad = 7\cdot78\%$

3. **The curve is symmetric.**

   What about finding the percentage of a value to the left of a negative value of z? There are no
   negative values for z in the tables.

   ▶ Find $P(z \leq -0\cdot86)$.

   $P(z \leq -0\cdot86) = P(z \geq 0\cdot86)$

   $\quad = 1 - P(z \leq 0\cdot86)$

   $\quad = 1 - 0\cdot8051$

   $\quad = 0\cdot1949$

   $\quad = 19\cdot49\%$

   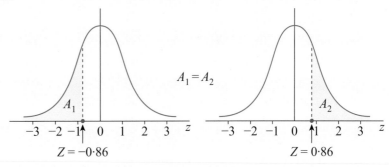

   ▶ Find Z, if $P(z \leq Z) = 0\cdot2327$.

   As $0\cdot2327 < 0\cdot5$, Z is negative. Put $Z = -w$.

   $P(z \leq -w) = P(z > w) = 1 - P(z \leq w) = 0\cdot2327$

   $\therefore P(z \leq w) = 1 - 0\cdot2327 = 0\cdot7673$

   From the tables: $w = 0\cdot73$

   $\therefore Z = -0\cdot73$

4. **Finding the percentage of values between two positive z-values.**

   ▸ Find $P(0·87 \leq z \leq 1·32)$.

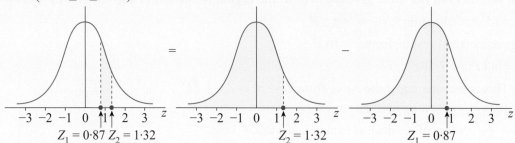

$$P(0·87 \leq z \leq 1·32)$$
$$= P(z \leq 1·32) - P(z \leq 0·87)$$
$$= 0·9066 - 0·8078$$
$$= 0·0988$$
$$= 9·88\%$$

5. **Finding the percentage of values between one negative value of z and one positive value of z.**

   ▸ Find $P(-1·36 \leq z \leq 1·1)$.

   $$P(-1·36 \leq z \leq 1·1)$$
   $$= P(z \leq 1·1) - P(z \leq -1·36)$$
   $$= P(z \leq 1·1) - P(z > 1·36)$$
   $$= P(z \leq 1·1) - [1 - P(z \leq 1·36)]$$
   $$= 0·8643 - 1 + 0·9131$$
   $$= 0·7774$$
   $$= 77·74\%$$

6. **Finding the percentage of values between two negative values of z.**

   ▸ Find $P(-1·4 \leq z \leq -0·8)$.

   $$P(-1·4 \leq z \leq -0·8)$$
   $$= P(0·8 \leq z \leq 1·4)$$
   $$= P(z \leq 1·4) - P(z \leq 0·8)$$
   $$= 0·9192 - 0·7881$$
   $$= 0·1311$$
   $$= 13·11\%$$

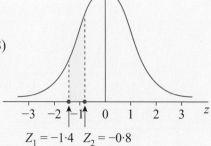

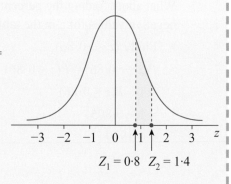

7. **The 50th percentile has a z-score of 0.**

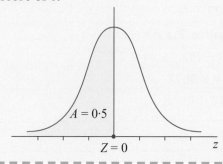

EXAMPLE 11

A test has a mean mark of 240 and a standard deviation of 60, assuming a normal distribution.

(a) Find what test score is the 80th percentile.

(b) Find what test score is the 25th percentile.

(c) Find the 50th percentile on this test.

Give all answers correct to the nearest whole number.

Solution

(a) The 80th percentile means that the area to the left of the z-value is $0{\cdot}8$ on the normal standard distribution curve.

Therefore, it is a positive value. Call it Z and look up $0{\cdot}8$ in the table to get Z. The closest value is $0{\cdot}7995$, which gives a Z-value of $0{\cdot}84$.

$P(z \leq Z) = 0{\cdot}8 \Rightarrow Z = 0{\cdot}84$

Now transform back to the normal curve with mean 240 and standard deviation 60.

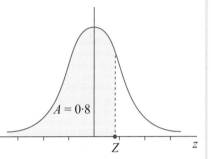

$z = \dfrac{x - \mu}{\sigma} \Rightarrow 0{\cdot}84 = \dfrac{x - 240}{60}$

$60(0{\cdot}84) + 240 = x$

$x = 290{\cdot}4$

290 is the test score.

(b) The 25th percentile means that the area to the left of the z-value is $0{\cdot}25$.

As $0{\cdot}25 < 0{\cdot}5$, the z-value is negative. Call it $-Z$.

$P(z \leq -Z) = P(z \geq Z) = 1 - P(z \leq Z) = 0{\cdot}25$

$\therefore P(z \leq Z) = 0{\cdot}75$

As $0{\cdot}25 < 0{\cdot}5$, the nearest value to $0{\cdot}75$ is $0{\cdot}7486$.

Therefore, $Z = 0{\cdot}67$.

Therefore, the z-value $= -0{\cdot}67$.

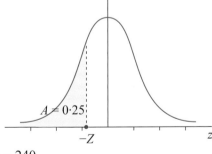

$-0{\cdot}67 = \dfrac{x - 240}{60}$

$x = 199{\cdot}8$

200 is the test score.

(c) The 50th percentile is always $Z = 0$ in a standard normal distribution:

$0 = \dfrac{x - 240}{60} \Rightarrow x = 240$

EXAMPLE 12

The results of a Physics exam are normally distributed. The mean percentage mark is 60% with standard deviation of 10%.

(a) What is the probability that a randomly selected student scores above 80%?

(b) What score, correct to the nearest whole number, separates the top 40% from the rest?

(c) What range of scores would form the middle 60% of the distribution, correct to the nearest whole number?

(d) There is a prize for the mark that is greater than that obtained by 91% of all the students. Find this mark, correct to the nearest whole number.

(e) If two students scored 90%, did they cheat given there are 200 students in the class?

Solution

$\mu = 60$, $\sigma = 10$

(a) $x = 80 \Rightarrow z = \dfrac{80 - 60}{10} = 2$

$$P(x > 80) = P(z > 2)$$
$$= 1 - P(z \le 2)$$
$$= 1 - 0.9772$$
$$= 0.0228$$

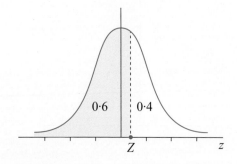

(b) $P(z > Z) = 0.4 \Rightarrow P(z \le Z) = 0.6$

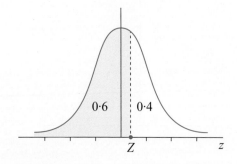

0.5987 is the closest number to 0.6.

Therefore, $Z = 0.25$.

$0.25 = \dfrac{x - 60}{10} \Rightarrow x = 62.5$

63 is the mark.

(c) Middle 60% of distribution:

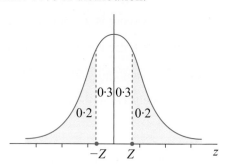

$P(-Z \le z \le Z) = 0.6$

$P(z \le Z) = 0.8$

0.7995 is the closest number to 0.8.

Therefore, $Z = 0.84$

$0.84 = \dfrac{x - 60}{10} \Rightarrow x = 68.4$

$-0.84 = \dfrac{x - 60}{10} \Rightarrow x = 51.6$

$51.6 \le x \le 68.4$

$52 - 68$ is the range of marks.

(d) $P(z < Z) = 0.91$

0.9099 is the closest number to 0.91.

Therefore, $Z = 1.34$.

$1.34 = \dfrac{x - 60}{10} \Rightarrow x = 73.4$

73 is the mark.

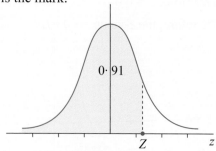

(e) $x = 90$

$z = \dfrac{90 - 60}{10} = \dfrac{30}{10} = 3.0$

$$P(x \le 90) = P(z \le 3.0)$$
$$= 0.9987$$

It looks likely that the students did cheat, as only

0.13% of 200 students

$= \dfrac{200 \times 0.13}{100} = 0.26$ of a person scored 90 or more!

EXAMPLE 13

The following are the test scores for two age groups:

	12-year-olds	14-year-olds
Mean	46	54
Standard deviation	6	10
Number of students	400	700

Assuming both sets of results are normally distributed:

(a) estimate how many 12-year-olds do better than the average for 14-year-olds,

(b) estimate how many 14-year-olds do worse than the average for 12-year-olds.

Solution

12-year-olds: $\mu = 46$, $\sigma = 6$, $N = 400$

14-year-olds: $\mu = 54$, $\sigma = 10$, $N = 700$

(a) Average 14-year-old score = 54

Where does this figure lie on the 12-year-olds' distribution?

$$x = 54: z = \frac{54 - 46}{6} = 1\cdot333$$

$$P(z > 1\cdot33) = 1 - P(z \leq 1\cdot33)$$
$$= 1 - 0\cdot9082$$
$$= 0\cdot0918$$

∴ $0\cdot0918 \times 400 \approx 37$ students

(b) Average 12-year-old score = 46

Where does this figure lie in the 14-year-olds' distribution?

$$x = 46: z = \frac{46 - 54}{10} = -0\cdot8$$

$$P(z < -0\cdot8) = P(z \geq 0\cdot8)$$
$$= 1 - P(z \leq 0\cdot8)$$
$$= 1 - 0\cdot7881$$
$$= 0\cdot2119$$

Number = $0\cdot2119 \times 700 = 148$

EXERCISE 17

1. Use the z-score tables to find:

   (a) $P(z \leq 1\cdot5)$

   (b) $P(z \leq 1\cdot96)$

   (c) $P(z \geq 1\cdot3)$

   (d) $P(z \geq 0\cdot65)$

   (e) $P(z \leq -1\cdot21)$

   (f) $P(z \leq -0\cdot56)$

   (g) $P(0\cdot41 \leq z \leq 1\cdot32)$

   (h) $P(-0\cdot73 \leq z \leq 0\cdot58)$

2. Use the z-score table to find Z, $Z > 0$, correct to two decimal places:

   (a) $P(z \leq Z) = 0\cdot8023$

   (b) $P(z \geq Z) = 0\cdot0721$

   (c) $P(Z \leq z \leq 2\cdot3) = 0\cdot125$

   (d) $P(z \leq Z) = 0\cdot4168$

   (e) $P(-Z \leq z \leq 2\cdot7) = 0\cdot695$

3. If x is a random variable in a normal distribution with mean μ and standard deviation σ, find $P(\mu - 3\sigma \leq x \leq \mu + 3\sigma)$.

4. Find s, correct to two decimal places, in a normal distribution with a mean of 4 and standard deviation of 2, if $P(4 - s \leq x \leq 4 + s) = 0\cdot5934$.

5. In a city, the maximum daily temperature in July is normally distributed with mean 22 °C and standard deviation of 5 °C. Calculate the number of days in July in which it is expected to reach a maximum temperature of between 20 °C and 26 °C, correct to the nearest whole number of days.

6. The test results of a class follow a normal distribution with $\mu = 78$ and $\sigma = 30$. What is the probability of a student scoring higher than 72? What is the probability of a student scoring higher than 84? What percentage, correct to the nearest percentage, of students who scored higher than 72 scored higher than 84?

7. An intelligence test has a mean of 32 and standard deviation of 6. Assuming scores are distributed normally:

   (a) What is the *z*-score for a raw score of 38? What percentile is this?

   (b) What raw score is the 62nd percentile, correct to the nearest whole number?

   (c) What is the probability of getting a raw score between 25 and 37, correct to two decimal places?

8. SAT scores form a normal distribution with a mean of 500 and standard deviation of 100.

   (a) What is the minimum score needed to be in the top 20%, correct to the nearest whole number?

   (b) Find the range of values that defines the middle 80% of SAT scores, correct to the nearest whole number.

9. A normal distribution has a mean of 20 and a standard deviation of 4.

   (a) Find the percentile rank of a value of 15.

   (b) Find the data value that approximates 65% of values below it, that is, find the 65th percentile, correct to two decimal places.

   (c) Find the data value for which 87% of the values are above it, correct to two decimal places.

   (d) Find the range of data values, correct to two decimal places, corresponding to the middle 50% of the distribution of values.

10. A researcher is examining the reaction times of animals to a stimulus. The mean time is 1·2 seconds with a standard deviation of 0·2 s. However, she believes that 5% of the scores farthest from the mean are due to error. What is the range of reaction times that should be ignored, correct to two decimal places?

11. A manufacturer makes bulbs with lifetimes that are normally distributed with a mean lifetime of 1500 hours and standard deviation of 140 hours. After how long would you expect 5% of them to burn out, correct to the nearest whole number?

12. The mean height of women in a country is distributed normally with a mean of 1·65 m and standard deviation of 0·05 m. In that country, the minimum height requirement for women to join the police force is 1·70 m. What percentage of women, correct to the nearest percentage, are eligible to join the police force in the country?

13. The diameters of ball bearings for a job must be 2·5 ± 0·02 cm. Any ball bearing outside this range cannot be used. What percentage of bearings will be acceptable if the manufacturer says they are normally distributed with a mean of 2·5 cm and standard deviation of 0·008 cm, correct to two decimal places?

14. A teacher wants to boost the lowest marks in his class by adding 5 marks to the lowest 15% of the scores. The mean test score is 140 with standard deviation of 21. What is the highest score you can get to obtain the extra marks, correct to the nearest whole number?

15. A recent survey of second-level students reported their attitudes to homework. The boys' scores were normally distributed with a mean of 105 and standard deviation of 15. The girls' scores were also normally distributed with a mean of 110 and standard deviation of 10. A score higher than 90 indicates a very positive attitude to homework.

   (a) What percentage of boys had a very positive attitude to homework, correct to the nearest percentage?

   (b) Between what two scores are the middle 70% of girls, correct to the nearest whole number?

   (c) Jack has a score of 75. What is his percentile rank?

   (d) If there are 500 girls, how many had a very positive attitude to homework, correct to the nearest whole number?

Inferential Statistics

CHAPTER 22

Learning Outcomes

- To understand what is meant by statistical inference.
- To understand the difference between populations and samples.
- To distinguish between population proportions and population means.
- To use the central limit theorem to make predictions about the population from a simple random sample.
- To carry out hypothesis testing.

22.1 The concept of statistical inference

KEY TERM

Statistical inference is a set of mathematical techniques that enable you to make scientifically defensible statements about a population (a large number of objects) based on information obtained from a sample (simple random sample).

Populations

KEY TERM

A **population** is the set of all possible objects about which information is required.

▸ If you are measuring weights of children in Irish schools, the population is every child in an Irish school.

▸ If you are measuring the voting preferences of Australian citizens, the population is every Australian citizen who is registered to vote.

Surveying or measuring a whole population can be very difficult and expensive. It is only done occasionally, as in a **census** or a **general election**.

KEY TERM

Numbers that give us information about the population, like mean and population proportion, are called **population parameters**.

Measuring populations

In this course, we will concentrate on two population parameters:

1. Population proportion p
2. Population mean μ

1. Population proportion p

You are asked the question: 'Do you support the upcoming referendum on reducing the voting age to 16?' The answer will be either yes or no. The data being collected is categorical data. When the referendum takes place, the population proportion p of those who support the referendum will be known. Let's say that this value turned out to be 65%. This is the **true** population proportion of those who support the referendum.

Population proportion $p = 0.65$

2. Population mean μ

You were asked the question in a survey in 2015: 'What is your yearly income?' The answer will be a number. The data being collected in this case is numerical data. If a census had taken place that year, the mean income and the spread of income (standard deviation) of the population would be known. Let's say the average income is €40 000 with a standard deviation of €5000. €40 000 is the **true** population mean.

Population mean μ = €40 000

Incomes in most countries have a positively skewed distribution of wealth with a small number of people earning very large incomes.

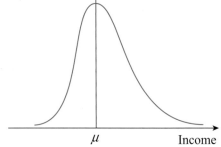

Samples

Instead of surveying everybody in a population, it is far less expensive and time consuming to survey just a **sample** of the population – maybe 100 people. The numbers like mean and sample proportion that we get from a sample are called **statistics**. You will see that accurate predictions about population parameters can be made from a sample by choosing the sample carefully.

The sample chosen should be **representative** of the population. In most cases, this can be achieved by taking a simple random sample where every member of the population has an equal chance of being picked to be part of the sample.

Suppose you want to find the percentage p (proportion) of students in a university of 20 000 students whose height is less than 1·78 m.

The answer is $p = \dfrac{\text{Number of students in the university with height less than } 1\cdot78 \text{ m}}{\text{Total number of students (population) in the university}}$

$= \text{Population proportion}$

In practice, this is very difficult and expensive to do. What you could do instead is estimate the population proportion by taking a simple random sample (SRS) of, say, 50 students and calculating the **sample proportion** $\hat{p}$.

$\hat{p} = \dfrac{\text{Number of students in the sample with height less than } 1\cdot78 \text{ m}}{\text{Number of students in the sample}}$

If $\hat{p}$ turns out to be 0·47, say, this value can be used as a **point estimate** of the true proportion p (which you don't know), because if you took nine more samples of 50 students, you would get a different value of $\hat{p}$ each time. How accurate this estimate is depends on many factors, including:

1. Sampling error and sampling variability
2. How representative the sample is
3. The size of the sample

1. Sampling error and sampling variability

If the true population proportion p (which you don't know) in the previous example of students with heights less than 1·78 m was 50%, then the sampling error is:

$\hat{p} - p = 47\% - 50\% = \text{point estimate} - \text{true value} = -3\%$

If you took nine more samples of 50 students, you would get nine more sampling errors for $\hat{p} - p$.

The 10 sampling errors in all might be as follows: 3%, 2%, 5%, −4%, −3%, 1%, −4%, 3%, −6%, −2%

> **KEY TERM**
> The variation in sampling error is known as **sampling variability**.

▶ In a census of the Irish population, the mean annual income μ per person was €40 000. For five samples of 100, find the sampling error, given sample means of €40 600, €40 780, €39 650, €41 230 and €39 750.

Sample mean $\bar{x}$	Population mean μ	Sampling error $\bar{x} - \mu$
€40 600	€40 000	€600
€40 780	€40 000	€780
€39 650	€40 000	−€350
€41 230	€40 000	€1230
€39 750	€40 000	−€250

Each answer you get from a sample is an **estimate** of the true population proportion or mean. Nearly every sample will give you a different estimate of the true value. Sampling variability is usually due to the fact that not all samples truly reflect the characteristics of the population but may also be due to pure chance. Clearly, the smaller the spread of sampling errors, the better the estimate will be for the true value p of the population proportion.

2. Representative samples

Generalising results from a sample to the whole population is only valid if the data is representative of the population.

> **KEY TERM**
>
> A **representative sample** is one in which the relevant characteristics of the sample members are generally the same as those of the population.

▸ To estimate the mean weight of the adult Japanese male, you do not take a sample of 50 professional sumo wrestlers!

3. Size of the sample

It is important to realise that if you take larger and larger samples (100, 1000, etc.), the sample proportion $\hat{p}$ or sample mean $\bar{x}$ will get closer and closer to the population proportion p or population mean μ. This is known as the law of large numbers.

Sample	Population	Law of large numbers
size n	size N	$n \to N$
mean $\bar{x}$	mean μ	$\bar{x} \to \mu$
proportion $\hat{p}$	proportion p	$\hat{p} \to p$

Simple random samples (SRS)

> **KEY TERM**
>
> A **simple random sample** of objects of size n is a group of n objects chosen from a larger set N (population) of objects in such a way that every set of n such objects has an equal chance (probability) to be the set selected.

The process of simple random sampling has the following characteristics:

1. There is no favouritism or bias.
2. Each object has an equal chance of being selected.
3. Each group of n objects has an equal chance of being selected.

▸ Every five-card hand has an equal chance of being selected.

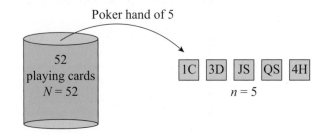

Poker hand of 5

52 playing cards $N = 52$

1C 3D JS QS 4H

$n = 5$

EXAMPLE 1

Three students in a school decided to investigate the average number of hours that sixth-year students study per week in their school. The number of students in sixth year was 120.

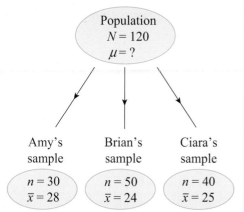

(a) Amy conducts a survey of her sixth-year English class of 30 students and gets an average of 28 hours of study per week.

(b) Brian asks the school secretary to randomly generate the names of 50 sixth-year students from the school computer records and interviews each of these. This gives an average of 24 hours of study per week.

(c) Ciara cuts up the names of all 120 students in sixth year and picks 40 of these names out of a hat to interview. This gives an average of 25 hours of study per week.

(i) Which of these, if any, are simple random samples? Why?

(ii) Which average is the most likely to be closest to the actual (true) mean?

Solution

(i) Brian's and Ciara's samples are simple random samples, as any group of 50 or 40, respectively, from 120 was equally likely to be selected. Indeed every student out of the 120 was equally likely to be selected. Amy's sample is not a simple random sample because this group of 30 was not as equally likely as any other group of 30 that could have been selected, nor was any student in the 30 equally likely to be selected as any student in the 120. Indeed, Amy's group may not be representative of the whole year group in terms of study habits.

(ii) The mean most likely to be closest to the population mean is 24, as this comes from the simple random sample with the biggest size ($n = 50$), because of the law of large numbers.

Sampling distributions

WORKED EXAMPLE
Looking at sampling distributions

Two Economics teachers asked their fifth-year classes of 25 students each to carry out a project. Each student was to ask the school secretary to randomly generate 50 samples of the names of 35 sixth-year pupils, one sample for each student. Each fifth-year student asked each sixth-year student in their sample of 35 how many hours they spent studying per week. Each fifth-year student then worked out the average study time for their own group. The results were set out as follows:

Mean study time $\bar{x}$ (hours)	Number of means
21–22	4
22–23	6
23–24	8
24–25	14
25–26	8
26–27	6
27–28	4

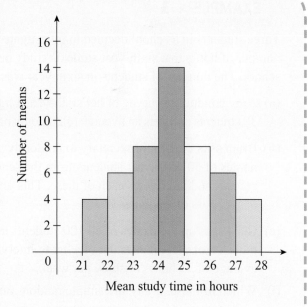

A histogram of the results was drawn, leading to a frequency distribution of the sample means (sampling distribution).

The frequency distribution of the sampling means formed a normal distribution with mean $\bar{\mu} = 24 \cdot 5$ hours ($\bar{\mu}$ = mean of the means) and standard deviation $\bar{\sigma} = 1 \cdot 65$. At the end of the year, every sixth-year student filled out a questionnaire administered by the class teachers. One of the questions was: 'How many hours did you study per week during the past year?' The mean worked out as $\mu = 24 \cdot 5$ hours and the standard deviation σ was $9 \cdot 76$ hours.

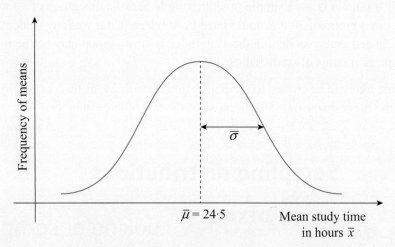

One of the class teachers, who is a Maths teacher, noticed that $\bar{\mu} = \mu = 24 \cdot 5$ and $\bar{\sigma} = 1 \cdot 65 = \dfrac{9 \cdot 76}{\sqrt{35}} = \dfrac{\sigma}{\sqrt{n}}$,

where n was the size of each sample of the fifth-year project. Was this a fluke?

This idea that the frequency distribution of the means of a large number of simple random samples is a normal distribution is the basis of inferential statistics and is known as the **central limit theorem**.

KEY TERM

The **central limit theorem** states that the sampling distribution of any statistic will be normal or nearly normal, if the sample size is large enough.

Central limit theorem

Suppose you want to find out the mean daily time spent by all Irish second-level students on social network sites.

> Population = all Irish second-level students = N
>
> Mean = μ
>
> Standard deviation = σ

$$\mu = \frac{\text{Total amount of time spent by all Irish second-level students on social network sites per day}}{\text{Number of Irish second-level students}}$$

This is a huge population, too big to observe or access in any way. It could be a normal distribution but more than likely it is skewed to the right. Suppose, for argument's sake, the mean of this population is $\mu = 42$ minutes with standard deviation of $\sigma = 10$ minutes and has a positively skewed frequency distribution.

The only way you can get any sort of estimate of this mean time is to take a simple random sample of, say, size 100 students, and find its mean and standard deviation.

Another sample of 100 would probably give a different mean and a different standard deviation. If 50 such samples are taken, you would expect each sample to be positively skewed to reflect the population and to have different means.

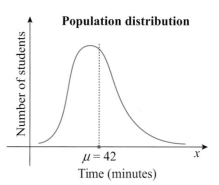

Population distribution

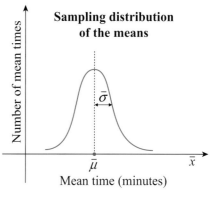

Sampling distribution of the means

$$n = 100 \quad n = 100 \quad n = 100$$
$$\overline{x}_1 \qquad \overline{x}_2 \quad \dots \quad \overline{x}_{50}$$

However, if a frequency distribution of these 50 means is plotted, this sampling distribution turns out to be normal, with a mean of $\overline{\mu} = \mu$ and a standard deviation of $\overline{\sigma} = \dfrac{\sigma}{\sqrt{n}}$, where μ is the population mean, σ is the population standard deviation, and n the sample size of each sample.

This is the idea behind the central limit theorem for a sample mean. There is also a central limit theorem for a sample proportion.

Statement of the central limit theorem

1. Sample mean

For samples of size $n \geq 30$, the shape of the frequency distribution of the sample mean $\bar{x}$ for any population with mean μ and standard deviation σ is approximately a normal distribution with mean $\bar{\mu} = \mu$ and standard deviation $\bar{\sigma} = \dfrac{\sigma}{\sqrt{n}}$ (standard error).

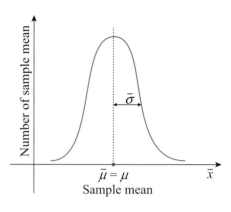

2. Sample proportion

For samples of size $n \geq 30$, the shape of the frequency distribution of the sample proportions for any population with proportion p is approximately normal with mean p and standard deviation

$$\hat{\sigma} = \sqrt{\frac{p(1 - p)}{n}} \text{ (standard error).}$$

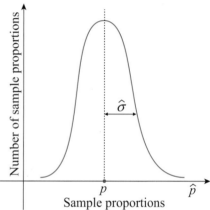

TIP

If the population distribution is normal, then the sampling distribution will also be normal, irrespective of the size of the samples. For any population distribution, the sampling distribution will be approximately normal for sample sizes $n \geq 30$. The bigger the value of n, the closer the sampling distribution resembles a perfectly normal distribution.

Population to sample

You can deduce results about samples from information about a population. Like all normal curves, a sampling distribution curve can be transformed into a standard normal curve, with its properties enabling you to work out $\bar{z}$-scores for sample means and $\hat{z}$-scores for sample proportions.

1. For a sample means distribution

$$\bar{z} = \frac{\bar{x} - \bar{\mu}}{\bar{\sigma}}, \text{ where } \bar{\mu} = \mu \text{ and } \bar{\sigma} = \frac{\sigma}{\sqrt{n}}$$

This enables you to deduce results about sample means obtained from a population.

EXAMPLE 2

Samples of size 50 are drawn from a population of mean 35 and standard deviation of 14. What is the percentage of samples that have a mean less than 33?

Solution

Population: $\mu = 35$, $\sigma = 14$

Sample: $n = 50$, $\bar{\mu} = 35$, $\bar{\sigma} = \dfrac{14}{\sqrt{50}}$

$$\bar{z} = \dfrac{\bar{x} - \mu}{\bar{\sigma}}$$

$$= \dfrac{33 - 35}{\dfrac{14}{\sqrt{50}}}$$

$$= -1{\cdot}01$$

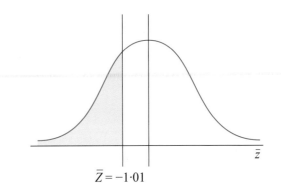

$\bar{Z} = -1{\cdot}01$

$$P(\bar{z} < -1{\cdot}01) = P(\bar{z} \geq 1{\cdot}01)$$

$$= 1 - P(\bar{z} < 1{\cdot}01)$$

$$= 1 - 0{\cdot}8438$$

$$= 0{\cdot}1562$$

$$= 15{\cdot}62\%$$

EXAMPLE 3

The IQ scores of students in a school are normally distributed with a mean of 100 and a standard deviation of 8·4. If a sample of 16 students is selected, what is the probability that the mean IQ of the sample will be less than 105?

Solution

Given that the population is normal, the sample size does not matter.

Population: $\mu = 100$, $\sigma = 8{\cdot}4$

Sample: $n = 16$

$$\mu = \bar{\mu} = 100$$

$$\bar{\sigma} = \dfrac{\sigma}{\sqrt{n}} = \dfrac{8{\cdot}4}{\sqrt{16}} = 2{\cdot}1$$

$$\bar{z} = \dfrac{\bar{x} - \bar{\mu}}{\bar{\sigma}} = \dfrac{105 - 100}{2{\cdot}1} = 2{\cdot}38$$

$$P(\bar{x} < 105) = P(\bar{z} < 2{\cdot}38)$$

$$= 0{\cdot}9913$$

$$= 99{\cdot}13\%$$

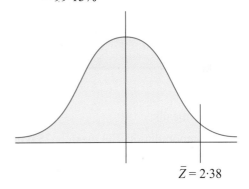

$\bar{Z} = 2{\cdot}38$

2. For a sample proportion distribution

$$\hat{z} = \dfrac{\hat{p} - p}{\hat{\sigma}}, \text{ where } p = \text{population proportion and } \hat{\sigma} = \sqrt{\dfrac{p(1 - p)}{n}}$$

EXAMPLE 4

In a television survey it was reported that 37% of people believe in ghosts. If 100 people are selected at random, what is the probability that more than 50% of these 100 people believe in ghosts?

Solution

Population: $p = 0.37$

Sample: $n = 100$

$$\hat{\sigma} = \sqrt{\frac{0.37 \times 0.63}{100}} = 0.048$$

$$\hat{z} = \frac{\hat{p} - p}{\hat{\sigma}}$$

$$= \frac{0.5 - 0.37}{0.048}$$

$$= 2.71$$

We need to evaluate $P(\hat{p} > 0.5)$.

$$P(\hat{p} > 0.5) = P(\hat{z} > 2.71)$$

$$= 1 - P(\hat{z} < 2.71)$$

$$= 1 - 0.9966$$

$$= 0.0034$$

$$= 0.34\%$$

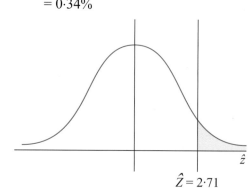

$\hat{Z} = 2.71$

The discovery that the distribution of the sample proportions and means is normal with a mean similar to the population is called the central limit theorem. It is a fundamental principle underlying how statistics operates. So far we have been dealing with populations and making predictions about samples. It is far more useful to use the central limit theorem the other way around. In other words, to make predictions about a population based on a sample.

EXERCISE 18

1. Sample means:

    (a) In a population, the mean is 25 with a standard deviation of 4·2. Samples of size 50 are chosen. Find the mean and standard deviation (correct to one decimal place) of the samples.

    (b) In a population, the mean is 54 with a standard deviation of 8. Samples of size 100 are chosen. Find the mean and standard deviation of the samples.

    (c) In a population, the mean is 5 with a standard deviation of 2·8. A sample of 75 is chosen. What is the probability, correct to two decimal places, that the sample mean is less than or equal to 5·5?

    (d) In a population, the mean is 15 with a standard deviation of 7. A sample of 30 is chosen. What is the probability, correct to

    three decimal places, that the sample mean is greater than 16·5?

    (e) In a population, the mean is 156 with a standard deviation of 40. A sample of 32 is chosen. What percentage, correct to one decimal place, of values in the sample lie between 150 and 175?

2. Sample proportions:

    (a) A population proportion is 0·6. A random sample of 32 is chosen. What is the probability that the sample proportion is greater than 0·68?

    (b) A population proportion is 0·35. A random sample of 49 is chosen. What is the probability that the sample proportion is less than or equal to 0·31?

(c) A population percentage is 45%. A random sample of 100 is chosen. What is the probability that the sample proportion is less than or equal to 48%?

(d) A population proportion is 0·224. A random sample of 50 is chosen. What is the probability that the sample proportion lies between 0·2 and 0·3 and includes these values?

(e) A population percentage is 64%. A random sample of 60 is chosen. What is the probability that the sample percentage lies between and 60% and 65% and includes these values?

Give all answers correct to two decimal places.

3. The test scores in an examination are normally distributed with a mean of 67 and standard deviation of 13. For random samples of size 50, find the mean and standard deviation, correct to two decimal places, of the distribution of sample means.

4. The statistics after a General Election showed that 33% of the electorate voted for a certain political party. If a sample of 1000 had been polled before the election, what is the probability that more than 36% would have said they were going to vote for the political party in the upcoming election, correct to three decimal places?

5. Samples of 100 adults were surveyed on their salary. The mean of the sampling distribution was €32 000 with a standard deviation of €800.

(a) Is this sampling distribution normal? Why?

(b) Can you apply the central limit theorem?

(c) Find the mean and standard deviation of the population.

(d) Do you think the population distribution of salaries is normally distributed?

6. Samples of size 25 are drawn from a normally distributed population with a mean of 18 and standard deviation of 4. Find the mean and standard deviation of the sampling distribution of the sample means $\bar{x}$. Find $P(\bar{x} < 16)$.

7. A new car model went on sale but 8% were recalled because of steering problems. A dealership in Galway sold 180 of these cars. What is the probability that fewer than 4% of the cars from the Galway dealership experience steering problems, correct to three decimal places?

8. The mean weight of an adult male in a country is 77 kg with a standard deviation of 6·8 kg. The weight of adult males is normally distributed. Sixteen male adults enter a lift with a maximum weight restriction of 1300 kg. Find the probability that the cable snaps. Comment on this 'random' sample.

9. The maximum daily temperatures in a town are normally distributed with a mean of 20·4 °C and standard deviation of 5·1 °C.

(a) Find the percentage of maximum daily temperatures between 12 °C and 22 °C, correct to the nearest percentage.

(b) Find the percentage of days with a maximum daily temperature less than 24 °C, correct to the nearest percentage.

(c) In a random sample of 25 maximum daily temperatures, what is the probability, correct to two decimal places, that the mean maximum daily temperature of this sample is between 18 °C and 22 °C?

10. Of all the computer chips produced by a certain factory 8% are defective. A sample of 324 is selected for inspection. What is the probability, correct to two decimal places, that the sample contains between 19 and 26 chips (19 and 26 included) that are defective?

11. To invest in the stock market or not? Based on past performance, a stock index has a mean annual return of 10·2% with a standard deviation of 21·3% on its stock listing on a particular date. What is the probability that the mean annual return over the next 40 years will exceed 13% based on previous performance, correct to two decimal places?

12. A bulb manufacturer claims its bulbs last an average of 800 hours with a standard deviation of 80 hours. If a sample of 50 bulbs were tested, what is the probability that the mean life of the bulbs in this sample would exceed 780 hours, correct to two decimal places?

22.2 Confidence intervals

A poll suggests that a political party has 37% support with a margin of error (ME) of 2%. This means that the actual (true) support is in the interval (35–39)%. This is an example of a confidence interval (CI).

Confidence intervals in statistics

What are they? A health organisation measures the cholesterol level of 50 adults in each of 100 different locations across the country. It discovers that in 95% of the samples, the mean cholesterol level is between 4·5 and 6·5. In the other 5% of the samples, it is outside the interval 4·5–6·5. The organisation reports that at the 95% confidence level, the mean adult cholesterol level is in the interval 4·5–6·5. This interval is known as a confidence interval and 95% is the corresponding confidence level.

A 95% confidence level is the success rate of the method that produces the confidence interval. The organisation is claiming that it is '95% confident' that the population mean adult cholesterol level is between 4·5 and 6·5.

KEY TERM

▲ A **confidence interval** is a range of values within which a true population value (mean or proportion) is likely to lie, subject to a given level of confidence.

Properties of confidence intervals

Any confidence level can be set by an experimenter and the corresponding confidence interval found or vice versa.

1. Most confidence intervals are quoted at the 95% confidence level because it is the area of the normal distribution curve between $-1\cdot96$ and $+1\cdot96$ standard deviations of the mean.

2. The confidence level can affect the confidence interval width:

   ▸ A health organisation reports that at the 95% confidence level, the mean adult cholesterol level is in the interval 4·5–6·5. In the small print of its findings, the health organisation reported that at the confidence level of 99%, the cholesterol level was in the interval of 4–8. This means in 99% of the samples, the cholesterol level was between 4 and 8.

TIP

▲ The **bigger** the confidence level, the wider the confidence interval and so the less precise the estimate of the true value of the population mean or proportion.

A **lower** confidence level gives a smaller confidence interval and so a more precise estimate of the true value of the population mean or proportion.

3. The sample size can affect the confidence interval width:

   Larger sample sizes mean more precise results for the true population values and so narrower confidence intervals.

   ▸ Two surveys on the mean height of university students in a country were carried out:

Survey **A** used 30 random samples each of 30 university students around the country. It reported the mean height of university students was in the interval (173–183) cm at a 95% confidence level.

Survey **B** used 30 samples each of 60 university students. It reported a mean height in the interval (175–181) cm at a 95% confidence level.

Confidence intervals for population proportions and population means

1. A population proportion (percentage) at 95% confidence level

Suppose you want to find the true proportion p of Irish adults that are in favour of giving the vote to 16-year-olds.

$$p = \frac{\text{Number of Irish adults that favour giving the vote to 16-year-olds}}{\text{Total number of Irish adults}}$$

The population is too big to survey in its entirety. So the true proportion p can be estimated by taking a simple random sample. The sample proportion $\hat{p}$ will be given by:

$$\hat{p} = \frac{\text{Number of Irish adults in the sample that favour giving the vote to 16-year-olds}}{\text{Size of the sample}}$$

For argument's sake, suppose the population proportion is 53% ($p = 0.53$). If a sample of 80 adults is randomly selected from the population and, of these, 48 adults favour giving the vote to 16-year-olds, then $\hat{p} = \dfrac{48}{80} = 0.6$.

Another random sample of 80 would be unlikely to get the same value for $\hat{p}$. Indeed, if 100 different samples of 80 people were selected, you would be unlikely to get the same value of $\hat{p}$ from all such samples.

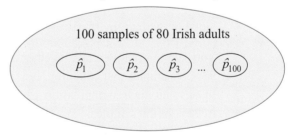

The central limit theorem for a sample proportion states that if you take lots of samples of the same size n from a population that contains a proportion p of successes, the frequency (sampling) distribution of the sample proportion $\hat{p}$ of successes is approximately normal with a mean of p and standard deviation of $\hat{\sigma} = \sqrt{\dfrac{p(1-p)}{n}}$ for $n \geq 30$.

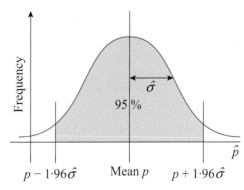

Because the sampling distribution is normal, 95% of the sample proportions are in the interval: $p - 1 \cdot 96 \hat{\sigma} \leftarrow \hat{p} \rightarrow p + 1 \cdot 96 \hat{\sigma}$.

This means p lies in the interval: $\hat{p} - 1 \cdot 96 \hat{\sigma} \leftarrow p \rightarrow \hat{p} + 1 \cdot 96 \hat{\sigma}$ (Can you show this?)

The interval of numbers between $\hat{p} - 1 \cdot 96 \hat{\sigma}$ and $\hat{p} + 1 \cdot 96 \hat{\sigma}$ is called a 95% confidence interval for p.

TIP

The confidence level of 95% means that in 95% of the samples the true population proportion p lies between $\hat{p} - 1 \cdot 96 \hat{\sigma}$ and $\hat{p} + 1 \cdot 96 \hat{\sigma}$, where $\hat{\sigma} = \sqrt{\dfrac{\hat{p}(1 - \hat{p})}{n}}$.

At a 95% confidence level, $\hat{p} - 1 \cdot 96 \hat{\sigma} \leftarrow p \rightarrow \hat{p} + 1 \cdot 96 \hat{\sigma}$ is the best estimate for p, where $\hat{p}$ is the sample proportion.

At a 95% confidence level, $\hat{p} - 1 \cdot 96 \hat{\sigma} \leftrightarrow \hat{p} + 1 \cdot 96 \hat{\sigma}$ is the best estimate for a population proportion p and is the 95% confidence interval for p, where $\hat{p}$ is the sample proportion and $\hat{\sigma} = \sqrt{\dfrac{\hat{p}(1 - \hat{p})}{n}}$.

As p is unknown in many cases, $\hat{\sigma} = \sqrt{\dfrac{\hat{p}(1 - \hat{p})}{n}}$ is taken as an approximation for $\hat{\sigma} = \sqrt{\dfrac{p(1 - p)}{n}}$.

KEY TERM

The margin of error (ME) for a population proportion is given by:

$$\text{ME} = 1 \cdot 96 \hat{\sigma} = 1 \cdot 96 \sqrt{\dfrac{\hat{p}(1 - \hat{p})}{n}}$$

The maximum value of $\hat{p}(1 - \hat{p}) = 0 \cdot 5 \times 0 \cdot 5 = 0 \cdot 25$. Therefore, the maximum value of the margin of error is $\dfrac{1 \cdot 96 \times \sqrt{0 \cdot 25}}{\sqrt{n}} = \dfrac{0 \cdot 98}{\sqrt{n}}$.

You cannot say for certain whether or not any single random sample is one of the 95% of samples that contain p, but you believe it does 95% of the time. This means that the true population p lies in the interval $\hat{p} - 1 \cdot 96 \hat{\sigma} \leftrightarrow \hat{p} + 1 \cdot 96 \hat{\sigma}$ in 95% of the samples.

EXAMPLE 5

In a simple random sample of 144 adult females in Ireland, 75 are single.

(a) Find the margin of error for this sample proportion.

(b) Construct a 95% confidence interval for the percentage of adult females in Ireland that are single.

Solution

$n = 144, \hat{p} = \dfrac{75}{144} = 0 \cdot 52$

(a) $\text{ME} = 1 \cdot 96 \times \text{SE} = 1 \cdot 96 \times \sqrt{\dfrac{\hat{p}(1 - \hat{p})}{n}}$

$= 1 \cdot 96 \times \sqrt{\dfrac{0 \cdot 52 \times 0 \cdot 48}{144}}$

$= 0 \cdot 082$

(b) Confidence interval: $\hat{p} - \text{ME} \leftrightarrow \hat{p} + \text{ME}$

$= 0 \cdot 52 - 0 \cdot 082 \leftrightarrow 0 \cdot 52 + 0 \cdot 082$

$= 0 \cdot 438 \leftrightarrow 0 \cdot 602$

$= 43 \cdot 8\% \leftrightarrow 60 \cdot 2\%$

TIP

As you increase the sample size n, the margin of error ME $= 1.96 \sqrt{\dfrac{\hat{p}(1 - \hat{p})}{n}}$ decreases. Hence, the width of the confidence interval decreases, giving a higher precision for the population proportion.

EXAMPLE 6

In a survey conducted by a student, the margin of error was $\pm 6\%$ at the 95% confidence level. What was the sample size if the sample proportion was 50%?

Solution

$\hat{p} = 50\% = 0.5$

$\text{ME} = 1.96 \sqrt{\dfrac{(0.5)(0.5)}{n}} = 0.06$

$\sqrt{\dfrac{0.25}{n}} = \dfrac{0.06}{1.96}$

$n = 267$

EXAMPLE 7

The margin of error for a sample of size 144 at the 95% confidence level in a survey was ± 0.0784. What was the sample proportion in this sample?

Solution

$n = 144$

$\text{ME} = 1.96 \sqrt{\dfrac{\hat{p}(1 - \hat{p})}{144}} = 0.0784$

$\dfrac{1.96 \sqrt{\hat{p}(1 - \hat{p})}}{12} = 0.0784$

$\sqrt{\hat{p}(1 - \hat{p})} = 0.48$

$\hat{p}(1 - \hat{p}) = 0.2304$

$\hat{p} - \hat{p}^2 = 0.2304$

$\hat{p}^2 - \hat{p} + 0.2304 = 0$

$\hat{p} = \dfrac{1 \pm \sqrt{1 - 4(0.2304)}}{2}$

$= \dfrac{1 \pm 0.28}{2}$

$= 0.64 \text{ or } 0.36$

TIP

When $\hat{p}$ is not given in a question on sample proportions, $\hat{p}$ is assigned the value 0.5. In this case, the margin of error is $\dfrac{0.98}{\sqrt{n}}$.

EXAMPLE 8

A researcher wishes to estimate with 95% confidence the proportion of students who own a car. She wishes to be accurate to within 10 percentage points of the true proportion. What is the minimum sample size required to carry out this analysis?

Solution

Margin of error $= 1.96 \sqrt{\dfrac{0.5 \times 0.5}{n}}$

$\text{ME} = \dfrac{0.98}{\sqrt{n}} = 0.1$

$\sqrt{n} = 9.8$

$n = 96.04$

The minimum sample is 97 people.

2. A population mean at 95% confidence level

The central limit theorem for a sample mean states that if you take lots of samples of the same size n from a population with mean μ and standard deviation σ the frequency (sampling) distribution of the sample means $\bar{x}$ is approximately normal with a mean μ and a standard deviation $\bar{\sigma} = \dfrac{\sigma}{\sqrt{n}}$ for $n \geq 30$.

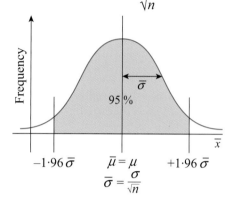

Because the sampling distribution is normal, 95% of the sample means are in the interval $\mu - 1{\cdot}96\,\bar{\sigma} \leftarrow \bar{x} \rightarrow \mu + 1{\cdot}96\,\bar{\sigma}$. This means that μ lies in the interval $\bar{x} - 1{\cdot}96\,\bar{\sigma} \leftarrow \mu \rightarrow \bar{x} + 1{\cdot}96\,\bar{\sigma}$. This is the central limit theorem for a population mean.

The interval of numbers between $\bar{x} - 1{\cdot}96 \times \dfrac{\sigma}{\sqrt{n}}$ and $x + 1{\cdot}96 \times \dfrac{\sigma}{\sqrt{n}}$ is called a 95% confidence interval for μ.

TIP

The confidence level of 95% means that in 95% of the samples the true population mean μ lies between $\bar{x} - 1{\cdot}96 \times \dfrac{\sigma}{\sqrt{n}}$ and $\bar{x} + 1{\cdot}96 \times \dfrac{\sigma}{\sqrt{n}}$.

This means that the true population mean μ lies in the interval $\bar{x} - 1{\cdot}96\,\bar{\sigma} \leftrightarrow \bar{x} + 1{\cdot}96\,\bar{\sigma}$ in 95% of samples.

At a 95% confidence level, $\bar{x} - 1{\cdot}96 \times \dfrac{\sigma}{\sqrt{n}} \leftarrow \mu \rightarrow \bar{x} + 1{\cdot}96 \times \dfrac{\sigma}{\sqrt{n}}$ is the best estimate for μ, where $\bar{x}$ is the mean of the sample and σ is the standard deviation of the population or the sample and is the 95% confidence interval for μ.

KEY TERM

The margin of error (ME) for a population mean is given by:

$$\text{ME} = 1{\cdot}96\,\bar{\sigma} = 1{\cdot}96 \times \dfrac{\sigma}{\sqrt{n}}$$

You cannot say for certain whether or not any single random sample is one of the 95% of samples that contain μ, but you believe it does 95% of the time. This means that the true population mean μ lies in the interval $\bar{x} - 1{\cdot}96\,\bar{\sigma} \leftrightarrow \bar{x} + 1{\cdot}96\,\bar{\sigma}$ in 95% of the samples.

EXAMPLE 9

A survey of the heights of Irish adult males was carried out. The mean height of the sample of size 100 was 1·76 m. If the standard deviation of the population height of Irish adult males is 12 cm, construct a 95% confidence interval for the height of these men.

Solution

$n = 100$

$\bar{x} = 1·76$

$\sigma = 0·12$

$\bar{\sigma} = \dfrac{\sigma}{\sqrt{n}} = \dfrac{0·12}{\sqrt{100}}$

$\phantom{\bar{\sigma}} = \dfrac{0·12}{10} = 0·012$

$ME = 1·96\bar{\sigma} = 0·0235$

Confidence interval:

$1·76 - 0·0235 \leftrightarrow 1·76 + 0·0235$

$= (1·74 \leftrightarrow 1·78)$ m

TIP

As you increase the sample size n, the margin of error $ME = 1·96 \times \dfrac{\sigma}{\sqrt{n}}$ decreases and so the width of the confidence interval decreases, giving a higher precision for the population mean.

EXAMPLE 10

A 95% confidence interval is to be constructed for the population mean from a single random sample of 225 with a standard deviation of 10.
If the sample mean is 20, find the confidence interval.

Solution

$n = 225$

$\sigma = 10$

$\bar{x} = 20$

Confidence interval:

$20 - 1·96 \times \dfrac{10}{\sqrt{225}} \leftrightarrow 20 + 1·96 \times \dfrac{10}{\sqrt{225}}$

$18·7 \leftrightarrow 21·3$

EXAMPLE 11

If the standard deviation of the monthly rent for an apartment in Dublin is €150, what is the size of the sample that would give a confidence interval of €880−€930 at the 95% confidence level?

Solution

$\bar{x} + 1·96 \times \dfrac{150}{\sqrt{n}} = 930 \dots \textbf{(1)}$

$\bar{x} - 1·96 \times \dfrac{150}{\sqrt{n}} = 880 \dots \textbf{(2)}$

$\textbf{(1)} - \textbf{(2)}: 1·96 \times \dfrac{300}{\sqrt{n}} = 50$

$n = \dfrac{(1·96 \times 300)^2}{50^2} = 138·3$

139 is the sample size.

EXERCISE 19

1. A survey is conducted on the support a certain political party has in the electorate. A simple random sample of 1212 voters was surveyed. In this survey, 253 people stated that they supported the party.

    (a) Is this a sample mean or a sample proportion question?

    (b) Find the sample proportion $\hat{p}$, correct to four decimal places.

    (c) Find the standard error, correct to four decimal places.

    (d) Construct a 95% confidence level to estimate the party's percentage support. Give your answer correct to one decimal place.

2. In a simple random sample of 1000 students at university, 200 favour a return to a non-semesterisation system. Construct a 95% confidence interval to estimate the percentage of students at university that favour a return to non-semesterisation. Give your answer correct to one decimal place.

3. In order to estimate the diameter of a variety of orange, a sample of 35 oranges was selected. The sample mean diameter was 7·3 cm and the standard deviation of the variety of orange was 1·6 cm. Find a 95% confidence interval for an estimate of the mean diameter of this variety of orange, correct to one decimal place.

4. In a randomly selected sample of 500 Irish people, they were asked if they thought the minimum wage should be raised or not. Of this sample, 336 said yes. Construct a 95% confidence interval to estimate the percentage of Irish people who believe the minimum wage should be raised. Give your answer correct to one decimal place.

5. In a television survey, 305 of the 400 people surveyed agreed that the Junior Certificate exam should be abolished. Find a 95% confidence interval for an estimate of the percentage of the population that believes the Junior Certificate exam should **not** be abolished. Give your answer correct to one decimal place.

6. The mean number of text messages sent by people over 15 years of age in a country per week is 125 with a standard deviation of 20. A sample of 300 texters over 15 years old is randomly chosen from the population.

    (a) Find the standard 'error' of $\bar{x}$ in the sample, correct to four decimal places.

    (b) About 95% of all such samples will capture the population mean in a certain interval. What is this interval? Give your answer correct to the nearest whole number.

7. One thousand people are randomly selected for a cheese-tasting of two cheeses A and B. If 60% indicate a preference for A, what can you conclude about the percentage of individuals in the population that preferred cheese B with 95% confidence?

8. A newspaper published the results of an opinion poll that showed 45% would vote for Fine Gael (FG) in an upcoming election. The following week a new poll showed 42% support for FG. The paper stated that this was a significant decline in support for FG. If a simple random sample of 1000 was surveyed for each poll, what is your opinion of the newspaper's view, assuming a 95% level of confidence, correct to the nearest percentage?

9. In a random sample of drink drivers, the 95% confidence interval for the proportion of drink drivers that was male was $0\cdot68 \leftrightarrow 0\cdot76$. Find:

    (a) the sample proportion that was male,

    (b) the standard error, correct to four decimal places,

    (c) the sample size.

10. The heights of students in a university are assumed to have a normal distribution with a standard deviation of 10·7 cm. If a 95% confidence interval is to be constructed for the population mean that is accurate to within 1·27 cm, what is the minimum sample size?

11. Show that if $\hat{p} - 1\cdot96\,\hat{\sigma} < p < \hat{p} + 1\cdot96\hat{\sigma}$, it can be deduced that $p - 1\cdot96\hat{\sigma} < \hat{p} < p + 1\cdot96\hat{\sigma}$.

22.3 Hypothesis testing

One day in class after a test, Jenny claims that 'girls are more intelligent than boys'. This claim is called a **hypothesis**. It is a statement about a parameter (mean or proportion) of a population. Rather than dismiss the claim as ridiculous, and to be scientific and objective, the teacher suggests that the class conducts a hypothesis test.

KEY TERM

A **statistical hypothesis** is a statement about a population that can be tested using data from one or more samples.

The statement that the mean or proportion of a population has a certain value based on evidence **from a sample** can be rejected or not. In the case above, the statement is about the IQ of boys and girls.

Setting up a hypothesis test (significance test)

The teacher then explains to the class how to go about setting up a significance test. There are two hypotheses in a significance test:

1. The null hypothesis (H_0)
2. The alternative hypothesis (H_1)

The null hypothesis (H_0)

This is the term used for any hypothesis that is set up primarily for the purpose of seeing whether or not it can be **rejected**. It is usually a statement of no difference, no change or no effect. The null hypothesis can be either:

(a) A stand-alone claim that is made without any reference to any existing situation or standard and stated as if it were true. It is regarded as the prevailing situation (status quo).

 ▸ An airline claims that it has 80% customer satisfaction. This is stated by the airline as if it is a fact and is regarded as the status quo by the airline.

or

(b) A statement of no change, no difference or no effect in an existing situation or standard (status quo).

 ▸ A car manufacturer claims that its new model has greater engine efficiency than its old model, which has an engine efficiency of 57%. The null hypothesis here is that the new engine has the same efficiency of 57% as the old engine. (It is not a more efficient engine than the old one.)

 ▸ For the IQ claim:

$$H_0: \begin{array}{c} \text{Average IQ} \\ \text{of girls} \end{array} \quad \mu_g = \mu_b \quad \begin{array}{c} \text{Average IQ} \\ \text{of boys} \end{array}$$

The null hypothesis assumes no difference between the IQs.

The alternative hypothesis (H_1)

The alternative hypothesis is the alternative to the null hypothesis. It is the hypothesis to be accepted when the null hypothesis is rejected. The alternative hypothesis is either:

(a) A statement that a stand-alone claim is not true.

▸ Be sceptical: 'I don't believe it.'

▸ The airline's customer satisfaction is not 80%.

(b) A claim about a population that there is a difference in an existing situation or standard.

▸ The efficiency of the engine of the new model is greater than 57%.

The burden of proof is always to show a stand-alone claim is not true or there is a difference in an existing situation or standard.

▸ For the IQ claim, the alternative hypothesis is:

$$H_1: \begin{array}{c} \text{Average IQ} \\ \text{of girls} \end{array} \quad \mu_g > \mu_b \quad \begin{array}{c} \text{Average IQ} \\ \text{of boys} \end{array}$$

Acceptance or rejection

Remember that it is always the null hypothesis that is under scrutiny by asserting an alternative to it. If you produce enough evidence in favour of the alternative hypothesis, then you reject the null hypothesis as being true. If you do not produce enough evidence in favour of the alternative hypothesis, then you simply do not have enough evidence to reject H_0.

For the IQ claim:

Reject H_0	Do not reject H_0
$H_0: \mu_b = \mu_g$	$H_0: \mu_b = \mu_g$
$H_1: \mu_g > \mu_b$	$H_1: \mu_g > \mu_b$
Reject H_0 in favour of H_1.	Do not reject H_0 in favour of H_1.
Girls are more intelligent than boys.	There is not sufficient evidence to conclude that girls are more intelligent than boys.

TIP

▲ If any variation from the null hypothesis is due to chance (sampling variability), the null hypothesis must not be rejected. If the variation is unlikely to have occurred by pure chance, the null hypothesis is rejected because it is fundamentally flawed.

EXAMPLE 12

A television station claims that at least 32% of the population tuned in to watch its blockbuster movie on Tuesday night. State the null and alternative hypotheses to test this hypothesis.

Solution

This is a stand-alone claim about a population proportion stated as if it were true.

$H_0: p \geq 0.32$

The proportion of the population that tuned in was $\geq 32\%$.

$H_1: p < 0.32$

The proportion of the population that tuned in was $< 32\%$.

This is a left-hand, one-tailed test as p is strictly less than 0.32. $p < 0.32$ in H_1.

EXAMPLE 13

A tyre company claims that its tyres are safe for an average of 70 000 km. State the null and alternative hypotheses to test this claim.

Solution

This is a stand-alone claim about a population mean stated as if it were true.

$H_0: \mu = 70\,000$

The mean safety distance of the tyres is 70 000 km.

$H_1: \mu \neq 70\,000$

The mean safety distance is not 70 000 km.

Note: This is a two-tailed hypothesis test because $H_1: \mu \neq 70\,000$ means that μ could be greater or less than 70 000 km.

EXAMPLE 14

A new cancer drug claims an 85% success rate. A researcher suspects that this is too high. State the null and alternative hypotheses to test this claim.

Solution

This is a stand-alone claim stated as if it were true.

$H_0: p = 0.85$

$H_1: p < 0.85$

EXAMPLE 15

A generic drug that has been used for years has an established, proven success rate of 62%. A new drug claims that it is more successful than the generic drug. State the null and alternative hypotheses for this claim.

Solution

This is a question of a claim of a change in an existing situation.

H_0: There is no difference between the new drug and the generic, $p = 0.62$.

The success rate of the new drug is 62%. It is no more successful.

H_1: The new drug is more successful than the generic, $p > 0.62$.

This is a right-hand, one-tailed test as p is greater than 0.62 in $H_1: p > 0.62$.

EXAMPLE 16

A TD suspects that the actual average yearly wage is different from the official national average of €35 800. She intends to carry out a significance test on a sample of her constituents to test if this is the case. State the null and alternative hypotheses for her test.

$H_0: \mu = €35\,800$

There is no difference between the average yearly wage and the official yearly wage.

$H_1: \mu \neq €35\,800$

There is a difference.

Solution

This is a claim about a difference from a standard population mean.

General points about the null (H_0) and alternative (H_1) hypotheses

1. H_0 must be written with the symbols $=, \leq, \geq$
2. H_1 must be written with symbols $\neq, >, <$
3. H_1 is the negation (opposite) of H_0.
4. H_1 is a statement that must be true if H_0 is false.

Types of hypothesis testing

A **hypothesis test** is a statistical method for testing the truth or otherwise of the null hypothesis.

We will consider two types of tests:

1. A margin of error test (confidence interval) for a population proportion.
2. A z-test for a population mean.

1. Conducting a hypothesis test for a population proportion using a confidence interval

Step 1: Establish the null hypothesis H_0 for the population proportion p.

Step 2: Establish the alternative hypothesis H_1 (opposite to H_0).

Step 3: Note the confidence (significance) level at which the test is to be carried out (95%).

Step 4: Using the data provided (SRS), find the sample proportion $\hat{p}$ in support of the alternative hypothesis and the standard error $\hat{\sigma} = \sqrt{\dfrac{\hat{p}(1-\hat{p})}{n}}$.

Step 5: Construct a confidence interval $\hat{p} - 1{\cdot}96\hat{\sigma} \leftrightarrow \hat{p} + 1{\cdot}96\hat{\sigma}$.

Step 6: Make a conclusion:

If p is **in** the confidence interval, H_0 cannot be rejected, as $\hat{p}$ has come from a population with proportion p in 95% of samples of size n.

If p is **not in** the interval, H_0 is rejected and H_1 is accepted, as $\hat{p}$ did not come from a population with proportion p in 95% of samples of size n. $\hat{p}$ must have come from a population with a different proportion.

TIP

A confidence level of 95% is often stated as a significance level of 5%.

EXAMPLE 17

A television company claimed that 50% of UK citizens believe the euro will fail. A newspaper carried out a survey to test this hypothesis. In the survey of 1200, 680 people said they thought the euro would fail. State the null and alternative hypotheses and conduct a significance test by finding the confidence interval at the 95% confidence level.

Solution

Step 1: $H_0: p = 0.5$ [Stand-alone claim]

Step 2: $H_1: p \neq 0.5$ [Opposite to H_0]

Step 3: Confidence level: 95%, $n = 1200$

Step 4: $\hat{p} = \dfrac{680}{1200} = 0.567$

$\hat{\sigma} = \sqrt{\dfrac{(0.567)(0.433)}{1200}} = 0.0143$

Step 5: Confidence interval: $\hat{p} - 1.96\,\hat{\sigma} \leftrightarrow \hat{p} + 1.96\,\hat{\sigma}$

$0.539 \leftrightarrow 0.595$

$\therefore 53.9\% \leftrightarrow 59.5\%$

Step 6: The true population proportion is in the interval $53.8\% \leftrightarrow 59.5\%$ in 95% of samples of size 1200. This is unlikely to have come from a population with proportion 50%. Therefore, reject H_0 and accept $H_1: p \neq 0.5$.

EXAMPLE 18

A researcher claims that 90% of people trust DNA testing. In a survey of 225 people, 200 said they trusted DNA testing. Test the researcher's claim at a 5% level of significance.

Solution

Step 1: $H_0: p = 0.9$ [Stand-alone claim]

Step 2: $H_1: p \neq 0.9$ [Opposite to H_1]

Step 3: Confidence level: 95%, $n = 225$

Step 4: $\hat{p} = \dfrac{200}{225} = 0.889$

$\hat{\sigma} = \sqrt{\dfrac{0.889 \times 0.111}{225}} = 0.021$

Step 5: Confidence interval: $\hat{p} - 1.96\hat{\sigma} \leftrightarrow \hat{p} + 1.96\hat{\sigma}$

$0.848 \leftrightarrow 0.93$

$\therefore 84.8\% \leftrightarrow 93\%$

Step 6: The true population proportion is in the interval $84.8\% \leftrightarrow 93\%$ in 95% of the samples of size 225. You cannot reject $H_0: p = 0.9$ because 90% lies in this interval.

EXAMPLE 19

A survey is carried out on 1000 randomly selected people with the result that 60% support the government. The following month, another survey of 1000 people was conducted and the results showed that 58% now support the government. Conduct a hypothesis test at the 95% confidence level to see if there is any evidence for a change in government support.

Solution

This is a comparison hypothesis test. The first month is the status quo.

Step 1: For the second month we assume nothing has changed.

H_0: Government support is 60%. $p = 0.6$

Step 2: $H_1: p \neq 0.6$

Step 3: Confidence level: 95%, $n = 1000$

Step 4: $\hat{p} = 0.58$

$\hat{\sigma} = \sqrt{\dfrac{0.58 \times 0.42}{1000}} = 0.0156$

Step 5: $\hat{p} - 1.96\hat{\sigma} \leftrightarrow \hat{p} + 1.96\hat{\sigma}$

$0.549 \leftrightarrow 0.61$

$\therefore 54.9\% \leftrightarrow 61\%$

Step 6: Since 60% is between 54.9% and 61%, there is no evidence for a change in government support.

2. Two-tailed z-test of significance for a population mean

The z-test is based on the test statistic $\bar{z} = \dfrac{\bar{x} - \mu}{\overline{\sigma}}$ that measures the distance between the measured sample mean $\bar{x}$ and the null hypothesis mean (population) μ in units of standard deviation $\overline{\sigma} = \dfrac{\sigma}{\sqrt{n}}$, where σ is the standard deviation of the population or sample, whichever value is given.

- The null hypothesis is not rejected if the sample (measured) mean $\bar{x}$ is close enough to the null hypothesis (population) mean μ.
- The level of **closeness** is determined by a value known as the level of significance α (set by the experimenter.)
- The null hypothesis is rejected if the sample (measured) mean $\bar{x}$ is **too far** from the null hypothesis (population) mean μ.
- The distance of the sample mean $\bar{x}$ from the null hypothesis μ (population mean) is measured in standard deviation units (the z-statistic) based on the hypothesis being true.
- Large values of $\bar{z}$ ($\bar{z} > 1 \cdot 96$, $\bar{z} < -1 \cdot 96$) at a 5% level of significance indicate the estimated sample mean is too far from the population mean to support the null hypothesis being true.

Level of significance

The level of significance of a hypothesis test is the border for deciding between the null and alternative hypotheses. A $0 \cdot 05$ level of significance is the same as a 95% confidence level.

A 95% confidence level z-test is a test based on the fact that any measured $\bar{x}$ which is less than $1 \cdot 96 \overline{\sigma}$ from the null hypothesis mean μ on the standard normal sampling distribution curve is likely to have occurred by sampling variability/error and not because the null hypothesis H_0 is wrong.

On the standard normal distribution curve, H_0 is not rejected for z-values between $-1 \cdot 96$ and $1 \cdot 96$.

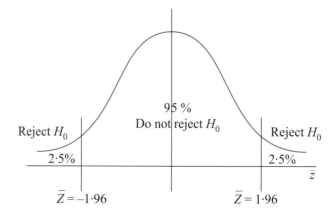

Notes

1. The $\bar{z}$-values that separate the non-rejection region from the rejection regions are known as critical values.

2. For a 5% level of significance, these critical values are $\overline{Z} = \pm 1 \cdot 96$.

3. For $-1.96 < \bar{z} < 1.96$, the null hypothesis is not rejected, corresponding to the central 0.95 of the area of the standard normal sampling distribution curve. This is because these values indicate that in 95% of samples the only difference between the sample mean and the population mean is due to pure chance.

4. For $\bar{z} < -1.96$ or $\bar{z} > 1.96$, the null hypothesis is rejected, corresponding to the area of 0.05 in the left and right tails of the standard normal sampling distribution curve. Values of $\bar{z} < -1.96$ or $\bar{z} > 1.96$ at a 5% level of significance indicate that the measured sample mean $\bar{x}$ is too far from μ to support the null hypothesis being true. The sample mean could not have come from a population with mean μ. So the null hypothesis is rejected. You believe your alternative hypothesis to be true.

p-values

Instead of comparing the $\bar{z}$-value with the critical values, you can get a specific probability p for $\bar{z}$. This p-value is the probability that the measured $\bar{x}$ is within 1.96 standard deviations of the null hypothesis mean on the normal sampling distribution curve.

Consider a $\bar{z}$-value in the two shaded regions shown on the standard normal distribution curve.

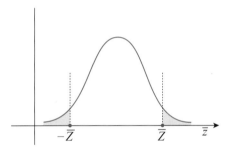

The probability p of a $\bar{z}$-value in either of these two regions is given by:

$$p = P(\bar{z} < -\overline{Z}) + P(\bar{z} > \overline{Z})$$

$$= 2P(\bar{z} > |\overline{Z}|)$$

$$= 2\{1 - P(\bar{z} < |\overline{Z}|)\}$$

For a 5% level of significance hypothesis test, the null hypothesis H_0 is rejected for $\bar{z}$-values in the shaded regions shown below.

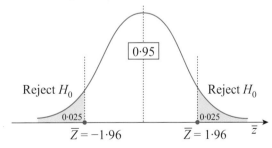

The biggest possible area of this rejection region is $0.025 + 0.025 = 0.05$.

This means that H_0 is rejected for values of $\bar{z}$ such that $p < 0.05$,

where $p = 2\{1 - P(\bar{z} < |\overline{Z}|)\}$.

> **TIP**
>
> If $p < 0.05$, the null hypothesis is rejected, but if $p \geq 0.05$, the null hypothesis is not rejected, where $p = 2\{1 - P(\bar{z} < |\overline{Z}|)\}$.

Notes

1. $p < 0.05$ means the probability of $\bar{x}$ coming from a sample of a population with mean μ (the null hypothesis mean) by pure chance is so small that it cannot be believed. It could not have come from a population with mean μ. It must have come from a population with a different mean. The null hypothesis mean is rejected.

2. If $\left|\bar{Z}\right| = 1.96$ in the formula $p = 2\{1 - P(\bar{z} < \left|\bar{Z}\right|)\}$, you get $p = 0.05$. Try it.

EXAMPLE 20

A population has a mean of 0. From a sample of 100, the p-value for a mean of $\bar{x} = 11$ is **(a)** 0·23 and **(b)** 0·04. Comment on these p-values at a 5% level of significance.

Solution

(a) This implies that a value of a mean as far from 0 as $\bar{x} = 11$ would happen in 23% of the samples of size 100 when the true mean is 0. This is not good evidence against rejecting the mean of the population as 0, because the level of rejection is set at less than 5%.

(b) This implies a value of a mean as far from 0 as $\bar{x} = 11$ would happen in only 4% of the samples of size 100 when the true mean is 0. This is good evidence that it is unlikely your sample mean came from a population whose mean is 0. It gives strong evidence against the null hypothesis.

> Large $\bar{z}$-values mean small p-values.
>
> Small $\bar{z}$-values mean large p-values.

Steps for conducting a two-tailed z-test for a population mean and finding the p-values

Step 1: Set up the null hypothesis H_0.

Step 2: Set up the alternative hypothesis H_1.

Step 3: State the following:

    (i) Significance level $\alpha = 0.05$

    (ii) Sample size $n \geq 30$

    (iii) Sample mean $\bar{x}$

    (iv) Population standard deviation or the sample standard deviation σ.

Step 4: Calculate the $\bar{z}$-value: $\bar{z} = \dfrac{\bar{x} - \mu}{\dfrac{\sigma}{\sqrt{n}}}$

Step 5: If $-1.96 < \bar{z} < 1.96$, do not reject H_0.

If $\bar{z} > 1.96$ or $\bar{z} < -1.96$, reject H_0.

Step 6: Find the p-value from the standard normal distribution table.

$p = 2\{1 - P(\bar{z} < \left|\bar{Z}\right|)\}$, where $\bar{Z}$ is the value in **step 4**.

If $p < 0.05$, reject H_0.

If $p \geq 0.05$, do not reject H_0.

ACTIVITY 27

ACTION
Understanding hypothesis testing

OBJECTIVE
To define the null hypothesis based on a claim and to learn how to test its truth

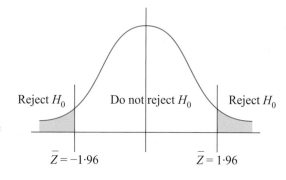

Reject H_0 Do not reject H_0 Reject H_0

$\bar{Z} = -1.96$ $\bar{Z} = 1.96$

EXAMPLE 21

A consumer watchdog suspects a shop is selling poor-quality Top bars. Genuine Top bars have a mean weight of 103 g with standard deviation of 3·2 g. The watchdog tests a sample of 36 bars from the shop and gets a mean weight of 101·5 g for the sample. Conduct a hypothesis test on this sample at a 5% significance level to see if the shop is selling genuine Top bars.

Solution

The idea of the test is to investigate whether or not the sample data is consistent with the population of Top bars. In other words, could this sample of 36 bars come from a population with a mean of 103 g and standard deviation of 3·2 g within the limits of sampling variability?

Step 1: Null hypothesis H_0: $\mu = 103$ g

Step 2: Alternative hypothesis H_1: $\mu \neq 103$ g

This is an example of a **two-tailed hypothesis** test because 'is not equal to 103 g' implies μ could be either **greater or less than** 103 g (two possibilities).

Step 3:

 (i) $\alpha = 0\cdot05$ is the significance level.

 (ii) $n = 36$ (>30)

 (iii) $\bar{x} = 101\cdot5$

 (iv) $\sigma = 3\cdot2$

Step 4: The central limit theorem states that $\bar{x}$ is $\bar{z}$ standard deviations μ in a sampling distribution with mean $\mu = 103$ g and standard deviation $\bar{\sigma} = \dfrac{\sigma}{\sqrt{n}}$,

where $\bar{z} = \dfrac{\bar{x} - \mu}{\bar{\sigma}} = \dfrac{101\cdot5 - 103}{\dfrac{3\cdot2}{\sqrt{36}}} = -2\cdot81$.

Step 5:

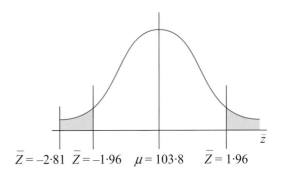

$\bar{Z} = -2\cdot81$ $\bar{Z} = -1\cdot96$ $\mu = 103\cdot8$ $\bar{Z} = 1\cdot96$

Because of the 95% confidence level, any $\bar{z}$ -value between $-1\cdot96$ and $+1\cdot96$ supports the null hypothesis.

As $\bar{z} = -2\cdot81 < -1\cdot96$, the null hypothesis is rejected.

Step 6: $p = 2(1 - P(\bar{z} < \left| -2\cdot81 \right|))$

$\quad\quad p = 2(1 - P(\bar{z} < 2\cdot81))$

$\quad\quad\quad = 2(1 - 0\cdot9975) = 0\cdot005 < 0\cdot05$

This means the probability of the sample mean coming from a sample from a population with a mean of 103 g is very small. It is very unlikely than it can be accounted for by sample variability (chance). So reject the null hypothesis; the Top bars are suspect.

EXAMPLE 22

Anna claims that the average rental income for a room in a city is €600 per month. The mean rent paid by a sample of 35 people was €620 per month with standard deviation of €50.

 (a) Calculate a 95% confidence interval for the mean monthly rent paid by all tenants in the city.

 (b) Is there evidence to support Anna's claim? Test this hypothesis using a 5% level of significance. Clearly state the null and alternative hypotheses and give your conclusion.

 (c) Give a p-value for this test and interpret this value.

Solution

(a) $\bar{x} = 620$, $\sigma = 50$, $n = 35$

Confidence interval:

$$620 - 1\cdot96 \times \frac{50}{\sqrt{35}} \leftrightarrow 620 + 1\cdot96 \times \frac{50}{\sqrt{35}}$$

$$= 603\cdot43 \leftrightarrow 636\cdot57$$

The mean monthly rent paid by all tenants in the city lies between €603·43 and €636·57 with 95% certainty. This range does not include €600.

(b) Step 1: $H_0: \mu = 600$

Step 2: $H_1: \mu \neq 600$

Step 3:

   (i)   Two-tailed test $\alpha = 0\cdot05$

   (ii) $n = 35$

   (iii) $\bar{x} = 620$

   (iv) $\sigma = 50$

Step 4: $\bar{z} = \dfrac{620 - 600}{\frac{50}{\sqrt{35}}} = 2\cdot37$

As $2\cdot37 > 1\cdot96$, reject H_0.

Therefore, Anna's claim is wrong.

(c) $p = 2\{1 - P(\bar{z} < 2\cdot37)\}$

$= 2\{1 - 0\cdot9911\}$

$= 0\cdot0178$

As $p < 0\cdot05$, reject H_0.

EXAMPLE 23

The mean hourly wage in a certain EU country is €11·50 with standard deviation of €3 per hour. A sample of 40 workers in a town called Alice has a mean hourly wage of €10·80.

(a) Calculate a 95% confidence interval for the mean hourly wage in Alice. Interpret this interval.

(b) Is there evidence to suggest that hourly wages for workers in Alice are different from the national hourly wage? Test this hypothesis using a 5% level of significance. State the null and alternative hypotheses clearly and give your conclusion. Give a p-value for this test and interpret this p-value.

Solution

(a) $\bar{x} = 10\cdot8$, $\sigma = 3$, $n = 40$

Confidence interval:

$$10\cdot8 - 1\cdot96 \times \frac{\sigma}{\sqrt{n}} \leftrightarrow 10\cdot8 + 1\cdot96 \times \frac{\sigma}{\sqrt{n}}$$

$$10\cdot8 - 1\cdot96 \times \frac{3}{\sqrt{40}} \leftrightarrow 10\cdot8 + 1\cdot96 \times \frac{3}{\sqrt{40}}$$

$$= 9\cdot87 \leftrightarrow 11\cdot73$$

The mean hourly wage of workers in Alice lies between €9·87 and €11·73 with 95% certainty. The range includes the hourly mean wage of the country.

(b) Step 1: $H_0: \mu = 11\cdot5$

Step 2: $H_1: \mu \neq 11\cdot5$

Step 3:

   (i)   Two-tailed test $\alpha = 0\cdot05$

   (ii) $n = 40$

   (iii) $\bar{x} = 10\cdot8$

   (iv) $\sigma = 3$

Step 4: $\bar{z} = \dfrac{10\cdot8 - 11\cdot50}{\frac{3}{\sqrt{40}}} = -1\cdot48$

$\bar{z} = -1\cdot48 > -1\cdot96 \Rightarrow$ Do not reject H_0.

Therefore, the mean hourly wage for workers in Alice is the same as the rest of the country.

$p = 2\{1 - P(\bar{z} < 1\cdot48)\}$

$p = 2\{1 - 0\cdot9306\}$

$= 0\cdot1388$

As $p \geq 0\cdot05$, do not reject H_0.

EXERCISE 20

1. Write down H_0 and H_1 for the following problems and state whether the test is a one-tailed (left or right) or two-tailed test:

   (a) A company makes bulbs with a mean lifetime of 600 hours. A retailer suspects that her supplier is not supplying her with these bulbs and wants to carry out a significance test.

   (b) The mean score of an adult in a psychological test is 5·2. A research student suspects that retired adult men score higher than adult men in general and he carries out a significance test.

   (c) A supermarket states in its literature that 78% of its customers are satisfied with its services. A rival carries out a significance test of this claim.

   (d) A broadband provider claims average download speeds of 20 MB per second or more. A consumer does not believe it and suspects that the broadband speeds are slower.

   (e) Spain claims a higher survival rate than all other EU countries for a particular type of cancer. The survival rate in the other EU countries is 82%. A hypothesis test is carried out to test this claim.

2. A book publisher believes that its new Geography book will capture 80% of the market. In a market survey of 120 people, 80 said they would use the book. Conduct a hypothesis test at the 95% confidence level to test the publisher's claim.

3. Your teacher read in a newspaper that 60% of sixth-years students buy fizzy drinks. You conducted a survey of 122 students in sixth year and 78 said they buy fizzy drinks. Conduct a hypothesis test at the 95% confidence level to test this claim made in the newspaper using your data.

4. A political party believes its support has changed from 40%. It conducts a survey of 500 people and finds that 216 say they support the party. Conduct a hypothesis test at the 95% confidence level to test its suspicion.

5. Coillte believes that 10% of the pine tree population in Ireland are infested by a particular species of beetle. It samples 1200 trees and finds that 127 are infected. Conduct a hypothesis test at the 95% hypothesis level on the Coillte claim.

6. The percentage of properties in negative equity in Ireland in 2010 was 31%. The Economic and Social Research Institute (ESRI) conducted a survey in 2013 to see whether or not this had changed. It found that in a sample of 300 properties, 85 were in negative equity. Conduct a hypothesis test at the 95% confidence level to test if there is a change.

7. In a certain year, 7% of job applicants who were tested for drugs failed. Five years later, the same test was conducted on a sample of 1650 job applicants. There were 68 failures. Conduct a 95% confidence level hypothesis test to see if the failure rate had changed.

8. It is claimed that 50% of first-time brides are younger than their husbands. A test is conducted at the 5% significance level on a simple random sample of 125. Of this sample, 61 said that they were younger than their husbands. What can you conclude?

9. An established drug A has a 57% success rate. For another drug B, a pharmaceutical company claims that its new drug is more successful than the established one. In a clinical trial of 500 patients, the results showed that drug B was successful in 320 cases. Use a hypothesis test at the 5% significance level to decide if there is sufficient evidence to justify the company's claim.

10. A newspaper claims that 32% of Irish second-level students are 180 cm or taller. In a survey of 200 students, 38 are 180 cm or taller. Is there sufficient evidence to reject the claim at the 5% significance level?

11. A pharmaceutical company claims that its new gel relieves backache 75% of the time. A consumer agency investigates this claim by getting 100 backache sufferers to try the new gel. Sixty-eight of them say that it works. Use a hypothesis test to examine the company's claim at the 5% significance level.

12. A random sample of $n = 100$ observations is drawn from a population. The sample mean is 120, while 60 is the sample standard deviation. Test at a significance level of $\alpha = 0.05$; $H_0: \mu = 110$; $H_1: \mu \neq 110$. State if the test is two-tailed or not. Find the p-value for this hypothesis test and state what it means.

13. It was reported that a certain population had a mean of 26. To test this claim, a random sample of size 100 was selected. The computed sample mean and standard deviation were 24 and 8, respectively. At the 0.05 level of significance, test the validity of the reported mean.

14. The mean systolic blood pressure for males over 60 is 130 mm Hg with standard deviation of 15 mm Hg. A sample of 80 retired males over 60 was selected. Their mean blood pressure was 127 mm Hg. Carry out a hypothesis test using a significance level of 5% to see if there is evidence to suggest that the mean systolic blood pressure of retirees over 60 is different from the population average by finding the p-value.

15. A company that makes tyres for tractors claims that the mean life of their tyres is 17 500 km with standard deviation of 880 km. A consumer watchdog wants to investigate the company's claim. A test on a random sample of 35 tyres gives a mean life of 16 000 km. Carry out a hypothesis test using a 5% level of significance to see whether or not there is evidence to support the company's claim by finding the z-statistic.

16. The mean weight of king penguins in an Antarctic colony in 2013 was 15·5 kg. In a sample of 36 penguins in the same colony in 2014, the mean weight was 14·8 kg. Assuming the population standard deviation is 2·4 kg, test if the mean weight has changed at a 0·05 significance level by finding the p-value.

17. A doctor in one Irish county suspects that the mean level of cholesterol of children in that county differs from the national mean. In 2013, the national mean cholesterol level was 6 with a standard deviation of 1·5. In that year, she found the mean of a sample of 100 children was 5·8. Test her hypothesis at the 5% level of significance by calculating the p-value of her sample.

REVISION QUESTIONS

1. The table below shows the measurements of the arm spans x and the heights y in cm of 20 sixth-year students.

x (cm)	y (cm)
166	165
173	172
153	159
98	96
154	149
178	173
180	180
169	164
129	131
174	172
135	128
101	107
162	164
165	163
182	174
153	160
141	142
128	124
135	137
163	161

(a) Find $\bar{x}$, the mean arm span of the sample, and $\bar{y}$, the mean height of the sample using your calculator.

(b) Find σ_x and σ_y, the standard deviations of the arm spans and the heights using your calculator.

(c) Draw the scatter plot of y against x.

(d) Calculate the correlation coefficient r and comment on its value using your calculator.

(e) Use your calculator to find the equation of the line of best fit in the form $y = A + Bx$.

(f) Show $(\bar{x}, \bar{y})$ is on the line of best fit.

(g) Plot the line of best fit with $(\bar{x}, \bar{y})$ as one of the points on the line.

(h) Use the equation of the line of best fit to find y, when $x = 110$, correct to one decimal place.

2. (a) Illustrate the empirical rule by giving the percentages of the shaded areas in the normal distribution curves shown.

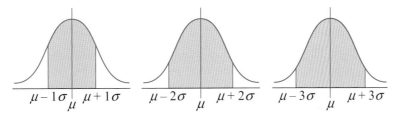

(b) In a school, the ages of all new teachers employed over the last 10 years were normally distributed. 95.46% of the ages centred about the mean were between 23.4 and 37.8 years. Find the mean age and the standard deviation of teachers employed over the past 10 years, correct to one decimal place.

(c) What is the median age of this group?

(d) (i) What is the 75th percentile of this group, correct to the nearest year?

(ii) What is the 25th percentile age of this group, correct to the nearest year?

(iii) What is the interquartile range, correct to the nearest year?

(e) What percentage, correct to the nearest percentage, of this group was:

(i) over 35 years of age,

(ii) between 25 and 35 years old?

3. (a) Explain the following terms:

  (i) Confidence level

  (ii) Confidence interval

 (b) A manufacturer claims that 75% of all their chocolate bars have a weight equal to 100 g. In a sample of 100 bars, 62 have a weight of 100 g. Conduct a hypothesis test at the 95% confidence level to test the manufacturer's claim.

 (c) An airline claims that a mean turnaround time on one of their routes is 25 minutes. A travel consumer watchdog conducts a survey of 50 flights on this route and finds a mean turnaround time of 28 minutes with a standard deviation of 5 minutes. Conduct a hypothesis test at the 95% confidence level to test the airline's claim.

4. (a) State the central limit theorem:

  (i) for the sampling distribution of means of random samples of size $n \geq 30$ selected from a population of mean μ and standard deviation σ,

  (ii) for the sampling distribution of proportions of random samples of size $n \geq 30$ selected from a population with proportion p.

 (b) A population has a mean of 48 and standard deviation of 6. Simple random samples of size 40 are selected from this population.

  (i) What is the mean of the sampling distribution?

  (ii) What is the standard deviation of the sampling distribution?

 (c) The proportion of people that eat fast food more than once a week is 32%.

  (i) If simple random samples of size 100 are selected from the population, what is the mean and standard deviation, correct to four decimal places, of the sampling distribution?

  (ii) In a sample of 100, what is the probability that more than 40 eat fast food more than once a week?

5. (a) Explain what is meant by a simple random sample. Give an example to illustrate your answer and give an example of a sample that is not random.

 (b) A random sample of 980 voters was interviewed. Of that sample, 585 said that they approved of means testing for child benefit. Construct a 95% confidence interval for the true percentage population of voters that approves of a means test for child benefit. Give your answer correct to the nearest percentage.

 (c) A school wants to know how much its 16-year-old students know about EU institutions. A standard EU-wide test given to 16-year-old EU students gave a mean score of 50%. A random sample of 80 16-year-olds in the school gave a mean of 54% with standard deviation of 6%. Construct a 95% confidence interval and use it to test the claim that the school's 16-year-old students are better informed about EU institutions than the average 16-year-old EU student.

6. A supermarket sells bags of potatoes in 2·5 kg, 5 kg and 10 kg bags. The actual weight of potatoes in a 2·5 kg bag can be modelled by a normal distribution with a mean of 2·7 kg and standard deviation of 0·16 kg.

 (a) Find the probability that a 2·5 kg bag weighs:

  (i) less than 2·8 kg, correct to two decimal places,

  (ii) more than 2·5 kg, correct to two decimal places.

 (b) The actual weight x of potatoes in a 5 kg bag may be modelled by a normal distribution with a mean of 5·2 kg and standard deviation of 0·25 kg.

  (i) Find $P(5\cdot1 < x < 5\cdot3)$, correct to two decimal places.

  (ii) Find the probability, correct to two decimal places, that if a random sample of four 5 kg bags is selected that none have a weight between 5·1 kg and 5·3 kg.

7. In a Midlands town there is a boys' secondary school and a girls' secondary school. The boys' school has six transition year (TY) classes with 20 students in each class. The girls' school has four TY classes, with 20 students in each class. In fifth year in the girls' school, three TY students, Eva, Margaret and Isolde, decide to conduct a survey of 50 TY students in the town on their attitude towards TY by giving the year a rating out of 1–5, where 5 is excellent.

(i) Eva decides to get the names of all 200 TY students in both schools from the school secretaries, put them into a hat, and draw out 50 names to survey.

(ii) Margaret puts the 10 TY classes into a hat and labels them B1, B2, B3, B4, B5, B6, G1, G2, G3 and G4. She picks out five classes from the hat and then randomly selects 10 from each class list by lottery.

(iii) Isolde decides to select a number of students randomly from the boys' school and a number from the girls' school in proportion to the number of girls and boys in both schools.

(a) What type of sampling is conducted in each case?

(b) How many boys and how many girls did Isolde interview?

(c) Give one advantage and one disadvantage of each sampling method.

(d) Which sample do you think is the most representative sample?

(e) If 40 students in Eva's sample gave TY a score of 5, at a 95% confidence level, give an estimate of a range for the percentage of the country's TY students that would give TY a 5, correct to the nearest percentage.

8. The distribution of the minimum pressures (in millibars) of all recorded hurricanes since records began is shown as follows:

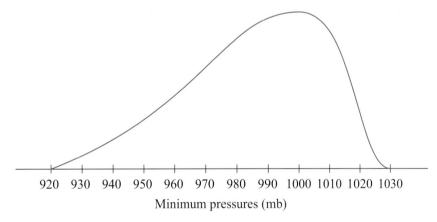

Minimum pressures (mb)

Mean minimum pressure = 985 mb

Standard deviation = 40 mb

Median minimum pressure = 1000 mb

Lower quartile = 957 mb

Upper quartile = 1012 mb

(a) What shape is this distribution? Mark the positions of the mode, mean and median on the graph.

(b) What is the probability that a hurricane had a minimum pressure greater than 957 mb?

(c) In a computer simulation, many random samples of 100 hurricanes are repeatedly selected from this population and the sample mean minimum pressures are recorded for each sample.

    (i) Describe the expected shape of the distribution of the sample means.

    (ii) What is the standard deviation of this distribution?

    (iii) What percentage, correct to the nearest percentage, of the samples has mean minimum pressures greater than 990 mb?

SUMMARY

Statistics

1. Organising data:

   (a) Tally frequency tables

   (b) Grouped frequency tables

   (c) Stem-and-leaf plots

2. Types of graphs:

   (a) (i) Pie **(ii)** Line **(iii)** Bar **(iv)** Trend

   (b) Histograms:

   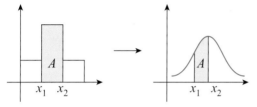

   A = area = frequency of data between x_1 and x_2

3. Central tendency:

   (a) Mode = the most frequent value

   (b) Mean = the average of a set of numbers

   Formulae for mean:

   (i) List:

   $$\mu = \frac{\sum x}{N}$$

   where x is a data value and N is the number of data values.

   (ii) Frequency or grouped frequency distribution:

   $$\mu = \frac{\sum fx}{\sum f}$$

   where x is a data value for a frequency distribution or x is the mid-interval value for a grouped frequency distribution.

   (c) Median = the numerical value in the middle of a set of data when arranged in order of increasing value

   (i) Odd number n of data values in increasing size:

   Median = value of $\left(\frac{n+1}{2}\right)^{\text{th}}$ result

   (ii) Even number n of data values in increasing size:

   Median = average of $\left(\frac{n}{2}\right)^{\text{th}}$ and results $\left(\frac{n}{2}+1\right)^{\text{th}}$

   (d) Shapes of frequency distributions:

   (i) Symmetrical distribution:

   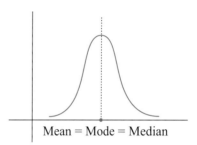

   Mean = Mode = Median

   (ii) Positively skewed distribution:

   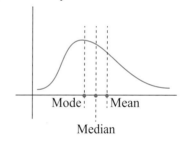

   Mode Mean
   Median

   (iii) Negatively skewed distribution:

   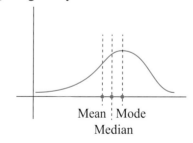

   Mean Mode
   Median

   (e) Scatter plots:

   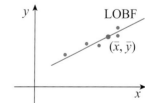

(i) Line of best fit (LOBF):

  I. Equation of LOBF: $y = A + Bx$ where A, B are found using a calculator.

  II. $(\bar{x}, \bar{y})$ is on the LOBF.

(ii) Correlation coefficient r from calculator:

- Strong positive correlation: $0\cdot7 < r < 1$

- Moderate positive correlation: $0\cdot4 < r < 0\cdot7$

- Weak positive correlation: $0 < r < 0\cdot4$

- Strong negative correlation: $-1 < r < -0\cdot7$

- Moderate negative correlation: $-0\cdot7 < r < -0\cdot4$

- Weak negative correlation: $-0\cdot4 < r < 0$

4. Spread:

  (a) Range = upper extreme (UE) – lower extreme (LE)

  (b) Interquartile range (IQR):

  $$IQR = UQ - LQ$$

  UQ = median of the upper half of data values greater than the median

  LQ = median of the lower half of data values less than the median

  (c) Standard deviation (σ):

  (i) List: $\sigma = \sqrt{\dfrac{\Sigma d^2}{N}}$

  (ii) Frequency distribution or grouped frequency distribution:

  $$\sigma = \sqrt{\dfrac{\Sigma fd^2}{\Sigma f}}, \; d = (\text{data value } x - \text{mean } \mu)$$

5. Normal distribution:

(i) Bell curve:

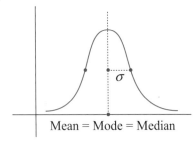

Mean = Mode = Median

50% of total area | 50% of total area

Mean μ

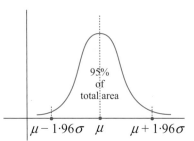

95% of total area

$\mu - 1\cdot96\sigma$ μ $\mu + 1\cdot96\sigma$

(ii) Empirical rule: 68–95–99·7:

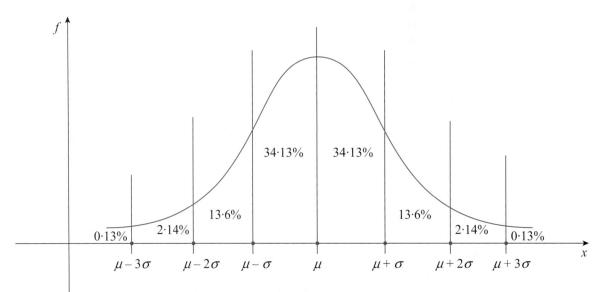

6. Position:

(a) Percentiles:

The pth percentile is the data value with $p\%$ of the data values less than or equal to it.

(b) z-scores: $z = \dfrac{x - \mu}{\sigma}$ for standard normal distribution

---

7. Inferential statistics:

(a) 95% confidence intervals:

  (i) Population proportion p:

$$\hat{p} - 1 \cdot 96\hat{\sigma} \leftarrow p \rightarrow \hat{p} + 1 \cdot 96\hat{\sigma}$$

where $\hat{\sigma} = \sqrt{\dfrac{\hat{p}(1 - \hat{p})}{n}}$ or $\sqrt{\dfrac{p(1 - p)}{n}}$

  (ii) Population mean μ:

$$\bar{x} - 1 \cdot 96 \,\frac{\sigma}{\sqrt{n}} \leftarrow \mu \rightarrow \bar{x} + 1 \cdot 96 \,\frac{\sigma}{\sqrt{n}}$$

where σ is the standard deviation of the population or the sample.

(b) Hypotheses:

  (i) Null hypothesis H_0:

A stand-alone claim stated to be true.

or

A statement of no change or difference in an established situation or standard.

  (ii) Alternative hypothesis H_1:

The opposite of the null hypothesis.

(c) Hypothesis testing:

  (i) Population proportion using a 95% confidence interval:

$$\hat{p} - 1 \cdot 96\hat{\sigma} \leftarrow p \rightarrow \hat{p} + 1 \cdot 96\hat{\sigma}$$

Conclusion:

- Do not reject H_0 if p is inside this interval.

- Reject H_0 if p is not inside this interval.

  (ii) Population mean at 5% level of significance:

Calculate $\bar{z} = \dfrac{\bar{x} - \mu}{\sigma}$, where

$\bar{\sigma} = \dfrac{\sigma}{\sqrt{n}}$ is the standard deviation of the population or the sample, and then

$p = 2\{1 - P(z < |\bar{Z}|)\}$, if required.

Conclusion:

- Do not reject H_0 if $-1 \cdot 96 < \bar{z} < 1 \cdot 96$ or $p \geq 0 \cdot 05$.

- Reject H_0 if $\bar{z} < -1 \cdot 96$ or $\bar{z} > 1 \cdot 96$ or $p < 0 \cdot 05$.

Answers

Section 1

Chapter 1

Exercise 1

1. (a) $x = 30°$, $y = 150°$, $z = 130°$ (b) $x = 70°$, $y = 40°$, $z = 70°$ (c) $x = 46°$, $y = 70°$, $z = 64°$ **2.** (a) No. $75° \neq 82°$. Alternate angles not equal. (b) Yes. Corresponding angles are equal. (c) $G \Rightarrow F$ (d) F true implies G true (e) $F \Leftrightarrow G$ (f) Equivalent **3.** (a) $x = 59°$, $y = 11°$ **5.** (a) $x = 2\sqrt{10}$, $y = 2\sqrt{19}$ (b) $x = 4$ **6.** (a) $r = 2\sqrt{2}$ cm (b) $4 \cdot 2$ m^2 (c) $h = 2 \cdot 35$ m (d) $d = 2049$ km (e) $|AC| = 5$ km, Total time $= 1\frac{1}{4}$ hours (f) (i) $l = 135 \cdot 88$ m (ii) $d = 148 \cdot 5$ m **7.** (b) $|\angle BCP| = 45°$ (d) $|AC| = 225$ m (e) $223 \cdot 6$ km **8.** (a) $x = 15°$, $y = 20°$

Chapter 2

Exercise 2

1. $[AB]$ because it is opposite the bigger angle.

2. z because $|\angle BAC|$ is the smallest angle in $\triangle ABC$ and $z = 180 - |\angle BAC|$, making it the biggest exterior angle.

3. (a) (i) $|\angle ADB| = 80°$ (ii) $|\angle BAD| = 80°$ (iii) $|\angle ABD| = 20°$ (iv) $|\angle DAC| = 50°$ (v) $|\angle BAC| = 130°$; $[BC]$ because it is opposite the biggest angle $\angle BAC$; $[AC]$ because it is opposite the smallest angle $\angle ABC$. (b) (i) $34 \cdot 7$ m (ii) $\angle CAB$ (iii) $\angle ABC$ **4.** (a) $|\angle ABD| = 75°$ (b) $|\angle ADB| = 75°$ (c) $|\angle BDC| = 105°$ (d) $|\angle BCD| = 60°$; $[AC]$ because it is opposite the biggest angle $\angle ABC$ of size $90°$.

Exercise 3

1. (a) Yes (b) Yes (c) No, $|AB| + |AC| = |BC|$ (d) No, $|AB| + |AC| < |BC|$ (e) Yes **2.** $|AC| = 5$

3. Because $|AB| + |BC| = 6$ cm $< |AC| = 8$ cm

4. (a) $x + 8 > 12 \Rightarrow x > 4$ (b) $x + 12 > 8 \Rightarrow x > -4$ (c) $x < 20$; $4 < x < 20$; $x \in \{5, 6, 7, 8, 9, 10, 11, 12, 13, 14, 15, 16, 17, 18, 19\}$ **5.** 71 m

Exercise 4

1. $|BC| = 3$, $|EF| = 4$ **2.** (a) $|BC| = 2 \cdot 5$ cm (b) Not equally spaced **3.** 125 m **4.** (a) $|AC| = 4$ (b) $|AE| = 2$ (c) $|DE| = 1 \cdot 5$ (d) $1 \cdot 5$ (e) 6 (f) 4 **5.** $28 \cdot 23$ m **6.** (a) $|FG| = 4$ (b) $|GH| = 4$ (c) $\frac{1}{2}$ (d) $\frac{1}{2}$ **8.** $\frac{4}{3}$

Exercise 5

1. (a) $x = 4 \cdot 5$ (b) $x = 2 \cdot 5$ (c) $x = 2 \cdot 4$ (d) $x = 10 \cdot 5$ (e) $x = 6 \cdot 4$ (f) $x = 21$ **2.** (a) $x = 6$, $|\angle ABC| = 90°$, $\frac{4}{9}$ (b) $x = 5$, $y = 7 \cdot 5$ (c) $x = 3$ (d) $x = \frac{2}{3}$, $y = \frac{5}{3}$ **3.** (i) 10 cm (ii) $7 \cdot 5$ cm (iii) $\frac{4}{5}$ **5.** (b) 3 cm

Exercise 6

1. (a) $x = 8$, $y = 12$ (b) $x = 3$, $y = 6$ (c) $x = 6$, $y = 4 \cdot 5$ (d) $x = \frac{8}{3}$, $y = \frac{4\sqrt{13}}{3}$ **2.** (a) $x = 9 \cdot 6$, $y = 2 \cdot 4$ (b) $x = 4 \cdot 5$, $y = 9$ (c) $x = \frac{8}{3}$, $y = 2 \cdot 4$ **3.** (a) $x = 7 \cdot 2$ (b) $x = 12$, $y = 13 \cdot 5$ **4.** (a) $x = 9$, $y = 18$ (b) $x = \frac{19}{4}$ (c) $x = \frac{2}{3}$ **5.** $|DC| = 9$ **6.** $x = 6 \cdot 25$, $y = 9$ **7.** $|BC| = 9$, $|AD| = 2\sqrt{5}$ **8.** 296 m **9.** $h = 2 \cdot 7$ m **10.** $14 \cdot 7$ m **11.** $187 \cdot 5$ m **12.** $h = 40dl$, 20 cm **13.** 142 m **14.** $4 \cdot 1$ m **15.** (a) $1 \cdot 6$ m (b) $4 \cdot 8$ m **17.** (b) $\frac{2}{3}$

Exercise 7

1. (a) 27 (b) $21 \cdot 6$ **2.** (a) Area $\triangle ABC = 150$; Area $\triangle DEF = 37 \cdot 5$ (b) Area $\triangle ABC = 18$; Area $\triangle ACD = 30$ (c) Area $\triangle ABC =$ Area $\triangle BCD =$ Area $\triangle CDE = 75$ **3.** (a) $x = 5$ (b) $x = 11 \cdot 2$ (c) $h = 6$ **4.** (a) 315 m^2 **5.** (a) 48 (b) 50 **6.** 20 **7.** (a) $x = 22$ (b) $x = 6$, $h = 23$ **8.** (a) Area $\triangle AFD = 18$ (b) Area $\triangle FDC = 6$ **9.** $x = 6$ **10.** (a) $h = 4$ (b) $x = 7$ (c) Area $= 40$ **11.** $8\sqrt{3}$

Chapter 3

Exercise 8

1. (a) $x = 92°$ (b) $x = 41°$ (c) $x = 77°$ (d) $x = 260°$, $y = 100°$ (e) $x = 26°$ (f) $x = 50°$, $y = 60°$ (g) $x = 55°$ (h) $x = 58°$ (i) $x = 45°$ (j) $x = 80°$, $y = 40°$ **2.** (a) $x = 90°$, $y = 58°$ (b) $x = y = 41°$; $w = z = 49°$ (c) $x = 30°$ (d) $x = 37°$, $y = z = w = 53°$ (e) $x = 80°$, $y = 50°$, $z = 40°$ (f) $x = 54°$, $y = 54°$, $z = 90°$ (g) $x = 8$ (h) $x = 1$, $y = 1 \cdot 3$ (i) $x = 30°$ (j) $x = 60°$ **3.** (a) $x = 110°$, $y = 80°$ (b) $x = 35°$, $y = 145°$ (c) $x = y = z = 43°$ (d) $x = 72°$, $y = 36°$ (e) $x = 64°$ (f) $x = 70°$, $y = 35°$, $z = 140°$ (g) $x = 105°$ (h) $x = 108°$, $y = 80°$ (i) $x = 67°$ (j) $x = 30°$, $y = 40°$ **4.** (a) (i) $x = 180° - y$; (ii) $z = 180° - y$; $z = x$ (b) (i) $x = 90° - y$ (ii) $z = y$ (c) It is a diameter

Exercise 9

1. (a) $x = 52°$ (b) $x = 45°$ (c) $x = 124°$ (d) $x = 58°$
(e) $x = 34°$ (f) $x = 52°$ (g) $x = 30°, y = 28°$ (h) $x = 79°$
2. 8 **4.** 6 cm, 3 cm **5.** 4 cm, 9 cm **6.** 4 m, 9 m

Exercise 10

1. 17 **2.** 7 **3.** (a) 7 cm (b) 25 cm **4.** 9 cm **5.** (a) 4 cm
(b) 4 cm (c) $2\sqrt{5}$ cm (d) $2\sqrt{5}$ cm; Yes, AB is a chord and
$|BO| = 2\sqrt{5} = r$ **6.** Yes, because C_1D and C_2D are both
perpendicular to $[AB]$, i.e. centres of s_1 and s_2 are both on
perpendicular bisector of $[AB]$. **8.** (a) 13 (b) 5 (c) 12
(d) 25; $k = 5$ **9.** (a) 8 (b) 48 (c) 20 **11.** (b) 30°

Chapter 4

Exercise 11

2. (a) Altitudes (b) The orthocentre **3.** $|\angle BAD| = 75°$
4. (d) 4 cm **5.** (a) 30° (b) 120° (c) 35° (d) 110° (e) 130°
(f) 25° (g) 25° **6.** (a) 12 (b) 24 (c) 18; $6\sqrt{13}$ **8.** (c) 1·5 cm
9. $|\angle AOB| = 90°$ **11.** (a) 5 (b) 6 (c) 1 **12.** 2
14. (c) $|\angle POQ| = 60°$ (d) $9\sqrt{3}$ cm²; $(6\pi - 9\sqrt{3})$ cm²
15. (c) $|CG| = 4$ cm; $|GD| = 2$ cm

Exercise 12

4. (a) 12 cm (b) 6 cm; yes, because $|FE| = |AB| \times 2 \times \frac{1}{2} = |AB|$.
6. (b) (i) $k = 2\cdot5$ (ii) 5 cm; $|A'B'| = 12\cdot5$ cm (c) 90°; 6 cm²;
37·5 cm² **7.** (c) 100 cm²; 75 cm² **8.** (b) $k = 3$
(c) $|AD| = 1$ cm, $|B'C'| = 9$ cm **9.** (a) O (b) $k = 3$
(c) $|DE| = 7\cdot5$ cm (d) 800% **10.** (a) $k = 1\cdot5$ (c) $|BC'| = \frac{10}{3}$
11. (a) $k = 2$ (c) Area $\triangle ABC = 21$ (d) $|AB| = 5\cdot25$
12. (c) 6·25 (d) $k = 4\cdot5$ **13.** 11 mm **14.** $k = \frac{4}{3}, x = \frac{16}{3}$ cm
15. $k = 2, x = 8$ cm **16.** (a) $k = \frac{5}{3}$ (b) $|OB| = 35\sqrt{2}$ cm;
$|OF| = 21\sqrt{2}$ cm **17.** (a) $k = 2$ (b) $|AC| = 3$ (c) $|DE| = 10$
(d) $|DF| = 6$ (e) $x = 5$ **18.** (a) (i) 90°, since OA is a
tangent to s_1 at A. (ii) 90°, since OE is a tangent to s_2 at E.
(b) (ii) $|DE| = 3$ cm, $|OE| = 4$ cm (iii) $|OD| = 5$ cm
(c) (i) 9 cm (ii) $|OC| = 15$ cm (iii) $|DC| = 10$ cm
(d) (i) $|\angle DOE| = 36\cdot87°$ (ii) $|AB| = 14\cdot4$ cm
(e) (i) 14·4 cm³ (ii) 4·86, €243

Revision Questions

1. (a) $x = 3, y = \frac{54}{7}$ (b) 21·5 m **2.** (a) $|\angle DCB| = 30°$
3. (a) (i) $|\angle BAE| = 70°$ (ii) $|\angle BCE| = 110°$ **4.** (a) (i) 64°
(ii) 64° **5.** (a) 5 (b) 24 cm **6.** (a) (i) x (ii) $180° - x$
(iii) $180° - x$ (b) y **7.** (a) $x = 3$ (b) 36°, 48°, 96°
8. $|\angle BAK| = 20°$ **9.** (b) $|BQ| = \frac{10}{3}$ (d) $|RC| = 8, |AR| = 4$
12. (a) (ii) $|\angle BED| = 90°; |\angle DEC| = 90°$ (b) $x = 37$ cm

14. (b) (i) $\sqrt{2}r$ (ii) 45° **15.** (b) $|BE| = 2\sqrt{14}$;
(b) $|AD| = 16\sqrt{\frac{2}{15}}$ **16.** (d) (i) 2 km (ii) $|FD| = 2\sqrt{2}$ km;
$|FE| = 2\sqrt{10}$ km; $|FC| = 2\sqrt{5}$ km (e) At circumcentre,
which is halfway between C and E. (f) $2\cdot1 \times 10^{-5}$ s
17. (a) $|AC| = 17$ km (c) $x = 10\frac{2}{3}$ (e) 20 km
18. (b) (i) 64 mm² (ii) 64π mm² (c) $6\cdot4\pi \times 10^{-3}$ cm³
(d) 0·11 g (e) €11 (f) 144π mm² **19.** (b) 2

Section 2

Chapter 5

Exercise 1

1. (a) 14 cm, 12 cm² (b) 16 cm, 16 cm² (c) 26·5 m, 40 m²
(d) 48 cm, 112 cm² (e) 28 cm, 48 cm² (f) 24, 28 (g) 11·2, 3·9
(h) 54, 168 (i) 24, 33·9 (j) 41·8 cm, 57·5 cm² **2.** (a) 60 cm²
(b) 60 cm² (c) 32 cm² (d) 18 m² (e) 48 cm² (f) 112 cm²
(g) 154 cm² (h) 84 cm² (i) $(40\sqrt{2} - 16)$ cm² (j) 513 cm²
3. (a) 10 cm (b) 5 cm (c) 12 cm (d) 5 m (e) 2 cm (f) 5 cm
(g) 5 cm (h) 2 cm (i) 10 cm (j) 25 cm **4.** (a) 0·8844 m²
(b) 100 m (c) 23 cm, 161 cm² (d) $\sqrt{3}$:4 (e) $9\sqrt{3}$ cm²,
$54\sqrt{3}$ cm² (f) 24·6 m²

Exercise 2

1. (a) 20π cm, 100π cm² (b) 10π cm, 25π cm²
(c) $2\sqrt{3}\pi$ m², 3π m (d) πx units, $\frac{\pi x^2}{4}$ square units
2. (a) 164·53 cm, 1608·50 cm² (b) 10·71 cm, 7·07 cm²
(c) 21·78 cm, 29·45 cm² (d) 134·25 cm, 942·48 cm²
3. (a) 12π cm² (b) 5 cm, 25π cm² (c) 3 cm, 6π cm (d) (i) 120°
(ii) 4π cm (iii) 12π cm (e) 86° **4.** (a) 76·5 m² (b) 772·83 m
(c) 40212 km (d) 67°, 1·36 m/s (e) 306 m, 7466 m²
5. (a) 42 m, 119 m² (b) 42 cm² (c) 13·73 cm² (d) 392π cm²
6. (a) (i) 251 km, 565 km (ii) 20420 m² (b) (i) 0·684 m
(ii) 1·564 m (iii) 0·4 m² (c) (i) 45 c (ii) 6 (iii) 88 cm²
(d) (i) 100·3 m² (ii) 299·7 m² (iii) 3330 (iv) €5994
(e) (i) 53·4 m² (ii) 72·6 m²

Exercise 3

1. (a) 98·25 cm² (b) 567 cm² (c) 315 cm²
(d) 195 cm² (e) 48·7 cm² (f) 164 cm² **2.** (a) 164
(b) 35 (c) 94

Chapter 6

Exercise 4

A. Polyhedra

1. (a) 12 cm (b) 752 cm² **2.** 54 cm² **3.** 27 cm³ **4.** 336 l
5. (a) 40 cm² (b) 800 cm³ (c) 760 cm² **6.** (a) 3 m²
(b) 12 m³ (c) 38 m² **7.** (a) 112 m² (b) 4480 m³

8. (a) 162·5 m² (b) 2600 m³ **9.** (a) $2\sqrt{2}$ cm
(b) $4(9\sqrt{2} + \sqrt{3})$ cm² **10.** $3\sqrt{2}$ cm **11.** $8\sqrt{21}$ m²,
$32(2 + \sqrt{21})$ m² **12.** 336 m²

B. Curved surfaces

1. (a) 130π cm², 200π cm³ (b) 96π cm², 96π cm³
(c) 144π cm², 288π cm³ (d) 243π cm², 486π cm³
2. 36π cm³ **3.** (a) 144π cm³ (b) $6\sqrt{5}$ cm (c) 253 cm²
(d) 366 cm² **4.** (a) 20 cm (b) 312π cm² **5.** (a) 6 cm
(b) 192π cm² **6.** (a) 21 cm (b) 1649 cm³ **7.** 14 cm
8. 7·5 cm **9.** 2 cm **10.** 432π cm² **11.** (a) 8π m²
(b) 96π m³ (c) 48π m² **12.** (a) 3 m (b) (i) 1·5 m
(ii) $2\cdot97\pi$ m² (iii) $\dfrac{81\pi}{100}$ m³ (iv) 0·25 m³ **13.** 8 cm
14. $9\pi(h-1)$ cm³, 5 cm **15.** (a) 9 cm (b) 20 cm
(c) 144π cm³, 50% **16.** (a) 6 cm (b) 3·2 cm
(c) 36 cm (d) 2·29 cm **17.** (a) 40π cm³/s 160 s
(b) 160 s (c) 4 minutes

Exercise 5

1. (a) 112 cm² (b) 111·6 cm² (c) 90π cm² (d) 168π cm²
(e) $100\sqrt{3}$ cm² **2.** (a) (i) 48π cm² (b) (i) 84 cm²
(c) (i) 300 cm² (d) (i) 200π cm² **3.** 10 365·44 cm²

Revision Questions

1. (a) 24 m², $4(4 + \sqrt{2})$ m (b) (i) 8·25 m², 10 m² (ii) $\dfrac{15\sqrt{5}}{2}$ m²
(iii) 41·25 m³ (c) (i) 12 mm (ii) 100π mm³ (iii) 2 cm,
1·885 cm³ (iv) 663 **2.** (a) 395 m, 9219 m² (b) (ii) 30 m²
(c) $\dfrac{32\pi}{3}$ cm³, 24 **3.** (a) 4324·5 cm² (b) (i) 504π cm²
(iii) 20 cm (iv) 16 cm **4.** (b) (i) 42·8 cm² (ii) 42·8 cm³
(c) (i) 230 400π cm³ (ii) $\dfrac{32\pi}{3}$ cm³ (iii) 21 600 (iv) 3 cm
5. (a) 27·47 cm² (b) 18 m (c) (i) 46·25 m² (ii) 370 m³
(iii) 270 kl **6.** (a) $\dfrac{3}{8}$ (b) (i) 7·17 m² (ii) 2·868 l (c) 576π cm³
7. (a) $\dfrac{4}{9}$ (b) (i) 869 m² (ii) €6952 (c) 10·5π m², €396
8. (a) 2:1 (b) (i) 0 m/s (ii) 0 m/s (iii) 60 m (iv) 6 m/s
(c) $|FC| = 10$ m, 153·67 m² **9.** (a) (i) 0·93 l (ii) 23·7 cm
(b) (i) 171·5π cm³ (ii) $\dfrac{1029\pi}{4}$ cm³ (iii) 33$\frac{1}{3}$%
10. (a) 1·92 m³ (b) 29·4 cm (c) 59 **11.** (a) $150\sqrt{3}$ cm²
(b) (i) $h = 4$ cm, (ii) $\dfrac{416\pi}{3}$ cm³ (c) 84 cm²
12. (a) 4×10^{-3} m³/s (b) 500 s (c) (i) $0 \leq d \leq 18$ (iv) 38·4 m²
(v) 115·2 m³/s

Section 3

Chapter 7

Exercise 1

1. (a) $\dfrac{5}{13}$ (b) $\dfrac{12}{13}$ (c) $\dfrac{12}{5}$ (d) $\dfrac{15}{13}$ (e) $\dfrac{2}{13}$ (f) $\dfrac{1728}{125}$ (g) $\dfrac{432}{169}$ (h) $\dfrac{13}{5}$
(i) $\dfrac{13}{6}$ (j) $-\dfrac{5}{36}$ **2.** (a) $-\dfrac{3}{5}$ (b) $\dfrac{4}{5}$ (c) $-\dfrac{4}{3}$ (d) $\dfrac{9}{25}$ (e) $-\dfrac{8}{5}$ (f) $-\dfrac{27}{64}$
(g) $-\dfrac{9}{10}$ (h) $-\dfrac{108}{625}$ (i) 1 (j) 1 **3.** $P(-4, -3)$ (a) $-\dfrac{4}{5}$ (b) $-\dfrac{3}{5}$ (c) $\dfrac{3}{4}$
(d) $-\dfrac{16}{5}$ (e) $-\dfrac{3}{10}$ (f) $\dfrac{9}{16}$ (g) $\dfrac{9}{20}$ (h) $\dfrac{3}{4}$ (i) $-\dfrac{5}{4}$ (j) $-\dfrac{7}{24}$

4. (a) $\dfrac{3}{\sqrt{13}}, \dfrac{2}{\sqrt{13}}, \dfrac{2}{3}$ (b) $\dfrac{\sqrt{39}}{8}, \dfrac{5}{8}, \dfrac{5}{\sqrt{39}}$ (c) $\dfrac{2\sqrt{6}}{7}, \dfrac{5}{7}, \dfrac{5}{2\sqrt{6}}$
(d) $\dfrac{\sqrt{105}}{11}, \dfrac{4}{11}, \dfrac{4}{\sqrt{105}}$ (e) $\dfrac{\sqrt{2}}{2}, \dfrac{\sqrt{2}}{2}, 1$ **5.** (a) 45·6° (b) 33·7°
(c) 55·2° (d) 15·8° (e) 33·6° **6.** (a) $\dfrac{4}{5}, \dfrac{4}{3}, \dfrac{5}{4}, \dfrac{5}{3}, \dfrac{3}{4}$
(b) $-\dfrac{4}{5}, -\dfrac{3}{4}, -\dfrac{12}{5}, -\dfrac{27}{65}$ (c) $\dfrac{\sqrt{3}}{2}, -\sqrt{3}, 1$ (d) $-\dfrac{3}{\sqrt{10}}, \dfrac{1}{\sqrt{10}}, \dfrac{1}{19}$
(e) $\dfrac{12}{13}, \dfrac{5}{12}, \dfrac{5}{12}, \dfrac{5}{13}$ (f) $-\dfrac{1}{\sqrt{17}}, -\dfrac{4}{\sqrt{17}}, 4, 4$ (g) $\dfrac{35}{6}$
(h) $\dfrac{12}{13}, -\dfrac{12}{5}, -\dfrac{125}{864}$ (i) $-\dfrac{3}{\sqrt{58}}, \dfrac{7}{\sqrt{58}}, \dfrac{18}{17}$ (j) $\dfrac{17}{7}$ **7.** (a) $\dfrac{\sqrt{3}}{2}$
(b) $\dfrac{\sqrt{2}}{2}$ (c) 3 (d) 2 (e) 1 (f) 0 (g) 0 (h) ∞ (i) $\dfrac{\sqrt{3}}{9}$ (j) $\dfrac{1}{4}$
8. (a) (i) 1 (ii) 1 (iii) ∞ (b) (i) -1 (ii) -1 (iii) $-\infty$
9. (a) 90°, 270° (b) 0°, 180°, 360° **10.** (a) $\sin\theta$ (b) $\cos\theta$
(c) $-\sin\theta$ (d) $\sin\theta$ (e) $-\tan\theta$ (f) $\dfrac{1}{\tan\theta}$ (g) $-\cos\theta$ (h) $-\dfrac{1}{\tan\theta}$
(i) $\sin\theta$ (j) $-\cos\theta$ **11.** (a) (i) $-\dfrac{1}{2}$ (ii) -1 (iii) $\dfrac{1}{2}$ (iv) 3 (v) 1
(vi) $-\dfrac{3\sqrt{3}}{8}$ (vii) $-\dfrac{1}{2}$ (viii) $-\dfrac{3\sqrt{3}}{8}$ (ix) $\dfrac{1}{3}$ (x) $\dfrac{3}{4}$ (b) (i) $-\dfrac{1}{2}$
(ii) $-\sqrt{3}$ (iii) $\dfrac{\sqrt{2}}{2}$ (iv) $-\dfrac{\sqrt{3}}{2}$ (v) $\dfrac{1}{2}$ (vi) $\sqrt{3}$ (vii) $\dfrac{\sqrt{3}}{2}$ (viii) $\dfrac{3\sqrt{3}}{8}$
(ix) $-\sqrt{3}$ (x) -1 **12.** (a) $\dfrac{3}{5}$ (b) $\dfrac{4}{5}$ (c) $-\dfrac{3}{5}$ (d) $-\dfrac{4}{5}$ (e) $-\dfrac{3}{4}$ (f) $-\dfrac{4}{3}$
(g) $-\dfrac{64}{125}$ (h) $\dfrac{3}{4}$ (i) $\dfrac{3}{5}$ (j) $\dfrac{4}{5}$ (k) $-\dfrac{64}{27}$ (l) $\dfrac{4}{5}$

Exercise 2

1. (i) (a) $\dfrac{5\pi}{3}$ cm (b) $\left(\dfrac{5\pi}{3} + 20\right)$ cm (c) $\dfrac{25\pi}{3}$ cm²
(ii) (a) $\dfrac{16\pi}{3}$ cm (b) $\left(\dfrac{16\pi}{3} + 16\right)$ cm (c) $\dfrac{64\pi}{3}$ cm²
(iii) (a) $\dfrac{40\pi}{3}$ cm (b) $\left(\dfrac{40\pi}{3} + 60\right)$ cm (c) 200π cm²
(iv) (a) 24 m (b) 36 m (c) 72 m² **2.** 6702 km
3. (a) 0·5 rads (b) 2 rads (c) $4\frac{1}{3}$ rads **4.** $\dfrac{25\pi}{4}$ cm²
5. (a) $\dfrac{11\pi r}{6}$ (b) $\dfrac{11\pi r^2}{12}$ **6.** $\dfrac{4\pi}{3}$ m, $\dfrac{2\pi}{3}$ m² **7.** π cm, $\dfrac{3\pi}{2}$ cm²
8. (a) 1·2 rads (b) 4·8 cm (c) 50·4 cm² **9.** (a) 139·3 cm²
(b) 128·5 cm² (c) 127·5 cm² **10.** (a) 84·8 cm² (b) 54·9 cm²
(c) 164·4 cm² (d) 8·7 m² (e) 69·5 cm² **11.** $36\sqrt{3}$ cm²,
5·8 cm² **12.** (a) 8π m² (b) 6·87 m² (c) 161 cm²
13. (a) 2356 km² (b) 16·6 km **14.** (a) 13 cm (b) 13 cm
(c) 10π cm (d) 138·46° **15.** (b) 5·53 hours **16.** $\phi = \left(\dfrac{r_1}{r_2}\right)\theta$
17. 95·4 m² **18.** 14 cm, 279 cm² **19.** 339 m²

Exercise 3

1. (a) $3\sqrt{5}$ cm (b) $16\sqrt{3}$ cm² (c) $12\sqrt{2}$ cm (d) $\dfrac{5\sqrt{2}}{2}$ cm
(e) 6 cm **2.** (a) $4\sqrt{2}$ cm (b) 13 cm (c) 0·21 m (d) 2·5625 m
(e) 9·386 m (f) $|SQ| = 75$ m **3.** 308 m **4.** 300·5 m
5. 93·4 m **6.** (a) 90° (b) 36·87° (c) 53·13° **7.** 14·3°

8. 286·54 km, 2·2°   **9.** (a) 24·62° (b) 43·34° (c) 18·72°
(d) 1·96 cm   **10.** $\dfrac{\sqrt{15}}{4}$

Exercise 4

1. 6·46 m, 5 m   **2.** 31·8°, 10·5 m   **3.** (a) 553·38 m
(b) 107·35 m   **4.** (a) 58·22 m (b) 84·56 m   **5.** 249 m
6. (a) 16·4 m (b) 19·8 m (c) 30 m   **7.** (a) 866 m
(b) 185 m   **8.** 2·76 cm, 6·9 cm   **9.** 6·565 km
10. (a) 15·07 m (b) 12·3 m   **11.** 10·63 m,
$|PQ| = 3·76$ m, $|QR| = 16·24$ m   **12.** 28·7 km
13. 29·7 km, 32·6°   **14.** (a) 30 km/h (b) 85 km
15. (a) 8 m (b) 63°   **16.** (a) 8·00 cm (b) 21·54 cm
(c) 42·44 cm   **17.** (a) 60° (b) 40° (c) 12 cm
(d) $12\sqrt{3}$ cm (e) 15·4 cm (f) 18·4 cm   **19.** 25 m
20. 17·6 m   **21.** $r = \dfrac{k}{2\cos\theta}$, $h = \dfrac{k\sin\theta}{\cos^2\theta}$
22. $l = \dfrac{k}{\sin\theta}$, Area $= \dfrac{k^2}{\sin^2\theta}$ **23.** (a) $|PQ| = k\tan\theta$
(b) Area $\Delta OPQ = \dfrac{k^2}{2}\tan\theta$ (c) Area sector $OPQ = \dfrac{k^2\theta}{2}$
(d) Area shaded region $= \dfrac{k^2}{2}(\tan\theta - \theta)$
25. (a) $\left(20\sqrt{3} + \dfrac{70\pi}{3}\right)$ cm (b) 60°, $\left(60 + \dfrac{70\sqrt{3}}{3}\pi\right)$ cm,
175·3 cm² (c) $\left(32\sqrt{3} + \dfrac{76\pi}{3}\right)$ cm (d) $\left(10\sqrt{3} + \dfrac{32\pi}{3}\right)$ cm
(e) $(18\sqrt{3} + 14\pi)$ cm

Chapter 8

Exercise 5

1. (a) 15·32 cm² (b) 16·44 cm² (c) 128·57 mm²
(d) 43·92 cm² (e) 62·35 cm²   **2.** (a) $\sqrt{3}$ (b) 12·5 (c) 2·5
(d) $7\sqrt{3}$ **3.** (a) 2·7 cm (b) 17·8 m (c) 4·2 cm (d) 4 cm
(e) 5 cm (f) 3 cm (g) 6·5 m (h) 8 cm   **4.** (a) 30°
(b) 60°, 120° (c) 53·1° (d) 19·4°, 160·6°   **5.** (a) (i) 11·5 cm²
(ii) 1·9 cm² (iii) $10\sqrt{3}$ cm² (iv) 570 km² (b) 9·0 cm
(c) 23·6°

Exercise 6

1. (a) $x = 7·5$ cm (b) $A = 49·3°$ (c) $x = 7·6$ cm
(d) $A = 43·5°, 136·5°$ (e) $A = 68·0°, 112·0°$
2. (a) (i) $B = 59·5°, 120·5°$ (ii) $C = 82·5°, 21·5°$
(b) $A = 49·5°, B = 22·5°$ (c) (i) $A = 60·3°, 119·7°$
(ii) $C = 75·7°, 16·3°$ (iii) $c = 5·6$ cm, 1·6 cm
3. $C = 60°, 120°$ **4.** 8·08 m   **5.** (a) 10·9 km (b) 6·4 km
(c) 4·8 km   **6.** (a) $|GS| = 129·2$ km, $|FS| = 104·8$ km
(b) 21 mins   **8.** (a) $b = 23·0$ cm (b) $b = 2·6$ cm
(c) $b = 7·5$ cm, $c = 2·3$ cm (d) $B = 43·1°$ (e) $C = 38·5°$
9. $|\angle PQR| = 59°$ or 121°, $|\angle PRQ| = 81°$ or 19°,
$|PQ| = 9·2$ cm or 3·0 cm   **10.** $\dfrac{\pi}{6}$ m²   **11.** $7\left(\dfrac{\pi}{3} - \dfrac{\sqrt{3}}{4}\right)$
12. (a) 9θ cm² (b) $\left(\dfrac{9}{2}\sin 2\theta\right)$ cm²   **13.** $|\angle QPR| = 48°, 132°$

Exercise 7

1. (a) 15·7 cm (b) 12·3 m (c) 137·9° (d) 94·8°
2. (a) 103° (b) 30°   **3.** $|QR| = 426$ m, $|\angle PQR| = 77°$
4. 10·45 cm, 17·05 cm   **5.** 58 km   **6.** (a) $c = 7·1$ cm
(b) $b = 3·8$ m (c) $a = 113·6$ m (d) $A = 47°$ (e) $B = 30°$
7. $|\angle PRQ| = 76·787°, |\angle RPQ| = 55·692°, |\angle PQR| = 47·521°$,
Area = 340·7 m²   **9.** $|\angle PRQ| = 120°, |\angle RPQ| = 41°$,
$|\angle PQR| = 19°$ **10.** (a) $|\angle PQR| = 82°, |\angle PRQ| = 60°$,
$|\angle RPQ| = 38°$ (b) $|\angle PQR| = 103°, |\angle PRQ| = 47°$,
$|RQ| = 4·1$ **11.** $\sin\theta = \dfrac{4}{5}$, Area = 84   **12.** $|HF| = 7·9$ cm,
$|EG| = 12·8$ cm   **15.** $|AB| = t\sqrt{x^2 + y^2 - xy}$

Exercise 8

1. (a) $|QS| = 11·6$ cm (b) $|\angle SRQ| = 125°$ **2.** (a) $|SP| = 5·7$
(b) $|RQ| = 18·8$ **3.** (a) $|SQ| = 10$ m (b) $|\angle RSQ| = 53·13°$
(c) $|PQ| = 6·3$ m   **4.** (a) $|QR| = 7$ cm (b) 22 cm²
5. (a) $|\angle RPQ| = 41·5°$ (b) $|RS| = 7·3$ cm   **6.** (a) 14·2 cm
(b) 19 cm   **7.** (a) $|\angle RSQ| = 45°, 135°$ (b) $|PR| = 4·2$ cm,
9·3 cm   **8.** (a) $|SP| = 8·45$ cm (b) $|QR| = 11·39$ cm
(c) Area = 34·4 cm²   **9.** (a) $|PR| = 66$ km (b) $|PS| = 58$ km
10. (a) $|SQ| = 28·6$ m (b) $|PS| = 40·8$ m   **11.** (a) $x = 5$
(b) 35°   **12.** (a) (i) $|RS| = 5$ (ii) $|RQ| = \sqrt{34}$ (b) (i) $x = l\sin\theta$
(ii) $y = l\cos\theta$ (iii) $z = k - l\cos\theta$ (iv) $r = \sqrt{k^2 + l^2 - 2kl\cos\theta}$
13. (a) $\theta = \beta - \alpha$ (b) $l = \dfrac{h}{\sin\beta}$ (c) $x = h\left(\dfrac{1}{\tan\alpha} - \dfrac{1}{\tan\beta}\right)$
14. $h = d(\tan\theta - \tan\varphi)$ **15.** 5·34   **16.** (a) $|QR| = \dfrac{2h}{\sqrt{3}}$
(b) $|SQ| = \dfrac{4h}{3}$; $|\angle PQS| = \sin^{-1}\dfrac{3}{4} = 48·6°$

Exercise 9

1. $|PQ| = 73·1$ m, $|PS| = 50$ m   **2.** $|PR| = \dfrac{h}{\sqrt{3}}, |QR| = h\sqrt{3}$,
$|PQ| = \dfrac{2h\sqrt{2}}{\sqrt{3}}$ **4.** (a) $|SR| = \dfrac{10}{\sqrt{3}}$ m (b) 49° (c) $|PR| = 5\sqrt{5}$ m
(d) $|\angle SPR| = 27·3°$ **5.** (a) $|PQ| = 25\sqrt{3}$ cm
(b) $|RQ| = 25$ cm (c) $|UQ| = 99·87$ cm (d) $|\angle RUQ| = 14°$
6. $\theta = 21·8°$ **7.** $|SQ| = \dfrac{4}{\sqrt{3}}$ m, $|SP| = 4·1$ **8.** $|PS| = 17$ m,
$|SQ| = 19$ m, $|TQ| = 2\sqrt{34}$ m   **9.** $|PS| = 2·5$ m, $|PR| = 3·1$ m
10. (a) $|SR| = 10\sqrt{3}$ (b) $|SQ| = 10\sqrt{6}$ (c) $|TQ| = 10\sqrt{7}$
11. (a) $|RQ| = 3$ (b) $|RS| = \sqrt{3}$ (c) $|PS| = \sqrt{19}$
12. (a) $|PR| = 24·57$ m (b) $|SP| = 21·89$ m (c) $|SR| = 16·1$ m
13. (a) $|RQ| = 10$ m (b) $|RU| = 3\sqrt{29}$ m (c) $|QU| = 17$ m
(d) $|\angle URQ| = 77°$ **14.** (a) $|RQ| = 1·50$ m (b) $|RT| = 2·66$ m
15. $9\sqrt{3}$ cm   **16.** (a) 20 m (b) $|\angle PTQ| = 116·42°$,
$|\angle PTR| = 143·61° |\angle QTR| = 99·97°$ (c) $|QR| = 30·6$ m

17. $|PR| = 65$, $\angle PQR = 120°$ **18.** $|UP| = 5$ cm,
$|UQ| = 13$ cm, $\theta = 134\cdot76°$ **19.** $\theta = 30°$
20. $|\angle PRQ| = 120°$

Chapter 9

Exercise 10

1. (a) $\frac{56}{65}$ (b) $-\frac{16}{65}$ (c) $-\frac{33}{65}$ (d) $\frac{63}{65}$ (e) $-\frac{56}{33}$ (f) $-\frac{16}{63}$ **2.** (a) $\frac{77}{85}$

(b) $\frac{13}{85}$ (c) $\frac{36}{85}$ (d) $\frac{84}{85}$ (e) $\frac{77}{36}$ (f) $\frac{13}{84}$ **3.** (a) $-\frac{77}{85}$ (b) $\frac{84}{85}$ (c) $-\frac{77}{36}$

4. (a) $\cos 28°$ (b) $\cos 75°$ (c) $-\sin 8$ (d) $\sin 5°$ (e) $\frac{\sqrt{3}}{2}$

5. (a) $\sqrt{3}\cos x$ (b) $\sqrt{2}\sin x$ (c) $\sqrt{2}\sin A$ (d) $\sqrt{3}\cos x$

7. (a) $\frac{56}{65}$ (b) $-\frac{12}{13}$ (c) $-\frac{4}{5}$ (d) $\frac{56}{65}$ (e) $-\frac{56}{65}$ **8.** $\frac{3}{5}, -\frac{4}{5}$ **9.** -2

10. (a) $\frac{161}{289}$ (b) $\frac{240}{289}$ (c) $\frac{240}{161}$, First quadrant because $\cos 2A$
and $\sin 2A$ are positive **11.** (a) $-\frac{7}{25}$ (b) $-\frac{24}{25}$ (c) $\frac{24}{7}$, Third
quadrant because only $\tan 2A$ is positive

12. (a) $\frac{3}{\sqrt{13}}, \frac{2}{\sqrt{13}}, \frac{2}{3}$ (b) $\sqrt{\frac{5}{6}}, \frac{1}{\sqrt{6}}, \frac{1}{\sqrt{5}}$ (c) $\frac{3}{\sqrt{10}}, \frac{1}{\sqrt{10}}, \frac{1}{3}$

13. (a) $\frac{24}{25}$ (b) $\frac{7}{25}$ (c) $\frac{117}{125}$ (d) $\frac{336}{625}$ **14.** (a) $-\frac{119}{169}$ (b) $\frac{120}{169}$

(c) $-\frac{239}{28\,561}$ **15.** (a) $\frac{4}{3}$ (b) $\frac{11}{2}$ (c) $-\frac{24}{7}$ **16.** $\frac{24}{7}$ **17.** $\frac{3}{4}$

18. (a) $\sin 8\alpha - \sin 2\alpha$, (b) $\cos 5A + \cos 3A$
(c) $\sin 10x + \sin 2x$ (d) $\cos 2B - \cos 2A$ (e) $\sin 7A + \sin A$
(f) $\cos(2A + 6B) - \cos(6A - 2B)$ (g) $\frac{1}{2}(\cos 2B + \cos 4A)$
(h) $\frac{1}{2}(\cos 8x + \cos 2x)$ (i) $\sin t$ (j) $\frac{1}{2}(1 - \cos 2A)$

19. (a) $2\sin\left(\frac{9B}{2}\right)\cos\left(\frac{5B}{2}\right)$ (b) $2\cos 4\theta \sin\theta$

(c) $2\cos\left(\frac{3x}{2}\right)\cos\left(\frac{x}{2}\right)$ (d) $-2\sin 4x \sin 3x$

(e) $-6\sin\left(\frac{7A}{2}\right)\sin\left(\frac{3A}{2}\right)$ (f) $-\frac{1}{2}\sin 6A \sin A$

(g) $2\cos 40° \sin 10°$ (h) $-2\sin 40° \sin 20°$
(i) $2\cos A \sin B$ (j) $\sin x$

Exercise 11

1. (a) $\frac{2\pi}{3}, \frac{4\pi}{3}$ (b) $120°, 150°$ (c) $20°, 100°, 140°$

(d) $\frac{\pi}{3}, \frac{5\pi}{3}, \frac{13\pi}{3}, \frac{17\pi}{3}$ (e) $38°, 142°, 218°, 322°$

(f) $62°, 118°, 242°, 298°$ (g) $11°, 33°, 191°, 213°$

(h) $0°, 120°, 240°, 360°$ (i) $\frac{\pi}{2}, \frac{3\pi}{2}$

(j) $33\cdot75°, 56\cdot25°, 123\cdot75°, 146\cdot25°$

2. (a) $x = \begin{vmatrix} \dfrac{\pi}{18} + \dfrac{2n\pi}{3} \\ \dfrac{5\pi}{18} + \dfrac{2n\pi}{3} \end{vmatrix}, \quad n \in \mathbb{N}_0$

(b) $x = \begin{vmatrix} \dfrac{3\pi}{8} + n\pi \\ \dfrac{5\pi}{8} + n\pi \end{vmatrix}, \quad n \in \mathbb{N}_0$ (c) $x = \begin{vmatrix} \dfrac{\pi}{8} + \dfrac{n\pi}{2} \\ \dfrac{3\pi}{8} + \dfrac{n\pi}{2} \end{vmatrix}, \quad n \in \mathbb{N}_0$

(d) $x = \begin{vmatrix} \dfrac{2n\pi}{5} \\ \dfrac{\pi}{5} + \dfrac{2n\pi}{5} \end{vmatrix}, \quad n \in \mathbb{N}_0$ (e) $x = \dfrac{\pi + 2n\pi}{3}, \quad n \in \mathbb{N}_0$

3. (a) $x = 0°, 90°, 180°$ (b) $x = 0°, 30°, 90°, 150°, 180°$

(c) $x = \frac{\pi}{6}, \frac{\pi}{2}, \frac{5\pi}{6}$ (d) $x = 0, \frac{2\pi}{7}, \frac{\pi}{3}, \frac{4\pi}{7}, \frac{6\pi}{7}, \pi$

4. (a) $19\cdot5°, 160\cdot5°, 210°, 330°$ (b) $x = 19\cdot5°, 90°, 160\cdot5°$
(c) $x = 90°, 210°, 330°$ (d) $x = 45°, 135°, 210°, 225°,$
$315°, 330°$ (e) $x = 0°, 36°, 108°, 120°, 180°, 240°, 252°,$
$324°, 360°$ (f) $P\left(\frac{\pi}{3}, 0\right), Q(\pi, 0), R\left(\frac{5\pi}{4}, 0\right)$

5. $15°, 75°; 60°$

Exercise 12

1. (a) $[-3, 3], 2\pi$ (b) $[-1, 1], \frac{\pi}{2}$ (c) $[-p, p], 2\pi$ (d) $[-2, 2], 180°$
(e) $[-5, 5], 720°$ (f) $[-7, 7], \pi$ (g) $[-\infty, \infty], \frac{\pi}{9}$ (h) $[-\infty, \infty], \frac{\pi}{5}$
(i) $[-1, 5], \frac{\pi}{2}$ (j) $[-1, 9], \frac{2\pi}{7}$ (k) $[-\infty, \infty], \frac{\pi}{4}$ (l) $[p - q, p + q], \frac{2\pi}{k}$
(m) $[p + q, p - q], \frac{2\pi}{k}$ (n) $\left[-\frac{5}{2}, \frac{7}{2}\right], 4\pi$ (o) $[-5, 3], \pi$

2. (a) $y = \cos x$ (b) $y = 3\cos x$ (c) $y = \frac{5}{4} + \frac{3}{4}\cos x$

(d) $y = -1 - 4\cos x$ (e) $y = -\frac{5}{2} - \frac{9}{2}\cos x$ **3.** (a) $a = 0, b = 5$

(b) $a = 0, b = 7$ (c) $a = -1, b = 3$ (d) $a = -1, b = -3$

(e) $a = -\frac{3}{2}, b = \frac{11}{2}$ **4.** $P = 3$, Range $= [0, 2]$, $f(0) = 0$,

$f(5) = 2, f(7) = 1$ **5.** $P = 2\pi$, Range $= [-2, 2], f(\pi) = 0$,

$f\left(\frac{\pi}{2}\right) = 2, f(4\pi) = 0, f(10\pi) = 0$ **6.** $P = 8$, Range $= [-4, 4]$

$f(2) = 4, f(4) = 0, f(7) = -4, f(10) = 4, f(19) = 4$

7. $P = 8$, Range $= [-3, 1], f(2) = 1, f(4) = -3, f(8) = -3,$

$f(34) = 1$ **8.** $P = \pi$, Range $= [-1, 1], f(0) = 1, f(\pi) = 1,$

$f\left(-\frac{\pi}{2}\right) = -1, f\left(\frac{3\pi}{4}\right) = 0, f(10\pi) = 1, f\left(\frac{3\pi}{4}\right) = 0$

9. $k = 3, r = 4$ **10.** $k = 2, r = 5$ **11.** (a) $r = 1\cdot5, k = 1$
(b) $Q(30°, 0\cdot75), R(150°, 0\cdot75)$ **12.** $k = 5, a = 2, b = 0\cdot5$
13. $k = 3, a = -1, b = 0\cdot5$ **15.** Period of $f(x) = 180°$,
Range $[-4, 4]$; Period of $g(x) = 360°$, Range $[-3, 3]$
16. $x = 45°, 225°$ **17.** $x = 38°, 142°$ **18.** $x = 30°, 150°$
19. (a) $f(x) = 4\sin 2x$ (b) $g(x) = 2\sin 4x$ (c) $h(x) = \sin 4x$

20. (a) Period $= \frac{2\pi}{3}$ (b) $[-4, 4]$ (c) $b = 4$ (d) $k = 3$

21. (a) $r = 7$ (b) π (c) $P(0,0), Q\left(\frac{\pi}{4}, 0\right), R\left(\frac{3\pi}{4}, 0\right), S\left(\frac{5\pi}{4}, 0\right)$

22. $g(x): b = 2, k = 3, f(x): b = 1, k = 3$ **23.** $b = 3$
24. (a) $h = 1\cdot82$ m, $2\cdot18$ m (b) (i) $1\cdot82$ m (ii) $2\cdot18$ m (c) $\frac{2}{3}$ s
25. (a) $2\cdot35$ m (b) $1\cdot825$ m (c) 2 s **26.** (a) $k = 0\cdot986$
(b) $a = 12, b = 6$ (c) 17 hrs 9 mins (d) 225th day, 323rd day

27. $h = 2 + 0\cdot5\sin\left(\frac{\pi}{6}t\right)$ (a) $h = 2$ m (b) 9 a.m., 1 p.m.

28. (a) $h = 0\cdot75\cos\left(\frac{\pi}{5}t\right)$ (b) $h = 0$ m (d) 24 times

29. (a) $1\cdot07$ m (b) $1\cdot2$ s (c) $7\cdot6$ m/s (d) $14\cdot5$ s

Exercise 13

1. (a) $\frac{\pi}{4}$ rad = 45° (b) $\frac{\pi}{3}$ rad = 60° (c) $-\frac{\pi}{2}$ rad = −90°

(d) $\frac{1}{2}$ (e) $\frac{\pi}{4}$ (f) $\frac{2\pi}{3}$ (g) $\frac{\sqrt{2}}{2}$ (h) $\frac{\pi}{6}$ rad = 30° (i) $-\frac{\pi}{6}$ rad = −30°

(j) 0   **2.** (a) $\frac{\sqrt{3}}{2}$ (b) $\frac{2}{3}$ (c) $\frac{1}{\sqrt{10}}$ (d) $\frac{24}{7}$ (e) $-\frac{161}{289}$

4. (a) $x = 1$ (b) $x = \frac{5}{6}$

Revision Questions

1. (a) Period = 12, Range = [37·2, 40·2]

(b) $k = \frac{\pi}{6}$, $a = 38·7$, $b = 1·5$, $T = 38·7 + 1·5\sin\left(\frac{\pi t}{6}\right)$

(c) $t = 0$: $T = 38·7°$ C (d) 40·2 °C (e) On the ninth day
2. (a) 0 TW (b) 1980 TW (c) 2800 TW (d) 2010
(e) 1970 (g) 2070   **3.** (a) $x = 44·4°$, 135·6° (b) (i) $\left(\frac{3\pi}{2}, -1\right)$

(ii) $(\pi - \theta, k)$ (iii) $|\pi - 2\theta|$ **4.** (a) (ii) 14 cm (iii) 6 cm

(iv) 4 s (v) $\frac{1}{4}$ s^{-1} (vi) $-\sqrt{3}\pi$ cm/s (b) $P(90°, 0)$, $Q(120°, -0·5)$,

$R(240°, -0·5)$ **5.** (a) $|PQ| = 4·566$ cm, $|PS| = 10·057$ cm

(b) 7 cm   **6.** (a) $6\cos^2 x - \cos x - 2 = 0$, $x = 48°$, 120°,

240°, 312° (b) (i) $|\angle RQU| = 113·76°$, $|\angle PQU| = 66·24°$

(ii) $|\angle QUT| = 106·92°$, $|\angle QUP| = 73·08°$ (iii) $|PQ| = 88$ m,

$|PU| = 84$ m (iv) 81 m   **7.** (a) $x = 75°$, 105°, 255°, 285°

(c) (i) 60° (ii) 16 cm (iii) 60° (iv) $8\sqrt{3}$ cm (v) 60°

(vi) 120° (vii) $\left(16\sqrt{3} + \frac{16\pi}{3}\right)$ cm   **8.** (a) (i) Period = π,

Range = [−7, 1] (ii) $k = 6$, $a = \frac{1}{2}$, $b = -2\frac{1}{2}$ (b) (ii) 4 m

9. (a) (i) $h = r\left(\frac{1}{\cos\theta} - 1\right)$ (ii) $d = 2r\theta$ (iii) 325·74 km

(iv) 4900 km (b) (i) 8578 m (ii) 5·7 mins   **10.** (a) $|AK| = 2$ m

(b) $\sin x = \frac{1}{3}$ (c) $\tan x = \frac{1}{2\sqrt{2}}$ (d) $|FC| = 2\sqrt{2}$ m

(e) $(16\sqrt{2} - 5\pi)$ m^2 **11.** (a) $100\left(1 + \sqrt{3}\right)$ m ≈ 273·21 m

(b) $|PR| + |SQ| = 200\sqrt{2}$ m ≈ 282·84 m

12. (a) $-\frac{4}{3}$, $2x$ is obtuse (b) (i) $2\sin 2x \cos x$ (ii) $x = 0$, $\frac{\pi}{3}$, $\frac{\pi}{2}$,

π, $\frac{3\pi}{2}$, $\frac{5\pi}{3}$, 2π **13.** (b) $|QR| = 8$ (d) $30\sqrt{3}$ **14.** (b) (i) 106°

(ii) 108 cm^2 (iii) 126 cm^2 **15.** (a) $2r^2$ (b) $r^2\left(2 - \frac{\pi}{2}\right)$

(c) $r^2\left(\sqrt{3} - \frac{\pi}{2}\right)$ (d) $r^2(6 + \sqrt{3} + \pi)$

Section 4
Chapter 10

Exercise 1

1. (a) $|PQ| = 4$, $|RS| = 6$ (b) $|PS| = 8$, $|QR| = 6$

2. (a) Same y co-ordinate of 0: $y = 0$

(b) Same x co-ordinate of −2: $x = -2$

(c) Same y co-ordinate of −7: $y = -7$ **3.** (a) 8; 80 m
(b) 500 m   **4.** P: 4th, Q: 3rd, R: 2nd, S: y-axis,
T: 1st, U: x-axis   **5.** They all form straight lines when
joined

Exercise 2

1. (a) $2\sqrt{5}$ (b) 5 (c) $\sqrt{17}$ (d) $\sqrt{13}$ (e) $\sqrt{17}$ (f) $\sqrt{2}$ (g) $\sqrt{11}$
(h) $3z\sqrt{5}$ **2.** (a) (i) $|AC| = 15$ (ii) $|BC| = 10$
(b) (i) $|AB| = \sqrt{13}$ (ii) $|BC| = 2\sqrt{13}$ **3.** (a) Isosceles
(b) Scalene (c) Equilateral (d) Isosceles   **4.** (a) $|AB| = 5$
(b) $|BC| = 5$ (c) $|AC| = 5\sqrt{2}$ (d) $|AB| = |BC|$ (f) $|\angle ABC| = 90°$,
$|\angle BAC| = |\angle ACB| = 45°$ (g) $\frac{25}{2}$ **5.** (a) (i) 6·1 km
(ii) 5·8 km (iii) 11·2 km (b) 11:17 a.m.   **6.** (a) −3, 5
(b) −3, 15 (c) ±4 (d) 1, 3 (e) 1, −3   **7.** $\left(\frac{13}{6}, \frac{3}{2}\right)$ **8.** $D(2, -4)$,
64   **9.** (a) (i) 10 km (ii) 10 km (iii) $10\sqrt{2}$ km (c) Halfway
between P and R, i.e. midpoint of $[PR]$ (d) $5\sqrt{2}$ km

Exercise 3

1. (a) $C(1, 3)$ (b) $C(3, 4)$ (c) $C\left(-\frac{1}{2}, -2\right)$ (d) $C(0, 2)$

(e) $C(-4, -5)$ (f) $C\left(\frac{3}{4}, \frac{1}{4}\right)$ (g) $C\left(3\sqrt{2}, 3\sqrt{3}\right)$

(h) $C(z, z)$ (i) $C\left(z, \frac{5z}{2}\right)$ (j) $C\left(\frac{x_1 + x_2}{2}, \frac{y_1 + y_2}{2}\right)$

2. (a) $A(-4, 3)$ (b) $(-4, 4)$ (c) (i) $D(6, 7)$ (ii) $6\sqrt{2}$ km

3. (a) $C(-6, 5)$, $\sqrt{2}$ (b) $2\sqrt{82}$, $B(7, 29)$ (c) $E\left(\frac{17}{2}, 0\right)$,

$D(11, 0)$ **4.** (a) (i) $D(1, 3)$ (ii) $E(0, 0)$ (iii) $F(2, 1)$; Yes;

Because $\triangle ACB$ is similar to $\triangle DFB$ (b) (i) $E(-7, -3)$

(ii) $F(1, 0)$ (iii) $G(-5, 1)$ (iv) $H(-1, -4)$ (c) $D(11, 13)$,

$C(7, 10)$, $E(15, 16)$ (d) (i) $P(2, 2)$ (ii) $|AB| = 2\sqrt{10}$

(iii) Radius = $2\sqrt{5}$ (iv) $D(7, 7)$ (v) $|DB| = 2\sqrt{10}$

(e) $G(3, 12)$, $|OG| = 148\,431\,803$ km

5. (a) $|EB| = \frac{\sqrt{41}}{2}$ (b) $|EC| = \frac{\sqrt{45}}{2}$ (c) $|AD| = \sqrt{26}$

(d) $|AB| = \sqrt{17}$ (e) $|ED| = \frac{\sqrt{41}}{2}$ (f) $|EA| = \frac{\sqrt{45}}{2}$

(g) $|BC| = \sqrt{26}$ (h) $|DC| = \sqrt{17}$ **6.** (a) $B(20, -21)$

(b) 339 m (c) 361 911 m^2 (d) 648 m

Exercise 4

1. (a) 7 (b) 21 (c) 1 (d) $\frac{a^2 + b^2}{2}$ (e) 22 (f) 4·5   **2.** (a) 18

(b) 10 (c) 9   **3.** (a) $\left(\frac{5}{2}, 2\right)$, $\left(\frac{5}{2}, 2\right)$; Area = 11 (b) $\left(\frac{1}{2}, \frac{1}{2}\right)$, $\left(\frac{1}{2}, \frac{1}{2}\right)$;

Area = 56   **4.** 27·5   **5.** (a) 650 m^2 (b) 4150 m^2 (c) 25·5 m

6. (a) 22, −46 (b) ± 5 (c) −6, 22 (d) $-\frac{1}{5}$ (e) $x - 2y + 12 = 0$;

$x - 2y + 10 = 0$ **7.** (a) 500 m (b) 200 000 m^2 (c) 24 minutes

8. 5036 m^2 **10.** (a) (ii) $r = 1·31$ (b) (ii) $\cos\theta = -\frac{3}{5}$;

$\sin\theta = \frac{4}{5}$; Yes

Exercise 5

1. (a) $\sqrt{3}$ (b) $\dfrac{1}{\sqrt{3}}$ (c) $0\cdot445$ (d) -2 **2.** (a) $\dfrac{5}{8}$ (b) $\dfrac{3}{4}$

(c) Rise $= 99\cdot5$, Run $= 995\cdot0$ m **3.** (a) -4 (b) 4 (c) $\dfrac{8}{9}$

(d) 0 (e) ∞ (f) $-\dfrac{1}{\sqrt{3}}$ (g) $\dfrac{3}{2}$ (h) -2 (i) 0 (j) $-\dfrac{1}{\sqrt{3}}$

4. (a) 3 (b) 1 (c) 32 **5.** (a) $\dfrac{2}{3}$; Acute angle $= 33\cdot7°$ (b) -2;

Obtuse angle $= 116\cdot6°$ **6.** (a) 16 (d) They are the same

line (e) 5 **7.** (a) (i) Yes, $AB \perp CD$ (ii) No, AB is not $\perp CD$

(iii) Yes, $AB \perp CD$ (b) (i) $-\dfrac{2}{5}$ (ii) $\dfrac{3}{10}$ (iii) ∞ (iv) $-\dfrac{1}{4}$

(c) (i) 5 (ii) 4 (d) $-\dfrac{19}{2}$ (e) (i) $-\dfrac{14}{3}$ (ii) 11 **8.** Slope $AB = \dfrac{5}{4}$,

Slope $AC = -9$, Slope $BC = -\dfrac{4}{5}$; $\angle ABC$ **9.** (c) 3 **10.** (a) 7

(b) $\left|RQ\right| = 10$ m (c) $\left|QP\right| = 10$ m; Q is midpoint of RP

11. (a) $90°$ (b) $-\dfrac{8}{5}$ (c) $\dfrac{5}{8}$ (d) $90°$ **12.** (a) $\dfrac{1}{3}$ (b) x-axis

(c) $18\cdot4°$ **13.** $a = 8$, $b = 6$ **14.** (a) $0\cdot15$ m/m (b) $10\cdot5$ m

15. (a) Increased (b) $20\,000$ per year (c) $5\,000\,000$

16. (a) (i) 60 km/h (ii) 60 km/h (iii) 100 km/h (iv) 85 km/h

(b) Total distance $= 630$ km, total time $= 9$ hours, average

speed $= 70$ km/h **17.** (a) 1 g/°C (b) 100 g

Exercise 6

1. (b) Independent variable $= n$, dependent variable $= P$

(d) Yes, slope $=$ constant (e) $P = 5n + 220$

(f) No, discrete variables **2.** (b) Dependent variable $= V$,

independent variable $= t$ (d) Yes (e) Yes,

the variables are continuous (f) $V = -0\cdot8t + 140$

(g) $110\cdot41$ **3.** (a) On (b) On (c) Not on (d) On

(e) On (f) Not on (g) On (h) On **4.** (a) 7 (b) -1 (c) -2

(d) 2 (e) -16 (f) -13 (g) 9 (h) 0 **5.** (a) 3 (b) $-\dfrac{5}{11}$

(c) -5 (d) $\dfrac{1}{2}$ (e) 0 (f) ∞ (g) $\dfrac{3}{2}$ (h) $-\dfrac{7}{3}$ **6.** (a) Linear: slope

2, y-intercept 0 (b) Linear: slope 2, y-intercept $+3$

(c) Non-linear (d) Non-linear (e) Linear: slope $\dfrac{1}{2}$,

y-intercept 0 (f) Linear: slope $\dfrac{1}{3}$, y-intercept $+\dfrac{1}{3}$

(g) Linear: slope R, y-intercept 0 (h) Linear: slope m,

y-intercept 0 (i) Non-linear (j) Linear: slope $= 1\cdot5$,

y-intercept $-23\cdot5$ (k) Linear: slope $\dfrac{1}{273\cdot15}$, y-intercept V_0

(l) Linear: slope I^2R, y-intercept 0 **7.** (a) $y = 3x$

(b) $y = -\dfrac{3}{2}x + 4$ (c) $l = \dfrac{T}{20} + 5$ (d) $v = at + u$

8. (a) $3x - y - 1 = 0$ (b) $5x + y + 11 = 0$ (c) $4x - 7y + 17 = 0$

(d) $6x + 10y + 17 = 0$ (e) $x - 2y = 0$ **9.** (a) $2x - y = 0$

(b) $3x - 2y - 1 = 0$ (c) $3x + 4y - 1 = 0$ (d) $4x + 7y + 5 = 0$

(e) $4x + 4y + 5 = 0$ (f) $5x - 2y - 7z = 0$

10. (a) $x - 2y + 5 = 0$ (b) $2x + y - 12 = 0$ (c) $2x - y + 8 = 0$

(d) $x - 2y = 0$ (e) $6x - 5y + 8 = 0$ **11.** (a) $2x + y - 13 = 0$

(b) $x - 2y - 2 = 0$ (c) $3x + 4y + 11 = 0$ (d) $3x - 4y - 35 = 0$

(e) $8x + 7y - 2 = 0$ **12.** (a) $y - 2 = 0$ (b) $x + 6 = 0$

(c) $y - 11 = 0$ (d) $x + 1 = 0$ (e) $x - 3 = 0$ (f) $y + 7 = 0$

13. (a) $3x - 4y - 24 = 0$ (b) $4x - 3y - 3 = 0$

(c) $3x - 2y + 7 = 0$ (d) $x - y + 3 = 0$ (e) $x + y - 1 = 0$

(f) $x + y - 7 = 0$ (g) $2x + 3y - 4 = 0$ **14.** (a) $(2, 3)$

(b) $(-1, 4)$ (c) $(6, -3)$ (d) No solutions (e) An infinite

number of solutions, e.g. $(-11, 0)$ (f) $(-2, 5)$

15. (a) $3x - 4y - 1 = 0$ (b) $B(-1, -1)$ **16.** (a) $x + 3y + 1 = 0$

(b) $C(2, -1)$ (c) $B(-1, 0)$ **17.** (a) x: $(6, 0)$, y: $(0, -3)$

(b) x: $(-6, 0)$, y: $(0, 4)$ (c) x: $(8, 0)$, y: $(0, 2)$ (d) x: $(9, 0)$,

y: $(0, -6)$ **18.** (c) A: $h = -3t + 250$, B: $h = -t + 150$

(d) 50 hours (e) A; After 66 hours and 40 mins

19. (a) $x - y + 3 = 0$ (b) $x + y - 7 = 0$ (c) $5x - 3y + 8 = 0$

(d) $\sqrt{3}x - y - 2 = 0$ (e) $7x + 2y - 7 = 0$ **20.** (a) $y - 10 = 0$

(b) $x = 0$ (c) $x + 4y = 0$ (d) $3x + y - 2 = 0$ (e) $x + y - 5 = 0$

(f) $5x - 4y - 27 = 0$ (g) $2x - 3y + 8 = 0$ (h) $5x - 2y - 26 = 0$

21. $x - 5y + 25 = 0$ **22.** $x - 2y + 1 = 0$

Exercise 7

1. (a) 3 (b) $\dfrac{1}{2}$ (c) $\dfrac{2}{3}$ (d) 7 **2.** (a) $A(-2, -1)$, $B(2, -1)$, $C(2, 3)$,

$D(0, 5)$, $E(-2, 3)$ (b) $A'\left(-1, -\dfrac{1}{2}\right)$, $B'\left(1, -\dfrac{1}{2}\right)$, $C'\left(1, \dfrac{3}{2}\right)$,

$D'\left(0, \dfrac{5}{2}\right)$, $E'\left(-1, \dfrac{3}{2}\right)$ **5.** (a) 3 (b) $\dfrac{\text{Area } A'B'C'D'}{\text{Area } ABCD} =$

$\dfrac{324}{36} = 9 = (3)^2$ (c) $2x - 3y - 4 = 0$ (d) $P'(-3, -6)$

Chapter 11

Exercise 8

1. (a) $(2, 6)$ (b) $(2, -2)$ (c) $(-4, 9)$ (d) $\left(\dfrac{x_1 + x_2}{2}, \dfrac{y_1 + y_2}{2}\right)$;

Midpoint of $[AB]$

2. (a) $D\left(3, \dfrac{1}{2}\right)$; $[BD]$ is a median (b) $G(3, 3)$ (c) $E(1, 6)$

(d) $(3, 3)$ (e) Centroid of ΔABC (f) The centroid of a

triangle divides each median in the ratio $2{:}1$

3. (a) $A(0, 4)$, $B(10, 6)$ (b) $C\left(6, \dfrac{26}{5}\right)$ (c) $5\cdot2$ m (d) 4 m

4. $(3, 5)$, $(8, 7)$ **5.** (a) $D\left(\dfrac{x_1 + x_2}{2}, \dfrac{y_1 + y_2}{2}\right)$

6. q: $5x + 2y - 9 = 0$ **7.** l: $3x + y - 20 = 0$ **8.** (a) $C(4, 1)$

(c) 15 (d) $\sqrt{10}$ **9.** (a) $(0, -7)$ (b) $\left(\dfrac{21}{2}, \dfrac{27}{2}\right)$

Exercise 9

1. (a) $\theta = 60°$, $\phi = 120°$ (b) $\theta = 57°$, $\phi = 123°$

(c) $\theta = 7°$, $\phi = 171°$ (d) $\theta = 90°$, $\phi = 90°$ (e) $\theta = 90°$,

$\phi = 90°$ (f) $\theta = 45°$, $\phi = 135°$ (g) $\theta = 20°$, $\phi = 160°$

(h) $\theta = 48°$, $\phi = 132°$ **2.** (a) $74\cdot7°$ (b) $45°$

3. $\left|\angle ABC\right| = \left|\angle ACB\right| = 81\cdot9° \Rightarrow \left|AB\right| = \left|AC\right| = 5$

4. $58°$ **5.** (a) $\dfrac{1}{2}$, -2 (b) $-\sqrt{3}$, 0 **6.** (a) (i) $\dfrac{3}{2}$ (ii) $-\dfrac{1}{2}$ (iii) $83°$

(b) (i) 2 (ii) -3 (iii) $3x + y - 10 = 0$ (iv) $C\left(\dfrac{10}{3}, 0\right)$ (v) 2404 m

(c) (i) $-\dfrac{3}{2}$, $\dfrac{2}{3}$; Slope $AB = \dfrac{2}{3}$, Slope $AC = -\dfrac{3}{2}$

(ii) AB: $2x - 3y + 1 = 0$, AC: $3x + 2y - 5 = 0$

(iii) $B(-2, -1)$, $C(-1, 4)$ (iv) $\left|BC\right| = \sqrt{26}$

Exercise 10

1. (a) $\frac{6}{5}$ (b) $\sqrt{2}$ (c) $\frac{3}{5}$ (d) $\frac{4}{5}$ (e) $|c\cos\alpha + d\sin\alpha - a|$

2. (a) $\frac{6}{5}$ (b) $\frac{11\sqrt{41}}{82}$ (c) $\frac{|d-c|}{\sqrt{a^2+b^2}}$ **4.** (a) $2x+y+1=0$,

$2x+y-29=0$ (b) $3x+4y+4=0$, $3x+4y-26=0$

(c) $7x-y+18=0$, $7x-y-2=0$ (d) $12x+5y+36=0$,

$12x+5y-42=0$ (e) $x-2y+8=0$ (f) $\sqrt{3}x-y+10=0$,

$\sqrt{3}x-y-6=0$ (g) $2x-3y+42=0$, $2x-3y-10=0$

(h) $x-y+7=0$, $x-y-5=0$, $x+y+1=0$, $x+y-11=0$

5. (a) $2x-y+5=0$ (b) A: 6·26 km, B: 0·45 km

6. (a) $4x+5y=0$ (b) $4x+5y+15=0$ (c) 23·4 m

(d) $C\left(\frac{95}{16}, -\frac{31}{4}\right)$ **7.** (b) $A(1,1)$ (c) $x+3y-4=0$,

slope $m_1 = -\frac{1}{3}$, $3x-y-2=0$, slope $m_2=3$, $m_1 m_2 = -1$

(d) There are two bisectors of the angle between p and q

because there are two angles between p and q

8. $B(9,0)$ (a) $3x+4y+13=0$ (b) $|BD|=10$ (c) $\left(-\frac{13}{3}, 0\right)$

9. $\left(1, -\frac{7}{5}\right), \left(-3, -\frac{3}{5}\right)$

Chapter 12

Exercise 11

1. (a) $x^2+y^2-16=0$ (b) $x^2+y^2-4y-5=0$

(c) $x^2+y^2+2x-8y-32=0$ (d) $x^2+y^2+10x+4y+27=0$

(e) $16x^2+16y^2-96x+135=0$ (f) $x^2+y^2+10x+16y+64=0$

(g) $x^2+y^2+2ax-2ay+a^2=0$ (h) x^2+y^2+2ax+

$2ay-2a^2=0$ (i) $2x^2+2y^2-6x-2y-3=0$

(j) $8x^2+8y^2+20x-12y-7=0$ **2.** (a) $C(0,75)$

(b) $x^2+y^2-150y+2025=0$ (c) 0·75 km/h

3. (a) Not a circle, no x^2 and y^2 terms (b) Not a circle,

no x^2 and y^2 terms (c) Circle (d) Not a circle, has an xy

term (e) Not a circle, no x^2 term (f) Not a circle, no y^2 term

(g) Not a circle, no x^2 and y^2 terms (h) Circle

(i) Not a circle, coefficient $x^2 \neq$ coefficient y^2

(j) Circle **4.** $x^2+y^2=0\cdot0036$, $10\,000x^2+10\,000y^2-36=0$

5. $x^2+y^2-3y+2=0$ **6.** Front: $100x^2+100y^2-9=0$,

Rear: $100x^2+100y^2-520x+667y=0$

7. (a) $25x^2+25y^2-100x-60y+127=0$

(b) $25x^2+25y^2-1000x-60y+10027=0$

8. (a) $C(0,0)$, $r=\sqrt{10}$ (b) $C(0,0)$, $r=\frac{1}{2}$ (c) $C(3,-1)$, $r=\sqrt{2}$

(d) $C(2,-1)$, $r=\sqrt{7}$ (e) $C(-2,3)$, $r=\sqrt{17}$ (f) $C\left(\frac{1}{3}, \frac{4}{3}\right)$, $r=1$

(g) $C\left(\frac{3}{2}, \frac{3}{2}\right)$, $r=\frac{\sqrt{30}}{2}$ (h) $C\left(\frac{3}{4}, \frac{5}{4}\right)$, $r=\frac{\sqrt{34}}{4}$ (i) $C(1,0)$, $r=\sqrt{\frac{5}{3}}$

(j) $C\left(\frac{1}{3}, \frac{1}{2}\right)$, $r=\frac{\sqrt{13}}{6}$ **9.** s_1: $C_1(0,0)$, $r_1=1$; s_2: $C_2(5,8)$,

$r_2=2$; $|C_1 C_2|=\sqrt{89}$ **10.** (a) Out (b) Out (c) In (d) Out

(e) On (f) Out

Exercise 12

1. (a) $3x-y=0$ (b) $x-4y+17=0$ (c) $x+4y-11=0$

(d) $y-2=0$ (e) $9x+4y-5=0$ **2.** (a) $4x-3y+15=0$,

$4x-3y-25=0$ (b) $5x-12y+61=0$, $5x-12y-43=0$

(c) $3x-4y+15=0$, $3x-4y-5=0$ (d) $8x-3y-3=0$,

$8x-3y-76=0$ (e) $x+y+3=0$, $x+y-1=0$

3. (a) $y=0$, $4x+3y=0$ (b) $x+2y+4=0$, $2x-y-2=0$

(c) $2x-3y-13=0$, $3x+2y-13=0$ (d) $7x-y-50=0$,

$x+y-6=0$ **4.** (a) (i) $\sqrt{11}$ (ii) $2\sqrt{6}$ (iii) 10 (b) (i) -15

(ii) 2, 6 (c) 8, -22 (e) It is a tangent

5. (a) $2x-3y-13=0$; $4\sqrt{17}$ (b) $3x+2y-18=0$; $2\sqrt{19}$

(c) $x+y+3=0$, $x+y-1=0$ (d) (i) $C\left(3, \frac{7}{8}\right)$, $r=\frac{25}{8}$ (ii) $\frac{15}{8}$

(iv) $m=\pm\frac{4}{3}$ **6.** (a) $(2,0)$ (b) $(1,1)$, $(6,2)$ (c) $\left(-\frac{1}{13}, -\frac{34}{13}\right)$,

$(3,2)$ **7.** (a) x: $(3-\sqrt{21}, 0)$, $(3+\sqrt{21}, 0)$, length of

chord $=2\sqrt{21}$; y: $(0,-2)$, $(0,6)$, length of chord $=8$

(b) x: $(2,0)$, $(6,0)$, length of chord $=4$; y: $(0, 5-\sqrt{13})$,

$(0, 5+\sqrt{13})$, length of chord $=2\sqrt{13}$ **8.** (a) $x+4y-11=0$,

$13x-16y-75=0$ (b) $53°$ (c) $2\sqrt{17}$

9. (a) l_1: $x+y-8=0$, l_2: $x+y-2=0$ (b) l_1: $(8,0)$,

l_2: $(2,0)$ (c) $2x^2+2y^2+12x-32y+137=0$

(d) $N\left(-\frac{9}{2}, \frac{13}{2}\right)$

Chapter 13

Exercise 13

1. (a) $x^2+y^2+2x-6y-6=0$

(b) $36x^2+36y^2-24x+36y-239=0$

(c) $x^2+y^2-2x-6y+5=0$ (d) $x^2+y^2+x-2y-55=0$

(e) $x^2+y^2-10y=0$ (f) $x^2+y^2-2x-2y+1=0$

(g) $x^2+y^2-6x+4=0$ **2.** (a) $x^2+y^2-12x=0$,

$x^2+y^2+12x=0$ (b) $x^2+y^2+6y-16=0$, $x^2+y^2-10y=0$

(c) $x^2+y^2-8x-6y+16=0$, $x^2+y^2-14x-12y+76=0$

3. (a) $x^2+y^2-4x+10y+4=0$

(b) $x^2+y^2-10x+8y+16=0$, $x^2+y^2-10x-8y+16=0$

(c) $x^2+y^2+4x+4y+4=0$ (d) $x^2+y^2-4x-4y+4=0$,

$x^2+y^2-20x-20y+100=0$ (e) $x^2+y^2+4x+14y+28=0$,

$x^2+y^2-8x-2y-8=0$ **4.** (a) $x^2+y^2+6x-8y-40=0$

(b) Centre $(-3,4)$ (c) $\sqrt{65}$ (d) 50·66 m (e) No

5. $x^2+y^2-6x-10y+9=0$ **6.** $x^2+y^2-x-4y+20=0$;

$(8,0)$ is not on this circle; $r=4\cdot47$ m; Speed $1\cdot52 \times 10^8$ m/s

7. (a) $x^2+y^2-10x-2y+1=0$ (b) $C(5,1)$

8. (a) $x^2+y^2-10x-8y+25=0$ (b) 4 m

Exercise 14

1. $(-2,0)$; $x+2y+2=0$ **2.** $(3,4)$; $x-3y+9=0$

3. $c=-71$ **4.** $c=-20$ **5.** $5x^2+5y^2-2x-36y-60=0$

6. $D(4,5)$ **7.** 4 **8.** (a) s_1: $C_1(4,-1)$, $r_1=2\sqrt{10}$;

s_2: $C_2(-3,-2)$, $r_2=\sqrt{10}$ (b) $7x+y+13=0$

(c) $F\left(-\frac{8}{5}, -\frac{9}{5}\right)$, $E\left(-\frac{6}{5}, -\frac{23}{5}\right)$ **9.** (a) $C_1(0\cdot25, 0)$

(b) $C_2(0\cdot6, 0)$ (c) $|C_1 C_2|=0\cdot35$ m (d) 0·25 m

(e) 0·6 m; Yes

Revision Questions

1. $b = 4$; $\left(0, \frac{11}{4}\right)$ 2. $(0, -5)$ 3. (b) $b = 32$
4. (b) $5x + y - 55 = 0$ (c) $C(10, 5)$ 5. (a) $C(2, 2)$ (b) $\frac{7}{5}$
(c) $-\frac{5}{7}$ (d) $5x + 7y - 24 = 0$
6.

Equation of line	Slope	x-intercept	y-intercept
(a) $3x - 2y - 12 = 0$	$\frac{3}{2}$	4	-6
(b) $4x + y - 4 = 0$	-4	1	4
(c) $y = -2x + 3$	-2	$\frac{3}{2}$	3
(d) $y = -3$	0	None	-3
(e) $x = 4$	∞	4	None

7. (a) $7x - 3y + 9 = 0$ (b) $(0, 3)$ (c) $(1, -3)$ (d) 25
8. (a) $(2, 0)$ (c) $3x - 4y + 14 = 0$ (d) $4x + 3y - 48 = 0$
(e) $(12, 0)$ 9. (a) $D(1, 1)$ (b) p: $x + 3y - 4 = 0$ (c) $(4, 2)$
(d) q: $x - y - 2 = 0$ (e) $F\left(\frac{5}{2}, \frac{1}{2}\right)$ 10. (a) $5x - 12y = 0$
(b) $17x - 7y = 0$ (c) $\frac{13\sqrt{2}}{2}$ km   11. (a) $(4, 2)$ (b) $\sqrt{5}$
(c) $2\sqrt{5}$ (d) $(2, 1)$ (e) $(6, 3)$ 12. (a) $C_1(-1, 2)$, $r_1 = 5$
(b) $C_2(8, -10)$, $r_2 = 5$ (c) $\left|C_1C_2\right| = 15$ (d) $-\frac{4}{3}$
(e) $4x + 3y - 27 = 0$ (f) $H(3, 5)$ (g) $G(12, -7)$ 13. (a) $\left(\frac{1}{2}, 4\right)$
(b) $\left(\frac{25}{2}, 7\right)$ (c) $\left(\frac{13}{2}, \frac{11}{2}\right)$ (d) $C_1\left(\frac{7}{2}, \frac{19}{4}\right)$ (e) $C_2\left(\frac{19}{2}, \frac{25}{4}\right)$
(f) $r_1 = \frac{3\sqrt{17}}{4}$ (g) $4x^2 + 4y^2 - 28x - 38y + 101 = 0$
14. (a) $x^2 + y^2 - 8x - 8y + 16 = 0$ (b) $x + y - 8 = 0$
(d) $x + y - 8 \pm 4\sqrt{2} = 0$ 15. (a) $x^2 + y^2 + 2x - 14y + 40 = 0$
(b) Centre $(-1, 7)$, radius $= \sqrt{10}$ (c) $3x - y = 0$
16. (a) $x^2 + y^2 + 8x + 12y - 156 = 0$ (b) Centre $(-4, -6)$,
radius $= 4\sqrt{13}$ km (c) $6\sqrt{13}$ km (d) $(-12, -18)$
17. (a) $x^2 + y^2 - 10x + 2y + 1 = 0$ (c) $\frac{3}{4}$ (d) $\frac{4}{3}$ (e) $\frac{7}{24}$
(f) $\frac{117}{44}$ (g) $117x - 44y - 804 = 0$ (h) $\left(\frac{85}{12}, \frac{9}{16}\right)$
18. (b) $x^2 + y^2 - 6kx - 2ky + 9k^2 = 0$
19. (a) $C_1(0, 0)$, $r_1 = 10$ (b) $3x + 4y - 50 = 0$
(c) $C_2(21, 3)$, $r_2 = 5$ (d) $4x - 3y - 75 = 0$ (e) $Q(18, -1)$ (f) 15

Section 5
Chapter 14

Exercise 1

1. $S = \{(G, 1), (G, 2), (G, 3), (P, 1), (P, 2), (P, 3),$
$(R, 1), (R, 2), (R, 3), (Y, 1), (Y, 2), (Y, 3)\}$
2. $S = \{(1, A), (1, B), (1, C), (2, A), (2, B), (2, C),$
$(3, A), (3, B), (3, C), (4, A), (4, B), (4, C), (5, A),$
$(5, B), (5, C), (6, A), (6, B), (6, C)\}$
3. $S = \{(1, A), (1, B), (2, A), (2, B), (3, A), (3, B),$
$(4, A), (4, B) (5, A), (5, B)\}$
4. $S = \{(F, B), (F, P), (F, C), (G, B), (G, P), (G, C)\}$

5. $S = \{(H, H, H), (H, H, T), (H, T, H), (H, T, T), (T, H, H),$
$(T, H, T), (T, T, H), (T, T, T)\}$ 6. 6   7. 12   8. 4   9. 10
10. 6   11. 12   12. 18   13. 21   14. 36   15. 10000
16. 60   17. 60   18. 94 109 400   19. 72   20. 210   21. 81
22. 676   23. 338   24. 104   25. 32   26. (a) 120 (b) 48
27. (a) 234 000 (b) 216 000   28. (a) 900 (b) 648 (c) 90
(d) 64 (e) 450   29. (a) 9 (b) 90 (c) 90   30. (a) 36 (b) 36
(c) 36   31. (a) 260 (b) 260 (c) 520   32. (a) 90 (b) 45
33. (a) 25 (b) 36 (c) 61   34. 114 244   35. (a) 24 (b) 24
(c) 36 (d) 216 (e) 32   36. 900

Exercise 2

1. (a) 120 (b) 360 (c) 5040 (d) 24 (e) 60 (f) 336 (g) 1320
(h) 3 628 800 (i) 362 880 (j) 30 240   2. 6720   3. 120
4. 1680   5. 5040   6. 2520   7. 151 200   8. 59 280
9. 720   10. 360   11. (a) 24 (b) 18 (c) 6 (d) 6   12. (a) 6
(b) 840 (c) 64 864 800 (d) 420 (e) 140   13. 4200
14. 630 630   15. 6   16. 48   17. (a) 720 (b) 360
(c) 360 (d) 60   18. (a) 720 (b) 120 (c) 240 (d) 480
19. (a) 362 880 (b) 80 640 (c) 282 240 (d) 2880
20. (a) 40 320 (b) 336 (c) 4320 (d) 36 000
21. (a) 479 001 600 (b) 21 772 800   22. (a) $(n - 1)! \times 2$
(b) $(n - 1)! \ (n - 2)$ 23. 325   24. (a) 5040 (b) 840
(c) 120 (d) 20

Exercise 3

1. (a) 1365 (b) 120 (c) 120 (d) 6435 (e) $^{70}C_{15}$ (f) $^{50}C_{20}$
(g) 220 (h) 2002 (i) 1326   2. 55   3. 35   4. (a) 56
(b) 20 (c) 21   5. (a) 5005 (b) 715 (c) 1716 (d) 1287
6. 2 598 960 (a) 249 900 (b) 19 600 (c) 1287
7. (a) 3060 (b) 1260 (c) 70   8. (a) 924 (b) 105 (c) 350
(d) 455   9. (a) 34 (b) 35 10. 381   11. (a) 21 (b) 35
12. 6048   13. 38 798 760   14. 3 421 322 190   15. 15
16. 35, 15   17. 40   18. 135 19. 20   20. $\frac{n(n - 3)}{2}$

Chapter 15

Exercise 4

1. (a) 2 (b) H, T (c) $S = \{H, T\}$ (d) Yes (e) Coin is
unbiased (f) 300 (g) $\frac{1}{2}$ (h) Gender: boy or girl (i) $\frac{1}{2}$
2. (a) $S = \{RA, RB, RC, B\}$ (b) 4 (c) $E = \{RA, RB, RC\}$
(d) 3   3. (a) No (b) Biased in favour of red (c) 570
(d) 0·75 (e) 0·25   4. (a) 36 (b) (i) $\{(1, 1), (2, 2), (3, 3),$
$(4, 4), (5, 5), (6, 6)\}$(ii) $\{(6, 3), (5, 4), (4, 5), (3, 6)\}$
(iii) $\{(1, 1), (1, 2), (2, 1), (4, 1), (3, 2), (2, 3) (1, 4), (6, 1),$
$(5, 2), (4, 3), (3, 4), (2, 5) (1, 6), (5, 6), (6, 5)\}$ (c) $\frac{1}{12}$
(d) 15   5. (a) 8 (b) 216 (c) 24   6. (a) $S = \{(1, H), (1, T),$
$(2, H), (2, T), (3, H), (3, T), (4, H), (4, T), (5, H), (5, T),$
$(6, H), (6, T)\}$ (b) 12 (c) (i) 12 (ii) 12 (d) Yes
(e) $E = \{(1, H), (2, H), (3, H), (4, H), (5, H),$
$(6, H)\}$; 6 (f) $E = \{(2, H), (4, H), (6, H)\}$; 3
(g) $E = \{(1, T), (2, T), (3, T), (4, T)\}$; 4 (h) 1000

(i) (i) $P = \frac{1}{3}$: Rolling a number less than 5 and tossing a tail (ii) $P = 0.25$: Rolling an even number and tossing a head (iii) $P = 1$: Tossing a head or a tail (iv) $P = \frac{1}{2}$: Tossing a head

Exercise 5

1. $\frac{1}{7}$ 2. $\frac{1}{40}$ 3. (a) $\frac{1}{6}$ (b) 0 (c) $\frac{1}{2}$ (d) $\frac{2}{3}$ (e) $\frac{1}{2}$ 4. (a) $\frac{3}{8}$ (b) $\frac{1}{4}$
(c) $\frac{3}{8}$ (d) $\frac{3}{4}$ 5. (a) $\frac{3}{10}$ (b) $\frac{1}{4}$ (c) $\frac{1}{5}$ (d) $\frac{9}{20}$ 6. (a) $\frac{1}{6}$ (b) $\frac{1}{3}$
(c) $\frac{1}{3}$ (d) $\frac{2}{3}$ 7. $\frac{1}{3}$ 8. (a) $\frac{4}{13}$ (b) $\frac{2}{13}$ (c) $\frac{1}{13}$ 9. (a) $\frac{1}{6}$ (b) $\frac{1}{6}$
(c) $\frac{1}{3}$ 10. $\frac{1}{3}$ 11. (a) $\frac{1}{11}$ (b) $\frac{2}{11}$ (c) $\frac{2}{11}$ (d) $\frac{9}{11}$ 12. (a) $\frac{1}{8}$ (b) $\frac{3}{8}$
(c) $\frac{1}{8}$ (d) 0 (e) $\frac{3}{8}$ (f) $\frac{7}{8}$ 13. (a) $\frac{1}{7}$ (b) $\frac{6}{7}$ (c) $\frac{5}{7}$ (d) $\frac{2}{7}$ 14. (a) $\frac{5}{32}$
(b) $\frac{1}{32}$ (c) $\frac{13}{16}$ (d) $\frac{1}{16}$ 15. (a) 4 (b) 8 (c) $\frac{2}{5}$ 16. (a) $\frac{33}{50}$ (b) $\frac{17}{50}$
(c) $\frac{9}{25}$ (d) $\frac{16}{25}$ (e) $\frac{1}{5}$ (f) $\frac{6}{25}$ 17. 6 18. 6 19. $S = \{(H, H)$,
$(H, T), (T, H), (T, T)\}$ (a) $\frac{1}{4}$ (b) $\frac{1}{2}$ (c) $\frac{1}{2}$ (d) 1 (e) $\frac{3}{4}$ (f) $\frac{1}{4}$
20. (a) $\frac{1}{12}$ (b) $\frac{1}{4}$ (c) $\frac{1}{4}$ (d) $\frac{1}{4}$ 21. (a) $\frac{1}{6}$ (b) $\frac{1}{12}$ (c) $\frac{1}{4}$ (d) $\frac{2}{9}$
22. (a) $\frac{1}{6}$ (b) $\frac{1}{3}$ 23. (a) 0 (b) 1 (c) $\frac{1}{16}$ 24. (a) $\frac{1}{4}$ (b) 0
(c) $\frac{11}{16}$ 25. (a) $\frac{1}{8}$ (b) $\frac{1}{8}$ (c) $\frac{3}{8}$ (d) $\frac{7}{8}$ (e) $\frac{3}{8}$ 26. (a) $\frac{1}{8}$ (b) $\frac{3}{8}$ (c) $\frac{1}{8}$

Exercise 6

1. (a) 24 (b) $\frac{5}{24}$ (c) $\frac{7}{24}$ (d) $\frac{1}{3}$ (e) $\frac{5}{6}$ (f) $\frac{1}{6}$ 2. 6 (a) $\frac{2}{5}$ (b) $\frac{9}{10}$
(c) $\frac{1}{5}$ 3. 0.8 4. $\frac{1}{12}$ 5. $S = \{1, 2, 3, 4, 5, 6\}$ (a) $\frac{1}{3}$
(b) $\frac{1}{2}$ (c) $\frac{1}{6}$ (d) $\frac{2}{3}$ (e) $\frac{2}{3}$ 6. No $P(D$ or $S) = 0.09$ 90
7. 0 (a) $\frac{17}{35}$ (b) $\frac{1}{7}$ (c) $\frac{6}{35}$ (d) $\frac{2}{35}$ (e) $\frac{6}{7}$ 8. (a) No: $F \cap H \neq \{\}$
(b) Yes: $F \cap T = \{\}$ (c) $\frac{1}{8}$ (d) $\frac{3}{4}$ 9. (a) $P(A \cap B) = 0$
(b) $P(A \cap B) \neq 0$ 10. (a) 0.14 (b) 0.86 (c) 0.14
11. $P(A$ and $B) = 0.3$, No, $P(A \cap B) \neq 0$

Exercise 7

1. (a) $\frac{1}{2}$ (b) $\frac{2}{5}$ (c) $\frac{1}{10}$ (d) $\frac{4}{5}$ (e) $\frac{4}{5}$ (f) $\frac{4}{5}$, not mutually exclusive
2. (a) $x = 15$ (b) $y = 75$ (c) $z = 120$ (d) $\frac{1}{4}$ (e) $\frac{3}{4}$ (f) $\frac{1}{8}$ (g) $\frac{7}{8}$ (h) $\frac{7}{8}$,
not mutually exclusive 3. (a) $\frac{3}{10}$ (b) $\frac{1}{2}$ (c) 0 (d) $\frac{4}{5}$
(e) $\frac{4}{5}$, mutually exclusive 4. (a) $x = 47$ (b) $y = 58$
(c) $z = 120$ (d) $\frac{47}{120}$ (e) $\frac{29}{60}$ (f) 0 (g) $\frac{7}{8}$ (h) $\frac{7}{8}$, mutually exclusive
5. 16 (a) $\frac{1}{15}$ (b) $\frac{7}{30}$ (c) $\frac{1}{6}$ (d) $\frac{8}{15}$ (e) $\frac{5}{6}$ 6. (a) $\frac{2}{3}$ (b) $\frac{1}{6}$ (c) $\frac{4}{13}$
(d) $\frac{11}{26}$ (e) $\frac{1}{3}$ (f) $\frac{5}{8}$ (g) $\frac{4}{13}$ (h) $\frac{3}{5}$ 7. 1 8. $\frac{9}{20}$ 9. (a) $\frac{1}{2}$ (b) $\frac{7}{12}$
(c) $\frac{5}{12}$ 10. $\frac{3}{4}$ 11. $\frac{7}{12}$ 12. (a) 1 (b) $\frac{18}{25}$ (c) $\frac{11}{25}$ 13. $\frac{6}{7}$ 14. $\frac{10}{17}$
15. (a) 900 (b) 90 (c) 90 (d) $\frac{1}{10}$ (e) $\frac{1}{10}$ (f) $\frac{1}{5}$ 16. (a) 40 320
(b) 25 200 (c) 5040 (d) $\frac{3}{4}$ 17. (a) 9000 (b) 900 (c) 4500
(d) $\frac{3}{5}$ 18. (a) $\frac{99}{54\,145}$ (b) $\frac{1}{270\,725}$ (c) $\frac{496}{270\,725}$ 19. $\frac{7}{10}$ 20. $\frac{5}{18}$
21. (a) $\frac{1}{36}$ (b) $\frac{1}{12}$ (c) $\frac{1}{169}$ (d) $\frac{1}{243}$ 22. (a) $\frac{1}{169}$ (b) $\frac{1}{221}$ 23. $\frac{1}{3}$
24. (a) $\frac{1}{24}$ (b) $\frac{1}{24}$ (c) $\frac{1}{56}$ 25. $\frac{1}{220}$ 26. $\frac{3}{10}$ 27. $\frac{1}{7\,893\,600}$
28. (a) $\frac{1}{6}$ (b) $\frac{1}{3}$ 29. (a) $\frac{1}{8}$ (b) $\frac{1}{8}$ (c) $\frac{3}{8}$ 30. (a) $\frac{1}{49}$ (b) $\frac{30}{49}$
31. $\frac{91}{400}$ 32. 0.95 (a) $\frac{361}{400}$ (b) $\frac{6859}{8000}$ (c) 0.358
33. 7.6×10^{-11} 34. (a) $\frac{9}{80}$ (b) $\frac{3}{32}$ 35. $\frac{5}{28}$ 36. 8

Exercise 8

1. (a) $\frac{15}{56}$ (b) $\frac{15}{56}$ (c) $\frac{3}{28}$ (d) $\frac{5}{14}$ (e) $\frac{15}{28}$ (f) $\frac{13}{28}$ 2. $\frac{3}{8}$ 3. $\frac{1}{18}$
4. $\frac{625}{3888}$ 5. $\frac{91}{190}$ 6. (a) $\frac{9}{20}$ (b) $\frac{11}{40}$ (c) $\frac{1}{20}$ (d) $\frac{31}{40}$ 7. $\frac{19}{24}$ 8. $\frac{3}{4}$
9. (a) $\frac{5}{72}$ (b) $\frac{2}{27}$ 10. 3

Chapter 16

Exercise 9

1. (a) $\frac{63}{256}$ (b) $\frac{45}{1024}$ (c) $\frac{165}{512}$ (d) $\frac{11}{1024}$ (e) $\frac{7}{128}$ (f) $\frac{1013}{1024}$
2. $\frac{768}{3125} = 0.24576$ 3. 0.1237 4. 0.258 5. 25
6. (a) 0.226 (b) 0.739 (c) 0.997 7. 0.25 8. (a) 0.402
(b) 0.737 (c) 0.067 9. (a) $\frac{384}{3125}$ (b) $\frac{4}{3125}$ (c) $\frac{128}{625}$ (d) $\frac{64}{3125}$
10. $1.857 \times 10^{-4} = 0.0001857$ 11. (a) $\frac{35}{128}$ (b) 0.109
12. (a) Yes, only two independent outcomes win (red) or lose (not red) with constant probabilities (b) (i) 8.9×10^{-4}
(ii) 0.117 13. (a) 0.0625 (b) 0.6063 (c) 0.2533 (d) 0.0026

Exercise 10

1. $\frac{32}{45}$ 2. $\frac{43}{320}$ 3. $\frac{19}{23}$ 4. $\frac{4}{7}$ 5. $\frac{43}{55}$ 6. $\frac{10}{17}$ 7. $\frac{25}{52}$
8. 36.57% 9. (a) $\frac{7}{24}$ (b) $\frac{21}{64}$ 10. (a) $\frac{9}{100}$ (b) $\frac{79}{100}$ (c) $\frac{1}{100}$
(d) $\frac{2}{9}$ 11. (a) $\frac{17}{25} = 0.68$ (b) $\frac{8}{25} = 0.32$ (c) $\frac{1}{25} = 0.04$ (d) $\frac{17}{64}$
(e) No, $P(S|G) \neq P(S)$ (f) No, $P(G \cap S) \neq 0$
12. (a) $\frac{17}{50}$ (b) $\frac{27}{100}$ (c) $\frac{2}{29}$ (d) No: $P(C \cap F) \neq 0$
(e) Probably independent 13. (a) 0.9 (b) 0.6 (c) No,
$P(A) = 0.7 \neq P(A|B)$ 14. (a) $\frac{3}{5}$ (b) $\frac{1}{2}$ (c) $\frac{12}{25}$ (d) $\frac{2}{5}$ (e) No
(f) $\frac{7}{25}$ (g) No 15. (a) $\frac{19}{100}$ (b) $\frac{3}{5}$ (c) $\frac{31}{100}$ (d) $\frac{19}{60}$ (e) $\frac{19}{31}$
16. (a) $\frac{33}{500}$ (b) $\frac{7}{22}$ (c) Probably, $P(B|D) = 0.31\dot{8}$,
$P(B) = 0.3$ (d) $\frac{7}{100}$ 17. (a) $\frac{1}{10}$ (b) $\frac{8}{15}$ (c) $\frac{3}{16}$ (d) $\frac{2}{7}$
18. (a) $\frac{3}{10}$ (b) $\frac{7}{10}$ (c) $\frac{1}{20}$ (d) $\frac{1}{10}$ (e) $\frac{17}{200}$ (f) $\frac{3}{17}$
19. (a) $\frac{31}{1250}$ (b) $\frac{49}{248}$ 20. (a) $\frac{637}{40\,000}$ (b) $\frac{1997}{3185}$
21. (a) (i) $P(H) = \frac{7}{10}$ (ii) $P(M) = \frac{3}{10}$ (b) $\frac{2}{5}$
22. 0.2518

Exercise 11

1. (a) $\frac{2}{5}, \frac{23}{5}$ (b) 0.2, 300 (c) 0.2, 20.75 2. (a) 0.11 (b)
0.75 (c) 0.88 (d) 1.74 3. (a) 0.4 (b) 0.6 (c) 0 4. 3.4
5. 12.88c, €15 456 6. 520 7. €31 250 8. €9000, invest
9. 1 hour per week 10. −€0.50, you would expect
to lose €50 11. €450 12. (a) (i) $\frac{1}{8}$ (ii) $\frac{3}{8}$ (iii) $\frac{3}{8}$ (iv) $\frac{1}{8}$
(b) €3 (c) (i) €3 (ii) €1 13. (a) $\frac{1}{38}$ (b) $\frac{37}{38}$, €0.50, No
14. (a) (i) $\frac{1}{6}$ (ii) $\frac{1}{6}$ (iii) $\frac{1}{6}$ (iv) $\frac{1}{2}$ (b) €5 15. (a) (i) $\frac{1}{25}$ (ii) $\frac{1}{250}$
(iii) $\frac{1}{1000}$ (iv) $\frac{191}{200}$ (b) €0.70 16. (a) (i) 0.001 (ii) 0.003
(iii) 0.996 (b) €50 17. 1.50 boys 18. The average
number of children the Ryans will have is 1.31; no
19. 0.98, −€6.80 20. €50, €60 21. 1.77 22. 1 23. $\frac{1}{3}$

24. (a) S = {B, GB, GGB, GGGB, GGGG}
(b) $\frac{1}{2}$, $\frac{1}{4}$, $\frac{1}{8}$, $\frac{1}{16}$, $\frac{1}{16}$ (d) 1·875   **25.** 0·9375   **26.** 7
27. (a) €50 (b) €0 or €200 (c) €40; No, it will cost him €50

Revision Questions

1. (b) (ii) No, the outcomes of the games are not independent and the probability of a win of either player varies from game to game because the server has an advantage (c) (i) 0·114 (ii) 0·953
2. (b) $-€\frac{1}{6}$; no, it's not fair   (c) €46·40, Yes
3. (a) No, $P(J \cap F) \neq P(J) \times P(F)$ (b) (i) $\frac{1}{16}$ (ii) $\frac{9}{16}$ (iii) $\frac{1}{4}$
4. (a) $\frac{15}{64}$ (b) Financially, the expected loss to the customer is $30·40. If you live in an earthquake zone buy it for peace of mind. (c) x = 5 (i) $\frac{51}{295}$ (ii) $\frac{247}{925}$ (iii) $\frac{11}{111}$
5. (a) (i) $\frac{2}{27}$ (ii) $\frac{26}{27}$ (b) $\frac{3}{4}$ (c) $\frac{260}{267}$ = 0·974   **6.** (a) (i) 0·327
(ii) 0·9998, Yes (b) (ii) $\frac{49}{115}$ = 0·426 (iii) $\frac{49}{106}$ = 0·462
(iv) $P(M|D) = \frac{104}{137}$ = 0·76, $P(F|D) = \frac{33}{137}$ = 0·24; Male
7. (a) 3 (b) (i) 0·2746 (ii) 0·44, 1·05 (c) $\frac{1}{7}$ (i) 0·242
(ii) 0·44 (iii) 0·8   **8.** (a) 0·883 (b) $\frac{101}{625}$ = 0·1616
(c) (i) 400 (ii) $\frac{1}{200}$ (iii) $\frac{1}{20}$ (iv) $\frac{1}{25}$ **9.** (a) 0·836 (b) $\frac{3}{10}$
(c) (i) 0·01 (ii) 0·0056   **10.** $\frac{2}{3}$, switch

Section 6
Chapter 17

Exercise 1

1. (a) Age (b) Yes; Only one variable   **2.** Hair colour
(i) 40% (ii) 10%   **3.** Value on face of die showing
4. Score on a die and head or tail on side of coin showing   **5.** (a) Name of political party (b) 47%
6. (a) Hair colour and eye colour (c) 10% (d) 5%
7. (a) Nominal categorical data (b) Gender
(c) Univariate   **8.** Ordinal categorical data (natural order); Condition of patient   **9.** Continuous; Time can take on all real positive values   **10.** Discrete;
The number of pencils can only be a natural number
11. Discrete; The number of bottles can only be a natural number   **12.** (a) Continuous; Height can have any real positive value (b) Nearest cm (c) 1·725 m ≤ h < 1·735 m
(d) 1·595 m ≤ h < 2·315 m   **13.** Because a person's age is always rounded down to the year of their last birthday, even though their age increases continuously
14. (a) Continuous (b) Discrete (c) Discrete

Exercise 2

1. (a) Population: all Irish households; sample: 2000 Irish households (b) Population: all American elementary schoolchildren; sample: 1000 American elementary schoolchildren (c) Population: all people at the venue; sample: every tenth person entering the venue
(d) Population: all tyres produced in one week at the factory; sample: 150 tyres (e) Population: all Liverpool season ticket holders; sample: 50 Liverpool season ticket holders (f) Population: all Leaving Certificate students; sample: 240 Leaving Certificate students who took the questionnaire   **2.** (a) The air inside all aeroplanes that fly domestically (b) The air inside 175 domestic flights
3. (a) All drivers (b) The drivers stopped on the M7 between 8:30 a.m. and 9:30 a.m. on 9 September (c) No, not every driver in the country has an equal chance of being surveyed   **4.** (a) All people in the country over 30 (b) 100 of its listeners over 30 (c) Not every 30-year-old in the country has an equal chance of being surveyed
5. (a) All fifth years in the school (b) 40 fifth years generated from the database (c) Because every student has an equal chance of being selected for the survey
6. (a) (i) No (ii) Quota sampling; She splits the population into two categories in proportion to the size of each category in the population and then selects the members of each category by convenience (her year group)
(iii) 21 (vi) 19 (b) (i) Quota sampling; The size of the groups are in proportion to their representation in the overall population at his convenience; No; It is biased in favour of young men and women (ii) 40 (iii) 30
7. (a) (i) 45 (ii) 455 (iii) 20 475 (b) (i) 3 (ii) 2
(iii) Fatima, Lucy, Gráinne (iv) Peter, Haroon (v) Fatima, Lucy, Gráinne, Peter, Haroon (c) Manon, Siobhán, Helen, Ben, Adam   **8.** 18 nurses, 10 doctors, 4 administrative staff, 8 theatre staff   **9.** (a) 7 males, 9 females
(b) Females: numbers 31, 22, 43, 24, 25, 28, 48, 38, 39; Males: numbers 21, 27, 30, 6, 19, 42, 33
10. (a) Cluster sampling (b) It is far too expensive to travel all over the country   **11.** (a) Assign a number to each of the 300 households and select them using a random number generator (b) Randomly select five blocks from 20 and then randomly select households in each of these five blocks   **12.** (a) Cluster (b) Stratified (c) Cluster (d) Random (e) Stratified (f) Cluster (g) Random

Exercise 3

1. (b) 137 cm, 205 cm; They are significant, as students could have these heights (c) Numerical continuous; Heights can have all positive, real values   **4.** (a) 2 (b) 12 (c) 3
(d) 35%   **5.** (b) 50–59 (c) 22·7% (d) Ronald Reagan
6. (b) 75% (c) 2008   **7.** (b) A very big range from 75 mg/dl to 220 mg/dl with a fairly symmetric distribution (c) Yes, 380 mg/dl (d) No, only 30% of the group have fasting plasma glucose levels between 90 mg/dl and 130 mg/dl

8. (b) Biskies, 14 g   **9.** (b) Week 4 (c) One Direction was more popular than Cher in 7 out of 10 weeks
10. (b) Yes, 600; An outlier; No; It was probably misrecorded and should be included as 60 (c) Yes. Girls study for longer times on average than boys
11. (b) Yes, there are more good acting parts for 40–80-year-old males than females (c) Yes, as most good acting parts for under 50-year-old actresses are concentrated in the 20–40-year-old group

Chapter 18

Exercise 4

2. (a) 32° (b) 80 (c) 180 (d) 400   **3.** (a) 6%
(b) 3505 billion dollars (c) 701 billion dollars
4. (a) Monday (b) 30%   **5.** (b) Yes, 20; Someone may have given a false answer (c) Yes, between 8 and 10
(d) 60%   **6.** (b) Yes, in class A all students scored 6 or more, whereas in class B many students scored 6 or less
(c) There are a number of students in class B that have a problem with the material   **7.** (a) Add a try to Wales
(b) England; 13 (c) Ireland and France: 10; Scotland, Wales and Italy: 6 (d) 19·6%   **11.** As study time decreases English marks decrease, and as study time increases English marks increase

Exercise 5

1. (a) 32 (b) (i) Asymmetrical (ii) Bimodal
2. Positively skewed   **3.** (b) 24%   **4.** (a) A is negatively skewed and B is positively skewed (b) A is people whose main source of news is radio, TV and newspapers, as the frequency is high at an old age; B is people whose main source of news is the internet, as the frequency is high at a young age   **5.** (a) Heights from 75·0 cm up to but not including 80 cm; 75 cm $\leq h <$ 80 cm (b) (85–90) cm
(c) 89·4 cm (d) Symmetrical   **6.** (a) Negatively skewed
(b) (60–70) years (c) 35%   **7.** Unimodal, negatively skewed

Chapter 19

Exercise 6

1. (a) 6, unimodal (b) 6, 8, bimodal (c) None (d) 3, 5, 7, multimodal   **2.** (a) 7 (b) 8   **3.** Mode   **4.** 8, 10   **5.** (a) 36 (b) 74 (c) 70–79   **6.** (b) Slightly negatively skewed
(c) 30 °C

Exercise 7

1. (a) 5; No mode (b) 2; Mode = 5 (c) $\frac{a+b+c+d}{4}$;
No mode (d) 4; No mode (e) $a + 4d$; No mode (f) $x + 5$;
No mode (g) 58·5; No mode (h) 25; Mode = 24·7 (i) 58;
Mode = 43 (j) $\frac{13}{36}$; No mode   **2.** Mean = 4·5, mode = 3
(a) Mean = 3·5, mode = 2 (b) Mean = 13·5, mode = 9

(c) Mean = 10, mode = 7   **3.** (a) 2 (b) 13 (c) 6
4. (a) €11·20 (b) 42 years (c) 1·62 m (d) €42 000
(e) 87 (f) 8 (g) 15   **5.** (a) Mean = 55·25, mode = 54
(b) Mean = 3·325, modes = 2, 3, 4 (c) Mean = 54, mode = 48   **6.** (a) 3·5 (b) 6 (c) 1   **7.** (a) 15
(b) $\frac{5a + 7b}{12}$ (c) $3q + p$ **8.** (b) 10 (c) Bimodal
9. 12·5; Unimodal   **10.** (a) (i) €114 500 (ii) €130 000
(b) Unimodal, negatively skewed   **11.** 1   **12.** (a) 97·35
(b) Multimodal (c) 46%   **13.** (a) 4·32 hours
(c) 3·5 hours (d) (i) Unimodal (ii) Positively skewed
14. (a) 29 years (b) Unimodal, positively skewed;
Mode = 27 years   **15.** (a) 215·18 lbs (b) Bimodal

Exercise 8

1. (a) Mean = 5, median = 5, modes = 3, 7 (b) Mean = 7, median = 4, mode = 3 (c) Mean = 4·3, median = 4·05, mode = none (d) Mean = 23·75, median = 11·5, mode = 7 (e) Mean = −4, median = −3, modes = −7, −3
(f) Mean = $\frac{43}{160}$, median = $\frac{1}{4}$, mode = $\frac{1}{4}$ (g) Mean = 50·5, median = 25·5, mode = none (h) Mean = $\frac{n+1}{2}$, median = $\frac{n+1}{2}$, mode = none   **2.** A: median = 5, mean = 6, mode = 5; B: median = 9, mean = 10, mode = 9; C: median = 15, mean = 18, mode = 15; D median = 16, mean = 19, mode = 16
3. (a) Median = 4·55, mode = 2·5, mean = 4·4
(b) Median = 6, mode = 3, mean = 8·2
(c) Median = 6, mode = 8, mean = 6·5   **4.** (a) 31 days
(b) Median = 32 per day, mean = 31·6 per day, mode = 29 per day   **5.** Mean = $\frac{64}{7}$, median = 8, mode = 8; Mean = $\frac{67}{7}$, median = 8, mode = 8; Only the mean has changed   **6.** (a) 11 (b) Median = 12, mode = 12, mean = 15·5   **7.** Mode = 2 points, median = 2 points, mean = 2·56 points   **8.** 0·5 mg/ml
(b) 0·5 mg/ml (c) 0·4 mg/ml   **9.** (a) 37 years (c) 36 years
10. (a) 397 minutes (b) 40% (d) 396 minutes
11. (a) 52·4 points (c) 51 points (e) 16   **12.** (b) 7:41 p.m.
(d) 7:44 p.m.   **13.** 32·5   **14.** 8 seconds

Exercise 9

1. (a) Modes = 6, 7, mean = 6, median = 6; Mean
(b) Mode = none, mean = 4·1, median = 2·7; Median
(c) Mode = none, mean = 150·8, median = 143·5; Mean
(d) Mode = none, mean = 25·0, median = 24·9; Mean
(e) Modes = 0, 48, mean = 51·1, median = 56; Median
2. (a) Mean (b) Mode (c) Median (d) Mean (e) Median
(f) Mean (g) Median (h) Median (i) Mean (j) Median
(k) Mode   **3.** €100 000; High earners skew the mean per capita income giving a misleading result. The median income is more representative of the actual annual income of a household of four   **4.** No; Because the four senior

solicitors have annual salaries in excess of €90 000 and this skews the mean **5.** Median vs mean **6.** No. The mean electrical consumption per household

$$= \frac{\text{Total countrywide consumption of all households}}{\text{Number of households}}$$

$$\neq \frac{\text{Sum of means for each county}}{26}.$$

Some counties may have a high mean consumption, i.e. lots of consumption for a small population **7.** Median age: 21 years **8.** 27 **9.** Median = 16 °C; Because 27 °C skews the mean **10.** 1, 1, 1, 1, 1, 1, 8; median = 1, mean = 2 **11.** 85·5 **12.** Mean vs median **13.** (a) 66 (b) 63 (c) 65, 63 **14.** (b) Mode = 3·3 kg, mean = 3·4 kg, median = 3·3 kg (c) Mean; Because lots of results are close together with no outliers (d) Unimodal, symmetric **15.** (a) Mean = 13·5 = Median; Unimodal, symmetric (b) Mean = 7·7, median = 8·2; Mean to the left of the median and mode, skewed left (c) Mean = 15·4, median = 13·4; Mean to right of median and mode, skewed right **16.** (a) A: unimodal, positively skewed; B: unimodal, negatively skewed; C: unimodal, symmetric (c) A: well under 50%, B: well over 50%, C: about 50% **17.** (a) Positively skewed (b) Mode = mean = median = 50 (c) 30 (d) Class B: 50% scored over 50; Class A: 50% scored over 30–40 (e) No evidence to make this conclusion **18.** A is 50 years or less, small median savings; B is 50 years or more, large median savings; Young people don't save as much as older people do **19.** A is Mozambique, B is Japan; Because Mozambique has a much lower median age for the number of deaths per 10 000 of population than Japan

Exercise 10

1. (i) (b) $r = 1$, perfect positive correlation; $(\bar{x}, \bar{y}) = (3, 6)$ (c) $y = 2x$ (ii) (b) $r = 0·54$, moderate positive correlation; $(\bar{x}, \bar{y}) = (2·5, 5·67)$ (c) $y = 0·91x + 3·38$ (iii) (b) $r = -0·98$, very strong negative correlation; $(\bar{x}, \bar{y}) = (2·5, 5)$ (c) $y = -1·49x + 8·71$ **2.** (a) (i) Very strong (ii) Positive correlation (b) 90 years **3.** (a) 90·4 (b) 35·6 (c) Positive; Because slope of LOBF is 0·8 **4.** (a) $r = -0·86$ (b) A strong negative correlation means that as the average number of TV viewing hours increases the average mark in the summer exams decreases (c) No; Other factors may influence the marks in the summer exams, e.g. diligence, intelligence, memory, preparation, etc. **5.** (b) (i) Moderate (ii) Curved **6.** (a) $r = -0·73$, strong negative correlation (b) $y = -8x + 102·56$ **7.** (b) Mean time = 65 minutes, mean length = 7·68 cm (c) $l = 0·14t - 1·61$ (d) $r = 0·99$ **8.** (b) Yes, 0 in test 2 is an outlier. So exclude (90, 0) in finding r (c) $r = 0·99$, $y = 0·71x + 36·94$ **9.** (b) Although there is a strong correlation between cancer deaths and the number of cigarettes smoked,

you cannot conclude smoking causes lung cancer as there may be many other factors involved like genetics, diet, environment, etc. (c) $r = 0·80$ (d) $y = 0·50x + 7·52$ **11.** (a) 0·997 (b) 340·4 parts per million (c) 419·6 parts per million **12.** (b) 5·5 million km^2 **13.** (a) $\bar{x} = 3·42$, $\bar{y} = 391.67$ (c) $r = -0·92$, strong negative correlation (d) Yes, as the strong negative correlation seems to indicate that increasing the number of oil changes per year reduces the annual repair costs (e) $-90·15$ (f) $y = -90·15x + 700$ (g) €69 (h) No, because other factors have not been taken into account, such as age of car, mileage, state of roads, driver behaviour, accidents **14.** (a) $r = -0·93$ (b) Mean of $T = 15·50$, mean of $F = 4·25$; $F = -1·5T + 20$ (c) (i) 29 (ii) 18·5 (d) No; Strong negative correlation **15.** (a) Slope $= -\frac{1}{4}$, equation: $y = -\frac{1}{4}x + 10·2$ (b) (i) $x + y = 10$ (ii) $y = 10 - x$ (iii) $r = -1$ **16.** (a) No, high ice-cream sales depend on many factors: air temperature, advertising events (pop concerts/football matches), number of outlets, price, etc. (b) No, homelessness has many causes, such as alcohol/drug abuse, unemployment, economic downturn, mental health (c) It is irresponsible because the station is implying that playing a certain video game causes people to steal cars. There are many lurking variables why car theft might be on the increase, such as downturn in the economy at the same time as the game was released and the reduction in the number of police, etc. (d) No, it is nonsense; Children with more fillings tend to come from a high-income family that can afford to visit the dentist regularly and provide access to more books

Chapter 20

Exercise 11

1. (a) 12 (b) 14 (c) 23 (d) 23 (e) 1020 **2.** (a) Range = 7, mean $= \frac{14}{15}$, mode $= -1$, median = 1 (b) (i) 44 (ii) 15 (iii) 24 (iv) 13 (v) 24 (c) (i) 6 (ii) 6·2 (iii) 6 (iv) 7 **3.** (a) Mean = 17·5, mode = 17·5, range = 35 (b) Symmetric, unimodal **4.** (a) (i) €1176 (ii) €1350 (iii) €2200 (b) The median; Because the range is so big **5.** (a) (i) 22·325 metric tonnes per person (ii) 19·25 metric tonnes per person (iii) 39·9 metric tonnes per person (b) Mean; Because it gives a measure of pollution to each person in these countries and hence a number that each has to reduce for themselves in order to lower CO_2 levels in the world

Exercise 12

1. (a) 53 (b) 98 (c) 45 (d) 75 (e) 65 (f) 88 (g) 23 **2.** (a) 16 (b) 57·5 (c) 55 (d) 62 (e) 7 **3.** (a) 8 (b) 4 (c) 2·5 (d) 6 (e) 3·5 **4.** (a) €60 000 (b) €40 000 (c) €73 000 (d) €33 000 **5.** (a) 7 mins (b) 4 mins

(c) 9 mins (d) 5 mins (e) 12 mins   **6.** (a) 54 (b) 100
(c) 37 (d) 71 (e) 34   **7.** (a) 37 (b) 20·5 (c) 16·5 (d) 30
(e) 13·5; None   **8.** (a) Mean = 47·75, mode = 45
(b) (i) 49 (ii) 36 (iii) 61 (iv) 25   **9.** (a) (i) 7·5 hours
(ii) 6·3 hours (iii) 9·3 hours (iv) 3 hours
(b) Mean = 7·3 hours, mode = 7 hours   **10.** (a) 36·5
(b) 17 (c) 50 (d) 33 (e) 107; Yes, 105, 109

Exercise 13

1. (a) $\mu = 8$, $\sigma = 3·7$ (b) $\mu = 4$, $\sigma = 4·3$ (c) $\mu = 2a$,
$\sigma = a\sqrt{\dfrac{2}{3}}$ (d) $\mu = 4·8$, $\sigma = 2·4$ (e) $\mu = 9x$, $\sigma = 4x$
2. $\mu = 3·71$, $\sigma = 2·25$ (a) $\mu_B = 6·71$, $\sigma_B = 2·25$
(b) $\mu_C = 7·42$, $\sigma_C = 4·5$ (c) $\mu_D = 13·13$, $\sigma_D = 6·75$
3. $\mu = 3$, $\sigma = 1·38$ **4.** $y = 10$, $\mu = 2·8$, $\sigma = 1·6$ **5.** 4
6. 44–72   **7.** *A* and *B* have the same standard deviation;
C has a bigger standard deviation than *D*. The results
are more spread out in *C* about the mean than in *D*
8. (a) Mean increased by €1000; No effect on standard
deviation (b) Mean increased by 20%; Standard
deviation increased by 20%   **9.** A: range = 80,
standard deviation = 20·5; B: range = 80,
standard deviation = 25·0; Yes; It indicates that both
classes have the same range of ability; It gives the
spread of the marks about the mean; Class A marks
are more clustered about their mean than class B marks
are about their mean   **10.** $\mu = 10$, $\sigma = 4·5$
11. (a) (i) Class B: most marks furthest from the mean
(ii) Class C: fewest marks furthest from the mean
(b) Class A: $\mu = 25$, $\sigma_A = 9·7$; Class B: $\mu = 25$, $\sigma_B = 14·1$;
Class C: $\mu = 39·7$, $\sigma_C = 6·2$ **12.** (a) $\mu = 22$ (b) $\sigma = 4·9$
(c) (i) 26·9 (ii) 17·1 (d) 3 days; 58%   **13.** (a) Fairly
symmetric (b) 1·65 m (c) 1·35 m (d) 5810 (e) 1210
(f) 6790, 97%

Chapter 21

Exercise 14

1. (a) Not normal or approximately normal,
positively skewed (b) Approximately normal
(c) Not normal or approximately normal, positively
skewed   **2.** (a) Symmetric; Mode = 14,
median = 14, mean = 14 (b) Negatively skewed;
Mode = 30, median = 30, mean = 25 (c) Positively
skewed; Mode = 35, median = 35, mean = 37·7
(d) Approximately normal; Mode = mean = median = 50
(e) Negatively skewed; Mode = 95, median = 80·7,
mean = 76·3   **3.** (a) (i) 34·13% (ii) 68·26% (iii) 2·27%
(b) 1683   **4.** 97·6%   **5.** 15·87%; 0·1587 **6.** (a) 11 days
(b) 3 days   **7.** (a) 9·0 °C, 2·6 °C (b) (3·8–14·2) °C
8. (a) (233–297) days (b) 217 days   **9.** (10·5–13·5) litres;
81·86%

Exercise 15

1. 99th   **2.** 9   **3.** 54   **4.** 10   **5.** True   **6.** (a) Median
(b) Lower quartile (c) Upper quartile **7.** 4   **8.** 13; 11
9. 99th percentile   **10.** 35 years   **11.** Yes; In Kilanor,
80% of the scores were below 70, but in Ballygan 80%
of the scores were below 53

Exercise 16

1. 1·6   **2.** 73·4   **3.** The actual score is the mean score:
$x = \mu$ **4.** −2   **5.** (a) True (b) True (c) False (d) True
(e) True   **6.** (a) −2 (b) −1 (c) 1·5 (d) −3
7. It gives $\sigma = -5$, which is impossible   **8.** $\mu = 79$, $\sigma = 3$
9. Physics   **10.** 8, as you would be placed higher
in the test   **11.** 6th year was more pro-uniform
12. $\mu = 25$, $\sigma = 16$ **13.** $z = +2$; 16th

Exercise 17

1. (a) 0·9332 (b) 0·9750 (c) 0·0968 (d) 0·2578
(e) 0·1131 (f) 0·2877 (g) 0·2475 (h) 0·4863
2. (a) 0·85 (b) 1·46 (c) 1·10 (d) −0·21 (e) 0·52
3. 0·9974   **4.** 1·66   **5.** 14 days   **6.** 0·5793; 0·4207;
73%   **7.** (a) 1; 84th (b) 34 (c) 0·68   **8.** (a) 584
(b) $372 \le x \le 628$, $x \in \mathbb{N}$ **9.** (a) 11% (b) 21·56
(c) 15·48 (d) $17·32 \le x \le 22·68$, $x \in \mathbb{R}$ **10.** $x \le 0·8185$,
$x \ge 1·535$, $x \in \mathbb{R}$ **11.** 1270 hours   **12.** 16%
13. 98·76%   **14.** 118   **15.** (a) 84% (b) 100 to 120
(c) 3% (d) 488

Chapter 22

Exercise 18

1. (a) 25, 0·6 (b) 54, 0·8 (c) 0·94 (d) 0·121 (e) 79·9%
2. (a) 0·18 (b) 0·28 (c) 0·73 (d) 0·56 (e) 0·31   **3.** 67, 1·84
4. 0·022   **5.** (a) Yes; $n \ge 30$ (b) Yes, $n = 100 > 30$ (c) €32 000,
€8000 (d) Unlikely. Generally salaries are skewed
with larger numbers on lower salaries   **6.** 18, 0·8;
0·0062   **7.** 0·024   **8.** 0·0062; You must assume the
sample reflects the population and does not consist of 16
heavyweight boxers   **9.** (a) 57% (b) 76% (c) 0·93
10. 0·43   **11.** 0·20   **12.** 0·96

Exercise 19

1. (a) Sample proportion (b) $\frac{253}{1212} = 0·2087$ (c) 0·0117
(d) 18·6% $\leftrightarrow$ 23·2%   **2.** 17·5% $\leftrightarrow$ 22·5%
3. 6·8 cm $\leftrightarrow$ 7·8 cm   **4.** 63·1% $\leftrightarrow$ 71·3%
5. 19·6% $\leftrightarrow$ 27·9%   **6.** (a) 1·1547 (b) 123 $\leftrightarrow$ 127
7. *B*: 37% $\leftrightarrow$ 43%   **8.** 1st poll A: 42% $\leftrightarrow$ 48%,
2nd poll B: 39% $\leftrightarrow$ 45%; Poll A shows support could
have been as low as 42%, hence Poll B does not

necessarily show a decline   **9.** (a) 0·72 (b) 0·0204
(c) 484   **10.** 273

Exercise 20

1. (a) H_0: $\mu = 600$ hours, H_1: $\mu \neq 600$ hours; Two tailed
(b) H_0: $\mu = 5\cdot2$, H_1: $\mu > 5\cdot2$; Right, one tailed
(c) H_0: $p = 0\cdot78$, H_1: $p \neq 0\cdot78$; Two tailed
(d) H_0: $\mu = 20$ MB, H_1: $\mu < 20$ MB; Left, one tailed
(e) H_0: $p = 0\cdot82$, H_1: $p > 0\cdot82$; Right, one tailed
2. Reject H_0; CI: 58% $\leftrightarrow$ 75%   **3.** Do not reject
H_0; CI: 56% $\leftrightarrow$ 72%   **4.** Do not reject H_0;
CI: 39% $\leftrightarrow$ 48%, as no change in support   **5.** Do not
reject H_0; CI: 9% $\leftrightarrow$ 12%   **6.** Do not reject H_0;
CI: 23% $\leftrightarrow$ 33%   **7.** Reject H_0, as failure rate has changed
8. Do not reject H_0; CI: 40% $\leftrightarrow$ 58%
9. Reject H_0; CI: 60% $\leftrightarrow$ 68%. There is evidence that
drug B has a success rate between 60% $\leftrightarrow$ 68%,
i.e. it is more successful than drug A **10.** Yes, reject H_0;
CI: 14% $\leftrightarrow$ 24%. There is evidence to suggest the
proportion is much lower   **11.** Do not reject H_0;
CI: 59% $\leftrightarrow$ 77%   **12.** Do not reject H_0; $\bar{z} = 1\cdot67 < 1\cdot96$;
Two tailed; $p = 0\cdot095 \geq 0\cdot05$, Do not reject H_0
13. $\bar{z} = -2\cdot5 < -1\cdot96$; Reject H_0; $\mu \neq 26$
14. $\bar{z} = -1\cdot79 > -1\cdot96$; Do not reject H_0 as
$p = 0\cdot0734 \geq 0\cdot05$ **15.** $\bar{z} = -10\cdot08 < -1\cdot96$;
Reject H_0 **16.** $p = 0\cdot08 \geq 0\cdot05$; Do not reject H_0.
There is no change in weight   **17.** $p = 0\cdot1836 > 0\cdot05$;
Do not reject H_0. There is no difference

Revision Questions

1. (a) $\bar{x} = 151\cdot95$ cm, $\bar{y} = 151\cdot05$ cm (b) $\sigma_x = 23\cdot965$ cm,
$\sigma_y = 22\cdot977$ cm (d) $r = 0\cdot9854$ (e) $y = 7\cdot4852 + 0\cdot9448x$
(h) 111·4 cm   **2.** (a) 68·26%, 95·46%, 99·74%
(b) 30·6 years, 3·6 years (c) 30·6 years (d) (i) 33 years

(ii) 28 years (iii) 5 years (e) (i) 11% (ii) 83%
3. (a) (i) CL: The success rate (probability) of the method
that is specified by the experimenter (ii) CI: The range
of values of a statistic (mean or proportion) of interest
constructed so that this range has a specified level of
probability (95%) of including the true value of the
statistic in the population (b) CI: 53% $\leftrightarrow$ 72%; Reject H_0;
It is unlikely. The manufacturer's claim is true as in 95%
of samples of size 100, the percentage with weight 100 g
is between 53% and 72% (c) $\bar{z} = 4\cdot24 > 1\cdot96$; Reject
airline's claim   **4.** (a) (i) The sampling distribution is
normal with mean μ and standard deviation $\dfrac{\sigma}{\sqrt{n}}$
(ii) The sampling distribution is normal with mean
p and standard deviation $\sigma = \sqrt{\dfrac{p(1-p)}{n}}$ (b) (i) 48
(ii) $\dfrac{3\sqrt{10}}{10} = 0.95$ (c) (i) 0·32, 0·0466 (ii) 0·0427
5. (a) A simple random sample is a sample of n objects
chosen from a larger set of N objects (population) in
such a way that every set of n such objects has an equal
chance to be the set selected; SRS: selecting five cards
from a pack of 52; Not SRS: in measuring the heights of
6th-class students the basketball team would not
be a simple random sample (b) CI: 57% $\leftrightarrow$ 63%
(c) CI: 53% $\leftrightarrow$ 55%. As 50% < 53% the claim is justified
6. (a) (i) 0·74 (ii) 0·89 (b) (i) 0·31 (ii) 0·23
7. (a) (i) Simple random sample (ii) Cluster sampling
(iii) Stratified sampling (b) 30 boys, 20 girls
(c) (i) SRS: Highly representative/time consuming
(ii) Cluster: Quick/high sampling error (iii) Stratified:
Very representative/slow (d) Stratified, as it is very
representative and ensures gender balance
(e) 17% $\leftrightarrow$ 23%   **8.** (a) Negatively skewed (b) 0·75
(c) (i) Normal distribution, bell shaped (ii) 4 mb
(iii) 11%